HAL CHASE

HAL CHASE

*The Defiant Life and Turbulent Times
of Baseball's Biggest Crook*

by
Martin Donell Kohout

McFarland & Company, Inc., Publishers
Jefferson, North Carolina, and London

Library of Congress Cataloguing-in-Publication Data

Kohout, Martin Donell, 1959–
    Hal Chase : the defiant life and turbulent times of baseball's biggest crook / by Martin Donell Kohout.
      p.   cm.
    Includes bibliographical references and index.
    ISBN 0-7864-1067-1 (softcover : 50# alkaline paper) ∞
    1. Chase, Hall, 1883–1947. 2. Baseball players—United States—Biography. I. Title.
GV865.C434K64   2001
796.357'092—dc21   2001031273
[B]

British Library cataloguing data are available

©2001 Martin Donell Kohout. All rights reserved

No part of this book may be reproduced or transmitted in any form or by any means, electronic or mechanical, including photocopying or recording, or by any information storage and retrieval system, without permission in writing from the publisher.

Manufactured in the United States of America

On the cover: Hal Chase from the December 16, 1909, issue of *The Sporting News* (Thomas Carwile Collection)

McFarland & Company, Inc., Publishers
   Box 611, Jefferson, North Carolina 28640
      www.mcfarlandpub.com

Acknowledgments

This work, such as it is, would not exist without the assistance of a number of people, none of whom should be held responsible for its faults. Among those who selflessly shared with me their research or insights into the enigmatic character of Hal Chase are Lynn Bevill, Gib Bodet, Roy Drachman, David Frishberg, Cappy Gagnon, Lester Grant, Robert Hoie, A. Marguerite Peck, Arturo Soto, Renwick Speer, Steve Steinberg, Mark Stewart, and Betsy Tunis.

Among the many who offered guidance or encouragement are Mark Alvarez, the late Red Barber, Peter C. Bjarkman, Ken Burns and Susanna Steisel of Florentine Films, Tom Carwile, Pete Cava, Bill Conlin of the Sacramento *Bee*, L. Robert Davids, Ed Dinger, Frank Eakes, John B. Holway, Donald Honig, Philip Cate Huckins, Milton Jamail of the Lyndon B. Johnson School of Public Affairs at the University of Texas at Austin, Peter Levine, Sheldon Meyer of Oxford University Press, the late Paul F. Otis, Douglas Payne, Tom Simon, Richard L. Wentworth of the University of Illinois Press, and George Will. Several of the aforementioned individuals are members of the Society for American Baseball Research (SABR), which provided many opportunities for discussion and reflection on Chase and his place in baseball history.

Bill Deane and Dan Cunningham of the National Baseball Library in Cooperstown, N.Y.; Steve Gietschier of *The Sporting News*; Cindy Hayostek of the Cochise County (Arizona) Historical and Archaeological Society; Anne-Marie Kern of the Office of the Commissioner, Major League Baseball; Leslie Masunaga of the San Jose Historical Museum; Jorge C. Menendez of the Leones de Yucatán; Julia O'Keefe and Anne McMahon of the Santa Clara University Archives; Bob Johnson of the California Room at the Martin Luther King Jr. Library in San Jose; Emerson N. Shaw of the Forbes Mill History Museum in Los Gatos, Calif.; John E. Spalding; and Jerry Vaughn responded promptly and generously to my requests for information. In addition, John Leidy, the grandson of Chase's former teammate Ray Fisher, graciously shared with me the transcript of an interview with his grandfather as well as a copy of a magazine article on Chase which I had somehow missed.

Various relatives and descendants of Hal Chase shared with me memories of their notorious forebear, and while they may disagree strongly with my conclusions, I am deeply indebted to the kindness and patience of his son, the late Hal E. Chase Sr., and grandson, Hal E. (Casey) Chase Jr.; his granddaughter, Barbara Lee Chase; Frank and Roxanne Cloak; Corinne Kunkel; Mary Jane Reilly Nichols; Esther Wright Madden; and Thomas Wright.

Richard Ribb read pieces of this manuscript with a close and scholarly attention to detail, and inspired me to think more deeply about historiographical issues. Sarah Bird, Debbie Mauldin Cottrell, Bill Crawford, Mark Odintz, Janice Pinney, Gabriel Schechter, John Taliaferro, Allen Turner, and George B. Ward provided moral support and useful advice. Stieg and Nancy Klein unhesitatingly opened their home to me when my research took me to San Jose. Linda Webster did a wonderful job of indexing the book.

Finally, and most important to me on a personal level, I must pay tribute to the patience and encouragement of my wife, Heather Catto Kohout, who now knows a hell of a lot more about baseball in general and Hal Chase in particular than she ever imagined she would.

Contents

Acknowledgments	v
Introduction	1
One — A Great Fun-Loving Boy	9
Two — A More Brilliant Player Does Not Wear a Uniform	27
Three — Chase Has Been Too Highly Praised in New York	53
Four — It Is a Business with Me	78
Five — We Will Find a Place for Hal All Right	105
Six — The King of the Leapers	124
Seven — I Want to Square Myself with the Public	153
Eight — A Severe "Black Eye" for the Game	187
Nine — I Beat Them in Court Every Time	211
Ten — A Long Way to the So-Called "Big Town"	249
Epilogue	281
Chapter Notes	283
Bibliography	313
Index	325

Falstaff: O, thou hast damnable iteration, and art indeed able to corrupt a saint. Thou hast done much harm upon me, Hal, God forgive thee for it! Before I knew thee, Hal, I knew nothing, and now am I, if a man should speak truly, little better than one of the wicked....
— Shakespeare, *1 Henry IV,* I.ii

... Farewell happy Fields
Where Joy for ever dwells: Hail horrors, hail
Infernal world, and thou profoundest Hell
Receive thy new Possessor: One who brings
A mind not to be chang'd by Place or Time.
— Milton, *Paradise Lost,* I, 249–253

Introduction

The boy used to bring Uncle Hal groceries and cigars and sometimes five or ten bucks from Grandma Jessie. Because Uncle Hal was Grandma Jessie's brother, Grandpa Frank couldn't throw him off the ranch entirely, but he'd be damned if he'd let him in the main house. Building Uncle Hal his own little shack had been a compromise. His health was shot; the booze and hard living had left him thin and weak, and his liver and kidneys and heart were all giving him trouble. Occasionally the boy would drive Grandma Jessie out to the cabin, and occasionally Uncle Hal would drag himself down to Sacramento to cadge drinks in some bar, but for the most part the boy was his only companion. It was wartime, and they didn't have such luxuries as balls and gloves, but oranges were plentiful on the ranch, and when Uncle Hal was feeling good he'd challenge the boy to try to throw an orange past him. No matter how hard he tried, the boy never succeeded. Uncle Hal's wracked body would, for a few moments, throw off the years of illness and abuse, and he would spring, catlike, to snare the bright fruit before it got past him.

In those moments the boy caught a glimpse of what Uncle Hal must have been like when he was young and healthy and strong and famous, when he wore the colorful flannels of a major leaguer with unmatched swagger, before the money and the contracts and the gambling got in the way. Perhaps for Uncle Hal these games with the boy were a return to play just for the fun of it. Perhaps this was the way it should have been all along.[1]

The decades surrounding the turn of the twentieth century were a period of considerable upheaval in the United States. The nation's population increased by 279 percent between 1870 and 1920, from 38 million to 106 million. The gross national product, adjusted for inflation, more than quadrupled between 1869 and 1914, while per capita income rose 250 percent. One historian estimates that the number of millionaires in the United States increased tenfold in the thirty years after the Civil War.[2]

All the news, however, was not good. More and more wealth concentrated in the hands of a relatively small urban elite, and the gulf between them and rural Americans and the urban poor, both native-born and immigrant, grew ever wider. In 1900, for example, a scant 0.35 percent of the population held three-fifths of the nation's wealth, and 25,000 to 40,000 families controlled $31 billion, or half of the nation's total. This was the age of the corporation, the trust, the holding company, and the plutocrat, of men who accumulated vast personal fortunes with little or no regard for their fellows.[3]

Traditional ethical and moral standards buckled under the strain of this fantastic economic growth. Latter-day historians have written of the "quantitative ethic" that came to dominate America, of "the grotesque competition of the rich," of "the pure capitalist rapacity" of the era's businessmen. It was "a long national carnival of fraud and bribery," and, as one scholar has noted, "Increasingly, the worth of everything—even beauty, friendship, religion, the moral life—was being determined by what it could bring in the market."[4]

Such judgments were by no means limited to those with the benefit of hindsight. The iconoclastic Thorstein Veblen noted in 1899 that wealth, rather than achievement, had become "the conventional basis of esteem," and was "now itself intrinsically honourable and confers honour on its possessor." Brooks Adams wrote that the American capitalist "looks upon the evasion of a law devised for public protection, but inimical to him, as innocent or even meritorious." "Get money—honestly if you can, but at any rate get money! This," lamented Henry George, "is the lesson that society is daily and hourly dinning into the ears of its members." Not even the world of sport was immune: Grantland Rice wrote of this period, "The new law of life is not Make, but Take—and yet the world wonders at its growing troubles." John Jay Chapman surveyed his countrymen and passed judgment even more succinctly: "The most heartless people in history—that's what we are."[5]

Chapman's condemnation was understandable in the face of William H. Vanderbilt's notorious retort to protests that the public needed a rail line he had decided to discontinue ("the public be damned!"); Jay Gould's response to the threat of a strike by the employees of his railroad ("I can hire one half of the working class to kill the other half"); and Milton Smith's definition of society (it "was for the purpose of one man's getting what the other fellow has, if he can, and keep out of the penitentiary").[6]

It was an era of crude and brutal tactics, of grabbing for the main chance and devil take the hindmost. In the words of one historian, "No personal feeling or humanitarian consideration should be allowed to interfere with the duty of making a profit." In such a society, "The ideal of abiding by the rules of the game was weakened. Only success counted, and the game had no rules. To contend for fair play was to expose yourself as weak and effeminate." Yet the nation was still sufficiently moralistic to require "a host of ethical evasions no more subtle than the evils they were meant to hide."[7]

Organized baseball, which in fact benefited more from urbanization and industrialization than many other institutions (major league attendance doubled between 1901 and 1908), shrewdly positioned itself as the symbolic repository of those traditional American virtues which seemed to be in eclipse. The self-styled "National Pastime" became an island of nostalgia for those — and there were many — who yearned for a return to slower, simpler times. "Baseball elevates, and it fits the American character," proclaimed Albert Spalding, a former player and executive, in 1910. "There is no chance for secret cheating, therefore there is no tendency in that direction.... Drunkards and all other moral undesirables are barred from real success upon the base ball field by the very nature of the sport." Three years later, an article in *Outlook* magazine insisted that baseball aided "powerfully in physical and moral development." Charles Comiskey, the president of the Chicago White Sox and, like Spalding, a former major leaguer, made the same argument more pithily when he declared that "Crookedness and baseball do not mix."[8]

In fact, like many other national institutions, the reality of baseball had little in common with its public image. Veblen grasped something of that reality as early as 1899, when he insisted that "Chicane, falsehood, brow-beating, hold a well-secured place in the method of procedure of any athletic contest and in games generally." Indeed, wrote baseball historian Harold Seymour, "to call professional baseball a sport and the players and owners sportsmen is to use language so loosely as to divest it of meaning. Games played for money are not played for fun." Greed and venality were as much a part of the game as the hit-and-run and the stolen base, but the governing structure of the game was loath to acknowledge the extent to which money, both legitimate and illegitimate, controlled the game.[9]

Given the paradoxical, if not hypocritical, climate of the game, and of the nation at large, it is no surprise to learn that baseball's promoters repeatedly hushed up scandals involving gambling, bribery, and throwing games, and that professional baseball players seemed as unconcerned with ethics as did their counterparts in other industries. The most notorious of them all was Hal Chase.

Chase was an incredibly graceful athlete, and handsome and charming to boot. Unsurprisingly, he became a favorite of newspaper reporters, who proclaimed him a star almost immediately upon his arrival in the major leagues in 1905. He was a breathtaking fielder, repeatedly making defensive plays that no other first baseman would even attempt, and a dangerous hitter and baserunner. Perhaps more than any other player before Babe Ruth, Chase ensured the survival of the New York franchise of the upstart American League, then known as the Highlanders but later renamed the Yankees, in the nation's largest city, where they had to compete for fans with the New York Giants and Brooklyn Dodgers of the established National League. The consensus of those who saw him play was that he was, as Frank Graham wrote almost thirty years after Chase's last major league game, "the greatest first baseman that ever lived ... greater than [Lou] Gehrig or [Bill] Terry or [George] Sisler or anyone you care to name."[10]

Chase's peers generally shared Graham's assessment of his talent. Babe Ruth,

Walter Johnson, Napoleon Lajoie, and Ed Barrow, all members of the National Baseball Hall of Fame, picked Chase as the first baseman on their all-time all-star teams—said Ruth, "For my dough, Hal Chase was the greatest first baseman who ever lived"—as did *Baseball* magazine in 1930.[11] When George Kelly, another Hall of Famer and Chase's successor as first baseman of the New York Giants, was asked years later whom he believed to be the greatest first baseman of all time, he responded, "Oh, Gehrig and Terry were good. But Chase could do everything they could—and better." Hughie Jennings, who was the great Ty Cobb's manager with the Detroit Tigers, insisted that "As a player, there is nobody who can touch Chase for holding down first base. Not only is he a superb fielder, but he is one of the most intelligent men in the game up at the plate." And after Chase's death, Clark Griffith, his first manager in New York and later the manager and owner of the Washington Senators, said, "You wouldn't believe a man could do all the things on a ball field Chase could do. There wasn't a modern first baseman who could come close to him. There wasn't any 'second Hal Chase.' He was in a class by himself."[12]

While such testimonials are compelling, the statistical record does not support them. Chase's career fielding percentage was .980, while those of Sisler, Gehrig, and Terry were .987, .991, and .992 respectively. Of course, fielding percentage alone is a poor measure of a player's defensive abilities, because an agile player with great range will naturally get to more difficult balls, and thus commit more errors, than a less gifted player, who restricts himself to only the easiest chances. Even so, the most sophisticated calculations of latter-day sabermetricians indicate that only twelve men in major league history who played more than one thousand games at first base have had a worse composite fielding-runs total than Chase's.[13]

How to square these admittedly crude statistical measures with the adulatory accounts from so many of Chase's peers? Perhaps those who saw him play were misled by his lithe grace and ability to make the spectacular look routine (or vice versa). Or perhaps he really was the best first baseman ever—when he was trying to win, which was not always the case. Jack Martin, a young infielder with the Highlanders in 1912, recalled Chase with unabashed admiration: "When I came up I fielded a grounder at third and then held up on my throw because Chase wasn't on the bag. Chase told me, 'Kid, just throw the ball to the bag and I'll be there,' and he always was. Great player." But others, including shortstop Roger Peckinpaugh, who joined the team in 1913, told a different story. "I remember a few times I threw a ball over to first base, and it went by to the stands, and a couple of runs scored," recalled Peckinpaugh. "It surprised me. I'd stand there looking, sighting the flight of the ball in my mind, and I'd think, 'Jeez, that throw wasn't that bad.' Then I'd tell myself that [Chase] was the greatest there was, so maybe the throw was bad. Then later on when he got the smelly reputation, it came back to me, and I said, 'Oh-oh.' What he was doing, you see, was tangling up his feet and then making a fancy dive after the ball, making it look like it was a wild throw."[14]

Similarly contradictory are the accounts of Chase's personality. Baseball historian Bob Hoie believes that "the closest approximation of his personality is Paul Newman in *The Sting*"—that is, a rogue, a liar, and a cheat, but ultimately an irresistible character. Early in Chase's career, one contemporary wrote that his "unassuming way has made him a popular favorite among his teammates, and the well-deserved praise showered upon him has left no sign of a swelling of the cranium with this young player," while another called him "a mannerly, gentlemanly fellow."[15]

This may be exaggeration—the sporting press in the early twentieth century was more interested in creating than discrediting heroes, and frequently served as little more than an unofficial public relations department for the teams it covered—but many found Chase "charming, witty, well-spoken, and altogether an enjoyable companion—a man among men."[16] One former teammate, Ray Fisher, recalled Chase as "a nice fella ... such a likeable guy," and remembered gratefully how Chase, during his tenure as Yankee manager, allowed Fisher to leave a Sunday game early so he could pick up a little extra money pitching for a semipro team in Bennington, Vermont: "He *wanted* me to go up there and get the money."[17] During his years in New York, Chase was the toast of Broadway's sporting and theatrical demimonde, a grinning, cigar-chomping, back-slapping dandy who numbered Al Jolson, George M. Cohan, and Will Rogers among his pals.

Others could not stand him, and portrayed him as an arrogant, boastful prima donna who despised, and was despised by, his fellows. Once, when a writer complimented him on a particularly spectacular play, Chase grinned and said, referring to his teammates, "I could make plays like that every day, only I am afraid to turn the ball loose because I might hit one of those dopes in the head."[18] Of course, a sterling character is not necessarily a prerequisite for success in the major leagues; as one sympathetic biographer of Chase has noted, "The Hall of Fame in Cooperstown, New York, is generously sprinkled with bigots, drunkards, and, perish the thought, even a few fixers."[19] No less an iconoclast than the curmudgeonly Bill James allowed that "Chase would probably be in the Hall of Fame had he been honest."[20]

Of course, had Chase been honest, he would not have been Chase; he would have been some other, considerably less interesting person. His son insisted, with some plausibility, that "money never seemed to mean anything to him,"[21] yet Chase was implicated in at least half a dozen bribery and fixing schemes, including the infamous Black Sox conspiracy, before he was quietly blacklisted following the 1919 season. Indeed, Chase had ties to at least thirteen of the eighteen other active major leaguers either banned or blacklisted during the early 1920s, including the Black Sox.[22] Unlike Cobb, however, whose financial acumen was legendary,[23] as soon as Chase got money, he spent it, and he rarely spent it wisely. It was the getting, not the keeping—the means, not the end—that seems to have excited him, and he seems not to have minded very much when he lost it. He was incorrigibly irresponsible as a player, dissipating his breathtaking talents in a series of scandals, and as a man, failing at least twice as a husband and virtually abandoning his only (legitimate) son; yet that son continued to defend his father almost fifty years after his death, and he persists as a strangely sympathetic character. Certainly, if you had to choose one ballplayer to win a game, you would choose Cobb over Chase. If, however, you had to choose one ballplayer with whom to spend a night on the town, you would choose Chase over Cobb, even though you knew he was cheating you.

According to one student of his life, "Chase was known as a petty thief, a gambler and a carouser" as far back as his college days. "But his talent and charm always won him through his troubles, and his indiscretions were always excused to youthful exuberance and, perhaps, over-active glands." His activities may indeed have been common knowledge, or at least widely suspected—said one contemporary, "He was a cheater right from the beginning and everybody knew it," and the fact that five teams in fifteen years decided that they would be better off without so great a star is otherwise inexplicable—but no crime was ever officially attached to his name.[24]

That such a man could spend fifteen years in the major leagues, however, reveals much about the game, and the nation, at that time. Did Chase lie, cheat, gamble, bribe, throw games? Almost certainly he did; the evidence, though circumstantial, is overwhelming. Yet Chase was merely doing, more or less, what a number of his contemporaries, both players and owners, were doing. The official version of the game's history sought to portray Chase as the lone serpent in the Edenic grass of early twentieth-century baseball, but we must remember that, in the words of one student of the game, baseball itself in Chase's day "was as crooked as a barrel of snakes." Consider that the owner of the Highlanders during Chase's tenure with the team was Frank Farrell, whom the New York *Times* identified as the "dictator of the poolroom syndicate." His gambling house on 33rd Street, just a few doors from the Waldorf Hotel, was among the most luxurious in New York, featuring an interior designed by Stanford White. Farrell's partner in the ownership of the Highlanders was William S. (Big Bill) Devery, the former New York police chief who was Tammany Hall's most notorious graft collector, a figure so egregiously corrupt that he became an embarrassment even to Boss Croker.[25]

Farrell and Devery were hardly unique among the game's magnates. Charles A. Stoneham, owner of the New York Giants, was "a curb market broker of dubious integrity"; he was arrested for fraud in 1908, and later indicted for perjury and mail fraud. For a time he owned a Havana racetrack and casino in partnership with Giants manager John McGraw, and was an intimate of Arnold Rothstein, the so-called "Banker to the Underworld" and mastermind of the Black Sox scandal.[26] McGraw himself had jumped his contract with Baltimore of the American League to join the Giants in 1902, an ethically dubious move about which he remained extremely sensitive for the rest of his career, and close associates of his were charged more than once with attempting to bribe players on other teams. McGraw was also "an inveterate gamester"—he was arrested in

1904 and charged with illegal gambling—and Rothstein was his silent partner in a New York pool hall.[27]

Moreover, Charles Weeghman, owner of the Chicago Cubs, was an intimate and unabashed friend of Monte Tennes, a prominent Chicago gambler. And August (Garry) Herrmann, president of the Cincinnati Reds and longtime chairman of baseball's governing National Commission, was an associate of George B. Cox, the notorious political boss of Cincinnati, which Lincoln Steffens described as "one great graft." In 1906 Herrmann admitted having bet $6,000 that the Pittsburgh Pirates would not win the National League pennant.[28] Yet baseball insisted publicly that its integrity was unimpeachable. Charles Comiskey's confident assertion that "baseball and crookedness do not mix" was published in 1919, the same year that eight of his star players—the infamous "Black Sox"—allegedly agreed to throw the World Series to the Cincinnati Reds in return for secret payments from gamblers (possibly including Chase). Comiskey's first impulse upon learning of the fix was to attempt to hush it up; only later did he adopt the role of outraged defender of baseball's purity.

In such a milieu, the various scandals to which Chase was linked seem considerably less than shocking. In fact, the owners probably intended the appointment of federal judge Kenesaw Mountain Landis as baseball's first commissioner in the wake of the Black Sox scandal more as a cosmetic gesture to reassure the public than as a sincere attempt to clean up the game. Landis, despite his celebrated reputation for uncompromising rectitude, seems to have applied justice only when publicity made it unavoidable. For example, while he expelled the Black Sox from organized baseball despite their acquittal in a jury trial, he never officially banned Chase (who had avoided extradition to face charges in the trial) from organized baseball, although Prince Hal "was about as welcome as a mouse in a kitchen."[29] Instead, Chase was informally blacklisted, which had the advantage of keeping secret the reasons for his departure. But he refused to play the penitent, at least at first; after being eased out of organized baseball, he became a mercenary semiprofessional ballplayer, first in his native California and then, after his implication in more fixing scandals, in Arizona, a rough and dusty frontier where several disgraced ex–major leaguers (including some of the Black Sox) found employment for a time. By the time a group of New York writers rediscovered him in Tucson in 1933, he was obviously in decline, a long, slow process that ended only with his death just over thirteen years later. During these years Chase had to support himself by working a variety of menial jobs as well as through the charity of pitying friends and relatives. He finally began to pay the price for a lifetime of irresponsibility and drinking and was hospitalized several times for a variety of ailments. Despite these troubles, however, he seems to have remained essentially cheerful. His son remembered that "For all the things that happened to him, he was not bitter," and one man who befriended him during his later years echoed this assessment: "He didn't seem to be a guy who had a lot of resentment about him.... He seemed like a happy-go-lucky guy. He didn't cry about his bad luck or anything." In fact, in the words of one baseball man, "This guy seemed to *love* every minute he was alive."[30]

In various interviews during his final years Chase finally admitted some responsibility for his sordid reputation, though he continued to insist that he was innocent of the worst allegations against him. In 1941, for example, he told one reporter, "I knew years ago—and I know it more clearly now—that my life has been one great big mistake after another." But such statements sound more like the final con of an inveterate con man than the sincere regrets of a true penitent. Prince Hal finally died of kidney and heart ailments in 1947; thus the year "all hell broke loose in baseball," as one book would have it, actually marked the passing of the game's most notorious demon.[31]

We will probably never know the full extent of Chase's illegal activities, or the motives behind them. One man who knew Chase early in his career held that he had "a corkscrew brain," while a later observer insisted that "Chase was a mental case. There was no question but what his mind was greatly disordered."[32] Perhaps this is true, but the implication that Chase was somehow not responsible for his actions is unconvincing. Perhaps his old teammate Roger Peckinpaugh summed him up best: "Any way you look at him, he was the greatest—the greatest first baseman and the greatest scoundrel."[33]

One

A Great Fun-Loving Boy

"Men who have no province, wanderers without a community, sojourners with a dwelling place, but with no home, citizens of the world, who have no local attachments, — in these days," wrote the philosopher Josiah Royce in 1909, "we all know of the existence of far too many such beings."[1] Royce, like many thinkers of his age, was concerned about the future of an increasingly urbanized, secularized, industrialized, and bureaucratized America, an America in which men were alienated from the land.[2] He and others like him wondered whether, in the words of Alan Trachtenberg, "the America fashioned on the frontier," the traditional, virtuous America celebrated by Frederick Jackson Turner in his famous 1893 address to the American Historical Society, could "survive the caldrons of the city."[3]

Though Royce himself, like Hal Chase, was a product of the frontier, a California boy who moved east to find fame in his chosen field, it seems unlikely that the bookish Harvard philosopher had ever heard of the celebrated baseball star. Yet Royce's gloomy description of the new American fits Chase to a tee. While Chase in some respects seemed the personification of the best of the American character — handsome, well-spoken, and a preternaturally gifted athlete — he was in other respects Royce's worst nightmare brought to life — a self-centered and incorrigibly corrupt mercenary whose only loyalty was to himself. In the cities which made possible his career in professional baseball, traditional notions of honesty, sportsmanship, and integrity seemed increasingly irrelevant.

Chase left California in 1905, only four years before Royce's lament, at the age of twenty-two. When he died, in 1947, he left behind, in addition to a reputation as the most crooked player in baseball history, two, or possibly three, ex-wives; one estranged legitimate child; and apparently at least one unacknowledged illegitimate offspring. His checkered career had taken him, as both hero and villain, to New York, Chicago, Buffalo, Cincinnati, New York again, his native Bay Area, Tucson, and Reno, before he finally ended his days as a lonely alcoholic on his sister and brother-in-law's ranch in rural northern California.

His peregrinations had some precedent in the Chase family. Two cousins,

Stephen Hall Chase and Josiah W. Chase, arrived in San Francisco on May 18, 1859, having taken passage on the schooner *Golden Rucket* from Boston and around Cape Horn. Stephen, known as Si, was twenty-five, and Josiah was twenty-three. Both were natives of Washington County, the easternmost part of the United States, where their fathers were farmers and loggers. They joined the thousands of fortune-seekers flocking to the West, of whose ambition the disgusted stay-at-home Henry David Thoreau wrote, "It matches the infatuation of the hindoos, who cast themselves under the car of Juggernaut."[4] The cousins were too late for the great Gold Rush, of course, and when they first reached California, they struggled; Josiah's first job was digging ditches in Mountain View, south of San Francisco, and they spent four years as laborers in the lumber camps around Lexington and Alma, south of San Jose. But California was booming, and they seem to have been ambitious and hard-working young men; a 1915 biographical sketch described Josiah upon his arrival in California "as a poor boy from the East, but with a bounteous supply of vigor and spirit, determined to make his way in the new western land."[5] The cousins saw their opportunity in the lumber business, with which they had some experience in Maine. Many farmers were settling in the Santa Clara Valley, which had already been adjudged excellent cropland, and their growing communities created a demand for redwood lumber from the Santa Cruz Mountains, which the cousins resolved to help fill.

Some of the early settlers in those mountains had cut and split timber, but mostly for their own use. Josiah and Stephen were the first full-time lumbermen in the area,[6] and Josiah was the first to bring lumber from the other side of the Santa Cruz Mountains into the Santa Clara Valley. The cousins bought 146 mountainside acres for $100 from Lyman Burrell, and in 1863 they built a mill and lumberyard on Summit Road. Soon there were eight sawmills in the Los Gatos vicinity, producing 600,000 board feet of lumber a day.[7] Josiah and Stephen founded the S. H. Chase Company in Lexington, south of San Jose, then moved it to Fourth and St. John Streets in San Jose in 1878. By the time of Hal Chase's birth, five years later, it was one of the most successful firms in Santa Clara County, and it remained a fixture in San Jose until 1960. The Chases provided much of the millwork for many fine houses in the area, including the famous Winchester mansion, which remains a tourist attraction as the Winchester Mystery House.[8]

The news of the cousins' success in the West convinced other family members to brave the long journey west from Maine. Josiah's brother Foster came out and ran the steam-powered sawmill in Lexington, which by 1867 was producing four thousand board feet of lumber a day, and had a small fruit ranch there as well. Josiah and Foster married sisters, the daughters of the neighboring Watkins F. Howell family.

News of Josiah and Si's success on the Pacific Coast inspired another pair of brothers, Elmer and James Edgar Chase, to follow in their footsteps. James Edgar, known by his middle name, was born on September 11, 1846, in East Machias, in Washington County. He was the son of Ephraim Chase, a descendent of Israel Chase, and Mary Gooch.[9] Edgar and Elmer set out from nearby Chase's Mill and traveled to California by way of the Panama isthmus. A third brother, Ephraim, a Mormon elder, arrived in 1882.

Edgar Chase was twenty-three when he arrived in California. He quickly showed enough ambition and drive to make starting a family seem practical and married Mary Cavenee in 1870. Mary was born on January 23, 1844, in Ohio to James Cavenee and Eliza Montgomery, originally from Alabama, but her family moved to Maine when she was a girl. Apparently she and Edgar had come to an understanding there before she journeyed out by covered wagon to meet him in California.

By February 13, 1883, when their fourth son Harold was born,[10] Edgar and Mary were renting a comfortable house at 321 University Avenue in Los Gatos. Edgar had worked his way up to become the manager of the Alviso branch of S. H. Chase, a post he held for the next seventeen years.[11]

The 1900 United States Census recorded Mary Chase as the mother of six children, although only four were living at home: Albert, or Bert, born in October 1872; Clifford, born in August 1877; Edwin, born in March 1881; and Harold. Edgar and Bert, the two oldest males, were day laborers; the younger boys were in school.[12]

Edwin was considered the best athlete in the family, but he died of appendicitis at the age of twenty-three. Two of Hal's other brothers, Oscar and Bert, followed the family tradition by entering the lumber business. Bert worked for S. H. Chase, while Oscar began his own firm, the Loma Prieta Lumber Company, in Pacific Grove, near Monterey. The last Chase brother, Clifford, was born with a crippled left leg, but even that handicap could not quench the physical vigor that ran so strongly in the family; for years he hunted and trapped in the Santa Cruz Mountains.[13]

Hal showed his athletic ability at an early age. He first played baseball while the family was living in Alviso, and San Jose baseball historian John E. Spalding wrote that "Hal Chase's first brush with authority over a baseball game came when he was twelve and his father disciplined him for accepting fifty cents to play in a Sunday game."[14] A University Avenue neighbor, Dorsey Purviance, later recalled that the boy was seldom without a ball, rock, or apple to throw at a nearby fence or post.[15] Another who knew young Hal remembered a mischievous teenager. "[A] great fun-loving boy was Hal," said Bill Robertson. "[H]e worked in a fruit stand for three dollars per week. Every time a butcher or grocer boy delivering went by, Chase, with the deft aim of a tail gunner, would throw an apple, banana, or any edible to hand, right to the bulls-eye between the first and third rib of the horse they were driving, causing the animal to about jump out of its harness and provoking great mirth for all onlookers plus despair to the owner [of the fruit stand], seeing his profits thrown away."[16]

Not all observers found such antics amusing, however. In 1896, the Los Gatos *Mail* editorialized huffily, "Los Gatos is just now the possessor of as mean

Chase at bat as a young player in California, wearing the uniform of the Mayer Bros. team. Chase's supposed amateur status as a student at Santa Clara College did not prevent him, at the age of twenty, from playing for money with the semipro team sponsored by a local clothier. *Santa Clara University Archives.*

a gang of young toughs as can be found anywhere. The gang consists of a number of young boys who go about breaking windows in unoccupied houses, stealing fruit and whatever else may be close at hand and rendering themselves nuisances in a general way."[17] The newspaper named no names, but it does not require much imagination to imagine a thirteen-year-old Chase as part of such "a gang of young toughs."

Hal became a star pitcher and second baseman for the Los Gatos High School baseball team, though he apparently paid more attention to baseball than to academics, for no record exists of his graduation.[18] It was around this time that Charles (Doc) Strub, later the president of the San Francisco Seals of the Pacific Coast League, first noticed Chase. "I was just a youngster myself," Strub recalled decades later, "and here was this boy, a farmer boy, he was wearing blue overalls, and he was catching, a left-handed catcher, mind you — well, I could scarcely believe my eyes...."[19]

The Bay Area was a hotbed of baseball activity in those days, and promising players had plenty of opportunities to test themselves in fast company. Young Hal played on weekends with the semiprofessional Soquel Giants, also known as the Grover Gulch Wildcats, a team "known as a rugged lot, made up of mainly loggers and ranch hands."[20] At the age of twenty he was asked to join the semi-pro team run by local clothier Emil Mayer. The Mayer Brothers team held its own against some top competition, including teams of local professionals.[21]

The weaknesses of his academic transcript and his participation in semi-pro games did not prevent nearby Santa Clara College, founded in 1851 as an outgrowth of the old Mission Santa Clara de Asis,[22] from recruiting him. At Santa Clara, according to the school's historian Gerald McKevitt, "baseball soared to a new zenith of popularity at the turn of the century — testimony perhaps to the continued presence of the high board fence that forced students to seek their entertainment within the college walls."[23] The school's academic reputation and Jesuitical discipline had little to do with Chase's decision to enroll in the fall of 1902. Santa Clara had established itself as arguably the best collegiate baseball program on the Pacific Coast, and in the spring of 1903 would defend the "inter-scholastic championship" against the University of California, Stanford University, and Belmont. "Everywhere there seems to be an intense desire to take from old Santa Clara College the pennant that has floated over her campus for so many years," noted the monthly campus magazine the *Redwood*, but the school did not intend to yield its dominance without a struggle.[24]

The choice of baseball coaches at Santa Clara showed how seriously the school took the sport. The coach when Chase arrived was Joe Corbett, the brother of boxing champion Jim Corbett and a former pitcher for the Baltimore National League team in the late 1890s. He resigned as coach in 1903 "through stress of business" and made a brief and unsuccessful comeback attempt with the National League team in St. Louis the following year. Corbett was followed as coach by twenty-five-year-old Charlie Graham, "an old boy [alumnus] and captain and catcher of the Sacramento League Team,"[25] and later the co-owner, with fellow alum Doc Strub, of the San Francisco Seals.[26] With men like Corbett and Graham in charge, and with games against professional and semiprofessional teams in addition to contests against its collegiate rivals, playing at Santa Clara was a superb preparation for professional baseball. This fact was apparently not lost on Chase. He supposedly studied civil engineering but again, as in high school, he apparently devoted more attention to baseball than to his studies; years later he supposedly bragged that he never attended a single class.[27] Indeed, the university has no record of his graduation, and a biographical form prepared years later by the Santa Clara athletic department includes the notation, "While Hal

Chase is listed in the 'Registry of Students' printed in the College catalog, I do not find him listed in the Registrar's Book or in the 'Librum Voti' (grade book) for the year."[28] He appears in the "Register of Students" in the official Santa Clara catalogues for 1902-1903 and 1903-1904 as "Harold E. Chase," and in a ledger book in the Santa Clara archives listing students registered for the 1902-1903 session as "Chase, Harold Erle."[29]

Chase's cavalier disregard of the rules ostensibly governing the student-athlete was hardly unique. One of his teammates at Santa Clara was Tom Feeney, who received his Bachelor's degree from Santa Clara in 1904, played for the San Jose Prune Pickers of the professional California League in 1906, and a year later returned to the college ranks to play on the St. Mary's College team that Chase coached.[30] Indeed, so pervasive was the practice of hiring mercenary ballplayers that in 1909 Santa Clara and St. Mary's, its principal athletic rival, felt compelled to negotiate an agreement which specified more stringent rules of eligibility for those seeking to play sports for the schools: "To discourage the recruitment of 'ringers,' 'deadheads,' and 'baseball bums' who traveled from team to collegiate team," noted McKevitt, "the two schools agreed that no student who at any time during the college year played on a team other than those representing his own college would be allowed to compete in any collegiate contest. Moreover, no student would be eligible to compete for more than six years, nor would he participate in any sport if he were taking fewer than three hours of college work daily."[31]

Such rules were not in force during Chase's time on campus, however, and he was the regular second baseman for Santa Clara in 1903 and 1904, even though he was lefthanded. Most baseball experts believe that a lefthanded second baseman is at a disadvantage, as he has to turn his whole body to throw to first base, whereas a righthander does not. Lefthanders have traditionally been restricted to pitching and playing first base or the outfield, where which arm they threw with was immaterial.

But Santa Clara already had a good player, Bill Whalen, at first base in the spring of 1903, and Chase's remarkable quickness and agility seemed to make up for any disadvantage which he might have suffered as a southpaw at second base. He also pitched and played catcher in several games, an early display of the athletic versatility which he would display for the rest of his baseball career. Time and again, even in the major leagues, Chase would delight in playing positions other than first base: second, shortstop, the outfield, even occasionally pitching. Perhaps the game came so easily to him that he had to invent challenges for himself, either by playing new positions or, less benignly, by seeing how much he could get away with in the way of cheating. At any rate, Chase seldom seems to have lost his sense of baseball as only a game, and it was this attitude which allowed him to cheat, to break with impunity the rules that others regarded as sacrosanct.

Another of Chase's college teammates was Bobby Keefe, who later pitched in the major leagues. With Cincinnati, Keefe was briefly a teammate of a

One—A Great Fun-Loving Boy

The 1903 Santa Clara College baseball team. Chase is third from the left in the top row, with his cap pushed back at a jaunty angle. Coach Charlie Graham is seated third from the right. *Santa Clara University Archives.*

mediocre lefthander named Sleepy Bill Burns; in fact, the two were related by marriage. Chase and Burns would later figure prominently in the Black Sox scandal, and Keefe, however innocently, may have been the initial link between the two.

At Santa Clara in 1903 Chase quickly set about winning a reputation for timely hitting, speed on the bases, and flashy, if occasionally erratic, fielding. He made significant contributions as Santa Clara beat the All-Stars, "an aggregation of Leaguers from San Jose and the suburbs," twice, and the Independents, a professional team from San Francisco, as well as collegiate rivals Stanford and California, the latter in a game in which Keefe outdueled future major league star Orval Overall.[32]

The *Redwood* called a 4–2 victory over the Pacific National League team from Butte, Montana, "without a doubt the greatest feat of the season." The game was played at Cycler's Park in San Jose, where Butte was training for the beginning of the Pacific National League season. Keefe limited the professionals to three hits and struck out nine, and was ably assisted by the fielding of his teammates: "These, the infield, Merle, Chase, Farry and Keleher, formed a Gibraltar of defense, so that nothing passed them, nothing frightened them.... Monaghan, the Butte secretary, an ex–Notre Dame man, and therefore able to judge, said that never before had he seen a college team that could outclass the Santa Clara organization."[33]

Chase finished the twenty-game season with a batting average of .302, only the fifth-best on the team, but led the team in stolen bases with sixteen and was second in hits and runs. Defensively he committed a team-high seventeen errors in 134 chances, for a fielding average of .873.[34]

Chase had apparently made plans for the summer long before the end of the college season, plans that reflected some of the changes in turn-of-the-century baseball, which was becoming an increasingly important activity in many American towns, and quite a few Canadian ones as well. Chase and Stanford pitcher Elmer Emerson announced that they planned to visit Emerson's relatives in Victoria, British Columbia.

Victoria had been the most important city in the province for a number of years, and its town baseball team was the unofficial provincial champion for thirty-three of the thirty-five years from 1866 to 1901. But the city's location on the southern tip of Vancouver Island, separated from the mainland by the Strait of Georgia, had become a distinct liability. After Vancouver, on the mainland, was selected as the western terminus of the Canadian Pacific Railway in 1885, Victoria's dominance began to wane. In the next fifteen years Vancouver's population had grown from 300 to 26,000, surpassing that of Victoria, and Vancouver's baseball team, the Terminals, won the first two championships of the newly reorganized British Columbia Amateur Base Ball League in 1901 and 1902. The backers of the Victoria team were determined to reestablish their city's preeminence, at least on the baseball field.[35]

On February 4, 1903, the Victoria *Daily Colonist* reported that the Victoria Baseball Club had decided to retain its amateur status and not to join a professional league proposed by L. H. Cohn, the owner of a team in Vancouver. At the end of the story a brief summary of the Victoria team's personnel noted that its catchers would include "a new player from California, who has lately decided to make Victoria his home."[36]

The unnamed new player was probably Chase, who joined the team in April along with Emerson, although he would spend more time at third base than at catcher. Chase later admitted that he had been paid $75 a month in Victoria, a figure later raised to $90, but neither he nor Emerson bothered to use a pseudonym.[37] College players of the time frequently played under their own names for semipro or even professional teams during the summers[38]; during his career at Santa Clara, Chase made a little money on the side by playing on Sundays in Hollister, about forty miles southeast, for four or five dollars a game. His association with Victoria was different, however. Chase was one of only two players on the club receiving a salary, while the others were to divide the team's profits, if any, at the end of the season.[39]

Before his debut with Victoria Chase participated in a game between two lower-level Victoria clubs, pitching for the Hillside Intermediates in their 8–7 victory over the Wanderers on April 25. His participation prompted a protest, later disallowed, by the Wanderers—perhaps the earliest, but by no means the gravest, controversy of his baseball career. An account of the game in the local newspaper mentioned Chase's "very tricky curves" and predicted that he would "prove himself a great addition to the senior team."[40]

On May 9, as Victoria beat the strong semipro team from Whatcom 7–5, Chase had two hits in three at bats, but had problems at third base, as he committed two errors. The *Daily Colonist* grumbled about the new man's performance in language that anticipated later complaints against him as a major leaguer: "Chase was not in the best of form yesterday.... Chase's every movement is the acme of grace, but style is not everything, and there were a couple of grounders which he might have at least stopped."[41]

Two weeks later, however, after Victoria had won five games in a row, the same newspaper was calling Chase "Victoria's star third baseman." He was still adjusting to his new position, but his remarkable abilities were obvious, and the *Daily Colonist* turned Victoria's relative isolation into a positive, as it kept Chase from the attention of professional teams: "As for Chase, it is lucky that we are a few miles away from the cities on the Sound, else he would have a contract coming his way that would keep him busy this summer traveling the circuit from Seattle to Los Angeles. He gets the ball across the diamond with the speed of an aeronaut dropping from a balloon just before the parachute opens."[42]

Chase got an opportunity to show his skills as "an all-around man" in Victoria's next game. Catcher Jack Smith suffered a hand injury in practice, so Chase moved to catcher against the Tacoma Athletic Club. After helping Victoria to two straight wins over Tacoma, his throwing inspired the *Daily Colonist* to yet another labored figure of speech: "Chase is certainly a whirlwind behind the bat, the Tacoma runners hugging the first bag with all the fear and trembling of a fledgling on its first attempt to cleave the air with its untried pinions."[43] His baserunning was dazzling, too. On July 2, as Victoria beat Portland's Multnomah Athletic Club 11–2, Chase stole second and third base on consecutive pitches in the first inning, then scored when the rattled Multnomah pitcher made a wild pickoff throw.

When star pitcher Jimmy Holness quit the Victoria team two days later, Chase had another opportunity to show off his versatility. On the day before he was scheduled to pitch against Everett, the *Daily Colonist* assessed the Californian's style on the mound: "His delivery is a most peculiar one, and the way he mixes up his fast and slow ones is a revelation...."[44]

Chase gave up ten hits and seven runs in his debut as a pitcher, but Victoria beat Everett 8–7. He walked two batters, hit two with pitches, and was charged with four wild pitches, but he also had six strikeouts and only one of the seven runs against him was earned. The *Daily Colonist* pronounced his pitching "most satisfactory" and added that "Chase's fielding was of the phenomenal order."[45]

On the next day, when Victoria beat Everett 9–7, Chase played yet another new position: left field. He had two hits, including a bases-loaded double, and one play he made in the outfield moved the *Daily Colonist* to extravagant prophesy: "Away hence in the dim futurity, say about in 1954, when Chase shall have earned the repose which comes to septuagenarians, he will often close his eyes and lapse into a daydream of the glory galore which came to him in the days when he was a sun among lesser orbs on the field of play. To the grandchildren (for who does not wish that he will leave a numerous progeny to hand down his fame to future ages) who will cluster around his knees and hang on his shoulder, he will recite his marvelous feats on the diamond and arouse their speechless wonderment. He will have many exploits to narrate, and among them will be the story of a one-handed catch taken on the sprint, with two men out and two runners stampeding for the home plate, but whose cherished hopes of butting into the run column proved to be of the stuff of which dreams are made."

By now he was unquestionably the brightest star on the team. "Fortune singles out certain individuals for especial distinction," reported the *Daily Colonist*. "Put Chase in any position in the field and it is a safe gamble that the sphere would be constantly hovering around him, and inviting him to do things, which never fail to win the very best going in the line of plaudits."[46]

The vision of Chase telling his grandchildren of his exploits would never come true, of course. By 1954 Hal Chase had been in his grave for seven years. He died estranged from his only son and never met his five grandchildren. He never even knew that the son who bore his name, the son who had tried and failed to get close to his famous, ill-starred father, would name his own first-born son Hal, or that his son and grandson would insist for years, in the face of overwhelming circumstantial evidence, that their infamous forebear was innocent of the charges that still stain his reputation and in all likelihood cost him election to the Hall of Fame.

Apparently Chase's stint as a pitcher was not achieved without cost, for a week later the *Daily Colonist* reported that he would fill in for the injured regular first baseman, Bernie Schwengers, despite "a very sore arm."[47] Ironically, in light of his future career, this assignment was considered a temporary expedient while Schwengers was out and his arm recovered: "It is understood that the management will put Chase behind the bat as soon as he is in shape...."[48]

Despite his struggles, Chase's abilities had begun to attract the attention of professional teams. On August 11 the *Daily Colonist* reported that Dan Dugdale, manager of the Seattle team in the Pacific National League, had "had his eyes on two of the Victoria team for some time," and on July 10 had extended formal offers to Chase and Emerson.

Dugdale's offer was delivered in dramatic fashion, according to the *Daily Colonist*. Emerson had been fishing peacefully on Foul Bay when his reverie was disturbed. "On the shingle a telegraph messenger stood waving a handful of paper like the pardon in the last act of a cheap melodrama. At the same time he kept his voice going like a juvenile fog alarm, until Emerson came to shore and received the message."

The 1904 Santa Clara College baseball team. Chase is standing second from the left. He clearly regarded college as merely a jumping-off point for his professional baseball career, as during his two years on campus he is not known to have attended a single class. *Santa Clara University Archives.*

Dugdale apparently assumed that the two young players would leap at the chance to join a full-fledged professional team. His telegram to Emerson read, in its entirety, "Send me your terms at once. Have Chase do likewise."

Chase and Emerson's answer to Dugdale was similarly pithy: "Thank you for offer. Victoria good enough for us."[49]

It was unlike Chase to decline an opportunity to make more money. Perhaps this was the point at which Victoria raised his salary from $75 to $90 a month.[50] The *Daily Colonist,* of course, attributed his dismissal of Dugdale to his sense of loyalty: "Emerson and Chase have become attached to Victoria ... and didn't care to leave, not even to play ball at a good salary offered by Dugdale." The *Daily Colonist* also revealed that Chase, Emerson, and a third Victoria player, Burnes, had earlier declined an offer from Cohn to play for Vancouver.[51]

Victoria won three of its last four games of the season. On August 12 Emerson pitched a one-hit, eighteen-strikeout effort against Port Angeles, winning 5–0. Catcher Chase chipped in with two hits and two runs batted in and erased the only Port Angeles runner who attempted to steal with "a beautiful throw." Nine days later Victoria beat a "Picked Nine" of local players 19–3. Chase "caught his usual good game, and amused the audience by making a couple of good slides."

On September 1 the Victoria Baseball Club announced that it had concluded the season $304 in the red. The season was a greater success artistically than financially, however. Victoria won twenty-three games and lost only ten. In the twenty-nine games for which box scores survive, Chase batted .353, scored 29 runs, led the team with 3 home runs, and posted a slugging percentage of .563.[52] He had become the star of the team, overshadowing local favorites Holness and Schwengers and even his fellow import Emerson, who pitched a no-hitter, and went back to California having established himself as a player with a bright professional future. He returned to the Santa Clara team in 1904, but he would not remain in the amateur ranks for long.

In February 1904 hopes were high on the Santa Clara campus. The *Redwood* reported that "if we succeed in winning the series arranged with St. Vincent's College, Los Angeles, the present team will perhaps become historic," and the season began encouragingly. Santa Clara won three out of five from Mayer Brothers, beat Stanford once to even their season series (a third game ended in a tie) and on February 5 beat the Reliance Club, "the fastest aggregation of semi-professionals in the state," 9–2.

Chase, back for his second varsity season, was no longer exclusively a second baseman. Against Reliance he played catcher, and contributed a triple and a sacrifice to the Santa Clara offense. Defensively, he was a sensation: "The two double plays of catcher Chase deserve special notice and especially the heretofore unheard of stunt of securing a bunted ball, tagging the runner and catching a man on second."[53] Chase's victim on this unprecedented play was his old acquaintance Doc Strub, who was trying to lay down a sacrifice bunt to advance a runner on first base. The cat-quick Chase, anticipating the tactic, stepped around Strub and grabbed the ball just as it left the bat, then threw to first base to double up the runner. Three decades later, after fifteen years in the major leagues, Chase would still remember "the day I caught a bunt off Doc Strub's bat" as his biggest thrill in baseball.[54]

But Chase was not through demonstrating his all-around ability. In his next game he excelled as the other half of Santa Clara's battery, pitching an 8–4 complete-game victory against Stanford. He also had two hits, including an inside-the-park home run to right-center in the second inning, and a stolen base. He gave up just four hits and two walks and struck out eight, and probably would not have yielded even four runs if not for Santa Clara's five errors. He nearly hit another home run in the fifth inning, but loafed on the bases and was thrown out; according to "a local reporter" quoted in the *Redwood*, "Chase put the ball over the chapel in left field, scoring Farry, but he was caught going second [sic]."[55]

On February 7, against his former team Mayer Brothers, second baseman Chase had two of Santa Clara's four hits off his Victoria teammate Elmer Emerson and scored the only run of the game on a long home run. His winning blow gave another old friend some exercise: "Bill Whalen, Mayer's left fielder was seen dashing madly toward the Senior's tennis court, while our reliable hitter was making the entire circuit, landing safe at home just as the perspiring fielder secured the heavy drive and was turning to throw out the runner who had already taken his seat among admiring comrades."[56]

On March 1, against Stanford in Palo Alto, Chase was back on the mound, and his "star-pitching ... aroused the other players" to an 11–0 blowout. "The explanation was brief; Stanford could not find Chase; only once did they succeed in making the necessary connections and not even once did they go to first on balls." As if his one-hit, no-walk, seven-strikeout performance were not spectacular enough, he added four hits in five trips, including a triple, and scored two runs.[57]

Once again, as during the previous summer in British Columbia, Chase's exploits attracted the attention of the professionals. On March 5 Santa Clara went to Los Angeles to play St. Vincent's (later Loyola Marymount University[58]), the Southern California champion and winner of nineteen straight games. The eagerly anticipated clash between the two top college teams did not live up to expectations; Santa Clara led 11–1 after seven innings and coasted to a 13–8 victory. Second baseman Chase had three hits, including a double, in six trips, scored three runs, and had three of his team's remarkable total of sixteen stolen bases.

The Los Angeles *Times*, reporting on Santa Clara's smashing triumph, declared that "The second baseman for the victors is the fastest ever seen in an amateur game in Los Angeles," a judgment with which James Morley, the manager of the defending champion Los Angeles Angels of the professional Pacific Coast League, evidently agreed. After the game, which Morley had umpired, he quietly signed Chase to his first professional contract. By doing so he got the jump on a Pacific Coast League rival; Henry Harris, owner of the San Francisco Seals, had had his eye on Chase for some time and had reportedly told manager Charlie Irwin to sign the youngster.[59]

At the time, however, the biggest baseball story in Los Angeles was the upcoming exhibition series between the Angels and the visiting Chicago Colts (later renamed the Cubs) of the National League.[60] Perhaps the Colts' best player was team captain and first baseman Frank Chance, a California native who was well known to Los Angeles fans. "The Peerless Leader," as he was known, would later play a significant role in Chase's career.

The series was rich in symbolic value. The Pacific Coast League was officially a minor league, but until that spring it had been an independent, or "outlaw," league, and a thorn in the side of organized baseball. The major leagues had no franchises further west than St. Louis, and the Pacific Coast League, with its milder weather and longer playing season, provided the majors with some real competition for desirable talent, thereby driving up player salaries. Organized baseball's efforts to bring the Pacific Coast League into its fold finally bore fruit on February 2, 1904, at a meeting in the San Francisco office of Pacific Coast League president Eugene Bert. Bert, Morley, and Harris represented the Pacific

Coast League, while Byron Bancroft (Ban) Johnson, the founder and president of the American League; Ned Hanlon, the sly manager of the National League Brooklyn Superbas; and James A. Hart, president of the Colts, represented organized baseball.

Hanlon and Morley were already locked in a struggle over the services of Frank (Pop) Dillon, the Angels' first baseman and captain. Dillon, who had flopped in earlier major league trials in Pittsburgh, Detroit, and Baltimore, had batted .360 and stolen forty-three bases in leading Los Angeles to the 1903 pennant.[61] Hanlon, figuring that Dillon would be an improvement over his incumbent first baseman, the aging Jack Doyle, signed Dillon to a contract for the 1904 season. But Morley revealed that shortly before signing with Brooklyn Dillon had signed a contract to remain in Los Angeles in 1904.[62]

The dispute threatened to disrupt the harmonious tone of the meeting, but the conferees voted to submit all such disputes to arbitration rather than hold up negotiations. The Pacific Coast League agreed to sign the National Agreement and submit to the governance of the National Commission, of which Johnson was a member. With the agreement, the empire of organized baseball had achieved its manifest destiny, stretching from sea to sea. The series between Morley's Angels and Hart's Colts was to be the first visible symbol of the new peace.

That peace, however, was threatened almost immediately, as Morley and Hanlon renewed their dispute over Dillon. Initially, Morley had every reason to believe that he would triumph over Hanlon. A sympathetic columnist in *The Sporting News* noted that "Manager Morley has a contract with Player Frank Dillon, which antedates the one signed with Brooklyn and how anybody can award this player to Hanlon is more than I can see." Ban Johnson himself admitted that Los Angeles had first claim to the player.[63] But "Foxy Ned" Hanlon had no intention of losing Dillon on a legal technicality. In late February, but before the settlement with the Pacific Coast League had been formally ratified, Hanlon convinced the National Association of Minor Leagues to demand that the Pacific Coast League yield Dillon as a condition of admission to organized baseball. Morley refused, whereupon Hanlon warned that "If Dillon does not play with Brooklyn there will be no national agreement."[64]

Hanlon's brinkmanship succeeded. An editorial in *The Sporting News* noted that "The expenses of the war of 1903 were enormous," and predicted that the other Pacific Coast League magnates, led by Bert and Harris, would not wish to renew their costly campaign against organized baseball. Morley's peers decided that Dillon was a small price to pay for peace and blandly voted to waive claim to him without Morley's consent, thereby quashing what *The Sporting News* called "the spirit of sedition" exemplified by Morley's stubbornness.[65]

Morley, of course, was furious. He insisted that the National Association had no jurisdiction in the Dillon case, since it involved a dispute with a major league club, and that the other Pacific Coast League owners had no right to dispose of one of his players. "I can see the fine Italian hand of Ned Hanlon in this business," fumed Morley, "and that name of Foxy Ned is certainly well earned and served."66

Morley still insisted that Dillon would be in the Angels' starting lineup on opening day, but he was obviously fighting a lost battle. Bert had instructed umpire Jack O'Connell not to let Dillon play, despite an injunction obtained by Morley, but Los Angeles beat Oakland anyway, by a score of 4–3. Shortly thereafter the National Commission officially awarded Dillon to Brooklyn, the peace settlement was duly ratified, and Morley had to find a new first baseman.67

Initially, at least, few observers envisioned Chase as that man. The Los Angeles *Times,* seeking to compare Chase to one of the visiting Colts, picked not first baseman Chance, but the man who played beside him in the Chicago infield: "The newcomer is very much such a looking lad as Johnny Evers, the sensational second baseman of the Chicago Nationals." Chase was described as "a loose-jointed fellow with considerable ground-covering ability," traits which seemed more appropriate to a middle infielder than a first baseman. The Los Angeles *Herald* predicted that Chase "may be given a try out on the initial sack," but placed more emphasis on the youngster's athletic versatility. One report called him a potentially outstanding pitcher and catcher, but made no mention of the position which he would play so spectacularly for fifteen major league seasons: "Chase is said to be a first-class addition to the team in several ways, as he can perform in a creditable manner in the box and behind the bat as well, and is likely to become one of the stars of the league before the season is over." The *Herald* saw him primarily as a "general utility man," suggesting that his versatility might make him more valuable as a reserve: "Chase is an all-round man.... He is said to be a good man with the stick and has played every position on the diamond.... He is fast and shifty on his feet, uses his head at all times and should make good in any position."68

In Santa Clara the news of his defection was greeted philosophically, especially since Santa Clara beat St. Vincent 7–3 and 17–3 without him. The *Redwood* celebrated the end of a successful season ("To say that we are entirely satisfied with the work of the season, is to put it mildly") and argued that the ability of the team to keep winning despite the loss of Chase and various other misfortunes merely "aroused us to a realization of our hidden strength.... The team of '04 will long be remembered in baseball circles."69

Chase made his debut for Los Angeles on March 27. He was hitless in three at bats but drove in a run on a sacrifice fly as the Angels beat Oakland 5–2. The *Herald* raved about the newcomer, although the story contained one of the first examples of what was to become a persistent confusion about his age: "Chase, the Santa Clara college player who won Morley's heart in the college game here a month ago [*sic*], created a favorable impression. Chase is just a boy, not yet out of his 'teens, but he bats and fields as though he had seen a ball game before. He accepted all his chances at first, and while his stick work did not cut much figure in the percentage column, it helped to win the game. His first effort was a neat sacrifice, and twice he went out on long flies to the outfield that the swift northern runners literally picked off the Chutes fence." Even the man whose place he had taken was impressed: "Dillon, who has been coaching Chase during his practice here, says the boy has the making of a National leaguer."[70]

After his second game, a 3–0 victory over Portland on March 29, Chase gained a brief notice in the national press. *Sporting Life* noted that "Chase, Los Angeles's new first baseman, played a star game and got two doubles."[71] Soon he was recognized as one of the brightest young stars in the Pacific Coast League. On May 7 *Sporting Life* reported that "Los Angeles has unearthed a rising young first baseman named Chase, who is a hard hitter." In late June the same publication reported that "Los Angeles has in first baseman Chase one of the most promising young players brought out this season. He is a fine fielder and a hard and timely hitter."[72] Back in Santa Clara the *Redwood* noted with vicarious pride that Chase had been "called away to astonish the State by filling Captain Dillon's shoes with such wonderful success," and argued that Chase's performance with the professionals reflected glory on the whole team: "We may judge of all from one, from Chase who solved the Dillon controversy by going to Los Angeles and winning universal admiration."[73]

Still, despite the presence of this bright new star the Angels had problems defending their championship. They finished the first half of the Pacific Coast League's split schedule with a 59–52 record, behind Seattle and Tacoma. In the second half of the season Los Angeles posted a 60–45 mark, finishing in a virtual tie for first place with Tacoma.[74] Morley, seeking every advantage in the race with Tacoma, signed Frank Chance after the end of the National League season.[75] Chance hit .274 for Los Angeles and split his time between first base and catcher, his original position. Perhaps his most notable moment with the Angels came when he assaulted an umpire in the eighth inning of a loss to Seattle.[76]

When Chance played first base Chase usually played second base, though he also saw action in the outfield. Nine years later, perhaps remembering their time together in Los Angeles, Yankee manager Chance would again move Chase to second base, with disastrous results, but in 1904 Chase seemed to have little difficulty readjusting to the position he had played so well in college. On September 4 the *Herald* reported that he played second base "faultlessly" and did "some fast work as middle man in a double play." Two days later, against San Francisco, "Hal Chase was the star of the day...." On September 8, in reporting a Los Angeles defeat, the *Herald* nonetheless pointed out that Chase, "as usual, put up a star game."[77]

Chase's statistics in his first professional season were unspectacular. He batted a mediocre .279 with only two home runs and finished eleventh in fielding and second in errors among Pacific Coast League first basemen, although he was third in putouts and assists.[78] But his speed (thirty-seven stolen bases) and agility marked him as a player of extraordinary promise and attracted the attention of a major league team some three thousand miles away. In mid–October *Sporting Life* reported that the New York Highlanders of the American League had drafted pitcher Eustace James (Doc) Newton and first baseman Hal Chase of the Los Angeles club.[79]

The Highlanders were the newest members of the American League. Ban Johnson, the president and founder of the American League, had boldly claimed major league status for his new circuit in 1901, but knew that it would never be considered a true major league until it had a successful team in New York.[80] The National League, unsurprisingly, had attempted to block all attempts to place an American League rival in the city, thanks largely to the efforts of Andrew Freedman, who owned the Giants until 1902. Freedman, taking full advantage of his ties to Tammany Hall, threatened to have the city cut a new street through any site on which the American League expressed interest in building a ballpark.[81] It had taken Johnson some time to line up backers with the necessary clout to overcome such threats, and when they finally appeared, in 1902, he was none too choosy about their reputations.

Johnson's old friend Joe Vila, a New York sportswriter, put him in touch with Frank J. Farrell, a former bartender who was now the owner of a racing stable and a notorious racketeer. His luxurious "House with the Bronze Door" at 33 West Thirty-third Street was one of Manhattan's best-known gambling establishments.[82] Farrell's establishment was thought to be largely immune from police raids thanks to his intimate friendship with the legendary policeman William S. (Big Bill) Devery, by general consensus perhaps the most corrupt public official in the city.

Farrell and Devery: these were the men to whom Ban Johnson, "the sworn foe of every kind of baseball crooks and of gambling on baseball,"[83] entrusted the most important franchise in his league. He sold them the troubled Baltimore franchise for $18,000, shifted it to New York, and arranged for Clark Griffith, a longtime National League star who had earlier jumped to the Chicago American League team, to take over as player-manager. Farrell and Devery agreed to buy a piece of property belonging to the New York Institute for the Blind at 165th Street and Broadway and build a new ballpark. At first the trip from City Hall took almost an hour, but in 1906 the long-awaited West Side Subway reached the park. Because the site was one of the highest in Manhattan, and because Farrell and Devery's frontman as president was the respectable coal merchant Joseph W. Gordon (the Gordon Highlanders were one of the most famous regiments in the British army), the new team was nicknamed the Highlanders.[84]

They finished a mediocre fourth in 1903, their inaugural season, but in the following year they narrowly missed winning the pennant, thanks in large part to an extraordinary effort by pitcher Jack Chesbro, who won an astonishing forty-one games. Now they hoped that the addition of Newton and Chase would bring them their first championship.

Newton, a lefthander, was arguably the best pitcher in the Pacific Coast League, having won seventy-four games in two seasons, but had already had inconclusive major league trials with Cincinnati and Brooklyn.[85] He would win only nineteen games in five seasons with the Highlanders. Chase was the real prize, even though he was still an unknown quantity to many Eastern baseball fans. William F. H. Koelsch, who covered New York's major league teams for

Sporting Life, initially reported that the Highlanders had drafted a first baseman named "Sam" Chase, and reported that he was nineteen years old when he was in fact already twenty-one, thereby perpetuating the confusion about Chase's age.[86]

Despite such confusion the dour Griffith had heard plenty about the young first baseman from sources who might be expected to know major league talent when they saw it. Chase had been highly recommended by Bill Lange and George Van Haltren, two former teammates of Griffith's in Chicago now playing out their careers in the Pacific Coast League; Lange even compared Chase to Frank Chance, with whom Chase would cross swords years later. Griffith's friend Danny Long, another former major leaguer, went even further, telling Griffith that "Chase is the best young player I have seen in a lifetime, and I have no fear about him not making good."[87]

Other experts shared Long's enthusiasm. *The Sporting News* reported that Jake Beckley, the star first baseman of the St. Louis Cardinals, had seen Chase in action and had been impressed: "He says Chase is a sure enough wonder, and he predicts that Chase will make good in the East next season. [Oakland manager] Pete Lohman says the 'kid' is the best first-baseman on the Coast today, barring none. Several other old-timers who know a ball player when they see one, join in predicting a great career for Chase as a ball tosser. And to think that Manager Morley, who practically discovered Chase, has to lose him. Isn't that hard luck?"[88]

In fact Morley had no intention of giving up so easily. Had it not been for the provisions of the National Agreement which called for the orderly drafting of minor league players by major league clubs, he stood to make thousands of dollars off Chase and Newton. The Los Angeles *Times,* remembering the Dillon affair, called the National Agreement "that instrument of graft by which the Pacific Coast League has been buncoed out of everything good that it ever had and ever hopes to possess," and called the draft "a big league scheme to steal two players from each Coast League team."[89] The San Francisco *Chronicle* reported that the Los Angeles manager was "greatly exercised" over the loss of his two stars, having planned to keep them until the interest of major league teams had peaked, then sell them to the highest bidder, as would have been standard practice before the Pacific Coast League signed the National Agreement. He had earlier refused an offer of $2,500 for Newton, but under the new drafting laws would get only $750 for his star pitcher. "Chase, too, could have been disposed of next year for a round sum," noted the *Chronicle,* "and the draft of the two means a substantial loss for the Los Angeles magnate in money and for his team in material."[90] Morley, however, still smarting over the loss of Dillon the year before, had one more ace up his sleeve.

Two

A More Brilliant Player Does Not Wear a Uniform

Chase may already have had the seeds of corruption in him when the Highlanders drafted him, but no city in America was more calculated to turn the head of a young man from the provinces than New York, "the diamond stick-pin on the shirtfront of America."[1] No other city in America, or indeed in the world, could match its growth — the city's population grew 66 percent, from just over three million to almost five million, in the first decade of the twentieth century[2] — or its flash and glamour. "There is a great movement going on about you, a surge of struggling humanity," commented one observer; "and there is a great roar, the metallic-electric hum of power in action...." Another contemporary observer exulted, "The thrill, the life, the movement, the strength of the city — how they stand for the most representative Americanism!"[3] New York was the nexus of the worlds of finance, art, sport, journalism, and politics; frequently, it seemed, the only thing New Yorkers had in common besides an obsession with money was an obsession with risking it, as gambling "flourished, unimpeded, in every quarter of the city." Rupert Hughes's intrepid reporter "Ananias" Blake comments in *The Real New York*, published in 1904: "'Is there any gambling in New York?' you ask. Why, there's almost nothing else."[4]

Blake exaggerated only slightly, at least as far as New York's wealthy were concerned, and in the Gilded Age they were so much wealthier and more plentiful than ever before that the traditional standard for determining a truly wealthy man had to be raised. "Up to this time for one to be worth a million of dollars was to be rated as a man of fortune, but now bygones must be bygones," observed Ward McAllister, the arbiter of Gotham's high society, in 1890. "New York's ideas as to values, when fortune was named, leaped boldly up to ten millions, fifty millions, one hundred millions; and the necessities and luxuries followed suit." Highrollers, swells, hustlers, plungers, dandies, con men, gangsters, and tycoons mingled in the illegal casinos in New York and, during the summer, in Saratoga, betting huge sums of money on horses or cards or dice or pool. John W. "Bet-a-Million"

Gates, the Wall Street plunger who ran a brokerage company with his son out of the Waldorf-Astoria, explained his philosophy thusly: "For me there's no fun in just betting a few thousand ... I want to put down enough to hurt the other feller if he loses, and enough to hurt me if I lose." Apparently he felt some pain one August afternoon in 1902 when he lost several hundred thousand dollars at the race track in Saratoga, for he repaired to Richard Canfield's Club House that night to recoup his losses at faro. By ten o'clock he was down an additional $150,000, but by dawn he had won back that sum plus another $150,000.[5]

Saratoga became the regular summer haunt of New York sportsmen, who were attracted to the rural setting by the famous race track and Canfield's equally famous casino. Saratoga's popularity was such that in the early 1900s New York's bookmakers arrived en masse every summer on a special train called the Cavanagh Special, named after John Cavanagh, bookie to the rich and famous.

Among those arriving on the Cavanagh Special in 1904 was twenty-one-year-old Arnold Rothstein, nicknamed "the Brain," a pool hustler and crap shooter who amassed a considerable fortune and became a leading figure in organized crime in New York. Rothstein found Saratoga a congenial spot. He spent every summer there from 1904 to 1909, when he married a showgirl named Carolyn Greene; the journalist Herbert Bayard Swope, later the editor of the New York *World*, was his best man. On their wedding night, Rothstein supposedly borrowed his bride's jewelry as collateral for his gambling. Rothstein eventually opened his own gambling club in Saratoga, the Brook, which was a huge success, though one August night, when the notorious plunger Sam Rosoff got up $400,000, Rothstein was sufficiently concerned to call his good friend Charles Stoneham, who had a cottage in Saratoga, for emergency backup funds. Stoneham immediately took $300,000 from his wall safe and sent it to Rothstein, though by the time the money arrived Rosoff had lost his winnings and an additional $100,000.

Rothstein also ran a casino on West Forty-sixth Street in New York, where Bet-a-Million Gates's son Charles reportedly lost $40,000 one night in 1910 betting on roulette and faro to celebrate his recovery from an appendicitis operation. Among those who worked for Rothstein in Saratoga were Charles (Lucky) Luciano, Meyer Lansky, Frank Costello, Legs Diamond, Waxey Gordon, and Dutch Schultz, all of whom went on to notable careers in organized crime. Rothstein's name was linked with Chase's in the fixing of the 1919 World Series, but "the Brain" was never formally accused in the case. He was shot dead in 1928 when he was slow paying a $340,000 debt incurred in a card game which he insisted had been rigged.[6]

Another notable inhabitant of this world was the *bon vivant* Diamond Jim Brady. With his personal fortune of $12 million; his collection of 26,000 diamonds, including those decorating his underwear; and his gift of a $10,000 gold-plated bicycle to Lillian Russell, Brady raised what Thorstein Veblen derided as conspicuous consumption almost to an art form. "Diamonds larger than door knobs," Brady advised, "should never be worn except in the evening."[7] One of his typical post-gambling repasts included three dozen bluepoint oysters, a quart of *potage ambassadeur,* a whole roast chicken *demi deuil,* and two four-pound lobsters, plus a cake for dessert. Diamond Jim — who might have been expected to know — insisted that Frank Farrell's "House with the Bronze Door" on West Thirty-third Street served the best steaks and broiled lobster in town.[8]

When Farrell opened his place in the fall of 1891, his only other business was a saloon on Sixth Avenue. In 1897, however, when his friend Asa Bird Gardiner was elected district attorney on an anti-reform platform, Farrell branched out, opening a string of three hundred pool halls which served as fronts for bookmakers taking illegal bets on horse races. A few years after opening on Thirty-third Street, Farrell and his partners hired Stanford White, the most celebrated architect of the age and an arch-hedonist in his own right, to make the place even more sumptuous. White demolished the interior and went to Europe and Asia with half a million dollars to buy furnishings. Among the fixtures he brought back was the huge door, supposedly from the palace of a Venetian doge, which gave the place its name.[9] Farrell, whose discretion was reflected in "a bland fleshy face that concealed everything he knew,"[10] reportedly spent some $25,000 a year on food and refreshments for his patrons, which was apparently money well spent: according to one historian, "The casino was conducted with the quiet decorum of a gentleman's club. Patrons were served an elaborate buffet supper at midnight; the finest cigars, wines and liquors were continuously available for those who wished them; no money was accepted for any of these refreshments. It was said that at least fifty thousand dollars changed hands every night."[11] One June evening in 1898, a wealthy Englishman supposedly won $165,000 at roulette there, then gave the entire sum to charity. On December 1, 1902, Gardiner's successor, the crusading William Travers Jerome, led a raid on the place, but White's massive portal held the police at bay long enough for Farrell's guests to escape through the tunnel connecting the house to the property next door.[12]

Crusading district attorneys aside, Farrell profited from his cozy relationship with those sworn to uphold the law. Among these was the cartoonish figure of Big Bill Devery. Devery had joined the police force in 1878 and within fifteen years, thanks to the influence of Boss Croker's Tammany Hall, had worked his way up to the rank of captain. In 1894 the owner of an East Side brothel testified before the Lexow Committee that he had paid Devery $500 when he opened his house; Devery was subsequently indicted on criminal charges, but acquitted on a technicality and reinstated. In 1898 he was promoted to inspector and then, after some political chicanery by Mayor Robert A. Van Wyck, to chief.[13] "Under Devery," wrote one historian, "the police department of New York was transformed into a shakedown and blackmail ring for the benefit of Tammany politicians."[14] Even Tammany admitted that he "was responsible for the evils in the 'Red Light' district, and also for the open protection by the police of poolrooms, policy shops, gambling houses, and other dens of vice." So egregious was his administration that in 1901 the state government was moved to pass a law replacing the office of police chief with that of a police commissioner.

The effect of this legislation was muted somewhat when Michael G. Murphy, the newly appointed commissioner, immediately named Devery his first deputy. Calling Devery "a foolish and vulgar person" and noting "his illiteracy, his impudence, his coarse vanity," the reform-minded New York *Times* editorialized that "To aquiesce in Devery's retention at the head of the force would be for the State administration to consent to the practical nullification of the legislation which it has enacted to improve the conditions in New York."[15] A not entirely unsympathetic account of Devery from 1901, shortly after he had returned to power under Murphy, described him as "an individual with the face of a retired pugilist.... a flesh-and-blood ruffian with the humors belonging to a man of Hibernian descent and a weight of some twenty stone."[16] When the reformer Seth Low was elected mayor, his first official act after his inauguration on January 1, 1902, was to remove Murphy and Devery from office.[17]

When Ban Johnson decided to move the Baltimore franchise to New York, to compete directly with the Giants, he knew he needed friends in high places to counter the power of Andrew Freedman, the owner of the Giants and a Tammany Hall insider, who had vowed to use his political connections to build a road through any site on which the American Leaguers attempted to build a ballpark. Sportswriter Joe Vila, sympathetic to Johnson's plight, hooked the American League magnate to Farrell and Devery, whose pull at Tammany was equal to Freedman's and who had the cash to give the transplanted Orioles a realistic chance of survival.

Johnson had secretly leased property belonging to the New York Institute for the Blind in Washington Heights, the highest part of Manhattan Island. There, just off Broadway between 165th and 168th Streets, nine blocks beyond the Polo Grounds, the home of the Giants, the American League hurriedly built a new ballpark, called Hilltop Park. The contractor was Thomas F. McAvoy, a former police inspector and Tammany leader.

Johnson announced that the president of the club was Joseph W. Gordon, a bland and respectable coal merchant and another Tammany stalwart. The team would be known as the Highlanders, in part because of the new ballpark's location, and in part because of the team president's surname: the Gordon Highlanders were a famed Scottish regiment. But Gordon was just a figurehead; the principals among the seven stockholders were Farrell and Devery. After the 1903 season, Farrell ended the sham; Gordon disappeared from the team hierarchy and Farrell became the president in title as well as in fact.[18]

This, then, was the milieu into which Chase would be plunged upon joining the Highlanders. The team was desperate for a star attraction who could win fans away from the Giants, who still had much the upper hand in the affections of the city's fans. As one man who grew up near Hilltop Park recalled, "The Highlanders weren't baseball—the Giants were baseball in those days."[19] The Giants boasted stars like Joe McGinnity, Roger Bresnahan, Mike Donlin, Bill Dahlen, and—most notably—two men who were to figure prominently in Chase's later career, the pitcher Christy Mathewson and the pugnacious manager

John McGraw. The Highlander roster boasted such well-known talents as Jack Chesbro, Willie Keeler, and Kid Elberfeld, but they had first risen to prominence with other teams in other cities. Chase was to be the first star to make his major league debut with the team. Moreover, John Ganzel, the veteran whose position he would be trying to win, had announced that he planned to buy and play for a minor league team in Grand Rapids, in his native Michigan, unless the Highlanders gave him a $600 raise. The Highlanders refused either to grant him the raise or release him from his contract, so Ganzel became a holdout. The situation seemed ideal for Chase's debut.[20]

In late January 1905 Griffith, whose nickname "the Old Fox" testified to his sly nature, was characteristically cautious in discussing his hopes for Chase: "Should Ganzel decide to stay away, I have [John] Anderson to fall back on, and if Chase lives up to his reputation the club will be well taken care of as regards first base." In reality, though, the first base job was Chase's to lose; even Griffith admitted that Anderson, primarily an outfielder, was "not the best at the initial sack."[21]

With every indication that he would be able to step right into New York's starting lineup, Chase agreed to a $2,000 salary plus his expenses in traveling east. But when the team assembled for spring training at Montgomery, Alabama, in early March, Chase was absent.

Initially his absence caused little concern. Griffith assumed that Chase and veteran shortstop Norman (Kid) Elberfeld, who was holding out for a higher salary, would soon join the team. In an uncharacteristic burst of optimism he even predicted that the Highlanders, with the addition of young talent like Chase, Newton, and pitcher Bill Hogg, would win the pennant that had barely eluded them in 1904.[22] The Ganzel situation remained unresolved, but by this time Griffith was willing to predict publicly that Chase would be more than an adequate replacement when he finally showed up.

The Highlanders attempted to downplay the youngster's absence. They announced that Griffith had granted him permission to remain out West "until after the spring trip" due to the death of his brother Edwin.[23] But when several weeks passed with no word from their new first baseman the club began to panic. *Sporting Life* reported that Griffith was trying to trade the rights to Chase's services to Portland of the Pacific Coast League in return for veteran first baseman Dirty Jack Doyle, a onetime star with Baltimore and the New York Giants whose best days were far behind him, and the man whom Ned Hanlon had let go in favor of Pop Dillon, giving Chase his big break in Los Angeles.[24] No such deal was forthcoming, although Griffith maintained sufficient interest in Doyle to sign him in an emergency a few months later.

Speculation about Chase's absence increased. Some wondered if the youngster had "lost his nerve," but those who had seen him play in California insisted "that the kid has already shown his ability to make good, by his brilliant work with the Los Angeles Club." Others suspected that Morley was behind Chase's nonappearance.[25]

The speculation ended on March 14, when Griffith received a telegram from Chase in which the young first baseman indicated that Morley was indeed preventing him from reporting to the New York camp. Griffith promptly wired Ban Johnson, asking the American League president to take immediate action against Morley. No one doubted the truth of Chase's story, especially after Newton admitted that Morley had tried to persuade him to remain in California as well.

The pitcher had ignored the Los Angeles owner; Chase, however, seemed more inclined to listen.[26] Perhaps he sincerely did not want to leave the West Coast; apart from his summer in Victoria Chase had never lived outside California.[27] Perhaps he hoped to play Morley off against the Highlanders with the aim of landing a bigger contract. In fact, though, Chase was merely a pawn in a deeper game between the Pacific Coast League, which was already wondering whether giving up its independent status had been wise, and the rest of organized baseball, which was determined to avoid a return to the costly bidding war for talent which had prevailed before the February 1904 peace conference.

The Highlanders got off to a good start without Chase. They won their first four exhibition games against local teams in Montgomery and in Vicksburg, Mississippi, using Anderson and catchers Red Kleinow and Jim McGuire at first base. Elberfeld finally reported for duty, and most observers believed that it was only a matter of time before Chase eluded Morley and joined the team as well.[28]

When the Highlanders reached New Orleans on Tuesday, March 21, the New York *Times* reported that Chase had left California on the previous Friday. The relief in the Highlander camp was short-lived, however, because on the following day the *Times* reversed itself and reported that Chase had "decided to remain on the Pacific Coast and has signed a contract to play with the Los Angeles team during the coming season."[29]

R. G. Arrington, writing in *Sporting Life*, predicted a quick end to such foolishness. He reminded his readers that the Pacific Coast League was now bound by the rulings of the National Commission, which had the power to expel a player from organized baseball for failing to honor a legal contract. "Chase has accepted $200 advance money, and he took up the railroad ticket sent him by the New York Club to come east," wrote Arrington. "As he belongs to the New York Club it is only a matter of time before he will have to report to New York or not play ball."[30]

The audacious Morley, however, disputed this assertion. He claimed that when New York drafted Chase and Newton it had violated the terms under which the Pacific Coast League had consented to become a part of organized baseball. At the February 1904 peace conference, said Morley, the men representing organized baseball, one of whom was Ban Johnson, had agreed that no Pacific Coast League players would be drafted by major league teams before November 1 of each year. This concession, a deviation from the September 1–October 15 drafting season specified in the National Agreement, was supposedly adopted in deference to the Pacific Coast League's eight-month playing schedule, the longest in the nation. Because they had been drafted in October, Morley argued, Chase and Newton were not legally the property of the Highlanders. By the same token, the St. Louis Browns had no legal claim to Seattle outfielder Emil Frisk and Oakland pitcher Jim Buchanan, nor did the Cincinnati Reds have any right to Seattle catcher Cliff Blankenship.

The other Pacific Coast League owners initially seemed willing to fight for the rights that Morley claimed had been ignored by the major league teams. Indeed, Morley sought to justify his actions in signing Chase by claiming disingenuously that he believed "that war had [already] been declared between the American League and the Class A minor leagues."[31] Under the circumstances, then, Morley was within his rights in asking Chase to stay in Los Angeles. For his part, according to a sympathetic writer, Chase was merely waiting to see what the National Commission decided before reporting to the Highlanders: "Chase has no idea of ignoring the draft as long as the National Agreement is in effect, but as there is, at this writing, a prospect that he can play on the Coast, Chase will remain in Los Angeles until the National Commission makes a ruling in the case."[32]

While dismissing Morley's argument the Highlanders were careful to blame Chase's recalcitrance on the Los Angeles owner, who was said to be filling the ear of the innocent young player with lies: "Griffith says Morley wants to keep Chase and that he has been deluding the young man into the belief that he can be retained.... Griffith harbors no resentment against Chase for playing fast and loose with New York, excusing the young man on the ground of youth and inexperience, but he does not feel so kindly toward Morley, to whose influence he attributes Chase's actions."[33]

Others followed Griffith's lead. New York sportswriter Joe Vila was outraged, invoking President Theodore Roosevelt's favorite rhetorical weapon in his column in *The Sporting News*: "Is there no way this man Morley of Los Angeles, can be punished for tampering with First Baseman Chase of the New York Americans? From what I have heard he needs to feel a few whacks from the 'Big Stick.'" Vila, like Griffith, portrayed Chase as the victim of the villainous Morley, who had "withheld Chase's railroad ticket and would not let him leave Los Angeles on his life, telling the boy that he could remain there, when at the time the Pacific Coast League was under the protection of the National Agreement." The baseball establishment, speaking through an editorial in the same issue of *The Sporting News*, charged that Morley had acted "in violation of the spirit of the National Agreement and in defiance of the National Commission, which had adjudged Chase to be an asset of the New York Club of the American League."[34]

The skirmish seemed likely to escalate into the outright war that Morley had shrewdly anticipated. The other Pacific Coast League magnates announced that this time, in contrast to their behavior in the Dillon controversy of the previous year, they would stand by Morley.[35] They threatened to secede from the National Agreement and even negotiated briefly with the other Class A minor leagues. Some sought to defuse the potentially explosive situation. "Just Keep Cool," pleaded an editorial in *Sporting Life*, which attributed the talk of a new war to "hysterical or ill-informed scribes." But organized baseball braced for a resumption of hostilities. William F. H. Koelsch warned that "Unless the rebellious Mr. Morley, of Los Angeles, has backed down the top-line minor leaguers who are monkeying with the National Agreement buzz saw will likely get all the war they seem to be aching for."[36]

Ultimately, of course, the crisis passed. The proposed alliance with the other minor leagues never got off the ground, and the other Pacific Coast League magnates thought twice about launching what was sure to be a long and costly war against organized baseball on their own. They withdrew their support of Morley, who was left with no choice but to abide by the decision of the National Commission.

That decision was a foregone conclusion. The members of the commission would never rule in Morley's favor, although a close reading of their carefully evasive language suggests that a drafting concession was indeed discussed at the February 1904 peace conference, as Morley claimed. But Johnson and the other negotiators from organized baseball never intended to implement the concession, a fact of which Morley was almost certainly aware: "If the agreement referred to by the Pacific Coast League representatives was under discussion at the time the conference referred to was held, the same was never reported to either the National or American Leagues for their consideration and approval, and as it involves a change of the National Agreement, could not have been put into effect without the approval of all parties to the agreement; nor was the matter ever reported to the National Commission."

Indeed, the commission had "always been under the impression that the drafting season of the Pacific Coast League was the same as fixed by the National Agreement." Furthermore, "From the correspondence it is evident that the Pacific Coast League realized that even if a change in the drafting season had been talked about at the conference referred to it had not been put into effect."

Therefore, and especially since the Los Angeles, Seattle, and Oakland clubs had accepted without protest the draft money offered by the major league clubs at the time of the draft, "Our finding is that the players in question were properly drafted and belong to the clubs by which drafted."[37] Once again, as in the Dillon case the year before, Morley had been shut out.

His legal status clarified, Chase finally joined the Highlanders in Jackson, Mississippi, on March 28, "looking as fit as could be."[38] On the following day, Chase played in his first game in a major league uniform, a 5–0 victory over Jackson.

His performance in that game went far toward answering any questions that might have remained about his abilities. Although he committed an error, he also had a base hit and a sacrifice bunt, stole a base, and scored a run. *Sporting Life* reported that Chase "made a decidedly favorable impression from the moment he reported to Griffith, and from all accounts he is a player of unusual promise.... He took up his station at first base and at once gave evidence of possessing all the qualities that earned for him such a wide reputation while with

A cabinet portrait of the young Highlanders star, taken by Horner Studios of Boston during Chase's rookie season of 1905. *Thomas Carwile Collection.*

the Los Angeles Club." The Highlanders' star outfielder Willie Keeler told a reporter that "he never saw a more likely man than Chase break into fast company."[39]

In stark contrast to later years, Chase was said to be popular with the other Highlanders: "In the training camp in the Southland his gentle, unassuming manners and the utter absence of any signs of swelled head and his willingness to take the advice and profit by the teachings of older players soon made him a prime favorite with his teammates."

Certainly those who knew him best would find this description laughable, but the Highlanders, and those members of the New York press who were loyal to the American Leaguers, saw in Chase an opportunity to win a few more fans away from the National League. Thus the team, and the sympathetic press, sought to idealize him. During this time the press tended to lionize all professional athletes regardless of their actual character, but Chase, with his good looks and pleasant manner, lent himself more readily to this process than many of his peers. He was "a tall, handsome-looking chap, with light hair and complexion, and has the appearance of an athlete.... He bears himself confidently and like the well-bred college boy he is." In a comparison aimed directly at Giant fans he was even said to resemble Christy Mathewson, the star pitcher for McGraw's team.[40]

Years later, when Mathewson had become Chase's manager with the Cincinnati Reds, this comparison would have seemed grotesque. In 1905, it still seemed reasonable enough, if a trifle presumptuous. Mathewson was quite simply the most revered professional athlete in America. He was, in the words of one historian, "the first professional athlete to function as a role model for America's youth."[41] "Handsome, clean-cut, intelligent, clean-living, and heroic," he was a graduate of Bucknell University, where he had sung in the glee club, and his genteel collegiate demeanor differentiated him from the majority of his colleagues, who were crude, ignorant roughnecks, "lower even than circus clowns, itinerant actors, and train robbers."[42] Like Chase, he was handsome, articulate, and phenomenally talented, but he was also honest and modest, although his piety was doubtless exaggerated. He was accidentally exposed to poison gas while serving in the military in France in 1918 and never fully recovered his health. His death from tuberculosis seven years later, at the age of forty-five, made him a martyr as well as a saint in the eyes of the American public.

Mathewson and Chase would be linked throughout their careers. They were both tragic characters, one the personification of honest American sportsmanship and the other the avatar of duplicitous avarice. Each was the negative of the other. Indeed, in his novel *The Celebrant* Eric Rolfe Greenberg capitalized on their strange and awful relationship, using the two as diametrically opposed symbols of good and evil.[43]

Although they were still strangers in the spring of 1905, Chase and Mathewson almost certainly met early in Chase's career. New York in the first years of this century was a much smaller city than it is today, and ballplayers tended to move in the same social circles. In the spring of 1906, Giant manager John McGraw and his wife Blanche moved to the Washington Inn, a residential hotel at 155th Street and Amsterdam Avenue. Chase was among their new neighbors, and the "well-mannered, pleasant twenty-two year old Californian" quickly charmed the McGraws. Mathewson was John McGraw's protegé; before the McGraws moved to the Washington Inn, they had shared an apartment with Mathewson and his wife.[44] Any friend of McGraw's would have known Mathewson as well.

The two athletes seem to have genuinely liked each other at first; in fact, Matty autographed a presentation copy of his book *Won in the Ninth,* a thinly veiled *roman à clef* about a gallant young first baseman named "Harold Case," for Chase in 1910.[45] A clash between the two was inevitable, though, and when it finally occurred, after they had followed their different paths to Cincinnati, it was spectacular indeed.

In the spring of 1905, however, the ironies of his relationship with Mathewson were still in the future, and Chase quickly set about living up to his advance notices. He hit safely in his first six exhibition games, five of which New York won, but his defense was what really excited his teammates and the press. William F. H. Koelsch wrote in *Sporting Life* that "Chase handles himself like a veteran in the field and Griffith is satisfied that he has landed a future star performer."[46]

By the time the Highlanders returned to New York in early April to prepare for the start of the regular season Chase had established himself as the team's top attraction. After New York beat Jersey City of the Eastern League on April 8, giving local rooters their first look at the new first baseman, his status was officially confirmed in the local press: "The work of Chase, the Californian, who was secured to take Ganzel's place at first base, was accounted the best of the game. His display in the field was the work of an artist, and the opinion of old baseball 'fans' was that he was undoubtedly the greatest 'find' seen on a baseball field in a long time."[47]

Two days later, following a win over Newark, the *Times* reported that "There was much curiosity to see Chase, the Californian, who made a deep impression at first base, the place formerly occupied by John Ganzel. The newcomer is young, active and uses excellent judgment, something not often seen in a minor league player.... He is lively on the bases, and at the bat stands like a man who should be able to hit."[48]

Vila in *The Sporting News* agreed: "I took a look at Hal Chase, the Americans' new first baseman, today and was impressed with his style. He is a natural ball player, as fast as greased lightning, easy, confident and brainy. He is the counterpart of Fred Tenney [the star first baseman of the Boston Braves] in the way he goes after grounders, widely thrown balls and bunts. Better still, he seems to know what is meant by inside ball. As he is only a boy he will improve steadily from year to year and will always be a star. Chase will be a great drawing card all over the American League circuit. He has already made the fans forget all about Long John Ganzel."[49]

Optimism was the order of the day, both for Chase and the Highlanders. New York had won fourteen of its seventeen exhibition games and began the season in Washington by sweeping three games from the Senators. Chase got his first major league hit, a double, in the first game, and three more in the third; his fielding drew notice in all three contests. On April 22 the Highlanders beat the Senators 5–3 in New York's first home game before an excited crowd of more than 25,000; the attendance was boosted by Farrell's decision to admit all fans to the ballpark free of charge after the previous day's scheduled home opener had been rained out.[50]

Two weeks into the season New York was tied with Connie Mack's Philadelphia Athletics for first place, but the Highlanders' pennant hopes soon evaporated. They played eight games in a row against the Boston Red Sox, who had edged them for the 1904 pennant, and lost six. By the middle of May New York had fallen to seventh place. Chase was struggling offensively — on May 6 he was batting just .209 — and fielding erratically, committing seven errors in his first sixteen games. *Sporting Life* sniffed that "Chase still has much to learn in modern first base playing," and reported a rumor that the Highlanders would send either Chase or John Anderson to Grand Rapids in return for Ganzel.

This rumor "brought a warm denial from Griffith," and several writers defended the youngster. Vila argued that Chase's "fielding and base running fairly balance his temporary weakness with the stick," a judgment with which Koelsch concurred: "Chase has done some great fielding and has shone some as a base runner. As a batter he has not cut a wide swath, but many, including Connie Mack, think he will improve as a batter."[51]

By late May, with the Highlanders on an extended trip to the American League's westernmost cities, Chase began to show why Griffith had been so anxious to get him. He had three hits in a loss to the Detroit Tigers on May 20 and made "a sensational one-handed catch that saved one, and possibly two runs."[52] He was even attracting favorable attention from opposing fans: "His work in Chicago and St. Louis was praised universally, and in Detroit he startled the natives.... According to reports, Chase was quite a hero with the Windy City fans. Judging by the way Chase started in Detroit when he made three hits and some lightning plays, the young Californian has struck a very fast gait."[53]

In at least one game, however, Chase's revolutionary approach to playing first base backfired. Years later, in an article in *Outing* magazine, Mack Whelan recalled a 1905 game between the Highlanders and Athletics in which Philadelphia had a runner on second with shortstop Jack Barry at the plate. "Chase watched Barry closely," recalled Whelan. "A hit meant a run and possibly the game. Just as the pitcher started his delivery, Chase advanced rapidly toward the plate with his typical cat-like stride. Barry bunted, but Chase was only a few feet away from the slowly rolling ball. Picking it up with his left hand, the new first baseman made a sweeping throw toward third base. The ball crossed the bag accurately, but the station was completely vacant."

Both the runner on second and Barry scored on the play, as Chase's throw went rolling down the left field line. "Ninety percent of the crowd and most of the American League teams thought that the new player was either temporarily crazed by the heat or lacking in all baseball sense. Only Griffith and a very few of the discriminating followers of baseball saw anything but stupidity in the action of the first baseman, and throughout the rest of the contest he had to endure the frank remarks of the bleachers and some caustic comments from fellow players.

"When Griffith entered the clubhouse after the game, he found Chase the silent target for a general attack. 'Wait a minute,' said the manager, then to Chase, 'What was the reason for your throw?'

"'I watched Barry when he came to the plate,' said Chase. 'I knew that he'd probably try something unexpected. When he came up I saw from the way he held his bat that he was going to bunt so I ran in for it. I thought someone would have enough sense to cover third.'

"'Suppose Barry had seen you start your run in?' asked the manager. 'Don't you think you took big chances leaving first base open ?'

"'No,' answered Chase, 'I thought of that. If Barry had seen me and tried to change his grip on the bat, he'd have missed the ball.'

"'That's about enough for you fellows,' said Griffith, turning to the men who had been criticizing the new player. 'From now on I want every man on this team to watch Chase and act accordingly.'"[54]

Despite such praise from his manager, the rookie still stumbled occasionally. On May 26 in Cleveland Chase was sent in to replace second baseman Jimmy Williams toward the end of a scoreless tie. His first major league appearance at his old college position was not an auspicious one. Chase was doubled off first base in the top of the tenth inning on a fly ball, then dropped George Stovall's popup in the bottom of the inning. Stovall, who reached second base on the play, eventually scored the winning run.

Still, most observers realized that in Chase the Highlanders had something special. In early June Koelsch wrote that "Hal Chase has shown marked improvement in his batting since the early games of the season. In twenty-one games on the road and beginning May 5, Chase's batting average was .333. While he needs seasoning, that record is encouraging, especially as his fielding and base running have been excellent." A week later Koelsch noted smugly that "Local fans are now satisfied that in Hal Chase Griffith has picked up a player of considerable value and that Ganzel's return would not add strength to the team."[55]

Perhaps Ganzel was not the answer, but the Highlanders clearly needed something. Chesbro had been ill and the other pitchers had been hurt or ineffective; then several regular players went down with injuries. At one point New York lost twelve out of fifteen games and plunged to eighth place, although it quickly climbed back up the standings. On July 12, after a win in Detroit, the Highlanders found themselves in fifth place with a 31–35 record, .001 ahead of

Boston. But on the following day Chase was struck in the eye by a batted ball during pregame practice. He missed the next twelve games, and the Highlanders dropped back in the standings. "The loss of the young Californian was Griffith's greatest misfortune," reported Koelsch, "as he was showing form that was a revelation for a youngster in his first year in fast company."[56]

Griffith sent Chase back to New York to recuperate and gave Jack Doyle, the veteran for whom Chase was supposedly to be dealt in the spring, a trial. In his only game with the Highlanders the thirty-six-year-old Doyle was hitless in three at bats and committed two costly errors in a 6–3 loss to the Tigers. It was his last game in the major leagues. Then, in a move of dubious legality, the Philadelphia Athletics "loaned" Mike Powers to New York. Powers batted only .182 for the Highlanders in eleven games before being sent back to Philadelphia, but Koelsch reported that president Charles Comiskey of the Chicago White Sox raised "a decidedly uncalled for howl" about the presence of Powers in the New York lineup, and the unfortunate player became the target of bottles thrown from the stands in Chicago. "Considering the badly crippled condition of the New York Club on the recent Western trip," wrote the chauvinistic Koelsch, "Comiskey's attitude in the Powers matter was despicable."[57]

Chase finally returned to the lineup on Saturday, July 29, when the Highlanders swept a doubleheader from the Cleveland Naps at Hilltop Park. His return was a heroic one; in the first game he stole home and singled in the winning run in the bottom of the ninth inning and finished his afternoon's work with four hits in eight at bats. The doubleheader sweep gave New York a 39–41 record, good for fifth place, and marked the beginning of a nine-game winning streak.

Chase had not grown rusty during his layoff. After New York beat Cleveland 3–2 on August 1 the *Times* said that both teams had played "sensational" defense, "but the most wonderful exhibition of fly catching was performed by Chase in the sixth inning, when he ran a long distance into right field with the ball, then twisted himself around and caught it."[58] On August 5, in a doubleheader against the St. Louis Browns, Chase registered the astonishing total of thirty-eight putouts, including twenty-one in the first game. Five days later, with the Highlanders having moved up to fourth place, his batting average was up to .260.

Griffith still believed that the Highlanders could win the pennant, but the rest of the season was a disaster. On August 20, during a 2–1, eleven-inning loss to the White Sox in Chicago, Chase replaced Wid Conroy in center field when the latter came in to play shortstop after Elberfeld was ejected for fighting with the umpire.

The loss would prove doubly costly for the Highlanders; Ban Johnson suspended Elberfeld indefinitely, and Chase broke a bone in his right wrist while playing the outfield.[59] He played briefly in the first game of a doubleheader in St. Louis on August 24 and again in a loss in Detroit on August 29; failed as a pinch-hitter in a loss to the Tigers on the next day; and succeeded in the same role on September 4 as New York won the second game of a doubleheader against Boston.

He finally returned to the lineup on September 5 with his wrist still bandaged. His determination drew admiring comment in *Sporting Life*, which insisted that "Nothing but praise should be showered on Hal Chase" for trying to play even though "he is unable to grasp the bat while at the plate." In fact Chase was managing all right as a hitter, but his defense once again became erratic, as he committed six errors in one twelve-game span. By then other demons seemed to be pursuing the Highlanders as well. New York won only fifteen of its last forty-five games and four of its last sixteen. Injuries forced Griffith to play outfielder Keeler at second base, players were fighting on the bench, and Detroit and Boston were both threatening to push the Highlanders out of fourth place and into the second division.[60]

On September 30 Elberfeld and outfielder Dave Fultz collided while chasing a fly ball off the bat of Cleveland's Bill Bradley. Elberfeld sustained cuts on his nose and above his eye and was sent home for the rest of the season. Fultz was hospitalized with a broken nose, a broken jaw, and a concussion; he never played in the major leagues again. After the accident Griffith moved Chase to shortstop and installed Joe Connor, a catcher borrowed from Newark, at first base. The experiment lasted only one game before Griffith signed Rube Oldring, later a star outfielder for the Philadelphia Athletics, from Montgomery of the Southern League to play shortstop.

The Highlanders' nightmare season finally ended on October 7. They finished in sixth place with a 71–78 record, having been passed by Detroit, Boston, and Cleveland in the last month of the season. Chase finished with a batting average of .249, the lowest of his major league career, although he did steal twenty-two bases, second-best on the team. He also finished ninth among American League first basemen in fielding percentage, although he stood fifth among those who played in at least one hundred games.

Despite the Highlanders' disappointing showing Frank Farrell reportedly turned a profit of $40,000 for the 1905 season,[61] and the Highlanders pronounced themselves well satisfied with the performance of their new first baseman. Griffith had already predicted that Chase would be the best first baseman in baseball in 1906, and after the season praised the youngster's poise and mental agility: "He went through the season without once missing a signal. That is something remarkable for a man in his first experience in fast company. When Chase reported to us in the spring I showed him what signals we were using for our plays, and he did not have to be told again. He always was watching for the signals and always did his part in pulling off the play that was signalled for. He runs the bases with his head on a pivot—has his head turned or in position to see what is coming off. I saw him get fooled only once in judging what a hit was good for, and that was in Chicago. He was thrown out at third trying to stretch a hit, and wouldn't have been caught then but for a good relay by [White Sox shortstop] George Davis."

With Griffith's words of praise echoing in his ears Chase was offered a $500 raise for 1906 and "signed readily, at the same time expressing gratitude for his fair treatment at the hands of Farrell and Griffith."[62] He returned to California after the season to play for a club in San Jose, although his wrist was still troubling him. In San Jose, at Griffith's request, he tried batting lefthanded. The early reports on the experiment were highly encouraging, although he had abandoned it by the time he reported to the Highlanders' spring training camp in Birmingham, Alabama.[63]

In Birmingham Chase began to dispel any doubts about his ability that may have lingered after the previous season's disappointment. He excelled in all aspects of the game, and Koelsch noted his poise with admiration: "The California wonder worked with that entire confidence that means so much to a ball player," he wrote in the middle of April. "There is almost no doubt but that Chase will further startle the fans this year." Two weeks later, he reported that "Of Chase nothing need be said except that a more brilliant player does not wear a uniform. To youthful energy he has added the confidence of the veteran."[64]

The year 1906 was an unsettling one for the nation in general, what with the San Francisco earthquake and the coal strike, but the 1906 baseball season was a watershed for Chase, as he emerged as perhaps the most exciting player in the American League and the favorite of the New York fans. On opening day, April 14, Chase drove in the winning run in a 2–1, twelve-inning win over Boston's Cy Young. Earlier in the game, when umpire John B. Sheridan dared to call a strike on Chase on a close pitch, one leather-lunged fan yelled, "It's worse than the coal strike!"[65]

Early in the season Chase was already acknowledged as the best player at his position in the major leagues and drawing raves from Koelsch for his all-around play: "About Hal Chase, the child wonder, do you ask? Well, let it be said that that lad is the most brilliant first-base guardian in the biz to-day. Lands on a few, too, and can bunt with the best of them, allowing no grass to grow under his feet as he dashes around the white sacks. On the squeeze play Chase is a jewel. To see Keeler dash in as Chase puts one down for 'the squeeze' is an inspiring play." Chase was "an incomparable artist" as a bunter and "to see him play is alone worth the journey up in the sweltering subway," which had just opened.[66]

In early June, Koelsch waxed even more enthusiastic. "The brilliant work of Hal Chase, the youthful first baseman, has been the talk of the town and there's a reason," wrote Koelsch. "One year ago this husky kid came from Los Angeles heralded as the boy wonder of the Pacific Coast. It was not long before it was evident that Chase was far above the average beginner in big leagues [sic]. He was new in fast company and inclined to be somewhat fussy"—perhaps an oblique reference to Chase's temperamental nature—but soon began "to open the eyes of the fans by his brilliant work." Now, wrote Koelsch, "the kid has 'come' and we beg to make the assertion that a more brilliant ball player never broke into baseball. As a first baseman Chase is in a class by himself. As a batter the big boy looms up stronger as the season progresses." Koelsch predicted that "before the season closes he will be regarded as the sensation of the base ball year," and suggested that he would not trade Chase "for even the great Napoleon Lajoie. Pretty big talk this, Mr. Editor, but you can throw it back at us if the future does not prove Hal Chase the most valuable man in the game. Not the distant future either. If success do [sic] not turn that boy's head, with youth and natural brilliancy to aid him, he should shine as a leader in his profession for many years to come."[67]

But success did turn Chase's head, success and the prospect of making easy money by bending or breaking the rules. Ultimately, of course, his activities cost him his career. But in 1906 his future seemed limitless. The tentativeness and timidity that had occasionally marked his rookie season were gone. Sure now of his ability to hold his own in fast company, he began to display a willingness to ignore the letter of the laws governing on-field conduct. On May 8, for example, in the third inning of a game against Washington, the Senators' Lave Cross hit what looked like a sure triple to left-centerfield. The *Times* described what happened to the unsuspecting runner: "In circling first base he ran into Chase, the latter's elbow striking Cross in the side of the head. The Washington third baseman fell to the ground senseless, but after a few minutes revived and was able to continue." One month later, in the first inning of a win in Chicago, White Sox catcher Billy Sullivan was the victim of Chase's new ferocity: "With only one man out Chase knocked out Sullivan, spiking his hand in addition, in an unavoidable collision at the plate."

The suspicious elbow that knocked Cross out and the "unavoidable collision" which forced Sullivan from the game put the baseball world on notice that Chase had arrived as a major leaguer, in full and confident command of his remarkable skills. Chase was inclined to take every advantage he could, legal or illegal.

His play in 1906 caused a sensation around the American League — "Nothing like it has ever been seen in St. Louis, and, for that matter, in any city," was the reaction of one admiring Western fan — and in New York. After a dramatic 4–3 victory over the White Sox on July 12, in which Chase drove in three of the Highlanders' runs, he was carried off the field on the shoulders of the jubilant New York fans. The July 28 issue of *Sporting Life* published Chase's photograph on the front cover and gave a brief summary of his career, although the magazine perpetuated the confusion about his age by asserting that he had been born in 1884.[68]

Chase was earning recognition as perhaps the most exciting player in the league; but Ira Smith, looking back fifty years later, described a bump in Chase's otherwise smooth road. In 1906 Frank Farrell owned a racehorse named Clark Griffith, after the New York manager. According to Smith, Clark Griffith (the horse) was entered in the Withers Stakes at Belmont Park on July 20 and Chase was sure the horse would win. He convinced a number of his teammates to bet their spare money on the horse, which finished third, several lengths back.

The next day, wrote Smith, the Highlanders, unsettled by the outcome of the race and the loss of their money, dropped a sloppy 6–1 decision to the Detroit Tigers. New York managed only four hits and committed four errors, one of them by Chase. After the game Chase supposedly walked up to his manager and said, "I wish, and I think you do, too, that this world had never seen a four-legged Clark Griffith."[69]

Smith's version of the story is, alas, apocryphal. The loss to the Tigers on July 21 took place just as he described it, but the Withers Stakes had been run two months before, on May 19. Clark Griffith did indeed finish third in that race, doubtless occasioning much consternation in the Highlander camp. But the team did not respond with a distracted effort on the next day, because May 20 was a Sunday, and professional baseball was banned in New York on the sabbath. On Monday, May 21, the visiting White Sox did beat New York 7–6, thanks to four Highlander errors, including one by Chase, and eight bases on balls issued by three New York pitchers, including Griffith himself; but it seems a stretch to attribute this display to the outcome of a horse race run two full days before. The aspects of Chase's personality that Smith, writing fifty years after the fact, wished to point out — Chase's fondness for gambling and his easygoing charm and humor — are well-documented, but the extent of the former would not become common knowledge for some years yet.[70]

The July 21 loss to Detroit dropped the Highlanders into a third-place tie, this time with Cleveland; however, New York came back to sweep the next four games from Detroit. On July 24, according to the *Times*, "Chase practically won the game for the New Yorks" with a pair of splendid fielding plays: "In the eighth inning, with the fleet-footed [Davy] Jones at second base and only one out, [Sam] Crawford smashed the ball terrifically toward Chase, but the Californian made a remarkable one-handed stop, and caught the runner at first. In the ninth inning he ran nearly to the seats at right field, and caught Charley O'Leary's fly ball, which ended the game...." In addition, Chase's speed and aggressiveness on the basepaths allowed him to score the only run of the game. In the bottom of the eighth he beat out an infield hit, moved up on a sacrifice, and scored all the way from second base on another infield hit by Frank Delahanty.[71]

But along with such heroics Chase also showed the fragility that would become another trademark of his career. On the next day, in the fourth inning of a 9–0 rout of Detroit, Chase stumbled and fell awkwardly while trying to catch a foul popup; "for a few moments," reported the *Times*, "the indications were that the great player had either broken his arm or twisted an ankle." In fact he had sprained his ankle, although he remained in the game until the eighth inning.[72]

Chase missed only three games, although his ankle was far from healed when he returned. The Highlanders were locked in a close pennant race with the White Sox and Athletics; on August 12, after a loss in Chicago, New York was in third place with a 57–41 record, just .005 behind the front-running White Sox. Chase was struggling a bit offensively, but his defense sparkled. On August 16, during an eleven-inning loss in Detroit, he showed why he was considered the best first baseman in baseball at handling bunts. In the first inning, with Davy Jones on second base, Pinky Lindsay tried to sacrifice. Chase pounced on the ball and fired it to third base in time to retire the surprised Jones. Four days later, however, with New York having lost seven of its last eight games, Chase committed two errors in a 4–1 loss to the White Sox. "The trouble was entirely with the infield," complained the *Times*, "and Chase, who is playing with an injured ankle, was one of the principal offenders."[73]

Still the Highlanders refused to quit. Beginning on August 23 they won nineteen of their next twenty games, including one stretch of fifteen in a row. Probably the most exciting was a 9–8, ten-inning win against the Senators in the second game of a doubleheader on August 30. Washington had piled up an 8–1 lead by the fifth inning, but New York came storming back largely on the strength of Chase's remarkable offensive performance; he finished with three triples and a double in five at bats. The Highlanders won the last seven of those fifteen games without the tempestuous Elberfeld, who had been suspended again after the park police had twice prevented him from attacking umpire Silk O'Loughlin during a game against Philadelphia.[74]

When the Red Sox finally ended the fifteen-game streak on September 10, New York was in first place with a 77–49 record, one game ahead of the White Sox. The Highlanders hung on to first place until September 15, when they split a doubleheader with the Senators while the White Sox beat the St. Louis Browns. When the Highlanders came to Chicago on Friday, September 21, they trailed the White Sox by one game. Before the second-largest crowd in Chicago history New York swept a doubleheader, 6–3 and 4–1 against Ed Walsh and Frank Owen. Chicago came back with a 7–1 win the next day, but the Highlanders beat Walsh again on Sunday, this time by 1–0, to leave Chicago with a one-game lead.

That weekend in Chicago was to prove the high-water mark of the Highlanders' season. On Monday they lost to Detroit while the White Sox beat Boston, and the two teams were tied again atop the standings. On Tuesday New York fell back to second place as the Tigers won again while Chicago again beat Boston. Chase missed that game due to "an operation for the removal of several pernicious corns,"[75] but was back in the lineup on Wednesday, when his wild throw on a first-inning bunt helped the Tigers to a 2–0 victory.

The Highlanders won five of their last nine games, but Chicago's "Hitless Wonders" clinched the pennant on October 3 when Philadelphia beat New York in the second game of a doubleheader. New York finished with a 90–61 record, three games behind the White Sox and two games ahead of third-place Cleveland.

Despite its disappointing conclusion the 1906 season was a most successful one for Chase and the Highlanders. The handsome young Californian had established himself as one of the brightest stars in the game. His batting average of .323 was the third-best in the league, and he finished second on the team in stolen bases and runs batted in. For his performance, the club reportedly rewarded him with a new contract calling for a salary of $3,000 or $3,500, but "whatever it was you can gamble that Chase will not find fault."[76]

Chase had also apparently found a measure of personal fulfillment as well. On September 18 the *Times* printed the announcement of his engagement to Nellie Heffernan, the brown-haired, blue-eyed daughter of Mr. and Mrs. Thomas Heffernan, Irish Catholic immigrants who owned a grocery store in Bayonne, New Jersey.

Nellie and her three sisters were all beautiful and high-spirited, and inclined to coquettishness. They enjoyed showing off the clothes made by May, the eldest. Nellie was particularly fond of an ornate hat which inspired her sisters to serenade her with a song of their own composition titled, "You don't know Nellie like I do, said the saucy little bird on Nellie's hat."[77] Nellie loved baseball, and had caught Chase's eye during an exhibition game in Bayonne in 1905; their wedding was set for April 1907 in that city.[78]

Chase, however, proved unwilling or unable to abide by such schedules. By early March 1907, when the Highlanders were to report for spring training in Atlanta, stories had reached New York to the effect that Chase had been offered a $4,000 salary, plus half interest in a local cafe, to play for the Los Angeles club in the outlaw California State League.

Griffith tried to downplay the controversy. "There is about as much truth in the story that Chase will not play with the Greater New Yorks this year, as there is that I will not be with the same team," announced the manager on March 1. "I am not at all worried about Hal Chase. In the first place, he has never intimated that he had a grievance against the club, and if he has one now I would be the first to know it. It has only been a short time since I received a letter from Chase, in which he stated that he was in splendid health and ready to begin play, and recommended what he considered a promising catcher to me."[79]

In fact Chase had been playing with the local team in San Jose, where his teammates included his New York teammate and fellow Santa Clara product Harry Wolter and such former or future major leaguers as Norman (Kitty) Brashear, Elmer Stricklett, Frank Arellanes, and George Hildebrand. Despite this array of talent San Jose had lost a five-game series to the Stockton team, which included Chase's future nemesis and former Los Angeles teammate Frank Chance and major leaguers Lefty Leifield, Mike Mitchell, Danny Shay, and Tommy Sheehan.[80]

Chase had also been coaching the baseball team at St. Mary's College in Oakland,[81] which he led to a 26–0–1 record in 1907. His success at St. Mary's, where his players included future major leaguers Harry Hooper, Harry Krause, and Ed Burns,[82] may have first ignited his desire to manage in the big leagues, which would result in one of the most controversial episodes of his career. Under Chase's guidance St. Mary's won the Midwinter Intercollegiate League and the California-Nevada College League championships, beating the Stanford and Cal teams, a Pacific Coast League all-star team, and the Chicago White Sox along the way. Doubtless Chase enjoyed this opportunity to disprove those who said he did not have the makings of a manager. Not everyone was convinced, however; Hooper, noting his former manager's addiction to stealing cigars and other small items, later insisted that Chase "just wasn't all there."[83]

Griffith realized the need to handle his temperamental star with kid gloves. He even implied that spring training was not mandatory for Chase, who was sure to be in good condition already; indeed, said the manager, "if he did not report at Atlanta by the time we got there on next Tuesday night, it would not matter very much."

Griffith was obviously trying to put the best face on a delicate situation. He made a statement that seemed designed to appeal to Chase's sense of loyalty but concluded matter-of-factly by boiling the issue down to its economic basics: "For the benefit of those people who think that Chase can be induced to cut loose from legitimate baseball, I wish to say that the San Jose boy is one of the fairest and most sensible persons that I have ever met during my connection with the game. In my opinion he would not transfer his allegiance from major league ball, in which he has been satisfactorily treated, to outlaw ball of an uncertain character. It's farcical to think, anyhow, that an outlaw club in Los Angeles can afford to pay $4,000 salaries."

In short, predicted Griffith, "Chase will be at first base for the New York team next year just as sure as he is alive. He has received a contract and a railroad ticket for his passage from his home, at San Jose, to Atlanta, by way of New Orleans, and I expect to meet him when the New York contingent gets to the Georgia capital next Tuesday."[84] Several New York baseball writers shared Griffith's optimism, theorizing that Chase was threatening to play in California simply to scare the Yankees into raising his salary to $5,500, although other reports said that he was asking only for $4,000.[85]

Years later his son would argue that Chase's fondness for California played a major role in this and later conflicts between Chase and management. Of course the climate on the West Coast was ideal for baseball almost the entire year, without the grinding heat and humidity of eastern summers. Moreover, baseball in New York was serious business. In California it remained the game that had given him such joy in his boyhood. "He always seemed the same old Hal," recalled Bill Robertson, who grew up in Los Gatos at this time. "The younger boys all knew him, for after playing a Sunday [game], he would line us up under the old incandescent arc light on the corner of Main and Santa Cruz by the hotel and play catch."[86] By the same token, by abandoning New York for California Chase may also have been seeking a way out of his impending marriage to Nellie Heffernan.

But at the same time Chase found New York irresistible, and it is difficult to reconcile the view of Chase as a homesick innocent with the picture of Chase the swaggering boulevardier and Broadway dandy, the back-slapping, cigar-chomping habitué of saloons and pool halls, seldom seen without a chorus girl on his arm.

Griffith held the first practice of the spring on Wednesday, March 6, and reiterated his belief that Chase would show up soon; indeed, reported the *Times*, "the entire squad is looking for him to arrive within a short time."[87] But as each day passed with no sign of Chase the Highlanders began to plan for life without their star, working utility infielder George Moriarty at first base. "He appears to be at home at the position," reported the *Times*, "and Griffith believes he will make an acceptable substitute in event of the non-appearance or disability of Chase."[88]

Moriarty was a competent ballplayer; but on March 10, in a preview of the upcoming season, the *Times* predicted that the loss of Chase would be a grave blow to New York's pennant hopes, "for Chase is one player in a hundred in skill and an easy man to handle." Griffith and Farrell might have disputed the latter assessment, but could only agree with the gloomy conclusion: "Moriarity [*sic*] might be an acceptable man on the bag had Chase not played it, but Moriarity will never be a Chase."[89]

Griffith continued to downplay the situation, saying only that he was "puzzled" by his star's absence, and predicted that Chase would join the team in time for the start of the regular season. The *Times* reported that the opinion of the other New York players was that Chase was merely seeking to avoid the drudgery of spring training. Moreover, "This appears to be all right with the manager, as he realizes that the first baseman is keeping in good condition by playing in California and will be as fit as any of those who came South when the season opens." Such an attitude would hardly seem conducive to the development of a well-disciplined, unselfish club, but at least one of Chase's teammates shared the manager's lack of concern. "He has been playing ball all winter and must be in great condition," said this player to sportswriter Sid Mercer. "By the time the rest of us have ironed out the kinks and knuckled down to hard work Chase will come along, hop on that old first base and buckle down to it, as if he had done nothing else since last fall."[90]

Griffith might have been excused for not sounding too concerned about Chase, because he had plenty of other worries. The spring of 1907 was an unsettling time for the Highlanders, and not just because of Chase's absence. Jack Chesbro, who had won eighty-five games over the past three seasons, had announced in late February that he was retiring to work on his farm in North Adams, Massachusetts; his loss would hurt the Highlanders, whose other pitchers, aside from Al Orth, were largely untested. New York won its first five exhibition games, but Elberfeld, Jimmy Williams, and Frank LaPorte, who along with Chase made up the starting infield, were all nursing injuries. In a loss to Macon, Griffith was forced to use a catcher, Red Kleinow, at second base and play third base himself. Neither was the grim news that spring restricted to the Highlanders' camp. On March 28 Chick Stahl of the Red Sox, reportedly distraught over a scandalous love affair, committed suicide by drinking carbolic acid. On the next day Patrick (Cozy) Dolan of the National League Boston Braves died of typhoid fever.[91]

The Highlanders finally got some good news on April 2. Chase wired sportswriter Walter St. Denis that he had decided to rejoin the team, but had been delayed by "a slight sickness" that had "grown a little worse."⁹² The *Times* portrayed the resolution of the crisis as a victory for management: "it is almost certain that the Californian's demand for an increase of salary was not acceded to. It is well known that Chase asked for something like $2,000 more than he received last season. The contract he was asked to sign this year is said to have specified a voluntary increase of $1,000, but Chase seemed obdurate, and the report was circulated that he intended to open a cafe in San Jose [*sic*] and play with an outlaw club in that city. This did not seem to affect the Greater New York Club officials. In fact, it is believed that Mr. Farrell told his first baseman that his demand was unreasonable, and under no circumstances would it be considered. His letter, therefore, which Manager Griffith received at Atlanta on Monday [stated] that he had made a mistake, and was willing to rectify it."⁹³

Farrell later confirmed that "Chase refused to join the club, and threatened to join an outlaw league unless I paid him $4,000 a year." Unwilling to risk losing his biggest gate attraction, the New York owner said that he acceded to the first baseman's demands, contrary to the reports in the press at the time.⁹⁴ Chase signed a three-year contract, but the 1907 season would not be a happy one in New York.

By the time the Highlanders left Atlanta on April 7, four days before the start of the season, Griffith was predicting that Chase would miss the opener against the Senators but would join the team before it left Washington. On Thursday, April 11, with Moriarty at first base, the Highlanders won the first game of the season 3–2 before the largest crowd in Washington history, including President Roosevelt. The next day's game was rained out, and the game on Saturday was called after ten innings with the score tied 4–4. But Griffith did not mind, for on Saturday Hal Chase finally appeared in Washington.

He looked tired, and explained that he would have arrived sooner but for late trains which twice caused him to miss connections and added two days to his journey from California. "I'll be all right, boss, just as soon as I get a night's rest," he told Griffith. "Just hand me a uniform tomorrow and put me to work." His teammates, too, were relieved. "We just had to have that boy," said one. "He puts new life in the infield. We can just throw them over any old way, and there will be somebody there to get them."⁹⁵ He had also missed his April wedding date, although the newspapers did not report this fact. If Nellie was upset, she apparently forgave him, for events later that summer indicated that he and Nellie had apparently begun living together as man and wife anyway.

Chase made his 1907 debut on Sunday, April 15, in a 9–4 loss to the Senators. He batted fourth in the New York lineup, the cleanup position usually reserved for a team's most dangerous hitter, and despite his lack of preparation had two hits in three at bats. On defense he handled ten chances flawlessly, but committed six errors in his next eleven games, plus another two in an exhibition against Newark of the Eastern League.

Still, despite Chase's apparent rustiness and minor injuries to Keeler and Williams, the New York team, which some were beginning to call the Yankees, played well. After an 8–0 defeat of Philadelphia on May 4 New York had eleven wins and six losses, good for second place. And as Chesbro had signed a new contract on May 1, ending his short-lived retirement, the Yankees had hopes of a lofty finish in 1907.[96]

But Griffith knew that his pitching staff was thin, even with the return of Chesbro. New York picked up two veteran pitchers in May, securing Earl Moore from Cleveland in a trade and then buying Frank Kitson from Washington. Moore had won twenty games in 1903 and Kitson had had some good years with Brooklyn in the National League, but neither contributed much to the Yankees. New York began to lose, dropping eighteen of twenty-four games and falling back to fifth place.

Even the Yankees' few wins were not without their embarrassing moments. In the sixth inning of a 9–3 win against the Tigers on June 10, with two out and a man on base, Detroit's Charley O'Leary rapped a sharp grounder to the right side. Chase made a sensational stop and sprinted to the bag in time to retire O'Leary for the final out of the inning—or so he thought. He nonchalantly tossed the ball back toward the pitcher's mound and prepared to head for the bench, only to discover that the umpire had called O'Leary safe. A chagrined Chase retrieved the ball and threw it to second in time to get O'Leary, who had kept running, but not before Germany Schaefer had crossed the plate with a run for Detroit.[97]

Such a blunder was out of character for Chase, who had already shown himself one of the headiest and most poised players in baseball. One possible explanation for his lapse surfaced after the Yankees committed an astonishing eleven errors, including four by Elberfeld, in a 10–4 loss to the Tigers two days later.

In reporting on this appalling spectacle the *Times* raised publicly the possibility that certain Yankee players, dissatisfied with Griffith's leadership, were deliberately trying to lose: "In years gone by there have been instances in baseball of games having been 'thrown.' Such things, of course, have passed away. But the old-time enthusiast, unacquainted with modern baseball, who happened to drop in at American League Park yesterday might have suspected that he was witnessing a revival of the old customs."

The story stopped short of actually accusing the players of trying to lose, but the implication was clear: "There has been some talk of dissatisfaction among the players. Disaffection with Manager Griffith has been freely hinted. Some of the players have been particularly unfortunate in making mistakes at critical times, and have committed errors of omission that were very costly. These [players] have been pointed out as the leaders of the malcontents. Of course it is preposterous to suppose that a conspiracy could exist to oust the manager, but the circumstantial evidence happened to coincide with this view."

The strain of internal dissension was apparently starting to tell on the normally placid Griffith as well; following the game he assaulted a fan, a dry-goods merchant named Frank, who had been chatting with Detroit's Ty Cobb, then ran to hide in the clubhouse before the man's friends could retaliate.[98]

After this crisis the rumors of dissension on the team seemed to recede. Throughout the rest of June and in early July Chase's breathtaking defensive play continued to draw comment in the newspapers,[99] and he put together a twenty-two game hitting streak. But still the Yankees stumbled along in fifth place, losing as many games as they won, and below the surface the team's problems continued to fester.

Finally, on July 26, matters came to a head. Cleveland beat the Yankees 7–5 in the first game of a doubleheader, aided to no small extent by Elberfeld, who committed three errors and "nearly stood First Baseman Chase on his head a couple of times diving after wide throws." Griffith benched Elberfeld for the second game, which Cleveland won anyway, 8–3, and then Farrell announced that he was indefinitely suspending the veteran shortstop without pay. The *Times* applauded the move: Farrell had "struck a heavy blow at the disaffection in the ranks of the Yankees" with his stern treatment of Elberfeld, who had reportedly "been nursing a 'grouch' for some time."[100]

As if all this were not enough distraction for Chase and his teammates, on that same day Nellie and her friend Ethel Martin, the wife of the Highlander trainer, were arrested in Suffern, New York, and charged with unlawfully disposing of the body of an infant.

The story is as pathetic as it is gruesome. Mike Martin and Ethel Monroe had been married only a few weeks before, on July 3. According to the police, Mrs. Martin had given birth to a stillborn child on July 19, although one newspaper reported a rumor that the baby had actually been born alive. At any rate, Ethel and Nellie tried first to burn the body and then placed it in the Martins' back yard, where it was found and "torn" by a stray dog. The police, acting on a tip from neighbors, discovered the remains, and subsequently arrested the two women, who were said to be "astounded" upon their arrest.

Elberfeld, who had apparently returned home to serve out his suspension, and his wife posted the $1,500 bail for the unfortunate pair. Perhaps thanks to the influence of Farrell and Devery, the affair was quickly hushed up and no account of its ultimate disposition subsequently appeared in the newspapers. Still, while trumpeting the news of the arrests, the newspapers discreetly avoided raising another scandal. They repeatedly identified Nellie as "Mrs. Hal Chase," even though she and Chase had not yet married. The implication seems to be that she and Chase were already living together.[101]

The suspension of Elberfeld had no immediate effect on the team's fortunes. On Saturday, August 3, Chase was spiked in the arm by Chicago shortstop George Davis on an attempted steal of second base. He missed the next twenty-two games, during which the Yankees continued to lose as often as they won.

Chase finally rejoined the team on August 29, contributing a hit and two stolen bases and scoring a run as New York beat the Athletics 5–2. He received ovations from the New York fans at his first at-bat and after a fine running catch of Danny Murphy's fly ball in the second inning. On the following day, however, Philadelphia's Rube Waddell beat the Yankees 6–3. After striking out Chase in the ninth inning the irrepressible Waddell yelled, "It makes no difference, for they all look alike to me!"[102]

In the first four games after his return Chase played left field, away from the wear and tear of infield play, "so that there would be less chance of hurting his injured arm."[103] He made three errors in his first seven games after returning to first base, but quickly began playing with his accustomed brilliance.[104] The Yankees nevertheless finished the season in fifth place, with a 70–78 record. Chase's batting average fell to .287, considerably less spectacular than his mark of the year before but still the highest on the team and the tenth-best in the league. He also led the Yankees in runs batted in, hits, and doubles, and was second on the team in stolen bases and runs. At the age of twenty-four he seemed to have every reason to believe that the 1908 season would be his best yet.

Three

Chase Has Been Too Highly Praised in New York

Chase's activities after the 1907 season, however, threatened to end his major league career almost before it had fairly begun. The controversy once again involved his participation in the outlaw California State League. Chase doubtless enjoyed his time in the CSL, as he got to play at home, in relatively relaxed surroundings, with and against many familiar faces, including his former Santa Clara teammates Frank Farry and Carmel Martin and his old Victoria sidekick Elmer Emerson.[1] By 1907, however, the Pacific Coast League, alarmed at the number of quality players who had signed on with the outlaws, began to look upon the CSL as a serious competitor. Whereas in previous years the participation in the CSL of Chase and his fellow moonlighting major leaguers had aroused little or no comment, now one national magazine criticized their "base and petty greed" in seeking to augment their incomes.[2] In October, acting on the complaints of the Pacific Coast League, the National Commission announced that all players who had jumped existing contracts to play in the CSL would be declared ineligible to play in organized baseball, while those who had violated the reserve clause had thirty days in which to return to their original clubs. All other National Agreement players who played with the outlaws would be fined $100 on the first offense and suspended on the second.[3]

When asked if he intended to abide by the ruling, Chase responded, "Yes, I will observe the rule. There is nothing else to do. The ruling is an unjust one and it is hard for the men in the big leagues, for it deprives them of an opportunity to make some money after their contracts with the Eastern clubs have expired. Still, the Commission is powerful enough to enforce the penalties, and the best thing we can do is to obey the rule."[4]

Chase's resentment of the ruling was probably sincere; in a letter to his friend Mike Martin, the Yankee trainer, Chase claimed that he had been playing winter ball to finance the purchase of a house for his parents, but had quit after playing in only two games for San Jose as soon as he heard of the commission's ruling.[5] In reality, he continued to play for San Jose into mid–November under the name of Schultz, dividing his time between shortstop and the pitcher's mound. "Schultz" batted .478 and split two decisions in twenty-one innings for San Jose, but the ruse fooled no one; the box scores and accounts of the games in the newspapers continued to call him "Chase."[6]

In early January 1908 he reportedly wrote a letter to his Yankee teammate George Moriarty "to the effect that he has decided to remain permanently in California and will do all he can to help the outlaws along."[7] The baseball establishment initially put little credence in these rumors: after all, Chase had two years left on his Yankee contract, and "he does not intend to lose this plum by getting himself into trouble among the Coast outlaws."[8] Moreover, Farrell claimed that he had received a letter from Chase in late January in which the first baseman had written, "I have been most liberally treated by you, Mr. Farrell, and I am not an ingrate. I will come East in time to report to Griff at Atlanta the first week in March, and I will do my best to earn the handsome salary which I am to receive." Chase added that he had never considered quitting the Yankees for outlaw ball, and again denied that he had played in any games after the commission's ruling.[9]

Publicly, the Yankees sought to minimize the entire affair. "Hal is a fellow who likes to make friends, and he is easily led," explained Farrell lamely. "He hates to say no to the California people, with whom he has been brought up, and there is such a demand for him out there that he has to stall, possibly, to get rid of them and their talk." In remarks that revealed much about the patronizing relationship between owners and players in the early twentieth century, Farrell went on to compare Chase to one his stable of racehorses. "He had played the entire twelve months without any rest at all, and on that account I am glad he has been obliged by the National Commission's ruling to take a rest this winter. There is such a thing as a player having too much base ball, and if I were one I think I should welcome the layoff that a winter affords. What if I should race my horses all winter? They would become stale, wouldn't they? Well, a ball player is just the same — they need a rest, too."[10]

Privately, Farrell knew full well the gravity of his star player's refusal to abide by the ruling. "Chase ignored this action of the commission and continued to play," Farrell later admitted, "and it was only through my continued efforts that he was not blacklisted."[11] Doubtless the owner pointed out to Ban Johnson that his team, coming off a difficult season, would be even less likely to win fans away from the Giants if it were deprived of its only star player. Whatever his arguments, Farrell succeeded in convincing the National Commission not to suspend his errant star. This decision may have had unforeseen longterm effects, as Chase had publicly defied the authority of organized baseball and had gotten away with it virtually unscathed. One biographer has postulated that this episode "may have assured him that he would be able to break the rules again," in far more serious ways.[12]

Chase himself eventually issued a mildly penitent statement in which he admitted the deception regarding his last name: "I have quit the outlaws for good and all, though I played with them for some time under the impression that I had a right to do so. But I am now through and I will send you the newspapers when they play their next games, showing that the names of Schultz and Chase will be absent from the San Jose line-up."[13]

With this crisis averted, Griffith was again issuing optimistic predictions in the spring of 1908. Chase was, in fact, among the first players to report for spring training, but his early arrival was not the only novelty awaiting the Yankees in Atlanta that spring, for Georgia had recently become a dry state. "It's pretty odd to not be able to buy a drink," mused Griffith. "However, as a manager I rather like it. I won't have much trouble keeping the boys straight."[14]

Keeping Chase straight was a perennial problem, but not because of alcohol. He had finally married Nellie Heffernan at St. Joseph's Church in San Jose on the first day of the new year. If Griffith and Farrell hoped that marriage would settle the youngster down, however, they were mistaken.

The young couple set up housekeeping in Leonia, New Jersey, and at least initially seemed to be happy; three years later, a newspaper story noted that "Since her marriage to Chase Mrs. Chase has never missed a [home] game...."[15] The marriage soon turned sour, however. Chase was an incorrigible philanderer, and marriage seems to have done little to curb his wandering eye. Moreover, their first child died suddenly while still an infant; their second son, also named Harold, was born in 1910,[16] but Chase was as irresponsible a father as he was a husband.

Despite his shortcomings, however, many found him irresistible. More than eighty years later, Nellie's niece Esther Wright Madden still remembered Chase fondly. "We loved Hal," she recalled, "because he was just one of those lovable people." She described him as "charming and handsome" and "a big kid," and recalled riding on his back when she was a girl of ten or eleven, before the marriage fell apart.[17]

Chase's reinstatement and new marital status did not help the Yankees much in 1908, as the internal problems that had plagued the team during the previous season resurfaced and grew even worse. This time they not only cost the team any chance at a pennant, they cost Griffith his job.

At first the manager's spring optimism seemed justified, as the team began the season playing well and was in first place in early June. But then the Yankees left New York on what was to be "the most disastrous trip of recent years."[18] They won only four of seventeen games over the next three weeks and by June 23 had fallen all the way to seventh place amid rumors that Griffith had lost control of his team.[19] New York sportswriter Mark Roth's attempt to dismiss these rumors merely seemed to confirm them. "Certain individuals, perhaps, have not behaved themselves at times," wrote Roth, "but the slump of the team can hardly be laid to that."[20]

Griffith was stunned and demoralized by this abrupt reversal in the team's fortunes and on June 24, in Philadelphia, announced his resignation as manager. The *Times* reported that he had actually submitted a letter of resignation to Farrell a week before, "asserting that luck was against him, and that it was useless for him to continue." Farrell had joined the team in Philadelphia, supposedly hoping to change Griffith's mind, but the manager "was obdurate." Griffith reportedly told Farrell that "there were no dissensions on the team, and that the players were willing to fight to the last ditch for him," but he felt that "there was some hoodoo following him."[21]

In fact, the "hoodoo" plaguing Griffith was probably Kid Elberfeld. Baseball historian Harold Seymour insisted that Chase, who had managerial aspirations, was "instrumental" in Griffith's departure,[22] but the two remained friendly thereafter, and Chase apparently saved his most mutinous activities for later managers. One account says that Griffith's departure was precipitated by pitcher Bill Hogg, who complained to Farrell that Griffith was not using him enough. Farrell ordered Hogg to pitch against the Browns, who hammered him. The irate owner ordered the pitcher suspended, but Griffith objected and refused to enforce the suspension, whereupon Farrell dumped him.[23]

Elberfeld, however, whose managerial ambitions were well known, had no great fondness for the Old Fox and reportedly put his own interests above those of the team. One writer subsequently attributed the team's problems to a feud between the hot-headed shortstop and second baseman Jimmy Williams. Elberfeld came out on top when Williams was traded to St. Louis, but then embarked on a systematic campaign to discredit Griffith in the eyes of the management. Obviously, that campaign succeeded; Farrell allowed Griffith to pretend that he was leaving voluntarily, but the owner had determined that a change was necessary.[24]

Publicly Griffith said only that for him to continue as manager "was simply useless," and so he had resigned "in justice to Mr. Farrell." He said he had become "disheartened" over the team's recent performance and hoped that it would improve under a new manager. "I do not know who my successor will be," said Griffith, "but I understand Elberfeld is mentioned for the place. If that is so, I wish him the best of luck, and I hope my successor will pull the team out of the rut and place them where they belong."[25]

It was not to be. Farrell did indeed appoint Elberfeld to replace Griffith, but the team continued to lose. Two days after Elberfeld took over, Chase injured his ankle while playing second base during another Yankee loss. At first the ankle was thought to be broken, but the injury was later diagnosed as a bad sprain. As Chase was carried from the field, the beleaguered Farrell, who was watching the game from the pressbox, sighed and said, "Well, for hard luck, that is the limit."[26]

Chase missed ten games while his ankle mended, and the Yankees lost eight of them. The most embarrassing defeat occurred on June 30, when forty-one-year-old Cy Young of the visiting Red Sox pitched the third no-hitter of his career while collecting three hits and driving in four of his team's eight runs.

Chase's return to the lineup on July 7 made little difference in the team's fortunes. He played left field in his first three games, but had a difficult time,

Three—Chase Has Been Too Highly Praised in New York

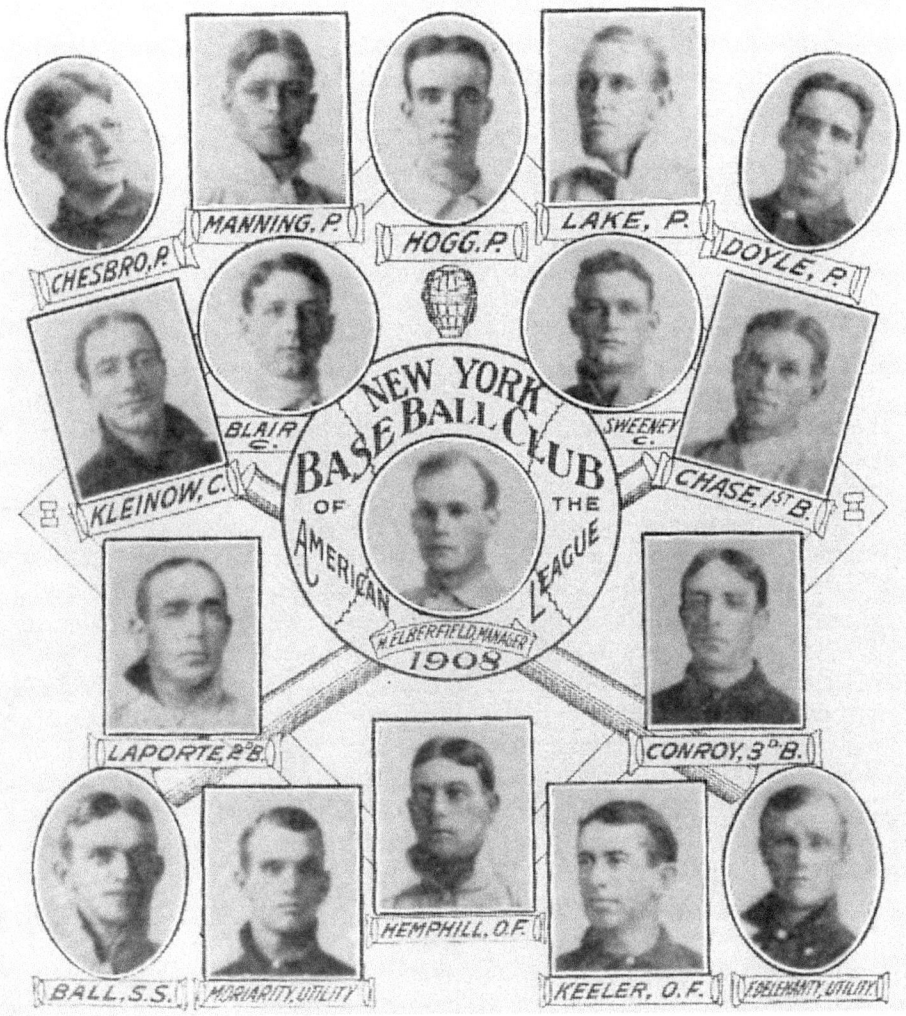

The 1908 Highlanders, the worst team in the American League. In 1908 Chase had a dismal season, batting .257 with just 36 runs batted in and feuding with shortstop Kid Elberfeld (here incorrectly identified as "Elberfield"), who replaced Clark Griffith as manager in June. Chase jumped the club in September to play in the outlaw California State League. *Author's collection.*

misjudging a couple of fly balls. He was back at first base on July 9, when he collected three hits and stole two bases, but came out of the next day's game after four innings, complaining that his ankle was still sore. The Yankees went on to lose their fifth game in a row to the Tigers.[27]

So desperate was Elberfeld that he even allowed Chase to make his long-awaited debut as a major league pitcher in Detroit on July 25. Chesbro was pitching for

New York and went into the bottom of the eighth inning with a 3–2 lead, but one-out singles by Germany Schaefer and Sam Crawford and a triple by Ty Cobb gave the Tigers a one-run lead and brought Claude Rossman to the plate. Elberfeld knew that Rossman always hit well against Chesbro, but the Yankee bullpen was in sorry shape. He decided to discuss the situation with Chesbro.

As Elberfeld made his way to the pitching mound Chase joined him and begged for a chance to pitch. Elberfeld decided to let Chase pitch to Rossman and kept Chesbro in the game by moving him to first base. Chase's major league pitching career lasted just one pitch; Rossman hit his first delivery for a long sacrifice fly to center field, scoring Cobb, and Elberfeld yelled for Chase and Chesbro to resume their former positions.[28] The Tigers went on to win the game 5–3, dropping the Yankees' record to 32–56.[29]

Chase never got another chance to pitch in the major leagues, but he made another, even more remarkable switch before the end of the season. On September 3, with over a month remaining on the schedule, he jumped the club and returned to California. At the time he was batting just .257.[30]

He denied that he had left because Farrell had passed him over in favor of Elberfeld, but rumors persisted that Chase had long coveted Griffith's job. The *Times* noted that "There has been trouble between Chase and Elberfeld extending over a year," but Chase attributed his departure to an article in another newspaper accusing him of giving less than his best on the field.

The article, written anonymously by Ernest J. Lanigan, appeared in the New York *Press* on August 23, almost two months to the day after Griffith's departure. Headlined "Chase's Play Now Surprise to Fans," it accused Chase of selfishness and laziness. "Chase has been too highly praised in New York," wrote Lanigan; he had "had his head swollen by the advice of his supposed friends and has failed to fit in with the idea of team work that produces a winning combination." Chase had sulked since Elberfeld was named to succeed Griffith; but Chase should "realize that Frank Farrell engaged him to play first base and that Mr. Farrell is perfectly competent to select his manager."

This was strong stuff, but there was more. Lanigan quoted an unnamed American League manager who said he would not want Chase on his team, despite his immense talent, because of his inflated sense of his own worth.

Said this manager, "It will take Chase just about six months to realize the right angles in the national game, and then he'll be the boy for a pennant winner. Just at present he's not, because he gets sore at his infielders when they're not able to cope with his remarkable speed. Moreover, self-appointed managers never are successful. There are men in baseball to-day who have forgotten more than Chase ever knew, and he should get down off his perch, stop sulking and play the ball which he is capable of playing."

The article concluded with the news that Farrell had fired Yankee trainer Mike Martin, "Chase's fast friend," at Elberfeld's request. Elberfeld was reportedly upset because Martin "was paying too much attention to Chase and not enough to the other players on the team."[31] Perhaps Elberfeld was also influenced by an incident that occurred during a loss to the Tigers a few days before, when Martin picked up and tossed away an overthrown ball that was still in play after it had rolled to the Yankee bench. Umpire Silk O'Loughlin waved two Detroit runners across the plate on the play, and one reporter commented caustically of Martin, "If this is the sort of training he's been imparting to the Yanks, everything is explained."[32] Other observers agreed that Chase's ego, perhaps thanks to Martin's attentions, had gotten out of control: "They tell me that the young Californian, when he saw himself pictured and boomed in the newspapers, became so inflated that he thought he was a human balloon. He began to look around him and in his own opinion he was playing with a lot of mutts.... He is a very young and unsophisticated person."[33]

Unsurprisingly, Chase took umbrage at these attacks. He claimed that the Yankees themselves had planted the story in the *Press* and announced that he was through with the team. "I am not satisfied to play under a management that sees fit to give out a story detrimental to my character and questions my integrity and honesty," he said. "I feel that I could not do myself justice under such conditions, and therefore I have decided to quit. I never had managerial ideas." He also issued a vague but ominous threat: "If any attempt is made by the management of the club to roast me, I will tell a story which will rip the baseball world wide open."[34] The threat may have been an empty one, simply designed to give Farrell something to think about; or Chase may have had some inside information about his boss's less respectable business activities, or about some of Farrell and Ban Johnson's less than absolutely ethical attempts to ensure the survival of the American League's New York franchise.

Farrell came out swinging against Chase's accusations, denying that anyone associated with the team had had anything to do with Lanigan's article and claiming that Chase was only using the article as an excuse. In fact, said Farrell, Chase had been planning for some time to leave the Yankees and return to the California State League. The owner said that before the jump he had confronted the player with rumors of his imminent departure and Chase had given "his word of honor as a man that he had no intention of leaving the New York Club." Upon learning of the first baseman's departure, Farrell said, he told Elberfeld to telephone Chase. Chase told the manager, said Farrell, "that he had been thinking of going for a long time." (A California newspaper reported that Chase had been negotiating with Cy Moreing for at least a month, but had not wanted to announce his switch before picking up his last paycheck from the Highlanders on September 1.) His complaints about Lanigan's article in the *Press* were meant "to overshadow this unmanly action." Furthermore, in reference to Chase's threat to "rip the baseball world wide open," Farrell concluded coolly, "I will welcome any statement he may see fit to make."[35]

No such statement was forthcoming, but Chase's days as a Yankee seemed to be over. A rumor in Philadelphia had the Yankees trading Chase to the Athletics for veteran first baseman Harry Davis, who would become the new player-manager in New York, but Connie Mack immediately denied the rumor and

Davis stayed put.³⁶ Joe Vila, who generally reflected the Yankee management's point of view, blamed the Yankees' poor showing on "Chase and a gang of cowardly knockers who have done all sorts of low-down things to ruin the American League in this city," although he refused to elaborate, and called Chase "a very foolish, misguided young man." He also noted the "strange fact that ever since Hal Chase deserted the Yankees, the team ... has played fifty per cent better ball.... There is no longer any reason to hide the fact that Chase was a disturbing element."³⁷ Vila thus may have been the first to imply publicly that Chase was trying to throw games, although he would certainly not be the last.

The figures seemed to support Vila's conclusions. The Yankees had won only fifteen of their first sixty-four games under Elberfeld, a winning percentage of .234, but won twelve of their remaining thirty-four games after Chase's departure, a winning percentage of .353. The latter figure is almost exactly fifty percent higher than the former. But overall the team played even more poorly under Elberfeld than under Griffith, winning only twenty-seven of its last ninety-eight games and finishing the season in last place. Elberfeld's tenure as manager would clearly be brief. The day after Chase's desertion Sid Mercer, who was a friend of Prince Hal's, wrote that "it is an indisputable fact that Elberfeld has failed as a leader of men. His players not only have no confidence in him, but the team is divided into factions, neither of which is especially strong for the 'Kid.'"

Mercer viewed Chase's departure as primarily a comment on Elberfeld's deficiencies as a manager, and added that he and the other writers had known about the team's internal troubles for some time, but had chosen to keep silent: "There are many stories of dissension among the Yankees that probably never will come to light, but any fan who is personally acquainted with the players has known for some time that trouble was coming. It was known to the baseball writers also, but nothing was said because it was hoped that the affairs of the club might be adjusted without any unpleasant publicity. But Chase's action exposes the dissatisfaction, and there are mutterings from certain other players."³⁸

One of the most remarkable things about the comments of Vila and Mercer is their admission that they knew about the problems on the team but chose not to write about them. It is hard to imagine today's media finding "any reason to hide the fact" that a player was causing problems in hopes "that the affairs of the club might be adjusted without any unpleasant publicity," but the relationship between the press and the teams they covered was much cozier then. Muckrakers Lincoln Steffens and Ida M. Tarbell had already begun to expose the seamier side of the American institutions of government and industry, but the practice would not spread to the sports world until the 1970s. In Chase's day, the newspapermen assigned to cover a major league team were frequently little more than shills for the team's management; they were, after all, dependent upon the team for their livelihood.

After the season Farrell lost little time in relieving Elberfeld of the managerial duties and naming the hardnosed Georgian George T. Stallings to replace him. Ban Johnson had clashed with Stallings during the latter's tenure as the first manager of the Detroit Tigers, and years before had reportedly vowed never to allow Stallings to return to the American League — a vow which he supposedly reiterated at a meeting of the National Commission in mid-October — but Farrell was confident that the feud was over: "So far as I know there is no opposition in the American League to Mr. Stallings, and stories to the effect that he is being opposed by President Johnson are without foundation and detrimental to his reputation."[39]

Meanwhile, Chase was making good money in California. He had accepted Cy Moreing's offer of $1,000 to play twenty-three games with the Stockton Millers, who had won four California State League pennants in a row. (Moreing, always on the lookout for promotional possibilities, had invited star Pittsburgh shortstop Honus Wagner to join the Millers when Wagner held out at the beginning of the season, but Wagner had declined the offer and rejoined the Pirates.) If Chase expected to be free of further controversy, however, he was soon disappointed, for he immediately became the subject of a dispute between Stockton and San Jose.

When Moreing first announced his intention to sign Chase, the San Jose Prune Pickers, with whom Chase had spent the previous winter, objected strenuously. Moreing claimed that San Jose had released Chase when he left to rejoin the Yankees before the 1908 season. San Jose manager Al Jarman disagreed, insisting, "We want Hal Chase and we're going to have him, too." The dispute prompted Jarman to threaten to join the Pacific Coast League in 1909 rather than play another season with the thieving Moreing.[40]

Chase played for San Jose in an exhibition game against the Chicago Ladies' Club,[41] but the league ultimately awarded his services to Stockton, and Chase immediately set about showing why both teams had coveted him. He made his first appearance for the Millers on September 9 as Stockton split a doubleheader against the Sacramento Senators. Chase had two hits, including a double, in the first game, a 9–1 Stockton victory, and defensively he was, as usual, spectacular. Reported the San Francisco *Examiner*, "The immense crowd gave him a royal welcome."

With the dispute over his services resolved, Chase soon found himself at the center of another controversy, one that was uncharacteristic of the usually easygoing star. A Sacramento sportswriter reported that Stockton's 11–5 loss to the host Senators on October 17 was distinguished by "incompetency, dirty ball playing, rowdyism, and lack of decency." The same writer insisted that "the only redeeming feature in it was the magnificent tackle made by Charlie Enwright when he grabbed 'Rowdy' Hal Chase as the coward was running away" after starting a bench-clearing brawl. (Enwright had been one of Chase's St. Mary's players in 1907.)

The fun began when Chase fielded a chopper hit by Sacramento's Charlie Doyle about halfway up the first base line. He and Doyle collided, and Doyle fell to his knees. "Chase then struck Doyle with the ball, and as he was rising to his feet slammed a vicious uppercut on Doyle's mouth." As players from both

George Tweedy Stallings, celebrated as the manager of the 1914 "Miracle Braves," had an earlier and less successful stint as manager of the Highlanders. *National Baseball Hall of Fame Library, Cooperstown, N.Y.*

teams rushed onto the field the Senators' Joe Nealon went after Chase, who quickly decided that, in this case at least, discretion was indeed the better part of valor, and attempted to evade Nealon. Chase's strategic retreat was foiled, however, by Sacramento's shortstop: "Charlie Enwright saw the move and tackled him, holding Chase until the police gained the point and prevented a riot." The officers took Chase into custody, which probably saved him from a beating by the outraged Sacramentans.[42]

Chase's skill as a ballplayer was undeniable, and he still had great personal charm. No longer, however, could he be plausibly portrayed as a second Mathewson, a mild-mannered, self-effacing, reluctant hero. As hero or villain, though, Chase was a great attraction for the California fans, who could hardly have expected to see so great a star in action in his home state before the end of the American League season. Away from the troubles and tensions of New York, playing baseball was fun again. Chase helped the Millers win their fifth pennant in a row by batting .385, with twenty-one hits in eighty-one at bats. He hit five doubles, three triples, and two home runs, stole five bases, scored twenty runs in twenty-one games, and played his usual spectacular defense.[43]

He did not achieve this remarkable record against wholly inferior competition. The California State League, despite its outlaw status, attracted a handful of prominent athletes, including several former or future major leaguers. Among Chase's Stockton teammates were Bill Moriarty, George's brother, who would have a brief trial with the Cincinnati Reds in 1909; Danny Shay, who had played for three teams in a four-year major league career; Doc Moskiman, who would have a brief trial with the Red Sox in 1910; and Jim McHale, who had played 21 games with the Red Sox earlier that year. With Sacramento were Chase's former coach at Santa Clara, Charlie Graham; Nealon, who had spent two years with the Pittsburgh Pirates and in 1906 led the National League in runs batted in; and Enwright, who would have a three-game trial with the St. Louis Cardinals in 1909. Spider Baum, who never played in the major leagues but whose path would again cross Chase's several years later, pitched for Fresno, while Harry Wolter, later Chase's teammate with the Yankees; Frank Arellanes, soon to join the Boston Red Sox; and Elmer Stricklett, a former spitballer for the Brooklyn Dodgers, were stars for San Jose.[44]

Despite Chase's insistence that he was through with the major leagues ("No more of the big bush for me. They can go as far as they like, I'm done"[45]), at least two American League teams apparently believed that he could be convinced to change his mind. The Boston Red Sox asked Sacramento manager Graham, their representative on the West Coast, to intercede with Chase on their behalf before his first game for Stockton, in Sacramento on September 9. The Red Sox hoped that Graham, as Chase's former college coach, would prove a persuasive figure. They said that they were ready to buy Chase's contract from New York or make a trade if he would agree to play for Boston, and also hinted at a hefty raise and even an appointment as manager.

When Graham told Chase of the Boston offer, however, Chase merely replied, "Nothing doing. I have had enough of the East." He added that his health, which had suffered in New York, was more important to him than any glory that the Red Sox could offer. At least one reporter, observing Chase's physical condition, found his explanation plausible: "He has grown taller and thinner and does not look to be in the rugged health which he enjoyed last year. His playing, though still fast, lacks the ginger he has been showing."[46]

Several weeks later, while the Detroit Tigers were in the process of losing the World Series to the Chicago Cubs, several newspapers reported that the Tigers were offering five players to the Yankees in return for Chase and either Wid Conroy or George Moriarty. The five players included three-fourths of Detroit's starting infield—Claude Rossman, Red Downs, and Bill Coughlin—plus a young utilityman named Wade Killefer and righthander George Mullin, one of the Tigers' best pitchers.[47] Mullin had won seventeen games in 1908, third-best on the Detroit staff but three more than any New York pitcher, and had won at least twenty games in each of the previous three seasons. If true, the rumor that the Tigers, who had just won their second pennant in a row, would consider trading a top pitcher, three regulars, and another player for Chase and a utilityman indicates something of the esteem in which Chase was held. The rumor also indicates that most of organized baseball did not expect Chase's participation in the outlaw league to result in serious disciplinary action.

In fact, organized baseball may have decided that it needed Chase more than Chase needed organized baseball. According to another rumor, Ban Johnson himself supposedly came out from Chicago in mid-October to plead with Chase to rejoin the Yankees, although this story cannot be confirmed.[48]

Johnson and his National League counterpart Harry Pulliam did travel to San Francisco in December in an attempt to convince the California State League to give up its outlaw status and sign the National Agreement, but the negotiations foundered when the two sides could not agree on how to dispose of those players who had jumped contracts with teams in organized baseball to play with the outlaws.

While that was exactly what Chase had done, Johnson went to some lengths to excuse him. The American League president, noting Chase's "good record with the New York club," implied that the National Commission would look kindly on an application for reinstatement from Chase, and attributed his abrupt abandonment of the Yankees to his feud with Elberfeld.

A few days later an article in the San Francisco *Examiner* predicted that Chase would indeed return to the Yankees in 1909. Apparently merely playing with the outlaws was considered a minor offense; actually jumping a contract was the "unpardonable offense," and thus far Farrell had not preferred such charges against Chase, or even complained officially to the National Commission about Chase's participation in California State League games.[49]

While Johnson and Farrell were preparing a graceful way for Chase to rejoin the Yankees, Cy Moreing vowed to escalate his war against organized baseball. He issued a statement on January 1, 1909, announcing that he would move his Stockton team to San Francisco, where Chase would be his major drawing card while receiving more money than any two players in the Pacific Coast League. "Speaking of Chase," wrote Moreing, "it brings a smile to his face whenever he reads all of the rot being sent out of the East about his returning [to the Yankees]."[50]

Moreing's statement was mere wishful thinking. Chase was shrewd enough to realize that the California State League had no chance of surviving a war against organized baseball. He later claimed that Moreing had offered him a salary of $9,000 for the 1909 season, but said he had told Moreing of his doubts about the league's future and advised the rebellious manager to give up his struggle (to no avail; Moreing reportedly lost $45,000 in the California State League).[51] Chase dutifully applied to the National Commission for reinstatement, claiming that poor health had made a move to California seem advisable (he later said that the tension between him and Elberfeld had caused him to drop to a mere 154 pounds, the lowest weight of his career).[52] The commission could have suspended him for five years, but Farrell begged Johnson to go easy on Chase and he was duly reinstated upon payment of a $200 fine.[53] Once again, Chase had beaten the rap, and proven that organized baseball was unwilling to enforce the letter of its own law, at least where a major gate attraction was concerned.

Why did Farrell take his part? Perhaps he had come to share Chase's rumored dislike of Elberfeld; the hot-tempered infielder lasted only one more season in New York. Perhaps Chase's reputation as a troublemaker scared off other teams to whom the Yankees might have traded him. Perhaps Chase was simply too great a favorite with the New York fans; Farrell knew that no other Yankee could match Prince Hal as an attraction.[54]

Whatever the reason, the Yankee management tried to downplay the previous year's problems. "There are no cliques in my team," insisted Stallings. "How could any one say that Hal Chase caused trouble in a ball club? He is the greatest ball player I have ever seen." Joe Vila immediately revised his opinion of Chase, writing that there was "no hard feeling on the part of President Farrell towards Chase, who has already been forgiven and will be received with wide open arms by the fans, who appreciate his worth." Vila noted approvingly that Prince Hal's first action upon arriving at the Yankee spring training camp in Macon, Georgia, "was to shake Elberfeld's hand and in a few moments these star ball players were off in a corner chatting confidentially as if there had never been the slightest friction." In early April Chase and Elberfeld were said to "smoke the pipe of peace constantly."[55]

All did not continue smoothly for Chase and the Yankees that spring. In early April, while Chase was nursing a minor ankle injury, several newspapers reported that he had come down with "a touch of malaria."[56] One reporter noted that he was "thinner in the face than he was several days ago, and his usual exuberant spirits are not with him at present," while another added that he had "broken out with some sort of rash." A day later, after an examination by a local physician, he was confined to the "pesthouse" in Augusta with smallpox, apparently contracted from two bellboys at the Yankees' hotel in Macon.[57]

Chase later claimed that he had had "a great time" during his three weeks in the hospital in Augusta, but they must have been frustrating. When the Yankees played Augusta of the South Atlantic League on April 5 Chase was in the hospital cupola, about a half-mile away, "frequently waving his hand at his teammates."[58] Nellie came down from New Jersey to be with him, although she was only allowed to talk with him over the telephone. His illness threw a scare into the other Yankees, who had to be vaccinated, with often unpleasant results, and were delayed three times by zealous health inspectors on their way north to New York. Joe Vila insisted that Chase's condition was not serious ("He's had an attack of varioloid and a slight one at that"), but it created sympathy for the prodigal first baseman.[59] By the time he rejoined the Yankees Chase was again a hero; when the Yankees announced preparations for a Hal Chase day early in the season, one reporter predicted that Chase's "thousands of admirers and hundreds of close personal friends in New York" would welcome him so enthusiastically "that the noise will drive all the fancy offers he had from the Pacific coast outlaws out of his brain."[60]

Chase reached Jersey City on Sunday afternoon, April 25, and went straight to his in-laws' house in Bayonne. That night he went to Grand Central Station to see the Yankees off on the 10 p.m. train for Boston. His welcome was warm; his teammates "let out a whoop" when they saw him, and one fan said, "Gee! If it'd been in the papers that he was going to be here there'd ha' been 10,000 people here!"[61]

At the station Chase said that he had been practicing for the last ten days and felt in fine fettle. "All things considered, I did not have such a bad time in Augusta," he said. "I chafed, of course, at having to be away from the team, but evidently while I was missing I wasn't missed [the Yankees were off to a good start without him]. Manager Stallings wired me the results of the games, and I was unhappy only on the first day of the season, when the Senators trimmed us. The doctor in Augusta is a warm friend of Manager Stallings, and I had the best care and attention while I was laid up.

"Besides taking an hour's practice every day, I used to sit on the fence in the afternoon and watch the South Atlantic League team play ball. That's a fast little league. I will call on President Farrell in the morning. I appreciate being back in the American League and am grateful for the plan of my friends who thought of the Hal Chase Day scheme. I hope on that afternoon I won't do as Hans Wagner did when the Pittsburgh fans honored him. Wagner struck out once, did not make a hit and his team was beaten besides."[62]

On the morning of May 3 the New York *Globe* published a poem by the Yankees' George Moriarty. Relief that he would not after all face a season of being compared unfavorably to Chase as a first baseman undoubtedly contributed to Moriarty's exuberance. A single stanza will perhaps suffice to give an idea of the whole:

> Old New York is a cheery place
> Most everyone seems glad
> The heavy hearts are happy now
> Where once they were so sad
> It's not because Jim Jeffries said
> He'd fight that smoke next year
> We're soused with joy and bliss because
> Our old friend Hal is here![63]

That afternoon a crowd variously estimated at nine thousand and twelve thousand braved cold, wet weather at Highland Park "to pay tribute to the young first baseman after his trying time."[64] Before the game Chase caused a scare in the Yankee clubhouse by pretending to pick scales off his hands and toss them around the room, adding casually that when they reached that stage they were dangerous.[65] Once upon the field, however, a more decorous atmosphere prevailed. Vila reported, without a trace of irony, that "The first time Chase came to the bat his fellow players walked to the plate and Norman Elberfeld in a speech of fifty words, all well chosen, presented Prince Hal with a $600 silver loving cup. It was a gift on the level and showed just what the Yankees thought of this mild-mannered, modest baseball star." Chase's "little speech" in reply "was made in such modest tones that nobody in the stands heard it."[66] Still, despite such public attempts to smoothe over the controversy, Chase's desertion of the team the previous season had irreparably tarnished his standing among the fans. He might still be the best first baseman in the game, but from now on many would feel that the Yankees would be better off without him.

The skeptics were still in the minority in 1909, however, as under Stallings and with Chase back in the fold the Yankees improved to fifth place, winning twenty-three more games than they had the previous year. The Big Chief, as Stallings was nicknamed, overhauled the team's roster, and Chase, who was one of only three 1908 regulars to retain his job in 1909, batted a solid .283 and finished second on the team in runs batted in and stolen bases despite missing most of the month of August with a sprained ankle.[67]

Chase was clearly the best and most popular player on the team, and he enjoyed the perks that accompanied that status. In 1910 his salary was $5,500, at a time when only a handful of players earned more than $4,000.[68] He was also popular with the fans. In January of that year he was in Ogdensburg, New York, on the St. Lawrence River, on a barnstorming tour with an indoor baseball team. On January 8 the temperature in Ogdensburg was twenty below zero. As Chase walked from the hotel to the train station a man confronted him outside the town drugstore.

"You're Hal Chase," said the man. "I know you from your pictures." Chase confirmed the man's suspicion, whereupon the stranger abruptly reached down and picked up a handful of snow, which he proceeded to rub in Chase's face. Chase naturally took exception, and began to fight the man. A small crowd gathered quickly, and another man explained that the stranger had merely been trying to save Chase's nose.

Everybody went into the drugstore, where the townspeople continued to rub his face with snow. "Sure was a good thing I stared at you," said the stranger. "Otherwise I wouldn't have noticed that you was well along to getting a badly frostbitten nose."

Chase related this story when he returned to New York. "Chances are that I wouldn't be sitting here with a healthy nose on my face if I wasn't a ballplayer," he concluded. "Sure pays to be sort of famous."[69]

Andy Cava, a pretty fair sandlot first baseman in New York at the time, offered another testament to Chase's popularity. He named his eldest son, born in 1911, Harold Cava in tribute to his ballplaying hero.[70]

Another taste of fame came in a different form. Chase's friend and doppelganger Christy Mathewson had become so famous that in 1910 a New York publisher initiated a series of fictional sports books for boys, ostensibly written by Matty and "edited" by W. W. Aulick. The first book in the series, titled *Won in the Ninth*, was a *roman à clef* in the style of the popular Frank Merriwell and Dink Stover books. The story involves a shy young Californian named "Harold

Case" who tries to win a spot on the varsity baseball team at Lowell University, "the greatest University in the East." Mathewson/Aulick made sure that any baseball fan would recognize the other characters, all of whom were thinly veiled versions of actual major league stars, as well. The team is managed by Hughie Jenkins (Jennings), and includes such players as Johnny Everson (Evers), Ty Robb (Cobb), Honus Hagner (Wagner), Tris Talkington (Speaker), Babe Radams (Adams), and Miner Black (Brown). Last year's first baseman, Fred Penny (Tenney), has graduated, and Jenkins is planning to try a couple of newcomers named Dill and Ross in Penny's place.

The description of Case seems lifted from the newspaper descriptions of the younger Prince Hal himself: "He was a well built fellow, but modest and somewhat backward about pushing himself forward. His hair was brown and his features were good although no one would call him handsome. His eyes were light blue and clear, his mouth was firm, and if the other fellows only knew it, he was as quick as a flash in any game he was familiar with, and he was as graceful as a deer in motion. He could run almost as fast as a deer, too." Later in the book Everson describes him in language which was often applied to the real-life Chase as well: "He is a quiet chap and unassuming."[71]

The lefthanded Case is determined to make the team as a pitcher — perhaps a nod to Chase's well-known infatuation with pitching — even though his friend Hagner suggests that he might make a better first baseman. Case makes the team as a substitute pitcher, but sees little action until both Dill and Ross have proven unreliable first basemen. Then, in a game against Armour, a desperate Jenkins sends Case in to play first base. Of course he immediately makes a sensational catch: "Nothing like it had ever been seen before on any ball ground."[72]

The story proceeds predictably to the championship game against Lowell's archrival, Jefferson College, whose baseball team is managed by Frank Church (Chance) and features such stars as Tommy Beach (Leach), Larry La Joy (Lajoie), Eddie Hollins (Collins), Sam Warcford (Crawford), and George Mellen (Mullin). As the Lowell team travels west by train for the first game of the series with Jefferson, Mathewson/Aulick writes: "Hal ... did wear his cap on the train and just before he went to bed he took a wad of chewing gum out of his mouth and stuck it on the top of his cap. There may have been no superstition connected with that, however. He probably only wanted to put it where he could find it."[73]

Of course the two teams split the first two games of the series, and the third and deciding game is played at the Polo Grounds in New York. Jefferson takes a 5–3 lead at the end of eight innings, and has the bases loaded with two out in the top of the ninth. Then Church hits a grounder to Lowell's third baseman Arthur Delvin (Devlin), whose throw to Case is extremely high. The result is a collision that in some ways prefigures the real-life Chase's future relationship with the real-life Chance: Case "ran three steps, made a mighty leap into the air, his back to the ball, and then that right hand of his shot up one, two, maybe four feet higher, and he got it. He was as far from the bag almost as the runner,

A picture of Chase in action, from the December 16, 1909, issue of *The Sporting News*. *Thomas Carwile Collection.*

only he was up over it. He came to earth feet on the base and as the umpire waved his hand for the out, Hal and Church came together and the breath was knocked out of both of them."

Lowell wins the game in the bottom of the ninth inning on a home run by Hagner, but Case's sensational catch is the key play of the game. By the end of the book Mathewson/Aulick has conveniently dispersed the fictional players to the major league teams for which their real-life counterparts played: Case to the Highlanders, Jenkins and Robb to the Tigers, Church, Everson, and Black to the Cubs, Hagner to the Pirates, and so on.

The book, of course, is a wholly undistinguished work of literature, designed primarily to capitalize on the fame of its alleged author. But the fact that Mathewson (or Aulick) decided to make "Harold Case" the hero of the very first book in the series indicates something of the esteem in which Chase was held, and suggests that Matty and Prince Hal were on good terms at this time. In fact, Mathewson gave Chase a signed presentation copy of the book.[74]

In March 1910 Stallings appointed Chase the first captain in the history of the Yankees. Perhaps the manager hoped that the new title would lead to a new attitude on the part of his star player. Chase did indeed seem to be in a good mood in spring training; he played the ninth inning of New York's first exhibition game, against the University of Georgia, in his stocking feet, holding his baseball shoes in his throwing hand while he retired the side. But a few days later he hurt his ankle, and in late March he returned to New York to await the birth of his son.[75]

The Highlander infielders during spring training in 1910 in Georgia. Team captain Chase is third from the right. *Thomas Carwile Collection.*

Young Harold was born on April 6, and his famous father rejoined the team three days later for an exhibition game in Jersey City, shortly before opening day, and early in the season was playing outstanding baseball again. Yankee fans expected their team to continue to improve in 1910. Their optimism still seemed justified in early July; the Philadelphia Athletics led the league by a comfortable margin, but Stallings had the Yankees in second place.[76] Beneath the surface, however, were the stirrings of the same kind of disaster that had befallen the team in 1908. The temperamental Elberfeld was gone, sold to the Washington Senators the previous winter, but once again Chase would play a central role in the Yankees' ongoing soap opera.

Despite the characterization in Mathewson's book, Chase's behavior showed that he was well aware of his status as a celebrity. No longer was he the popular, mild, modest young man who had charmed his teammates six years earlier — if, indeed, he ever had been; while some of the other Yankees found him a likeable companion,[77] for the most part he was earning a reputation as a selfish prima donna who made little effort to conceal his scorn for his teammates. A relatively mild example of such behavior occurred on September 30, 1909. The Yankees held a 4–2 lead over visiting St. Louis with two out in the top of the ninth inning when Hobe Ferris of the Browns lofted an easy fly ball to outfielder Clyde Engle. "Almost all the players on the diamond and the benches began their dash for the clubhouse before the ball, high in the air, quivered in its turn for the descent," reported the *Times*. "Chase sped so swiftly toward his shower bath and street clothes that he was close to the clubhouse gate ere the ball came to earth." But the unfortunate Engle dropped the ball, and the players were called back to the field. "Chase hardly could believe he was wanted again on first base. He grinned at those who first called him back, and when he did return he stared at Engle as if at a strange specimen of the genus ball player." St. Louis went on to tie the Yankees by scoring two runs before the game was called because of darkness.[78]

More troubling was an incident during the 1910 season that third baseman Jimmy Austin recalled years later. Yankee infielder Jack Knight had been hitting extremely well with a new bat. Chase, who already "had a thousand bats himself," according to Austin, wanted to try it. He asked Knight, "You don't mind if I borrow your bat, do you, Jack?"

"I'd rather you didn't," replied Knight, "because it's the only one I've got."

At this, recalled Austin, "Chase got so mad that he took Jack's bat and slammed it up against the dugout wall as hard as he could."[79]

Such actions did not exactly endear Chase to his teammates, but their attempts to punish him backfired: "Some of the other infielders, in their dislike of him, tried to make him look bad by whipping the ball across to him at bad angles," recalled Frank Graham, "but succeeded only in making themselves look bad, because he would snare the throws with the greatest of ease."[80]

Chase's relationship with his teammates was not the only problem plaguing the Yankees in 1910. In late July Ban Johnson announced that he would investigate Chicago manager Hugh Duffy's charges that the Yankees had been stealing opponents' signals during the 1909 season. Johnson seems to have seized upon the sign-stealing charges as an excuse to renew his war on Stallings.[81] And once again Chase's health betrayed him; this time he came down with malaria, missing two crucial series against the Red Sox and Tigers at the end of July.[82] He returned to New York to recuperate; then, while he and pitcher Jim "Hippo" Vaughn, his closest friend on the team, were traveling to Cleveland to rejoin the team, their train was involved in a wreck, and Chase suffered a wrenched neck.[83]

And once again ominous stories were circulating about dissension on the team. Ernest J. Lanigan in *The Sporting News* reported a rumor "that Hal Chase was well enough to play with the Highlanders against the Tigers and the Red Sox and that the reason he didn't was because he was peeved at Stallings." Lanigan added casually that "Chase will undoubtedly be the next manager of the Highlanders, but there is slight chance of George T. Stallings being canned just to elevate Prince Hal to the leadership."[84]

Lanigan's prediction, as subsequent events would prove, was only half right. By August 8, following a loss to the Tigers in Detroit, the Yankees had fallen to fourth place, and Chase felt compelled to address the rumors of dissension. "All that talk about me sulking seems to be an invention of the papers, which I think is ridiculous. I have not been in the best of health for some time. I have felt good some days and the next would have to just force myself to make some plays around first base that would ordinarily be easy for me. It was first thought that I had malaria, but upon examination the doctor said that there was no signs [sic] of malaria and that all I needed was a rest. I will take that rest until the team returns home and then get back in the game. There is absolutely no truth in the sulking story. If I wanted to sulk I would not have joined the club in Cleveland from New York. I think a rest will do me good, and then I will get in the game and give the club my best, as I have always tried to do."[85] He was absent for more than a week, during which time the *Press* reported that he took "ocean baths daily at Rockaway" on the advice of his doctors.[86]

Years later, however, Austin claimed that Chase's departure in late July had a more devious explanation. He recalled that when the Yankees left Cleveland, their previous stop, "Nobody could find Hal Chase.... he'd just disappeared. The next day we found out what had happened. When we had gotten on the boat for Detroit, he had taken the train to New York. He'd gone to Mr. Farrell ... and complained about Stallings and a lot of other things."[87]

When Chase finally rejoined the team on August 18 the *Press* reported that he was ready "to see if he cannot have something to say about who is going to capture the automobile offered [by the Chalmers company] for the country's leading hitter."[88] By the end of August, however, Chase was batting only .285 — a respectable average, but far behind the league leaders. Still, the Yankees had been playing well. In early September they passed the Red Sox and briefly moved into second place before immediately losing three games in a row in Boston and dropping back into fourth. Shortly thereafter, in Chicago, the internal dissension finally boiled over amid charges by Stallings that Chase was deliberately "laying down" on the field.

The trouble started on Sunday, September 18, in St. Louis, where the Yankees lost 6–3 to the Browns. With one out in the eighth inning, New York had runners on first and third while trailing by three runs. Chase called for a squeeze bunt but missed the ball, and Bert Daniels was an easy out at home. After the game Chase claimed that he had accidentally given the signal for the squeeze play, and had then been forced to try to go through with it. Stallings claimed that Chase had deliberately changed the signals in order not to be interfered with from the bench, and had called for the squeeze on his own.[89]

The Yankees lost the opening game of their next series, in Chicago on September 19, when Chase and Yankee pitcher Jack Quinn got tangled up trying to field a bunt. Quinn eventually picked up the ball, but too late to keep Chicago's Bruno Block from scoring the only run of the game. The play overshadowed a botched hit-and-run play on which Bert Daniels again was thrown out, this time at third base, when Chase missed a pitch.[90]

The loss touched off a week of controversy and chaos for the Yankees, and once again Chase was in the middle of it. This time he was locked in a power struggle with Stallings, and the charges and countercharges taxed even Farrell and Ban Johnson's considerable expertise in spin control. When the dust finally settled Chase had not only emerged unscathed from another potentially major scandal, but had replaced Stallings as manager.

Initially, however, the outcome seemed anything but certain. The New York *Globe* reported that after the loss to the White Sox Chase had been "the storm centre" of a fight on the bus carrying the Yankees back to the Lexington Hotel, "the other players blaming him for the loss of the opening battle here." The team was being "torn asunder by internal dissensions," and Chase's managerial aspirations were the cause.[91] "Speaking frankly," an anonymous source told *The Sporting News*, "the team accuses Chase of laying down on the club for the reason that he expects to be made manager next year and wants the credit of boosting the club into a pennant." Vaughn was accused of "being in league with Chase in an effort to make the latter manager," while the other Yankees, "almost without exception," sided with Stallings.[92]

Two days later, after another White Sox victory, Farrell summoned Stallings to New York. The manager left team secretary Tom Davis, Farrell's brother-in-law, in charge; Davis immediately turned control of the team over to Chase.[93] The significance of this move was not lost on the Yankee players, who were not happy about it. "With the exception of possibly four men, the players on the team are lined up solidly against Chase, and say openly that they would not play their best ball for him," reported the *Globe*. "Immediately several players said that they would ask Mr. Farrell to trade or sell them to other clubs...."[94]

With Stallings gone, Chase went on the offensive. He announced that he had already signed a $10,000 contract to manage the Yankees in 1911, and added, "The most outrageous stories have been printed concerning me, and I am going after some of the people who have been spreading them. If Stallings says that I have tossed games away I will force him to apologize. My playing and my record speak for themselves, and I am quite willing to leave it to the public as to what sort of a ball player I am or what I am worth to a team."[95]

Chase said that the trouble between him and Stallings began when Chase made a routine error during the series in St. Louis: "One day I dropped a ball, a thing which any player might do, and I drew a 'roast' from Mr. Stallings. If the 'roast' had been brought on by a boneheaded play I would have felt that I deserved it." Things came to a head, said Chase, after the first game in Chicago, as a result of the bungled hit-and-run play on which Daniels was thrown out. Stallings said nothing about the play at the time, according to Chase, but that night the first baseman ran into a New York reporter who told him, "I have an interview with Mr. Stallings to the effect that you are laying down on the team."

According to Chase, "Mr. Stallings later verified the statement and admitted that he was quoted correctly. Of course," he added drily, "such events could not put one in a pleasant frame of mind. Stallings has always shown a tendency to go behind a man's back. I feel and know that in this trouble I have the support of every member of the New York team."[96]

This was, to say the least, an exaggeration; Jimmy Austin and Jack Knight, for example, would not seem likely supporters of Chase.[97] But Farrell, according to one newspaper report, "does not believe Chase has caused any trouble in the team and ... is sure that the talk of internal dissension has been exaggerated." According to team secretary Davis, "there was no truth in the report that there had been a battle in the New York players' bus after the game in Chicago on Monday," said Farrell, who added that he had not spoken to Chase about managing the team "next year or any other year."

Publicly, Farrell made a great show of maintaining a pose of judicious objectivity with regard to Stallings's accusations: "George and I will have a long conference tomorrow, but I will not decide on anything until I have carefully considered all the angles and found out just what are the differences between Chase and Stallings and what has brought about the present situation.... I want to give Stallings's requests the consideration they deserve and shall take Davy Crockett's advice: 'Be sure you're right, then go ahead.'" In actuality, Farrell and Devery had never liked the abrasive Stallings,[98] and may have been glad of an excuse to get rid of him.

Stallings, though "his perfectly good eyes enabled him to read the handwriting on the wall, the bench, and everywhere else,"[99] resolved to go down fighting. He admitted that he had been an unpopular leader, at least initially, but insisted that he had won the players over when they realized that his methods got results: "I beat and drilled baseball into them until almost every man on the team hated me, but now that they see what I have made of them I think every man except two are [*sic*] for me strong." Stallings insisted that the idea of Chase replacing him as manager was absurd: "As for Chase, he is one of the grandest ballplayers in the world, but so far has never shown that he knows anything about running a club. He has never suggested or taken part in a single decision regarding possible new plays which have come up in our meetings in the clubhouse, and he has not been to morning practice but twice all season. Teamwork can only be brought about by talking over plays and then getting out in the morning and trying them and keeping at them until they are ready to be sprung."[100]

After two meetings with Stallings on September 22, the Yankee owner pronounced himself shocked at the manager's story: "To my surprise, Mr. Stallings made grave accusations against Hal Chase.... Mr. Stallings charges that Chase has not been giving his best services to the club, and that he has been guilty, in baseball parlance, of 'laying down.'" Farrell promised a prompt and thorough investigation of the charges. "If Chase is guilty of Stallings's charges, there is no place on the New York American League team for him, or any other team, in my judgment. If he is not guilty, he should be promptly cleared of the charges, that he may stand vindicated before the public."

Farrell's spin control campaign was in full swing now. The New York *Tribune* called the situation "so one-sided that it is hard to understand how [Stallings] could invite almost certain banishment [by forcing Farrell to choose between him and Chase].... First basemen like Chase are born, not made, and not born very often, either, while managers like Stallings, so successful as he has been, can be replaced." The *Tribune* praised Stallings's ability to judge baseball talent, but noted delicately that "the rather strenuous way in which he handles his men is quite likely to cause dissatisfaction and bring about a revolt."[101]

W. M. Rankin in *The Sporting News* echoed this assessment of Stallings, with a veiled reference to the old sign-stealing charges: "No one will question his knowledge of the game, or his ability to get together a winning team, but his methods have not always been of a nature desired by others interested with him in the success of the game, in which honorable dealings, conforming to upright principles, peace and harmony in its ranks are more essential to its welfare than in the mere developing of a pennant-winning team."[102]

Farrell announced that he would go to Cleveland, where the Yankees had gone to play the Naps, to investigate Stallings's charges personally, though he ordered Stallings himself to stay in New York. The press, which had initially reported that the players sided with Stallings, now reported that to a man his teammates stood by Prince Hal. Meanwhile Chase, no doubt at Farrell's urging, backed off his earlier statements in Chicago. "I am not trying to supplant Stallings as manager," he insisted. "I am perfectly satisfied to go about my own business and try to do it conscientiously. I am not desirous of assuming managerial control of the team, for I think I have all I can do to play first base, and were I manager I should be hampered in my work."[103]

When American League president Ban Johnson joined Farrell in Cleveland, Stallings realized his goose was cooked. Johnson revealed that he had summoned the Yankee manager to his office four days earlier — the day of the first game against the White Sox — to discuss the Chase situation. At that time, said

Johnson blandly, "I explained to Mr. Stallings the position that the American League took in the matter...." The New York *Times* reported that at their meeting Johnson had told Stallings that "he must get out of the league at once," and had come to Cleveland merely "to make known his ultimatum to Farrell personally. Stallings knew he was through when he left Chicago for New York Wednesday afternoon."[104]

The acerbic Ring Lardner probably summed up the feelings of many in an imaginary monologue by Farrell in verse form, which began, "I am tired of this stalling and chasing,/And chasing and stalling again."[105] The denouement finally came on September 26, when Farrell formally announced that Chase had been appointed the new manager of the Yankees. "I have found the charges presented against Chase by Stallings absolutely unfounded," said the Yankee owner. "I presented them to Byron B. Johnson, president of the American League, and he decided the matter. Beyond that I have nothing to say."[106] Johnson's statement was even sharper: "Stallings has utterly failed in his accusations against Chase. He tried to besmirch the character of a sterling player. Anybody who knows Hal Chase knows that he is not guilty of the accusations made against him."[107]

The active role which the American League president had played in the drama was no surprise to baseball insiders. "Johnson has been after Stallings ever since the New York Manager became mixed up in the alleged tipping scandal of a year ago," reported the *Times,* but the animosity between the two went back farther than that. "Johnson has had it in for me for years," Stallings told a friend. Johnson's hostility apparently dated from 1901, when Stallings supposedly tried to sabotage the brand-new American League by selling the Detroit Tigers to the National League, a charge which Stallings denied: "I did not then know Fred Knowles, who is named as the man with whom it was said I carried on negotiations. Besides, it would have been an impossibility for me then to have sold the Detroit club, as Mr. Johnson had the lease of the grounds in his possession and also fifty-one percent of the stock."[108]

Despite the fact that he had lost the power struggle, Stallings refused to back down: "I can only say that I saw what was my duty and acted accordingly. I firmly believe that every charge I made against Chase not giving the club his best services, is true."[109] After Farrell's announcement on September 26, Stallings said only, "Farrell may be able to find a better manager, but not one who worked harder to make the team a success."[110] Stallings gained some measure of vindication four years later, when he led the heretofore lowly Boston Braves to the most improbable championship in baseball history. That team would forever be remembered as the "Miracle Braves," and Stallings as the "Miracle Man."[111] The Yankees would not win their first pennant until 1921, by which time neither Chase nor Farrell was associated with the team.

When Chase stepped up to home plate for his first at-bat as a player-manager in New York, against Washington on September 30, the game was halted and he was presented with two huge floral horseshoes and two large baskets of flowers. When the flowers had been cleared and the game resumed, Chase provided an ironic sequel to the tribute by grounding out to his old nemesis Kid Elberfeld, now playing third base for the Senators.[112] Chase was hitless in four at-bats and committed an error in that game, which the Yankees lost 6–3, but the team won nine of its last eleven games under his leadership to finish in second place and played well in losing a postseason exhibition series to John McGraw's Giants.

Despite all the distractions Chase finished the season with a batting average of .290, tenth in the American League. He led the team in stolen bases with forty and tied for the team lead in runs batted in. His salary was raised to $8,000 when Farrell appointed him manager, and the team had high hopes for the 1911 season. Still, many feared that Chase would never make a successful manager because he would be unable to discipline his players, and that his own playing would suffer under the added responsibilities.

An article in the *Times* summarized these concerns. Chase was "the greatest player that ever covered the initial cushion," but "the weight and worry of the duties of manager" might "affect Chase's brilliant work as a player ...." While the season would present a difficult test the fans should remain optimistic: "Discipline and harmony among the men are the things that Chase will have to work for, and the players as a body may make the task easy or hard. His standing among his team mates is high, and it is believed by Yankee enthusiasts that Chase will make a name for himself this season."[113]

Four

It Is a Business with Me

Mark Roth, one of Chase's biggest boosters among the local sportswriters, caught up with him in late February. The new Yankee manager was playing billiards with Turkey Mike Donlin, the star outfielder and notorious bon vivant of the Giants, at Jack Doyle's parlor. Donlin was hardly the sort of company a dignified leader of men would be expected to keep. In the spring of 1902, while playing for the Orioles, a drunken Donlin had attacked a chorus girl named Mamie Fields, blackening both her eyes outside a Baltimore saloon co-owned by John McGraw. He had received six months in jail.[1]

"Yes, I know the tip is out that I will blow as a manager, while there are a few who think I will be successful," Chase told Roth. He believed that any manager was only as good as his players: "A good club will no doubt help considerably to make a good manager. If you have a bad looking team, why, the manager looks like three cents."

Chase shrugged off the issue of whether he could handle the additional responsibilities. "Aside from the fact that we have a corking looking ball club I am not worried about my new position, which is one of the hardest in baseball. It is generally the policy to predict that a player will lose his standing as a player just as soon as he is nominated to be a manager." No doubt at this point he allowed himself a small smile. "I am going along in my old way, and I think you will find me playing the same old game."

Obviously Chase already knew the kind of confident pronouncements expected of major league managers in the spring. "I don't think we have any lemons in our club. We have young players who have been well-seasoned, and I think our pitching staff looks almost invincible. We seem to have all live ones on the club. All the boys are well pleased with their berths, and, old boy, harmony will go to the bat hitting .300 for our team all season, if I know anything about it." He also sounded optimistic about the Yankees' chances in the coming season. "The Yankees will be up there," he told Roth, "stick a spike in that."[2]

Roth, at least, was willing to believe. He favorably, if implicitly, compared Chase's style of leadership to that of the hot-tempered Stallings: "Chase is easy-going

Chase succeeded Stallings as manager of the Highlanders just before the end of the 1910 season but was not a success as a leader. Perhaps in part because of pictures like this, the team soon changed its name to the Yankees. *Thomas Carwile Collection.*

and will not bully his men, and will get along with them. He has a pleasing personality, and will be patting the men on the back and getting the best there is in them."

Chase himself acknowledged the pressure he faced. "It's up to me, sure," he told Roth. "The manager must make good or 'can him' will be the slogan of the fans. It won't be long now before the big show will be on. Now that is all I have to say on the matter."

Still, not all observers shared the optimism of Chase and Roth. Jimmy Austin had been the Yankee third baseman in 1910 but was traded to the St. Louis Browns in January 1911. Austin loathed Chase, but his public comments were discreet. "Hal Chase is a fine fellow," he said, "but I think he has a tough job ahead of him this season." Austin acknowledged that the Yankees had looked good in 1910, but warned that expectations were higher. "Now it is up to Chase to win the pennant next season to be a real howling success as a manager. He has to finish at least second in the race or his debut as a team leader can hardly be called prosperous. From what I have been able to figure out, he hasn't much of a chance to win the pennant, and his prospects for finishing second are not very bright."[3]

Austin's assessment of the team's chances was exactly right. In 1911 the Yankees fell from second place to sixth, twenty-five-and-a-half games behind the first-place Athletics, and won twelve fewer games than they had in 1910. Although the Yankees won as many games as they lost, the season was a major disappointment, and many blamed Chase for the team's poor showing. Like many other great players, including his contemporaries Mathewson, Lajoie, and Cobb, Chase would be considered a failure as a manager.

The Yankees held spring training in the resort town of Hot Springs, Virginia. The press reported that Chase would run a relaxed camp featuring "mountain climbing, baths, and a little practice with the baseball."[4] Chase seemed to be enjoying his new duties, and took advantage of every opportunity to display his athletic versatility.

He tried his hand at golf for the first time and was less than a complete success; according to the *Times* he "showed as much skill in sending away wild ones from the tee as he does at stopping wild ones on the diamond." He soon turned to more familiar pursuits: the *Times* carried an account of his exploits on horseback, reporting that "The many-sided Chase is a veteran at this pastime. If anybody doubts that he is an accomplished rider he has leather puttees, khaki breeches, and a cavalryman's shirt to prove it."[5] When the capricious Virginia weather kept the team indoors, "Chase, [Bert] Daniels, and [Charlie] Hemphill went swimming ... and had a fine time in the big warm water pool. Chase swims as well as he plays baseball. He did some long-distance diving."[6]

Between these pleasant pursuits the Yankees also got in some baseball practice, but even here Chase seemed not to be entirely serious about preparing for the coming season. He pitched two innings in an exhibition game in Chattanooga on March 30 and held the Lookouts hitless, although eight men reached base against him on two walks, one hit batsman, and various Yankee miscues. None of the eight scored, however, although the Yankees lost 2–1. The *Times* was pleased to report that "Chase is as spry as ever, and so far the management has not dimmed his lustre as a performer."[7] Indeed, the 1911 season was to be his best in several years as a player, as he batted .315, drove in eighty-two runs, and stole thirty-six bases. But the rest of the team was troubled. With Austin and second baseman Frank LaPorte traded to St. Louis, the New York infield remained unsettled all season. Chase tried Jack Knight, Otis Johnson, Roy Hartzell, and even outfielder Birdie Cree at shortstop, all with an equal lack of success.

Moreover, as many fans and reporters pointed out, he seemed too relaxed to be an effective manager. A manager, they argued, needed to be tough with the players and the umpires; he had to impose discipline on his men and let the umpires know that they could not get away with calling close plays against his team. Chase was too softhearted and too easygoing for the job, said the skeptics. Indeed, before the season he told his players not to argue with the umpires. The men in blue were no doubt grateful for this policy, but it did the Yankees no good on the field.[8]

Despite his placid exterior, however, there were signs that Chase was feeling the pressures of his new position even before the start of the regular season. In the first inning of an exhibition game in Indianapolis on April 6 Chase doubled to drive in a run, but "thought the ball had been caught and didn't know he had made a two-bagger until a coacher shouted to him and he collected his wandering wits."[9]

Four days later, when the Yankees won an exhibition game in Scranton by a score of 10–0, Chase could not resist another opportunity to show off his athletic versatility. "The game was so easy for New York," reported the *Times*, "that Hal Chase resigned from his post at first and pitched for a while himself."[10]

The Yankees cruised through their exhibition schedule, winning eleven of their fourteen games, and seemed primed for the start of the season. "The men are in fine condition and full of go and are delighted to have the season open and get a chance to test their strength against the best teams in the league," reported Chase the day before the regular season began. "We have, I believe, the best pitching staff in the league, a fast fielding and a hard-hitting team, and I expect we will finish either first or second."[11]

The Yankees' first home game, against the Senators on April 21, was halted while Chase had to pretend to be surprised once again by a floral tribute, this time a five-foot-high basket of flowers mounted on a float which required six men to carry out onto the field.[12] Despite the high hopes symbolized by the display the Yankees soon fell far behind the Athletics and Tigers, who opened up a big lead on the rest of the league. After Boston beat New York 14–6 on May 5, the *Times* complained that the Yankees were playing "dull baseball" and noted "a few painful incidents which showed that the Yankees were not exercising the least bit of intelligence at their command. A glaring error of judgement was

Player-manager Chase, at right, participating in the flag-raising ceremony with captain Harry Davis of the Athletics at Philadelphia's Shibe Park on opening day, April 12, 1911. During Chase's tenure as manager the team plummeted from second place to sixth. *Thomas Carwile Collection.*

made in the base running, and most surprising of all, Hal Chase allowed three runs to go to the Boston side of the ledger by an illuminating bit of bad work on a high fly, which belonged to the right fielder." The miscue occurred in the third inning, when Duffy Lewis of the Red Sox hit a lazy fly ball toward Gene Elliott. Chase, not trusting the twenty-two-year-old rookie to handle the ball and perhaps remembering Clyde Engle's blunder in St. Louis in September 1909, tried a running, over-the-shoulder catch, but dropped the ball. All three baserunners scored.[13]

Mental mistakes continued to plague the Yankees. On May 12 in Detroit the Tigers won 6–5 when Ty Cobb doubled in the seventh inning to drive in Donie Bush with the tying run, then stole third base and home "under the noses of almost the entire New York team" as the Yankees argued with the umpire that Bush had been out.[14]

Perhaps if Chase had been there, he would have enforced his no-arguing policy, but he missed that game, and the next seventeen as well. At first he was reported to be suffering from nothing worse than a bad cold, but on May 15 Roth wrote that "Manager Chase is a very sick man, and it may be weeks before the fans will see him moving about the first sack for the team." Chase was now rumored to have contracted erysipelas, an acute infectious disease. Although the diagnosis was later changed to bronchitis he was confined to his bed in Cleveland's Colonial Hotel and allowed no visitors. When the Yankees left Cleveland for St. Louis they left their ailing manager a bouquet of roses.[15]

Chase was back on the Yankee bench on May 27, as New York split a doubleheader in Philadelphia, although he did not play for another four games. When he finally returned to the lineup on June 1 the Yankees had won eighteen games and lost twenty, including their last four in a row. On that day, however, they beat the Browns as Chase had two hits, scored a run, stole a base, and "cavorted as nicely as of yore."[16] New York promptly went on a tear, winning sixteen of its next nineteen games and climbing to third place.

Eventually, of course, the Yankees cooled off. The low point of the season came in early July, when they lost four out of five games to the visiting Athletics. In the last of those four defeats Chase himself played shortstop, but committed a costly mental error when he failed to cover second base on a throw from catcher Ed Sweeney. Almost immediately rumors began to circulate that the Yankee players were chafing under Chase's management.

Mark Roth moved quickly to Chase's defense. "There has been some gossip floating around the baseball way to the effect that some of the Yankee players were laying down on Chase," wrote Roth in mid–July. "This subject has to come up every year in order to keep up with the baseball times. Chase is getting along with his players in first-class style. Perhaps he has made some blunders in handling his club, like the best of managers will do. The way the Yankees were handled in the Athletic's [sic] series started the story. The truth of the matter is that the Yankees were outclassed in those games, but of course a slump of that kind is always put up to the manager."[17]

Even the faithful Roth, however, soon acknowledged that something was wrong with the Yankees. The team was locked in a fight with Chicago and Boston for third place but seemed unable to win more games than it lost. Four days later, with the Yankees in the midst of a six-game losing streak, Roth warned that "Chase will surely have to get a move on or he will find his club having hard work to keep up in the race."[18]

A couple of weeks later, with the Yankees in fifth place and the grumbling increasing, Roth again tried to defend Chase, pleading with the fans to have patience with the twenty-eight-year-old manager: "Of course Chase comes in for a great deal of criticism, and is blamed for the slump his team is having at the present time. But Chase is not to blame. He is doing the best he can under the circumstances. A young fellow like Chase can't break in and tear the league up right off the bat.... He has made mistakes just like all baseball managers, and has been criticized and roasted for it." But Roth had to admit that "there is no pepper scattered around the Yankee lot, and the ship seems to be sinking."[19]

Chase continued to issue optimistic pronouncements. "There is no doubt that we will have to skip along pretty fast to finish in third place," he said in late August, while the Yankees were winning eleven out of thirteen games without managing to pass Cleveland in the standings, "but I think we can do it."[20]

For the most part, Chase the player seemed unaffected by the cares of being a manager, making plays that astonished even those who had grown to expect the extraordinary from him. Perhaps his exertions on the field provided his only respite from the worries and frustrations of managing an inferior team. At any rate Chase may never have played better than he did in the midsummer of 1911. In mid–July he was batting .347, best on the team and eleventh-best in the American League. He was also playing spectacular defense. In the ninth inning of a game in St. Louis on July 12, for example, the fastest Brown, Burt Shotton, was on first base when Jimmy Austin hit a grounder to the right side. Chase scooped up the ball and, astonishingly, outsprinted Shotton to second base, preserving a Yankee victory. After the game a St. Louis newspaper called Chase the "greatest first baser of all time."

Similarly, in the ninth inning of a game against the Tigers on August 8, with one out and Detroit's Davy Jones on second base, Ty Cobb lashed a hard liner toward right field. Chase, who had been moving toward second base, leaped and caught the ball one-handed, then fired it to second to double off Jones and end the game.

Even the great Cobb was impressed: "I have seen many a good play on the ball field since I have been in the big league, but there is none which one could say was any better than that.... How in thunder he ever got over there to make a play on that ball—one of the hardest I ever hit—I don't know." Cobb shook his head. "You have to take your hat off to that guy."[21]

Roth wrote that managers Hughie Jennings of the Tigers and Connie Mack of the Athletics said "that they never had seen any playing around [first base] such as Chase has put over the board this season."[22] But such moments of individual glory could not compensate for the problems of the rest of the team.

As late as September 12 the Yankees were still in third place, just ahead of Cleveland, and on October 1 they were only one game behind the Naps. But the season ended disappointingly for Chase and the Yankees. Chase injured his leg on September 22[23] and missed the next three games. When he returned to the lineup, he put himself in center field for seven games, then moved back to the infield to play second base after Earle Gardner was beaned.

By this time the fans and the players had given up. The Yankees won only six of their last twenty games, and fewer than two hundred fans showed up to watch their last home game, a 6–4 loss to the Red Sox. The most enthusiastic among them, according to the *Times,* was little Hal Jr., "who was continually calling out to his illustrious papa."[24]

On October 5 Philadelphia beat New York 1–0, dropping the Yankees to fifth place. On the next day, after a 5–4 loss to Philadelphia and Boston's victory over Washington, the Yankees fell to sixth place.[25] They finished the season with a 76–76 record and twelve fewer wins than in 1910. Clearly, Chase had proven a failure as a manager. The pitching staff, which he had predicted would be a strong point, was not nearly as effective as it had been the previous season. In fact the Yankee pitchers finished the season with a 3.54 earned run average, well above the league average of 3.34, and only ninety-one complete games, as opposed to one hundred and ten during the previous season. Russ Ford, who had won twenty-six games in 1910, was only slightly less superb in 1911, winning twenty-two. But Jack Quinn and Hippo Vaughn, who had combined for thirty-one wins in 1910, won only eight games apiece in 1911.

Moreover, the team's defense was spotty. Only one team, the last-place Browns, made more errors than the Yankees. The major factor in the poor defense was Chase's inability to find a satisfactory infield combination. On August 29, in what the *Times* called "the biggest travesty in the history of the National

A relaxed Chase, second from the right, with Naps first baseman George Stovall, Red Sox president Jimmy McAleer and Browns shortstop Bobby Wallace, on July 24, 1911, at the game played to benefit the family of Addie Joss. Joss died from tuberculosis at age 31 shortly after the start of the 1911 season. *National Baseball Hall of Fame Library, Cooperstown, N.Y.*

game," the Yankees beat St. Louis 7–4 despite being charged with seven errors, although "as many more escaped official tabulation." On September 20 the team committed twelve errors, including five by second baseman Jack Knight, and "acted like minor leaguers most of the way" in splitting a doubleheader with Cleveland. The next day Chase replaced Knight with Earle Gardner, but Gardner committed two errors, as did shortstop Otis Johnson. The day after that Chase benched Johnson and put Hartzell at shortstop.[26]

Some observers felt that such shuffling was counterproductive. They argued that no team could win putting a different lineup on the field every game, but the plague of physical ills that struck the Yankees meant that Chase could rarely have put the same starting lineup on the field two days in a row even had he wanted to do so. Knight, Johnson, Gardner, Sweeney, Vaughn, Birdie Cree, Harry Wolter, Ray Fisher, and Chase himself all missed time because of injuries or illness.

But the fans and, increasingly, the newspapers were not interested in such excuses. Chase had made some blunders in assessing the team's talent, perhaps most notably in the case of Gene Elliott. During spring training Chase had predicted that the twenty-two-year-old rookie third baseman would be an immediate star. "Elliott is as fast as a flash," said Chase in mid–March. "He is also full of the stuff which makes a big league ballplayer shine. He can pound the ball. I think he is a finished ballplayer right now." A few days later he reiterated his assessment: "I believe that Elliott is a finished big league player right now and the best I have seen hatched out of the minors.... There is no doubt in my mind that he will deliver the goods."[27] Elliott played in only five games for the Yankees in 1911, managing but one hit in thirteen at-bats, and never played in the major leagues again, which certainly did little to enhance Chase's reputation as a judge of talent.

Before the end of the season even Roth, who in the spring had praised Chase's "easy-going" nature, began to wonder whether Prince Hal was tough enough to be a manager. "Perhaps Chase is too easy with his men," Roth wrote in early September. "It has been often proven that a manager in order to be a success must have the right temperament and discipline must be enforced." He cited Chase's old friend, the ferocious John McGraw, as an example.

A few days later Roth again raised the issue of Chase's handling of the team: "Some believe that Chase is too kindhearted, and perhaps he has made mistakes. Then again all those mistakes this season may benefit him next season." Roth assured his readers that Farrell intended to give Chase another chance: "All the friends of the great first sacker are anxious that he be given another trial, and he will get it."[28]

A couple of weeks later Roth reported that Chase had signed a contract to return as manager in 1912, but the writer seemed not to share the popular assumption that things would be better the following year. "It has been passed around that he is too good a fellow to make a success as a manager," wrote Roth, "but the experience he has had this season will make him different, *say the majority.*" A few days later Roth's reversal was complete: "The writer coincides [*sic*] with those who say Chase is too good a fellow to lead a ball club."[29]

Years later Joe Vila articulated the complaints of many players and reporters about Chase's leadership: "As a manager Chase was a failure, because he didn't take his position seriously. There was no discipline on the team and Chase finally assigned himself to center field, where he was far away from trouble."[30]

At least one of Chase's former players, however, remained an admirer eight decades after Chase gave him his first taste of major league action. Chet Hoff had never played organized ball, but in the summer of 1911 his brother convinced him to pitch for the local semipro team in their native Ossining, New York. A New York banker by the name of Al Buckout, who knew Chase, happened to see Hoff pitch, and was impressed by the youngster's ability. Shortly before his hundredth birthday, Hoff recalled what happened next: "[Buckout] took me to New York and introduced me to Chase. And [Chase] called one of the big catchers over and said, 'Take this young boy down and give him a tryout.' The catcher warmed me up out there about fifteen minutes. He must have made a good report to the manager because Chase said to me, 'Come down tomorrow morning and practice with us.'"

Hoff spent a couple of days working out with the Yankees, and Chase continued to like what he saw. "I came back again the next day and he says, 'See that locker over there? Your uniform is over there. Put it on and come out with the regulars for this afternoon's game.'"

Hoff never developed into a star, appearing in only twenty-three games in four major league seasons. Perhaps the high point of his career was striking out the very first batter he faced in the majors, a fellow by the name of Ty Cobb. He remained eternally grateful to Chase, however, for giving him his opportunity. "Hal Chase was a wonderful man," said Hoff. "Oh, I loved him! ... Chase was the biggest man in New York City when he was managing. They called him Prince Hal. Everybody loved him. He was a great person. He was very easy to get along with. I always thought he was tops. Hal seemed to take a liking to me and he invited me up to his home for dinner. I met his wife and she was a very nice woman."

Perhaps because of his personal affection for and gratitude to Chase, Hoff refused to believe that Prince Hal was guilty of the crimes of which he was later accused. "That was only a rumor about Chase throwing ball games. I never saw anything suspicious going on. I never knew anything about it. I never saw him make an error."[31] Of course, it is possible that Chase would have been less interested in throwing games when he, as manager, would be held personally responsible for the team's showing.

By mid–October the World Series between the Giants and Athletics occupied the attention of the baseball world. Chase, who had agreed to lend his name to a ghostwritten column on the Series for the *Globe*, predicted that Philadelphia would beat the Giants in seven games, although he (or his ghostwriter) had kind words for Mathewson: "I think that Matty is the greatest pitcher in the land."[32]

The 1911 World Series will forever be remembered as the Series in which Philadelphia third baseman Frank Baker earned the nickname "Home Run" Baker. Baker hit two home runs in the Series, one off Rube Marquard to win the second game and one off Mathewson to send the third game into extra innings. In the tenth inning of that third game the Giants' Fred Snodgrass was on second base when a pitch by Jack Coombs got away from Philadelphia catcher Jack Lapp. Snodgrass tried to reach third base, but Lapp recovered the ball and threw to Baker in plenty of time to get the runner. When he reached the base Snodgrass slid into Baker spikes first.

Although Baker sustained only a slight cut many observers, including Chase, were convinced that Snodgrass had deliberately tried to put the Philadelphia star out of the game. "I have seen ball players who would deliberately maim an opposing player to gain an advantage, and I have seen many mean and dirty tricks pulled," wrote Chase in the next day's *Globe*, "but there never was one which I could compare to the work that that same Fred Snodgrass, centre fielder of the Giants, tried to 'pull' in yesterday's game." The plays on which Chase himself had knocked Lave Cross cold and broken Billy Sullivan's ankle evidently could not compare with Snodgrass's "fiendishness": "As I said before, it was the most cowardly and dirty piece of ball-playing I ever witnessed."[33]

Such comments were bound to be controversial in New York, which was probably what the editors of the *Globe* had had in mind all along. The city's vociferous Giant fans did not hesitate to tell Chase what they thought of his condemnation of Snodgrass. "My statement concerning the Snodgrass-Baker incidents seem [sic] to have caused more or less of a commotion in the baseball world," Chase wrote two days later. "I stick to what I originally said, and that is, that it was a deliberate attempt to injure Baker so that he could not take part in any more of the games.... I hope that I am mistaken as to Snodgrass' intentions, but it will take more than a flood of anonymous letters at the *Globe* office from baseball fans to convince me that it was an accident."[34]

The controversy continued for several more days. Roth wrote that Chase's comments had "stirred up a veritable hornets' nest," and that the Yankee manager had "been flooded with letters since the story appeared." Some of the letters were favorable, or at least polite, but others were "most venomous in their denunciation of Chase," wrote Roth. "The language used in them would make the champion long distance cusser of the world slink away in disgrace." Roth added that other players who had seen the play, including George Stovall and Tris Speaker, agreed with Chase's assessment.[35]

Just when the Snodgrass controversy was dying down Chase found himself in hot water again. This time his sense of humor, rather than his sense of sportsmanship, was the culprit. On October 24 in Philadelphia the Athletics won the fourth game of the Series 4–2, scoring three runs off Mathewson in the fourth inning. Roth described what happened next: "Hal Chase nearly caused a riot coming home from the ball park when he got mixed with some Philadelphia fans and started discussing the Athletics' hitting in that fourth inning, which were all clean hits. Chase looked at [his companion] Al Reddy and said: 'I think they were all punk hits.' Chase had to laugh it off or he might have been mobbed."³⁶

Chase also used an incident in the sixth and final game of the Series to flash his wit. In the fourth inning Philadelphia shortstop Jack Barry bunted and was beaned by the throw from Giant pitcher Red Ames. The ball bounced into right field and the Athletics went on to score four runs in the inning en route to a 13–2 rout. After the game Chase complimented Barry on his "great head work."³⁷

In the *Globe* Chase praised both teams and concluded philosophically: "So pay your bets and forget it. Baseball is a hard game to dope out."³⁸ At the time no one suspected the irony in those words, but in the aftermath of the Black Sox and other gambling scandals that rocked baseball, Chase's casual references to bets on the World Series and "doping out" baseball games would no longer seem so innocent. Indeed, just a few years later John McGraw could piously insist that "Baseball is different from other forms of professional sport. It does not need betting to add spice to it, like horse racing, for instance. In fact those who really enjoy the game most — get worked up over it — seldom bet."³⁹ The assumption in 1911, however, was that a dedicated baseball fan would as a matter of course put a little money on the World Series.

With the World Series over, the attention of the New York baseball world returned to Chase's managerial future. Roth reported that Chase, still seeking ways to improve the Yankee infield, was considering playing second base himself in 1912. While conceding that Chase could play any position on the field, Roth hoped and expected that Chase would change his mind before the season. The story indicated that Chase was planning to manage the Yankees again in 1912, and Farrell stood by him publicly. "Chase thinks he will be better as a manager next year, due to his experience this season," wrote Roth. "He will get the chance and be backed up to the limit."⁴⁰

A little over a week later a rumor circulated that Farrell wanted Harry Wolverton, manager of the Oakland Oaks of the Pacific Coast League, to take over the Yankees in 1912. The rumor had some historical precedent; Farrell had hired Wolverton to manage the Newark Indians of the International League in 1909, but Wolverton had resigned shortly thereafter when Farrell sold the club. Now, however, Farrell denied any interest in Wolverton and insisted that he still supported Chase as manager.⁴¹

Chase himself acknowledged that he had made mistakes in 1911, but clearly expected to be given a second chance. "I know that I was not the best manager in the world last season, and perhaps far from being a good one," he admitted. "I have been told by my friends that I was too good a fellow to handle a ball club, and that I did not have the right temperament to be at the helm. However, I think I will do better next season. I observed a great many things while I was on the job last season. The experience did me a great deal of good. Yes, we have the talent, and if we land another good man to play second base I think we will be playing up around the leaders all next season. I may as well take the blame for not being up there last season."⁴²

Within a few days, however, Farrell, with the help of the press, began preparing a graceful way out for Chase. On November 17 Roth reported that Chase might be considering resigning as manager: "The writer doesn't think Chase is crazy about the position, and it may be that he will tell Frank Farrell that he would rather step out and just do duty at first base. Chase can get as much money for playing first base as he can for managing the club. It's up to Chase whether he wants the job or not. At the present writing he is the manager." The message was unmistakeable; Chase was being eased out.[43]

Three days later he announced his resignation as manager at a press conference. He professed to be relieved: "I'm the happiest ball player in the world. It's a better thing for the club, and I'm sure I can hit .400 next season." Farrell maintained that Chase's decision was a surprise to him, although he conceded that "Chase is too big hearted to make a good executive." The Yankee owner also promised that Chase's salary would not be cut: "He's the greatest first baseman in the country, and I'm glad to give him the same amount as he had for managing the team, just to have him in his old position."

Chase's wounded pride was evident in a subsequent conversation he had with Roth. "I have found that a star ball player, who can get a big salary, is foolish to take up the responsibilities of leading a ball club," said Chase. "I am not crazy for the job." A touch of bitterness crept into his voice. "I have been regarded as a joke when I was manager. Perhaps I was. They tell me I was too soft, and did not have the right temperament for the leader of a ball club. Perhaps that's right, too. As I have said before, it would be better for me to lose that part of the game and attend to my duty at first base."

He no longer pretended to be the carefree young man who played ball just for the love of the sport. "I will get out of baseball long before the average player," he predicted. "It's my aim to make all the money I can now, so when I get out I can go in some other line of business." Chase was cool when discussing Farrell's promise not to cut his salary, choosing not to refer to his boss by name. "I have been treated all right by the owner of the New York club, and will stick by him. There seems to be no doubt in my mind that we will fix up the matter satisfactorily."[44]

In fact Farrell apparently offered him a $6,000 contract but kept the cut secret, allowing Chase to save face. The Yankee owner also addressed the suspicions that he had engineered Chase's removal, insisting that the resignation had been Chase's idea: "I want to make it strong that Chase was not forced out as the manager of the team. I had my mind made up to go ahead with Chase, but he thought it would be better for the club if he resigned, which would leave him nothing to do but play next season. I think he did a wise thing. There isn't any trouble. Chase stepped out of his own free will."[45]

Most of the New York newspapers expressed satisfaction with the move. The *World* said that Chase's decision to play center field, although he was the greatest first baseman in the game, had been a sure sign of his poor judgment: "At that time baseball wiseacres declared that Hal was not 'long for the managerial world.'"[46]

The *Daily Tribune* agreed. Chase had chosen to play other positions in order to keep Jack Knight's bat in the lineup when first base seemed the only position that Knight could play. As a result "many of the patrons of the park were denied the pleasure of watching [Chase] cover the initial sack," and Knight's presence in the lineup seemed to make little difference in the team's fortunes. Chase "could probably lead the team again and give a good account of himself, but as for building up a pennant winner which can meet the Athletics and fight them to a finish he is hopeless, in the opinion of most of the 'fans.'"[47]

Others were more sympathetic. The *Times* admitted that Chase had made mistakes but attributed the Yankees' disappointing season primarily to "happenings which he could not forestall."[48] The *Herald* hinted that Chase's biggest problem as manager was not his inability to discipline his players but interference from the front office, and implied that similar problems had led to Griffith's departure: "There are some who say that Chase, expecting to be the real manager, found himself entangled with the same dominating influences which entangled Griffith." If Farrell was not meddling, wondered the *Herald*, then why had the Yankees gone through three managers in less than ten years while during that same time the Giants had thrived with just one?[49]

Meanwhile the subject of Chase's replacement as manager was inspiring all sorts of rumors. At various times the list included Connie Mack, then only ten years into his fifty-year tenure with the Athletics; Yankee scout and factotum Arthur Irwin, who had managed National League teams in Washington, New York, and Philadelphia before the turn of the century; former White Sox manager Fielder Jones; former Red Sox and Braves manager Fred Lake; former Red Sox manager George Huff; Jack Dunn, president of the Baltimore International League team; and even Chase's old teammate Willie Keeler. Ban Johnson was reportedly trying to arrange a deal whereby Hughie Jennings of the Tigers would take over the Yankees, thereby competing directly with his old friend and former Baltimore teammate John McGraw of the Giants.[50] But Wolverton's name was seldom far from the top of the list, and finally, on December 11, Farrell ended the suspense by announcing that he had signed Wolverton to manage the Yankees.[51] His tenure would be even shorter and less successful than Chase's, however, and in another year Farrell would again be searching for a new manager.

Despite Farrell's assurances that there was no trouble between him and Chase many suspected that the way the "resignation" had been handled had embittered the first baseman. In early December a rumor circulated that the Yankees were seeking to trade Chase to the White Sox because he and Farrell were "not the best of friends." Roth dismissed the rumor with an example of the racist humor of the time: "There is as much chance of Chase getting away from the 'burg' as there is for a colored person refusing a piece of watermelon."[52]

The rumors, however, persisted on into the following spring. In March 1912 a rumor circulated that the Yankees would trade Chase to the Washington Senators for Walter Johnson. Johnson, arguably the greatest pitcher in baseball history, had won twenty-five games in both 1910 and 1911 while pitching for seventh-place teams and was still only twenty-five years old.

While Clark Griffith, the new manager of the Senators, might have welcomed a reunion with his former star, the trade was never made; Griffith was not about to give up Johnson, even to get Chase. Instead he used a young player named Arnold "Chick" Gandil at first base in 1912. Gandil had flopped in a trial with the White Sox in 1910 but blossomed into a star in Washington. Seven years later, after he had returned to the White Sox, his path would cross Chase's with fateful results.

Despite the unlikelihood of a Chase-for-Johnson deal, Wolverton, in Atlanta awaiting the beginning of spring training, chose to deny it publicly and at the same time dismiss rumors that an unhappy Chase would cause problems. "There is no foundation for that story," said the Yankee manager. "Chase will be with the Yankees, and I have not thought of trading him. He will be here this week with the rest of the players, and I want a man like him on my team to make it a winner. There will be no trouble with Chase, and I look for him to be as good a player the coming season as he has been in the past. That is all about the Chase story."[53]

Chase reported to the Imperial Hotel in Atlanta on Thursday, March 7, having remained in New York "to consummate a business deal" a few days after most of his teammates had departed.[54] He disclaimed any knowledge of trade rumors and promised to go all-out for Wolverton. The new Yankee manager soon showed that he intended to take a tougher line with his players than had Chase. He lectured the team on the dangers of petty internal jealousies and banned dice games in the clubhouse. Predicted Roth approvingly, "The fans will notice when the team answers the call of the bell at the opening game that there will be more ginger and aggressiveness on the ball field under Wolverton than there was under any previous manager."[55]

Chase seemed to have gotten over whatever grudge he might have had against the team, and Wolverton handled his star with kid gloves, pampering and praising him effusively at every opportunity. On March 14 a heavy rainstorm flooded the Yankees' regular practice field at Ponce de Leon Park, so the team worked out at the nearby Marist College field — all except Chase, who sat out with a sore arm. "It is something new for Chase to miss a day from Spring work," noted the *Times*, "but Wolverton thought it best for him to nurse the tender wing."[56]

Such enforced idleness made Chase restless. On the following day he came out to the Marist field again to watch practice and could not resist joining his teammates, even though he had not brought his uniform. Even with a sore arm, he put on a show: "His arm is improving, but still weak, and, barring the fact that he had no spikes on his shoes and looped his throws, he was as frisky as ever. He had not intended playing, but shed a few garments and jumped in. He was a dapper figure, with his monogrammed shirt and Nile green tie, transplanted from Fifth Avenue. Hal, be it known, is the modish dresser. Sartorially he trains with the bon ton."[57]

A pensive Chase, no longer the fresh-faced innocent, in his Highlander pinstripes ca. 1912. For the better part of a decade he was the team's biggest draw and one of the most celebrated stars in baseball. *National Baseball Hall of Fame Library, Cooperstown, N.Y.*

By March 20, when the Yankees played their first exhibition game against the Atlanta Crackers, Chase was back in the lineup, even though his arm was still bothering him. In the third inning he made a leaping bare-handed catch of a foul pop-up against the stands. The play, reported Roth, "had the colored folks in the bleachers just falling from their seats."[58]

The Yankees looked good that spring. Ty Cobb, who watched them lose to the Crackers on March 26, was impressed by the team's spirit. "Keep your eye on the Yankees," he warned. "Every one I have met tells me that Wolverton is a real live manager and will put a great deal of ginger in the club, something they lacked last season."[59]

Wolverton displayed some of his ginger on April 3 in Indianapolis, where the Yankees kicked off a brief barnstorming tour of the Midwest before returning to New York for the beginning of the regular season. The Yankees beat Indianapolis 4–3 in twelve innings, but Wolverton was ejected in the fifth inning when he raged at the umpire who had called Chase out for failing to touch first base on a triple. Wolverton "is without a doubt the most aggressive manager the New York American League club has ever had," wrote an admiring Roth. "It has always been known among the hilltop fans that things were not lively enough on the hilltop."[60]

Wolverton's attitude seemed to be contagious. On April 6 the Yankees beat Columbus 13–11 as Chase had three hits, including a triple which he stretched into a home run, and twice pressured the harried local fielders into wild throws. His 1911 policy of not arguing with the umpires had clearly been abandoned. "The pugnacious Yankees growled at the umpire a good deal," reported the *Times*, "and even Chase, usually sweet tempered on the field, fussed frequently with the arbiter. A bellicose lot, these Yankees are becoming."[61]

A crowd of some twelve thousand showed up to watch the Yankees host the Red Sox on opening day. Boston won 5–3 by scoring four runs in the ninth inning, but the New York fans still got a good show. At two o'clock, when the Yankees emerged from their clubhouse for pregame practice in brand-new white uniforms with black pinstripes, the fans looked in vain for Chase and Wolverton. Showing a fine sense of the dramatic, Chase finally appeared fifteen minutes later and received a huge ovation—"second only to that accorded to Wolverton," who also received a floral horseshoe from the Oakland Board of Trade.[62]

Unfortunately, whatever hopes the Yankees had for the 1912 season went down as quickly and completely as the *Titanic*, which sank in the North Atlantic on April 15. The Yankees lost their first six games of the season, and for good measure were beaten 11–2 by the Giants in an April 21 exhibition at the Polo Grounds to benefit survivors of the ill-fated liner.

The Yankees' game against the Athletics was rained out on the following day. This was probably the "cold, drizzly day" on which writer F. C. Lane interviewed Chase in the Yankee clubhouse. Their conversation, titled "A Half Hour with Hal Chase," was printed in the June 1912 issue of *Baseball* magazine.

Despite the occasional ugly incident with his teammates, Chase had obviously lost none of his ability to charm. Lane wrote that the first baseman "had the easy, disingenuous air of the man who is perfectly at peace with his surroundings and with life in general, the attitude of the happy-go-lucky individual who takes things as he finds them and can find gilded linings to every cloud." In a description that must have inspired a snort or two from George Stallings, for one, Lane found Chase "without any tinge of affectation or egotism, which might be easily overlooked in the case of so young a man who has attained such prominence in his chosen profession. But Chase is as free and open in his dealings with other humans as the most critical person could wish and has a kindly considerateness in his make-up which is particularly reassuring to the chance visitor."

Chase took issue with Ty Cobb's assertion that catcher was the most difficult position in baseball. "It may seem like a fellow's boosting his own game to say so but it seems to me that first base is the hardest job on the diamond. I know people may say I think so because I play that position myself but that isn't the reason. The first baseman may have fewer fielding chances than any other infield position. In fact he does, but the chances he does have are as hard as those of the third baseman's [sic]. Short, vicious drives which are coming red hot and teasing little bunts, just as the third baseman has, make his life full of trouble. But the main thing is the fact that the first baseman not only has his own troubles to look out for but he also has to handle all the chances of the other fellows [by receiving their throws]. So take it all in all and the first baseman is about the busiest person on the ballfield. First base is the natural pivot of the diamond and the art of fielding that position properly has grown wonderfully in the past few years."

Lane asked whether Chase occasionally found the throws of his teammates hard to handle, whereupon Chase smiled. "I do," he said, "but that isn't the main difficulty. The hardest part of the program is the fact that a first baseman has to study the batters all the time. If he gauges their hits rightly he can calculate the particular part of the diamond they are likely to go to and be pretty well on his guard for the throw that the fielder who gets the ball will make to first base. It is a great study, this study of the batter, and no one has begun to learn it yet."

Later in the conversation, while opining that Walter Johnson was the greatest pitcher in baseball, Chase made clear the esteem in which he still held his old friend Matty: "[Johnson] is the Mathewson of the American League and that is the highest praise anyone can give. For Mathewson was the peer of them all not long ago, though he may be going back a little now." In fact the statistical difference between the two was slight. In 1911 the thirty-four-year-old Mathewson had compiled a 26–13 record with a league-leading 1.99 earned run average, while Johnson, ten years younger, had compiled a 25–13 record and a 1.89 earned run average. But Chase's point was valid; Matty's greatest years were behind him now, even though he had three more twenty-victory seasons left, while Johnson was just embarking on an eight-year string that would see him win 214 games and four earned run average titles and lead the American League in strikeouts eight times.

Lane then asked Chase which pitch was the hardest for him to hit. "A low ball on the outside. Yes, that is my special weakness, though just at present I find them all pretty hard to hit." He chuckled modestly; on April 22 Chase was batting only .208, with five hits in his first twenty-four at bats. "I find them all hard to hit and my batting average grows leaner every day, but it won't last. Every player has slumps which he can't account for. He loses his batting eye and can't hit a balloon. They all have them, even the best, and I am far from the high water mark as a batter."

This may have been false modesty, but when Lane attempted to argue the point, "Chase only smiled and looked skeptical of my sincerity...." Lane then asked the first baseman the classic question: how does it feel to be a star?

"It isn't what people think it is," answered Chase. "The position is about all work and no play. There isn't much in it except hard work and the competition is very great. A man not only has to make good, he has to keep on making good. And the daily grind gets on a player's nerves after a while. Keeping in training all the time is a great drag to a man's energies and it is a hard life. I shall not be sorry when I am through with it all."

Lane expressed surprise at this response, but Chase insisted that he was sincere. "Yes, I mean it," said Chase, reiterating what he had told Mark Roth the previous winter. "As soon as I find that I am declining at all from my best pace I shall go out of the game for good. It is a business with me as it is with most ballplayers, nothing more or less. And when a man can no longer do himself justice in his particular brand of business, it is high time for him to get out. At any rate that is what I intend to do."

"Have you anything definitely in mind when that time comes?" asked Lane.

Chase smiled again. "No, nothing special. I studied civil engineering when I went to college and always thought I should like it. It appeals to me more than anything else I know of, at any rate, and so I should be inclined to give it a try if I had a chance."

Of course that chance would never come. Chase could not have been serious; he had never been much of a student, and even after his major league career ended he clung desperately to the one thing he truly knew how to do well, which was playing baseball.

After Chase had discussed, and dismissed, the possibility of a career on the stage, as had been attempted by his old billiards partner Mike Donlin, among others, Lane changed the subject. "Do you look for a good season?" he asked.

"The best ever," was Chase's cheerful response. "I know the boys have hit a slump just now, but Wolverton is one fine manager and the team hasn't found its stride yet. Yet we are going to play good ball before the pennant is won and plenty of it. And I think we are going to begin right away."

At this point, wrote Lane, Chase "laughed in his open, boyish way." Lane was not sure that he approved of Chase's easygoing attitude, but he was inclined to be forgiving: "If there is one fault about Chase it is that he takes himself a little too lightly, but the public must remember that in spite of his wonderful achievements he is still very young."[63]

In fact Chase was then twenty-nine years old, no longer young by baseball standards. For all his talk of retirement he was still only halfway through his major league career. But the 1912 season would continue to be difficult for him and the Yankees.

On April 27 the Senators beat the Yankees 5–0 in Washington, New York's ninth loss against only two wins. Chase, in poor health, sat out the game. Initially, his ailment was not believed to be serious: "Hal Chase woke up this morning with a bad cold, and asked to be relieved from the task of playing first base," reported the *Times*. On the following day, however, a headline screamed, "Chase Breaks Down." The article reported that Chase had been sent home to New York on a train late Sunday night. "He is suffering from a complete nervous collapse, and may not be in the Yankee line-up for several weeks."

The *Times* attributed Chase's condition to the poor showing of the team: "Although he is not worrying over the managerial troubles this season, Hal has been crumpling up under the strain of daily losses. He caught a severe cold in Philadelphia before coming to the capital, and this caused his downfall yesterday."[64]

As the Yankees continued to struggle without Chase, their fans began to turn ugly. On May 11 they showered umpire Silk O'Loughlin with bottles after Wolverton, Jack Quinn, and Gabby Street were ejected during a 9–5 loss to Detroit. Four days later Cobb went into the stands during the fourth inning of an 8–4 Tiger victory and beat a fan who had been leading what the *Times* delicately called a "chorus of mining camp talk."[65]

When Ban Johnson slapped Cobb with a suspension his teammates, on his side for once, decided to strike in protest. On May 18 in Philadelphia the Athletics won 24–2 over a Detroit team made up of local sandlot players, college boys, and dreamers. Among the Tigers-for-a-day was a former boxer named Billy Maharg, who played third base and went hitless in one at bat. Maharg would appear in only one other major league game, as an outfielder for the National League Phillies in 1916, but his name, like Gandil's, would later be linked with Chase's in the Black Sox scandal.

On the same day that the Athletics beat the ersatz Tigers Chase appeared in his first game since April 26. He pinch-hit unsuccessfully against Cleveland's Vean Gregg in the tenth inning of a 10–7 Cleveland win which dropped New York's record to seven wins and sixteen losses. Chase was back at first base for the Yankees' next game, another loss to the Naps. He went hitless in three at bats and the *Times* reported that he was "far from being the star player he is capable of being."[66] Chase committed three errors in his next two games, although his baserunning won one of those games. The Yankees and White Sox were tied 8–8 in the ninth inning when Chase reached third base and bluffed a steal of home. The disconcerted Chicago pitcher, Frank Lange, balked and Chase walked home with the winning run.[67]

The next day brought yet another outbreak of trade rumors involving Chase. This time he was supposedly on his way to the Red Sox in exchange for first baseman Hugh Bradley and outfielder Olaf Henriksen. Farrell and Red Sox president Jimmy McAleer both denied the rumor vigorously, although the *Times* reported that the Yankees had several weeks previously sought to trade Chase to Boston for the great outfielder Tris Speaker. McAleer had declined that deal, as he did this one.

In 1911 both Bradley and Henriksen had batted over .300 but had seen only limited action and had combined to drive in only twelve runs. The idea of such a trade seemed absurd, unless factors other than athletic skill and value were involved. The *Times* asserted "that Chase is on the outs with the New York management, and that he will play better baseball by far if he could get away from New York." McAleer continued to insist that no deal had been discussed. "The New York Club does not want to get rid of Chase, and I would give no players for him," insisted the Boston president. "There is no deal under consideration." Nevertheless, the simmering feud between Chase and Farrell once again seemed on the point of boiling over.[68]

All signs seemed to indicate that Chase had finally worn out his welcome in New York. On May 23, when the Yankees lost to the White Sox, 10–4, Roth reported that Chase laughed when the frustrated fans in the right field stands greeted his eighth-inning base hit with a sarcastic cheer. Roth blasted those who whispered that Chase was "laying down" on Wolverton. "Nowadays it's a crime to be sick," he wrote, but "Chase has been sick and is improving." Wolverton tried one more time to quash the trade rumors. "Chase will stay with the Yankees and we have not tried to trade him," he insisted. "Everybody seems to be trading Chase but the New York club."[69]

On June 6 the Yankees lost 8–3 at Cleveland, dropping their record to thirteen wins and twenty-seven losses. Chase had two hits, including a double, and scored a run but committed his sixth error in eight games. The next day the *Times* blasted him and his teammates. "Yanks Indifferent in Their Playing: Daniels Benched for Loafing," ran the headline. "Chase Lacks Ginger in His Work."

The article reported that Wolverton had removed right fielder Bert Daniels from the game when his lackadaisical pursuit of a first-inning Cleveland hit allowed a runner to score from first base. The *Times* also accused Chase of failing to put forth his best effort. "Chase is one of the players who has not put much ginger into his work here," it said. "To-day [June 6] he did not work out in practice, but played first. He did not put up the game of last season, however, nor does he show as much class on the bases."[70] Chase's batting average after the game was a puny .198.

A few days later yet another trade rumor surfaced in the newspapers. This time Chase and Russ Ford were supposedly on their way to the White Sox in return for Ed Walsh, second only to Walter Johnson among American League pitchers, and Rollie Zeider, a light-hitting but versatile player.[71]

Whether or not the criticism from the press and fans had stung him, Chase began to play better. After a 2–1 Yankee loss on June 9 in Chicago the *Times* noted that Chase's "all-around work" had been the highlight of the game. "It's no wonder the White Sox would like to have the services of Hal Chase," wrote Roth in the *Globe*. "If some of the fans who have been accusing him of laying down on Wolverton could have seen him yesterday they would have changed their minds. Chase is well again and 25,000 fans went wild over the play he made around the first sack."[72]

In the first eight games after the critical article in the *Times* he batted .344, raising his season's average to .232. Then on June 19, during batting practice before a game with the visiting Red Sox, a bat slipped out of Yankee outfielder Guy Zinn's hands and struck Chase in the chest. He missed the next two games and when he returned his bat had turned cold again. After Boston won the second game 15–8, dropping New York's record to seventeen wins and thirty-three losses, Roth wrote that "it was the consensus of opinion that there is something serious the matter with the Yankees."[73]

The Red Sox, storming to their first pennant in eight years, won six games in a row against the hapless Yankees by a combined score of 54–18. New York lost three out of four to the Athletics and five more in a row in Boston before finally eking out a win against the Red Sox.

Chase batted only .174 in those games. This time his poor performance may have had a psychological rather than a physical cause. "Chase is still being accused of not giving the New York club his best services," wrote Roth in late June. "Very true. The great first baseman has not looked like the great ball player he is. Sickness was one thing, but the real reason for his slump has just leaked out. New domestic troubles interfere. They have taken a great deal of the ginger out of him."[74] No doubt Nellie, left at home with their infant son, had tired of his philandering. She would divorce him less than a year later.

Perhaps seeking something to take his mind off his marital troubles, Chase sought a new challenge on the field. In the final game of the series in Philadelphia Chase convinced Wolverton to play him at second base when the regular, Hack Simmons, was sidelined with an injury. Chase went hitless in four at-bats and committed a costly error in the fifth inning, when his wild throw led to the last Philadelphia run in a 4–0 Athletic victory.

Most observers were skeptical of the switch. "Chase has said that he would like to play second base and that he could make a success of the job," reported Roth. "But there are others who do not think so.... First base is the place for Chase and he is making a mistake in shifting." The *Times* agreed: "The sight of a left-handed second baseman was a decided novelty to local cranks, but it failed to be impressive."[75]

On the following day in Boston Chase was back at first base, but had to leave the game after one inning when teammate Charlie Sterrett accidentally spiked him. He missed the next game, then played second base in six straight games. He committed three errors in a 13–6 loss to the Red Sox on June 29, but played faultlessly in the other five games.

Unfortunately the Yankees continued to founder. They won only two out of twenty games from mid–June to early July and once again had trouble putting a whole team on the field. Outfielder Harry Wolter had already been lost for the season; now Earle Gardner, Jack Martin, Gabby Street, Bill Stumpf, Pat Maloney, Birdie Cree, Roy Hartzell, and Simmons were all either hurt or slumping badly. Wolverton began shuffling players around desperately, much as Chase had the previous season. He even used Russ Ford in left field on June 29, a day after Ford had pitched in a 5–4 loss.[76]

By July 3, when they dropped a doubleheader to the Senators, the *Times* reported that the Yankees were "demoralized."[77] On the following day Chase was again out of the lineup, forcing Wolverton to use Ford at second base. Chase missed the next several games with a sprained ankle, but was back in the lineup — at first base — on July 13, when the Yankees split a doubleheader with the last-place Browns.

He had apparently put his marital troubles behind him, for he began playing with his customary flair. After the Yankees swept a doubleheader from Cleveland on July 20, with Chase tallying three hits and three of New York's nine stolen bases, the *Times* said that one reason for the team's "rejuvenation" was its aggressiveness on the bases. "Another reason is the change that has come over Hal Chase. His work yesterday was a revelation, for he has never shown the grace, ginger, and cleverness of play in a couple of seasons."[78]

After Chase had four hits in a 4–3 victory over the White Sox on July 24, raising his batting average to .247, the *Times* was even more effusive: "Chase again demonstrated his wonderful talent as a ball player, both at the bat, in the field, and on the bases." He "covered all the territory around his station with the swiftness of a shadow" and pulled off "a brainy play" in the fifth inning. The White Sox had two men on base and one out when Rollie Zeider bunted to the third base side of the pitcher's mound. Yankee pitcher George McConnell was about to field the ball when "Chase, with startling agility, rushed over and scooped the ball and made a rifle-shot toss to Hartzell, forcing the runner, Walsh, at third base."

Those at the ballpark knew that they had seen a stunning example of Chase's speed and ability to think quickly: "The crowd broke into a storm of applause, and after thinking it over every fan in the gathering of 4,000 wondered how Chase got from first base to the other side of the pitcher's box so quickly. To reach the ball in time, Chase, with all the intuition of a natural ball player, started just as soon as the bat met the ball, and seemed to know instinctively just where it was going."[79]

After the Yankees beat the White Sox 12–3 in Chicago a week later the *Times* headlined its account of the game "Hal Chase Makes Sensational Play." With two out in the seventh inning Ping Bodie hit a hard grounder off Russ Ford to the right of Chase, who could only deflect the ball and chase it into short right field. The *Times* reported what happened next: "With his back to Ford, who had run over to first, Chase grabbed the ball with one hand and threw it in the

Chase toward the end of his controversial tenure with the Highlanders, ca. 1912. *National Baseball Hall of Fame Library, Cooperstown, N.Y.*

general direction of the sack. Just as the scorers were about to credit Bodie with another hit, Ford caught the toss and [umpire John] Sheridan yelled 'You're out!'" Fans and players alike were astonished: "The Yankees were so surprised by this play that it was several seconds before they threw off their gloves and started for the bench, and Ford was so excited that he almost forgot to catch the ball."[80]

On September 20 Cleveland beat the visiting Yankees 9–8, but a play by Chase was again the highlight of the game. In the eighth inning, with Doc Johnston on second base, Cleveland shortstop Ray Chapman pushed a bunt down the third base line. Chase, who had crept in on the infield grass in anticipation of such a maneuver, "rushed almost to the foul line," picked up the ball, and fired it to Yankee third baseman Ezra Midkiff in time to get Johnston. "It was a most remarkable play," reported the *Times,* "and the crowd cheered lustily."[81]

Chase finished the season with a rush, batting .303 from mid–July to the end of the season. The fast finish raised his overall batting average to a respectable .274. His fifty-eight runs batted in led the Yankees, while his four home runs and thirty-three stolen bases were second on the team.

But again, as in 1911, his individual effort was not matched by more general success for his team. The day after his remarkable play on Chapman's bunt the Yankees lost 5–4 to Cleveland in ten innings. The defeat was their ninth in a row and dropped them into last place, behind even the traditionally awful Browns.

By October 5, when the Yankees beat the visiting Senators 8–6 to complete "The most disastrous season that a New York American League team has had," their opponents were no longer taking them seriously. In that game Washington coach Nick Altrock, utility infielder Germany Schaefer, and Clark Griffith himself all pitched in relief. The game was pure farce. The forty-two-year-old Griffith faced only one batter, his old friend Chase, who promptly hit a home run to deep right field. "That was too much for Altrock, and he promptly chased Grif off the mound and sent his fellow-comedian, Germany Schaefer, to the box," reported the *Times.* "The latter finished the game as pitcher, with Griffith playing second base and Altrock on first."[82]

Two days later the Yankees beat the Giants, who had again won the National League pennant, in an exhibition game at the Polo Grounds. Some fifteen thousand sailors, soldiers, and students, admitted free, were there; Chase was not.[83] Three weeks later, however, after the World Series, he was arrested at Olympic Park along with Josh Devore, Louis Drucke, and Cy Seymour for violating the New York law that banned Sunday baseball.

After the World Series, in which McGraw's team was beaten for the second year in a row, Giant second baseman Larry Doyle organized a team to play semiprofessional teams in and around New York. This was a common method for major league players to supplement their regular salaries during the offseason; indeed, on the same day that Chase was arrested Schaefer and Altrock of the Senators were arrested on similar charges at the Lenox Oval.

The players claimed that they had not known that they were violating the law, an unlikely defense since neither the Giants nor the Yankees had played home games on Sundays for a number of years. Magistrate Krotel of Harlem Court fined them five dollars apiece.

Besides Chase and Doyle himself, Larry Doyle's All-Stars also included Devore, Drucke, Red Murray, Moose McCormick, and Grover Hartley, all teammates of Doyle's on the Giants, and Seymour, an ex–Giant. Despite their array of major league talent they were beaten 6–0 by the Lincoln Giants, a perennially powerful black club, who managed only two hits in the game.

Black players would be barred from organized baseball until 1946, when Jackie Robinson joined the Brooklyn Dodgers' organization. Black baseball players were restricted to the so-called "Negro leagues" and a few independent black teams, where they were paid less and enjoyed less luxurious lives than did their white counterparts in the major leagues.

Occasionally a major league team would agree to play an exhibition game against one of these black teams, but most major leaguers discovered the talents of their black counterparts through less formal contacts. Major leaguers in search of extra cash would frequently compete under assumed names in local city league games, in which black teams regularly played white teams. White players such as Honus Wagner and Walter Johnson freely acknowledged that the best black players would have been stars in the major leagues, and when black teams took on teams that included major league talent the black teams frequently won, though of course the white players may not always have taken the contests seriously. Against the Lincoln Giants, for example, Chase began the game at first base, then pitched the last three innings, giving up two runs.[84]

Chase's late-season heroics for the Yankees had not gone unnoticed. "Chase in the concluding weeks of the season played a greatly improved game," wrote E. D. Soden in the November issue of *Baseball* magazine, "and his return to form was largely responsible for the increased effectiveness of the club."[85] Soden did not trouble to explain how that increased effectiveness was reflected in the fact that the Yankees won only six of their last thirty-one games.

Despite such praise, however, the 1912 season was a disappointment for Chase personally as it was for the Yankees generally. He would be thirty years old before the start of the next season, middle-aged for a major league baseball player. The month before Soden's piece appeared the same publication had published an article arguing that Philadelphia's Stuffy McInnis was now the best first baseman in the American League, because "the work of Chase at first base while brilliant at times is so marked by erratic playing as to yield to that of McInnis of the Athletics. Chase, during the latter part of the year, showed a fair return of his old powers, but even at the best his work was uncertain and by no means of that consistent standard to entitle him to first rank."[86]

And in the same issue in which Soden's piece appeared *Baseball* published a letter from a fan which showed even more clearly how far Chase's reputation had fallen. The fan, J. W. Dunwell of Plainfield, New Jersey, argued that Jake

Daubert of the Dodgers, who had just completed his third major league season, was "immeasurably superior" to Chase. Daubert was an excellent first baseman who twice led the National League in batting and compiled a lifetime average of .303 in fifteen major league seasons; nevertheless, he is seldom mentioned among the very best first basemen in major league history. But Dunwell was convinced of his superiority. Daubert was "a game, hard fighter and never lies down on anyone, something that cannot be said of Chase. The latter was once a wonder, but he has gone back more or less, and even at his best was not the equal of Daubert."[87]

Five

We Will Find a Place for Hal All Right

Farrell knew that he needed something spectacular to give the disappointed Yankee fans reason to look forward to the 1913 season, especially since the Giants had won the last two National League pennants. Conveniently, he was granted an opportunity to do just that when the Chicago Cubs of the National League unexpectedly dismissed their revered manager Frank Chance.

Chance had guided the Cubs to four pennants in seven seasons, earning the nickname of the "Peerless Leader." Injuries had limited him to thirty-three games as a player in 1911 and only two in 1912, but for years he had been one of the best first basemen in the National League, and he was still only thirty-four. He was unceremoniously fired by the Cubs' bumptious owner Charles W. Murphy after a third-place finish in 1912, provoking a "storm of disapproval" throughout the baseball world.[1] "There has never been a greater manager than Frank Chance," was the opinion of Chance's former teammate, second baseman Johnny Evers, who was named to succeed him as manager of the Cubs. "No man was more strongly, more deservedly popular than he."[2] Eventually Garry Herrmann, the owner of the Cincinnati Reds and the chairman of the National Commission, worked a deal with Murphy for Chance to spare baseball the embarrassment of seeing one of its greatest stars out of work, but Herrmann had no place for Chance on the Reds.

In late December 1912 Herrmann sold Chance to Farrell for $1,500.[3] By unloading Chance so cheaply, Herrmann may have been doing a favor for Ban Johnson, who had been a friend of Herrmann's since his days as a Cincinnati sportswriter and served with him on the National Commission; Johnson's biographer wrote that Johnson "masterminded" the series of deals that secured Chance for the Yankees, and certainly he and Farrell, still seeking ways to steal some thunder from the more successful Giants, were anxious to have the Peerless Leader join the American League's New York franchise.[4] The presence of Chance, "a treasure beyond all price," would give the entire league instant credibility. *The Sporting News* said Chance would be "the biggest drawing card that could be placed in New York opposite McGraw."[5]

William A. Phelon wrote in *Baseball* magazine that "The National League papers have gnashed their teeth and wailed bitterly over the departure of Frank Chance and the strange fact that all the clubs in the older league permitted him to depart without putting in a claim.... In New York, they think his coming means new life to the Highlanders...."[6]

Chance, however, still smarting over his treatment at the hands of Murphy, was not about to rush into anything. A Los Angeles newspaper reported that he was considering retiring from baseball and devoting himself to growing oranges at his ranch in Glendora, California, but he finally agreed to meet Farrell at the Congress Hotel in Chicago. Farrell was assisted in pressing his suit by Ban Johnson, who "got out of a sick bed" to attend the meeting, and White Sox owner Charles Comiskey, but Chance played it close to the vest until the very end. On the day before he finally agreed to terms with Farrell, in fact, Chance told the press, "I really will not play ball next season, at least not with a major league team. Neither will I manage a major league club."

But, said Chance, "Mr. Farrell's arguments were convincing," and on January 8 in Johnson's office he signed a three-year contract calling for an annual salary of $25,000, making him the highest-salaried manager in baseball, plus five percent of the club's net earnings. The total worth of the pact was estimated at $120,000.

The signing was front-page news in New York, where it was hailed as "a master stroke by the American League," and caused a sensation throughout the baseball world. W. J. McBeth in *The Sporting News* predicted that Chance would soon become "almost as priceless an object of adoration as the mighty McGraw himself," and noted that the Yankees "have received greater quantities and more favorable publicity since the name of Chance was first mentioned as Wolverton's successor than in almost any year of its former history."[7] Others agreed. "Chance's addition to the Highlanders," wrote Phelon in the March issue of *Baseball* magazine, "will mean a vast increase of revenue for the American League, and may mean a marked increase in the standing of the Hilltop club."[8]

Hundreds of fans greeted Chance upon his arrival at New York's Grand Central Station on Monday, February 10. He immediately announced that he planned to make a comeback as an active player: "Will I play next season? Sure, I will, if my legs hold out and I am able to come back."

His comeback would create a potential conflict with Chase, the incumbent first baseman and the acknowledged star of the team, but Chance, no doubt recalling their days as teammates in Los Angeles, claimed to have a solution already figured out. He was careful to compliment Chase in explaining it to the *Press:* "Well, we will find a place for Hal all right. Mr. Farrell tells me Chase wants to play first base, and Chase says he can play second. I think Chase also can play second, and see no reason why he should not be as much of a star at second as at first."

Frank Chance with the Chicago Cubs in 1909. Chase ran afoul of Chance shortly after the "Peerless Leader" became manager of the Yankees in 1913. Chance immediately traded Chase to the White Sox for "a bunion and an onion," in the contemptuous words of New York sportswriter Mark Roth. *National Baseball Hall of Fame Library, Cooperstown, N.Y.*

Chase had not distinguished himself in his brief trial at second base in 1912. Conventional baseball wisdom insisted that a lefthander could not play second base successfully on the major league level because of the extra time he would need to get into position for a throw to first base, but Chance predicted that Chase's athletic ability would more than compensate for this disadvantage: "Of course, it would be a big handicap to the average left-hander to play second, but Chase is no average player.... The situation is this: I can play only first base, and Chase can play almost any position. I think the team will be stronger with both of us in the game, so we must find a new position for Chase, and as Chase would much rather play second base we cannot well disappoint him."[9]

Chance sounded similarly upbeat in the *Tribune*, saying, "If Hal Chase can play second as he thinks he can, it will be plain sailing.... I think it will strengthen the team to have us both in the line-up." Then, in words that would soon come to seem ironic, Chance said breezily, "This managing a team is not hard if you know how to go about it.... It has been my practice to give every man an even break and then if he turns on me to get rid of him as quickly as possible."[10]

Chase had already been reported to be "greatly pleased" at Chance's signing, and had promised, wrote Fred Lieb in the *Press*, to "work his head off for the new manager."[11] Chase met with Chance several times that week, and the *Press* reported optimistically that "the two are mutual admirers of one another. Chance freely admits that he never was or could hope to be the first baseman that Chase is, and Hal, on the other hand, knows from actual experience that he is several thousand miles behind Chance as a manager." Moreover, said the *Press*, Chase would probably accompany Chance to Bermuda, where the Yankees would be holding their spring training camp. Chance seemed to have gone out of his way to get on the good side of his temperamental star; years later Joe Vila wrote that the Peerless Leader had told Chase that he would make Prince Hal his replacement when Chance's contract expired.[12]

Chance left New York on Saturday, February 15, aboard the steamer *Arcadian*, accompanied by Roy Hartzell and Arthur Irwin. Chase did not sail with them. In retrospect his absence seems an omen that his relationship with the Peerless Leader, despite the mutual admiration they professed in the newspapers, was not to be a smooth one.[13]

Still, the Yankee camp opened on an optimistic note. Chase arrived on March 3 and almost immediately glowing reports of his play at second base began filtering north. Chance told the *Times* that "Hal is making the most wonderful plays you ever saw" at his new position. "Whoever plays shortstop and third base will have to keep their eyes open, for in making plays to short and third Chase will beat any right-handed second baseman who ever covered the position."

McBeth in *The Sporting News* also confidently predicted that Chase would prove a success as a second baseman: "Chase has shown his adaptability many times. He is more than a mediocre pitcher; he can play the outfield with the best, and he would not hesitate at catching if he were permitted. So, why should he not be able to play second base with as much adeptness as a right-hander?... Hal's remarkable speed will make up for any infinitesimal fraction of a second he may lose in making a turn to throw to a bag."[14]

During the first week of March Chance and Irwin confirmed McBeth's prediction in letters to Farrell. "Chase is working out at second base and is making the most wonderful plays there you ever saw," wrote Irwin, while Chance told Farrell that "Chase already promises to be a revelation at second base. He is so fast on his feet and thinks so quickly that I do not see how he can be improved upon in this position."[15]

On March 8, however, in the Yankees' first practice game on the cricket field in Hamilton, the team received a major scare. Chase "strained his right leg so badly in trying to block off Harbison at second base in the third inning that he will be out of the game for at least two weeks, on the word of a physician. According to Frank Chance, Chase only escaped a broken leg because of a brace he was wearing."

Despite the best efforts of Doc Barrett the ankle took three weeks to heal. Chase "took his place among the other players in his street attire and tossed the ball around for some time" on March 18 but did not get back in uniform for nine more days. Upon his return he seemed to show few ill effects from either the injury or the lost practice time. "He danced about without the least sign of a limp, and made one sensational play after another," reported the *Tribune* after the Yankees beat Jersey City 10–1. "He said at the hotel this evening that as far as he could judge the ankle was as strong as ever." And again, on the following day, "Chase was a wonder at second and handled himself in a way to satisfy the most cautious that he will do his part, even though handicapped, as some contend, for the position by being left-handed."[16]

When the Yankees arrived back in New York on April 3, the *Tribune* reported that "Hal Chase came off the steamer without the sign of a limp," and quoted another hopeful prediction from Chance: "I think Chase will be ready to step in and take his place when the season starts. He has been handicapped greatly by lack of practice, but he is a remarkably natural player and undoubtedly will make as great a second baseman as he was a first baseman."[17]

All was still calm in the Yankee camp. Sportswriter Will Irwin captured a relaxed moment during a rainstorm which had cancelled an exhibition game against the Skeeters in New Brunswick. Chase and outfielder Harry Wolter, another Santa Clara product, were discussing the effects of the 1906 earthquake on their old college's baseball field.

"You remember the boys' chapel over by third base?" asked Wolter.

"Sure!" said Chase.

"That got cracked. Then after the fire they moved the priest's house—"

"The one in left field?"

"That's the one. Well, they took that and put it over by the home plate."[18]

Chase's unfamiliarity with these changes on his old college campus, seven years after the earthquake, symbolized the extent to which he had adopted New

York as his home. He would still winter in California, but the big cities of the east, with all their flash and glamour, were where he belonged now.

Those same qualities were factors in the breakup of his first marriage. In 1912 Chase brought suit against Nellie, basing his claim on an "alleged act" that had taken place a couple of months after their marriage, while she was in Jersey City.[19] But Nellie filed a countersuit charging that he had been having an affair with "a blonde young woman,"[20] and in October 1912 the referee recommended dismissing Chase's suit and granting Nellie the divorce.[21] After some more legal wrangling, she was finally granted a divorce on April 24, 1913. The decree forbade Chase from marrying in New York state again, and gave Nellie custody of young Hal and alimony of $100 a month (see page 112).[22] Nellie's devoutly Catholic family was shocked by the divorce,[23] so she decided to try her luck out west. She moved to San Francisco, found a job in a candy store, and gave Hal Jr. to her former in-laws, with whom she remained on good terms. In 1919 she married a welder named Bill Brown, and Hal Jr. moved in with his mother and stepfather.[24]

The Yankees' practice session at the Polo Grounds on April 4 provided "New York's first peek at Hal Chase as a second baseman." The *Times* reported that he was still favoring his ankle slightly, but "turns quickly in getting the ball to first base and gets the ball over to Chance fast."[25] In an exhibition game against the Brooklyn Dodgers the next day Chase "played a brilliant game in the field, digging them out of the ground, making one-handed stops and lightning throws with that same old ease and grace that the 'fans' have come to expect." Apparently, however, his ankle still bothered him: "Chase showed traces of lameness in running the bases, and twice his lack of speed cost his team runs."[26]

Chase was at second base on April 10 when the Yankees opened the season with a 2–1 loss in Washington, though Chance was unable to play first base due to a pulled hamstring. Before the Yankees' second game, against the Red Sox, Chase was hit in the arm by a thrown ball in practice. He left that game in the third inning, but on the next day "played a great game at second base." The Yankees won 3–2 as Chase "showed that a clever left-hander can play the keystone bag as well as a right-hander." After "an unusually brilliant play in the sixth inning," when he stopped a sharply-hit grounder and retired Larry Gardner at first base, the Boston fans gave Chase an ovation.[27]

A few days later the *Tribune* confidently asserted that "Hal Chase is no longer a doubtful quantity at second base," but on the very next day, after Washington beat New York 9–3 in the Yankees' first home game, was forced to admit that Chase had still not completely adjusted to his new position: "as experienced a player as he is, he looked a little green on the job. He was a trifle slow in getting to second when Gandil stole the bag.... He made a botch of this play and received an error." He also threw wildly in trying to catch George McBride off third base on an attempted double steal.[28] A day later, on April 18, Chase made two more errors in an 8–5 loss to the Senators.

Chance had seen enough; on April 19 Chase was back at first base with Bill McKechnie at second base. The *Tribune* reported that, contrary to what he had insisted all spring, "Frank Chance seems to have made up his mind that Hal Chase, with all his natural ability as a baseball player, is not capable of plugging up the gap at second base, because of the fact that he is slightly handicapped by being left handed."[29]

One wonders whether this is the whole story. Art Shires, who spent four years as a marginally talented but extremely colorful major league first baseman, played semipro ball with Chase in Arizona in the mid–1920s before beginning his own professional career. At that time, recalled Shires, Chase played second base so that Shires could play first. "I didn't believe a lefthander could play second base until I played alongside of him. I know he was the greatest first baseman there ever was. And I believe he could have been the greatest second baseman if he had wanted to."[30] Perhaps, under Chance, Chase simply didn't want to.

Chance finally made his debut as a player on April 22 in Philadelphia, with Chase moving to center field. "The changes seemed to be highly beneficial," reported the *Tribune,* but the Athletics beat the Yankees 7–4. Despite the great expectations that had accompanied Chance's arrival the Yankees were in last place, having won only one of their first eight games.[31]

As the season stretched on into May the Yankees continued to lose with discouraging regularity. Their own fans jeered them when they committed five errors during an 8–6 loss to the Athletics. Two days later Chase gave the home crowd more reason to laugh when he made an uncharacteristic mental blunder during an 8–1 loss to the Athletics. In the fourth inning, with one out and neither team having scored, Philadelphia managed to get Frank Baker on third base and Stuffy McInnis on first. The Athletic runners tried a double steal and thoroughly embarrassed the Yankee first baseman: "Chase raced toward second after the truant McInnis and while he was thusly engaged, Baker went home and McInnis beat Chase to second by an eyelash," reported the *Times.* The play provoked bitter laughter from the crowd, and "The guffaws were directed mostly at Prince Hal."[32]

The loss was the Yankees' fifteenth in seventeen games. On May 8, after the Yankees lost to the Tigers in Detroit, Chase's batting average had fallen to .179. A week later the Yankees celebrated Chance's return to Chicago by losing four in a row to the White Sox in Chicago. Thirty-six thousand fans turned out for the third game of the series, which Comiskey had declared "Frank Chance Day" in a not-so-subtle slap at the National League Cubs. Chance started that game, a 6–3 Yankee loss, at first base but gave way to Chase after one unsuccessful at bat.[33]

Despite those losses in Chicago the Yankees had begun to play slightly better ball. By May 20 they had won seven of their last thirteen games. Once again, however, Chase was about to become the focus of controversy. An article in the May 18 *New York Tribune* had quoted Chance's flattering assessment of Chase ("Great ball player, that")[34] but by then W. J. McBeth in *The Sporting News* had already warned of more trouble in New York.

McBeth hinted that the Yankees were looking to get rid of Chase, either by dealing him to another team or, if necessary, by suspending him: "Hal Chase is playing the worst ball of his career, which leads to rumors that he is not giving the club his best services and that Chance plans to trade him. However this may be, it is a moral certainty that Hal Chase will not get very far if he tries to 'kid' Frank Chance.... If Chase goes on the bench — unless he is as sick as his friends claim — he will go on indefinitely and without pay."[35] Just two weeks later the situation blew up.

The explosion came shortly after the *Tribune* reported Chase's impending marriage to Anna Marion Cherurg, the twenty-four-year-old daughter of a Bronx dentist. Chase was free to marry again because his divorce from Nellie had just become final. In September 1912 Chase had filed for divorce from Nellie, on the grounds that she had committed an "indiscretion" two months after their wedding in 1908. Nellie denied the accusation and filed a countersuit for divorce. Noting Chase's $8,000 salary, she asked for $300 a month in alimony and $1,000 for legal fees.

Chase responded that his current contract with the Yankees expired in mid-October and that he did not expect to receive more than $4,500 in salary in his next contract. He countered Nellie's demands by offering to pay her $15 a week, about one-fifth of what she sought. He presented no evidence at a hearing before referee Alvin Untermyer, claiming that his principal witness, a former tobacco company employee named McGrath, had left his job and was travelling in Pennsylvania. "I wish I could find him," said Chase. "I am very anxious to obtain this divorce."

A skeptical Untermyer suspected Chase of "collusion and connivance" in helping Nellie obtain a divorce. He recommended dismissing Chase's suit. After a second hearing before Untermyer, Supreme Court Justice Bijur granted Nellie an interlocutory decree of divorce on December 31 and set alimony at $1,200 per year.

No doubt the dissolution of her marriage caused great anguish for Nellie. Almost eighty years later her niece recalled that the divorce was never discussed in the Heffernan family, which was devoutly Catholic, because "That was a thing that just didn't happen," and it was a major factor in Nellie's subsequent decision to move with Hal Jr. to California.[36]

The divorce decree became final on April 24, 1913, about a month before the *Tribune* announced that Chase intended to marry Anna Cherurg.[37] The newspaper rather uncharitably repeated Nellie's accusations of an affair with "a blonde young woman" but noted gallantly that Miss Cherurg was "a very pretty brunette." She had been introduced to Chase by her brother, Rudolph Cherurg, an attorney of the firm of Cherurg & Falk.

On Monday, May 26, the couple had driven to Jersey City to apply for a marriage license, intending to be married on the following day. Chase, typically casual, had forgotten to bring a certified copy of the decree of his divorce from Nellie. Then he had to hurry back to New York in time for that afternoon's game, which the Yankees lost 3–1 to the Red Sox. Anna had to journey back to New York, fetch the missing document, and return to Jersey City alone before receiving the license.[38]

Three days later the Yankees lost to the Athletics again. Years later reporter Fred Lieb of the *Press* recalled that he and Heywood Broun of the *Tribune* were sitting in the press box about a half hour after the game when they were confronted by a furious Chance.

"Did you fellows see what went on out there today?" he demanded. "Chase let those throws go right through him. He's been doing that to me every day, throwing down me and the club."

Lieb and Broun knew that they had a hot story — a manager did not often publicly accuse one of his players of deliberately trying to lose — and hurried back to their respective newspapers. Lieb's editor at the *Press*, James Price, was a friend of Farrell and killed the story: "Chance popped off," he explained, "and he'll be sorry he made the charge in the morning." Broun's editor at the *Tribune*, George Herbert Daley, also downplayed the story but allowed a watered-down version into print.

Broun's story, recalled Lieb, sparked an immediate response from the Yankee management. Farrell issued a statement denying that Chance had said anything of the sort; Chance claimed he had been misquoted.[39]

Another writer attributed the final breach between Chase and Chance to a different episode, albeit one that also reveals something of Chase's essentially unserious attitude toward his profession. According to Frank Graham, Chase "took a perverse delight in Chance's rages" and took advantage of the fact that the Peerless Leader was deaf in one ear, the result of being hit by one too many pitches. Chase would sit on the manager's deaf side in the Yankee dugout and mimick him behind his back for the amusement of the other players. One day catcher Ed Sweeney could take it no longer and told Chance what Chase had been doing.

"I'm no stool pigeon," said Sweeney, glaring at Chase, "but you're not going to make fun of the big guy in front of me any more."

Chance was furious. "Get out," he told Chase. "Go to the clubhouse and take off that uniform."

Chase's eight-year career as a Yankee was over. The Peerless Leader was not the sort of man to take lightly insults to his dignity. "That night," said Graham, "he made a deal for Chase with the White Sox."[40]

On June 1 the Yankees announced that they had traded Chase to Chicago for infielder Rollie Zeider and first baseman Babe Borton. A jubilant Charles Comiskey called Chase "a smart ball player, an exceptionally brilliant fielder, and a strong hitter," and predicted that his acquisition guaranteed a pennant for the White Sox.[41] A little over a year later Comiskey would have reason to wish the trade had never been made.

On the face of it Comiskey was right to exult. The trade seemed hopelessly one-sided: Chase was one of the biggest stars in baseball, even though he had

had a miserable season thus far. While Zeider and Borton were promising players, neither was likely to develop into a star of Chase's magnitude, though Chance insisted that the Yankees had gotten the best possible return for Chase, as no other club had been interested in him.

Chance's statement contradicted rumors that had circulated a month earlier and were later repeated by I. E. Sanborn in the Chicago *Daily Tribune*. In April Red Sox president Jimmy McAleer acknowledged that Boston needed a first baseman to replace the veteran Jake Stahl, whom he had recently and unceremoniously dumped. Nonetheless McAleer denied reports that he was negotiating a trade with the Yankees for Chase. "I have no knowledge of any deal which would bring Hal Chase to the Red Sox," insisted McAleer, "and have not discussed the question with any one — not even with Robert McRoy, secretary of the club, who was supposed to be my emissary."

Despite the denials McAleer had admitted that he would love to have Chase on his team: "Needless to say, I would be glad to make a trade that would bring Chase to the Red Sox. Most any owner or manager would. He has few equals as a first baseman." If Chance was to be believed, however, only a month later McAleer had decided that he could do without Chase.[42] The White Sox got Chase almost by default.

The trade was analyzed extensively in the New York and Chicago newspapers, although Chase himself maintained a public silence. Most of the New York reporters dutifully echoed the Yankee party line; Chase may have been the biggest star in town, but their primary loyalty was to the club. While admitting that "As a fielder Chase has no superior in baseball," the *Times* attributed his departure to his "falling off in batting." The *Tribune* said the news of the trade "came like a clap of thunder out of a clear sky," but noted that Chance "long has had his eye on Zeider ... and confidently believes that he will develop into a star."[43] W. J. McBeth wrote in *The Sporting News* that "So far New York seems to have reaped all the benefit of the swap" and confidently described Borton as "a natural slugger."

Both assessments were highly debatable, but McBeth knew that the actual abilities of the players involved had mattered less to the Yankees than the opportunity to get rid of Chase. Baseball insiders knew exactly what he meant when he argued that "Chance would have done well to rid himself of Hal if he had to give him away.... Those who stop to reason should realize that Chase, as a winning factor for New York, was through some time ago. It is to be hoped for the good of base ball that he reforms under Callahan's command. Players like Chase come along once in a century. That he can play first as it never was and perhaps never again will be played is a well known truth. That he will is a different matter."[44]

An editorial in *Baseball* magazine, while acknowledging Chase's talent, concurred with McBeth's assessment that Chase had worn out his welcome in New York by his persistent refusal to take his career seriously: "It is not our aim to criticize Hal Chase. But his passing has been a significant lesson. No player is greater than the game. No player can live on records, however brilliant. Chase squandered the magnificent reputation he once enjoyed in Greater New York. He allowed some of the best years of his career to slip listlessly through his fingers. It is to be hoped that in his new surroundings he will display some of that old-time form which once made him the wonder of the diamond."[45] A month later, the same publication averred that "Chase, once undisputed sovereign of the initial sack, is no longer supreme even in his own league."[46]

Not all observers agreed. A letter to the editor of *Baseball* magazine called such assertions "Rubbish!" and asserted that "Chase is the best first-baseman that has ever played, or is now playing, the game.... Come now, Mr. Editor, be fair, your magazine is too good to be given over to belittling a great baseball player; one who taught them all how first-base should be played."[47] Mark Roth of the *Globe* accused the Yankees of knuckling under to pressure from the fans, who had begun to sour on Chase since his defection in 1908, in dealing the player to the White Sox. Roth wrote that the trade proved "that baseball fans can drive the best player on any ball club out if they get after him. In other words, the fan is the boss. Fans in this city were determined to get Chase out, and they have succeeded." Roth was one of the few to attribute Chase's recent poor performance to his physical problems: "Chase has not been the same ball player since he injured his ankle in Bermuda," wrote Roth, "but he stuck to the bag when he should have been out of the game."

Roth insisted that Chase had been made an undeserving scapegoat by the fickle Yankee fans: "Chase heard it all from the stands. He was not sensitive and went along doing his best. He has received bundles of mail telling him what a troublemaker he was. Every manager who has been with the Yankees has been told that it would be better to get Chase off the club," but "there are thousands of fans in this city who will never forget the plays he made around that first sack. What is more, we will never see his like again."[48]

Meanwhile the initial reaction to the trade in Chicago, despite Comiskey's enthusiasm, was cautious, though generally positive. Two limericks by Ring Lardner in the June 3 *Daily Tribune* summarized the city's feelings:

> We welcome the party named Chase,
> Who can certainly cover first base,
> Agreeing with Cal
> That he'll help us like Hal,
> If he plays at his speediest pace.
> But 'twould be the acme of folly
> To say that we won't miss our Rollie;
> And Babe Borton, you
> We hate to lose, too,
> But we're glad that Chance got you, b'golly.[49]

More seriously, I. E. Sanborn wrote in *The Sporting News,* "Both clubs appear satisfied with the swap and there is good logic in the opinion expressed that both clubs will benefit by the deal." He predicted that Chase, who was reported to be "satisfied" with the trade, would behave well in Chicago: "He and Manager [Jimmy] Callahan are good friends and there is no reason why he should not do his best work in his new uniform." The *Daily Tribune* noted that "Chase has fallen off considerably in his batting this year," although it failed to mention his ankle injury, but added hopefully that "A change of pasture probably will bring out Chase's real hitting ability."[50]

Callahan himself doubtless realized that even with Chase at his best the White Sox were not yet ready to challenge the Philadelphia Athletics, who were in the process of winning four pennants in five years, for supremacy in the American League. The White Sox were not without some good players; Buck Weaver, for example, then a hard-hitting but scatter-armed young shortstop, would soon develop into perhaps the best third basemen in baseball. Outfielders Ping Bodie and Shano Collins and third baseman Harry Lord, the team captain, were solid veterans; Ray Schalk, only twenty, was already considered one of the best catchers in the league. The pitching staff featured righthanders Jim Scott and Eddie Cicotte, a veteran who would shortly blossom into one of the best pitchers in baseball, and lefthander Reb Russell, a sensational rookie on his way to twenty-two wins.

But except for that deep and talented pitching staff the White Sox lacked the overall talent to compete with the very best teams. Second base and right field were persistent trouble spots, and the offense was, as usual, anemic; the 1906 Chicago team that had unexpectedly won the World Series had been nicknamed the "Hitless Wonders," and little had changed since then.

Callahan hoped that the addition of Chase would help his team score more runs and also tighten up the erratic infield defense, but his restrained comments showed that he was not unaware of the problems that had dogged Chase in New York. "There is no doubt about Chase being a great player," Callahan told the *Daily Tribune*. "That is admitted. If we cannot create conditions which will make him play good ball in Chicago that will be our own fault, will it not? I look for a change of scene and surroundings to do Chase a world of good." Still, the White Sox manager cautioned, "Any trade is a gamble and always will be, [and] time only can tell how it will pan out."[51]

Callahan was right to be cautious, although not even he could have foreseen the ultimate consequence of the trade. Six years later Cicotte and Weaver would be expelled from organized baseball for their involvement in the infamous Black Sox scandal, which their former teammate Hal Chase allegedly helped arrange. If Chase had never left the Yankees, perhaps the 1919 World Series would not have been fixed; perhaps the panicked owners would not have hired crusty Kenesaw Mountain Landis as commissioner; and perhaps baseball would have developed along very different lines. Of course, the Black Sox scandal was not the only scandal threatening baseball's reputation in the early 1920s; indeed, it was but one of many, and Chase seemed to be involved in most, if not all, of them, and the list of players whose careers were ended or tainted as a result of their association with him includes Heinie Zimmerman, Lee Magee, Babe Borton, Joe Gedeon, Jean Dubuc, Buck Herzog, Rube Benton, Benny Kauff, and several others.

Callahan ordered Chase to report to the fourth-place White Sox in Boston on Tuesday, June 3, where they were to begin a four-game series with the Red Sox, but before Chase could even join his new team baseball's tireless rumor mill had him on his way to yet another team. This time Chase was supposed to be on his way to the Tigers in a trade for Ty Cobb.

The tempestuous Cobb had won five of the last six American League batting titles, but had supposedly worn out his welcome in Detroit. He was unpopular with his teammates and had been suspended during the 1912 season after climbing into the grandstand and attacking a fan in Philadelphia. Still, the Tigers were not about to trade him away. Cobb, despite, or more likely because of, his sociopathic personality, was unquestionably a greater player than Chase, and the rumor seemed curious in light of Chance's statement that the Yankees had found no other team interested in Chase, but the fact that a Cobb-Chase trade seemed plausible indicates something of the esteem in which Chase was held at the time. Tiger owner Frank J. Navin moved quickly to quash the rumor: "The idea of such a trade is so silly that there is no use discussing it." Besides, argued Navin, "If we had wanted to trade Cobb for Chase I guess we would have made the deal with Chance direct, instead of waiting for him to send Chase to another club."[52] Cobb, of course, was a notoriously difficult man who alienated teammates and management alike, but if the Tigers were hoping to rid themselves of one headache they were well advised not to take on another, albeit a more congenial one, in Chase.

On Tuesday, the day that Chase was supposed to join the White Sox in Boston, Frank Farrell telephoned Callahan and told him that the first baseman had been unavoidably detained while tending to his personal affairs in New York. Several days passed with no sign of Chase, and then the story was given out that he had been resting the troublesome ankle that he had injured in Bermuda. Ring Lardner was skeptical: "With due respect to Hal Chase," he wrote, "New York is our notion of no place in which to rest the ankles."[53]

Chase missed all four Boston games, and rumors began to circulate in New York that he was dissatisfied with his contract. He finally reported for duty on the morning of Saturday, June 7, by which time the White Sox were in New York to play the Yankees. He denied that he was unhappy with his contract, although a year later the exact terms under which he joined the White Sox would become a bone of contention in a court of law.[54] In his first game with the White Sox, before the same fans who until a few days ago had considered him one of their own, Chase had two hits and scored a run, but the Yankees won 3–2. Ironically the winning run scored on a hit by Zeider in the ninth inning.

The New York fans greeted Chase warmly, even though he now wore an enemy uniform, when he walked to home plate for his first at-bat against Ray Keating, but their loyalties were mixed. Wrote I. E. Sanborn: "The big crowd seemed undivided in admiration for the former Yankee star until he missed the first strike. Then his detractors got in their work with a loud roar of delight." Chase had the last laugh, however, and "gave his fans another chance by rapping a clean single to center."[55]

On Monday the Yankees beat the White Sox again, this time by a score of 4–1, although they had to do it without Zeider. On the previous day the speedy infielder had undergone surgery for a bunion, the first in a series of physical problems that would plague him for the rest of the 1913 season. Even without Zeider, however, the Yankees were aided mightily by Chase, whose two errors on one play, a grounder by Roy Hartzell, helped the home team score four times in the fifth inning.[56]

Chase soon seemed to be settling in with his new team, although he had apparently been prepared to be unhappy: "You may say for me that I was agreeably surprised in the White Sox," he said in late June. "They are a fine bunch of fellows."[57] He could not have welcomed the trade; the glamor and excitement of New York suited him, especially since he had been almost without exception his team's only star; the Yankees, for most of his tenure with the team, had lacked other players even remotely in his class.

But Chicago was still the second-largest city in the nation, a thriving center of culture and commerce. Just four years later, in fact, that noted curmudgeon H. L. Mencken called Chicago "the most civilized city in America."[58] Chase must have looked forward to giving the lie to Chance and those who said that his best days were behind him. He batted .286 for the rest of the season, by far the highest average on the team, and played first base with his customary flair. Sanborn noted that "Chase has been as aggressive as in his former days and has been a different man entirely. It has needed a few men like Chase to instil the winning spirit into the Sox."[59] His arrival "made a pronounced difference in the work of the other infielders," as they had confidence that his ability to flag down errant throws would save them countless errors. Another Chicago writer commented in early July that Chase's presence had "gingered up the Sox infield considerably."[60] His performance seemed calculated to make Chance and the Yankees look foolish, especially in light of what happened to the two men they had received for Chase.

By early July Borton was gone, sent to Rochester of the International League. He had batted only .130 in thirty-three games with the Yankees, and never developed into the slugger that Chance had predicted. Zeider fared little better. He played in only forty-nine more games that season due to a succession of injuries; indeed, his physical condition became the focus of a dispute in mid–July between Chance and Callahan.

Supposedly Zeider had injured his foot during a game against the Tigers just before the trade was made; Chance suspected that Callahan had deliberately deceived the Yankees by keeping the injury a secret.

Chance announced that he would ask Ban Johnson to investigate. Johnson sounded sympathetic: "Callahan represented Borton and Zeider as being fit

Five—We Will Find a Place for Hal All Right

physically when he traded them to Chance. Zeider has been useless because of injuries and Borton has been sent to the minors. I shall certainly consider any appeal Manager Chance may make and it is quite possible that the National Commission will take action."[61]

Mark Roth, who had thought the trade a bad idea from the start, was unsympathetic; his caustic assessment of the deal—"The Yankees traded Chase to the White Sox for a bunion and an onion"—was quoted widely. Chance, however, relieved to have gotten rid of Chase, stressed repeatedly that he did not wish to have the trade rescinded. In late July, with Zeider hospitalized in St. Louis, the Yankee manager insisted, "I wouldn't trade Rollie Zeider right now for Chase, and I'm not meaning to discredit Chase a bit.... All I said was that I thought the Chicago club should pay [Zeider's] hospital bill and his salary until he was able to play ball for New York." He added, "I never intimated that I wished to have the deal rescinded in any way. I want no part of Chase's game. Zeider, in the hospital, is worth more to the New York Club than ten Chases."[62]

Callahan, for his part, professed ignorance of Zeider's physical problems. "I didn't know about any injury," said the Chicago manager. "Now it seems Zeider was bruised on the foot by [Detroit's] Sam Crawford in a play at third base only a few days before the trade. It wasn't bad enough for him even to call for time, and I knew nothing about our trainer treating Zeider's foot. The trainer evidently did not consider it serious or I would have heard of it."[63]

In fact, the White Sox could have pointed out that Chase's ankle was still bothering him, as it would for the rest of the season and on into the following spring. Lardner had some fun at Chance's expense when he suggested that "Commy might ask Frank Farrell to pay Hal Chase's salary," since Chase, like Zeider, was not one hundred percent at the time of the trade.

Meanwhile, despite Chase's resurgence, the White Sox were not living up to Comiskey's optimistic expectations. During one stretch in late July and early August they lost nine out of ten games, including six in a row. The first of those six consecutive losses, a 7–1 loss to the visiting Senators on July 23, provided what one reporter called "a horrible exhibition of the national pastime."[64] In that game Chase had one hit in three at bats, stole a base and scored the only Chicago run, but also committed four errors, still the single-game record for American League first basemen. In the second inning he fumbled Danny Moeller's grounder and then threw wildly past Jim Scott, who was covering first base. Two runs scored as a result. In the sixth inning, with a man on base, Chase booted consecutive bunts by Jack Calvo and George McBride to load the bases. One out later he fielded Joe Boehling's grounder cleanly, then threw wildly to catcher Ray Schalk, allowing one run to score and again loading the bases. Two more runs scored on the next play when Chicago outfielder Larry Chappell made a wild throw.

Such displays prompted Lardner to suggest that the team should be nicknamed the "Witless Blunders" rather than the "Hitless Wonders."[65] But the White Sox promptly got hot, winning twelve out of their next sixteen games.

In one of those four losses Chase was involved in an interesting play. On Thursday, August 14, the visiting Yankees beat the White Sox 2–0 as Chase had one of the five Chicago hits off Ray Fisher. In the fourth inning Yankee third baseman Fritz Maisel fielded Chase's grounder, then threw wildly to Harry Williams at first base. Maisel's throw brought Williams directly into the path of the onrushing Chase. Sanborn reported the outcome: "Hal could have cut the youngster's feet out from under him on the play if he had chosen to, but tried to dodge past and was tagged because of his consideration for a young rival's welfare."[66] Perhaps Chase was simply afraid of reinjuring his gimpy ankle in a collision; or perhaps his competitive fires now burned less intensely than they had eight years ago when he knocked Lave Cross cold and broke Billy Sullivan's ankle.

Nevertheless Chase's play still won the admiration of Chicago fans. Almost fifty years later the novelist James T. Farrell, a passionate follower of the White Sox, vividly recalled the pleasure he took as a boy in watching Chase. Prince Hal, wrote Farrell, "could pivot like a ballet dancer; in fact, it is not at all inappropriate to speak of his movements, his footwork and his throwing and fielding as though it were a dance."[67]

On August 15 Comiskey celebrated his sixty-fourth birthday and the White Sox beat the Yankees 3–2. The day also marked the arrival of a young White Sox outfielder named Edd Roush, who would later be a teammate of Chase's on the Cincinnati Reds and eventually a member of the Hall of Fame. In 1913, however, Roush was still an unknown; his name was spelled "Rousch" and "Rausch" in the *Tribune*.

Roush did not play on August 15, but Chase did, and his canny baserunning helped Cicotte win. Chase was on first base when the next Chicago batter singled to right field. Chase sprinted around second base, then slowed as if preparing to stop at third base. Instead, having lulled the Yankee defense, he suddenly accelerated again and slid safely into home plate ahead of the throw from Roy Hartzell, the embarrassed Yankee right fielder.[68]

Chase continued to play well for the White Sox. On September 2, in the second game of a doubleheader at Cleveland, he had four hits, including a triple and a home run, scored four runs and drove in three as the White Sox won 9–3. Chase "went crazy and ran wild in spite of a weak ankle," wrote an admiring Sanborn. "[H]e had to hit the ball a helova ways to get so many extra bases on his flat wheel."[69]

The win gave the White Sox a 67–63 record — not what Comiskey had hoped, of course, but not bad considering the state the team had been in a month ago. Sanborn wrote that "On all sides a lot of credit is given to Hal Chase for the reversal of form shown by the [White Sox]," especially in light of his ongoing physical problems: "Chase is given all the more credit because he is playing under a heavy handicap with a bum ankle which slows him up a lot. Between games the ankle gets enough rest to strengthen it up a little and he can start in all right, but before the ninth inning arrives Hal limps painfully."

Still, Chase refused to give up his spot in the lineup: "When Callahan mentioned giving Chase a rest by using Collins on first and Rousch [*sic*] in the outfield, Hal said he guessed he could stick to the bag for a while longer." Sanborn attributed Chase's grit to his determination to prove that the Yankees had been in the wrong in unloading him: "He does not intend to give his eastern enemies a chance to say, 'I told you so,' if he can help it."[70]

Despite their recent success the White Sox could not shake the pursuing Red Sox. When they lost 1–0 to the lowly Browns in St. Louis on September 7, the White Sox dropped to fifth place, .001 behind the Red Sox. Three days later, after beating the Athletics 5–3 in ten innings, Chicago moved up into a tie with Boston, but Philadelphia won the next two games and the White Sox were back in fifth place to stay.

The knowledge that they were well out of the pennant race may have contributed to yet another incident in which Chase seemed to be stretching the rules that bound other players. On Tuesday, September 23, after splitting a doubleheader with the Red Sox in Boston, the White Sox travelled to Portland, Maine, for an exhibition game on the following day. The game was to be played in honor of their captain, Lord, a Portland native, but Chase was the star of the day. The White Sox beat the local team 2–1 as Chase drove in one Chicago run with a double and scored the other himself. Even more impressive was his fielding in the pregame practice; Sanborn reported proudly that "Some of the feats he performed bewildered the local writers."[71]

On Friday, however, when the White Sox lost to St. Louis 3–2 in ten innings back in Chicago, they were without Lord, who had been given permission to stay in Portland and catch a fast train out of Boston on Thursday morning. Chase had gone to New York from Portland, intending to catch the same train when it passed through New York, but both men had missed their connections. On Saturday, September 27, Lord was back with the team as Chicago beat St. Louis 6–2. Chase was still missing, although he had telephoned to say that he had stayed in New York because his wife was ill.[72]

After beating the Naps in Cleveland on September 28, the White Sox embarked on a three-day exhibition tour through the upper Midwest. They beat the Michigan City (Indiana) Grays and played a ten-inning tie with the Milwaukee Brewers, champions of the American Association; a third game, in Madison, Wisconsin, was rained out.

Chase finally rejoined the team on October 4, in Detroit, where they finished the regular season by losing two out of three to the Tigers. Chicago finished the season with a 78–74 record, seventeen and a half games behind the first-place Athletics. Still, the White Sox finished more than twenty games ahead of the Yankees, whose 57–94 record put them only one game in front of the last-place Browns. Getting rid of Chase had not helped New York as much as Chance had hoped. The Peerless Leader himself, despite his brave words that spring, played in only eleven games and compiled a meager .208 batting average.

Most of the baseball world now turned its attention to the World Series, which would match the Athletics and the Giants for the second time in three years. In Chicago, though, the World Series took a back seat to the annual city series between the White Sox and the Cubs, who had finished third in the National League.

The Cubs, while they had lost two-thirds of their fabled Tinker-to-Evers-to-Chance double play combination, still had Heinie Zimmerman, the hot-headed third baseman who had led the league in batting and home runs in 1912, and a couple of other solid hitters in first baseman Vic Saier and left fielder Frank Schulte. Their pitching staff had been bolstered by the addition of Chase's old Yankee buddy, Hippo Vaughn, who posted a 5–1 record and 1.45 earned run average in seven late-season games. Vaughn would go on to become one of the best pitchers in the National League for the next several seasons.

Most experts believed that the Cubs would win the best-of-seven series, but the White Sox won the first game, lost the next two, and then won three in a row to claim the championship of Chicago. At bat Chase did little to help his team win, batting only .208. Evidently he did not take the games too seriously; the *Tribune* reported after the second game, in which Vaughn beat the White Sox, that Chase and the Cub lefthander "kidded each other every time they got within speaking distance."[73] The series may also have marked the first meeting of the gregarious Chase and Zimmerman; six years later, as teammates in another city, the two would be linked in a scandal that ended their major league careers.

The city series meant more than a chance to fraternize with other ballplayers, however, as each member of the winning team received $807.22.[74] But the season was still not over for the White Sox players. Two days after the last game of the city series they began the longest road trip in baseball history.

Comiskey and John McGraw had agreed in the winter of 1912 to take their teams on an around-the-world tour after the 1913 season. There was some precedent for such an undertaking; Albert Spalding had led his Chicago Nationals against an all-star team on a similar tour in 1888–1889. But this tour would be even more ambitious. The teams would play thirty-one games as they made their way through the Midwest and Southwest and up the Pacific Coast. From Victoria, where Chase had unofficially begun his professional career, they would sail on the Canadian Pacific liner *Empress of Japan*. Their itinerary would take them to Japan, Hong Kong, the Philippines, Australia, Ceylon, Egypt, Italy, France and England before they returned to New York in March 1914 — just in time for spring training.

Of course, not every player on the two teams was willing or able to spend the winter away from home; Chase, for example, hoping that a prolonged rest would finally allow his ankle to heal, agreed to play only until the two teams sailed for Japan.[75] To fill out their roster Comiskey and Callahan arranged for outfielders Tris Speaker of Boston and Sam Crawford of Detroit and infielder Germany Schaefer of Washington to become temporary White Sox. Only six of McGraw's men volunteered for the trip, so he recruited six members of the

St. Louis Cardinals and two Philadelphia Phillies, as well as Chase's old billiards partner, former Giants star Mike Donlin. One of the St. Louis players recruited by McGraw was utilityman Lee Magee, who three years later would be Chase's teammate on the Cincinnati Reds. As would be true for Cicotte and Weaver, and for Zimmerman, Magee's association with Chase would have fateful consequences.

The first game of the tour was played in Cincinnati on Sunday, October 18. Despite two hits by Chase the "Giants" beat the "White Sox" 11–2. The two teams played seven games in the next seven days; their itinerary included stops in Chicago; Springfield; Peoria; Ottumwa, Iowa; Sioux City, Iowa; Blue Rapids, Kansas; and St. Joseph, Missouri. Chase played well, with fourteen hits in those first eight contests, as the two teams won four games apiece.

In St. Joseph he had three hits in four at bats as the White Sox beat the Giants 4–3. The game ended painfully for Chase, however, as he injured his ankle in the top of the ninth inning. Ironically, the injury occurred on the same type of play on which he had avoided the Yankees' Harry Williams in August. Chase, the first baseman, reached for a wild throw from Weaver as the Giants' Fred Merkle thundered up the basepath. This time, however, fielder and baserunner collided. The *Tribune* reported that Chase's injury was "not considered serious,"[76] but he missed the next ten games on the tour. At least two of those games were of more than ordinary interest: on October 27, in Joplin, Missouri, Washington's great pitcher Walter Johnson made an appearance for the White Sox in a 13–12 Giant victory, and on the next day, in Tulsa, a section of the bleachers collapsed, killing one fan and injuring thirty-five.[77]

When Chase finally returned to the lineup the teams were in Douglas, Arizona, a copper-mining boomtown on the Mexican border. Chase marked his return by hitting one of the five home runs in the game, won by the Giants 14–5.[78] He had no way of knowing that ten years later, in enforced exile from organized baseball, he would end up back in this same dusty town, playing semiprofessional baseball and running a bar across the border in Agua Prieta.

The two teams played on into Southern California and up the coast, their contests marked by a certain amount of frivolity. In Oxnard, Hans Lobert of the Phillies, considered the fastest man in baseball, lost a race around the bases by a nose. His opponent was a horse. In rainy Medford, Oregon, Lee Magee, playing left field for the Giants, caught a fly ball with one hand while holding an umbrella with the other.[79]

Despite such lighter moments, however, storm clouds were gathering on the baseball horizon. Two days before Magee's clowning catch in Oregon James A. Gilmore of Chicago had been elected president of a little-known "outlaw" organization called the Federal League.[80] Few of the White Sox and Giants could have known that Gilmore's election signalled the start of a conflict that would turn their world upside down.

On Wednesday, November 19, their last two games in Tacoma and Seattle having been rained out, the "world tourists" sailed from Victoria. Hal Chase went home to San Jose to rest his ankle and await the spring.[81]

Six

The King of the Leapers

On Thursday, February 26, 1914, the White Sox beat the Giants 5–4 in eleven innings before a crowd of some thirty thousand, including King George, in London. The contest was the last of their world tour. On that same day the Chicago players who had remained behind (not including Chase) held their first practice of the spring in Paso Robles, California, under coach Kid Gleason.[1]

Most of them had come by train from the east and had had a difficult time reaching Paso Robles, a resort town about halfway between Los Angeles and San Francisco. Because spring floods had made the railroad tracks impassable, the players had been forced to spend several days in Los Angeles, during which they were visited by Frank Chance. No record survives of what they discussed on this occasion, but surely Chance must have been tempted to ask what the other White Sox thought of Chase. When the White Sox finally made it to Paso Robles they were surprised to find that Chase was not there waiting for them. At first they believed that he was simply waiting for traveling conditions to improve, but when two days passed with no word from their star first baseman they began to worry.[2]

On Saturday their worst fears were confirmed. A report from San Jose quoted "friends" of Chase who said that the Federal League had offered him a three-year contract "with a material raise of salary and a bonus." Chase himself "was missing from his accustomed haunts" and so could neither confirm nor deny the story, but Joe Tinker, Chance's former Cub teammate and the manager of the Chicago Federal League team, admitted that the new league had been after Chase. According to Tinker, however, the negotiations had collapsed because of Chase's unreasonable demands.

"We asked Chase what he wanted, and if I remember correctly he asked for a three years' contract at $10,000 per year. Then he wanted a bonus of $10,000 for signing, and he wanted $20,000 of his three years' salary paid him in advance," Tinker told the *Tribune*. "He never got an answer."[3]

The reports of Chase's negotiations with the Federal League were an indication of the unsettled state of professional baseball in the spring of 1914. Under

Gilmore's aggressive leadership the year-old Federal League was seeking recognition as a third major league. At first the Federals promised to respect existing National and American League contracts and sign only those major leaguers whose contracts had expired—whose services, in other words, were retained by their former clubs under the reserve clause.

The reserve clause was the controversial legal foundation on which organized baseball was built. It effectively gave a team, in Harold Seymour's words, "an exclusive and perpetual option on [a] player's services" for the duration of his career, and ensured that no other team would employ him while that team reserved its rights to him. By restraining the ability of players to sell their services to the highest bidder the reserve clause supposedly assured an equitable distribution of talent among all the teams in the major leagues. Without the reserve clause, argued its supporters, a small number of wealthy teams could corner the market on star players, destroying baseball's competitive balance.[4]

By announcing that they would respect existing contracts while ignoring the reserve clause, the Federals were being disingenuous. They knew that such a policy made war with organized baseball inevitable. Initially, however, the baseball establishment responded cautiously to the Federal League threat; no one in organized baseball really wanted to have the legality of the reserve clause tested in court, which would almost certainly be the result of open hostilities. Instead organized baseball tried to downplay the Federal League threat and convince those players who had already signed or were considering signing with the new league that they were making a serious mistake.

But the uneasy peace soon broke down. The Federal League was outraged when several players who had already signed contracts with the new league were induced to jump back to their old teams. The response, which came on March 3, was predictable. "Now we have declared war in earnest," said Gilmore in approving wholesale raids on National and American League rosters, "and I have the backing of every club owner in our league to go ahead with the firing." Moreover, he added, "There'll be more stars in the Federal League by July than in both the American and National put together, if this war has to go the limit."[5]

This turned out to be largely an empty threat. In 1914 the Federals boasted a few talented players, such as Tom Seaton and Claude Hendrix and Tinker himself, but most of the new league's other big names, such as Mordecai (Three-Finger) Brown, George Stovall, Danny Murphy, and Davy Jones, were former stars long past their primes. Still, Gilmore's message was clear: the Federals would no longer hesitate to throw big money at top players, regardless of the reserve clause. Once again, as in 1905, Hal Chase was a much-desired prize in a struggle between two competing organizations. This time he apparently stood to profit handsomely by the struggle.

On March 1 Chase watched Santa Clara, his old school, beat the visiting White Sox yannigans 7–0. Chase chatted with the Chicago players and admitted to them that he had replied to a Federal League offer to name his terms by asking for $30,000 for three years, but with a $5,000 bonus, not $10,000, as

Tinker claimed. Now, said Chase, he was waiting to hear Gilmore's response; if the Federals agreed to his terms he would sign with the new league.

Sanborn guessed that Chase was flirting with the new league because he was unhappy with the contract the White Sox had offered him for 1914. When the White Sox acquired Chase from New York, according to Sanborn, they had assumed the first baseman's unexpired contract with the Yankees, which supposedly still called for the $8,000 salary he had received as player-manager.[6] (In actuality, Farrell had cut Chase's salary to $6,000 when he forced Prince Hal out as manager, and that had been the contract that the White Sox had assumed.[7]) Now, however, the White Sox used the continuing weakness of Chase's ankle as an excuse to offer him less money. Sanborn cited the number of potential replacements the White Sox had invited to camp as evidence that Callahan "was not basing his hope on Chase for the whole season."

If the White Sox lost Chase, of course, they could no longer claim to have put one over on the Yankees. In fact, wrote Sanborn, "It looks as if the trade was an even break, for Borton was discarded quickly and Zeider has jumped to the Federals...." Mindful of the traditionally weak White Sox offense, however, Sanborn wrote that the loss of Chase would be hard to bear, "as he was one of the few members of the team to pull stuff in the attack."[8]

Remembering Chase's 1908 jump to the outlaw California State League, most observers took seriously his threats to sign with the Federals and assumed that there was little chance he would return to the White Sox. But on March 4 Gleason received a letter from Chase in which the first baseman said he would report to the White Sox by the end of the week. Chase made no reference in his letter to the Federal League or to his absence, but he did say that he had been doing outdoor work for several weeks and was in good shape physically.[9]

One possible explanation for the failure of Chase's negotiations with the Federals that spring was that the new league, despite its belligerent rhetoric, was not yet ready to risk open warfare with organized baseball on all fronts. On March 5 the Chicago *Daily Tribune* reported that president Charles Weeghman of the Chicago Federals, anxious to keep the peace in his overcrowded market, had told his fellow owners to keep their hands off players belonging to the White Sox and the Cubs.[10]

This explanation did not satisfy Ring Lardner, who had little faith in the ability of baseball executives to maintain a stand on principle alone. Lardner asked rhetorically, "If Hal Chase had offered to play for $2,000 a year, do you think the Feds' determination not to tamper with Sox and Cubs would have kept them from signing him?"[11] A more likely explanation, as Joe Tinker had implied, was that Chase's demands were simply too high.

During the first week of March the White Sox left Paso Robles and established temporary headquarters in Oakland, where they prepared for a series of exhibition games with the Oakland Oaks and across the bay with the San Francisco Seals, both of the Pacific Coast League. Early in the morning of March 7, a day after the "world tourists" arrived in New York on the *Lusitania,* Hal Chase reported to the White Sox in Oakland. He went hitless in the game that afternoon, although he did drive in a run with a sacrifice fly as the White Sox beat the Seals 5–3 in San Francisco. Sanborn noted that Chase was indeed in good physical condition, as he had said in his letter to Gleason. His ankle seemed to be stronger, although Sanborn suspected that it still bothered him, if only psychologically: "When he does not have to go at top speed he favors the bum wheel a bit, perhaps from force of habit."[12]

A couple of days later the White Sox travelled to Sacramento to play three games against the PCL Wolves, formerly the Senators but renamed after their manager, Harry Wolverton. The Sacramento *Union* featured Chase's photograph in promoting the games. Before the first game, which was won by the home team 2–1, Chase met his successor as manager for the first time since Wolverton's brief and unsuccessful tenure in New York. Sanborn called the meeting "interesting," perhaps recalling the rumors that Chase had given way to Wolverton only reluctantly. "There was no kidding exchanged," he noted, "but considerable sympathy and fellow feeling was expressed sarcastically."[13]

The White Sox were losing about as often as they won in these early games against the PCL teams, but since their manager and many of their best players had not yet arrived after the around-the-world tour no one, including Chase, took these contests very seriously. On March 13 the White Sox beat the Seals 4–0 in San Francisco, but they had to do it without Chase, who had left his uniform and glove at the hotel in Oakland. He claimed it was an accident, but some were suspicious. Sanborn noted that Chase had asked that morning to be excused from the game, "but did not have a reason good enough to satisfy Gleason." Sanborn added that Chase was scheduled to play a billiards match that night against Chick Wright at Wright's Billiard Palace, on Ellis Street, "and probably wanted the afternoon off to polish up his stroke."[14]

On the following day Callahan arrived in time to see his team play the Seals again. This time, perhaps coincidentally, Chase remembered his uniform. He had two hits and three runs batted in, including the game-winner, as the White Sox won 5–3 in ten innings. When he came to bat in the sixth inning with Harry Lord on first base, Chase gave an exhibition of "inside ball" at its best. When Lord took off on an attempt to steal second base Chase blocked San Francisco catcher Louis Sepulveda from making a throw. For this Chase "was heartily hissed and hooted." The San Francisco *Examiner* noted that "Chase was within his rights, but the crowd did not like his tactics and they cheered lustily when [Skeeter] Fanning struck him out."[15]

A week later the White Sox were in Los Angeles for a series of games against the Venice team, which included at least two familiar faces: former pitching star Doc White, who had quit the White Sox after the previous season, and Babe Borton. On March 22 Venice beat the White Sox 5–3, but the most important news of the day for Chicago fans was that Hal Chase finally signed a contract for the 1914 season late that night. The terms of the contract were not disclosed, although most assumed correctly that it called for a salary of less than $8,000.[16]

On the following day a number of Chicago players, led by Ed Walsh, took advantage of an off day to visit Frank Chance's orange ranch in Glendora. Chance himself was in Houston, where the Yankees were holding spring training that year, but the newspaper account of the visit did not say whether Chase was among the players who toured the Peerless Leader's orange groves.[17]

On March 30 the White Sox began the trip back to Chicago, playing local teams in Arizona, Texas, Oklahoma, Kansas, and Missouri along the way. Chase looked to be back to his old form; in Abilene he had four hits, including two home runs into the teeth of a fierce north wind. Sanborn reported that "in the opinion of Abilene fans, Hal easily will lead the American league in batting this year." A few days later, in assessing the team, Sanborn noted that Chase's ankle seemed to have healed completely and predicted optimistically that Chase and Lord, "working together, probably will pull off plenty of stuff on the bases this year."[18]

Sanborn's confidence was misplaced. The White Sox in 1914 were a troubled team. They started the season by winning their first five games, and as late as April 26 were still tied with Detroit for first place. But then things started to go wrong. The offense was again punchless. The pitching staff, annually among the best in baseball, was weakened by the continued absence of its leader, Walsh, still nursing the sore arm that had hampered him in 1913, and the failure of Reb Russell to duplicate his rookie success; he would win only eight games in 1914. By May 12, after a 3–2 loss to the Senators in Washington, Chicago had fallen all the way to seventh place, having won only three of its last thirteen games.

Not only had the White Sox been losing games, they had been losing them badly. They had reached the nadir the previous week in Chicago, when they committed sixteen errors in losing three games to the Tigers. Now, in Washington, the sloppiness seemed to be continuing. In the 3–2 loss to the Senators Chase was charged with two errors. One came in the sixth inning when, with two out, Washington's Clyde Milan tripled to right field. When Chase took the relay throw from the outfield he spun and fired the ball to third base, but Lord was not on the bag. Milan scored on the play and Chase was charged with the error, but Callahan and everyone else on the team knew that the fault had been Lord's.[19]

That night, after his teammates were in bed, Lord packed his bags, said goodbye to his roommate, Hal Chase, and boarded a midnight train out of Washington. He would never play in the major leagues again. Chase reported Lord's departure to Gleason the next morning. The White Sox were stunned, but tried to be understanding. Shortly after the third baseman's desertion, Sanborn wrote: "Lord is high strung, impulsive, and the toughest loser in the world." The newspaperman theorized that Lord had left the team because he was distraught over "the poor showing of the White Sox" and his mistake in the Washington game.[20] Perhaps that mistake was simply the straw that broke the camel's back; at the time of his departure Lord was batting only .188.

Callahan, who denied having chewed out the sensitive Lord about his misplay, quickly appointed Buck Weaver as the new team captain. On May 13, the day after Lord's departure, the White Sox beat Washington 9–2 as Chase had four hits, including a triple and a double, and stole a base. But the team quickly reverted to its losing form; on the next day Jim Scott pitched a no-hitter for nine innings, only to lose 1–0 in the tenth.

On May 16, having limped into Philadelphia to play the world champion Athletics, the White Sox lost 4–3. Chase cost Chicago the potential tying run in the fourth inning when he failed to slide while trying to score from third base on Ping Bodie's grounder to shortstop. "Manager Callahan called Chase's attention to the fact forcibly," noted Sanborn drily, "but at the present writing Chase is still with the team." As in the 1913 game when he went out of his way to avoid a collision with the Yankees' Harry Williams, Chase seemed not to be going all out, but another possible explanation for his failure to slide was reported the next day, when Sanborn noted that Chase was "bunged up with a lame wing and a softening of the ankle which gave him so much trouble last season."[21] Once again, however, as in 1913, Chase stayed in the lineup despite his physical problems, and for the next month the team played somewhat better ball.

While the White Sox were winning about as often as they lost, the Federal League was stepping up its campaign against organized baseball. League counsel Edward E. Gates announced that the Feds would file an antitrust action against organized baseball under the Sherman Act; the Brooklyn Federals reportedly offered Walter Johnson a three-year contract at an annual salary of $25,000, with a $25,000 bonus; and Cincinnati outfielder Armando Marsans informed club president Garry Herrmann that he would leave the Reds in ten days to join the St. Louis Feds.[22]

By invoking the so-called ten-day clause, a standard feature of most baseball contracts, Marsans turned the tables on management. The ten-day clause said that a team was required to give an unwanted player ten days' notice before terminating his contract. It was designed to protect players from being dumped without warning. The magnates had never anticipated that the same clause might be used by a player seeking to cut himself loose from a team. At the same time, rumors began to appear in the Chicago newspapers that Chase and Lord were both being wooed by Buffalo of the Federal League. The Buffeds, whose business manager Richard T. (Buck) Carroll had appeared in two games as a pitcher for the Yankees in 1909 and was said to be an old friend and former business associate of Chase's, reportedly offered Chase the highest salary ever paid to a first baseman.

On Sunday, June 14, the Athletics beat the White Sox 8–3 in Chicago. Two sensational news items relating to the Federal League, however, overshadowed the result of the game. The first was an offer by the Brooklyn Federals to the Athletics' Eddie Collins, the best second baseman in baseball, of a contract worth even more than that offered to Walter Johnson. Collins said he would consider it, although he refused to leave the Athletics during the season. The second was a report that Hal Chase had signed a contract with Buffalo.[23]

The Federal League would not be wholly unfamiliar to Chase. His old Yankee teammates Russ Ford and Walter Blair were already in Buffalo, as were former American Leaguers such as Billy Louden, Gene Krapp, and Fred Anderson. Two more of Chase's former Yankee teammates, Frank LaPorte and Bill McKechnie, were with the Indianapolis Federals, as was Edd Roush, the young outfielder who had had a brief trial with the White Sox in 1913. The veteran Davy Jones, a former Tiger who had begun the 1913 season with the White Sox, was with the Pittsburgh Rebels of the new league. Ex-Yankees Hack Simmons, Guy Zinn, and Jack Quinn had landed with the Baltimore Terrapins. And Rollie Zeider, the "bunion" traded to the Yankees for Chase, had joined Tinker's Chicago team.

Despite the presence of such players, and despite its claims to the contrary, the Federal League probably did not deserve major league status. It had attracted a handful of stars, including Ford, Tinker, Mordecai (Three Finger) Brown, and Eddie Plank, but its depth of talent could not compare with that of the American and National Leagues. Moreover, most of the big names signed by the Feds were well past their primes. The addition of a star player still in his prime such as Chase or Collins or Johnson would be a major coup for the Federals.

That night a reporter caught up with Chase at the Warner Hotel. The first baseman seemed surprised that the story had already leaked out and at first sought to deny any knowledge of such a deal, but finally admitted that he was about to cast his lot with the new league.

"Yes, it is true the Feds have been after me," said Chase, "and I have decided to serve the ten day notice on the Chicago American League owner."

Chase and Comiskey met privately on the following day, after another White Sox loss to Philadelphia. Just what went on at that meeting eventually became the subject of much dispute. Chase later claimed that he handed Comiskey written notice of his intent to leave the team in ten days. Receiving no response from the White Sox owner, Chase said, he believed that he was free to do as he wished.

Comiskey's memory of the meeting was very different. Chase had given no such written notice, said the White Sox owner; moreover, he had denied having any contact with the Federal League. Instead, according to Comiskey, Chase said that he had decided to quit baseball and go into business with a friend, rumored to be Lord, in Philadelphia.

"I advised Chase to remain in the game," related Comiskey, "but I told him I would not stand in the way to prevent his entering business, if he had fully made up his mind to leave baseball."

As always, Ring Lardner was skeptical. "It is said that Mr. Chase intends to quit the Sox and go into business with Harry Lord," he wrote in the *Tribune*, adding facetiously, "Federal league baseball is a business."[24]

For several days the baseball world swirled with rumors about Chase and the Federals, and White Sox fans did not know which to believe. Most observers shared Lardner's skepticism, assuming again, as they had that spring, that Chase had already signed with the new league despite his denials. They dismissed the retirement story as a ploy to avoid a confrontation with Comiskey.

In Buffalo feelings were mixed about the possible arrival of the best first baseman in baseball. On June 20 the Buffalo *Express* announced in a headline that "Chase Looks Sure to Come." The accompanying story was cool, due to Chase's run-in with a local hero, the former manager of Buffalo's International League club. "Probably owing to the difficulties Chase had with George Stallings, who has many friends in Buffalo, the local Feds could have picked a more uniformly popular star than Chase," noted the *Express*, "but, no matter what else, Chase is known as a ball player and if he can deliver star goods here he can probably earn a welcome." The story also hinted at another explanation for Chase's failure to sign with the Federal League that spring: "most of the Fed managers preferred to fight shy of Chase, because of his continuing reputation as a disturbing element. But no one would care to deny that Chase is a ballplayer, when he plays, and an asset to the playing strength of any club."[25]

The rumors of Chase's alleged jump sparked a new set of rumors that various other White Sox players, including Weaver, Scott, Russell, Joe Benz, Ray Demmitt, and Lena Blackburne, either had signed or were about to sign Federal League contracts. Supposedly Gilmore, angered by Ban Johnson's continued attacks on the Feds, had rescinded the hands-off policy with regard to Comiskey's players and declared the White Sox fair game.

This was seen as a dangerous move. Comiskey, nicknamed "the Old Roman," was an immensely popular figure, not just in Chicago but nationally as well. He was a notoriously tight-fisted employer, a fact which may have made his players more receptive to overtures from the Federal League and, later, to the Black Sox scheme, but he was considered one of the game's true aristocrats. William A. Phelon expressed a common view when he wrote in *The Sporting News* later that summer that "Raiding Commy's club is the one unpardonable offense, the one thing that cannot be forgiven or tolerated.... Attacking Comiskey was the most suicidal thing the rebels ever did." The dire consequences of their rash act were not immediately apparent, however; for his part Comiskey, fearing the loss of most of his best players, briefly considered buying the Baltimore Orioles of the International League to ensure an adequate supply of replacements.

Ban Johnson was apparently one of those who believed that the Federals had indeed signed Chase, and he was not about to let this challenge go unanswered. "Federal League teams will not get one single player from Charles A. Comiskey, owner of the Chicago White Sox, and if Hal Chase jumps his contract he will never play with a third league club," predicted the American League president. "All of Comiskey's players are bound by contracts that have no ten day clauses. Chase was the single exception. I know Chase had the ten day clause in his contract, but if he jumps he will never be permitted to play with a Federal League team — you can set that down as a certainty. Furthermore, any player in the American League who jumps his contract to play in the Federal League will never be permitted to appear on the rolls of an American League team again."

Johnson repeated this threat a few days later, this time calling attention to Chase's dubious past. This time the American League president made no reference to Chase's "sterling" qualities as he had during the Stallings controversy: "If anybody should have gratitude towards organized baseball, Chase is the man," he said. "His present behavior has taught me one good lesson. No one who quits my league in this fight will ever get back as long as I am president."[26] Such threats may have helped win over the other six Chicago players rumored to be dickering with the Feds, but they had no effect on Chase.

On Sunday morning, June 21, Hal Chase went to Comiskey Park, packed up his belongings, and showed up at Weeghman Park on the city's north side, the home of the local Federal League team. The ten thousand fans who came that afternoon to watch the Chifeds play Buffalo got an added surprise when the announcer informed them that Hal Chase would play first base for Buffalo.

Though Chase had two hits and drove in a run Chicago won 2–1, but more important than the result of the game was the mere fact of his participation. "Evidently," reported the Buffalo *Express,* "he was played today just to show that he had really, as he had promised, swapped horses crossing the stream of season play." The *Express* noted that the announcement of Chase's participation was greeted "with prolonged applause" by the Chicago fans, and that his every move during the game "was rewarded with outbursts of cheers and handclaps."[27]

The timing of the appearance was shrewd. Comiskey would not expect Chase to appear in a Buffalo uniform so soon — four days before the end of his ten-day waiting period, assuming that he had indeed given the White Sox owner such notice at their June 15 meeting. Moreover, because it was a Sunday, Comiskey was powerless to obtain a legal injunction barring Chase from playing. Chase and the Buffeds had stolen a march on Comiskey and Johnson. His point made, Chase left Chicago for Buffalo immediately after the game so as to be safely out of reach when the Illinois courts reconvened on Monday morning.

In New York, where the major league owners had assembled to discuss ways to fight the Federals, Johnson tried to downplay the Chase situation. "I notice Chase played with the Federals on Sunday, in open disregard of his own statements to Mr. Comiskey," said Johnson casually. "As it was Sunday that could not be helped, but action will be taken to keep him from playing with the Buffalo team, which is equally culpable with Chase." Meanwhile the owners, near panic, were seriously considering a proposal to elevate the International League to major league status, in hopes of crowding out the Federals. Fortunately, cooler heads prevailed before this scheme could be implemented.

The daring and impudence displayed by Chase naturally caused great excitement in Buffalo, and the Buffeds quickly made plans for Hal Chase Day, to be celebrated on Thursday, June 25, when Chase would play his first game before the Buffalo fans. The team announced that every fan attending Thursday's game would receive a four-page souvenir booklet with a photograph and biographical sketch of Chase and "a statement by the Buffalo (Federal league) club in connection with the Chase matter."

Chase in his Buffalo uniform in July 1914, shortly after he joined the Federal League upstarts. His abrupt abandonment of the White Sox caused an uproar in the baseball world. *Author's collection.*

Meanwhile the whereabouts of Chase himself were "a deep mystery." The ostensible reason for keeping him hidden was to foil Comiskey's process servers, although the Buffeds had no doubt realized that the cloak-and-dagger aspects of the situation could only heighten interest in Thursday's game. In fact Chase and his wife were safely stashed across the Canadian border, at the Queen's Royal Hotel in Niagara-on-the-Lake. There they had "rusticated beautifully for a couple of days," inspecting the golf course at Fort George and lounging on the shores of Lake Ontario. Supposedly Hal was overheard telling Mrs. Chase that their situation was "not so bad, at all."

The Chase affair quickly became the biggest story in the city. On Thursday the lead story in the *Express* was headlined "Hal Chase — Can He Do It?" The story indicated that the local fans, who had initially regarded the acquisition of Chase with some ambivalence, were now excited by the prospect of seeing Prince Hal in the home team's uniform. Stallings had been a popular figure with the city's baseball fans, but "Buffalo, including the staunchest friends of Stallings, is willing to forget and forgive. There never has been a disposition to regard Chase as other than one of the greatest ball players living and now that he is here and has declared himself as prepared to do his best for Buffalo, and willing to be judged by what he does and not on past reputation, there will be a warm place for him in the affection of the local fans."[28]

Meanwhile Johnson and Comiskey were reportedly in Buffalo, lawyers in tow, intending to keep Chase from playing. They planned to attend that afternoon's game, at which Chase would be served with papers. (In this the article was mistaken; Johnson did not come to Buffalo, although Comiskey was accompanied by White Sox attorney J. J. Healley; Robert B. McRoy, the secretary of the National Commission; and Ellis G. Kinkaid, the attorney for the National Commission.) The story also reported the rumors that Chase had been hiding in Canada, but took a dim view of the strategy: "Just what the object has been in spiriting Chase away, when he was not to be in action, and bringing him back at the eleventh hour, when he will be in the limelight and easy prey for the servers with no time for a legal fight, has not been set forth, but Owen B. Augspurger, attorney for the Buffalo Federals, who is now deep in baseball lore, betrays no particular anxiety as to what move the opposition may make."

In fact, the Buffeds were still seeking ways to play up the drama of Chase's Buffalo debut. They asked pioneer aviator Glenn Curtiss, based in Hammondsport, about sixty miles away, if he would fly Chase into the stadium; "Curtiss replied that he would have been happy to engineer the trick, but that the time was not sufficient."[29]

As it turned out Curtiss could hardly have added to the circus atmosphere of Chase's debut. The story of how he got to the ballpark was remarkable, combining elements of detective fiction and low farce. On Wednesday afternoon Carroll and Buffed vice president Walter Mullen drove to Niagara-on-the-Lake and picked up Chase and his wife. They drove south along the Canadian side of the river to Niagara Falls, where they dined at the Clifton, and then to Black

Creek, Ontario, where Chase boarded a motorboat owned by Ralph Sidway. Carroll and Mullen drove Mrs. Chase back to Buffalo while Chase spent the night at the Buffalo Launch Club on Grand Island. He arrived by motorboat in Buffalo on Thursday morning, had lunch at the Century Club, then was taken to the home of Tommy O'Grady, the head of a local detective agency.

At this point the story became even more bizarre. Chase left O'Grady's house in drag; the *Express* reported coyly that "Hal made a very pretty looking girl — heavily veiled." He was taken, in "full feminine costume," to the ballpark at about one o'clock in the afternoon. At the ballpark he went not to the clubhouse but to an empty toolshed down the right field line, where he changed into his uniform and "was left temporarily to ruminate on the vagaries of the national game, which left a stellar performer locked in a closet."

Meanwhile attorneys Healley and Kinkaid met with John W. Ryan of the local firm of Moot, Sprague, Brownell and Marcy. Ryan appeared before Justice Pooley of the state supreme court and was granted a temporary injunction on behalf of the White Sox restraining Chase from playing anywhere in the state of New York until the issue was settled in court.

With the scheduled game time of 3:30 p.m. approaching and the crowd of almost six thousand awaiting the denouement of the farce, a horde of photographers gathered around the toolshed door, which opened occasionally to admit a messenger to or from the Buffeds' bench. Soon the crowd was told that the game would begin a half hour late, at four o'clock. At 3:55 Deputy Sheriff William Crane, carrying the papers to be served on Chase, attempted to enter the ballpark; he was greeted and detained by Augspurger. Eventually Sheriff Becker telephoned and announced that he was on his way to take charge of the situation.

Finally, reported the *Express,* all the maneuvering appeared to be coming to a climax: "At 4 o'clock the announcer megaphoned the names of the batteries for the day's game to the spectators and an impressive after-announcement that 'Hal Chase will play first base for Buffalo' awoke a great cheer." The visiting Pittsburgh team unexpectedly took the field, allowing the home team to bat first. As the first Buffalo batter, Frank Delahanty, made his way to home plate the toolshed door opened. Out came "the tall athletic figure of Chase," preceded by a security guard.

"It was not a very dramatic entrance, after all," said the *Express*. Chase received an ovation as he made his way to the Buffalo bench; he "took to the ovation as a duck to water and doffed his cap," then grabbed two bats and began to loosen up while Delahanty continued his at-bat.

Finally, with Delahanty out of the way, came the moment for which all of Buffalo had waited. Chase made his way to the plate — and promptly struck out on three pitches. "Even this won a laughing cheer," according to the *Express*.

The Buffalo half of the inning ended without incident and the Rebels came to bat. By this time Sheriff Becker had arrived and went to the Buffalo bench with Augspurger. Becker wanted to go out on the field and get Chase after the first out of the half-inning, but Augspurger persuaded him to wait until the

A wary-looking Chase with Buffalo. *National Baseball Hall of Fame Library, Cooperstown, N.Y.*

inning was over. Thus, after the third out, as Chase dropped his glove on the field and headed for the bench, he was met by Becker, Crane, Police Captain Henry J. Griven, and McRoy. The latter pointed at Chase and told Becker, "There's your man." Becker handed Chase the papers and said, "For you, Mr. Chase."

Chase left the game without protest. He went to the clubhouse, where he ran into his old friend Carroll.

"How long will this thing last, Dick?" asked Chase.

"Oh, not long, I guess."

Outfielder Charlie Handford, who had come back to the clubhouse for a moment, interrupted. "Hal, me hearty, you can prepare to warm the bench for the rest of the summer!"

"No bench for that baby," laughed Carroll, with what must have been forced jocularity, "and he'll stick in Buffalo till the finish. Eh, Hal?"

"You bet," replied Chase.[30]

He was probably less enthusiastic than he sounded, for at the time Handford's prediction seemed entirely plausible. The legal battle over Chase, which the *Express* predicted would be "lengthy and tortuous," lasted more than a month. Initially the Federals hoped to have the case argued before Justice Harry Leonard Taylor. Taylor had played major league baseball in the early 1890s before commencing his legal career. In 1900, as counsel to the short-lived Players Protective Association, he had been a vociferous proponent of reforming baseball's contract. Among the views which had alarmed major league owners at the time had been Taylor's insistence that the ten-day clause should apply to the player as well as the team — the same argument that Chase had used in leaving the White Sox.

Taylor was no longer the wild-eyed radical of the Protective Association; indeed, organized baseball, perhaps innocently, had coopted Taylor by electing him president of the Eastern League, forerunner of the International League.[31] But his declining to hear the case still came as a relief to organized baseball and a disappointment to the Federals.

"Justice Taylor was perfectly willing to hear the case," explained the *Express*, "but inasmuch as he was at one time a professional ball player, a former president of the International League and part owner in the franchise of the [International League] Buffalo club, he thought it advisable to have Justice Bissell, who had expressed a willingness to hear the proceedings, preside."[32]

Taylor had lost his battle on behalf of the Protective Association in 1900 and, as his activities in the International League indicated, could now be considered one of the magnates whom he had fought so bitterly almost fifteen years before. But Chase's argument on the mutual applicability of the ten-day clause could be expected to find a sympathetic ear in Taylor's court. Judge Herbert P. Bissell, unlike Taylor, brought no extra baggage to the case.

The Buffeds departed on another road trip, leaving Chase in Buffalo until the case was decided. He hired Keene H. Addington of Santa Clara, "a personal friend," to represent him in cooperation with Augspurger. Also expected to participate were Augspurger's partner Michael F. Dirnberger and Edward E. Gates of Indianapolis, the chief counsel of the Federal League. They would be opposed by Ryan, Kinkaid, and Ryan's partners Moot and William H. Marcy.[33]

Meanwhile, the Federals tried to keep the pressure on organized baseball on other fronts. Carroll had earlier hinted to Buffalo reporters that the Buffeds were about to sign the Athletics' brilliant second baseman Eddie Collins. This rumor proved false, but on July 7 the *Express* reported that Collins and Walter Johnson were "as good as signed up to the Brookfeds for next year." And Chase's attorneys again threatened to attack organized baseball on the grounds that it was in violation of the Sherman Antitrust Act.

Such an argument could throw the entire structure of professional baseball into disarray: "Where organized baseball will be, or where any attempt to organize the game will be, if the contention carries, and the Federalites are confident it will, is a dubious question," noted the *Express*.[34]

Predictably *The Sporting News*, the voice of organized baseball, was outraged by the whole affair. An editorial in the July 2 issue headlined "Barnumizing

Buffalo" heaped scorn upon the handling of Chase's Buffalo debut: "There was no necessity for any of this hippodroming, for the sheriff was instructed not to serve notice on Chase until he had actually played, of course, but it was a great advertising stunt. That seems to be the main idea with the Feds now — rather than real ball playing." The editorial also implied that the version of Chase's biography handed out to the Buffalo fans had been heavily edited, hinting archly that some of Chase's past actions might not withstand close scrutiny: "Not having seen a copy of the booklet it can not be said if the true story of Hal's life, with all its particulars, was told or not."[35]

Such comments were mild compared to those of Chase's old nemesis Ernest J. Lanigan, who had written the article that had supposedly driven Chase to jump the Yankees in 1908. Lanigan argued that Chase should be barred permanently from organized baseball for his traitorous behavior. Chase, Marsans, and pitcher Dave Davenport, another of the "Ten-Day Boys," wrote Lanigan, "when peace is declared or the Federals go under, ought to be kept out of organized base ball. There may have been some excuse for Marsans and Davenport jumping, but for Hal Chase — none. He is the king of the leapers and the National Commission ought never to have reinstated him and neither should Frank Farrell have rewarded him for his disloyalty by making him manager of the Highlanders."

Lanigan returned to this theme again and again: "The Commish found extenuating circumstances for Hal the Hopper and so reinstated him — an act that smelt to the Heavens.... The Federals never will prosper if they get many more players of the Chase type. There wouldn't be so many of them if the National Commission had not acted so foolishly in the past."

In fact, wrote Lanigan, organized baseball was better off without Chase. "The Highlanders were strengthened immeasurably when Chase was traded to Chicago and the Sox struck a winning streak just as soon as the athlete with the peculiar streak left them."[36] Few would agree that New York was better without Chase — the Yankees in 1914 were on their way to their second consecutive seventh-place finish — but the White Sox had indeed begun to play better baseball since Chase's departure. Chicago won thirteen of its first fifteen games without him and rose from sixth place to fourth.

Such issues, however, were immaterial to the court battle. Chase argued in a thirty-page affidavit that he had fulfilled his contractual obligations in giving Comiskey ten days' notice, and that his salary had been illegally cut from $8,000 to $6,000 when he was traded to Chicago. Before the trade, said Chase (that is, before the Federal League began wooing major league players, before the players realized that the ten-day clause could work for them as well as against them), he had protested the inclusion of the ten-day clause in his contract to Farrell. Callahan had promised that the clause would be removed, but had failed to do so. In effect, the negligence of the White Sox was the reason that Chase had left Chicago. The affidavit also repeated the charge that organized baseball had acted as a monopoly in violation of the Sherman law when it sought to keep Chase and his fellow defectors from playing for the Feds.[37]

Publicly, organized baseball dismissed the Federal League's threats. "We are not restraining Marsans and Chase from playing, but are trying to get them to play," argued Garry Herrmann, in an admirable example of twisted logic. "It is the Federal League which is keeping them from playing if any one is."

Others followed Herrmann's lead. "Chase set up in his defense ... that he had been compelled through alleged trust methods to accept a smaller salary from Chicago than he received from New York and this was argued as a shameful case of peonage by his lawyers," editorialized *The Sporting News*. "In answer the plaintiff Chicago Club shows that Chase played with the White Sox under the same contract he accepted from New York. Chase received $5,000 a year prior to taking the management of the Yankees. As manager he was paid $8,000. He voluntarily resigned and upon becoming a player in the ranks again signed a contract for $6,000, an advance over his previous salary as a player." The conclusion was obvious: "It will be hard for any reasonable judge on the bench to reach a finding that the player is any great sufferer under Organized Ball's operations if the facts in the Chase case are to be used as a basis."[38]

Notwithstanding his team's recent success Comiskey was determined to fight Chase and the Feds every step of the way. The terms on which the legal battle would be fought were becoming clearer: the White Sox and organized baseball would argue that Chase had no right to invoke the ten-day clause; that he had illegally broken his contract; and that he should be barred from playing for any team other than the White Sox. Interestingly, Comiskey's claim that Chase had never given him ten days' notice was not mentioned. Neither was Johnson's vow that Chase would never play in the American League again.

At ten o'clock in the morning of Thursday, July 9, the attorneys began presenting their case before Bissell. As expected, Addington argued that organized baseball was a monopoly that violated the Sherman act because it constituted a traffic in players, although he and the other Federal League attorneys concentrated most of their energies on the argument that without mutuality in the ten-day clause the contract between Chase and the White Sox was void.[39]

This was the crux of the matter. If management was allowed to use the ten-day clause while the player was not, the contract was unconstitutional and therefore void, and Chase was free to sell his services to the highest bidder. If the player was allowed to invoke the ten-day clause, as was management, then Chase had legally fulfilled his obligations to Comiskey — and was free to sell his services to the highest bidder.

While Bissell was still weighing the arguments in the Chase case the Federal League won a victory in a similar case when an appellate court in Chicago ruled that pitcher George (Chief) Johnson, formerly of the Cincinnati Reds, could play with the Kansas City Feds. The Illinois court did not address the issue of the ten-day clause in reversing the order of a lower court.[40]

Bissell finally announced his ruling on Tuesday, July 21. He ruled that organized baseball was not a form of interstate commerce and therefore not subject to the Sherman act. "We are not dealing with the bodies of the players as commodities or merchandise," he said, "but with their services as retained or transferred by contract."

In all other respects the ruling was a smashing triumph for Chase and the Federal League. The structure of organized baseball, said Bissell, "would seem to establish a species of quasi-peonage unlawfully controlling and interfering with the personal freedom of the men employed. Organized baseball is now as complete a monopoly of the baseball business for profit as a monopoly can be made. It is in contravention of the common law in that it invades the right to labor as a property right; in that it invades the right to contract as a property right and in that it is a combination to restrain and control the exercise of a profession or calling."

The attorneys for Comiskey and organized baseball immediately announced that they would appeal Bissell's ruling,[41] but the battle was over. Hal Chase was free to play with the Buffeds.

The Sporting News, as always a dependable mouthpiece for the baseball establishment, was outraged. An editorial published shortly after the ruling flayed Chase for his ingratitude, referring sarcastically to "the terrible conditions under which the enslaved ballplayer is compelled to follow his calling" under "that monstrous institution, Organized Ball." In defense of the charges of monopoly the editorial argued that "This unlawful monopoly raised a sport that was a medium for gambling and fraud ... to the stage where millions are proud to declare their allegiance to it as the 'Only Game.'... This is the system that is indicted by Judge Bissell from the bench because it sought before him to compel a conscienceless creature named Chase — his record is known to every [unclear] who follows the game...."

Had organized baseball erred in trying to hang onto Hal Chase? "So be it, let Hal Chase go to the Federals and to liberty, and may he enjoy there the full freedom that his aspiring soul desires. And we say now what we said in the beginning of this fight with the Federals, let every other ball player who has no more conscience, who has no more appreciation of what Organized Ball has done for him and his profession, go likewise to liberty and the Feds. And good riddance."[42]

Lanigan, whose hostility toward Chase was a matter of record, also felt that the major leagues would be better off without Chase and the other defectors. "Organized Base Ball is big enough to fight unorganized Base Ball in the right away — not in the courts, but at the turnstiles," he argued. "Let the Feds have their George Johnsons, their Hal Chases, their Fred Blandings, their Bill Killifers, their Armando Marsans. Let the players who wish to violate contracts violate them, and do not employ contract jumpers."[43]

But organized baseball could not be reconciled so easily to the loss of one of its greatest stars. On August 6 *The Sporting News* predicted that "As soon as the Buffalo team leaves home and appears outside of New York State he will bump into another injunction suit." When that prediction did not come true the magazine reported petulantly that "Hal Chase has failed to make the great hit with the Buffalo Federals that was expected and fans who follow the Feds in that city are clamoring that Joe Agler looks better on first base than does the once famous Child Harold. They are suggesting that possibly Chase can be of help to the team at second, but at first they want Agler."[44]

This absurd statement was, of course, mere wishful thinking. Agler was a journeyman first baseman and outfielder who had gone hitless in his only major league at bat, with the Washington Senators in 1912. With Buffalo in 1914 he batted a respectable .272, but the idea that he was a better first baseman than Chase was laughable. The Buffeds wisely disregarded this unsolicited advice.

On August 4, during a 5–4 victory over Indianapolis, Chase put on a remarkable show for the Buffalo fans, even though he was hitless in three at bats. In the fourth inning Vin Campbell grounded to Buffalo third baseman Fred Smith. Smith's hurried throw was high and off line, forcing Chase to jump for the ball as the speedy Campbell sprinted past. "There was only one way in which the play could have been accomplished perfectly and Chase rose to the occasion," reported the *Express*. "While in the air with his back to the speeding Campbell, he whirled around and tagged him on the shoulder — both players being in midair when the play was made."

Jack McInerney, the former president of the Pacific Coast League Sacramento team who was attending the game, was duly impressed. "That play was conceived and executed by Chase in the fraction of a second," he said. "It was the quickest piece of baseball thinking that I have ever had the pleasure of witnessing."

Chase may have forced McInerney to revise his assessment with another spectacular effort in the sixth inning. Buffed pitcher Al Schulz lunged for a grounder off the bat of Al Kaiser but could only deflect the ball. Chase fielded it about six feet from first base, turned, and dove for the bag. His hand touched the base just before Kaiser's foot. "The applause which greeted the play was the greatest accorded any one play at Buffalo Federal league park this season," reported the *Express*.[45]

By August 8, however, after losing 8–2 before a crowd of eight thousand on Hal Chase Day in Kansas City, the Buffeds had managed only to split eighteen games since the return of their star. Chase was hitless in four at bats on his day, but in the next three games of the series, all of which Buffalo won, he caught fire with nine hits in fourteen at bats. On August 10, six days after Great Britain had declared war on Germany, Chase's four hits included a long triple, moving the *Express* to report that "The ball shot so high over [Kansas City center fielder Fred] Potts's bean that he thought it was a German dirigible."[46]

A week later the same paper enthused that "Since joining the Buffalo Feds, in batting, fielding and base running he has kept pace with the wonderful work which he accomplished in New York city from 1905 to 1910, when his all around play was the sensation of the baseball world."[47] The Buffeds, however, continued to struggle along at the .500 mark. They moved past Brooklyn into fourth place after beating Chicago on August 22, but promptly lost five of their next eight games with the Brookfeds and fell back into fifth place.

Even more disheartening was the loss of Ford, the Buffeds' best pitcher with a 15–5 record and one of their most popular players, with a back injury that reportedly would require surgery. Still, their brief move into the first division was heartening, as was Ford's unexpectedly early return on September 5 — he would win six more games before the end of the season — and the signing of Clyde Engle, another of Chase's former Yankee teammates, on the following day.[48] And Chase himself continued to excel. On September 7, in the first game of a doubleheader against Baltimore, he went five-for-five with a home run and a double and made a bare-handed stop of a grounder. He went hitless in the second game, but hit home runs in each of the next two games.[49]

September 12 was proclaimed Greater Buffalo Day at the Federal League park. Although the Buffeds lost a doubleheader to Chicago the Buffalo fans were excited by the possible addition to the local team of pitcher Ray Caldwell, who sat on the Buffed bench in street clothes. Caldwell had won seventeen games for the Yankees before quitting the team in August after a dispute with Frank Chance. Now Chase had supposedly convinced his old Yankee teammate to join him in Buffalo, and Buffed business manager Dick Carroll announced that Caldwell had been signed for the 1915 season.[50] Unfortunately for the Buffalo fans the deal with Caldwell apparently fell through. Caldwell never pitched for the Buffeds, but returned to the Yankees and won nineteen games for them in 1915.

Coincidentally Chance chose this same day, September 12, to announce his resignation as manager of the Yankees. In a little less than two full seasons Chance's Yankees had won only 118 games while losing 170, and the Peerless Leader had feuded bitterly with the team's front office. Most recently he had accused Farrell and Devery of being unwilling to spend the money necessary to turn the team into a winner, while they had refused Chance's demand that longtime Yankee scout Arthur Irwin be fired. Things had come to a head when Devery took a swing at Chance in the Yankee clubhouse.

"If I had had Farrell to deal with alone I would have been successful," said Chance years later, after Devery's death. "Farrell knew baseball and was eager to do things on a big scale, but Devery was just the opposite. I couldn't get along with Devery, who was always butting in on Farrell, so I had to quit the management."[51]

On the field the Buffeds were finally starting to show the kind of form expected of them. By September 19, having won thirteen of their last nineteen games, they were back in the first division, only one game behind third-place Baltimore. But that was the high-water mark of the Buffeds' season. They would finish the season with a record of 80–71, seven games behind first-place Indianapolis and two and a half games behind the third-place Terrapins.

On October 7 Buffalo lost its last home game of the season by a score of 10–4. Chase had two hits in three at bats but his wild throw in the second inning allowed two Brooklyn runs to score. More interesting than the game itself were the pregame festivities, in which players from the two teams competed in various field events. Chase won the hundred-yard dash, in eleven seconds, and the sprint around the bases, in fourteen seconds.[52]

Four days later the Buffeds beat the Simon Pures, a top Buffalo semipro team, 15–3. Chase had five hits, including a double and a triple, in six at bats. So popular was he, reported the *Express,* that another exhibition game had been scheduled for Sunday, October 18, between the Simon Pures and "Hal Chase's All-Stars," just to give Buffalo fans "another chance to see Chase's wonderful work at first base."[53]

Chase's play during his half-season with the Buffeds had been wonderful indeed. In seventy-five games he batted .347, which would have been good enough for third place in the Federal League had he accumulated enough at bats to qualify among the official league leaders, and drove in forty-eight runs, which ranked third on the team. Chase seemed to have found a home in Buffalo; the *Express* even reported that he and his wife had bought a house in the city.[54]

Buffalo in the teens was a major American city. Thanks to the Erie Canal, it was the greatest grain port in the world, and was second only to Minneapolis as a milling center and to Chicago as a livestock center.[55] Still, Buffalo must have seemed small after the bright lights and glitter of New York and Chicago. On the other hand, the idea of being a big fish in a small pond must have had a powerful appeal for Chase. The Giants had overshadowed the Yankees throughout his tenure in New York, and he had been only one of several stars with the White Sox. In Buffalo he had no rival, with the possible exception of Ford, for the affection of the fans. Shortly after the season ended the *Express* called Chase "the most popular player that ever wore a Buffalo uniform" on the basis of his half-season with the Buffeds.[56]

The makeup of the "All-Stars" was the cause for much speculation over the next week. Among the players rumored to be joining Chase were former Giant and Tiger second baseman Heinie Smith, former Brave outfielder Jimmy Murray, and shortstop Natty Nattress, all longtime stars with the Buffalo Bisons of the International League. At one point Chase was also reportedly trying to get an unnamed White Sox pitcher to come to Buffalo for the game, but on the following day the *Express* reported that Buffed business manager Dick Carroll, whose major league career consisted of two games for the Yankees in 1909, would pitch for the All-Stars instead. For his one-game return to the managerial ranks Chase planned "to pull a few defensive plays and base-running tactics that he has advocated for a number of years."[57]

Perhaps inevitably the game was an anticlimax. Rain on October 18 caused the contest to be postponed for a week, allowing another seven days of hype in the local newspapers. The following Sunday was chilly and only about two thousand fans saw the Simon Pures defeat the All-Stars 6–4 in seven innings. Dick Carroll did not pitch after all; instead Chase prevailed upon Ray Caldwell to take the mound, but Caldwell gave up six runs in five innings and was hit in the head by a pitch from Paul Birtch of the Simon Pures. Chase replaced Caldwell as pitcher in the sixth inning and gave up only one hit in two innings of work. At bat Chase was hitless, and the account of the game in the *Express* makes no mention of any innovative defense or base-running by the All-Stars.[58]

More significant for the future of baseball was the long-threatened lawsuit filed on January 5, 1915, by the Federal League. In the suit Gilmore and his owners, encouraged at least in part by Bissell's ruling, charged the major leagues with restraint of trade in denying the Feds free access to the player market and asked for a nine-count federal antitrust injunction against the major leagues. The Feds filed the suit in federal court in Illinois, where they hoped that Judge Kenesaw Mountain Landis would be sympathetic to their cause.

Landis had made national headlines in 1907 by fining the Standard Oil Company more than $29 million, by a wide margin the largest fine ever laid against a corporation, for antitrust violations. Although a higher court had thrown out his verdict, the case had made him a popular hero for taking on big business, and established his reputation as a trustbuster.[59] He took the Federal League suit under advisement in late January, and most observers expected a ruling before the beginning of spring training.[60]

Chase spent the winter in Buffalo. In late February he attended an indoor baseball game between Company A and the Travelers at the 65th Infantry Armory, and was so intrigued by the game that he asked his host, Capt. Patrick J. Keeler, to schedule a game.

"If you want to play, bring on your big league players before their departure for spring training," said Keeler, "and my boys will show you a few stunts in indoor baseball which I think will surprise you."

"It's a go," replied Chase. "I'll do so."[61]

The game was scheduled for February 25, the day before Gilmore was to open a Federal League meeting in Buffalo. Once again the local newspapers were full of speculation about the identity of Hal Chase's All-Stars. Since all Federal League managers were expected to attend the meeting, the *Express* reported optimistically that Chase's team would include Joe Tinker at shortstop and Lee Magee, the umbrella-toting barnstormer of 1913 and the new player-manager of the Brookfeds, in left field. Magee's path would shortly cross Chase's again, with fateful results. The other "All-Stars" would reportedly include Chase's fellow Buffeds Larry Schlafly, Bill Louden, Gene Krapp, and Al Schulz, plus local favorites Fred Fischer and Norman McNeill. Chase himself would pitch.[62]

Once again the event failed to live up to expectations. Tinker, Magee, Schlafly, Louden, Krapp, and Schulz were all no-shows, but the "All-Stars" scarcely needed them, as they walloped Company A by a score of 13–3. Pitcher Chase "showed masterly skill at cutting the corners of the plate," reported the *Express*. "His control was perfect and his curves a mystery to the 65th boys." In nine innings he gave up only seven hits and two bases on balls while striking out five. He also had three hits, including a bases-loaded triple, in five at bats.[63]

By the time the Buffeds embarked for spring training in Athens, Georgia, a little more than a week later, Chase had gone to New York, promising to rejoin his teammates in Washington, D.C. The Buffeds had high hopes for 1915. They would have Chase and Engle for a full season, of course, and had added pitcher Hugh Bedient, who had won twenty games for the Red Sox three years before.

Schlafly had also signed another former Yankee teammate of Chase's, shortstop Roxey Roach of the International League Bisons, and lured Ivy Wingo, a promising young catcher, away from the St. Louis Cardinals.[64]

March, however, brought a succession of bad omens. Roach and Wingo both decided to jump back to organized baseball. When the Buffed travelling party of seventeen, including various reporters, team officials, players, and even some wives, left Buffalo on the evening of March 5, it did so in a howling blizzard that then followed the team all the way to Georgia.

Despite the wet and cold weather the Buffeds enjoyed their stopover in Washington. Some of the players met President Woodrow Wilson, while others visited the Capitol, the Navy Yard, the Library of Congress, Mount Vernon, and Arlington National Cemetery.[65] The team left Washington at 9:30 on Saturday night, with Mr. and Mrs. Chase on board. Walter C. Mason of the *Express* attributed the uncharacteristically civilized atmosphere on the train to the presence of several wives, including Anna Chase, who seemed to be in high spirits.

"Just to show you that my husband will be in good form this season I will try out his arm," she announced to Mason as she tossed pieces of rolled-up newspaper at the Buffed first baseman.

"Yes," responded Chase, lunging for her erratic throws, "but if any of our infielders ever make such wild heaves as you are now doing, I'm afraid that few will stop in my hands."[66]

On March 8, the Buffeds held their first practice at Sanford Field in Athens. Roach and Wingo were still missing, the weather was chilly, and Russ Ford was hit in the eye by a grounder during batting practice — more bad omens — but the mood was upbeat. On Thursday the regulars beat the yannigans 12–11 in seven innings as Chase had two hits in four at bats and stole a base. Despite his recent exertions against the men of Company A in Buffalo, however, he suffered some of the mishaps common to athletes trying to work out the kinks of a winter's relative inactivity. Mason reported that Chase "covered his territory, as he always does, with perfection," despite a sore foot. Another injury came to light on the next day when Mason reported that Chase had also strained his side while sliding.[67]

Neither injury was serious, as Schlafly made clear a couple of days later. "I look to see Hal Chase have the best year of his baseball life," the manager told Mason. "He has been injured or something else has always kept him from being at his best at the start of the season, but today there is nothing troubling him and he should play some grand baseball for Buffalo."[68]

Indeed, Chase was enjoying a relaxed spring. When the Buffeds went to Atlanta and twice beat Georgia Tech, Chase's "right hand scoops of low throws were revelations to the fans." Back in Athens, during a Buffed victory over the University of Georgia, he engaged in some banter, mostly good-natured, with the locals. Mason reported the outcome: "Chase had been having a lot of fun with the fans. When they became a bit too strong of voice about his batting ability [he had gone hitless in his first four at bats] he stepped into one that went so far over the left fielder's head that he had time to make the rounds closely on the heels of [teammate Tex] McDonald. It was a grand wallop and appeared to satisfy the natives that Chase had a hit in his bat after all."[69]

Still, the bad omens continued. In batting practice on March 25 Chase was almost beaned by a fastball from an overenthusiastic Buffalo pitcher. "That's about as close a shave as I've ever had," he said after barely deflecting the ball with his big new bat. "Better cut down that speed and try control," he called out to the mound. On the following day he injured a finger playing pepper and was unable to play first base in the infield drill that followed.[70]

And the weather continued to be a problem. Schlafly either cancelled or cut short several practice sessions due to cold and rainy conditions, and on the morning of March 31 snow drove the Buffeds into the local YMCA, where Chase played left forward for the losing side in an intramural basketball game. Anna Chase left Athens for New York on April 3. On the following day George Stallings visited the Buffeds on his way to the Boston Braves' camp in Atlanta.[71] No record of a meeting between Chase and Stallings survives.

Despite Schlafly's announcement that his team would now be known as the Blues[72] the new nickname never caught on entirely. The Blues, or Buffeds, opened the regular season in Brooklyn against Lee Magee's Brookfeds on April 10. The Brookfeds won 13–9 before a crowd of 15,441. Chase was hitless in four at bats, but scored a run with some tricky baserunning. He was on third base when Fred Smith hit a grounder to the pitcher. Chase started for home and the pitcher threw to catcher Mike Simon. Chase managed to scramble back to third, only to find the bag already occupied by Engle, who had moved up from second base. Without hesitating Chase turned back toward home and eluded Simon's tag with "the finest fadeaway slide that was ever produced."[73]

Despite that brief moment of excitement the Buffalo players were upset by their lackluster performance in the opener. "Just when we had our minds and hearts set on doing things up in proper style our feet slipped," said Chase. "But I'll wager it's the last poor exhibition the boys will put up this season."[74]

Such a wager would have been ill-advised. By May 3 the Blues were in last place with a 6–13 record. Despite his team's poor performance, however, Chase seemed to have picked up where he had left off at the end of the 1914 season. On April 22, when Buffalo beat the Baltimore Terrapins 3–0, Chase had three hits, including a home run, and also turned in a sparkling defensive play.

In the sixth inning Baltimore's Harry Swacina connected with a pitch from Hugh Bedient. "It was tearing and bounding down the first base line for the right field fence when Chase checked the ball's flight with a leap into space," reported Mason. "He nailed the ball with his bare left [hand]" and threw to Bedient, covering first, in time to retire Swacina. "It was a play that brought out the deserving cheers."[75]

After that April 22 game Chase's batting average stood at .342. But then he, like most of his teammates, began to slump. From April 23 to June 4 he batted only .182, bringing his overall average down to .217. The low point came on

April 25, in an incident that indicated that he was not universally popular in Buffalo. After a Buffed loss in Newark, Chase was walking along South Second Street in nearby Harrison. A fan named Billy Quinn began jeering him, and a brawl ensued. "Paddy McGuigan, a former pugilist and now a saloonkeeper here, landed a couple of stinging blows on Chase before the police broke up the fight. Chase aided Policeman Callaghan to capture Quinn, but the force of the two was insufficient to hold him against the mob."[76]

Schlafly insisted that the Blues would soon begin to play championship-caliber baseball. "One thing I can say, and that is that my team's going to be up there," he told Mason on May 19, when Buffalo's record was 8–21. "None of us is discouraged, and neither are the folks at home. Last place in May doesn't mean last place in October."[77] But the team's poor showing was obviously starting to wear on the manager; he was ejected twice in his team's next four games.

On May 24, the day after Schlafly's second ejection, the Blues lost a 4–3, fourteen-inning contest in Chicago. The big news, however, was the presence of Harry Lord in uniform on the Buffalo bench. Chase's former Chicago teammate, who had quit the White Sox so abruptly a year before, admitted that he had missed the game, but realized that his actions had precluded a return to organized baseball. He had no alternative but to join the Feds, he said: "I accepted terms from the Buffalo club because there were no other offers to accept."[78] By May 27 Lord had moved into the starting lineup to stay.

A few days later, after the Blues had been shut out in Pittsburgh, Schlafly again predicted that his team would rally. "The men are working like dogs to win, every man on the club has his heart and soul in the game to win and there isn't a man who isn't doing his level best," he insisted. "There will be a different story to tell in another month."[79]

Schlafly's prediction came true, but not in the way he had anticipated. The signing of Lord was only the first of several changes on the team. On June 1 the Blues traded Joe Agler, the man *The Sporting News* had said was a better first baseman than Chase, to Baltimore for outfielder Benny Meyer. Meyer, nicknamed "Earache" for his piercing voice, was better known for his antics on the coaching lines than his abilities on the field. The *Express* also reported a rumor that Hugh Duffy, a former star outfielder who had previously managed the Philadelphia Phillies and the White Sox, would replace Schlafly as manager.[80]

The rumor was half true. On June 3, after Brooklyn had swept a doubleheader from Buffalo, club president William E. Robertson announced that he was firing Schlafly. "We believe right now that we have the best team in the Federal League, and why it is not in a higher position we cannot understand," said Robertson. Catcher Walter Blair took over the team, but a day later, after the Blues had split another doubleheader with Brooklyn, Lord was appointed manager for the rest of the season.[81]

Though Buffalo won only five of its first ten games after the switch, the *Express* reported optimistically that "Under the leadership of Harry Lord every man on the team is playing his level best and there is more team spirit and real enthusiasm among the players than has been shown at any time this season."[82] The team did improve substantially under Lord; from June 5, when he took over, until the end of the season the Buffeds won fifty-nine games and lost only forty-eight. Had they posted that same .551 winning percentage for the full season they would have finished in fourth place.

Of course there were still rough spots, such as a June 18 game against the Chifeds. "The Buffeds started out gloriously," reported the *Express* after that game, "and were urged to do their prettiest by the members of Mrs. Hal Chase's box party."[83] But Chicago beat the Blues 8–0 as thirty-eight-year-old Three-Finger Brown allowed Buffalo only one hit.

The Buffalo fans had more reason to cheer three days later. Even though Kansas City beat the Blues 9–5, the long-awaited Roxey Roach finally joined the team. And Chase had three hits, including a triple, in five at bats.

That game marked the beginning of a remarkable streak for Chase and the Blues, although he missed four games in early July with an attack of lumbago.[84] Between June 21 and July 12 Chase batted .404 and flashed unaccustomed power. His twenty-three hits in fifty-two at bats included three doubles, four triples, and three home runs. On June 29, as Buffalo beat St. Louis 5–4, Chase hit two home runs and drove in four runs. His second home run, reported Mason, "was the longest clout ever registered on the Buffed park." The ball carried completely over the left field bleachers, "clearing the outer wall by at least seven or eight feet." He also turned in three defensive gems, including a one-handed stop of a hard-hit ball by another familiar face, Babe Borton, the failed "onion" of the 1913 trade who had resurfaced with the Federals.[85]

Borton was enjoying a successful season with the Sloufeds, batting .286 and leading the Federal League in runs. But his major league career was virtually over; he batted only .224 for the St. Louis Browns in 1916 before returning to the minor leagues for good. Four years later his name and Chase's would be linked again, as they had in 1913, but this time there would be no joking references to the "onion."

In 1915, however, Chase's rejuvenation gave the local press cause to celebrate. "Hal Chase is in again," wrote Mason. "Beware, Federal league pitchers. The famous Prince Hal has at last struck his stride — both in hitting and fielding and is now on the warpath — which should help the Buffalo Feds considerably in climbing out of the cellar."[86]

Indeed the Blues, perhaps inspired by the performance of their star first baseman, did begin to rise in the standings. They won eleven out of eighteen games and by July 10 had moved past Brooklyn and Baltimore into sixth place. On July 12 they lost 9–4 to Brooklyn, despite Chase's second bases-loaded triple in as many days, and dropped back into seventh.

Russ Ford was hit hard in that game, and a day later Robertson announced that the Blues were releasing their one-time star. Ford had won twenty-one games in 1914, but had struggled in 1915. "Ford has won but two games for us this season," said Robertson, "and we could not afford to carry him any longer at the salary he was getting." A week and a half later Buffalo re-signed Ford, reportedly for about half of his previous salary of $1,000 a month, but he would be released again before the end of the season, having totaled only five victories.[87]

Inevitably the Blues cooled off somewhat, although they continued to play much better ball than they had early in the season. But Chase was batting more ferociously than at any other point in his career. When Buffalo embarked on a road trip on July 16 he continued his one-man assault on Federal League pitching. In twenty games he batted .333, with twenty-five hits in seventy-five at bats. He also hit six doubles, two triples, and, in one two-game stretch in Kansas City, three home runs. This road trip also gave him more opportunities to show off his versatility. He pitched four innings in an exhibition game on July 26 in Ottumwa, Iowa, against a team from nearby Bloomfield — the Blues won 11–3 — and in a 10–1 loss to St. Louis on August 3 played right field, a less strenuous position than first base, due to the lingering effects of his lumbago.[88]

The Blues won eleven of nineteen games on the road trip and when they returned to Buffalo the club's management decided to hold "Harry Lord Day" on August 7. The Blues spoiled the celebration by dropping a doubleheader to Pittsburgh by the combined score of 20–5, but came back to beat the Rebels 6–3 on Monday. Chase hit a three-run home run in the eighth inning to win that game, which seemed only fair, since Pittsburgh left fielder Al Wickland had reached above the fence to rob him of another homer in the fourth inning.[89]

On the following day Chase went hitless in four at bats as St. Louis beat Buffalo 1–0, but Mason's account of his final plate appearance against Otis Crandall was a masterful example of the melodramatic journalism of the day, with all the elements of Ernest Thayer's "Casey at the Bat." The Blues had managed to get Benny Meyer to third base and Jack Dalton to first with two outs. "It was a confident stride that carried Chase to the pegging platform [home plate]. There was determination gleaming from his hazel eyes [actually Chase's eyes were blue]. There was a day's growth on his face. There was a hunk of gum receiving double action. There was a tight grip on the stick and a long swing of the arms denoted that something was about to be pulled off."

Unfortunately, with the situation ripe for heroic drama, the outcome was anticlimactic: "Doc Crandall took one look and backed away." After some discussion the Terriers decided to walk Chase intentionally, loading the bases for Billy Louden. "Four wide pitches sent Chase smiling to first," reported Mason, but Crandall retired Louden and St. Louis won the game.[90]

After another loss to the Terriers on the following day the Blues were in seventh place with a 47–61 record. Even so, team secretary Jack Kelly continued to talk of first place. "The manager who wins the Federal League pennant — if it isn't Harry Lord — can thank his lucky stars that Harry Lord did not take charge of the club one month before he did for the Buffeds would now be out in front and showing their heels to the present leaders," said Kelly. "Manager Lord has so imbued his men with the desire to win that many of the players have not given up the thought of landing in first place despite the present position of the club."[91]

A week later, after splitting a doubleheader with the Kawfeds, the Blues were back in sixth place. In the first game, a 3–2 Buffalo victory, Chase had three hits, including a double, and Mason claimed that a bad call by umpire William Brennan robbed Chase of a fourth. He also scored from second base on an infield out by Engle in the second inning and made a one-handed stop and dove into first base to retire Gene Packard in the seventh. His performance prompted the *Express* to headline its account of the game "Hal Chase Was In Everything."[92]

Two days later Buffalo beat Chicago 7–3 but received a scare when Chase hurt his foot sliding into second base in the first inning. He had to leave the game, but returned on the following day to register four hits, including a triple and another home run, as the Blues swept a doubleheader from the Chifeds. Despite the sweep the day was a disappointment for the Blues' management, for a morning rainstorm held the crowd down to only about seventy-five hundred on "Greater Buffalo Day."[93]

Chase's heroics in Buffalo were attracting attention elsewhere, at least along the shores of Lake Erie. On August 25 the *Express* published a poem, "To Hal Chase," by one John F. Herne of Cleveland. The poem makes up in enthusiasm what it lacks in artistry:

> A lot of good men play that bag
>   Just to the right of home,
> And though they aren't wont to brag
>   Nor none has a swelled dome,
> They cover the initial sack
>   But not like Mr. Chase
> The Buffed's top-notch crackerjack
>   Who stars around first base.
>
> The Californian has now
>   Begun to hit the pill,
> And he'll keep his team in the row
>   Which might yet win the mill.
> Hence every fan in this live town
>   Should pull for all he's worth
> For Chase, King Hal of great renown
>   And a much higher berth.[94]

Despite such enthusiasm, however, the Blues were in trouble. In early August Gilmore had decreed that all Federal League ticket prices should be reduced drastically, in an attempt to undercut the National and American Leagues. Despite the cheaper seats, rumors abounded that Buffalo, which had never attracted the sizeable crowds that league officials had anticipated, was in financial straits and might be in danger of losing its franchise.[95]

On August 27 Gilmore visited Buffalo and reiterated that the city's franchise would continue in the Federal League. On the next day the Blues beat visiting Brooklyn 7–2 in a game shortened to five innings by rain. The contest brought back yet another familiar face from Chase's past, as the Brookfeds had replaced Lee Magee as manager with John Ganzel, the man whose job Chase had taken with the Yankees in 1905.

On August 30, after Buffalo beat Brooklyn again, 2–1, the Blues announced that Lord had been rehired to manage the team in 1916. In the Buffalo victory Chase had three hits in three at bats, including a double, and "put up a stellar exhibition in the field," but his lack of hustle nearly cost the Blues a run in the second inning. Chase, on first base, was sure that Louden's long drive would clear the wall for a home run and strolled casually around the bases. But the ball failed to clear the wall and Chase, who would have scored easily on the play had he been running, was forced to stop at third base. He scored anyway when Engle followed with a sacrifice fly, but it was an embarrassing lapse.[96]

In late August and early September the Blues won eleven out of thirteen games, helping them even their season record at 69–69 on September 12 — the first time they had reached the .500 mark since April 22. Chase was red-hot again, batting .480 (twenty-four for fifty) with three doubles, five stolen bases, and four more home runs in those thirteen games. On Labor Day, September 6, Buffalo swept a doubleheader from Baltimore, winning the first game on Chase's home run in the bottom of the ninth. On September 8, when the Blues swept another doubleheader from the Terrapins, his two-run homer in the fourth inning of the second game tied the score at 4–4. On September 11, to complete the streak of four home runs in seven games, his enormous first-inning drive sailed completely out of Gordon and Koppel Field and into nearby Brush Creek as Buffalo beat the Kawfeds 2–0 in Kansas City.[97]

Chase managed the Blues in a 6–2 loss on the next day. Due to an anomaly in the Federal League schedule the Blues had five open days before their next scheduled league game in Chicago. Lord skipped the last game in Kansas City to go in search of opponents to fill the open dates with exhibition games. Buffalo beat the local team at Creston, Iowa, on September 14 and 15. In the latter game, a 10–3 laugher, Chase had three hits, including a home run, and pitched three innings, giving up only two hits, one walk, and a hit batsman while recording one strikeout. The Blues' game at Charlton, Iowa, on September 16 was rained out, but on the next day, in Bloomfield, Iowa, the local team beat the Blues 5–4. Chase had four hits in four at bats and stole a base, but had a rocky time on the mound. After replacing pitcher Cy Marshall in the sixth inning Chase struck out five men in four innings but gave up three runs on seven hits and two walks.[98]

By the time the Buffeds resumed their league schedule on September 18 they had cooled off. They won only two of their next twelve games in Chicago, Pittsburgh, and St. Louis, while Chase's booming bat turned cold again. He managed only five hits in the first eight games, a .156 average, before bouncing back with five hits in seven at bats in the next two contests. He missed the last two games in St. Louis but was back in the lineup as the Blues won their last two games of the season in Brooklyn.

The Blues finished the 1915 season in sixth place with a record of 74–78, twelve games behind the first-place Chifeds. Chase himself had enjoyed a superb season. His overall batting average of .284 was not up to his previous season's standard, but his seventeen home runs led the league. He also finished second in the league in total bases and third in runs batted in, doubles, and slugging percentage.

Those seventeen home runs may say as much about the quality of Federal League pitching as they do about Chase's abilities. In ten previous major league seasons Chase had never hit more than four home runs in a single season, and in 1915 Braggo Roth led the American League with seven. Also in 1915, however, a young Red Sox pitcher named George Herman Ruth began showing signs of extraordinary offensive firepower, hitting four home runs in only ninety-two at bats. Four years later Ruth, by then a full-time outfielder on days he did not pitch, would set baseball on its ear by hitting the unprecedented total of twenty-nine home runs. The year after that, in his first season with the Yankees, he exploded for fifty-four home runs. "Inside baseball," the game at which Hal Chase had excelled for so long, with its premium on craft and guile, was about to become obsolete.

Seven

I Want to Square Myself with the Public

The death on October 18 of Robert B. Ward, president of the Brookfeds and one of Gilmore's major financial backers, was seen by many as a sign that the demise of the Federal League was imminent. Rumors of secret peace negotiations again began to circulate, although publicly both sides continued to espouse the hard line. *The Sporting News* reported that four National League owners and all eight American League owners were implacably opposed to compromise with the Feds.[1] Gilmore insisted in turn that the Federal League would continue as an independent organization in 1916,[2] although the severe financial difficulties of at least two franchises had become common knowledge.

Both Buffalo and Kansas City had lost money during the 1915 season — one account put the totals at $50,000 and $35,332 respectively — and both had received advances from the league to meet their final payrolls of the 1915 season. The loans, of $40,000 in Buffalo's case, were due at the Federal League meeting in Indianapolis in early November. Failure to repay them would result in forfeiture of the franchises.[3]

The approaching deadline caused a flurry of activity in Buffalo. A group of local businessmen formed the Buffalo Federal League Booster Club at a Chamber of Commerce luncheon and pledged to raise $100,000 to bail out the team.[4]

On October 27 came rumors that the Federal League and organized baseball had reached an agreement by which the Federal League would be disbanded. Charles Weeghman, owner of the Chifeds, would buy the National League Cubs; Phil Ball and Otto Stifel, owners of the St. Louis Feds, would buy the National League Cardinals; and Harry Sinclair, the flamboyant Oklahoma oilman who had taken over the Indianapolis Feds and moved them to Newark before the 1915 season, would buy the Giants. Fans in the remaining Federal League cities would have to be content with minor league ball. The Buffalo Feds would merge with the International League Bisons and the Kawfeds with the Kansas City Blues of the American Association, while Baltimore would be granted an International League franchise.

Federal League and Buffalo officials disclaimed any knowledge of such a plan, and for a month and a half the rumors remained just that. Robertson insisted that the Blues were preparing for the coming season, although the team's financial situation showed no sign of improvement. He vowed, however, that if the Federal League stuck with its ten-cent admissions policy he would quit the league, claiming that the Blues could not turn a profit at the lower prices even if they drew record crowds. The point became moot on November 9 when Buffalo and Kansas City missed the deadline for repayment of their loans.[5]

Despite the forfeiture and a report that the franchise would move to Detroit, Robertson and Gilmore implied that Buffalo could still be a member of the league in 1916 if the citizens pledged sufficient support. Gilmore also announced that the Kansas City franchise would be shifted to New York. Organized baseball had survived a Federal League team in Brooklyn, but the prospect of a rival to the Giants and Yankees in Manhattan was frightening, especially since the move would supposedly be accomplished with the backing of Sinclair.[6]

Meanwhile Chase was preparing for another winter of barnstorming. On October 3, the Blues played the Linde Airs, a local semipro club, at Linde Air park on Genesee Street. Chase would play first base for the Federal Leaguers, reported the *Express*, "and that fact alone should attract thousands of fans...."[7] Once again Chase used the relatively relaxed atmosphere of an exhibition game to show off his versatility. This time he played first base, pitched the seventh and eight innings, and then switched to second base for the ninth inning as the Blues won 7–4. Although he was hitless in four at bats he pitched effectively, giving up only one hit and one walk in his two innings on the mound.[8]

On the following Sunday a reconstituted group of "Hal Chase's All-Stars," tuning up for a winter tour, played Harry (Ha Ha) Leavell's Cuban Giants, a travelling black team, at Doll's Park on Sycamore Street. The Cuban Giants beat the All-Stars 6–2. Chase, as usual, played first base and pitched, giving up only one hit in four innings.[9]

Two weeks later the All-Stars went to Rochester to play the Nationals, a local semipro team made up mostly of players of Polish extraction. Chase's men beat the Nationals 12–4 as Chase had three hits, including a pair of doubles. Once again he divided his duties between first base and the pitcher's mound, relieving starter Howard Ehmke in the sixth inning. In four innings Chase yielded two runs on four hits and three walks, but some of the Rochester players obviously found his deliveries puzzling. He struck out three and provoked the Nationals' second baseman into an unusual display of frustration: "Dernoga was so exasperated at being fooled by his slow ball," reported the *Express*, "that he threw his club at Chase."[10]

In mid–December the *Express* reported that peace negotiations between the Federals and organized baseball were on again. Gilmore and Sinclair had come to New York for the National League's annual winter meeting and hammered out a secret settlement. Barney Dreyfuss, owner of the Pittsburgh Pirates, went to Chicago, where Ban Johnson was presiding over the American League meeting, to present the proposals. On December 15 the American League owners agreed to the terms negotiated by the National League. "The end of the baseball war is in sight," announced Johnson.[11]

The general nature of the settlement, which was signed a week later in Cincinnati, soon became public knowledge, and largely confirmed the rumors that had circulated in October. Robertson conceded that the International League Bisons would be the only professional team in Buffalo in 1916. Although the Federal League was in dire financial condition, Gilmore succeeded in winning some remarkable concessions from the magnates of organized baseball, who were tired of the expensive war and feared the deep pockets of men like Sinclair. Weeghman was allowed to merge his Chifeds with the Cubs while Ball would do the same with the Sloufeds and the American League Browns. Sinclair was given the right to dispose of the contracts of all other Federal League players, thereby becoming, in the words of Harold Seymour, "the greatest trader in human merchandise since slavery was abolished."[12] If he could not sell them, Sinclair announced, he would put the players to work in his oil fields and allow them to play ball on Sundays. The Ward family of Brooklyn, which had served as the Federal League's de facto banker for most of the last two years, would be reimbursed $400,000, to be paid over twenty years. And all players who had jumped to the Feds, including Hal Chase, would be restored to good standing in organized baseball.[13]

The baseball establishment sought to portray the settlement as an unconditional surrender by the Feds, but in truth the American and National League owners were only too happy to see the hostilities cease. The Federal League had helped inflate salaries throughout baseball; indeed, many believed that the huge contracts offered by the Feds had finally driven the league to financial ruin. A story in the *Express* cited some examples of players whose salaries had risen astronomically when they left organized baseball for the outlaw league. Joe Tinker's salary had risen from $5,500 in organized baseball to $12,000 in the Federal League. Tom Seaton's pay had jumped from $2,600 to $8,200 and Benny Kauff's from $2,000 to $7,500. Hal Chase, whose salary with the White Sox was $6,000, made $9,000 in the Federal League.[14]

And of course even players who did not jump had benefited, as their teams offered them substantial increases to ensure their continued loyalty. The Tigers had raised Ty Cobb's salary from $12,000 to $20,000; George Stallings's Boston Braves boosted Rabbit Maranville's salary from $1,800 to $6,000; and many others got fat raises as well.[15] Thus the immediate effect of the peace settlement was predictable. With no competition for players from the Federal League, organized baseball began rolling back salaries.

The world champion Boston Red Sox struck the first blow, cutting the salary of their great center fielder, Tris Speaker, by fifty percent.[16] When Speaker objected the Red Sox calmly dealt him to seventh-place Cleveland. Other teams followed Boston's lead. Weeghman, the ex–Fed, showed that he could easily adapt to organized baseball by slashing the contracts of half a dozen of his newly acquired Cubs.[17] At least one baseball historian has suggested that the effect on salaries of the restoration of organized baseball's monopoly, coupled with the steep inflation of the war years, resulted in disgruntled players who were ripe for the kind of corruption later manifested in the Black Sox scandal.[18]

The return to the status quo antebellum was incomplete, however, as long as the Federal League lawsuit was still pending before Judge Landis. Dismissal of the suit was one of the conditions of the peace settlement, but the owners of the Baltimore Federal League team refused to go along. They were outraged that the settlement called for an International League team in Baltimore and insisted that the city deserved a major league club instead.

Jack Ryder of the Cincinnati *Enquirer* noted the irony of their stance: "The suit was brought on the ground that baseball as organized was a brutal and tyrannical trust and should be dissolved. Now the Baltimore Feds want to continue the suit solely because they have not be [sic] able to break into the iniquitous trust."[19]

The rebels had hoped and expected that Landis, the noted trustbuster, would crack down on organized baseball, but in this expectation they were mistaken. Landis was a baseball fan and had repeatedly made clear his dismay at seeing the game dragged through the muck of legal proceedings. At one point he said, "Both sides must understand that any blows at the thing called baseball would be regarded by this court as a blow to a national institution."[20] He refused to issue a ruling for over a year, supposedly because he wanted the two sides to settle out of court but conceivably because he knew that the Feds would not be able to hang on much longer and would eventually decide to drop the suit.

Finally, on February 7, 1916, Landis dismissed the suit without objection.[21] By the simple expedient of refusing to issue a ruling in the case for over a year he had shown himself to be a friend of organized baseball, and organized baseball would not forget him.

At last it seemed that baseball could get back to business as usual, although a few Federal League ghosts still remained. Shortly after Landis dismissed the Federal League suit, the Baltimore owners announced that they would file their own suit against organized baseball, asking for $500,000 in damages. The Baltimore suit eventually dragged on until 1922, culminating in a famous Supreme Court ruling upholding baseball's exemption from antitrust legislation.[22] And during the February meeting of the National League at the Waldorf Hotel in New York, several ex–Feds who had not yet found new jobs in organized baseball, including Tom Seaton, George Stovall, John Ganzel, and Bill McKechnie, haunted the lobby "wearing exceedingly hungry and anxious looks." Garry Herrmann had "declared himself as opposed to taking back contract jumpers," but unbent enough to sign several ex–Feds, including Chase's Buffalo teammates Billy Louden and Al Schulz.[23]

On February 2 Ban Johnson announced that Chase and Stovall, who had deserted the Cleveland Naps to become player-manager of the Kawfeds in 1914, would be banned forever from the American League. "There's no blacklist," said

Johnson, with typically mystifying logic, "but Stovall and Chase are not the kind of men the American League wants."[24]

At least one fan disagreed. "When the Federal League disbanded after the 1915 season," wrote James T. Farrell, "I remember how I hoped that Chase would be back in Chicago." The White Sox, however, had given first base to young Jack Fournier, who was not in Chase's class as a fielder but had batted over .300 two years in a row. When Fournier slumped to .240 and Chicago finished two games behind the first-place Red Sox, Farrell was inclined to think that Chase could have made the difference: "If the White Sox had had Chase in 1916, and he had played honestly, they might have won the pennant."[25] The second of those two conditionals was, of course, a substantial one.

Most major league teams seemed to share Johnson's dim view of Chase. After praising Chase's abilities as a player, Detroit Tigers manager Hughie Jennings added disapprovingly that, "for all his ability, I would not have him on my club.... He does not heed training rules and has a demoralizing influence on the younger players."[26] Sinclair admitted that no major league team had made an offer for Chase's services, in part because of his reputation as "a disorganizer."[27] At the age of thirty-two and coming off his two most successful seasons in professional baseball, Chase had apparently reached the end of the road in the major leagues. At home in California, he turned his attention to the Pacific Coast League, where he had officially begun his professional career twelve years before.

The PCL was still probably the best and most prestigious minor league in the country. In the spring of 1916 it included on its rosters a number of men whose paths either had crossed Chase's in the past or would do so again in the future. Frank Chance, the Peerless Leader, had just taken over the Los Angeles Angels, whose players included Chase's former Highlander teammate and fellow Santa Clara product Harry Wolter and a young outfielder named Harley Maggert. Pitcher Frank Arellanes, another Santa Claran, was with Vernon, as was a young infielder named Swede Risberg. And Harry Wolverton, Chase's successor as manager of the Yankees, was now leading the defending champion San Francisco Seals. Among his players were former White Sox outfielder Ping Bodie and pitchers Pol Perritt and Spider Baum, as well as Chase's first coach at Santa Clara, pitcher Joe Corbett, who was attempting yet another comeback, and, curiously, a young righthanded pitcher from Redwood City, also named Hal Chase but no relation to the first baseman.[28]

The Seals held spring training at San Jose's Luna Park in 1916, and in early March the San Francisco newspapers began implying that Chase might play for the home team. Seals owner Henry Berry hinted that his manager was planning to sign some "high-class players" for 1916. While he mentioned no names, Berry almost certainly had Chase in mind: "Wolverton has the men spotted, and I think they will be just a little bit classier than any our rivals have yet signed. We had a good team last season, but wait and take a look at the club Wolverton will place in the field on opening day."

Before signing Chase, however, Berry would have to figure out a way around the Pacific Coast League's salary cap, which strictly limited each team's total payroll. Berry argued that the cap hurt the PCL's chances of signing some of the ex–Federal Leaguers: "The majors have a number of players they cannot use hooked up to fancy contracts. By standing good for half the salary of these men they can turn them over to clubs in the American Association or International League. However, under our salary limit regulation, we are prevented from accepting players under these conditions. This rule was adopted before peace was arranged. It is not adequate to meet present conditions and should be revoked."[29] Berry realized that, as one reporter put it, "it is quite likely that Sinclair would willingly pay a large portion of [Chase's] salary in order to have what is to him a 'white elephant' taken off his hands."[30] But the salary cap remained.

Wolverton, continuing to hold out hope that somehow he could arrange "the biggest baseball transaction of recent minor league history," held several meetings with Chase at the Fourteen Mile House in San Jose,[31] but to no avail: "I doubt if there is any minor league club in the country that could afford to carry Chase at the salary that would have to be paid," said Wolverton on March 10. "He is a great baseball player, but it looks extremely doubtful just now about our getting him."[32]

Years later, Chase claimed that the Seals had offered him a $4,000 bonus and 10 percent of the stock in the club, and that he had been forced to turn them down because his contract had already been sold to Cincinnati.[33] In fact, his negotiations with San Francisco fell through long before Cincinnati acquired him, although he continued to work out with the Seals in March.

Chase's difficulties were the exception rather than the rule in the spring of 1916. Even those anxious players who had haunted the Waldorf found jobs in organized baseball: Tom Seaton with the Cubs, George Stovall with Toledo of the American Association, John Ganzel with Kansas City of the American Association, and Bill McKechnie with the Giants.[34] Buck Herzog, the shortstop and manager of the Reds, expressed the relief and optimism of many in organized baseball in the spring of 1916. "The failure of the Federal League is going to be a great help to us," he said shortly before leaving for the Reds' spring camp in Shreveport, Louisiana. "The players will all have their minds on their work and will not be bothered with offers from outlaws, which kept many of them up in the air during the past two seasons."[35]

Herzog, who had taken over as manager when Joe Tinker jumped to the Feds after the 1913 season, was a competent if erratic infielder who had played for John McGraw's Giants in three World Series. He had been less than an overwhelming success as a manager; in two years his teams had compiled a 131–177 record and finished last and seventh.

Now, however, with the addition of Louden and Schulz and a handful of others, the Reds felt they were ready to move up to the first division. One potential concern was the physical condition of Fred (Zip) Mollwitz, a moderately talented first baseman who had broken his arm during the 1915 season. The condition of Mollwitz's arm was the subject of numerous, often conflicting reports that spring. The early reports from Shreveport were encouraging,[36] but on March 8 Herzog found himself having to deny a report that the Reds had signed Hal Chase. "I am standing pat on my present lineup," insisted Herzog. "Moll's arm is good and he is in a class by himself at handling thrown balls."[37] A day later a story bearing a New York dateline reported that not only the Reds but the Giants as well were seeking to secure Chase's services. "Manager Herzog says he does not want Chase," admitted the story, "but the latter states that Herzog is mistaken, as the Reds have been dickering for his services."[38]

Although the rumors about Chase persisted while the Reds were losing four of their six exhibition games against the minor league Shreveport Gassers, Jack Ryder wrote in the *Enquirer* that Mollwitz was playing so well that he threatened "to be the class of the National League first basemen this year, not barring [Jake] Daubert [of Brooklyn] or any one else."[39]

Cincinnati continued to lose: to Shreveport, to the New Orleans Pelicans of the Southern League, to the Cleveland Indians, to the Yankees. After an 8–4 loss to the Yankees in Memphis on March 31, Ryder reported that Mollwitz was "a bit worried about his arm" and was considering consulting a specialist, probably the legendary John D. "Bonesetter" Reese, in Youngstown, Ohio.[40]

Once again the rumors about Chase intensified. Ryder noted that Pat Powers, Sinclair's partner in disposing of the Federal Leaguers, was concerned because Chase was still unsigned. "The Feds are obliged to pay Chase the neat sum of $8,000 this year, whether he plays ball or not, and naturally they are anxious to unload him on some club." Ryder acknowledged that Chase was "probably the fastest and most spectacular first baseman of the day," but recounted some of the less flattering episodes of Chase's career — his jumping the Yankees in 1908, his suspected role in the firing of Stallings, his abrupt departure from the White Sox — to explain why "no manager seems willing to dally with him." Once again Ryder said that Herzog and Herrmann were unwilling "to assume his contract and his disposition.

"The only possible reason for signing Chase," concluded Ryder, "would be the complete failure of Mollwitz's arm, which has been broken twice in the past two years and is none too strong. But Moll's wing has been doing efficient service so far and it looks as if he will be able to get through the season all right.... Unless Moll falls down completely, no further attention will be paid to the effort to land a berth for Chase with the Reds."[41]

Two days later, a presumably chagrined Ryder reported that the Reds had purchased Chase's contract from Sinclair and Powers. "Owners of the Cincinnati team are greatly worried over the condition of the throwing arm of Mollwitz, their star first sacker," explained Ryder lamely. "The member, injured some time ago, is not in first-class condition and the magnates immediately got busy in an effort to land Chase."

Mollwitz's days as a Red were numbered. Although Herzog insisted that both men would be given an equal opportunity to win the first base job, he

Chase with the Reds in 1916. After the Federal League collapsed, Chase was left without a major league job until the Reds signed him just before the 1916 season. He went on to enjoy his best season, winning the National League batting title. *Thomas Carwile Collection.*

"considers Mollwitz weak in throwing, hitting and on ground balls." Louden added helpfully that Chase was the best first baseman he had ever seen.[42]

Chase, who was still in California practicing with the Seals, initially sounded grateful at being granted another chance in Cincinnati. "I intend to do the right thing in the future," he told Joe Vila. "I want to square myself with the public."[43] But his subsequent actions were not calculated to endear him to his new ballclub or its fans. Once again, as in 1905, Chase seemed to have found an ideal situation in which to show off his skills; and once again, as in 1905, he threatened not to report, perhaps trying to extract a more lucrative offer from the team. "I have not made up my mind just what I am going to do," he said. "I suppose they can either force me to join the Reds or put me on the ineligible list, but it is possible that I would prefer to remain in California, even if there is no chance to play ball. At all events, I am in no hurry to decide, and will take all the time I want before reaching a conclusion."[44]

The Reds, gradually working their way north for the start of the regular season, professed not to be overly concerned. Herrmann, wrote Ryder, "thinks Chase is exhibiting some of his well-known temperament and independence, and that he will be right along as soon as he has expressed himself for a day or two in the manner of a big league star.... Chase likes to play ball, and it is likely that he will be along within a week or two. Meanwhile, Zip Mollwitz will continue to show the good form that he has displayed this spring, and it is possible that he might make such a good showing that he would hold the job, even against such a star as Chase."

The acquisition of Chase met with a mixed reaction in Cincinnati. Ryder reported "no great enthusiasm" for the move in the city, and chided the team's management for its reversal on Chase: "Red officials had repeatedly denied that Chase would be secured, and the sudden change of policy is not thoroughly understood." Herzog now sounded all in favor of the move: "Manager Herzog ... is confident that he can handle Chase, and that Hal will be of great assistance to the team in its fight for the first division.... Manager Herzog, while admitting the great ability of Mollwitz in handling thrown balls, believes that Chase will strengthen the team both on the offense and the defense and will make the Reds certain of the first division."

Such optimism was reinforced by Billy Louden, whose diplomatic comments provide a good indication of how his peers rated Chase. "Hal is a wonderful player in all departments," said Louden. "I played second base all last year, while he was playing first, and I have never seen a first baseman who could pull off the stunts that Chase repeatedly gets away with. He is a marvel at handling bunts and at breaking up the hit-and-run play. At times he seems to bob up right off the ground to grab a bunt that looked as if it was going to be perfectly safe. He is the most brilliant thrower I have ever seen. The other infielders will have to be strictly on their jobs or he will catch them napping with a snap throw to get a runner. He is also a very good hitter and is a sure man on the hit-and-run play, as he seldom fails to meet the ball squarely. He is fast and a live wire on the field. I have heard a lot of talk about Hal's disposition, but as far as I could see he is all right. He is a man of good habits and always playing to win. Mollwitz is a great reacher and a splendid mark to throw to. When he hooks up with Chase in a fight for the position it simply means that the Reds will have the best first baseman in the league, whichever man wins out."[45]

Chase was still in transit from California when the Reds opened the season on April 12 with a loss to the visiting Cubs. Mollwitz had apparently decided to make the most of Chase's absence. He had one hit in that game, then three more, including a triple, on the following day as Cincinnati beat Chicago 8–3. Ryder was impressed: "Zip Mollwitz had more than his share of the good old nervine," he wrote, "and it is going to be no easy matter for Hal Chase to drive him off first base."[46]

Chase finally reached Cincinnati on Saturday morning, April 15, in time to practice with his new teammates before their 2–0 victory over the Cubs. "He looks good and appears to be in fine shape," reported Ryder, but Mollwitz and the team were playing well and Herzog was reluctant to tamper with a successful combination: "No change will be made in the Red line-up so long as the Reds continue to remain on the winning side."[47]

Unfortunately for Mollwitz, however, he ran afoul of umpire Hank O'Day on the very next day and was ejected from the game. The ejection ultimately cost him his position as a starter; Ryder wrote gleefully that Mollwitz had been "Chased out of the regular lineup."

The ejection came while Mollwitz was batting in the bottom of the third inning against Carmen Hill of the Pittsburgh Pirates. When O'Day called a second strike on the Cincinnati first baseman, Mollwitz complained too vociferously and O'Day threw him out. Herzog sent Chase in to complete Mollwitz's at bat; the result was perhaps the most dramatic moment of Chase's entire career.

Chase strode to the plate, assuming Mollwitz's 0–2 count against Hill, and drove the first pitch he saw to left field for a stinging double. He stole third base while Hill was walking Tom Clarke, then crossed the plate on the front end of a double steal. The eighteen thousand fans on hand at Redland Field went wild; Chase, reported Ryder, "made a home for himself before he had been in the contest five minutes." Several decades later Lee Allen went even further: "If any player in the history of baseball ever made a more spectacular debut, it is not recorded. Chase had demonstrated immediately why he was regarded as a super player, and the galleries had a new hero—for a time."[48]

The Reds went on to beat the Pirates 6–1, as Chase got another hit and turned in his usual flashy performance at first base. In the ninth inning he made "a sensational stop of Max Carey's hot grounder ... a chance that very few first basemen would have handled at all." In sum, wrote Ryder, "Chase seemed as fast and as brilliant as when he was the star of the New York Americans.... And the big crowd was intensely pleased with his clever work."[49]

Chase went hitless on the following day, but came back on Tuesday, April 18, with three hits, including the game-winning home run off the center field

Chase in 1916, the year he won the National League batting title with the Reds and earned a temporary measure of redemption. Within two years, the Reds suspended him and accused him of offering bribes to teammates and opposing players. *The Sporting News Archives.*

wall in the tenth inning, and two stolen bases as Cincinnati beat Pittsburgh 4–3. Ryder reported after that game that the Reds would shortly send Mollwitz to the minor leagues, if they could secure waivers on him.[50] Within the space of seventy-two hours Chase had completely won over a skeptical city.

The Reds were still struggling, but Chase was a sensation in Cincinnati. "He outclasses all first sackers of ancient or modern times," wrote Ryder in late April. "Manager Herzog feels that the acquisition of Chase has insured a high place in the race for the Reds."[51] Chase seemed to be playing with the kind of fire and grit that belied his easygoing reputation. In the third inning of a game in Pittsburgh in late April he tore one of the fingernails off his left hand while stopping a pickoff attempt by Al Schulz and had to give way to Mollwitz, but told Herzog after the game that he would be ready to play on the following day.[52] Mollwitz played first base again the next day, although Chase scored the winning run in an 8–7 victory after pinch-hitting in the ninth inning. On the day after that Chase was back in the starting lineup, contributing a double and driving in two runs in a 3–0 Cincinnati win.

A few days later, in the first inning of a game in St. Louis, Chase again flashed the kind of brilliance that had awed the fans in New York, Chicago, and Buffalo. The Cardinals' Jack Smith, a speedy lefthanded batter, hit a slow grounder down the first base. "It was so slow in getting to [Chase] that he did not have time to get back to the bag," recounted Ryder, "but he made a flying leap through the air and just brushed Smith with the ball as he shot by." Such plays did not come without a price: "Chase fell flat and hurt his leg, but continued in the game, and his hitting was a feature."[53]

Despite such heroics, the Reds fell briefly to seventh place in the middle of May before rebounding slightly to the middle of the National League pack. Chase's hot bat also cooled off, but he was still capable of turning in an unusual performance at any time. On May 25, during an 8–4 victory over the Cubs, Chase played left field due to an injury to Wade Killefer and figured in a play that caused much embarrassment to Chicago's erratic third baseman Heinie Zimmerman.

In the first inning, with Greasy Neale on third base and Chase on second, Tommy Griffith hit a grounder to Cub second baseman Alex McCarthy, who threw home to get Neale. During the ensuing rundown Chase took third base, but Neale eventually scrambled back to third as well. Zimmerman, never renowned for his baseball intelligence,[54] blew it: "Zim touched Neale but forgot all about touching Chase, who had no right to the base, until Neale was put out or was scored." Neale immediately realized the blunder and took off for home plate again, scoring while a puzzled Zimmerman stood holding the ball and wondering what had happened. "It was the richest haw-haw of the year to date," wrote Ryder.

That game also marked the beginning of an experiment, as Herzog decided to try Chase in the outfield and return Mollwitz to the starting lineup at first base. Once again, as Frank Chance had done in 1913, a manager was attempting

Seven—I Want to Square Myself with the Public

to move the greatest first baseman in the game to a new position. Chase "looked quite natural out there," reported Ryder. "He has the speed, the arm and the ball playing instinct and is likely to make good in the garden."[55]

Chase played left or center field for the next month. Initially the move seemed to help; the Reds moved into fourth place after a win in Pittsburgh on May 29, and Chase "showed the bugs how left field should be played" with a running catch deep in the left field corner at Forbes Field. A few days later, Chase "held three or four hits to singles that would have been doubles with a slower man working out there," and in early June, with the Reds in New York, Ryder wrote that "He is covering his position in the outfield as if he had never played anywhere else in his life."[56]

The Reds, however, were still struggling for a position in the first division, and trouble signs were appearing. On May 30 Herzog was accidentally hit in the head by a throw from catcher Ivy Wingo during pregame practice. He was unconscious for nearly half an hour, and although he returned to the starting lineup on the following day the injury had some long-lasting effects. And in early June John McGraw, who knew both men personally, predicted trouble between Herzog and Chase, implying that Chase might covet the manager's job for himself. Ryder dismissed the story: "There is not a chance in the world that anything McGraw could say would stir up trouble between Hal and Herzie."[57]

Despite such distractions Chase had been playing superbly, although he was showing signs of fragility as well. His nineteen-game hitting streak ended in Boston on June 14, a day after his running catch of Ed Konetchy's fly ball ended a sixteen-inning scoreless tie with the Braves. On the next day, in Philadelphia, Chase had two hits in three at bats, but hurt his leg running out a double to left field in the sixth inning. The Reds' next game against the Phillies was rained out, but on June 17 Chase was back in center field and hit a double in Cincinnati's 1–0 victory, although his leg cost the Reds a run in the seventh inning, when he was thrown out trying to take third base on Tommy Griffith's grounder to shortstop Dave Bancroft.[58]

Chase did not play in three of the next five games and appeared as a pinch-hitter in the other two. Once again, however, he seemed determined to prove false his reputation as a malingerer. "The lay-off is giving Hal Chase's injured leg a lot of good," wrote Ryder on June 23. "Hal is one of those athletes who loves the game and hates to lie idle, so he will be in there just as soon as he is able."[59]

Chase returned to the starting lineup on June 24 in a doubleheader against the Cubs. In the first game, playing center field, he had four hits, including a home run and a double, in six at bats, stole a base, and drove in four runs in a 6–5 Cincinnati defeat. His leg was still not right, however, and he had to leave the second game in the seventh inning. Meanwhile Mollwitz was struggling at first base. He made three errors and several other misplays in the doubleheader.

On the following day, as the Reds dropped another doubleheader to the St. Louis Cardinals, Chase made his first serious mistake in the outfield, misplaying

Jack Smith's line drive into a home run in the first game. Ryder blamed the misplay on Chase's leg and the fierce sun, and Chase left the second game early, this time in the sixth inning.[60]

On June 26 Chase had two hits and a stolen base in Cincinnati's 5–4, eleven-inning win over the Cardinals, but left the game following his eighth-inning single when Herzog came on to run for him. Herzog passed out on the Cincinnati bench in the bottom of the eleventh, a victim of the heat and perhaps of the lingering effects of his accidental beaning, and thus missed his team's winning rally. The win lifted the Reds to fifth place and a 28–32 record, but the team promptly went into a prolonged slump, winning only seven of its next twenty-five games and falling all the way to eighth place. The Reds were clearly in trouble, and Herzog was feeling the pressure. On June 28, with the Reds leading 6–5, his error on Tommy Long's easy grounder with two out in the ninth inning opened the door for a four-run St. Louis rally that cost Cincinnati the game.

The team's troubles did not prevent Chase, Louden, Clarence Mitchell, and trainer Doc Hoskins from enjoying the horse races at Latonia, "over the river" in Covington, Kentucky, on the following day. Ryder reported that the four did reasonably well betting on the last two races. But while Chase and his friends were relaxing at the track Herzog's troubles continued. He admitted that his right eye was troubling him, probably as a result of his beaning a month before.[61]

On June 30 the Reds' team physician advised Chase to stay out of the regular lineup for a few days to give his leg a chance to heal completely. "The doctor fears that steady playing on the bum prop might result in serious complications for the athlete," reported Ryder. Chase appeared as a pinch-hitter in that day's game, but Herzog made two more ninth-inning errors, letting Pittsburgh score the winning run. After the game Herzog was "deeply worried and downcast over the failure of the team to make good on the home grounds," according to Ryder. Rumors were beginning to circulate that Herzog would not long continue as manager.[62] He started the next day's game but played only half an inning before deciding "that the extreme heat affected his bruised dome."[63]

On July 2, after splitting a doubleheader with the Pirates, the Reds were in seventh place, just .004 ahead of the last-place Cardinals. When the Reds left for St. Louis that night Chase remained in Cincinnati to rest his leg. A few days later he went back to New York to visit his wife, who was reportedly "quite ill."[64]

The Reds lost all three games in St. Louis and came home again firmly in last place. Herzog, "in the depths of despair," said that if he were relieved of his command he would quit baseball at the end of the season rather than continue only as a player: "It would be a great blow to my pride to continue as a player [only], after being a manager for three years," he told Ryder.[65]

On July 7 the desperate Herzog tried a new lineup against Brooklyn, playing third base himself, moving Heinie Groh to second base, and inserting Bobby Fisher at shortstop. The changes did not help, as the Superbas won 4–3. On the following day Chase was back in the starting lineup for the first time in almost a week. He played first base instead of left field, in order to minimize the strain on his leg, and had two hits. Nevertheless the Reds lost their sixth game in a row.

On the following day, Herzog's thirty-first birthday, they split a doubleheader with the Superbas. Chase had four hits in the doubleheader, including a pair of doubles, and in the second inning of the second game pulled off one of his patented plays to foil a Brooklyn squeeze attempt — "the first flash of that kind of form that the crack first-sacker has shown." His throw to the plate on Hy Myers's bunt just beat George Cutshaw. "He is still quite lame," acknowledged Ryder, "but seems to forget it when he has to put on a little extra speed."[66]

In the first inning of a Cincinnati win on the following day Chase pulled off a startling double play that "was impossible for any other first baseman in the league." With a runner on first base Chase took Casey Stengel's grounder near first base, snapped an underhand throw to Bobby Fisher at second base, and made it back to first in time to double up the speedy Stengel. Chase gave way to Mollwitz in the sixth inning to rest his leg, however, and watched the rest of the game from a seat in the upper grandstand. After the contest he had kind words for teammate Greasy Neale, who had made two sensational catches. "Let me tell you, those were great catches," Chase told Ryder. "I've never seen anything better in my life. Greasy is a winning ball player and I don't know of any center fielder in our circuit who has anything on him."[67]

By now Herzog's days in Cincinnati were clearly numbered. John McGraw had met with Garry Herrmann at an Elks convention in Baltimore to discuss the possibility of reacquiring Herzog, and after an 8–4 loss to the Giants on July 11 Ryder reported that the two met again to finalize the deal.[68] The Braves and Cubs were also reportedly interested in Herzog, but Ryder insisted that McGraw had the inside track.

Naturally all parties denied that any deal was in the works. "There is absolutely no truth in any statement to the effect that Manager Herzog will leave the Reds this season," said Reds treasurer Louis C. Widrig, the same official who had firmly denied that the Reds were interested in Chase the previous winter.[69] But the rumors persisted, and in a few days had even identified the man the Reds were to receive in return for Herzog. It was Chase's old friend Christy Mathewson.[70]

Matty's days as the best pitcher in the National League were behind him now. He had won twenty-four games in 1914, but had suffered through an 8–14 season in 1915 and thus far in 1916 had won only three games while losing four. But the Reds did not want him for his pitching. They knew that he had long been regarded as McGraw's heir apparent as manager in New York; since he had sat at the feet of the master for fifteen years, they reasoned, surely Mathewson had absorbed some of McGraw's tactical brilliance and skill at molding and evaluating players. Moreover, despite his recent difficulties, Matty was probably still the most popular man in baseball. He would be a great drawing card in Cincinnati even if he never pitched again.

Christy Mathewson, first Chase's friend, later his implacable enemy during his glorious career with John McGraw's New York Giants, ca. 1912. Matty, arguably baseball's first true superstar, later became Chase's manager with the Reds. His reputation for integrity gave added weight to his 1918 accusations that Chase had tried to bribe other players. *National Baseball Hall of Fame Library, Cooperstown, N.Y.*

To take Herzog's place in the Reds' infield, the Giants had reportedly been going to send shortstop Art Fletcher to Cincinnati with Mathewson, but Fletcher was injured. Instead, according to the newspapers, the Reds would now receive outfielder Edd Roush, who had briefly been a teammate of Chase's on the White Sox before going to the Federal League, and an infielder, either Bill McKechnie or Hans Lobert, in addition to Mathewson.[71]

The deal was supposedly all but done when the Giants threw a spanner into the works. First they insisted that the Reds give them an outfielder in addition to Herzog, a demand that Herrmann could easily meet. Then McGraw and Giants president Harry Hempstead insisted that New York retain the option to reclaim Mathewson after two years, thus confirming McGraw's intention eventually to yield control of the Giants to his protegé.

The Reds, understandably, were outraged. Why should they give up their manager and shortstop for a man whose services they would enjoy only for two years? Evidently the Giants regarded Cincinnati much as a Broadway producer regarded New Haven or Providence: a city of secondary importance, a place where Matty could have a tryout and gain experience as a manager before returning to a truly important job in New York. Herrmann immediately suggested that he might trade Herzog to the Boston Braves instead, for shortstop Rabbit Maranville, and name Chase the new manager of the Reds.[72]

When the deal with Boston fell through, Herrmann reportedly offered Herzog to Brooklyn for outfielder Zack Wheat and second baseman George Cutshaw, but Superbas owner Charles Ebbets nixed the transaction. Now Herrmann was said to be weighing competing offers from the Cubs and the Giants. If McGraw and Hempstead gave up their demand for the two-year recall, Matty would become Cincinnati's new manager. If Herzog ended up in Chicago, reported Ryder, Chase would be the Reds' new leader.[73]

The July 20 issue of the Cincinnati *Enquirer* boldly headlined "Hal Chase to Manage the Redlegs" above a photograph of Chase. "When the Reds take the field for a double-header with the champion Phillies this afternoon," read the accompanying article, "it is probable that Hal Chase, the star first baseman of the club, will be directing the affairs of the team." McGraw had refused to back down on the two-year recall; as a result Herzog was going to the Cubs in exchange for outfielder Max Flack and $25,000.

Chase's eventual appointment as manager had been predicted ever since he joined the Reds, said the article, "but Hal has not made any play for the position and really does not care about it. He will accept it only to help out the team in the present predicament." Chase's previous managerial stint with the Yankees had done little to inspire confidence in his leadership, but the Reds felt that they were in no position to be choosy. The article tried to put the best face on the situation: "Chase is playing such fine ball every day that he has the respect of the players and it is believed that he will be able to set the team on its feet and pull it out of the last hole.... He is well-liked by the other players and will have their confidence and support."[74]

All this carried the conviction of truth, but it was wrong. That day, while the Reds, under the temporary leadership of team captain Ivy Wingo, were splitting a doubleheader with Philadelphia, Herrmann and Hempstead finally pushed through a deal whereby Herzog and outfielder Wade Killefer went to New York for Mathewson, Roush, and McKechnie. Herrmann said that the Giants had finally dropped their insistence on the two-year recall.

Those who attended the doubleheader at Redland Field, of course, had read in their morning newspapers that Chase was to be the new manager, and they greeted him accordingly. "The fans at that time did not know of President Herrmann's change of mind with regard to Matty," wrote Ryder, "and they thought that Chase was the new leader of the team. The universal and hearty applause showed how popular the star first-sacker has become in this town." Chase professed not to be upset: "Hal recognized the mistake and took it all as a good joke."

He played three positions—first base, left field, and second base—in the doubleheader, and even batted lefthanded his last time up. He moved from left field to second base in the fourth inning of the second game, astonishing the crowd: "The sight of a left-handed second baseman was a big novelty to the bugs, and they were all pulling for some hitter to knock the ball down his way, but Hal did not have a single grounder to handle in the six rounds he was at second base."

Local fans hailed the acquisition of Mathewson. Said Ryder of the new leader, "He is popular and likeable, without being at all weak in character, and there is no doubt that he will command the respect of the players and will get the best work out of the team." Herrmann promised to support Mathewson without reservation: "We shall give him complete charge of the club and back him up to the last in any changes he may desire to make."[75]

On the following day Ryder reported the first of those changes: Mathewson would keep Chase at first base on a full-time basis, and so had decided to let Mollwitz go. The superfluous first baseman was sold to the Cubs on July 22. On that same day, however, Mathewson ordered Chase to rest until the following Tuesday. While most of the regulars would stop in Rochester for an exhibition game on Monday, Chase would be in charge of a small group of Cincinnati players, including Fred Toney, Pete Schneider, Tom Clarke, and McKechnie, who would leave Cincinnati after Sunday's game and go straight through to New York, where his wife would join him at the Ansonia Hotel on Monday night. Mollwitz played first base as the Reds lost to the Phillies on Sunday, but left after the game to join the Cubs in Boston. Mathewson would use pitcher Clarence Mitchell, a good hitter, as his backup first baseman.[76]

The Reds' game against the Giants on Tuesday was rained out, but on Wednesday, as the New York fans got their first look at the great Matty in an enemy uniform, Cincinnati beat the home team 4–2. Chase played first base and contributed one of his standard plays in the sixth, when he knocked down Dave Robertson's hot grounder, picked it up, and dove for the bag, just beating the runner. "Hal doesn't care what chances he takes," wrote Ryder admiringly. "He is a real ball player."[77]

Seven—I Want to Square Myself with the Public

The Giants came back and won the next two games in extra innings, but Herzog, still readjusting to life under McGraw, had a rough series, committing five errors in the three games, including four in the last.

The Reds moved on to Brooklyn, where they lost four of their five games with the Superbas. Chase had to leave the second game of a Saturday doubleheader in the second inning when his leg acted up again. Two days later he moved to second base when Heinie Groh was overcome by the heat.[78]

The Reds' next stop was Boston. Despite winning six of their seven games against the visitors the Braves appeared to be in even worse shape than the last-place Reds. In the absence of George Stallings, who had been suspended for arguing with an umpire, second baseman Johnny Evers had assumed command of the team. In the fourth inning of a game on August 3 Evers got into a fight on the bench with teammate Red Smith and was ejected by umpire Bill Byron. The excitable Evers immediately announced that he would be glad to accept his unconditional release, but Stallings said the second baseman would stay. "Evers is in a highly nervous condition," reported Ryder, "and the hot weather has affected him, too."[79]

On the following day the Reds lost 5–2 as Chase committed three errors. Ryder shrugged off the display: "That simply shows that even the best of them have a lot of trouble once in a while. Hal's troubles are few and far between, however, and his wobbles had nothing to do with the loss of the contest."[80]

Unlike Evers, Chase was normally among the most easygoing of players on the field. In the first game of an August 7 doubleheader, though, he too ran afoul of Byron. In the third inning, with one out and Earl Blackburne on third base, the Braves' Ed Fitzpatrick grounded back to the mound. Toney threw to Chase at first base for the second out, whereupon Blackburne decided to try for home plate. "Chase had the play right in front of him, and would undoubtedly have cut off Blackburne at the plate, but as he drew back his arm to throw the ball to Wingo Fitzgerald [sic] deliberately shouldered him and prevented him from throwing at all," wrote an outraged Ryder. "It was a clear case of unfair and intentional interference, and Chase made a legitimate kick, asking that Blackburne be called out for Fitzgerald's raw play."

Chase was arguing with Byron when the umpire called to Mathewson, "You'd better get this man out of here if you want him to play any more ball today." Chase turned back to his position when Mathewson came out of the dugout to discuss the matter with Byron, but the umpire ejected him anyway. "This raw deal deprived the Reds of the services of their best hitter in both games," wrote Ryder. "Chase is a power on the team, and his loss was keenly felt." Cincinnati was shut out in both games of the doubleheader for its fifth and sixth defeats in a row.[81]

The losing streak reached eight in Philadelphia, but then the team began playing a little better. Back in Cincinnati on August 13, Mathewson's birthday, the Reds beat the Cubs 4–3 in eleven innings thanks to some heads-up baserunning by Chase. After Tommy Griffith led off the bottom of the eleventh with a triple, Cubs manager Joe Tinker ordered Chase and Ivy Wingo walked intentionally to set up a force play at any base. Greasy Neale made the first out on a fly ball, then Louden hit what looked like a double-play ball to shortstop Chuck Wortman, who threw home to force Griffith. Catcher Rowdy Elliott immediately fired the ball to first base, but Louden barely beat the throw.

While all this was happening the Cubs forgot about Chase, who had taken off when the ball was hit and never stopped running. He scored the winning run unmolested, and so completely did he fool the Cubs that at first they did not even realize that the game was over: "They were hugely surprised and considerably annoyed when they perceived what Hal had put over on them," reported Ryder. "Zip Mollwitz, at first base, was so embarrassed that he did not even throw home. It wouldn't have done any good, anyway, for Chase had the play beaten a mile. He had outguessed the enemy and they were his."[82]

The Reds won again the next day, but then lost six more in a row, dropping their record to 43–74. On August 23, they travelled to Toledo for an exhibition against the amateur Rail-Lights. Cincinnati won 8–3 without Chase, who spent the day on the Miami River. "He will take a dip into the surging flood of this great stream, and, upon emerging, will be the guest at a fish fry," wrote Ryder. "Hal has been playing every day with a bum prop, and the rest will do him good, but it will be a little tough on the fishes."[83]

The Reds won three of their next seven games against the Superbas and the Giants, but the team was still unsettled. On August 28, in a 5–2 win over the Giants, Chase played second base when Heinie Groh had to move to shortstop due to injuries to McKechnie and Fisher. "Hal is one of those high-class performers who can play anywhere," wrote Ryder. "Just a natural artist, who fits in wherever he is put." Despite Ryder's praise, Chase committed two errors in the game. Meanwhile McGraw continued to reconstruct his infield, trading Larry Doyle, Herb Hunter, and Merwin Jacobson to the Cubs for Heinie Zimmerman. "The Great Zim," as he was only half-seriously referred to in Chicago, would finish the season as the National League leader in runs batted in, but a few years later his name would be linked with that of Chase, by then a teammate, in a scandal that would end their major league careers.

Chase remained at second base for ten games, six of them Cincinnati victories. He committed four errors during that period, but also batted .419, with eighteen hits in forty-three at bats. While the Reds were winning three of four games in Pittsburgh Chase had nine hits in thirteen at bats, even though he had complained of feeling ill before the first game of the series. Ryder attributed Chase's performance to his lingering dislike of the Pirates' manager: "To defeat Jimmy Callahan, with whom he had trouble in Chicago, is one of the most earnest purposes of the life of Mr. Chase." Ryder also made light of Chase's physical condition: "If the symptoms of illness in him always take the form of singles and doubles every time up he will get no sympathy should he become afflicted with gout, lumbago and housemaid's knee all at the same time."[84]

By early September Cincinnati fans began to realize that Chase was steadily creeping up on the top contenders for the league batting honors. With the Reds still mired in last place, Chase's batting average and the much-anticipated pitching debut of Mathewson in a Reds uniform were just about the only reasons for continuing to follow the team. "Hal has played wonderful ball this year, and has been of great help to the team, a fact which is thoroughly appreciated by the fans," wrote Jack Ryder. "He has a chance to lead the National League in hitting, and is making a great fight for the high honor, without letting down in his work in any respect." A few days later, after Chase had hammered out three hits in four at bats, Ryder reported, "The boys are all pulling for Hal to lead the league in hitting and he is game enough to keep on trying every day.... The beauty about Chase is that he gets so many of his drives in the pinches. He is the most reliable driver in of runs on the team."[85]

On September 4 Mathewson pitched for the first time in a Cincinnati uniform, opposing his old nemesis, Mordecai Brown of the Cubs, in the second game of a doubleheader in Chicago. The Reds won 10–8, but Mathewson, who gave up fourteen hits, was only slightly better than Brown, who surrendered eighteen. After the game Matty told his players, "Boys, I thought that I could pitch a few more games, but I find I haven't got the stuff any more. I shall never attempt to pitch a championship game again. If I ever go into the box again I will buy every one of you a suit of clothes."[86] He never had to make good on that promise.

Two days later the Reds beat the Henry Grays 13–8 in an exhibition game at Henry, Illinois. Chase played first base for seven innings, then succumbed to his old yearning and went in to pitch. "Hal had some trouble before he got through," noted Ryder, in something of an understatement. He gave up four hits and seven runs in the two innings, and saw his control evaporate completely. In the ninth, with one out and a runner on third, he walked three men in a row, forcing in a run. When his first three deliveries to the next batter were all wide of the plate, third baseman McKechnie had had enough. He called time, went to the mound and insisted on changing places with Chase. McKechnie's first pitch was ball four, forcing in another run, but he got the last two outs of the game on infield grounders.[87]

Chase was embarrassed again on September 8 in St. Louis, during a 6–1 loss to the Cardinals. In the seventh inning, with two outs and two runners on base, Jack Smith grounded up the first base line. Chase, playing first base again, fielded the ball cleanly and tagged Smith for the third out of the inning — or so he thought. He did not realize that umpire Pete Harrison disagreed, and nonchalantly tossed the ball back toward the pitcher's mound as Smith raced to second base and Lee Meadows scored.[88] Still, Chase managed six hits in the next three games against the Cardinals and concluded the series in first place in the batting race.

From St. Louis the Reds made an unusually long trip straight to New York, although Chase stopped for the morning in Buffalo to see his wife, who was staying there with her parents. He sounded confident about his chances of holding his lead in the batting race: "I have always hit well on all the Eastern grounds, with the exception of Boston. We are going to run up against tough pitching on this trip, but I think I can hold my own."[89]

The Reds lost nine of the thirteen games on this eastern trip, dropping their record to 57–93, but Chase continued his torrid batting. He hit .406, with twenty-six hits in sixty-four at bats, in those thirteen games, including seven hits in fourteen at bats in three games in Boston. After the first game, in which Chase had four hits, including a home run and a double, and drove in four runs in a 12–4 Cincinnati victory, Ryder reported that Chase had changed his mind about Boston: "Hal Chase rather dreaded this Boston series, as he has never felt that he could hit well on this field. He no longer feels that way, and now only wishes that all the rest of the games were to be played here. Hal is a game rooster."[90]

By September 25, when he went three-for-four in a 4–0 loss in Philadelphia, Chase had begun to put some distance between himself and the other contenders for the batting title. His .333 average led Brooklyn's Zack Wheat by thirteen points.

The Reds actually finished the season on an upbeat note, winning their last three games from the Pirates to move into a seventh-place tie with the Cardinals, thirty-three-and-a-half games behind the first-place Superbas. But those who had predicted an immediate change in the team's performance once Mathewson took over were disappointed. With twenty-five wins in sixty-eight games, Cincinnati's winning percentage of .368 under Matty did not compare favorably with the .410 compiled under Herzog.

Still, the fans were inclined to be patient. They knew that he had not had much voice in choosing the players on his team, a number of whom had had disappointing seasons. Cincinnati batters hit the fewest home runs in the league, while the Reds pitchers gave up more hits and more walks than any other staff in the league. The much-ballyhooed ex–Federal Leaguers Billy Louden and Al Schulz had been major disappointments; Louden batted only .219 and Schulz finished with an 8–19 record. Neither played in the major leagues again.

All these dismal figures made Chase's accomplishments even more outstanding. He finished the season with a batting average of .339, twenty-three points ahead of Jake Daubert, and eighty-two runs batted in, just one behind Zimmerman. Chase led the team in hits, home runs, runs batted in, stolen bases, and slugging percentage.

The Cincinnati fans appreciated his brilliance. Before the last game of the season, on Sunday, October 1, they presented him with a number of presents, which were carried out to home plate on a table. Actress May Buckley was on hand for the ceremony, which was recorded by motion-picture cameras. Jack Ryder grumbled about the distraction: "Miss Buckley insisted on getting in the picture so everybody would know her and took off her hat in order to be well seen. While she was presenting the vases and traveling bag to Chase, it reminded the band leader of a marriage ceremony, and the band struck up 'The Wedding March.' Miss Buckley made a presentation speech and Hal responded, but the words were lost in the air. Just why Miss Buckley was elected to do the presenting could not be found out, except that she added beauty to the moving picture scenes."[91]

By the following spring a modest optimism prevailed in Cincinnati, though there were signs that the war in Europe would soon encroach on baseball. "We don't look quite strong enough to do the Giants out of a pennant," admitted Mathewson in late February, "but you never can tell." Al Jolson, a baseball fan and old friend of Mathewson's, wired the Red manager just before the team left for spring training. "Give my regards to Hal Chase, Heinie Groh, Tom Clarke, Fred Toney, Bill McKechnie, Ivy Wingo and all the bunch," said Jolson. He added that he had dreamed three times within a two-week span that Cincinnati would win the pennant.[92]

The Reds seemed to be a happy team that spring. Their acquisition of Chase, which had seemed such a gamble the previous season, had paid handsome dividends. They held spring training at Shreveport again, and social activities were at a premium for Mrs. Chase and Mrs. Tommy Griffith, the only wives in camp, who were reported to be disappointed when Ivy Wingo reported for duty without his new bride. The two women returned to Cincinnati a couple of weeks later.[93] Chase himself announced that he would take his time getting ready for the season, though he seemed to be in fine shape already.[94] The 1,716 fans who saw the Reds win their first exhibition game against the Shreveport Gassers of the Texas League by a score of 7–0 gave the defending National League batting champion a big hand at his first at bat. "Hal gratified them with a splendid exhibition of fielding at the corner," reported Jack Ryder, but managed only a ninth-inning double against Shreveport's ace pitcher, a lefthander named Bill Terry. In a few years Terry would draw comparisons to Chase as the Hall of Fame first baseman of the New York Giants.[95]

After winning four out of five games from the Gassers the Reds began moving north. They beat John Ganzel's Kansas City Blues of the American Association and the Arkansas Travelers of the Southern Association en route to Memphis, where they hooked up with Clark Griffith's Washington Senators. Washington won 5–1 as the great Walter Johnson pitched three shutout innings, but the Memphis fans, like those in Shreveport, enjoyed seeing Chase in action. "Hal Chase and Walter Johnson, as the recognized leaders in their lines, were greeted with great applause by the fans, who seldom fail to show their liking for the real stars of the profession," reported Ryder.[96]

The Reds also beat the Memphis Chicks, managed by Chase's old billiard-hall sidekick Mike Donlin, and Toledo before hooking up with the Senators again. The Reds won two games in Louisville, but the Senators beat them in Cincinnati. On April 2 Matty received a surprising request from Ty Cobb, who had been training with the Tigers in Texas. The Tigers and Giants had been playing a series of exhibition games. During one of those games, furious at the savage insults being hurled at him from the New York bench, Cobb deliberately spiked Buck Herzog on an attempted steal. That night Cobb, accompanied by catcher Oscar Stanage and trainer Harry Tuthill, agreed to meet Herzog in single combat in Cobb's hotel room. Herzog arrived with Zimmerman, whereupon Cobb reportedly proceeded to beat Herzog senseless.

Now Cobb, "anxious to get away from unpleasant surroundings," asked Matty if he could come to Cincinnati and practice with the Reds. Mathewson was delighted; he hoped that Cobb could show his players a few base-running tricks. When Cobb arrived in Cincinnati, he labelled Herzog, Fletcher, and Zimmerman "wild men" and predicted that internal dissension would destroy the Giants. He also called McGraw "a mucker of the lowest type," a rather tactless remark given Mathewson's relationship to the New York manager. "If I ever get him alone in a nice, quiet place I shall be tempted to clean him up," warned Cobb, "but I understand he seldom moves without a bodyguard."[97]

Such petty disputes seemed insignificant on the following day, when President Woodrow Wilson officially declared war on Germany. Many people wondered what effect the war would have on baseball, but for the time being baseball tried to carry on with business as usual. On April 7 the Reds lost their last exhibition game to the Cleveland Indians 7–2. The press had made much of the meeting of the two reigning major league batting champions, but Cleveland's Tris Speaker went two-for-four while Chase was held hitless in three at bats.[98]

The season officially opened on Wednesday, April 11. Before a crowd of some twenty-five thousand in Cincinnati the Reds beat the Cardinals 3–1. Chase began the 1917 season as he had ended the last, as the subject of a pregame tribute. This time the Chase Motor Company, seeking to capitalize on Prince Hal's popularity and their shared name, gave him "a beautiful floral piece."[99] Chase rose to the occasion with two hits, including a triple, in three at bats.

Two days later, while she was watching her husband's team lose to St. Louis, someone stole a purple silk sweater belonging to Anna Chase. "She is quite sure that she knows the boy who abstracted it," warned Ryder, "and will expect him to return it to-day. She prefers not to prosecute him and will not do so if the garment is returned promptly and in good order."[100] No record of the sweater's return survives.

While the 1917 Reds were clearly better than their predecessors of the previous year, they still found interesting ways to lose. On April 20, in St. Louis, the Cardinals scored six runs in the first inning without hitting the ball out of the infield, thanks to four walks by Pete Schneider, three misplays by Chase, and two by third baseman Gene Getz. Mathewson was not present to witness this debacle, having been called home by the illness of his son. In Matty's absence Chase was in charge of the team. In light of future events, the weird inning is enough to raise suspicions about which team Chase hoped would win.

Schneider walked Bob Bescher leading off the inning and then hit Bruno Betzel with a pitch. Tommy Long put down a sacrifice bunt which Schneider fielded and threw to Chase for the first out, but the play turned out to be

Seven — I Want to Square Myself with the Public

anything but routine: "Chase, after taking the throw, stood with the ball in his hand, not noticing that Bescher was making the desperate play of trying to score from second base on the bunt." The St. Louis player crossed the plate safely. Dots Miller then topped a roller down the third base line, moving Betzel to third. Getz touched the ball in fair territory, then argued that it was a foul ball. While he held the ball and argued with the umpire, Miller took second base. Schneider walked Rogers Hornsby to bring up Walton Cruise with the bases loaded: "Cruise shot a grounder straight at Chase, made to order for a double play, but Hal let it go through him, and the official scorer kindly designated it as a hit." Betzel and Miller scored on the play and Hornsby advanced to third.

Schneider walked Jack Smith, and Frank Snyder got a hit on a ground ball that Getz should have stopped, but Hornsby had to hold third base. On the next pitch Schneider picked Hornsby off, but Getz dropped the throw and Hornsby scored. Mule Watson then hit another sure double-play grounder. This time the Reds got the forceout on Snyder at second base, but Chase dropped the relay throw and both Cruise and Smith scored. Bescher, up for the second time in the inning, thoughtfully grounded out to end the nightmare and manager Chase excused Schneider for the rest of the afternoon. Schneider's replacement was a promising youngster named Jimmy Ring, who was appearing in only his second major league game. Ring gave up six hits and only one run the rest of the way, but that one run was enough as St. Louis won 7–6.[101]

A couple of weeks later, by way of refreshing contrast, Cincinnati's Fred Toney and Chase's old Yankee teammate Hippo Vaughn, now the ace of the Cubs' staff, hooked up in what one historian has called "the greatest game ever pitched."[102] The game was played in near-freezing weather in Chicago before some twenty-five hundred hardy souls, who saw Toney and Vaughn pitch matching no-hitters through nine innings. The Reds finally got to Vaughn in the top of the tenth. With one out Larry Kopf drove a clean single to right field. One out later Chase lined a pitch to short center field, where Cy Williams dropped the ball. Chase held at first base on the error while Kopf moved up to third. On Vaughn's first pitch to Jim Thorpe, Chase stole second uncontested, as catcher Art Wilson held the ball in case Kopf tried to score on the play. Thorpe topped Vaughn's next pitch up the third base line. The Chicago pitcher raced over to field the ball just in front of the onrushing Kopf. Realizing that he had no chance to get Thorpe at first base, Vaughn shoveled the ball to Wilson, whereupon Kopf stopped dead in the basepath.

Wilson, however, apparently mesmerized, made no move to catch the ball. It bounced off his chest protector and rolled a few steps away. Kopf, seeing the ball roll free, raced across the plate with the first run of the game. Chase, too, saw Wilson's lapse and decided to try to score as well. When Vaughn looked back and saw his old friend rounding third base he yelled at Wilson, "Are you going to let him score too?" Wilson came out of his trance and picked up the ball just in time to tag the sliding Chase for the last out of the inning.

Toney quickly disposed of the demoralized Cubs in the bottom of the tenth, preserving his no-hitter and the 1–0 Cincinnati victory. After the game a furious Cubs owner Charles Weeghman visited his clubhouse and roundly cursed his players. Wilson, stricken with the enormity of his lapse, was in tears when he apologized to Vaughn: "I just went out on you, Jim — I just went tight." Vaughn tried to downplay his disappointment. "It's just another ballgame," he told a reporter. "Just another loss."[103]

Despite the presence of Toney and some other solid pitchers, Cincinnati was soon struggling again. By May 8, when the Reds played an exhibition against the International League Bisons in Buffalo, they were in fifth place with an 11–13 record. The occasion was proclaimed Hal Chase Day in Buffalo, and a crowd of more than two thousand saw the Reds beat the Bisons 10–5. Ryder managed simultaneously to praise Chase and demean the quality of play in the Federal League: "Hal put on some of his special fielding and base running stuff for his friends and showed them he has not gone back any since he left the *minor* leagues."[104]

The Reds went on to lose three in a row in New York and two of three in Brooklyn, dropping into sixth place. Chase had two hits in the last game against the Superbas, a 13–10 Cincinnati loss, but injured his leg in a collision with Ivy Olson in the fourth inning. He missed one game and then pinch-hit for Toney on May 19. Mathewson excused him from the Reds' trip to Newport, Rhode Island, to play a Sunday exhibition against the Newport Trojans, but Chase came along anyway — he had always wanted to see Newport, explained Jack Ryder — and played center field in a 4–1 Cincinnati victory.[105]

The Reds won two of three games from the Braves, but then lost three out of four in Philadelphia. After rapping out seven hits, including a home run, a triple, and a pair of doubles, in the four games against the Phillies, Chase's batting average was .278.

By this time the war in Europe had become impossible to ignore. On May 28, with their game against the Cubs rained out, every member of the Reds except Chase, Mathewson, and pitcher Elmer Knetzer, who were too old, registered for the draft at City Hall. A few days later Hank Gowdy of the Braves became the first major leaguer to enlist.[106]

The major league owners were terrified that the government might declare baseball a frivolous and superfluous institution in time of war and shut the game down. Consequently they lost no opportunity to stress the importance of the national game for the morale of the American troops. When President Wilson designated June 5 as Registration Day the owners, anxious to prove their patriotism, announced that baseball would celebrate the occasion with bands, speeches, and military drills in every major league park. "Organized baseball stands ready to do anything within its power to help along in the whole situation," wrote Garry Herrmann in a letter to Ohio Governor James M. Cox, who had recommended that all amusement parks and theaters be closed on June 5. "As you know, the game itself is particularly a soldiers and sailors' game.... Few men who enter our country's service but are intensely interested in professional baseball.... Baseball adds a necessary element of interest to military life and justifies its existence by that act alone.... In short, baseball is especially a war game, and its activities far from being curtailed should rather be stimulated by the present war." Cox amended his earlier stand in his reply to Herrmann, acknowledging "that patriotic services at amusement parks are in keeping with the desire for observation of registration day. We can see no objections therefore to your plans."[107]

While the Reds were bouncing between fifth and seventh place in the league standings, Ryder reported a social note that must have been of at least passing interest to Chase: Sleepy Bill Burns, now pitching in San Francisco, would marry Laura Carroll of Cincinnati, the sister of Mrs. Bobby Keefe. Keefe, now pitching in Sacramento,[108] had been a college teammate of Chase's at Santa Clara and for one year in New York before spending a couple of seasons with the Reds, where he was also briefly a teammate of the much-travelled Burns. If, as seems likely, he introduced Chase and Burns, he committed, however innocently, a fateful act.

On Registration Day the Reds beat the visiting Giants 6–5. They went on to win three out of four from New York, improving their record to 21–27 and climbing back into fifth place. The last Cincinnati victory, by 2–1 on June 8, sent McGraw into an uncontrollable rage. According to McGraw's biographer, the pugnacious Giant manager confronted umpire Bill Byron after the game, from which McGraw had been ejected by Byron's partner Ernie Quigley.

"Take your hands out of your pockets and I'll show you which is the better man," challenged McGraw.

"You're a fine one to talk, when you were run out of Baltimore and you know it," responded Byron. This answer, a reference to the less-than-completely honorable circumstances under which McGraw had left the old American League Baltimore Orioles and jumped to the Giants in 1901, set McGraw off. He took a punch at Byron, cutting the umpire's chin; before Byron could retaliate he was bundled into the umpire's dressing room by fans. Meanwhile Giants catcher Bill Rariden attacked Cincinnati groundskeeper Matty Schwab, who had attempted to intervene.[109]

McGraw, who immediately went to a notary public and swore out a statement, told a very different story. The Giant manager said he had been innocently walking past the umpire's dressing room when Byron yelled, "Keep walking!" at him.

McGraw said he responded, "No, I shall wait here and see what you are going to do," whereupon Byron answered, "You yellow streak, you were run out of Baltimore." McGraw said he asked Byron to repeat his statement.

"You are accused of it," said the umpire.

"Do you say I was run out of Baltimore?"

"Yes."

That was all the provocation McGraw needed. He concluded his statement, "Thereupon I hit him."[110]

Their success against the Giants seemed to awaken the Reds. For the next six weeks they played at a .667 pace, winning thirty-two of forty-eight games, including sixteen of twenty-two on the road. By July 27, when Fred Toney beat the Phillies for his eighteenth win of the season, they had hauled themselves into second place with an overall record of 54–43, .001 ahead of the Cardinals.

Chase, too, was playing much better; his four hits in a doubleheader in Brooklyn on July 21 raised his batting average to .298. He had hurt his right hand in Pittsburgh on June 30, the result of catching some hard throws, according to Ryder, and missed two games. He returned to the lineup on July 3 against the Cubs wearing an oversized mitt to protect his sore hand, but showed no ill effects from the injury. Ryder reported that Mrs. Chase joined her husband in New York on July 12, when the Reds swept a doubleheader from the Giants. "Hal celebrated the occasion by nicking Perritt for a single, a double and a triple, and his baserunning was exquisite. Hal is so far out in front of all other first basemen that they look like cart horses in comparison with him."[111]

This was a theme to which Ryder would revert repeatedly, especially at the expense of Jake Daubert, who was generally ackowledged to be Chase's only possible rival as the best first baseman in the National League. On July 23, when the visiting Reds beat the Superbas 5–2, Ryder crowed, "Chase showed Daubert up in the seventh inning, when the Brooklyn fans had to admit that Hal has it all over their former idol, who is now about through as a big leaguer."

With a man on first base Chase had hit into a forceout, and Daubert failed to pick up George Cutshaw's throw for an attempted double play. "The ball rolled not four feet from him, and Chase just kept on going, while Jake, half asleep, stood gaping and made no attempt to pick up the ball," reported Ryder. "The play showed the difference between a winning player and one who is more or less through. Chase is worth more to a ball club than a dozen Dauberts."[112]

Ryder's prediction that Daubert was "about through," however, was premature; Daubert would play six more years and bat over .300 in three of them. In 1919, ironically, following a contract dispute with Brooklyn owner Charles Ebbets, he would be traded to Cincinnati, where he would replace the disgraced Chase in the Reds lineup. He would enjoy his best major league season in 1922, at the age of thirty-six, batting .336 with twenty-two triples.

The streaky Reds cooled off in late July and early August, losing nine out of ten games and dropping back into fourth place. Chase, too, cooled off; between July 21, when his average reached .298, and August 11 he managed only thirteen hits in seventy at bats. His defense, too, seemed erratic. On July 14, when the Reds lost the first game of a doubleheader in New York, he dropped a throw in the third inning, allowing Benny Kauff to score. On August 4, again against New York, Chase dropped two throws in the fourth inning of a 4–1 Cincinnati win; a double play ended the inning before the Giants could score.[113]

In Boston on August 11 the Reds lost 5–4. Chase's error in the third inning gave the Braves a 2–1 lead. Boston's Ray Powell came to bat with runners on first and third and one out. "Powell lined straight into Chase's hands for a sure double play," reported Ryder, "but Hal muffed the ball and then seemed to lose track of what to do with it when he picked it up and got no one, [Ed] Tragresser scoring on the wobble."[114] On this occasion, at least, there was no crowing about Chase's superiority to Daubert.

Such lapses seemed to be aberrations, however, especially when Chase still pulled off brilliant plays with some regularity. One such moved Ryder to write, "It was a sensational piece of work, possible only to a player of the highest class, who thinks instantly and always knows just what to do with the ball. Hal is in something of a hitting slump, but he has too much nerve to allow it to interfere with his general play."[115]

On August 12, a day after his "wobble" in Boston, his defensive work helped Toney win his twentieth game of the season (and a $1,000 bonus). In the third inning the Cardinals had men on first and second with no outs. Pitcher Mule Watson was sent up to bunt the runners over, but Chase foiled the strategy: "Hal was right up under the bat when the Mule laid it down and had it over to Heinie [Groh, at third base] in time to beat [Doug] Baird by three full steps."[116]

The Reds won seven games and lost six on their final eastern trip of the season. The war again made its presence felt when the Reds played the Giants on August 19. The game was a benefit for the 69th Regiment of the New York National Guard, an Irish regiment with strong Tammany Hall connections that was soon to sail for France. It was the first regular-season National League game ever played on a Sunday at the Polo Grounds. A crowd of more than twenty thousand saw Toney win his twenty-second game of the season. On the following day, however, Mathewson and McGraw were summoned before Magistrate Frothingham of Washington Heights Police Court for violating New York's law prohibiting Sunday baseball. Frothingham dismissed the cases, and within a year New York had passed a law permitting Sunday baseball.[117]

After dropping two doubleheaders to the Phillies in late August the Reds found themselves back in fifth place with a 63–60 record, .001 behind the Cubs. Apparently disgusted by the losses, the Reds did not take seriously an August 26 exhibition in Jersey City, especially since Mathewson had taken the day off to play golf. When Cincinnati came out in the bottom of the first inning Chase went to third base and Groh, "decked out in Hal's big mitt," went to first. The crowd, hoping to see a serious contest, booed, and Jersey City manager Dave Driscoll came out of the dugout to complain. Eventually he convinced Chase and Groh to return to their normal positions, but Chase switched with left fielder Dutch Ruether in the fifth inning. The Reds lost 8–0 and committed four errors, and Driscoll stopped payment on the check for $408.75, their share of the receipts, on the grounds that they had not tried. "A farce like that of to-day hurts the Cincinnati Club and everybody connected with it," scolded a disapproving Ryder.[118]

By now Chase and his teammates were having a hard time taking even their regular-season games seriously. In the first inning of a 9–1 win in Boston on August 28 the Reds had some fun at the expense of the Braves' Wally Rehg. When Rehg failed to run out a ground ball, Chase began what is surely the only 3-4-6-9-1 putout in baseball history: "The foxy Hal did not touch first," reported Ryder, "but threw the ball to [Dave] Shean, who tossed to Kopf, who imparted it to Griffith, who finally threw to Schneider at first, Peter getting the put-out. Thus there were four assists on a play which did not really need any. Some fielding."[119]

Two days later Cincinnati won an exhibition game in Parkesburg, Pennsylvania. This time, with Mathewson in attendance, the Reds played hard, although Ryder suggested that Chase may not have been trying his hardest. "Hal Chase, a very intelligent performer, went out four times on bounders to the pitcher," noted Ryder. "Hal is saving them for an occasion when they will accomplish something for the club."[120]

The Reds played another exhibition on September 5 at New Kensington, Pennsylvania, but this time Chase did not participate. His replacement at first base, pitcher Clarence Mitchell, played so well that many of the fans assumed he was Chase, according to Ryder: "'Did you see Hal scooping them up around first base?' was a common query in the stand." On the following day another exhibition at Clarksburg, West Virginia, was rained out, which may have been just as well since local officials were reportedly upset that the Reds were missing several regulars. Chase missed another exhibition game in Parkersburg, West Virginia, the day after that, but the Reds won anyway.[121]

Against their National League opponents, however, the Reds continued to struggle. They lost four in a row to the Cardinals and Cubs, the last in particularly egregious fashion. In the second inning Chase booted Cy Williams's grounder, then threw wildly to Toney, who was covering first base. Williams moved up to second base on the error, took third on a passed ball, and scored when Kopf dropped Fred Merkle's fly ball. Art Wilson reached safely when Kopf dropped Toney's throw on an attempted forceout at second base, and Vaughn was given a hit when Kopf could not handle his grounder. With the bases loaded Max Flack hit a two-run single and Toney walked the next two batters to force in another run. He finally retired Morrie Schick and Charlie Deal to end the inning and then, perhaps understandably, quit for the day.[122]

On the following day the Reds bounced back to beat the Cubs 6–4. Chase had a couple of hits, but he was more of a hindrance than a help. In the third inning he came to bat with two Reds on base and one out. With the hit-and-run play on, Chase, known as the most adept practitioner of this art in baseball, swung and missed, and McKechnie was thrown out at third base. Chase then struck out to end the inning. In the seventh his wild throw to third base allowed Wilson to score the fourth Chicago run, and in the eighth he fumbled an easy grounder from Bill Marriott, but the Cubs could not take advantage.[123]

On the following day the Reds went through yet another exhibition-game burlesque, this time in Logansport, Indiana. Cincinnati beat the Ottos 4–2 as Chase played first base and pitched, surrendering four hits and both Logansport runs in the ninth inning. Wrote Ryder, "Hal Chase admitted after the game that he was a little worried when Kohler hit a long fly to left field in the ninth inning with two out, two men on and only two runs needed to tie," but Groh, playing left, made the catch. At that, Chase would have held the Ottos scoreless had Edd Roush, playing second base barehanded, not made an error.[124]

Two days later the Reds beat the Pirates to even their record at 70–70, but Chase missed the game with a finger injured "while tinkering with his automobile."[125] The finger kept him out of one other game, but seemed to be fully healed by September 18, when Toney beat Philadelphia 1–0. A fine play by Chase ended the game. With two out Dode Paskert grounded to McKechnie at shortstop. McKechnie's throw was high, "but Chase left the bag, grabbed the sphere in one hand and made a diving touch on Paskert's shoulder as he dashed by on his way to the base." Commented Ryder, "It was a grand wind-up to a wonderful battle."[126]

Chase slumped offensively in the last ten games of the season, managing just eight hits in his last forty-five at bats, and in the seventh inning of a win against the Braves on September 27 he threw the ball into the stands trying to get Wally Rehg at third base. A day later, during a loss to the Giants, he again botched a hit-and-run play, missing the ball as McKechnie was thrown out at third base.[127]

The Reds split those ten games to finish in fourth place with a record of 78–76, their first winning record in eight years. Chase's final batting average was .277, certainly a letdown after his brilliant 1916 record, but he again led the team in runs batted in, once more finishing second in the league to Heinie Zimmerman of the pennant-winning Giants. Chase also tied for the team lead in home runs and finished second on the team in stolen bases. But the Reds were no longer a one-man show. Cincinnati led the National League in team batting average as Edd Roush succeeded Chase as batting champion, posting a .341 average; Groh batted .304 and led the league in hits and doubles; and Toney and Schneider combined to win forty-four games. Certainly Reds fans had reason to look forward to 1918.

The last order of business in 1917, however, was a best-of-seven exhibition series with the Indians for the unofficial championship of Ohio. Cleveland, with stars such as Tris Speaker, Jim Bagby, Stan Coveleskie, and Ray Chapman, had finished third in the American League. The Reds won the first two games in Cincinnati and the third in Cleveland, but the Indians won the next two contests. After the Reds beat the Indians 8–1 in Cleveland on October 10 to win the series, the two teams agreed to play one more game for the soldiers at Ohio's Camp Sherman. In that game Chase played first base for five innings, then came on to pitch in the sixth. His presence on the mound provoked "many cries of disgust from the Cincinnati rooters, who had placed bets on the Buckeye champs," according to Ryder. "However, Chase, though walking four men, held the Indians safe." In fact, in three innings of work Chase held the Indians hitless and struck out four. Cleveland manager Lee Fohl, serving as umpire, called the game in the eighth inning with the Indians ahead 3–1 when Chase fouled off the last three baseballs in Fohl's possession.[128]

After this game the players departed for their various winter activities, the Reds players pocketing $2,989.78 apiece from the Cleveland series. Ryder reported that Chase, Groh, and Griffith would take a hunting trip together before returning to "camp out at their home firesides here till next spring."[129]

The 1917 season had been a gratifying one for Chase, although he fell short of his 1916 statistics. The baseball establishment, always eager for a happy ending, had welcomed back the chastened prodigal. His rehabilitation was celebrated in an article by J. C. Kofoed in the July issue of *Baseball* magazine and in two other works ostensibly written by Chase himself: an article in the October issue of *Baseball* and a book entitled *How to Play First Base.*

That Chase's name was chosen to appear on the book was a clear indication that he was again regarded as the best first baseman in baseball. Although the book, designed as an instruction manual for young players, was certainly ghostwritten, it seems to reflect some of Chase's own baseball philosophy, such as his conviction that his was as demanding a position as any in baseball: "First base is no longer a fielding sinecure for a heavy hitter. It is a position demanding speed, accuracy, a good pair of hands, quick judgment, fair throwing ability and plenty of nerve." Of course Chase himself had all of these qualities, especially the last, in abundance.

He reiterated his argument several times. "All in all, the first baseman must do all of the things that are required of the other infielders, and then some," he wrote. And again, although he quickly lapsed into predictable sermonizing on the traditional virtues of clean living and hard work: "There is no longer room on good ball clubs for the slacker or the slow thinker. Like all other players, the first baseman must be ever ready to do his part toward winning the game and this he cannot do unless he is in fine form, with a clear eye and muscles well trained and co-ordinated.... Any man who intends to excel as an athlete must take care of his body and train his mind to be always capable of its best efforts at critical moments. Only by keeping in perfect condition can he hope to achieve a high position in his chosen profession."[130]

Kofoed's article, titled "The California Comet," described Chase as "alive, vibrant in every atom," and attributed his earlier troubles to the actions of a brash, high-strung youth chafing under harsh management: "There was always much of the boy in 'Prince Hal.' He hungered for applause, and, as the most wonderful fielding first baseman the game ever saw, he won much of it. The hunger led him to play individual, rather than team ball. He became characterized as a 'grand-stand' player, and that reputation led to serious results."

But this was not all Chase's fault. "It is too bad that Chase never had the opportunity of playing under a calm, level headed, fatherly man like Connie Mack." When he joined the Yankees in 1905 Chase was "a finished, brilliant player, but a hot headed, inexperienced boy for all that." Griffith, while "a remarkable leader," was "not the type to understand or sympathize with a youth of Chase's temperament." Chase's subsequent managers had been "fighters, rather than students of men. In their eyes Chase was a marvel, but a trouble maker." In condemning their tactics, Kofoed compared Chase to a thoroughbred racehorse, a conceit which must have pleased a habitué of the track like

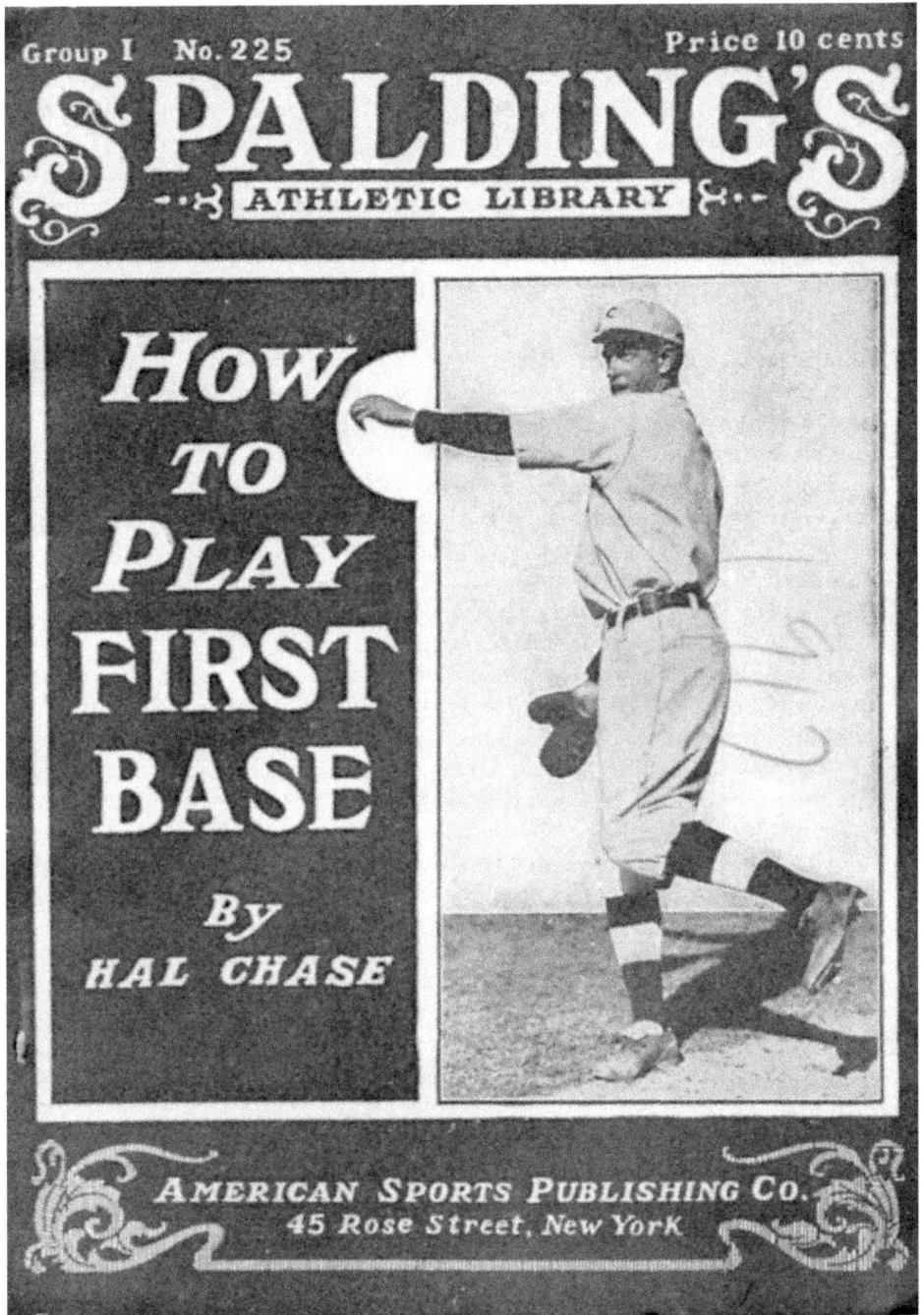

The cover of *How to Play First Base*, published in 1917. *Thomas Carwile Collection.*

Prince Hal: "They sought to curb and bit him. This was a tremendous mistake, for Hal is of that high-spirited, proud type that is easily led, but cannot be driven."

Chase's glorious 1916 season, however, had been "a vindication of the man ... a concrete exposition of the stuff that was in him." Kofoed argued that Chase had emerged from the controversies of his youth an older and wiser man: "Maturity has not taken away his speed or batting eye, but it has given him a grip on himself; a control that makes him a more valuable player today than he was a dozen years ago."[131]

In an article titled "Doing the 'Come-Back' Stunt" that appeared under his byline in the October issue of the same magazine, Chase could not resist taking a shot at those who had written him off when the Federal League folded. "I felt pretty good when the dope proved that an old 'has-been' who had been relegated to the junk heap was still good enough to lead the National League in batting," he wrote, with justifiable smugness.

Following Kofoed's lead Chase sought to disarm the skeptical by admitting that his past problems had been at least partially his own fault, while arguing that his previous managers were equally or more to blame. "I am not going to rehash a lot of stuff that is best forgotten," wrote Chase (or his ghostwriter). "The most I will say is that my career has not been altogether satisfactory to myself. But I am not taking the entire blame on my own shoulders."

He insisted that injuries and "managerial troubles" had been the two principal banes of his career. "I have had my full share of disagreements with the club boss," he admitted. "As I look back now, I can see that part of the fault, very likely, was due to myself, but I refuse to shoulder all the blame.... It has been my misfortune to be associated for several seasons, with managers with whose methods and policies I was wholly out of sympathy." Again following Kofoed's lead, Chase admitted that he was sensitive and temperamental: "It has also been my misfortune to feel and show these differences more than most players." But this was not a fault for which he should be condemned.

"I am not quarreling with managers as a class," Chase continued generously. "I have been one myself and well understand their difficulties. But I believe that where they have to deal with a player [like Chase himself, although he left this unwritten] who has shown that he has the ability to think for himself and play a good type of ball, they should let him follow his own lead with the minimum of interference."

He had only kind words for Matty. "My experience with Cincinnati has been a pleasant contrast with some of my former experiences. I consider Mathewson the ideal manager. I cannot conceive how any player could have trouble with Matty." The article concluded reflectively. "I guess I have about run the gamut of what can occur to a ball player," wrote Chase. "What will happen to me in the seasons that are left me in the big show? I can't tell. But I guess nothing that hasn't already happened; certainly nothing which will find me unprepared."[132]

Eight

A Severe "Black Eye" for the Game

While the spring of 1918 should have been a time of great optimism for the Reds, they were concerned about a number of factors beyond their control. For one thing, the war in Europe had not gone away, and increasingly baseball wondered whether the 1918 season would even take place. Equally serious were the legal problems facing big Fred Toney, the team's best pitcher, who had been charged in Nashville with entering false information on his selective service questionnaire in order to avoid the draft.[1]

One positive note was the acquisition of Lee Magee from the St. Louis Browns. Magee, a Cincinnati native whose real name was Leopold Hoernschemeyer, had suffered through a miserable 1917, batting only .200 for the Yankees and Browns, but was still only twenty-nine and seemed fully capable of recapturing the form that had made him a star in the Federal League. Magee himself looked forward to joining the Reds: "It has always been my ambition to play in my home town," he said, "and I am sure that I will deliver the goods to the satisfaction of my friends here."[2]

Once again, as the Reds prepared to leave for spring training in the south, a show-business friend of Mathewson and Chase's wished the team good luck. In 1917 it had been Al Jolson; this year it was Will Rogers, who was playing Cincinnati's Grand Theater, who called on Mathewson and Chase to wish them luck.[3]

The Reds held their spring camp in Montgomery, Alabama, in 1918. The first group of players left Cincinnati in a special car attached to the L & N on Monday, March 11. Despite the absence of Toney and the threat of the war spring training was, at least for Chase, a chance to relax. Mathewson divided the team into two squads captained by Chase and veteran Sherwood Magee (no relation to Lee). The "Hals" and the "Sherrys" played three games, all of which were won by the latter, but Chase claimed that his men could have won a best-of-seven series had the two kept playing.[4]

Chase's decision to grow a beard contributed to the general tone of hilarity. "Hal Chase is giving a lifelike imitation of Charles E. Hughes," wrote Jack Ryder. "He has not shaved for a week, but asserts that the camouflage does not interfere with his speed except in a high wind. Hal has one thing on Mr. Hughes. He wins when he sets out to."[5]

The Reds continued to enjoy themselves in their first exhibition games, beating teams from the University of Alabama and Auburn University, a couple of soldiers' teams, and the Waco Navigators of the Texas League. But then they joined the Detroit Tigers in Waxahachie, Texas, for a protracted tour. The two teams played thirteen games as they barnstormed through Texas, Oklahoma, Arkansas, and Tennessee on their way to Cincinnati, and the Tigers won ten. Not only did they beat the Reds, they hammered them, by scores of 11–0, 12–5, 11–4, 8–2 and 14–9.

Chase did little to further the Cincinnati cause in these games. He had three hits in four at bats at Waxahachie on April 1, but committed two errors as Detroit won 7–1. In the rest of the series he managed only four hits in twenty-seven at bats, and did not play at all in five of the contests. He missed one game, in Oklahoma City, with an upset stomach after giving himself an excessive dose of quinine to fight off a cold.[6]

These developments were depressing enough for Cincinnati fans, but Toney's situation was even worse. On April 10, while the Tigers beat the Reds 5–3 in Little Rock, Toney was indicted in Nashville for violating the Mann Act on the same afternoon that the jury in his draft case was discharged after failing to reach a verdict. Toney had been living with Gladys Strange as her husband in Cincinnati while still married to another woman in Tennessee. The fact that he had been separated from his wife for four years made no difference.[7]

The Reds opened the season without Toney on April 16, beating the Pirates 2–0 on a one-hitter by Pete Schneider. On April 22 Chase had two hits in three at bats and drove in the winning run as Cincinnati beat Chicago 3–2, but he injured his shoulder while sliding into second base on his game-winning hit. He missed four of the next six games and appeared in two as a pinch-hitter. On April 26 in Pittsburgh he pinch-hit for Hod Eller in the seventh inning and stayed in the game to play left field. This was not a wise decision, as his sore arm resulted in a home run for Casey Stengel: "It was a long blow to the left-field fence," reported Ryder, "but Hal could only toss the ball in so slowly that Casey made the full distance instead of being held at third."[8]

Chase returned to the starting lineup four days later in Cincinnati. Though his shoulder was still bothering him, he hit a triple, drove in two runs, and scored the winning run as the Reds beat the Cardinals 5–4. Two days later, however, he committed two errors in a 12–8 loss in Chicago. In the bottom of the second inning his "very careless and costly error" helped the Cubs score five runs. In the third, with two out and two runners on base, he failed to handle Paul Carter's easy grounder. "Hal picked up the ball after Carter had beaten it out and made a wild throw to third which let in two more runs and gave the Cubs the game." Ryder simply reported that "Chase had an off day at first base."[9]

Eight—A Severe "Black Eye" for the Game

Lee Magee, born Leopold Hoernschemeyer, was just one of several major leaguers tainted by association with Chase. Magee, here in the uniform of the Yankees ca. 1916, was Chase's teammate on the Reds in 1918. Magee and Chase apparently bet against their own team to lose a game to the Braves and the feckless Magee tried desperately but unsuccessfully to throw the game. *National Baseball Hall of Fame Library, Cooperstown, N.Y.*

He reported that his shoulder was still bothering him and was out of the lineup for the next nineteen games, missing fourteen altogether and appearing five times as a pinch hitter. He watched "from the shade of the grand stand" as the Reds beat the Cardinals 9–6 in St. Louis on May 8.[10] On May 15, which had been declared Bat and Ball Fund Day, a crowd of almost four thousand turned out to see the Reds beat the Giants 3–2. At the game the Reds presented baseball uniforms to the soldiers from the Fort Thomas and University of Cincinnati training detachments and auctioned off a ball autographed by Mathewson and McGraw. "A number of ladies, led by Mrs. Hal Chase," acted as ushers at Redland Field.[11]

On the following day, as the Reds beat the Giants 3–0, Ryder reported that "Hal Chase was out in uniform for the first time in several days and worked on the coaching lines with great gusto." Once again, however, the war was intruding on baseball. Ryder noted that major league owners would likely protest the actions of players like Joe Jackson of the White Sox and Al Mamaux of the Superbas, who had jumped their teams to sign on at munitions plants and shipyards in an effort to avoid military service.[12]

Chase finally was back in the starting lineup on May 23, but went hitless in four at bats as the Braves beat the Reds 4–3. He played in five games, then sat out the first game of a doubleheader in Chicago on May 30. He did not start the second game either, but was sent in to play right field after Greasy Neale was ejected for fighting. Chase went hitless in his only at bat and left for Cincinnati that night "for a treatment of an abscess in his ear."[13]

On June 10 in Boston Chase had Cincinnati's only hit off Dick Rudolph in a 1–0 loss, but committed a "wild-eyed wobble" on Ray Powell's grounder in the sixth inning. "Hal booted it a minute, but still had plenty of time to make the put-out, but he could not pick up the ball, which lay at his feet while he felt all around for it," wrote Ryder. "He was only two or three steps from the bag, but when he finally got hold of the elusive sphere Powell had arrived at the station." Powell eventually scored the only run of the game.[14]

That game was the second of nine consecutive Cincinnati losses. At least one of them featured another inexplicable defensive error by Chase. On June 18, when the Giants beat the Reds 7–1, Benny Kauff opened the second inning by grounding to Heinie Groh, but Chase "made a dead muff of the easy throw," and Heinie Zimmerman followed with a double to drive in Kauff with New York's first run.[15]

Four days later the Reds beat the Cardinals 9–7 in the second game of a doubleheader for their first win in almost three weeks. Chase had two hits in four at bats, but his eighth inning error led to the sixth St. Louis run.[16] After that game the Reds lost five more in a row, dropping their record to 24–35. Chase was batting a respectable .285, but had committed six errors in his last fourteen games.

The problems continued. Cincinnati beat the Cubs on June 30, then lost four more games. On July 2 in Pittsburgh the Reds lost 7–6 in ten innings when

Mike Regan walked Zip Mollwitz after yet another error by Chase had helped load the bases. Two days later the Pirates won 1–0 in the bottom of the eleventh when, with one on and one out, Pittsburgh's Buster Caton hit a grounder to Chase, "who was so anxious to make a double play that he kicked the ball away and it was scored as a hit."[17]

Chase was not the only member of the Reds who was struggling. Toney had rejoined the team, but had lost eight games in a row, and on July 6 Schneider pitched a one-hitter against the Phillies but barely hung on for a 10–9 win, thanks to his thirteen walks. Six of the passes came consecutively in the ninth, when Philadelphia scored all nine runs.[18]

The win may not have been pretty, but it did seem to turn the team around. The Reds won eleven of their next fourteen games and climbed back into fifth place. On July 11 Toney beat the Superbas for his first win since May 30; nevertheless, the Reds sold him to the Giants a week and a half later. Three days later Chase and Tommy Griffith attended services at Dr. Frederick McMillan's First Presbyterian Church in Walnut Hills. That afternoon Chase had four hits in five at bats to lead the Reds to a 9–5 win over the Giants, and on Monday Griffith had three hits in a 2–1 loss. "They intend to be regular churchgoers from now on," observed Ryder.[19]

After rapping out four hits in a doubleheader against the Giants on July 17, Chase had raised his batting average to .305. But two days later, in denying Washington catcher Eddie Ainsmith's appeal for an exemption from military service, Secretary of War Newton D. Baker officially ruled that baseball was a nonessential industry. The ruling meant that ballplayers of draft age must now either quit baseball for jobs in essential industries or lose such deferred draft classifications as they may have received through dependencies. The initial reaction in organized baseball was panic; indeed, wrote Ryder, "The decision is regarded in baseball circles as tantamount to the disbandment of organized baseball for the duration of the war."[20]

On the day after Baker's ruling the Reds dropped an 8–3 contest to the visiting Braves, for whom the much-travelled Buck Herzog was now playing second base. Lee Magee, who had established himself as Cincinnati's starting second baseman, had a horrible game. In the third inning, when Herzog hit an easy double-play ball to Cincinnati shortstop Lena Blackburne, Magee failed to touch second base and then threw wildly to first base. Boston went on to score four runs in the inning.[21]

On July 25 the Reds played a doubleheader in Boston. Chase had two singles in six at bats as Cincinnati won the first game 4–3 in thirteen innings, despite some highly questionable plays by Magee. Hod Eller of the Reds was trying to protect a 2–1 lead with two outs in the bottom of the ninth. With Roy Massey at first base and Al Wickland at bat, reported Ryder, "came one of the strangest plays ever seen at a ball yard, showing the high tension under which some of the athletes are working on account of the uncertainty of Government orders." Wickland hit an easy bouncer to Magee. "With plenty of time to run over to second and make the put-out himself, or to throw to first and end the game, he shot the ball with all his might far over Blackburne's head into left field, allowing Massey to score from first with the tying run. There was no need whatever for the play, which was a pure case of nervousness." Wickland reached third on the play, but Eller struck out Red Smith to end the inning.

The strange drama was far from over. Neither team could score in the tenth inning, or the eleventh, or the twelfth. Then, with two out in the top of the thirteenth, Magee hit what looked like an easy grounder to Boston shortstop Johnny Rawlings. But the ball took a bad hop and struck Rawlings in the face, breaking his nose; Rawlings had to leave the game, and Magee was given a single. Massey came in from the outfield to play shortstop and George Stallings sent pitcher Art Nehf in to play center field. With Edd Roush, Cincinnati's best hitter, at the plate, Magee stole second base. Then Roush smashed a long drive to left-center field, between Nehf and Hugh Canavan, another pitcher who had been pressed into service as an emergency outfielder. Magee circled the bases so slowly that Roush, hard on his heels, reportedly shouted, "Run, you son of a bitch!" and barely beat the throw home for a two-run, inside-the-park home run. The Reds now led 4–2.

In the bottom of the thirteenth, reported Ryder, "Lee came near throwing it away again but Blackburne stopped his mad heave." The game ended with the score still 4–2.

Magee's strange adventures were not over yet. In the third inning of the second game, his error put Lefty George on base, but that merely helped set up a remarkable play a few moments later. After Herzog singled Massey lined out to Blackburne, who caught the ball, touched second base to double up George, and threw to Chase before Herzog could get back to first base. It was that rarest of baseball events, a triple play, and helped the Reds to a 5–0 win.[22]

"Some of the Redlegs, particularly Lena Blackburne, showed a tendency to burlesque," wrote a disapproving Burt Whitman in the Boston *Herald*. "While the athletes still draw salaries, they should have sense enough to realize that the fans are entitled to the best playing possible." Whitman apparently confused Blackburne with his double-play partner Magee; while Blackburne managed only one hit in the doubleheader, he helped preserve the first-game victory by stopping Magee's "mad heave" in the bottom of the thirteenth, and started a triple play in the second game.[23]

On the following day Magee "had another bad off-day" as the Reds dropped a doubleheader to the Braves, 11–5 and 12–3. In the first game the Cincinnati second baseman went hitless in three at bats and committed three more errors. His performance did not please the notorious Boston gamblers; Cincinnati had been a two-to-one favorite to win the game when it was thought that Jimmy Ring would pitch. Instead the Reds sent young Adolfo Luque to the mound. Luque struggled in his first National League start, and Ryder noted the curious reaction of the Boston crowd: "There were huge howls of wrath from their backers when the Braves began pounding Luque all over the lot in the early rounds."[24]

Eight—A Severe "Black Eye" for the Game

Chase was hitless in four at bats. He left the game in the top of the eighth inning after cutting his hand in the dugout when the glass from which he was drinking shattered.[25] He did not play in the second game, in which Magee had two hits and was not charged with an error, nor in the doubleheader in Philadelphia on the following day.

The Reds won both games from the Phillies, lifting themselves into a fourth-place tie with their hosts. The Phillies, however, won the next game by a score of 5–4 in eleven innings on July 29. Chase pinch-hit unsuccessfully in the eleventh. Once again a defensive lapse by Lee Magee led to a Cincinnati defeat. He failed to cover first base on a bunt by Justin Fitzgerald in the bottom of the eleventh, and Fitzgerald scored the winning run a few moments later.[26]

The stumbling Reds lost three out of their first four games in Brooklyn. Chase played first base in two of the games, contributing two hits, a stolen base, and three runs batted in to the lone Cincinnati victory, a 10–1 decision on August 3, but left the game after being hit in the ribs by Rube Marquard in the seventh inning. Ryder noted that the billiard player Willie Hoppe was at Ebbets Field, cheering for the Reds: "He is a great friend of Hal Chase, and came over with that well-known performer, who goes some himself in the billiard line."[27]

After beating the Braves in a Sunday exhibition game in Montreal, the Reds returned to Brooklyn for the final game of their series with the Superbas on August 5. Ten minutes before the game Greasy Neale and Lee Magee got into a fight after Magee threw the ball over Neale's head during pregame practice. The pugnacious Neale floored Magee twice before their teammates separated them. Ryder treated the incident facetiously in the newspaper; the general attitude seemed to be that such incidents were inevitable, given the frustrations of playing for a struggling team under a hot August sun.[28]

Chase and Magee each had two hits in the game, a 5–0 Cincinnati victory, but Magee missed the Reds' next four games against the Giants. Chase had one hit in three at bats in the first game of the series, a 4–2 loss on August 6, raising his batting average to .301. There his average would remain, for on the following day Mathewson suspended Chase indefinitely for "indifferent playing" and ordered the star first baseman to return to Cincinnati.[29]

At first the press attributed the suspension to nothing more sinister than the first baseman's notorious lack of punctuality. Chase "lounged blithely in" just before the August 7 game at the Polo Grounds, explained William A. Phelon in *The Sporting News,* and "had been doing the same thing quite frequently of late around the circuit." Finally "the long-suffering manager" had had enough. "Matty doesn't bawl out his men, nor does he give them rough calls," noted Phelon, "but he does insist on everybody's showing up ready for preliminary practice."[30]

Chase's teammates were reported to be pleased with Mathewson's action; indeed, several felt that it was long overdue. "A number of the players have felt for some time that there were occasions on which Hal was not exerting himself to the limit of his well-known ability," wrote Ryder delicately in the August 8

Enquirer. A day later he wrote, "It is not a pleasant thing to say about so fine a natural player as Chase, but the other players on the team nearly all have expressed themselves as glad that he is out of the line-up." Phelon noted that Chase could still pull off the occasional sensational play, but "every now and then he has been letting easy rollers hit right at him, go past.... On several occasions these mishaps have hurt the team's chances, and caused more or less friction between Chase and the pitchers."[31]

Mathewson initially tried to downplay the significance of his actions, implying that he would eventually lift the suspension when he felt that Chase had learned his lesson. "We are trying hard to finish in the first division with a chance of slipping into third place," Matty explained. "Our pitching staff is very weak and we need the most earnest work on the part of every player on the team. I will not stand for indifferent or careless playing on the part of a man of such great natural ability as Hal possesses. I think a lay off will do him good."[32]

But the matter would not blow over so easily. First Chase characteristically refused to obey Matty's order to return to Cincinnati. He missed his train on the evening of August 8, even though business manager Frank Bancroft had given him his ticket, and announced that he would stay in New York until Mathewson reinstated him. The local press portrayed this decision as an insult to Cincinnati. "When Chase joined the Reds he brought his wife to Cincinnati and became a resident citizen, instead of going home to California [during the winter], as he had done in other years," wrote Phelon. "He became immensely well liked round town, making hundreds of friends, and is now counted as a real Cincinnatian." Now the fans were confused as they attempted to reconcile their devotion to Chase with their loyalty to the team. "One thing they didn't like: the fact that Chase stayed in New York, instead of coming home to Cincinnati."[33]

Soon the Chase affair no longer seemed to be merely a matter of a manager attempting to discipline a temperamental star. Although the Reds would not reveal the precise nature of Chase's alleged crime, their extreme reaction made clear the seriousness of his offense. "Hal Chase will never play another game for the Reds so long as Mathewson is manager or at any other time," reported Jack Ryder on August 10. Matty had long been suspicious of Chase, wrote Ryder, and had undertaken an investigation of the first baseman's actions. "Matty believes that he has absolute proof that Chase was not trying on several occasions, and he is done with him forever." Prince Hal's teammates were not sorry to hear the news: "Most of the players have been wise to Chase's methods for some time and they are tickled to death that he is through with the club.... After Matty has a conference with President Herrmann, it is probable that Chase's baseball career will be ended. It's a tough finish for a player of pleasing personality and great natural brilliance, but it is inevitable."[34]

More than forty years later one contemporary observer offered a different explanation for Mathewson's suspension of Chase. Tom Swope covered the Reds for the Cincinnati *Post* for forty-one years, beginning in 1915. In 1960 Swope claimed in a letter that "practically all the Reds knew Chase bet regularly on the club's games, sometimes that the Reds would win, more often, likely, that they would lose," but apparently Matty did not consider this eccentricity serious enough to warrant suspending Chase. The issue that finally brought the manager's wrath down on Chase, according to Swope, was a game of cards.

Swope wrote that Mathewson and Ryder, both of whom were "stingy and grasping in financial matters," were avid bridge players. Early in the season they recruited Chase and pitcher Mike Regan to make up a foursome, and proceeded to beat them regularly. "After a few sessions Chase, always a crook, told Regan that they were up against a bad situation in bridge and should do something to even the competition because they knew so little of the game." Chase devised a system of signals involving "the way he handled his ever present cigar." When Regan was drafted in August, however, the thought that he might die with his involvement in this dishonest scheme still on his conscience drove him to confess the plot to Matty. Only then, according to Swope, did Mathewson do "what other Reds had been asking him for weeks to do [i.e., suspend Chase]."[35]

Certainly this story, if true, reflects no great credit on Mathewson, whose honesty and integrity have always been considered above reproach. Swope was obviously no great fan of Matty's, and his account may not be entirely trustworthy. But Chase did have a reputation as a card-shark. "A strange character, a very strange character," former teammate Gabby Street called him when he heard of the suspension. "A fellow I never want to meet in a card game." Street had been an onlooker during a 1912 poker game between Chase and five or six other players: "Chase played his cards conservatively, frequently passing. But then, suddenly, when a big pot had built up, Hal raised every time it was his turn to bid. I noticed he had three kings. Then I looked again and he had four kings. The additional king must have come from a sleight-of-hand operation, for Chase was famous for his speed and agility. I never knew where that extra king came from, but later I saw a low card disappear out of Chase's hand with the speed of a magician's trick. He must have had the king early and whisked it out when it would do him the most good."[36]

Similarly, another former teammate, Ray Fisher, recalled Chase as a generous, if crooked, companion during poker games among the Yankee players: "if he wasn't playing, he'd sit right down next to you and see what you needed and he'd be trying to hand you the cards so you would cheat. Good fellow, but just wanted to do things that weren't right."[37]

After Herrmann and Mathewson met on August 10 the Reds president announced that Chase was officially suspended without pay for the rest of the season. "This is a case which will bear searching investigation," said Herrmann. "Matty is sure that he has the goods on Chase and we will go to the limit to find out the exact truth with regard to his action in certain games. It is a shame that a player of such great ability and brilliant qualifications should fail to give his best efforts on all occasions. He will never play another game of ball for us, and I rather think that his baseball career is completely over. There can be no halfway measures in a case of this kind." Again, just what kind of case that might be was not specified, although by now the implication that Chase was accused of having thrown ballgames was becoming clearer. Mathewson told Ryder that the Reds would have finished in second place, with an outside chance at the pennant, if not for Chase.[38]

Chase finally returned to Cincinnati on August 11 and watched the Reds split a doubleheader with the Cardinals "from a secluded nook in the upper stand." He claimed to have no idea why the Reds had suspended him and proclaimed his innocence of all charges, whatever they might be. Herrmann was asked if he would summon Chase for a meeting. "No," he replied starchily. "It is up to him to make a move, if he wants to. He has received his notice of suspension for the rest of the season, and I guess he knows what it means. I will be ready to see him when he calls, and to tell him what Manager Mathewson has discovered, but I shall not send for him."[39]

Chase met with Herrmann on the following day, and learned that Mathewson had compiled "a volume of evidence concerning Chase's action" which the club would forward to the National League. Only then would Chase be given a copy of the evidence. Chase continued to proclaim his innocence, and threatened to sue the Reds for his unpaid salary and for damages to his character.[40]

Herrmann shrugged and busied himself collecting affidavits from other players while continuing to express his shock and dismay at the charges against Chase. Yet Ryder let slip the fact that the charges were anything but news to the Reds president: "Mr. Herrmann had heard many rumors concerning Chase, both during the season and last year, but could hardly believe them. He was astounded when he read what Manager Mathewson had gathered." *The Sporting News* reported that "a man who has been traveling with the Reds" said that "the Chase matter has been developing since the first of June." Nevertheless Herrmann maintained his public show of surprised innocence: "I wish and hope that Chase can clear himself of the charges," he said on August 12. "Yet, I must say, the evidence against him looks damaging — there is a great deal of it, and it seems accurate and straightforward." A few days later he said, "The evidence is appalling. I would not have believed such things possible in the case of a player of the ability of Chase."[41]

While Herrmann was rounding up evidence and shaking his head in sorrowful wonder, Chase took the offensive. "Let's not dodge around the bush," he told *The Sporting News*. "I'm accused of betting on ball games and trying to get a pitcher to throw a game for money. I'm accused of frequenting pool rooms and making baseball bets. I've gone into pool rooms and made bets on horses, but I say right here [that I] have made no baseball bets and have never thrown the team. As a result, rumors have it that I was wagering $100 at a crack. Who would either take or offer a baseball bet running up into the hundreds? As a sample of the wild talk, I was accused in New York not of betting against the Reds, but of offering a certain Giant pitcher $800 to let us beat him."

An editorial in the same issue of the magazine, while acknowledging that he was "far from being a loveable character in spite of his talents," admitted to "a certain admiration for Chase" for having the courage to air the charges against him while his accusers were keeping them a secret. "A man who comes out like that makes a good point in his defense — even though there may be method in his boldness."[42]

Of course Chase was nothing if not bold. The "certain Giant pitcher" he referred to was William Dayton Perritt, a Louisiana native whose nickname, inevitably, was Pol. Perritt was one of McGraw's best pitchers, on his way to eighteen wins in 1918. He had probably met Chase in the spring of 1916, which both players spent with the San Francisco Seals. Chase had approached Perritt before a game at Redland Field and engaged him in a conversation, the exact details of which remained unclear. Perritt, however, reportedly assumed that Chase was attempting to bribe him, and reacted angrily. Another Giant player, outfielder Ross Youngs, also reportedly had had "serious talks with Chase," but refused to go on the record.[43]

The New York pitcher declined to discuss the matter after informing his manager of what had occurred. "Perritt refused to go into details," recalled McGraw, "except to say that he should have punched Chase in the eye for what he said. Perritt added that Chase should be put out of baseball." McGraw, however, seemed disinclined to take the matter seriously. "It is hard to believe the charges against Chase. He may have been kidding Perritt. He is a practical joker and says many things he doesn't mean."[44]

This explanation sounded rather far-fetched, however, and other bits of circumstantial evidence seemed to confirm the case against Chase. *The Sporting News* reported that several of Chase's teammates, including Sherry Magee, Groh, and Neale, had also accused him of offering bribes, and during the Reds' last Eastern trip opposing players had taken to yelling at Chase, "Well, Hal, what are the odds today?"[45]

Such ugly incidents were part of a larger and more ominous pattern. In 1918, with horse racing shut down for the duration of the war, gamblers and fixers increasingly turned to baseball. "The betting evil grew steadily during the past season in Cincinnati, and actually reached a point where it should have been summarily checked," wrote William Phelon in early August. He implied that many gamblers had inside information regarding the outcome of at least one game: "I was astounded Thursday at the magnitude of the bets offered on Brooklyn to beat the Reds." (On Thursday, August 1, Cincinnati lost 4–0 in Brooklyn.) Shortly thereafter he warned, "When the big house cleaning comes in baseball after the war, one of the first things to be tended to will be the gambling stuff. It has been growing stronger and more dangerous this season than ever." *The Sporting News* reported that "gambling cliques" based in New York and Boston "have been trying to corrupt big league players all season" and estimated that as many as fifty major league stars had been offered bribes.[46]

The same editorial that cautiously praised Chase for his openness in airing the charges against him reflected a strong nativist resentment of American involvement in European affairs. It issued a rather equivocal warning to the owners: "The magnates have been mighty careless about the gambling thing," admitted the magazine, although it stopped short of condemning all betting. Indeed, continued the editorial, the sporting wager was quintessentially American: "Our whole business system and everything else in which a dollar is involved as profit is more or less of a gamble. But there are gamblers and gamblers and there is gambling and gambling. Any man with an honest bone in his body and a bit of sportsmanship in his makeup knows where to draw the line either in business or wagering on the result of a deal of the cards or the direction of a batted ball." The true source of baseball's current trouble was "the pasty-faced and clammy-fingered gentry with the hooked noses"—that is, professional gamblers of foreign, specifically Jewish, extraction. No doubt the magazine had such men as McGraw's old chum Arnold Rothstein in mind when it published this description.

"The problem," concluded the editorial, "is to clean out the crooks and the would-be sure thing guys who don't make a bet for sport sake [sic] as gentlemen will, but seek to put something over by hook or crook, even to the point of bribing a ball player if they can."[47]

This argument reinforced Chase's strategy in defending himself. While admitting that he may have occasionally made "'piker' bets like $10 or $20" on his own team, as a true sport would, he firmly denied ever betting against his own team or attempting to bribe other players. William Phelon seemed inclined to believe him. While citing "unquestioned evidence" that Chase had twice bet "a flock of coin" during the postseason series between Cincinnati and Cleveland in 1917, Phelon wrote that Chase had backed the Reds each time, "betting honestly on his own team." Such bets were at worst minor sins, although they were not to be condoned: "When a player bets on his own club, he'll surely do his best to win, but, as Chase has acknowledged to me, it is a bad practice just the same. If you have money on your own club, and somebody's error loses both the game and your money, you can't help feeling grouchy and sore towards the unlucky error-maker, and that stuff doesn't tend towards harmony on the team."

Still, wrote Phelon, those bets were the worst that could plausibly be charged to Chase. He dismissed as "a skyrocket flight of romance" the story that Chase had offered Perritt $800 to throw a game: "If Chase could afford to give a hostile pitcher $800, he must have had several times $800 at stake—and where, in New York, would you find any such amount risked on any ball game? That sort of stuff looks impossible on the face of it, and all fair-minded fans will hope that the remaining charges against Chase will prove as gauzy."[48]

On August 21 Herrmann finally turned over to the National League the evidence that he and Mathewson had accumulated, which supposedly included affidavits from six policemen showing that Chase had bet against the Reds as often as he bet on them. Phelon reported that the Reds had spoken to a number of bookmakers and gamblers in Cincinnati seeking evidence that Chase had bet against the team, but still sounded skeptical: "For my own part, all I can say is that one man, whose place has long been counted as a handbook headquarters, claims that Chase bet and lost $100 in his resort, putting his money on the Reds to win, and that he also lost $100 on Chase's tip that the Reds couldn't lose."[49]

Chase had promised to stay in Cincinnati and fight to clear his name, so his supporters were surprised when Ryder reported on August 23 that Chase had "ducked out on the uncongenial climate of this vicinity," giving up his flat on Probasco Avenue and leaving for New York. Herrmann, attempting to serve formal notice of the charges on Chase a few days later, admitted to Heydler that he had been unable to find the player. "The story here is that he has gone to New York," wrote Herrmann, no doubt secretly relieved that Chase was no longer his sole responsibility.[50] Before skipping town, however, Chase had hired a Cincinnati attorney, Robert S. Alcorn, and filed suit against the Reds on August 26 for $1,670 in back salary lost during his suspension. He added that the affidavits collected by Herrmann were false, based on gossip or spite.

Herrmann met with his attorney, Howard Ragland, and announced that he welcomed the suit. "The trial will be a good thing for the game," said Herrmann, "as it will enable us to bring out all the evidence in legal form for the benefit of the public."[51] In fact, as his correspondence with National League president John Heydler revealed, Herrmann was less concerned with uncovering the truth than with concealing anything that might damage baseball's reputation for honesty. "I realize that the charges [against Chase] are serious and that everything connected therewith must be done in the most careful way," he wrote on August 29. Several weeks later he wrote that his old friend Ban Johnson "was strongly of the opinion that if the testimony warrants [Chase's] expulsion, that the reason for it should not be made public. The evidence is so damaging that [Johnson] believes, and I agree with him, that it would be a severe 'black eye' for the game if the details became fully known."[52]

Heydler shared Herrmann's concerns, but responded, with some exasperation, that "The charges against Chase have already received full publication in sporting columns of eastern papers. No one is in doubt as to what these charges are."[53] The Chase case had already caused Heydler a great deal of frustration. The National League president had tried to have formal notice of the charges served on Chase in Cincinnati in late August, but Herrmann had written back confessing that no one knew Chase's exact whereabouts. Eventually the league hired a detective agency that tracked Chase to New York. The papers were served on him at West Side Park in Jersey City on September 15.[54]

Meanwhile, as if to confirm Mathewson's statement that Chase had kept the team from contending for the pennant, the Reds were playing their best ball of the season without their star first baseman. On August 7, when Matty suspended Chase, they were in fifth place with a 43–52 record. Mathewson himself, disgusted with the events of the season, had applied for a captain's commission in the Chemical Warfare Service. Three weeks later, when the commission came through and Mathewson left for France, the Reds had won eighteen of their last twenty-three games. Under the temporary leadership of Heinie Groh they won seven of the last ten games of the season to finish in third place with a 68–60 record, five games behind the second-place Giants. "It makes a whole lot of difference when every man is trying his best to win every day," observed Ryder pointedly.[55]

After the season several Cincinnati players calculated that Chase had cost the Reds as many as twenty-seven victories, a total which would have put them far ahead of the first-place Cubs. "This is, of course, an absurd figure," admitted Ryder, "but there is no doubt that Chase was a serious handicap to the club at times, and that they would at least have beaten out the Giants and finished in second place if Sherwood Magee had been stationed at first base throughout the entire season."[56]

The Chase affair was not the only crisis afflicting major league baseball during that tempestuous winter. Recent events had convinced owners in both leagues that baseball's system of internal governance, based on the three-man National Commission, had outlived its usefulness. Those two old friends Ban Johnson and Garry Herrmann, who for so many years had sat together on the commission, were taking most of the blame.

Many already blamed Johnson for the shortened 1918 season, which had resulted in lower revenues than had been anticipated. In late October Johnson alienated them further by announcing that he would oppose any suggestion to resume play in the American League until 1920 or the end of the war. His statement drew heavy criticism from the owners, and he quickly backed down.[57]

Many owners also blamed Johnson for the resignation of National League president John K. Tener, the former governor of Pennsylvania. In June the Philadelphia Athletics and Boston Braves had locked horns in a dispute over the services of pitcher Scott Perry. Because Perry had previously been the property of a minor league team in Atlanta, the question of where he should play was to be decided by the National Commission, the secretary of the National Association, and the president of the minor league.

By a three-to-two vote they awarded Perry to the Braves, but manager Connie Mack of the Athletics refused to accept the decision. Instead, he broke with baseball's tradition of settling disputes in-house and took the matter to the courts, with, in the words of one historian, "at least the tacit approval" of Johnson, who had been one of the two votes in favor of awarding Perry to Philadelphia.

Mack gained an injunction preventing Perry from joining the Braves, thereby outraging the National League. Tener refused to resume his place on the National Commission until Mack surrendered Perry to Boston, and recommended cancelling the World Series unless the American League backed down. But the National League owners were unwilling to back him in this radical suggestion, and Tener resigned. He was replaced on an interim basis by league secretary John A. Heydler.

Heydler helped negotiate a compromise solution to the Perry case whereby the Athletics kept Perry, dropped the injunction, and paid the Braves $2,500

Eight—A Severe "Black Eye" for the Game

National League president John Heydler officially cleared Chase of Mathewson's charges in January 1919, although he later claimed to have had little doubt of Chase's guilt. *National Baseball Hall of Fame Library, Cooperstown, N.Y.*

compensation.[58] But the whole affair had besmirched baseball's image as a polite and self-patrolling society of sportsmen.

That image received another blow during the World Series, when the Red Sox and Cubs players decided to strike in protest of a National Commission vote reducing their shares of World Series money. The start of the fifth game in Boston was delayed for an hour as the members of the Commission, including an obviously inebriated Johnson, cajoled and threatened the players. Eventually the players gave in, having been promised that they would not be punished, but the Commission later spitefully announced that they would not be allowed to wear the traditional World Series badges on their uniforms.[59]

The Cincinnati *Enquirer* argued that Johnson's action in the Scott Perry case "unfits him to sit on any baseball court,"[60] and increasingly the American League owners were inclined to agree. In late November Harry Frazee, owner of the Red Sox, and Harry Hempstead, owner of the Giants, offered former President William Howard Taft the position of sole member of the National Commission. Taft expressed interest in such a position, but said that he would not accept the offer until his brother Charles sold off all his stock in the Cubs.[61]

Ultimately nothing came of the offer to Taft, but Frazee and Johnson continued as bitter enemies. In early December Frazee, disgusted with Johnson, talked of selling the Red Sox and buying the National League Giants. Johnson in turn charged Frazee with permitting gambling in Fenway Park and threatened to drive him out of the league. The charge was probably true, though Frazee was hardly the only guilty owner, but the attack backfired. The other owners felt that Johnson was overstepping himself, and no doubt resented his bringing the gambling issue out into the open. "I personally know that Frazee has taken measures, as has every magnate in the circuit, to keep the games of Fenway Park closed to the gambling crowd," said Charles Comiskey. "If Johnson has the good of baseball at heart he will lay off the gambling end of it and not be so interested in buying out owners in the American League. He has no authority to oust Frazee."[62]

Meanwhile, sentiment was growing in the National League that Herrmann should not be reelected to the National Commission. Barney Dreyfuss, owner of the Pittsburgh Pirates, held a grudge against Herrmann stemming from a National Commission decision awarding George Sisler to the St. Louis Browns instead of Dreyfuss's club in 1916. Other owners, including Harry Hempstead, pointed to the outcome of the Perry case as further evidence that Herrmann was too easily swayed to the American League point of view by his old friend Johnson. These men argued that a neutral National Commission chairman was a necessity.[63]

Herrmann was ultimately reelected to the National Commission for another year, thanks to some last-minute lobbying by Johnson, but the owners appointed a search committee to find a neutral chairman. The beleaguered Reds president was also experiencing problems on the home front in 1918. In early December Julius Fleischmann charged that the Reds had defaulted on interest payments on bonds he held, and threatened to take over the club unless its front office was reorganized. At the National League meetings in New York that month a rumor circulated that McGraw, who had long aspired to ownership of a ballclub, would buy the Reds, with the assistance of Fleischmann. Again, Herrmann survived; the McGraw rumor, of course, proved false, and Fleischmann was appeased.[64] Finally Herrmann could turn his attention to the problem of who would manage the Reds in 1919.

Matty's early departure in 1918 and association with the Chase affair, which was threatening to become a major embarrassment to the Cincinnati club, may have convinced Herrmann that a change was necessary, although he did not dare say so publicly. Perhaps Mathewson, disgusted with the atmosphere in Cincinnati, had already decided that he did not want his old job back. Another possible explanation is that McGraw never had actually dropped his demand for a two-year recall on Matty's services, and finally called in his chits; Mathewson eventually did rejoin the Giants as a coach for the 1919 season, although he never got the chance to succeed McGraw as manager.

Whatever the actual reason, Herrmann finally decided to seek a new manager after a number of well-publicized and unsuccessful attempts to contact Mathewson in France to find out whether he would be back in time for the start of the season. The Cincinnati newspapers reported that either Pat Moran, recently fired as manager of the Phillies, or Clarence (Pants) Rowland, former manager of the White Sox, would take over the Reds.[65]

Moran had just signed a contract as the Giants' pitching coach, but McGraw gave him permission to negotiate with Herrmann. Many assumed that McGraw's unaccustomed generosity of spirit had something to do with the Giants' unresolved first base situation. McGraw was through with Walter Holke, the young first baseman who had jumped the Giants in late July to play in the shipyard leagues.[66] Now McGraw needed a first baseman to take Holke's place. Two players appeared the most likely candidates: Jake Daubert and Hal Chase.

Brooklyn owner Charles H. Ebbets was willing to part with Daubert because the star first baseman was complaining loudly about not being paid the full $9,000 salary for which his contract called. When the owners had terminated the 1918 season prematurely they had also released all their players, using the ten-day clause, in order to avoid paying them the full salaries called for in their contracts.

Technically this maneuver meant that every major league player was now a free agent, but of course the owners had no intention of actually letting their players sell themselves to the highest bidder. In late December Detroit's Ty Cobb declared himself a free agent and announced that he would entertain offers from other teams, but the National Commission quickly ruled that all players had to return to their former clubs. "Thus the owners had it both ways," wrote Harold Seymour: "they saved an estimated $200,000 in payrolls and at the same time retained their monopsony control over their players, pending the reopening of business."[67]

Daubert, however, had threatened to sue to recover the salary he had lost through this ploy, and Ebbets decided to get rid of him. One rumor that circulated during the National League meetings in December held that McGraw had already acquired Daubert in exchange for Holke and pitcher George Smith. Other rumors held that Daubert would be dealt to the Reds, and that McGraw would sign Chase instead, assuming that Prince Hal was cleared of the charges against him. Releasing Moran to Cincinnati had supposedly been the price the Giants paid in return for the first option on Chase's services.[68]

"If McGraw is able to include Chase on the New York roster," predicted the New York *Times*, "his main problems will be solved."[69] But others saw two obstacles to this plan. For one thing, McGraw was supposed to be a hostile witness against Chase in the first baseman's hearing, corroborating Perritt's story. While McGraw's admiration of Chase's abilities was common knowledge, under the circumstances it seemed unlikely that he would care to have Chase on his team, even if the league cleared him.

Such an assumption failed to take into account McGraw's pragmatism. That he was not particularly choosy about his associates, as long as they enabled him to get what he wanted, was made abundantly clear on January 14, 1919, when he joined with Charles A. Stoneham and Francis X. McQuade to buy the Giants from Hempstead. Stoneham was the proprietor of a notorious "bucket-shop" who operated on the semilegal fringes of Wall Street. He "handled other people's money without scruple or responsibility," according to one historian, and his fondness for gambling was well known; in fact, one account says that McGraw and Stoneham put the deal together with the help of their mutual friend Arnold Rothstein. McQuade, the magistrate who had dismissed the case against Mathewson and McGraw for violating the state law banning Sunday baseball in 1917, was a prominent figure in Tammany Hall. If McGraw felt comfortable being in business with men like Stoneham, McQuade, and Rothstein, he could have no objection to employing Chase. Besides, McGraw had a long history of reclaiming veteran troublemakers, such as Heinie Zimmerman, from other clubs.[70]

The second obstacle to Chase's joining the Giants, of course, was the possibility that he might be thrown out of baseball. Herrmann sounded confident that the case against Chase was airtight: "We will have three men as witnesses against Chase. I am sorry to present such a spectacle, but these men are teammates of Chase on the Cincinnati club. They are Neale, Ring and Regan. One of the men who filed an affidavit against Chase is John J. McGraw, so I do not take much stock in the story that the New York Club is trying to clear Chase so as to sign him to play first base for the Giants."[71]

But McGraw frankly admitted that he doubted the charges against Chase. "I have no quarrel with Chase," he told Sid Mercer of the New York *Globe* about a week before the hearing. "I made an affidavit merely because I was asked to. There is nothing in it to prove anything except, perhaps, that Hal talked foolishly. He is still a great first baseman, and I would like to have him if he can clear himself. You can say that if he does and Garry Herrmann puts him on the market I will try to get him for the Giants."

Mercer was an old friend of Chase, and in his column he provided a forum for the suspended player to tell his side of the story. "I have already been put to great trouble and expense on this thing," complained Chase. "In the first place, my baseball income stopped suddenly last summer and I haven't drawn a cent since. I haven't had a fair deal. It looks like somebody is trying to get me for other things that have happened in my baseball career."

Mercer was openly scornful of the National League's handling of the affair. After dismissing the affidavits collected by the Reds as "nothing but 'hearsay' evidence," he noted that Prince Hal had already been all but tried and convicted in the court of public opinion: "Chase was pilloried in the public press and has never had a chance to combat the feeling against him."

Mercer's loyalty—he would serve as a character witness for Chase at the hearing, although he neglected to mention this fact to his readers—probably led Chase and his attorney to share with Mercer some of the documents in the case. Thus the newspaperman knew in advance the precise nature of the charges against his old friend, and attempted manfully to downplay their significance: "Ring swears that Chase attempted to give him a sum of money after he (Ring) had pitched and lost a game to the Boston Braves. He does not charge that Chase tried to influence him to throw the game.

"Regan's affidavit tells of a wager that Chase and himself made on the Reds to win a game—a thing that is done by major league players often. Perritt's brief statement deals with a conversation in which Chase asked Perritt whether he was going to pitch the second game of a doubleheader between the Giants and Reds.

"As far as is known there are no other charges. Mathewson's complaint is more or less of a general accusation that Chase was not playing his best game— that he was not trying."

After thus disposing of the charges Mercer concluded with a warning: "Chase has made his mistakes, but he is not on trial for them now. It is a serious thing to drive a star ball player out of baseball and brand him for life as a dishonest man. The National League should go slow and demand absolute proof of these charges."[72]

Heydler had originally set January 22 as the date of Chase's hearing but postponed it until January 30 at the request of Chase's attorney. As the date of the hearing drew closer Chase's allies in the press stepped up their campaign on his behalf. They portrayed the first baseman as a victim of petty jealousies and personality conflicts. Ever since the suspension, wrote Mercer on January 27, "the National League has attempted to link up a strong chain of evidence, but from all accounts it has failed. It seems to be fairly certain now that nothing more than a case of indifferent playing can be made out against Chase, if, indeed, that much can be proved. Chase says not. He declares Mathewson took a dislike to him and was only too willing to listen to the tales of other Cincinnati players who were not friendly to the first baseman."

Mercer also attacked the National League while carefully avoiding direct criticism of Heydler: "Probably President Heydler would not object to an open session, to which representatives of the press would be admitted, but the well known 'back stairs' policy of the National League is to cover up all its dirty linen and hand the public plausible statements that seldom do justice to both sides of a controversy." Mercer also called the hearing a "'star chamber' trial," although he continued to defend Heydler's personal integrity. While noting that the league would be "judge, jury and prosecution in this case," Mercer added that "John Heydler is an eminently fair official and can be depended upon to render a verdict in keeping with the evidence."[73]

Robert Ripley, the *Globe* cartoonist who later gained fame as the originator of "Ripley's Believe It or Not," was less tactful than Mercer. In a cartoon entitled "Keeping It Dark," Ripley depicted a baseball player, labelled "National League," sneaking down the "Back Stairs" of National League headquarters at night. Over his shoulder he carried a bag, labelled "Chase," from which emanated the yowls of an angry cat. The worried player was saying, "Wonder where the nearest river is?"[74]

Mercer's *Globe* colleague Harry Schumacher put in his two cents' worth as well: "The present writer was with the Giants throughout the trip on which Chase is supposed to have 'approached' Perritt and heard much of the players' gossip precipitated by the incident. Some of the Reds were extremely bitter in their critique of Chase, but not one could or would say that Hal had ever so much as suggested that they might profit through deliberately falling down in a pinch. Ring is expected to testify that Chase gave him $25 after he had blown a game at Boston, but will also testify that Hal made no dishonorable overtures either before or during the game in question. The rest of the evidence against Chase is understood to be of an equally circumstantial character."

Schumacher also reported that the Cubs might be interested in Chase, since they were looking for a replacement for Fred Merkle at first base, but probably would not be able to match whatever McGraw might offer in exchange for Chase. That the Cubs would want Chase seems unlikely, since Chase had supposedly driven their manager, Fred Mitchell, out of the American League when Mitchell was a backup catcher with the Yankees during Chase's tenure as manager. Schumacher concluded by predicting that "the case against [Chase] will collapse for want of supporting evidence."[75]

By the day of the hearing this point of view seemed to be gaining popularity. An editorial in *The Sporting News* proclaimed the magazine's "belief, unless the evidence is stronger than it appeared to be at the time the charges were made, that the only decision can be to clear Chase, and no admiration for him as a man influences that opinion." Joe Vila called the hearing "one of those secret affairs which never appeal to the public," and accused the National League of bungling the whole affair: "I hold no brief for Chase. He has nobody but himself to blame for his present troubles. But I do believe that the matter should have been investigated many weeks ago and that the National League should have wiped it off the books before it received so much unnecessary publicity." Walter St. Denis, Mercer's colleague at the *Globe,* added, "The league is to be censured for not conducting a quiet investigation last summer, when the charges could have been threshed out in a few days without subjecting the player to the humiliation he has endured."[76]

Vila and St. Denis were merely echoing Mercer, who wrote, "The whole affair now sizes up as just one more National League mistake. Instead of branding Chase as a dishonest player last summer the league should have immediately and in secret conducted the investigation and either expelled the player then or hushed up the matter."[77] Thus the National League was attacked for failing to handle the matter secretly back in August, as soon as Mathewson suspended Chase, and for attempting to handle the matter secretly in January.

Chase arrived in New York on January 29, still insisting that the flap against him was all a misunderstanding: "I am no longer a youngster, and I haven't very long to remain in baseball, but I certainly do not want to go out that way. I have said right along that if I could have a few minutes' talk with Heydler I could quickly convince him that I have done nothing wrong." On the following morning he showed up at Heydler's office with three attorneys — his brother-in-law Rudolph Cherurg; J. Franklin Tausch, "well-known as a cross-examiner"; and Harry Cherlet — and a stenographer.[78] Heydler was assisted by National League counsel John Conway Toole. Ring, Neale, and Regan were present, as was McGraw. Character witnesses for Chase included Mercer, I. O. De Passe, and L. E. Rich. Mathewson was still in France, and Perritt sent word from his Louisiana farm that he would be unable to attend. The Reds did not trouble to send an official representative; Herrmann was only too happy to dump full responsibility for the case in Heydler's lap.[79]

The absence of Mathewson and Perritt did not help the prosecution's case. Neither did McGraw's uncooperativeness. In fact, the Giant manager's involvement in the hearing raised a few eyebrows, given his admitted interest in Chase. "John McGraw's intentions may be the best in the world — if it is his plan to make use of Chase in case of a verdict of not guilty," editorialized *The Sporting News.* "He may be taking him on even out of the goodness of his heart to give him a fresh chance. But all these things considered, it would be far better if the former peer of first sackers were found employment elsewhere [than with the Giants]."[80]

Despite the absence of Mathewson and Perritt and the dubious presence of McGraw, however, many expected that the testimony of the three Cincinnati players would be sufficient grounds for expelling Chase from organized baseball. Indeed, the tales that they told did Chase little credit.

Ring said that Chase had offered him a bribe as he took the mound in relief of Regan during a game in Philadelphia on August 24, 1917. Ring refused the bribe, but gave up two hits and one run during two innings of work in a 6–5 Cincinnati loss. On the following morning, he said, Chase had casually dropped a roll of bills in his lap. That afternoon Cincinnati lost a doubleheader to the

Phillies, 4–3 in ten innings and 2–1. In the first game Chase had one hit, a sixth-inning home run off Grover Cleveland Alexander, to drive in all three Cincinnati runs. In the fourth inning Toney had been unable to handle his toss to first base on Bert Niehoff's grounder, allowing the second Phillie run to score. Regan had told Mathewson that Chase offered him $200 to lose the second game of that doubleheader, while Neale testified that Chase said that he had won $500 betting on that doubleheader. According to Neale, Chase said that he was particularly glad to win the $500 because he had recently lost $1,500 shooting craps.[81]

Curiously, Mercer reported that "The three Cincinnati players and John J. McGraw, manager of the Giants, gave testimony that was nearly all favorable to Chase." The league could produce no evidence substantiating the testimony of the players, so it was their word against Chase's, and Chase was nothing if not articulate. "He was quick witted, answered every question put to him without a second's hesitation, and stuck to his original story through a decidedly vigorous cross-examination," reported Harry Schumacher. "Many a trap was laid for him, for Mr. Heydler deemed it his duty to seek evidence that would corroborate rather than refute the charges, but he avoided all of them with the skill of a born witness for the defense." Schumacher was not the only reporter who admired Chase's performance: "Chase made a fine impression when he took the stand for two hours in his own behalf," wrote Joe Vila in *The Sporting News*. "He was straight-forward and enthusiastic in his replies."[82]

Chase's strategy was simple and effective. He sought to convince Heydler that the case against him was, in the words of one reporter, "the outgrowth of prejudice, careless talk, and a factional fight on the Cincinnati team." He said that the money he had given to Ring "was merely a gift." He insisted that Neale was the head of a clique on the Reds which "had it in" for him. He confessed to a couple of minor sins, admitting that he once made a bet with another player on a National League game while he was still in the American League, and that he had bet again during the Cincinnati-Cleveland series in 1917, but only that the Reds would win. He freely discussed some of his prior difficulties in baseball. The bulk of the charges against him he denied absolutely, entering his batting and fielding averages from his three seasons in Cincinnati as evidence of his honesty and effort.[83]

The hearing lasted some five hours, the majority of which Chase himself spent on the stand. After it was over Heydler announced that he would take a week to review the evidence before rendering his decision. That decision, announced on February 5, did not surprise those who had followed the case closely. "It is nowhere established that the accused was interested in any pool or wager that caused any game to result otherwise than on its merits," declared the National League president. "The testimony showed that Chase acted in a foolish and careless manner both on the field and among the players, and that the club was justified in bringing the charges in view of the many rumors which arose from the loose talk of its first baseman. Chase did not take his work seriously, and was entirely to blame for the position in which he found himself.

There was, however, no proof that he intentionally violated or attempted to violate the rules in relation to tampering with players, or in any way endeavored to secure desired results in the outcome of games.

"Chase testified that he had bet on the result of a baseball game with another player only twice in his professional career. The first case was many seasons ago when he was a spectator at a National League contest while a member of an American League team. The other wager was made in a post-season series of 1917, when he bet on his club to win a game.

"I do not know where Chase will play during the coming season but I wish to say now that he has been proven not guilty of the charges, I hope the fans and others will give him a fair chance to overcome the unpleasant impression which has been created. I feel sure that he realizes the position in which his foolish talk and actions have placed him and will endeavor to atone by taking his work seriously and playing the brilliant ball of which he is capable."[84]

The ruling seemed carefully designed to avoid offending anyone. Chase received a mild rebuke for his carelessness, although he was officially cleared of any wrongdoing: the worst that could be said of him, wrote Harry Schumacher, was that "despite his years, Chase is still a boy at heart and looks at life through a boy's eyes. He has absolutely no sense of responsibility and takes everything as a joke."[85] The Reds had been justified in suspending him, based on his suspicious behavior. Heydler had once again registered baseball's official opposition to gambling. And John McGraw's path was now clear to sign Chase for the Giants.

The ruling was not universally hailed, especially among those who deplored organized baseball's traditional reluctance to acknowledge its problems publicly. Dan Daniel wrote that the league had "whitewashed" Chase, but Joe Vila argued that Heydler's decision had been the only possible one, given the "flimsy" nature of the charges against Chase. Heydler "didn't 'whitewash' Chase, as some critics have told their readers," insisted Vila. "If the case had been tried in a court of law it would have been dismissed by the judge before the taking of testimony. It was nothing but hearsay, rumor, innuendo and ugly gossip."[86]

Heydler himself agreed. "There was no evidence whatever produced at the trial to show that Chase had made a bet, and the only direct evidence as to his crookedness was made by Player Ring," he wrote privately to Herrmann. "On the stand, however, Ring was a poor witness and made statements differing from what he had stated in his affidavit, so much so, in fact, that I brought him back here Monday for further testimony. To have found Chase guilty on this man's unsupported testimony would have been impossible."

Heydler made clear that he was unhappy with the verdict and that he held Herrmann responsible for the outcome of the hearing, and resented the manner in which Herrmann had washed his hands of the affair. "I feel that it is unfortunate that the Cincinnati Club could not, in any manner furnish me some direct evidence that Chase had placed a bet against his team," he wrote plaintively.

"If at any time in the future, any suspicion arises as to the honesty of a player, I feel that the same should be carefully investigated by the Club preferring the charges before they are made to the president of the League and publicity given to same. The repetition of similar charges without direct and positive proof to substantiate the same will do the game irreparable harm."[87]

Most observers were happy to put the controversy behind them. Heydler's ruling was reported to come as "a distinct surprise and jolt to Garry Herrmann," but even the Cincinnati *Enquirer* admitted grudgingly that "The verdict is a good thing for the life of the game, and the sports will accept the ruling as final, as the decision was made by John Heydler, one of the most honorable and competent men in baseball." An optimistic New York writer agreed: "President Heydler's sensible ruling provides a happy ending for a controversy that might have done baseball incalculable harm. The game's reputation for cleanness is established...."[88]

In fact, rather than providing "a happy ending," the ruling may have had exactly the opposite effect. Chase's good friend Joe Gedeon spent seven years in the major leagues, the last three as the starting second baseman for the St. Louis Browns, before being expelled by Judge Landis for his "guilty knowledge" of the Black Sox fix.

Gedeon blamed his expulsion on Heydler's verdict. "I probably would not have been in this trouble if the National League had handled the Hal Chase case differently," he told Ban Johnson years later.

"Why?" asked Johnson.

"Because if Chase had been punished, it would have put the fear of God into me. I would have realized what I was doing."[89]

Gedeon was not the first to suggest that Heydler's verdict in the Chase case had encouraged others to sin. In 1920 Heydler's response to such criticism was vigorous, if understandably defensive. He insisted that "the question was not did I personally consider Chase guilty, but did I personally consider the evidence against him sufficient to warrant his expulsion from the game.... To my mind, the expulsion of a player from baseball *at that time* demanded conclusive proof.... There is now no doubt of Chase's guilt. But there was a doubt at the time and on the strength of *the limited evidence that was placed in my hands*, I did not feel warranted in condemning this player."

The subsequent revelations of corruption in baseball had apparently obviated the need for due process. "Were I confronted with a similar dilemma today I should undoubtedly immediately banish such a player from the National League and cheerfully await any libel suit or suits for damage he might care to bring against us.... The player today against whom *any* material evidence can be lodged is doomed."[90]

Nine

I Beat Them in Court Every Time

The new year began with newspapers predicting that 1919 would be "the dawn of a new era on earth."¹ Soon, however, such confidence came to seem misplaced. After having won the war, America seemed to be losing the peace, and paying a steep price for its intervention in European affairs. Such transatlantic imports as the Spanish influenza, radical socialism, and organized labor were overwhelming traditional American optimism; underlying these questions, of course, was the question of the negotiations over the Treaty of Versailles. President Wilson, obsessed with his doomed and idealistic League of Nations, seemed to ignore the domestic problems facing the country. The mood at home grew dark, pessimistic, even cynical.² Violent confrontation seemed to govern relations between capital and labor, radical and conservative, black and white.

In late January, for example, twenty-five thousand shipyard workers walked off the job in Seattle, and the city's Central Labor Council voted to support them with the first general strike in the nation's history. In mid–April, eight thousand operators of the New England Telephone and Telegraph Company went on strike. On May Day, socialists and police clashed in Cleveland and Boston, and soldiers and sailors broke up the offices of the socialist newspaper *The Call*. The intended victims of a May Day bombing plot included, among others, Oliver Wendell Holmes Jr., John D. Rockefeller, J. P. Morgan Jr., and federal judge Kenesaw Mountain Landis, the erstwhile trustbuster who had more recently handed out stiff sentences to Socialist Victor Berger and Wobbly Big Bill Haywood under the Sedition Act. In early May, a race riot broke out in Charleston, South Carolina. In early June, bombs went off in eight cities, one on the doorstep of Attorney General A. Mitchell Palmer. Three weeks later, the first major race riot in American history broke out in Washington, D.C. And on June 28, the Treaty of Versailles was signed.

The treaty was seen by many as a betrayal of the principles for which the nation had gone to war, and as the ultimate expression of European cynicism and hypocrisy. "We had such high hopes of this adventure; we believed God called us," wrote Henry White, "and now at the end we are put to doing hell's dirtiest work, starving people, grabbing territory — or helping to grab it for our friends; standing by while the grand gesture of revenge and humiliation links this war up with the interminable chain of wars that runs back to Cain."[3]

And the bad news just kept coming. In Chicago on July 27, a young black boy was stoned to death after swimming across an imaginary color line off a Lake Michigan beach, setting off a five-day conflagration that left thirty-eight people dead and more than five hundred injured. On September 9, virtually the entire Boston police force went on strike, and mobs began looting the city until Governor Calvin Coolidge took over the city. On September 22, three hundred and fifty thousand steelworkers went on strike after Judge Elbert Gary, the chairman of the United States Steel Company, refused to meet with a union committee. And on September 28, a lynch mob in Omaha murdered a black man suspected of raping a white woman.[4] William Butler Yeats captured the spirit of the times on both sides of the Atlantic: "Things fall apart; the center cannot hold; / Mere anarchy is loosed upon the world...."[5]

This was the backdrop against which the 1919 World Series, between two of Hal Chase's former teams — the heavily favored White Sox and the surprising Reds — took place. Perhaps, given the general atmosphere of civilization in decline, a sense that one had better grab what one could while one still could, it should have been no surprise that a group of the White Sox players accepted bribes to throw the World Series.

The plot would not be revealed for almost another year, despite rumors at the time of the Series that all was not well; and even now, more than eighty years later, many of the details remain mysterious (witness the ongoing controversies over the involvement or noninvolvement of Joe Jackson and Buck Weaver). But in terms of its long-term effect on the nation's psyche, it is doubtful that any of the other disasters of 1919 had such a demoralizing effect on the nation as a whole. No longer could baseball present itself as the last bastion of traditional American virtues; no longer could the public look to the game for relief from the bad news which seemed to dominate the newspapers. Instead baseball was shown to be susceptible to the same cynical manipulation that seemed to characterize so many other facets of American life.

In the spring of the year, however, there were no ominous clouds on baseball's horizon. Indeed, most fans were relieved that the problems of 1918, including the shortened schedule and the Chase affair, were in the past. The Reds had decided that they did not want Chase back in 1919, regardless of the outcome of the hearing.[6] In fact, they had already acquired Jake Daubert from Brooklyn to play first base. With Heydler's verdict in hand, John McGraw could once again turn his attention to engineering a deal for Chase.

Initially most experts assumed that McGraw would give the Reds a pitcher in return for Chase, since pitching seemed to be Cincinnati's weak point. But when the deal was finally announced on February 19, the Reds received Holke

Legendary Giants manager John McGraw signed Chase for the 1919 season when no other team wanted him, even after McGraw's protégé Mathewson had publicly accused Chase of bribing other players. McGraw then inexplicably hired Matty as a coach. *National Baseball Hall of Fame Library, Cooperstown, N.Y.*

and catcher Bill Rariden. They immediately sent Holke on to the Braves for infielder Jimmy Smith. Rariden initially said that he would retire from baseball to work on his farm near Bedford, Indiana, rather than join the Reds, but eventually changed his mind.[7]

In effect, then, the Reds traded Chase for Rariden and Smith. On the face of it, this trade was perhaps even more one-sided than the famous "Bunion-Onion" deal in 1913. Rariden batted only .216 for Cincinnati in 1919 and retired a year later, while Smith played in only twenty-eight games with the Reds before being sold to Philadelphia in 1921. He retired after the 1922 season. Obviously the Reds had decided to accept any offer, no matter how absurd, rather than keep Chase on their roster.

Now that Chase was a member of the Giants, the local press took pains to reassure the fans that this time, finally, Chase would be on his best behavior: "Chase has learned a lesson, no doubt. He is coming to the end of his baseball days and can be counted on to give of his best for the Giants.... He ... said that he would be glad to play under McGraw, as he considers him one of the great managers of the game."[8] Of course, the fans in Cincinnati and Chicago, not to mention those New York fans who could recall Chase's tenure with the Yankees, had heard similar promises before.

In New York Chase would become one-fourth of the oldest and arguably the best infield in the National League. Third baseman Heinie Zimmerman had twice led the league in runs batted in, and while he was no longer the hitter he had been early in his career with the Cubs he was still a dangerous man at the plate. Second baseman Larry Doyle had led the league in batting in 1915, and while his range had decreased dramatically in recent years he was still one of the best second basemen in baseball. And shortstop Art Fletcher was a solid hitter and fiery team leader.

The Giants also had George Burns, Ross Youngs, and the ex–Federal League star Benny Kauff in the outfield; Lew McCarty and rookie Earl Smith at catcher; and a veteran pitching staff, including Toney, Perritt, Rube Benton, Jess Barnes, and Ferdie Schupp, though the latter was trying to come back from a sore arm. With the addition of Chase, the Giants seemed to be the team to beat in the National League. Harry Schumacher reported that one expert had gone "so far as to compare the Giants' inner line of defense with the Chance-Evers-Tinker-Steinfeldt combination of the old Cubs." To bolster this assessment, Schumacher quoted the Chicago *Daily News*: "The acquisition of Chase gives John McGraw the strongest hitting and fielding infield in baseball.... McGraw is to be commended for his cleverness in getting a man of Chase's talent."[9]

Pants Rowland, who had briefly been considered a possible successor to Mathewson as manager in Cincinnati, predicted that Chase and the Giants would be a perfect fit: "No one who knows either Chase or McGraw could doubt that Hal will play the very best ball of which he is capable this year and during every subsequent season of his career with the Giants. McGraw, a truly remarkable judge of human nature, will handle Chase as the somewhat temperamental

Californian should be handled, and Chase will repay him, unless I am greatly mistaken, by playing as brilliant ball for the Giants as he ever did in his life.

"I do not for one moment believe that Chase will run amuck under McGraw, as he may have under other managers. His recent experience has taught him a lesson that he will never forget and which will influence his conduct for as long as he remains in professional baseball. He is a somewhat moody player, however, and will require more intelligent guidance than most managers could give him. He likes to be petted, for one thing, and encouraged to believe that he is one of the brainiest players that ever lived. He likes to use his own judgment in emergencies and sometimes resents dictation. McGraw, I imagine, will allow him a lot of leeway in this respect and the result will be a greater Chase than ever we have seen since he was at the top of his game with the old Yankees.

"The acquisition of Chase gives McGraw another great ball club," concluded Rowland. "Add Chase and you have the most dangerous batting order in the National League to reckon with."[10]

The day after Rowland's comments were published, Chase announced that he had settled his suit against the Reds and signed a contract with the Giants. Astonishingly, Mathewson, finally back from France, signed on as McGraw's pitching coach three days later. Many wondered how Matty and Prince Hal would be able to coexist peacefully, given the events of the previous season, but McGraw smugly predicted that his firm management would forestall any problems between the two. "I do not anticipate a bit of trouble in that direction," said the manager. "Chase has told me within the past few days that his relations with Matty prior to the episode were always most cordial and that he does not feel the slightest resentment toward him now. Matty, too, is quite willing to let the dead past bury its dead. And even if they were still at swords' points I would not hesitate to have them both on the club, for while I remain as manager there can be no conflict between them."[11]

The first party of Giants left New York's Penn Station for spring training in Gainesville, Florida, on March 20. The group included team secretary John B. Foster, Zimmerman, Doyle, Burns, McCarty, and Rosie Ryan, as well as Mr. and Mrs. Hal Chase. Harry Schumacher reported en route that Chase seemed overjoyed to be with the Giants: "There is no happier individual in the Giant caravan to-day than Hal Chase, who is making his first southern tour as a member of the Clan McGraw. That he might one day join the Giants was for many long years the secret but none the less ardent hope of the brilliant Californian, and now that he is really one of them he is at no pains to conceal his elation. He acts and talks like a traveller who, after losing his way on many false trails, has finally struck the broad highway that leads to home."

Schumacher again insisted that Chase felt a new sense of personal responsibility in the wake of his suspension and hearing. "Hal realizes that he still has a long way to go before he can count himself safely re-established in the esteem of the festive fanatic but does not for one moment doubt that he can make the grade. He understands, at last, that life is something more than just a joke, whether in professional baseball or in any other sphere of human endeavor, and intends to conduct himself accordingly. 'No one will ever again have cause to say that I do not take my baseball seriously,' he said last night — and meant it."[12]

In Gainesville Hal and Anna boarded with a Major Thomas, a retired banker, along with the newspaper reporters accompanying the team and one or two of the rookies. Spring training got off to a frightening start. On March 22, Larry Doyle lost his grip on his bat, which struck Mathewson in the stomach. Doyle and the other Giants rushed to Matty's aid, but Chase, who had been awaiting his turn at the plate, did not move.

Although Matty was not seriously injured, Chase was no doubt delighted at the accident. "At least," said one witness, "he had the grace not to laugh out loud. But from now on Larry can get anything he wants from him."[13]

Chase looked good in early practices. On that same Saturday he "had the assembled Gainesvilleans gasping over the uncanny cleverness of his work. He raked in grounders and pulled down high ones in the old Chase manner, and did it all with an easy grace that can only mean that he is still just as young as he wants to be." A few days later, wrote Schumacher, "Chase surpassed himself in the brilliance of his play, making one spectacular stop after another, and retrieving an occasional wild heave with all the uncanny skill of ten years ago." Again, however, the reporter took pains to assure his readers that while Chase was still the same old Prince Hal physically, he had changed in other respects: "He is still the same carefree, happy-go-lucky Hal of old, but back of all his seeming indifference there is a perfectly obvious determination to make this the greatest season of his entire career if it is at all possible to do so. Hal has never worked harder on a spring training trip than he has during the past three days, and the natural consequence is that he is almost if not quite as fit now as he ever will be."[14]

Fred Lieb echoed Schumacher's assessment of Prince Hal's physical condition in the New York *Sun*: "Though Chase is the oldest of the New York infield he is playing the same dashing game of former years. He is one of the marvels of the sport. Despite his tempestuous career, the flight of time has had little effect on him. He still retains the same boyish face that was so popular at one time on the old Hilltop grounds. He may have slowed up just a trifle on the bases, but in the field he is just the same good player he was in his palmy days. On the training trip Chase had made plays that a fellow like Holke never would have attempted."[15]

On April 3 the Giants left Gainesville for Tampa, where they began a series of exhibition games against the American League champion Red Sox. McGraw's men were outscored 24 to 9 in losing four in a row to Boston; in the first game Boston's Babe Ruth hit what many still consider to be the longest home run in history, a mammoth shot estimated to have travelled 579 feet, and in the second game New York committed seven errors.

In retrospect, the series seems rich in baseball symbolism. A year later, the Red Sox would sell Ruth to the Yankees, who would win six pennants during the 1920s while surpassing the Giants as the most popular team in New York. Ruth was instrumental in lifting baseball out of the mess created by Chase and other corrupt ballplayers; his home-run-hitting heroics signalled a sea-change in the way the game was played. From now on teams would place increasing emphasis on the home run and the offensive explosion, and concern themselves less with the subtleties of "inside baseball." In 1919, however, McGraw, a firm believer in the scratch-it-out philosophy, sneered at Ruth. "If he plays every day," predicted McGraw, "the bum will hit into a hundred double plays before the season is over."

Thereafter, whenever Ruth smacked another impressive hit off the hapless Giant pitchers, he would yell over to McGraw, "How's that for a double-play ball, Mac?"[16]

Other incidents during the series were less amusing. Joe Bush, who had won fifteen games for the Red Sox in 1918, blew out his arm striking out Art Fletcher and pitched only three games in 1919, a major factor in Boston's disappointing fourth-place finish. After Larry Doyle tried to spike second baseman Mike McNally on a stolen base attempt, the Red Sox players targeted individual Giant players for retaliation, a plan which Boston manager Ed Barrow headed off with some difficulty.[17]

New York got some of its pride back when it won the last two games in the series, 7–3 at Columbia, South Carolina, and 4–1 at Spartanburg, South Carolina. "The festive old gentleman," as Harry Schumacher called Chase, batted .360 in the Boston series, tying Ross Youngs for the team lead in hits, and contributed a couple of sensational defensive plays. On April 10, as the Giants won 4–1, he made "the most sensational defensive play of the entire series to date."

With one out in the ninth inning Ruth hit "a skittish sort of bounder" toward Chase. The ball took a bad hop just as it reached Chase, who barely managed to knock it down. But he was not done yet, as Harry Schumacher reported: "Instead of quitting on the play, as most first basemen would have, Chase called for [pitcher] George Smith to cover the bag, and with a cat-like sweep pounced on the ball again, came up with it, and, without turning, flipped it back of him to where Smith should have been to receive it." Unfortunately, "the lanky and somewhat awkward pitcher" was unable to make the play and Ruth was credited with a hit.[18]

Such displays moved Schumacher to write that "Chase has shown the same superlative skill and cunning that made him the greatest of all first basemen and most, if not all, of his old-time speed and agility. He has been a constant source of wonder and amazement even to those who thought that they knew and appreciated the resources at his command.... In short, he has to all appearances been the Chase of old, chastened by time, but with his efficiency not at all impaired thereby."[19]

Chase continued to hit well during the rest of the exhibition schedule, as the Giants swept two games from the International League Baltimore Orioles and four out of five from the Washington Senators. After Chase collected four hits in a 9–7 win over the Senators at Richmond, Virginia, McGraw was moved to proclaim, "Chase rounds out our infield, and so far I have been highly pleased with him. I have found him a most agreeable chap, and I am sure we will get along without a hitch. Chase plays first base brilliantly, hits well and, more than that, thinks. That is what I want him for, to do some thinking on my infield."[20]

The Giants finished their exhibition season in New York with two games against amateur opponents, beating the Interborough Subway Guards 7–0 and Yale University 4–3. In the latter contest, reported Lieb, "the usually wide-awake Chase was the central figure in one of the most amusing blunders ever seen on a ball field." In the seventh inning, with New York leading the college boys 2–1, Chase threw to Fletcher to force out a Yale runner at second base, but Fletcher's return throw to Doyle covering first base was too late to complete the double play.

Doyle, however, in a typical bit of McGraw-inspired trickery, kept the ball hidden in his glove when pitcher Bob Steele returned to the mound. Doyle then fired the ball to Chase to pick the runner off, "but the first sacker evidently had not comprehended the signal and was away from the bag at the time the ball shot past him and rolled to the Giant dugout." The runner scored to tie the game.[21]

Such hilarity was put aside when the regular season began. McGraw had no doubt that the 1919 Giants would be at least as good as his 1918 team, which had finished ten and a half games behind the Cubs, and probably better: "Whether they are good enough to win a pennant is a matter of opinion, in which the fact that we have Hal Chase playing first base for us should receive serious consideration by fans and critics who unhesitatingly predict that the Cubs will repeat."[22]

Despite his optimistic public pronouncements, however, McGraw was concerned about his pitching staff. Ferdie Schupp, who had won twenty-one games in 1917 but had missed virtually all of 1918 with a sore arm, was still not right. Fred Toney was still serving out his prison sentence for violating the Mann Act; he would rejoin the club on May 31. And Chase's old accuser Pol Perritt was in Louisiana, holding out for more money.

To help fill in, the Giant manager bought righthander Jean Dubuc from Salt Lake City of the Pacific Coast League. Dubuc had spent several solid if unspectacular seasons with the Tigers before being released in 1917 because, he claimed, of a feud with Ty Cobb. Dubuc became a useful relief specialist with the Giants in 1919, but it was to be his last season as a player in the major leagues. Still, his tenure with the Giants would be significant for other reasons.

Despite their dubious pitching the Giants won twenty-four of their first thirty-two games. One of their few losses came on May 8 against the Braves, with Mathewson in charge of the club while McGraw was away trying to arrange a trade for St. Louis catcher Mike Gonzalez. In the eleventh inning of a 2–2 tie, with Boston's Rabbit Maranville on second base, Buck Herzog grounded to Heinie Zimmerman. Zimmerman had forgotten how many runners were on base and thought that Maranville would be forced to move up, so he stepped on third base and threw over to Chase, thinking he had completed a double play. Instead Maranville took third on the play and scored the winning run on an infield single. Had the Great Zim committed such a blunder in McGraw's presence he doubtless would have received a terrible tongue-lashing. But the Giants went on to win their next seven games in a row.

While the Giants were flying, however, Chase was struggling. By May 16 he was batting only .147, and by June 2, when the Giants swept a doubleheader from the Phillies, he had managed to raise his average only to .208. In the second game of that doubleheader Chase figured in perhaps the most unusual double play in baseball history.

The Phillies had Brad Hogg on first base and Hick Cady on third when Possum Whitted hit a fly ball to right field. Youngs made the catch and threw in to Chase. Chase, seeing that Hogg had tagged up and started for second, relayed the ball to Fletcher. Hogg retreated and Fletcher threw back to Chase, but Chase slipped and fell in the baseline. Hogg literally ran over him on his way back to first base, and Chase could only stick up his hand to slow Fletcher's throw. Youngs, backing up the play, saw Chase fall and raced in from the outfield. He slid into the bag, grabbed the ball, and tagged Hogg in the same motion. Thus the Giants' right fielder recorded two putouts on the same play.[23]

In June and early July the Giants won sixteen of twenty-nine games, a .552 percentage, but Pat Moran's Reds were now red-hot. After beating the Phillies on July 5 the Giants actually found themselves in second place with a percentage of .636, .001 behind Cincinnati.

In July and August the Giants and Reds battled atop the National League standings, with neither team able to gain much of an advantage. Despite the pressures of the pennant race, however, Chase was enjoying himself on the field. On July 25, in the fifth inning of a 5–0 victory over the Braves, Chase's bat slipped out of his hands and flew down the third base line after he fouled off a pitch. Boston pitcher Dick Rudolph, catcher Hank Gowdy, and shortstop Rabbit Maranville laughed at Chase, and, reported Fred Lieb, "Harold laughed with them." But he swung at the next pitch and pulled a home run into the left field bleachers. "To show there was no ill feeling Hal good naturedly poked Gowdy in the ribs as he completed his jaunt around the bases."[24]

Chase had reason to smile. He had batted .316 since May 15, hiking his overall average to .281. By the first week of August, when the Giants won one out of three games in the biggest series of the season in Cincinnati, Chase had his average up to .303.

The games in Cincinnati were almost unbelievably rowdy. The local newspapers had whipped the Reds fans into a howling frenzy of excitement and hatred of the Giants. During the first game umpire Bill Klem threatened to clear the Cincinnati dugout because the Reds were taunting the Giants unmercifully. Benny Kauff almost got into a brawl with Heinie Groh, Larry Kopf, and Morrie Rath. The second game, played before a crowd of some twenty-five thousand, including Ohio Governor James Cox, was somewhat more orderly. After the third game, however, played before a crowd of 32,121, "a horde of rabid fans" followed the Giants players and issued "threats of bodily harm."[25]

McGraw responded by yelling, "We beat you today and we'll be glad to get out of the home of the Huns." Such a retort in Cincinnati, a city with a proud and substantial German-American population,[26] was guaranteed to provoke, especially less than a year after the end of the war. A Cincinnati park policeman swung wildly at McGraw and hit Chase instead; Chase knocked the policeman's hat off. A riot was barely averted when a mounted policeman drove off the enraged Cincinnati fans; the New York players hustled into their waiting taxicabs and rode off.[27]

Chase, taunted mercilessly by the Cincinnati fans, managed only one hit in the three games. The series seemed to take some of the starch out of the Giants, who lost five of their next six games. McGraw knew his team needed a boost, so in early August he sent four players and $40,000 to the Braves for lefthander Art Nehf. Shortly thereafter he reportedly offered to send Zimmerman, Doyle, outfielder Lee King, and an undisclosed amount of cash to the Cardinals for Rogers Hornsby, whom he had long coveted, but the Cardinals declined the offer. Meanwhile the Reds reportedly offered Brooklyn $40,000 for outfielder Hy Myers, who would end the season as the National League leader in runs batted in. Charles Ebbets turned it down.[28]

On August 13 the Giants and Reds began another series, this time in New York. A crowd of some forty thousand, the largest in the history of the Polo Grounds, saw the Reds sweep a doubleheader, winning both games by one run. Errors by Chase and Fletcher in the fourth inning of the second game led to the only Cincinnati runs of the game.

Dan Daniel was appalled by what he had seen. "The Giant infield looked particularly bad in the early part of the second game when Chase, [pitcher Phil] Douglas and [second baseman Al] Baird could not reach an agreement as to who was to cover first on various infield chances in that direction. Douglas, who is a slow fielder, was at fault and soon McGraw got after him and told him where he belonged," but even then, "The infield did not move with its old speed and precision."[29]

On the following day McGraw replaced Baird with a promising rookie named Frankie Frisch and the Giants swept a doubleheader. They won the first game 2–1 in fourteen innings as Chase had two hits and drove in the winning run, but in the sixth inning, with the Giants leading 1–0, he cut in front of a perfectly positioned Frisch and grabbed Daubert's grounder. Daubert was safe because no one covered first base, and scored the tying run when Roush followed with a triple. Chase's double error on Larry Kopf's grounder in the top of the fourteenth — he booted the ball, then threw wildly to Toney — allowed the Cincinnati shortstop to reach second base and almost cost New York the game. The second game was marred by the ejection of Fletcher and fights between the Giants' Rube Benton and Cincinnati's Dolf Luque, and then between George Burns and Jimmy Smith.

Again, Daniel was appalled. "In the day's great triumph we will confess we suffered one big disappointment, and that was brought about by the work of Hal Chase at first base. As on Wednesday Chase was far from the nimble Hal of other days. His legs appeared to have gone back on him and he fell down on several plays—lapses which made fans hearken back to the days of Chase at the old Hilltop grounds and shake their heads. Chase will have to do a lot better if he is to help the Giants in the fight for the flag and if he is to be accepted as a New York fixture for next season. He was outdone in the field even by Jake Daubert, whose legs have been nothing to brag about these last three years. Chase played a great game in the West, we are told, and may be in only a temporary slump."[30]

On the following day the Reds came back and swept another doubleheader, 4–3 and 4–0. Chase went hitless in two at bats in the first game before McGraw sent Lew McCarty up to pinch-hit for him in the eighth inning, and in the second game was oh-for-three and committed an error before giving way to McCarty again in the ninth. The losses all but ended New York's chances of catching the Reds.

By now other New York writers were wondering about Chase's recent performances. "Chase was a drooping figure at bat all afternoon," wrote William B. Hanna in the *Herald*. "He made a few miracle catches of bad throws, but he couldn't hit and seemed to know it." Fred Lieb, Daniel's colleague at the *Sun*, agreed: "Chase has been playing through the entire series as though in a trance.... In the ninth inning of the second game McGraw sent Lew to bat for Hal, who is hitting close to .300, and permitted Frank Snyder, who is hitting under .200, to bat for himself."[31]

Obviously something was amiss. An explanation was offered on the following day when Chase sat out a win over the Cubs, pleading a sprained wrist suffered while sliding during the series in Cincinnati. Supposedly the wrist was the reason that he had played so poorly against the Reds in New York, although Daniel felt that Chase's legs were more to blame: "Chase's play previous to the series with the Reds was excellent, but against the Cincinnatis his legs were very bad and his work fell down most perceptibly."[32]

Chase sat out the first game of a doubleheader against the Cubs on August 19, then went hitless in two at bats in the nightcap. His legs seemed to be feeling better, as he scored on the front end of a double steal with Burns in the third inning. McGraw, however, was taking no chances, and summoned young George Kelly from Rochester of the International League.[33]

Kelly immediately took over at first base as Chase missed the next six games, five of which the Giants won. But the frustrations of the difficult season were beginning to show. Douglas and Fletcher got into a fight after the shortstop's three-run error cost Shufflin' Phil a victory over the Cubs, and a few days later the ill-starred pitcher jumped the club, earning a suspension from McGraw. Then a "listless" Benny Kauff loafed after a fly ball in a loss to the Pirates, letting the ball drop for a double.

Third baseman Heinie Zimmerman, Chase's teammate on the Giants in 1919, was another player whose association with Chase cost him his career. In September of that year, McGraw suspended "the Great Zim" for the rest of the season but took no official action against his old friend Chase, who was apparently equally guilty. Neither played in the majors again after the 1919 season. *National Baseball Hall of Fame Library, Cooperstown, N.Y.*

Chase got back into the lineup on August 26. Five days later he made "one of the most sensational catches ever seen at Ebbets Field" when he raced far down the right field line to catch a fly ball in the ninth inning of a 4–3 Giants victory, but he was in a batting slump and apparently his wrist was still sore. Brooklyn scored its only run in a 5–1 loss to the Giants when a poor throw by Fletcher pulled Chase off the bag. Chase made "a beautiful play of it," but "had to rest his arm a few minutes before he resumed."[34]

On the following day he was out of the lineup again. He appeared as a pinch-runner in the next game, then was back on the sidelines again. The Giants continued to play well, but they could not gain on the Reds. And then disaster struck.

In Chicago on September 10, Toney started for the Giants and pitched two shutout innings, then removed himself from the game with a 3–0 lead. Jess Barnes came on in relief to pick up the 7–2 win. Again Chase did not play, but Zimmerman had two hits, a run-scoring single in the first inning and a triple in the seventh.

On the following morning McGraw announced that he was suspending Zimmerman without pay for the remainder of the season, supposedly because the third baseman had stayed out with friends until early in the morning. McGraw claimed that Zimmerman had persistently violated club rules and made no attempt to stay in shape.[35]

In reality Zimmerman's suspension was for a far more serious breach of club rules, although what actually happened remains the subject of some dispute. Typically, it was hushed up at the time, and later the various men involved told contradictory stories, all of which seemed primarily intended to cast the tellers in the best possible light.

According to Toney, Zimmerman had tried to bribe him into losing the game against the Cubs. The pitcher said that he had been walking back to the dugout after the first inning when Zimmerman approached him.

"I'll give you $200 if you lose this game," said the third baseman. Toney said he had glared at Zimmerman but made no response. In the dugout he told Mathewson, "I'm through; you'd better put someone else in to pitch."

"What's the matter?" asked Matty. "Have you got a sore arm?"

"No, there's nothing the matter with me," replied Toney. He had simply decided that he did not want to be involved in a potentially crooked game. So Barnes came on in relief and picked up one of his twenty-five wins that season. Toney said that he saw McGraw at the team hotel that evening and delivered an ultimatum: either Zimmerman or Toney would have to go.

Other Giants later claimed that Zimmerman and Chase had worked together, offering bribes to various players to throw games. At the time, however, Chase's name was not mentioned publicly in connection with Zimmerman's suspension, though McGraw most certainly knew about the accusations against his first baseman. Chase must have felt the noose beginning to tighten around his own neck.

Chase sat out more than a week, then pinch-hit in the first game of a September 15 doubleheader in Cincinnati, which Moran's team swept to clinch the pennant. McGraw did not see the second galling defeat. He had already departed for New York, where he later claimed that he and Stoneham had confronted Zimmerman and exacted a confession, which supposedly implicated Chase as well.[36] Chase remained with the team, although he appeared only once, as a pinch-hitter, in the last twelve games of the season. The Giants concluded their difficult season by sweeping a doubleheader from the Phillies at the Polo Grounds, but Chase had left the club the night before. McGraw sought to deflect attention from his first baseman's absence. "He's sick," the manager told the press. "He hasn't been feeling well for a long time."[37] But Chase apparently recovered quickly, for he participated in the Giants' postseason barnstorming tour of the northeast.

McGraw's refusal to take public action against Chase is puzzling, even in light of the manager's genuine affection for the player. Restricting Chase to a pinch-hitting role may have effectively eliminated the threat of Chase's betting against the Giants and then playing to lose, since as a pinch-hitter he would never know in advance in which games he might see action. But as long as Chase was with the team, what was to keep him from trying to bribe his teammates? Perhaps with the pennant race already over McGraw wanted to allow his old friend to bow out relatively gracefully, with what was left of his reputation intact. No such solicitude governed McGraw's handling of Zimmerman, with whom he had clashed repeatedly and for whom he had no great liking. Perhaps McGraw simply did not want to admit publicly that he had after all erred disastrously in his assessment of Chase's character.

At any rate McGraw's problems were temporarily forgotten in the hoopla surrounding the upcoming World Series between the powerful White Sox and the underdog Reds. As usual, gambling was an intrinsic part of the World Series hype. The White Sox were early 7–5 favorites, though the Reds had some backing in Cincinnati. According to Dan Daniel, however, the Reds fans seemed reluctant to back their team with money: "The impression we get is that the fans [in Cincinnati] are very much elated over the present success of the Reds and are willing to go any verbal distance to praise the players and Pat Moran, but that way down in their hearts they have a strong feeling that the White Sox class above their favorites."[38]

The Reds found some support among National League managers, as McGraw and George T. Stallings picked them to win the Series.[39] But most of the nation considered the White Sox the best team in baseball and predicted a walkover for Comiskey's men. The Reds took advantage of uncharacteristically poor performances by Chicago pitchers Ed Cicotte and Lefty Williams to win the first two games, but most fans regarded those contests as flukes. The White Sox won the third game behind little Dickie Kerr, then lost two more as Cicotte and Williams again pitched poorly.

Now rumors of a fix began to circulate in earnest, and only increased in number after the White Sox beat the Reds in the sixth game. Some cynics argued that the two teams were seeking to prolong the series and thereby increase revenues from ticket sales.

Walter St. Denis, writing in the New York *Sun,* dismissed the rumors. He pointed out that any additional money would go to the owners, not the players. No ballplayer, argued St. Denis, would go out of his way to enrich an owner; instead, "He wants to clinch his dough as quickly as possible" and go home for the winter.

Besides, the very notion of throwing games was absurd: "There isn't any man in baseball who would dare approach the members of his team and ask them to toss off games. He'd have to interest the whole mob of them, and probably have to take in a few on the other side. Baseball cannot be decided with money. Its honesty has stood the test of scores and scores of years, and woe to the man who would even suggest the hippodroming of one game."

He concluded with an exhortation to the fans. "Banish the idea of any baseball game being crooked," he urged. Baseball "was built on honesty, has stood on honesty, and will rest on honesty as long as the world lasts. Its fields are no place for the crook to tread."[40]

Still, the stories about the 1919 World Series refused to die down completely. Two months later *The Sporting News* reported the rumor that "a New York gambler" had supplied the money for the fix, with "an ex–champion boxer" as his agent. And White Sox catcher Ray Schalk predicted that seven members of the team would not return in 1920.

Many refused to admit that the stories could be true. "Personally I don't believe for a moment that anything was wrong in the World's Series," wrote Joe Vila. "I figured that the Reds would win and I bet on them, too." Garry Herrmann also discounted the rumors of a fix, although he conceded that gambling was a problem: "Here's one thing I will announce: If I remain in the game, as I expect to, I will declare war on ball park gamblers. All baseball gambling takes its rise in the betting that is done in the stands, and I intend to drive all those people out of the parks, beginning with my own."[41]

Early in 1920, the baseball world seemed to be trying to put such matters behind it. Chase still enjoyed the esteem of his peers, despite the disappointing conclusion of the previous season. In the January 1 issue of *The Sporting News* umpire Billy Evans asked Kid Gleason, Hughie Jennings, and Willie Keeler, who had been McGraw's teammates on the great Baltimore Orioles teams of the 1890s, to compare contemporary players with their predecessors and name their all-time all-star team. "When it came to considering first base," wrote Evans, "the vote was unanimous in favor of Hal Chase. All three paid their respects to Fred Tenney, Tom Tucker, Frank Chance, Dan Brouthers, Pat Tebeau, Stuffy McInnis, and Jake Daubert, but to each one Hal Chase stood out as the last word in the art of first basing."

Evans concurred with their choice: "In selecting Chase the trio received my approval because to me it has always seemed that no human being other than Chase could possibly pull the remarkable plays I have seen him make. Chase was one of the first guardians of the initial sack to come in close on an intended bunt, and instead of being satisfied with getting the batsman at first, Chase was getting them at second and third with such frequency that clubs did not look on the sacrifice with much favor when Chase was playing first."

In fact, according to Evans, Chase was almost too good for his own good: "In a great many cases Chase was thinking a fraction of a second ahead of the rest of the infield, and very often he would be made to look foolish on some remarkable performance because the man at the other end was unable to execute his part of the play."[42]

No one, including Evans, realized that his column would serve as an epitaph for Chase's major league career. The same issue of *The Sporting News* predicted that Chase would again be the Giants' first baseman in 1920, and three weeks later Vila assured his readers that "McGraw has no idea of letting Chase ... get away from here. But he is through with Heinie Zimmerman."[43]

In fact the status of Zimmerman was of more concern to Giant fans than that of Chase. Zimmerman would clearly not be returning to New York, but two other National League teams were reportedly interested in him. *The Sporting News* reported in January that Zimmerman might be headed for Pittsburgh: "though Heinie is through as a Giant, he is not through as a ball player, and he no doubt would be a handy man for the Pirates, or for any other club for that matter, to have around." In February Vila reported that the Giants would trade Zimmerman, catcher Lew McCarty, and $25,000 to the St. Louis Cardinals for third baseman Milt Stock. Both rumors proved false, and McGraw refused to discuss the player[44]; as far as anyone knew, the Great Zim's fondness for the nightlife was still the only reason that he was "through as a Giant."

Meanwhile Chase was starting to hedge on reporting for the 1920 season. Vila reported in late February that Chase was "talking of going to his home in California to accept a business offer that looks like ready money.... He has no fault to find with his contract, but says he is tired of the game and soon must earn his livelihood in some other way."[45]

When the Giants assembled in San Antonio for spring training Chase and Zimmerman were absent, and for the first time McGraw implied that Chase had not left the team voluntarily. "I cannot talk about the matter," said McGraw. "If anything is to be said it must come from the players. As far as the Giants are concerned Chase and Zimmerman are through."[46]

McGraw's comments increased speculation that various ugly rumors about Chase and Zimmerman might be true. An editorial in *The Sporting News* attempted to dispel these rumors, at least insofar as they applied to the Great Zim: "Seems to us they are doing Henry Zimmerman an injustice when they couple his name with that of other players who are understood to have been dropped from baseball because of alleged too close connections with gamblers.... His suspension by the New York National League club last fall seems to have been for one of those more or less frequent indiscretions of his which, however much they are to be frowned upon, carry no reflections upon his honesty. We hope we are not mistaken when we say that Heinie Zim may be disorderly and a general bad actor, but not a crook."[47]

Among the "other players ... understood to have been dropped from baseball because of alleged too close connections with gamblers" was Lee Magee. In mid–February a Cincinnati newspaper had reported that the Cubs were about to give Magee his unconditional release. This seemingly innocuous action was the first link in the chain of events that eventually culminated in the revelation of the Black Sox scandal and, incidentally, sealed Hal Chase's reputation once and for all in the minds of most baseball fans. The Cubs' decision to release Magee initially seemed puzzling, since he had batted .292 in his half-season in Chicago and was still only thirty years old. Immediately, however, rumors spread that Magee was being let out for his involvement in a betting scandal, although no one would confirm them officially. Cubs owner William L. Veeck said only, "We don't want him on our team," which was a patently insufficient response. "There is more to it than this and it will all be given out in due time," wrote Oscar C. Reichow in *The Sporting News,* "but probably from the National League headquarters, and two other players will probably receive their unconditional releases also in this connection."[48]

Meanwhile, Chick Gandil, the first baseman of the White Sox, announced that he would not return to the American League champions and signed to manage a team in an independent league in Idaho. Gandil had batted a solid .290 in 1919 and led the league's first basemen in fielding percentage, but he had a reputation as a tough customer and Comiskey was not known for the warmth of his relationships to his players. Most observers probably attributed Gandil's decision to a contract dispute with the notoriously close-fisted owner. But the Magee situation continued to puzzle. By the time the truant Gandil dropped by the Cubs' training camp in Pasadena in early March, Magee had taken on the status of a nonperson. "He does not seem to be missed," reported Reichow, "and the ball players refuse to discuss his case. They do not even ask what happened to him or why he was released."[49]

Magee realized that he was being railroaded out of baseball, and resolved not to go quietly. Threatening to explode "the biggest bomb in baseball history," he announced that he would reveal the charges for which the National League had barred him "and let the public judge whether I've been fairly treated." But, he added, he would not take the fall alone: "I'm going to burn my bridges and then jump off the ruins. If I'm barred I'll take quite a few noted people with me. I'll show up some people for tricks turned ever since 1906. And there will be merry music in the baseball world."[50]

Magee's attorney Robert S. Alcorn announced that he had sent a letter to Heydler containing the names of four players involved in gambling. Heydler acknowledged receiving a letter from Alcorn, but said it contained no other names.[51] The identity of the four has never been established, although we may assume that Chase and Zimmerman were among them. The coming months would provide several other likely candidates.

Meanwhile Heydler responded coolly to Magee's accusations: "Magee is not under contract with any National League baseball club, and we, therefore, have no official connection or authority over him." Heydler wrote back to Alcorn that the league intended to ignore Magee until he produced "evidence implicating others with him, or showing them to be guilty of wrong doing in which he took no part."

Furthermore, Heydler told Alcorn, "No charges are pending in this office by, or against Mr. Lee Magee. If I understand the position taken by him ... he insists that charges have been made against him by some one; that they have to do with gambling and that he will expose himself and drag others into the matter with him. If there are any others implicated in the matters to which Mr. Magee seems anxious to plead guilty, the more quickly he names them and gives proof of their complicity with him or others, the better it will be for baseball."

In a statement to the press Heydler insisted, "Certainly more than 99 per cent of the ball players in this league are honest and are a credit to their profession. We do not intend that the one per cent of undesirables, if such exist, shall attach stigma to this honorable calling and so bring the game into disrepute."[52]

Of course Heydler was being disingenuous, but his stonewalling proved effective. Magee may have expected sympathy, but little was forthcoming. *The Sporting News* reported that Alcorn seemed to be "naming by inference players whose names were mentioned at the time charges were brought against Hal Chase, as knowing of Chase's alleged wrong doing, or being parties with him in such wrong doing." The editorial said that Alcorn had also represented Chase at his hearing before Heydler, although Alcorn was not one of the three attorneys reported to have accompanied Chase at that time, and noted that "if he means to indict players alleged to be involved with Chase then he takes the peculiar position of attempting to call to book co-defendants with the player who was his client, all of whom he at the time of the Chase hearing pleaded for as innocent of any such crimes as charged."

In light of Alcorn's actions, however, *The Sporting News* conceded for the first time that Heydler's ruling in the Chase hearing might have been a mistake, and also assumed that Chase's major league career was over: "Whatever miscarriage of justice there may have been in that case, Chase is now out of baseball, even those who were in a sense his sponsors when he was put on trial [i.e., John McGraw] having repudiated him, which is enough to say."

The editorial concluded with a call for Magee and Alcorn to make a clean breast of the situation, suggesting that Alcorn ignore the rules of his profession in the process: "If Magee knows anything, let him out with it. If the lawyer knows anything let him out with it, and baseball will not be disturbed by any ethics of his profession that he may violate in turning up anything he may have learned in preparing the case for any clients, past or present."[53]

On April 14, just two hours before the Cubs and Reds were to open the 1920 season at Redland Field, Magee and Alcorn took action. They filed suit against the Cubs in Cincinnati, asking for $9,500 in damages from the Cubs: $4,500 in salary and an additional $5,000 that Magee said he would have received if the Cubs won the pennant in 1920. He also sought the attachment of Chicago's share of the receipts, about $12,000, from the game at Redland Field.[54]

Organized baseball professed to be unconcerned. "We will fight Lee Magee's suit to a finish," promised Veeck, "and we fail to see where he has a legal chance to collect a red cent." Veeck also let slip, in passing, that he and other baseball officials had heard damning evidence against the player long before the matter had become public, though he did not explain why the matter had remained secret for so long: "He knows perfectly well why he was released and why we do not care to have him as a member of the club this season. His statement to President Heydler, of the National League, and myself, made in Chicago in February, covers the point. Our club will never weaken in his case to the slightest degree no matter what course he may decide to take." Garry Herrmann's comment was even pithier: "Magee's suit is a joke."[55]

Still, the suit laid baseball's basic integrity open to question, and *The Sporting News* was quick to respond. "Ball players as a whole do not like cheats," wrote Reichow reassuringly. "They will not sit in a poker game with a man who is known to be a cheat, therefore why should they stand for an associate who deliberately cheats in a ball game by throwing it away?"

Apparently Reichow could not see the difference between playing cards with a cheat, who would take the player's money, and playing ball with a cheat, who might very well cut his teammates in on the take. The rest of the article betrayed a similar naivete: "Throughout the year of 1919 I did not hear a single word of men attempting to throw ball games or associating with gamblers, despite the Hal Chase rumor of the year before," insisted Reichow. "I personally believe that 98 per cent of the players in the game today are honest and it is a shame to let the other two per cent do the harm that is possible."[56]

Meanwhile, in New York, the Giants and their fans seemed to be adjusting nicely to the absence of Chase and Zimmerman, thanks to the development of future Hall of Famers George Kelly and Frankie Frisch. In early May, when Frisch, then playing third base, was stricken with appendicitis, Vila noted that the Great Zim might have made a useful replacement, but added that the fans accepted McGraw's refusal to take him back: "McGraw wants to win, yet he is satisfied to worry along as best he can until Frisch is fit to resume work. McGraw and the owners of the Giants must be commended for their determination to rid the club of disloyal players and the metropolitan baseball public apparently understands why this policy has been pursued."[57]

On May 20 the Cubs asked U.S. District Judge John W. Peck to dismiss Magee's suit, claiming that on February 20 the player had admitted that before joining the Cubs he had bet "against the team of which he was a member, and sought to win bets by intentional bad playing to defeat the said team." Therefore Magee "was an unfit person to play baseball when he entered into the employ of the defendant" and the Cubs were justified in releasing him. Again, the team did not explain why it had kept Magee's confession a secret for so long.[58]

Peck refused to dismiss the suit and the trial began in Cincinnati on June 7. In his opening address to the jury Murray Seasongood, the Cubs' attorney, promised plenty of fireworks: "We will show that Magee and Chase on the night of July 24, 1918, conspired together and committed an act of treason against the Cincinnati club, their fellow players, the National League and the national game." Among the witnesses lined up by Seasongood were John Heydler, Christy Mathewson, and William Veeck, all icons of baseball's respectability, and a gambler named James Costello, identified as "the proprietor of a billiard room in Boston."[59]

Costello was the first to take the stand, and his testimony was indeed sensational. He testified that Magee had come to him on the evening of July 24, 1918, and said that he had a proposition to throw the Reds-Braves game on the following day. "Before Magee left he said that he would see me the next morning, with more details," said Costello. "The next morning Magee and Hal Chase, who then was the first baseman for the Reds, visited me. I told them that they would have to bet some of their own money, and that the gamblers would not bet unless they did. 'How much do you want to bet?' I asked them. They told me that they didn't have any money with them, but that they would give me checks. I accepted them.

"If the game was won [by the Braves] they were to get even money plus one third commission on all bets collected. They filled out two of my blank checks for $500 each. Magee and Chase both said that they had the pitcher fixed. They said that the pitcher's name was Schneider. I told them that between them and the pitcher it ought to be soft. The pitcher was changed, though, and when I went to the ticker I saw that the Reds had won." The game in question, of course, was the contest in which Magee had committed his egregious ninth-inning throwing error, allowing Boston to tie the score, and unwillingly scored the winning run in the thirteenth inning, ahead of Edd Roush's home run.

"Chase came to see me that night," continued Costello. "He told me that they tried hard and hoped for better luck next time." Magee did not return, testified Costello, and later stopped payment on his check, which provoked Costello to come to New York, where the Reds were playing the Giants, to confront Chase and Magee. "I threatened to expose them if the check was not made good," recalled Costello. "Magee offered to report to me on other games to be 'fixed' and also offered to fix that day's game with New York. I refused and again demanded my money. Finally after a conference between him and Chase, Magee said he would pay me in installments and Chase stood sponsor for him. A few days later I received from Chase $300, of which $250 was to be applied to the check transaction and $50 to cover my expenses to New York.

"I did not collect the balance on the check until after I brought suit in June, 1919, against Magee in the Boston Municipal Court."[60]

This testimony was bad enough, even though Costello was not necessarily the most credible witness. But there was more. Christy Mathewson testified that

Magee's play in that July 25 game, especially his wild throw in the ninth inning, had aroused his suspicions. "I was astonished at the play, and I wondered what excuse Magee could give for throwing to second instead of to first," recalled Matty. "When Magee got to the bench I said to him, 'You were a manager yourself. What would you say to one of your players if he made such a play?' Magee only mumbled, 'I don't know. I don't know.' The play was atrocious. It made me suspicious. I said nothing about my suspicion at the time. I wanted further knowledge and I kept him in the game to see."[61]

Veeck revealed that Magee's activities had been common knowledge among National League owners at least since the previous December, when Veeck, Garry Herrmann, and Charles Ebbets, Magee's last three major league employers, had agreed that the Cubs should unconditionally release the player for the good of the game. Herrmann and Ebbets agreed to pay Veeck $2,500 each in compensation for foisting a crooked player on the Cubs. "Magee would have been released had he not confessed his betting on ball games to President Heydler and myself," said Veeck, "but his confession caused the Cubs to release him sooner than he would have been."[62]

Heydler went into some detail about that confession: "He came to me and President Veeck about midnight, February 22, 1920, in my room at the Congress Hotel in Chicago and stated that he wished to make a clean breast of his whole trouble. He related to us that Chase came to him on a train bound for the east and threw a roll of money in his lap with the statement, 'I intend to clean up on the rest of the season, and those with me want you in on it.'" Then, said Heydler, Magee had admitted the whole sordid story: how he and Chase had bet against the Reds in the July 25 Braves game; how they had tried to make sure Cincinnati lost, with Chase cleverly mishandling several low throws, although he was not charged with an error; how Magee had stopped payment on his check after the game; how Costello had come to New York and demanded payment; how Magee had been arrested in Boston on June 3, 1919, and paid $250 to settle his debt with Costello out of court.

Much of Magee's confession, said Heydler, had involved Chase: "He told us that they had offered to let Costello in on other games they intended to throw and that Chase even went so far as to purposely cut his hand while at Boston so he could duck the Philadelphia trip and go right to New York to get ready for the big killing." At the time, of course, no one had thought anything about that injury, which had been attributed to his accidentally breaking a glass in the dugout.

Heydler continued, "[Magee] said that Chase informed him that Pete Schneider was in on the deal and that there was never a chance of the Reds winning when Pete was in the box. He stated that Matty had gummed things up when he sent in Hod Eller to pitch instead of Schneider, and that Roush's home run had finished them up." Magee's desperation led him into contradictory statements: "On being questioned he said he knew of no other players who were connected with the betting, but repeatedly told us that if he had to get out of baseball he would take others with him."[63]

"Is it your intention to bar Magee from playing with any National League club?" asked Alcorn.

Heydler reddened. "As long as I am president of the league Magee must not and shall not play on any of its teams."

"And why?" persisted Alcorn.

"Because it is actions such as his that hit at the very fundamental principles of the great national pastime," responded Heydler. "I should regard only the disintegration of our republic as a greater evil than that baseball should be polluted by men who stain and shame it by crooked playing with gain an object."

The National League president grew defensive when Alcorn questioned him about his handling of the Chase hearing. "The reason Chase was exonerated was because I could not get any direct evidence against him," insisted Heydler. For the first time, he publicly told the story of how Chase had approached Ring during a 1917 game and implied that the pitcher could make some easy money if the Reds lost. Ignoring Chase, said Heydler, "Ring went in and pitched his head off to win, but the breaks were against him and the Reds lost. Jimmy then declared that Chase came to him and stuck a fifty dollar bill in his lap. He said that he was only a rookie and did not know what to do in order not to get himself in bad with such a star as Chase. But Chase denied this, and it was one man's word against another, so I was forced to exonerate Chase."[64]

While such testimony did little to convince most observers that Heydler's ruling in the Chase case had been correct, neither did it help Magee much. Alcorn's primary strategy had been to convince the jury of two main points: first, that "there was betting right along between teams in the major leagues and between individual players," and second, that Magee and Chase had actually bet on the Reds to beat Boston in that July 25 game.[65] In the first part of this strategy Alcorn was partially successful, as he forced Mathewson to acknowledge that Greasy Neale had admitted betting on the Reds. Alcorn pointed out that Ring and Neale had kept quiet for over a year and had never been punished for doing so, an indication that such transgressions were not regarded as serious.[66]

The second part of his strategy depended upon whether Magee could plausibly refute the damaging testimony presented by Costello, Heydler, and Veeck. Magee admitted that he and Chase had placed bets on the July 25 game, but insisted that he had intended to bet on, not against, the Reds: "The first intimation I had that there was anything wrong and that I had lost while I had won was when I met Hal Chase after the game and he confessed to me that both my money and his had been bet, not on the Reds, as I had supposed, but against them. I became naturally indignant and informed Chase that at least I would save my check and was going to stop payment on it, which I immediately did. I also accused Hal of 'crossing' me, but he at a later date gave me his cancelled check for $500 in proof that he, too, had lost a like amount.

"Jim Costello, the man Chase and I had left the checks with to be bet, then came down to New York and demanded that I make good my check. Still feeling that I had been cheated, I again refused. In the fall of that year while in

Boston I was served with notice by a lawyer hired by Costello to appear in court there, and then I gave up and, placing the matter in the hands of an attorney, told him to settle the matter, which he did."

Magee contradicted Heydler and Veeck's account of his confession: "I told them what I have just related on the witness stand — that I had bet $500 on the Reds and had stopped payment on the check when I discovered I had been 'crossed' by someone," he insisted. "I most decidedly did not 'confess' to betting against my team, nor that I had done my best to help Boston win."[67]

Magee's testimony also might have led some to wonder why Garry Herrmann, the chairman of the National Commission, had failed to investigate Magee's involvement with a well-known Boston gambler. Costello had testified that he had contacted Herrmann about Magee's failure to make good on his check, and Magee testified that Herrmann had told him to clear the matter up. Magee told the Reds president that he had already done so, and Herrmann chose not to pursue the matter further.[68]

Still, the accumulated evidence against Magee was overwhelming. By the end of the trial Alcorn had been reduced to arguing that the Cubs should have waited until the season began before releasing Magee. In his closing argument to the jury, the desperate attorney first attempted to ridicule the notion that Magee and Chase had tried to lose the Boston game, pointing out that Chase had two hits and committed no errors in the game while Magee had scored the winning run. But then Alcorn reversed his field, implying that Heydler, by exonerating Chase after the 1918 season, had muffed a chance "to cleanse the game he so loudly pleads for."

This argument must have caused Heydler some discomfort. "This same Hal Chase," said Alcorn, "was on trial before Mr. John Heydler and was absolutely exonerated despite the fact that pitcher Jimmy Ring, whom Mr. Heydler so tearfully says is a man of undoubted integrity, swore to him that this same Hal Chase came to him and told him that if he pitched to lose it would mean money in his pocket. And Ring likewise swore that after the Reds did lose, Chase came to him and gave him $50, a part of the money he had won through the Reds' defeat. Jimmy Ring swore to these facts before this John Heydler, and yet this same Mr. Heydler claims that he had no evidence against Chase, was forced to believe him guiltless, and he went to New York to play for the Giants at a larger salary than he received here with the Reds. Mr. Heydler did all this in the Chase matter and yet he now cries loudly for baseball's integrity and claims that this integrity only can be obtained and maintained by the utter expulsion of Lee Magee, a man never before or since accused of a single shady act, a man accused of betting against the Reds in a game in which he made a hit in the last inning, stole a base and scored the winning run."[69]

Alcorn's diatribe was in vain. The Chase hearing was water under the bridge, and no one wanted to reopen an investigation that threatened further damage to baseball's already tarnished reputation. The jury took just forty-four minutes to find the Cubs innocent, and Magee's career was over.[70]

Pete Schneider, who by then was pitching for Beaumont in the Texas League, denied any involvement in the plot. He said that before the July 25 game Sherry Magee had told him that he had "better be careful" because Magee understood that some of the Cincinnati players had bet on Boston.

Schneider declared that his response to this news had been, "If that's so, I won't work today," and so Eller pitched instead.[71] Whether or not anyone believed Schneider was immaterial; the baseball authorities apparently thought it unnecessary to investigate his role in the affair. His major league career was over, even though he was still only twenty-seven. He had had only one winning season in five years with the Reds, who had sold him to the Yankees after the 1918 season. In New York he had appeared in only seven games, and his always-erratic control (he had led the National League in walks two years in a row) deserted him completely. With Schneider, as with so many others, baseball's policy was to let sleeping dogs lie.

The same impulse apparently governed the game's attitude toward Chase, who unsurprisingly denied all the charges against him. In May he had signed with the San Jose club of the Mission League, an independent organization in California. He was a part-owner of the club and commuted from Los Angeles, his new home, to play for San Jose every Sunday.[72] Magee's statement contained "absolutely no truth," he insisted. "I was exonerated of all charges of betting by the National Commission after it made a full investigation. I do not know what Magee did at the time of the game he mentions, but I do know that I did not place any bets."[73]

Still, in light of the testimony in the Magee trial, some observers wondered anew about that exoneration. Dan Daniel wrote that "the National League's hearing of the charges against Chase a year ago last winter was, to say the least, perfunctory. When Chase was whitewashed by the league a strong suspicion existed that many bits of evidence which should have been investigated thoroughly had been glossed over or ignored."[74]

The loyal *Sporting News* defended the National League president in an editorial. "No one would believe him capable of connivance in keeping Chase in baseball if he had evidence to prove the now discredited player guilty of dirty work," argued the editorial. "The facts are, and should be accepted without question, that Mr. Heydler did not have the evidence against Chase and there was no 'whitewash' of that player." The editorial went on to imply, however, that Heydler could have been more zealous in trying to unearth that evidence. Instead it was Ban Johnson, "while fighting enemies in his own league and out of it," who had found the time "to pursue an exhaustive investigation that he felt was required if the good name of baseball was to be preserved...."[75]

That good name had been taking a beating in both the major and minor leagues. In early May the San Francisco Seals of the Pacific Coast League released pitchers Tom Seaton and Casey Smith, charging them with gambling on games. *The Sporting News* noted that at the beginning of his professional career, while playing for an independent team in Oxnard, Seaton had been accused of accepting money to throw games, although charges were never pressed.[76]

In June Heydler held a secret hearing to investigate charges by Giants pitcher Rube Benton that Chase and Buck Herzog had offered him a bribe to throw a game during the previous season. Heydler interviewed Herzog and Benton before dismissing the charges and, still smarting from criticism of his handling of the Chase hearing, swore the players to silence, but word of the affair got out anyway.[77]

Then, in August, several players in the Pacific Coast League, including the unfortunate "onion," Babe Borton, were implicated in a bribery scandal. Salt Lake City pitchers Ralph Stroud and Charlie Baum, who had been with the Seals in the spring of 1916 when Chase practiced with the team, said that Borton and Chase had attempted to bribe them. Baum and Stroud also implicated their teammate Harley Maggert, who had received $300 from Borton. Maggert claimed the money was in payment of an old gambling debt, but was quickly released.

The Vernon Tigers suspended Borton "pending investigation." The player claimed that the charges were a plot concocted by Salt Lake City manager Ernie Johnson to disrupt the Vernon team. A few days later, however, Borton said that he and his Vernon teammates, including manager Bill Essick, had raised $2,000, which they had given to players on the Salt Lake City, Portland, and Seattle clubs to help Vernon win the 1919 pennant. Pacific Coast League president William McCarthy, shocked by the scope of Borton's accusations, sought to downplay the scandal. He called Borton's story "a mass of falsehoods from which the truth, if any, will be hard to extricate." Vernon quickly released Borton. Salt Lake City's Bill Rumler admitted having received $200 from Borton, but was "exonerated" by his team.[78]

On August 3 McCarthy issued a statement barring Chase from entering any Pacific Coast League ballpark. "If reports are true, Chase has done more to discredit baseball than any single individual," said McCarthy. "Chase will not hereafter be permitted in any park in our league. It is unfortunate that no further punishment can be imposed. Certainly there is no punishment too severe, but perhaps the contempt of men and women who love baseball and who believe in clean sport will prove sufficient penalty."

President James J. Nealon of the Mission League, not wishing to oppose the powerful PCL, quickly followed McCarthy's lead, though he doubtless was sorry to lose a star attraction; during Chase's brief Mission League career, he batted .442 in 14 games.[79] "The action of the Coast League directors in barring Chase admission to all Coast League games is sufficient proof to me that Chase is not a fit player for the Mission League," said Nealon. "The Mission League wants the friendship and cooperation of the Coast League and we stand ready to keep Chase and his element from infesting our parks."[80]

From Los Angeles Chase called Baum's accusations "foolish" and said that he would demand a hearing before McCarthy and Nealon, and if they failed to reinstate him he would take them to court. He also promised to come north as usual on Sunday, August 8, when San Jose was scheduled to play Hollister. And, as usual, he had an explanation for the controversy; as usual, he claimed that he was innocent and had been misunderstood.

"I have a friend who had been making small bets on the game," explained Chase, "and I thought he was foolish because I had heard that Coast League games were being 'framed.' I therefore went to Baum, whom I had considered a friend, and asked him about it. He told me that the games were on the square and added that [Walt] Leverenz would pitch the next day and usually won. 'If that will do you any good,' Baum said, 'you are welcome to the information.'

"The bets made by my friend were never more than $30 or $40 — simply a sporting proposition."[81]

Chase's defiant stance threatened to make a mockery of McCarthy and Nealon's ban. "The San Jose crowd cheered Chase madly when he appeared in uniform and again when he took the field" that Sunday. He tried to enter the game as a pitcher in the third inning, but his plans met a snag. "Acting under instructions from the league president the umpire refused to let Chase play," reported *The Sporting News,* "and when San Jose insisted the game was forfeited to the Hollister Club."[82]

Organized baseball seemed to be degenerating into chaos as well. McCarthy suggested that the Vernon club sue Borton for slander. Borton threatened to sue right back, saying that he had been slandered.[83]

Chase, too, was threatening legal action. On August 11 his attorney, James P. Sex of San Francisco, told a meeting of the Mission League directors at Gilroy that Chase would sue McCarthy for defamation of character. McCarthy was unimpressed. "So Hal Chase is suing me for defamation of character," he sneered. "I never knew he possessed such a thing."[84] The suit was never filed.

Doors throughout California were slamming shut on Chase. When the Lomoor club of the little-known San Joaquin Valley Baseball League expressed interest in signing Chase and Maggert, league president C. T. Buckman announced that no player who had been banned by organized baseball would be welcome in the league. Chase and Maggert played one game for the Madera team of the Northern San Joaquin Valley League, but league president J. C. Lesher quickly barred them from further participation.[85]

Inspired by the Magee case and the Pacific Coast League scandal, the press began investigating other suspicious events, as it seemed to be open season on organized baseball's carefully contrived reputation for integrity. An August 31 game between the Cubs and the last-place Phillies seemed particularly worthy of attention.

An hour before the game Cubs president Veeck received six telegrams and two long-distance telephone calls informing him that unusually large sums were being wagered against the Cubs in Detroit, implying that the gamblers had learned that the game was to be fixed for Philadelphia to win. Since no player has more control over the outcome of a game than the pitcher, suspicion naturally fell on the Cubs' scheduled starter, Claude Hendrix. Veeck ordered Chicago manager Fred Mitchell to replace Hendrix with Grover Cleveland Alexander, the

Cubs' best pitcher, and even promised Alexander, who had pitched three days before, a $500 bonus if he won. Aleck pitched reasonably well, but a second-inning error on a potential double-play ball by Buck Herzog led to two Phillie runs and the Cubs went on to lose 3–0. Despite the outcome Veeck was sure that Alexander had given him an honest effort.[86]

After the game Veeck hired the Burns Detective Agency to investigate the fix rumors. Having survived the public airing of the Lee Magee affair, the Cub owner wanted to make sure this potential scandal remained a secret. On September 2, however, the Chicago *Herald and Examiner* received a letter which declared, "The hotel lobbies [in Detroit] were crowded with gamblers wanting to bet any amount of money on the Phillies, despite unfavorable odds. Conditions were so openly rotten that I was prompted to write as I do. Every fellow mixed up with baseball gambling hung around the tickers chuckling over the returns of that game...."[87]

The story hit the front page on September 4. Immediately the press, having developed a keen taste for baseball scandals, began printing other rumors. The Chicago *Tribune* absolved Herzog of blame for the error that led to the Cubs' defeat: "It was rather a hard chance. Any player might have erred on the same play. There was nothing during the game to make it look suspicious." The same paper, however, determined not to be outdone by the *Herald and Examiner,* reported that local gamblers had linked four Cubs, three of whom had played in the game, to the plot. One local bookie, when asked about gambling on baseball, replied, "Say, thousands are bet every day within twenty-five yards of the city hall," and claimed that one man had lost $11,000 on the August 31 game.

The *Tribune* also reported a curious coincidence that had occurred in Philadelphia in early August. After sweeping three games from the Phillies, the Cubs had been 11–5 favorites to win the last game of the series, which Hendrix started, but the odds mysteriously shifted to 6–5 in favor of the Phillies shortly before the game. Hendrix gave up nine hits and four walks in seven and two-thirds innings. He was relieved after walking three in a row in the eighth inning, and the Phillies won 4–1.[88]

The rumors were threatening to get out of hand. Veeck launched a damage control effort: "The charges that there were 'fixed' players on the Cubs came as no surprise to me. If I had any regret at their publication at this time, it is merely that investigations which were being made might be hampered by publicity." He also announced that he was inviting the Chicago chapter of the Baseball Writers of America to investigate as well and offered to pay the writers' expenses. "Our unfortunate experience of last year [with Magee] made us feel doubly responsible to the great baseball loving public," intoned Veeck piously.[89]

But the Hendrix scandal, coming in the wake of the other rumors and revelations of the last year, was too much. The old pieties would no longer suffice. Joe Vila was disgusted by the spectacle. "For more than forty years the big league games enjoyed the absolute confidence of the sporting public," he wrote in

September. "Why? Because the players refused to be tempted and the gamblers devoted their attention to other sports.

"But the eyes of the fans were partially opened when Christy Mathewson lodged charges against Hal Chase in 1918 — charges that were dismissed because legal proof was lacking. Still the fact that ball players were betting on the games with bookmakers and gamblers, particularly in Boston, was a shock for those who never had dreamed that baseball wasn't on the square." Without even mentioning the mess in the Pacific Coast League, Vila ticked off the list of recent scandals: "The Magee case, the stories of sharp practice in the 1919 World's Series, the dropping of Chase and Zimmerman by the Giants, the charge made by a National League pitcher [Benton] that he had been offered $700 to throw a game to the Cubs in Chicago last September and the recent mess which President Veeck of the Cubs courageously exposed" all indicated that major league baseball had some hard work ahead if it wished to reestablish its reputation as an honest institution.[90]

Another commentator felt that much of the current mess in baseball could be attributed to Heydler's handling of the Chase hearing. I. E. Sanborn wrote in the Chicago *Tribune* that baseball had ignored repeated warnings of "the inroads of the betting fraternity," and thus had brought its troubles upon itself. "To take a concrete example," wrote Sanborn, "if the National league had acted firmly, fearlessly, even if unjustly, in the disposition of the Hal Chase matter several [sic] years ago there would have been comparatively little of the scandal that has developed since. Granting the alibi of the promoters at the time that the charges against Chase were not substantiated, the baseball public and the ball players never were convinced by the lack of evidence that there was not some fire where there was so much smoke.

"Granting, for the sake of the point, that Chase was wholly innocent of the charges made, it would have been better that one man suffer injustice for the good of the game than that scores of ball players should be made to suffer the injustice of suspicion, as has been the result of inaction in the Chase case."[91]

Vila and Sanborn were not alone in their disgust. James Crusinberry of the *Tribune* sought out Fred Loomis, a Chicago businessman and well-known baseball fan. Together they agreed that Crusinberry should write a letter in Loomis's name to call attention to organized baseball's persistent refusal to set its house in order.

The letter was published in the *Tribune* on Sunday, September 19. "Up to this time baseball has been accepted by the public as the one clean sport above reproach in every particular and engaged in by men, both owners and players, whose honesty and integrity have been beyond suspicion or reproach," wrote "Loomis." "At this time, however, it occurs to me that the game must be cleaned up at once ... if baseball is going to survive...." Crusinberry/Loomis suggested that, if baseball continued in its reluctance to clean itself up, other methods existed: "There is a perfectly good Grand Jury located in this county. The citizens and taxpayers of Illinois are maintaining such an institution for the purpose of investigating any alleged infraction of the law." Perhaps, he suggested, the time was right for that grand jury to get involved.[92]

Several other volumes, some more convincing than others, have purported to tell the true story of the Black Sox fix.[93] Such detailed analysis is beyond the scope of this work. Suffice it to say that Chase was repeatedly mentioned in connection with the fix, and was eventually indicted in the case. At the very least, as he acknowledged years later, he knew of the fix ahead of time. Grand jury testimony indicated that Chase won a large sum of money betting on the Series, although later in life Chase denied having done so; however, it is hard to imagine anyone, especially Chase, passing up such an opportunity.

The legal history of the Black Sox case begins with an insecure politician. Cook County district attorney Maclay Hoyne had angered many Chicago Democrats by forsaking the party to run unsuccessfully for mayor as an independent the year before, and in the fall of 1920 he faced a stiff challenge in the Democratic primary from Robert E. Crowe. Hoyne saw in an official investigation of the rumors of baseball corruption a potentially high-profile opportunity to guarantee his reelection. He discussed the rumors with his friend, Judge Charles A. McDonald.[94]

McDonald had succeeded Crowe as chief justice of the Cook County criminal court on September 7. As one of his first official actions he instructed the September grand jury to look into the rumors of dirty dealings in the national pastime, specifically the August 31 Cubs-Phillies game and the 1919 World Series.[95]

The investigation came too late for Hoyne, who lost the primary to Crowe, but the wheels of the judicial process had been set in motion. The grand jury hearings quickly became front-page news across the nation. The first player called to testify was Giants pitcher Rube Benton. "Benton knows a whole lot," said assistant state's attorney Hartley L. Replogle, whom Hoyne had placed in charge of the investigation. "We especially wish him to tell what a certain player on the Cubs team asked him to do."[96]

The identity of that certain player was an open secret: it was Buck Herzog, already suspected of being one of the three or four Cubs implicated in the August 31 fix. Cubs manager Fred Mitchell had sent Herzog, Hendrix, Fred Merkle, and Paul Carter home from Boston, claiming that they were not needed on the club's current road trip. Mitchell insisted rather unconvincingly that his action had nothing to do with the grand jury investigation.

Benton's appearance before the grand jury seemed to live up to Replogle's expectations, and even more than the Magee trial forced baseball to acknowledge publicly that corruption was a serious problem. Benton said that on September 11, 1919, the night before Heinie Zimmerman's suspension, Benton had met Chase and Herzog, who had been traded to the Cubs in midseason, for a few beers in a saloon near LaSalle and Madison Streets on Chicago's north side. There, Benton claimed, Chase and Herzog had suggested that he could make "some easy money" by letting the Cubs win the next day's game, since the Reds already had the pennant race sewn up. They told him that he would receive a substantial sum if he agreed to throw the game. Benton refused, and beat the Cubs 7–3 on the following day. After the game, he said, Zimmerman came up to him in the lobby of the Auditorium Hotel and said, "You poor fish, don't you know there was $400 waiting for you to lose that game today?"[97]

Benton also said that he had been in Jean Dubuc's room at the Ansonia in New York in late September 1919 when Dubuc received a telegram from Bill Burns telling him that the upcoming Series was fixed. Benton added that Chase had received similar telegrams from Burns and had won as much as $40,000 betting on the Series, but that as far as he knew Chase was an honest player.[98]

Benton's story was sensational, but Herzog quickly succeeded in raising doubts about the pitcher's reliability as a witness. Herzog testified that his friend Art Wilson of the Boston Braves had told him in May that Benton had been spreading the story that Herzog and Chase had tried to bribe him. Herzog said that he and Wilson had gone to see Veeck the next day. Veeck told them that he had already heard the rumors, whereupon Herzog demanded a hearing before Heydler to clear his name. At that hearing, held in June, Herzog told Heydler that Benton had carried a grudge against him since 1915, when Herzog was Benton's manager in Cincinnati, and suggested that Benton had concocted the bribe story to divert attention from his disciplinary problems with McGraw.[99]

Furthermore, Herzog told the grand jury he had shown Heydler affidavits from Wilson and Norman (Tony) Boeckel of the Braves stating that Benton had boasted of winning $3,800 betting on the 1919 World Series thanks to a tip from Hal Chase that the Series was fixed. Before Heydler, said Herzog, Benton said he had won $1,500, not $3,800.[100] After considering the various charges and countercharges, Heydler had cleared Herzog and instructed all parties to keep quiet about the matter.

Heydler corroborated Herzog's story. At the hearing, he recalled, Benton had backtracked rapidly, first claiming that he could not recall whether Herzog or Chase had offered the bribe, then that Chase was the guilty party. According to Heydler, however, Benton said that Bill Burns, not Chase, had told him about the World Series fix.

Heydler added almost casually that McGraw had gotten rid of Chase and Zimmerman because they offered Benny Kauff $500 to throw a game in St. Louis in September 1919: "John McGraw deliberately wrecked his pennant chances by getting rid of Chase and Zimmerman, because of their alleged gambling and game throwing." McGraw himself modestly concurred with Heydler's assessment of his selflessness: "I got rid of Chase and Zimmerman, even though I knew it would seriously injure my team, because I didn't want such men on the club."[101]

This was selfless indeed, "although it was not clear," as Harold Seymour pointed out, "just what risk McGraw was taking in ridding himself of the players who were jeopardizing his chances of winning the pennant."[102] McGraw explained that he had dropped Chase after Heydler told him that Lee Magee had implicated Prince Hal.[103] No one thought to wonder how Heydler had known of Magee's activities in the fall of 1919, six months before Magee's confession in Heydler's Chicago hotel room. Also unexplored was the issue of why the National League president for almost three months had suppressed the evidence from the Benton-Herzog hearing that the 1919 World Series had indeed been fixed.

Heydler's story of Chase and Zimmerman's departure from the Giants drew an angry denial from Zimmerman in New York. "No such thing ever happened," he insisted. "I guess they are trying to push me, Chase and Magee to the wall and make goats of us." He said that the Giants had sent him a contract for the 1920 season. He had not signed it, said Zimmerman, because it called for a salary cut and because of unspecified differences with McGraw.[104]

The Great Zim was small potatoes, however, compared to the fixing of the 1919 World Series. The first attempt to reconstruct the scheme in detail appeared in print on September 25 and gave Chase a central role in the scheme. According to the Chicago *Tribune*, Chase had approached Abe Attell at the Polo Grounds a few weeks before the end of the 1919 season and asked whether Attell could find backers willing to put up $100,000 to fix the World Series. Chase knew that Attell, a former featherweight boxer known as the "Little Champ," was one of Arnold Rothstein's lieutenants. Attell brought Chase's proposition to his boss, who turned it down; Attell, however, seeing an opportunity to make a little extra for himself, told Chase that Rothstein had agreed to put up the money. Chase then met with two members of the White Sox, most likely Gandil and Risberg, to confirm the scheme.

Anticipating a killing, Attell and Chase began placing bets on the Reds. Chase himself could not go to Cincinnati for the Series, as he had already committed to a barnstorming tour on the East Coast. In his absence another man, most likely Burns, was engaged to act as the middleman between Attell and the Chicago players.[105]

A different version of the fix appeared on September 28, when Jimmy Isaminger of the Philadelphia *North American* reported "the complete story of the most gigantic sporting swindle in the history of America." Isaminger had unearthed "a roly-poly man" named Billy Maharg, a former boxer and a well-known figure in Philadelphia sporting circles. He had officially appeared in two major league games, one with the Tigers when the team's regular players went on strike in sympathy for the suspended Ty Cobb in 1912 and one with the Phillies in 1916, and had lived with Grover Cleveland Alexander when Old Pete pitched for the Phillies.[106]

Maharg claimed that he and Bill Burns, not Chase and Attell, had set up the World Series fix after Cicotte approached them with the idea at the Ansonia in New York. Maharg said that he and Burns had met with Rothstein personally in New York, but Rothstein had turned them down. Maharg then returned to Philadelphia, but Burns wired him that he had run into Attell, who claimed to have "fixed things up" with Rothstein.[107]

Chase was conspicuously absent from Maharg's story, but he figured prominently in plenty of other incriminating stories. Larry Doyle told of an incident that occurred during the fall of 1919, when the Giants' barnstorming team played the Atlantic City Giants in Philadelphia. "Chase approached me before the game and told me there was a nice piece of change waiting for me if I booted a few and fanned in the pinches," related Doyle. "I told Chase I was Irish and that I had a peculiar way of answering offers like these. Chase walked away hurriedly."

The Giants' trainer, J. L. Mackall, testified that "All I know is that Mr. Hal Chase received a powerful lot of telegrams and phone calls just before the season ended last fall.... There used to be quite a few flashy dressed sports with diamonds as big as pigeon eggs palling around with Hal Chase and Bill Burns."

Dubuc testified that "Chase supplied all the information to Bill Burns about the series being fixed for Cincinnati to win. Burns wired me from Cincinnati to get down all I could beg, borrow and steal on Cincinnati to win the series." Dubuc claimed that he had not taken this advice, but had bet only a little.[108]

From Montreal, where he had gone to escape the proceedings, Attell claimed that he had first learned of the World Series fix from Chase and Burns. Attell said that he had first met Burns at a Phillies-Reds doubleheader in Philadelphia, during Chase's tenure with Cincinnati. Attell claimed that Burns and a friend of his named Mohawk (Maharg) "had Chase throw four games to Philadelphia, and I myself lost $4,000. At that time there was a boy on the field betting for Chase and Burns." Attell added that Rothstein had made as much as $70,000 betting on the series.[109]

By now the August 31 game between the Cubs and Phillies had been all but forgotten, but Chase's name was dragged into that relatively minor scandal as well. Ban Johnson produced a letter from a St. Louis newspaperman claiming that on the morning of the game a local gambler named Frog Thompson had received a wire, believed to be from Claude Hendrix, placing a $5,000 bet against the Cubs. The letter also charged that Chase had wired Thompson to tell him that the game was fixed. The upshot was predictable: "Thompson denied everything, and from then on the grand jury simply ignored the question of crookedness in the Philadelphia-Chicago game." Hendrix, however, was quietly expelled from organized baseball after the season.[110]

It was impossible to tell which of the conflicting versions of the truth was correct, and which rumors were deserving of credence, but one thing was clear: something was definitely rotten in baseball, and Hal Chase's name had once again been linked, however vaguely, to a scandal.

The novelist James T. Farrell was a high school student in Chicago at the time. He had been a great admirer of Chase's during the first baseman's brief tenure with the White Sox several years before, and the revelation of Chase's alleged dirty dealings came as "a shock" to him. Farrell vented his anguish in his English composition class: "I filled almost half a composition book sentimentally lamenting over the fall of 'Prince Hal,' as he was called. My teacher, Father Albert O. Dolan, O. Carm., who is now dead, got ten to fifteen times more than he had asked for, at least in volume."[111]

As if Chase's reputation had not already suffered sufficient damage in 1920 from the Magee trial, the Pacific Coast League scandal, and the grand jury revelations, Anna Chase sued him for divorce in Cincinnati in late November. The proceedings had more than their share of melodrama.

Anna, who was staying with friends in Avondale, a suburb of Dayton some fifty miles north of Cincinnati, charged him with cruelty and neglect, claiming that he had associated with other women and even introduced them into his home. Moreover, he had "been guilty of other immoral conduct to which publicity has been given from time to time in the press," causing her emotional distress and embarrassment. He was "given to gambling, dissipation and immoral conduct, wasting his money on other women and losing large sums gambling." Anna said that she had left Chase several times, but had returned each time when he promised to behave better. The last of these reconciliations had occurred in September 1919, but it did not last. Since the beginning of March, she said, Chase had contributed exactly $1.25 toward her support.[112]

Public sympathy was clearly on Anna's side: "Mrs. Chase is a comely woman," reported the Cincinnati *Enquirer,* "and she attracted considerable attention during her stay in the Domestic Relations Court." She produced a letter to Chase from an unnamed woman in Port Chester, New York, as evidence of his extramarital wanderings. It read in part: "My Own Sweetheart: I had planned to write you yesterday, but have been so very blue since you left that by the time C. B. left last night I was a nervous wreck and went to bed instead. There hasn't been a bit of sunshine since you left."

"C. B." was the woman's unsuspecting husband, who told her that she looked much more beautiful when Chase was in town. The letter was signed "Billy," and across the bottom of the page she had written, "Destroy this immediately."[113]

Anna also said that Chase had repeatedly lied to her about his salary with the Reds and Giants. He had been paid $9,000 with the Reds, she claimed, but allowed the club to reduce the figure on his contract to $7,000 and pocketed the difference. He told her initially that he made $6,000 with the Giants, but later admitted that his actual salary was $7,500.[114]

The Chases' Cincinnati landlord, Albert Dalker, testified that he had once found Anna crying and threatening legal action against her husband, but had dissuaded her from doing so. Dalker said that because of her husband's gambling Mrs. Chase always paid her rent months in advance during the summer, when he was employed, so that she would not be evicted during the winter.

"Chase was what is known as a crooked gambler," added Dalker. He related that Chase had once won $1,500 shooting craps by using loaded dice. When the other players in the game discovered his subterfuge, said Dalker, Chase escaped by jumping through a window and running away.[115]

Such sordid details were of secondary importance to baseball fans, however. For them, the real interest of the divorce involved the inside story of Chase's 1918 suspension. No doubt the Reds welcomed the trial as an opportunity to prove once and for all that they had been correct in suspending Chase in 1918; perhaps this explains the fact that the team's legal counsel, Howard Ragland, represented Anna Chase. Among the witnesses he called was Garry Herrmann, who recounted the events leading up to the suspension and formally identified the affidavits that Ring, Neale, Regan, and Mathewson had submitted to Heydler, which were entered as evidence. Anna herself testified that Chase had told her at the time of his suspension, "I guess they've got the goods on me." When Ragland asked her about Chase's activities with the Giants, she replied that she was "sure he was throwing games there, too." She added that she had asked Chase about the Black Sox fix, and he had told her, "I knew of it, and I did what I could to help it along."

Chase offered no defense to the suit, and Anna was granted her divorce on January 26, 1921.[116]

Despite his various troubles, Chase seems to have retained his sincere love of the game. Bill Schroeder, the longtime director of the Helms Athletic Foundation in Los Angeles, played baseball for Hollywood High School in 1920. He recalled that during one of the team's practices a man came up and asked if he could hit a few. The players agreed, whereupon the man took off his coat and proceeded to whack a series of long drives, in the neighborhood of four hundred feet. He then put his coat back on and thanked the awestruck boys. When they asked him if he had ever played pro ball, he replied, "Yes, a little." When they asked him his name, he replied, "Hal Chase," and walked on down the street.[117]

Meanwhile, in Chicago, the investigation of the Black Sox fix had been proceeding by fits and starts, amid rumors of political intrigue and tampering with the evidence. On October 22, 1920, the grand jury had indicted eight White Sox players: Chick Gandil, Eddie Cicotte, Swede Risberg, Lefty Williams, Happy Felsch, Fred McMullin, Buck Weaver, and Joe Jackson. The grand jury also indicted five gamblers: Abe Attell, Sport Sullivan, Bill Burns, Rachael Brown—and Hal Chase.[118] Judge William E. Dever set March 14, 1921, as the starting date for the trial; on March 10, however, the state's attorney's office announced that it would seek a postponement of six months in order to give the prosecutors time to prepare their case.

Organized baseball moved immediately to ensure that the indicted players would not be allowed to play in the meantime. Judge Landis officially placed them on the ineligible list on March 12. Four days later Comiskey notified them of their unconditional release. On the following day, after arguing unsuccessfully for a further delay, the prosecution moved for *nolle prosequi* in the cases against Cicotte, Risberg, Williams, Felsch, McMullin, Weaver, and Jackson, citing possible corruption of witnesses and rumors that a New York newspaper syndicate had offered the supposedly confidential grand jury testimony for sale. State's attorney Crowe announced that the seven would be immediately reindicted and added that the indictments against the other men in the fix—Gandil, Burns, Attell, Sullivan, Brown, and Chase—still stood. Their cases, however, were stricken from the call, meaning they would not come up again at least until the fall.

Nine—I Beat Them in Court Every Time

Arnold "Chick" Gandil, the first baseman and alleged ringleader of the so-called "Black Sox" who threw the 1919 World Series. Gandil was a rough customer who played semi-pro ball with Chase in Arizona during the 1920s. *National Baseball Hall of Fame Library, Cooperstown, N.Y.*

On March 26 the Cook County grand jury handed down eighteen new indictments. The eight Black Sox were reindicted, as were Attell, Sullivan, Burns, Brown, and Chase. Indicted for the first time were Carl Zork and Benjamin Franklin of St. Louis; Ben and Louis Levi, formerly of Des Moines; and David Zelser of Des Moines and San Francisco. According to the state's attorney's office, Zork and Franklin had organized the plot, the Levi brothers directed it in the Midwest and Sullivan in the East, while Attell had acted as a traveling agent.[119]

It seemed that the noose was drawing tighter around the alleged conspirators. In early April the New York *Times* reported that Jackson, Risberg, and Williams were organizing their own semipro team with the backing of several Chicago investment brokers, but the directors of the Chicago Baseball League quickly voted to expel any player or umpire who participated in a game with the Black Sox, as the new team was called.[120]

On April 25, Hal Chase was arrested by Detective Ray Starbird as he left a theater in San Jose. Crowe announced that extradition papers would be prepared immediately and said that Chase's arrest marked the beginning of a new phase in the case. Chase was held on $3,000 bond, which was posted by his father. Naturally Prince Hal denied any involvement in the conspiracy. "I know nothing about it and am not in any way connected with any baseball scandal," he insisted. "As far as I am concerned there is nothing to the charge against me."[121]

On the day after his arrest Chase aired an intriguing theory: he claimed that sexual jealousy on the part of John McGraw was responsible for his recent troubles. "When I was in that city [Chicago?] I knew a certain girl who was very friendly with me," he explained. "She was a good girl and a girl who confided in me more than once regarding the manner in which she was being pursued by John McGraw. McGraw thereafter thought that I had lessened him in the eyes of the girl and he started out to 'get me.'

"When you read about Benton and Dubuc of the Giants accusing me of crookedness it was McGraw getting even with me, that's all. And when Lee Magee accused me it was a case of a fellow in wrong trying to save his bacon by pulling another fellow down with him.

"The truth of the matter is, Ban Johnson, McGraw and others never forgave me for jumping to the Federal League, and they have been persecuting me ever since." Chase had apparently forgotten that McGraw had testified in his behalf before Heydler four years *after* he jumped to the Feds. "I beat them in court every time they started after me."

He then went on the offensive. "McGraw, who has been identified with racetrack gambling and who only the other day nearly killed an old actor, is a nice subject to be trying to send anyone to jail for crookedness in baseball.

"If I thought they had anything on me and I thought there was a chance of going to jail, don't you think I would be in Mexico before now? I know they have nothing."[122]

Chick Gandil was arrested in Los Angeles, where he had gone to work for a lumber company, the day after Chase's arrest, while Eddie Cicotte sent word from Detroit that he would come to Chicago to post bond. Some of the other indicted men, however, had already made other plans; Bill Burns was in Mexico, while Attell and Sullivan were reportedly in Canada, which had no extradition treaty with the United States. Ban Johnson, ready as ever with a grandstand play, announced that he would go to Washington, D.C., to seek federal support for asking Canada to deport the two as undesirables.[123]

There the situation rested for over a month, with the case seeming once again to have ground to a halt. And then, on May 27, another news flash hit Chicago: Hal Chase had been released on a writ of habeas corpus, his bail of $3,000 exonerated, on the grounds that a proper warrant for his arrest had not been sent from Chicago and no effort had been made to return him to that city.[124]

Eliot Asinof, the best-known historian of the Black Sox scandal, implied that William J. Fallon, the notoriously unscrupulous New York attorney known as "the Great Mouthpiece" and Rothstein's personal lawyer (as well as a friend of Stoneham and McGraw's[125]), pulled strings to get Chase released, hoping to

Trustbusting federal judge Kenesaw Mountain Landis became commissioner of baseball in 1921. He promptly banned the "Black Sox" from organized baseball, despite their acquittal by a Chicago jury. Chase had been indicted as a middleman in the fix but escaped extradition and never came to trial. Landis took no official action against Chase. *National Baseball Hall of Fame Library, Cooperstown, N.Y.*

minimize the scandal.[126] Chase himself later claimed that he had offered to go to Chicago to testify, but only on the condition that the state's attorney's office pay him $500 for his time and provide his transportation. The authorities declined his offer, he said, and that was the end of it: as he said, "They couldn't have wanted me very badly if they weren't willing to put up that small guarantee."[127]

In fact, Chase's exact role in the scheme remains unclear. One author, in a magazine article about Chase, concocted an apparently imaginary dialogue between Chase and his old teammate Bill Burns, who came to visit him in September 1919. According to this version, Chase declined Burns's invitation to play an active role in arranging the fix.

"You know the right players to approach," Burns told him. "If someone could raise a thousand bucks, the deal is a cinch."

"I've got trouble enough right now," Chase supposedly answered. "I don't want to get involved in anything else."[128]

Other versions of Chase's role seem equally, or more, plausible. Asinof wrote that Chase advised Burns to contact Rothstein personally, rather than use Attell as a middleman, to arrange financial backing for the scheme. According to Asinof, after Burns thanked Chase for the suggestion and asked what he wanted in return, Chase merely grinned and said he wanted only the right to bet on the series.[129] Rube Benton — hardly the most reliable witness — told Art Wilson and Tony Boeckel that Chase had tipped him off about the fix and that he (Benton) had subsequently won more than three thousand dollars betting on the Reds. Before the grand jury, however, Benton denied betting on the series himself, though he admitted knowing of the fix in advance. He testified that Dubuc and Chase had received telegrams from Burns advising them of the scheme, and that Chase had won $40,000 betting on the Reds.[130] Joe Gedeon said that he and Chase had bet on the Reds, winning a mere $600, on a tip from Swede Risberg.[131] Jean Dubuc, on the other hand, testified that Chase had told Burns about the fix, not the other way around.[132] Chase himself insisted for the rest of his life that he had indeed known about the fix in advance, but had not profited from it.[133] Given what we know of his character, however, it seems unlikely that he would pass up a chance for an easy killing.

Judge Landis officially took office as the sole commissioner of baseball in November 1921, and quickly won a reputation for his fierce and autocratic determination to rid the game of the taint of scandal. That Landis never publicly took action against Chase, as he did against several other players with considerably less redolent past records, is curious, but probably reflects the fact that Chase's career in organized baseball was already clearly over.[134]

Once again, Chase walked away from a major scandal officially untainted. Once again organized baseball had thought it had the goods on Chase, and once again he had beaten the rap.

Ten

A Long Way to the So-Called "Big Town"

Chase's victory, however, was in some respects a hollow one. His major league career was over, and he had been officially banned from pursuing his livelihood in his home state. Still, he seemed undaunted, and his character seemed basically unchanged. His son, who freely acknowledged that Chase was "a womanizer," thought he recalled having seen Mrs. Harvey S. Firestone among his father's visitors when the disgraced ex–major leaguer was briefly hospitalized in the 1920s; young Hal never learned if his youthful impression was correct, or what his father had to do with the spouse of one of America's leading industrialists.[1] For most of the rest of Chase's life he seemed content to live aimlessly, with little or no interest in settling down or planning for the future. In the early 1920s he bounced around the San Joaquin Valley before settling briefly in Watsonville, California, where he met a mining engineer who said he had connections in Nogales, Arizona, and could help set Chase up there.[2]

Arizona had attained statehood in 1912, and the proximity of the Mexican border and the get-rich-quick atmosphere of the copper-mining towns which dotted the state gave it a raw, frontier flavor. Sometimes the state barely seemed part of the United States; in fact, in many respects it resembled Chase's native California in the early stages of its development, when a different precious metal had attracted settlers, opportunists, and hustlers. In this setting, Chase's tarnished reputation mattered little, and even though he was almost forty he still found himself in some demand as a ballplayer.

At this time, a baseball team was considered a necessity for any town that wished to be taken seriously, and local boosters were prepared to pay handsomely for the services of a genuine big-league star, even if his career had ended rather ignominiously. Chase was much in demand, and received a flurry of attention when he was appointed manager of the Nogales Internationals in 1923. He had apparently lost none of his charm: "During his time here he became very well liked by everyone[,] especially the kids," remembered one man who grew up in Nogales at the time. "We use[d] to follow him around and watch him practice with great admiration."³ He may, however, already have begun the long slide into dissipation that made his later years such misery. Roy P. Drachman of Tucson, who played semipro ball at the time, recalled, "Hal Chase was a bum when I knew him. I met him the first time at the Cave Bar in Nogales. A friend said, 'Hal, let's see how you swing.' He was swinging pool cues at pieces of paper that were tossed to him. Everyone was drunk."⁴

The Internationals, as their name suggested, played on both sides of the border, and among their backers was the former governor of Sonora, Francisco Elias.⁵ According to *The Sporting News,* the news of Chase's appointment "came as unpleasant news to all honest men in the country, and as a distinct shock to President Ban Johnson of the American League." Johnson, "the sworn foe of every kind of baseball crooks and of gambling on baseball," was sufficiently alarmed to write to Manuel Tellez, the chargé d'affaires at the Mexican embassy in Washington, urging that Chase not be allowed such a prominent position. Tellez thanked Johnson for his concern but pointed out that the embassy had no authority over baseball.⁶

That Johnson sought to work through official government channels was not surprising. Baseball was seen as a significant diplomatic instrument. *The Sporting News* noted proudly that "largely through the friendly advice and assistance of President Johnson" baseball was supplanting bullfighting as Mexico's national sport, "and has thus become one more powerful medium of re-establishing friendly relations between these two peoples" after more than a decade of strained relations brought on by the Mexican Revolution and the ensuing problems along the U.S.-Mexican border.

"Under these circumstances the appointment of a man barred from every ball club in this country to any kind of executive position, or even employment as a player, in the new Mexican baseball institution is like a slap in the face to Organized Ball, must prevent any recognition by or assistance from the powers that be in this country, and is certain to impair the future progress and success of the game in Mexico." Chase's appointment was "a positive calamity" and "a grave mistake," and Johnson deserved "the thanks of every lover of clean and honest baseball" for taking the initiative when Commissioner Landis did not.⁷

Closer to home, E. D. Harrington, sports editor of the Arizona *Republic* in Phoenix, agreed that Chase's presence was a disgrace to the state. Harrington launched a bitter and lonely editorial campaign for "clean" sport. "Baseball is a profitable business for some," he wrote, "but the rank and file of fans in the city patronize the game as a sport." He noted approvingly that the Phoenix Tigers had asked Nogales president Sam Friedman to keep Chase out of the lineup until his eligibility could be determined.

Friedman agreed, but when Nogales swept a June 24 doubleheader from the visiting Tigers, Chase played under an assumed name. The Nogales papers jeered Harrington, who responded stiffly that "if trying to keep sports clean is going to make *The Republican* sports editor unpopular he is due to gather quite an adverse following down here." He chided the Tigers for their complicity in the charade: "There was no necessity for Chase using the name of 'Taylor' unless there was some doubt in the minds of Phoenix players as to the status of Chase; and if there was any doubt, the proper method would have been to keep Chase out of the lineup or refuse to play."[8]

On the same day that "Taylor" played for Nogales, another former major leaguer with a dubious reputation turned up in Arizona. Tom Seaton, who had been released "for the good of the game" by the San Francisco Seals in 1919, pitched the Tucson Motive Power team to a victory over Mesa, which protested his doctoring of the ball.[9]

Harrington was disgusted. "The game of baseball seems to have deteriorated to a do-as-you-please strata [sic] in Arizona," he wrote angrily. "Hal Chase must be laboring under the impression that he is now in 'the sticks.'... The Republican sports editor has no objection to Hal Chase playing in Nogales or Tom Seaton playing at Tucson, but it is proper to make suggestions for the home team to keep the game prosperous in Phoenix."[10]

Two weeks later Harrington attacked again. "Arizona is getting the spotlight on the sport pages—not as a spot where sportsmanship is given first call over financial gain—but as a haven for outcast athletes, men who have reached the end of the rope, and finding the doors locked in other parts of the country grasp at the last straw," he wrote. "It is nothing to boast, nothing to tell the world, that Arizona harbors Hal Chase, neither is it to the credit of semi-pro ballplayers to say they played with or against Hal Chase."[11]

Harrington quoted an article by I. E. Sanborn comparing Chase and his one-time friend Christy Mathewson, who had recently been named president of the Boston Braves. Matty's tenure would be brief and largely symbolic, due to continuing health problems stemming from his military service in France, but all of organized baseball was glad to see him back in the game again.[12]

Sanborn noted the irony that "these two stars were teammates, with equal opportunities to win fame and esteem.... It was Chase's own fault, however, that he does not stand out as preeminent among the first basemen of the past as Big Six does among the pitchers. The former had as much natural ability and skill as the latter. Chase had all the brains necessary to develop and use his ability to the limit.

"Otherwise they were exact opposites. Mathewson gave his best always to his team, his manager, and to the game. Chase worked always for himself and his own financial benefit. A written contract was a scrap of paper if he could better himself, and his friends were the wrong kind of bankers."[13]

A few days later Harrington returned to the topic. "It is not a question of Chase or Seaton, but the welfare of baseball in the southwest. If Chase and Seaton are not good enough to play in other cities why should Arizona come to the rescue?... So far as we are concerned Chase and Seaton can play in Nogales and Tucson just as long as the fans and promoters care to use them. But the fact remains that the record book does not show them good material for even the bushes. *The Republican* has presented the facts and sooner or later it will draw [*sic*] upon those involved that they have thrown a wrench into Arizona baseball and received nothing in return.

"Sport writers should not 'kid' Arizona fans into believing that Chase and Seaton are much abused ballplayers who have been 'railroaded' out of organized baseball and came all the way down here just to earn an honest living. It may be a long way to the so-called 'big town,' but so long as printing presses continue to roll and telegraph wires are in operation, Arizona fans will not stand for any 'kidding.' In fact the fans down here follow baseball just as close and are just as well informed as those who live in the big eastern cities."

Unsurprisingly, the Phoenix Tigers had grown weary of Harrington's constant scolding and complained about the lack of support from their hometown newspaper. Harrington took the high road in response: "*The Republican* has boosted baseball in this valley for years: carried eight column streamers for both Phoenix and Mesa — but we refuse to use the columns of the paper to advance the interests of Hal Chase and Tom Seaton.... [The Tigers] cannot expect us to act as publicity agents while they continue to deal with teams playing men who can not play in legitimate organized baseball."[14]

In Nogales, the local newspaper, the *Border Vidette*, dismissed such criticism. Chase was "a star ball player, and a thoro' gentleman. Que mas? No foolin', Nogales is for Hal, first, last and all the time."[15] Such enthusiasm reflected the great success of the Internationals; in 1923 "the team trumped all of its regular competitors" and concluded the season with "a rousing tour through Mexico."[16] Years later, however, Chase referred to an unspecified business opportunity he had lost and recalled being told in Ciudad Juarez not to proceed on to Mexico City, as planned, because yet another revolution had broken out.[17]

In 1924 Chase signed with the team in Williams, a lumber town in northeastern Arizona, but on June 20 jumped to the Jerome team, which had played Williams on the previous weekend.[18] Jerome's 1924 season culminated in the Labor Day defeat of its archrival, the Clarkdale Smelter team. After the season Chase returned to Nogales to tend bar, and did not return to Jerome in 1925. One local historian claimed that Chase had been fired from his job as an orderly at the local hospital for stealing supplies, although the same historian also implied that Chase was let go because of his success against Clarkdale at a time when local leaders sought to deemphasize the rivalry between the two neighboring towns and consolidate the Jerome and Clarkdale teams into one franchise.[19]

In the spring of 1925, a meeting of baseball boosters in Douglas voted to ask Chase, who was "now proprietor of a café in Agua Prieta, Mexico, just across the border from Douglas,"[20] to manage the local entry in the Southern Arizona League. Douglas was a company town, founded at the turn of the century when the Phelps Dodge Company of Bisbee selected a site for its new Copper Queen smelter and named after Dr. James Douglas, the president of Phelps Dodge. Before the war more than half of the state's copper had been processed in Douglas, but the postwar depression hit hard, and the smelters had only resumed operating in 1923.[21]

The prospect of Chase in Douglas aroused great excitement among the locals. The principal of the local high school, "a baseball player of considerable ability during his college days," posted an article from the March 8, 1924, Dearborn *Independent,* by "a veteran sports writer," on the school bulletin board. The article called Chase "the greatest fielder the position [first base] has known, also the greatest showman."[22] A local newspaperman wrote that "The whole world ought to be glad to attend a game just to see him cavort around first base." Nevertheless, some questioned the propriety of Chase's appointment. The Douglas *Daily International* responded testily: "We hear that there are people here who object to him as manager of the team. Funny they didn't go to the baseball meeting the other night and vote for someone else. We are beginning to wonder if anything will be done here without some one knocking the undertaking.... We would like to see the color of the man's hair who knows more about baseball than Chase does? We would like to know whether this thing that is being worked up is a winning baseball team or a knockers' battle."[23]

The newspaper's defensiveness seemed justified when an Eastern newspaper described Douglas in condescending terms: "A somewhat drab place is Douglas. Flat desert all around, big gloomy mountains in the distances, any way you look, and a smelter or two so close to the line that General Villa's bullets broke their windows when he attacked the Carranza garrison on the Mexican side in 1915. The dull, muddy main street of Douglas leads to a wire fence, which is the international boundary. Through the custom house, and you are in Agua Prieta, which is duller and muddier."[24]

The *Daily International* called the author of this article "either malicious or a poor ignorant sap to think that there was mud on the main street of Douglas which has been paved for two years and to think that there would be mud anywhere in a country where there has been no rain for a year."[25]

In the meantime, Chase found another opportunity to thumb his nose at organized baseball. He announced that he had been asked by the Mexican government to organize a proposed Mexican National Baseball League, an invitation which "would make him a Landis in Mexico." Chase foresaw a great future for the game in Mexico: "It won't be but a year or two now when any baseball team, before annexing the title of world's champions, will have to beat our best team," he predicted. "The Mexicans are natural ball players, and are developing a love for the game."

He admitted that he hoped to use the Mexican league to clear his name: "I feel I will have an opportunity here in Mexico of placing baseball on a sound and honest foundation and demonstrate to baseball fans of the United States that I was the Dreyfus and not the Benedict Arnold of baseball."[26]

Unsurprisingly, organized baseball failed to appreciate the rich ironies inherent in the idea of Chase becoming "a Landis in Mexico." John Wray in the St. Louis *Post-Dispatch* spoke for many when he wrote, "If we were the Republic of Mexico we would as soon think of putting a fox in charge of a hen house as Chase in charge of a ball league."[27]

Nothing came of the scheme. Perhaps Ban Johnson's diplomatic contacts paid off this time, as they had not when Chase had been named the manager in Nogales; perhaps Chase had simply made the whole thing up to annoy organized baseball. At any rate, he turned his attention to Douglas, where the situation had become confused. The team had been expected to play in the three-team Southern Arizona League, but when El Paso was denied membership in that league it offered to help finance Douglas's participation in a proposed new circuit, the Tri-State or Frontier League, which would also include teams in Juarez, Mexico, and Fort Bayard, New Mexico.

The Douglas *Daily Dispatch* predicted that such a move would mean that Chase would not manage the team after all, "as it is well known that the New Mexico and El Paso teams will not enter a league playing outlaw players."[28] Chase, who had been in Nogales, came to Douglas on March 31 to discuss the situation with the team's board of directors. Early the following morning, thieves stole the tires off the Chevrolet roadster he had borrowed from a friend and parked at the intersection of Railroad Avenue and First Street. Fortunately, they overlooked the suitcase he had left in the car.[29]

The directors voted to accept El Paso's offer to join the new league but with Chase as manager. Their decision was made easier when El Paso manager Frank H. Hodges sent a telegram saying, "Everything is O.K. to use Chase." Dr. T. J. McCamant of El Paso, who was about to be elected president of the league, also sent a letter heartily endorsing Chase's appointment. These men were doubtless motivated primarily by the thought of the crowds a star of Chase's magnitude would attract. As a Douglas businessman said at the meeting, "I am in favor of joining the Tri-State League because I feel sure we can be reasonably assured of good crowds when our team goes to El Paso or Fort Bayard, as both are good baseball towns."[30]

Chase's presence at the organizational meeting of the Tri-State League in El Paso was a popular success: "Chase was introduced to a crowd of approximately 3,000 fans at the El Paso park Sunday afternoon and the introduction was received with great favor, scores of the spectators throwing their hats in the air in welcoming the former major league star to the Frontier association."[31]

The fever for baseball was running high in Douglas as well. Appropriately, given Chase's fondness for booze and pool, a local bar and billiard parlor called the Smokehouse sponsored the team[32]; a Denver cigar company, perhaps seeking to capitalize on Chase's well-known weakness for cheroots, offered to supply uniforms; the Silver Dollar in Agua Prieta announced that it would give a new baseball glove to the first Douglas player to hit a home run[33]; and a local newspaper asked Chase to predict the outcome of the major league pennant races.[34]

Despite the high hopes, Douglas's season got off to a rocky start. Douglas lost its first two games to El Paso, and then Chase was called back to San Jose on April 22 by his mother's fatal illness.[35] He missed two games, but his return made little difference in the team's fortunes; Douglas lost nine of its first ten contests, and problems with a Mexican immigration official forced the cancellation of a game against the Juarez Indians and their star pitcher Tom Seaton.[36]

Part of the problem was that Douglas lacked the financial resources to buy competitive players. In May a group of Agua Prieta businessmen pledged $450 to support the team, and in early June the team announced a drive to raise $600 a month in subscriptions, but the financial problems continued: a few days later the team bought a bus from the Bisbee school system because travel by rail was too expensive.[37]

On June 17 Chase again left for California, this time on a recruiting trip to San Francisco. He did not return until early July, after the first half of the season had ended, and in his absence the team had continued to struggle. Chase himself, however, had been spectacular. At the age of forty-two, he ranked sixth in the league with a .375 batting average, with seven doubles, three triples, and three home runs in sixty-four at bats. He also led the league's first basemen with a .986 fielding percentage and had committed only two errors.[38]

Chase had revised his once-optimistic assessment of the local talent. Whereas before the season he had felt that the team would not have to look beyond Douglas,[39] now he and the directors announced that they would aggressively pursue as many former major leaguers as they could convince to come to Douglas. The rest of the season brought a series of rumors of ex–big leaguers about to be signed. Some of the rumors even proved to be true: on July 11 the *Daily Dispatch* trumpeted that Chase had invited Buck Weaver and Chick Gandil to join the team.[40]

Weaver played shortstop as Douglas swept a doubleheader from El Paso on the following day, and Gandil played first base on July 18 as Chase pitched a complete-game loss against El Paso. A week later, however, the final configuration of what one reporter labelled the "million dollar infield" had Gandil at first base, Chase at second, Weaver at shortstop, and Felix Ramirez at third base.[41]

But Chase was not through yet. In late July he signed pitcher Limb McKenry, who had pitched briefly for the Reds in 1915 and 1916, and shortly thereafter he tried unsuccessfully to lure Happy Felsch to Douglas from Scobey, Montana, where he was currently playing outlaw ball.[42]

The changes had a marked effect on the team's fortunes. By August 9 the Blues had moved into a first-place tie with Juarez. Six days later the Indians beat Douglas to break the tie, but the game was marred by a controversy. In the third inning an ejected Juarez player had refused to leave the field, and after a five-minute delay the umpire had allowed the game to continue with the ejected player still in the lineup. McCamant upheld Douglas's protest and ruled that the game would have to be replayed later. The Blues beat the Indians the next day and won seven of their last nine games to set up a season-ending series in Juarez to determine the second-half championship.

Juarez, needing to win all three games to clinch the title, won the first two. Douglas thereupon announced that the season had officially ended and then refused to play the third game, which was to have been the replay of the protested

August 15 contest. The Juarez team showed up at the ballpark at the appointed time, and after thirty minutes the umpire declared the Indians the winner by forfeit, leaving Douglas and Juarez with identical records of 14-11. The Blues, however, refused to acknowledge the forfeit, declared themselves second-half champions, and prepared to play Fort Bayard, the first-half champion, in a best-of-seven championship series.

The Blues split four games with Fort Bayard in late September, then agreed to a five-game series in Juarez on the following weekend. They insisted that this series with the Indians would not count in the official league standings, since several Douglas players, including Weaver, had already left for the winter, and the Blues were forced to fill out their lineup with volunteers from other teams, including Fort Bayard. Juarez won four of the five games, and the league declared the Indians the official second-half champions and ordered a three-game playoff series between Juarez and Fort Bayard. Juarez swept all three games, even though Fort Bayard had recruited Gandil for the series.[43] Despite its unsatisfactory ending, the 1925 season was something of a personal triumph for Chase. In 34 games he batted a resounding .424 with 21 extra-base hits.[44] Clearly, the old man still had something left, at least at this modest level of competition.

The messy ending of the 1925 season ushered in a tumultuous winter for the Frontier League. El Paso first tried to join another league, then offered the great Joe Jackson a contract. The negotiations reportedly ended when Jackson asked for the exorbitant salary of $500 a month. Fort Bayard withdrew from the league, but was replaced by the Chino club, representing the twin towns of Hurley and Santa Rita, New Mexico; Fort Bayard then rejoined the league, along with another new team representing Bisbee. And, in Douglas, rumors flew that Weaver would replace Chase as manager.[45]

These rumors proved to be true, although no explanation was given for the change; perhaps Chase simply tired of the responsibilities of the job. He announced that he would return to play first base for Douglas, however, and went on to post almost identically gaudy offensive numbers in 1926 as he had during the 1925 season. Gandil moved on to Fort Bayard, where he was joined by former Giants outfielder Jimmy O'Connell, who had been expelled from organized baseball for his alleged involvement in a 1924 bribery scandal.[46] The pain of losing Gandil eased considerably when Weaver showed up on April 1 with five new players, including Lefty Williams.

Chase arrived from San Jose a week later "with a fine crop of whiskers, a straw hat and lots of pep for the opening games in Bisbee." He also had his son with him, as Nellie and her second husband, a welder named Bill Brown, had given their permission for young Hal to accompany his father to Arizona.

Chase paid little attention to his son and made no attempt to alter his own nomadic lifestyle. Harry Ames, whose father owned the Smokehouse, claimed that Chase was the only player who never held a regular job in Douglas, preferring to spend his time at the Smokehouse or the neighboring B&P pool hall. The teenaged John Bernal and his friends, too young to go inside, used to watch

Chase play pool through the windows. "Damn right he was a good pool player," recalled Bernal. "But he couldn't make much of a living at it because nobody had any money back then."

Such a man would not seem to be the ideal father figure for a teenaged boy, and in fact Chase wasn't. "I was just an appendage, easy to get along without," his son recalled years later. "He put me in a rooming house, got me a meal ticket at a coffee shop and left me with a dollar. I had no idea when he would be back.

"When he did come back, ten days later, the first thing he said to me was, 'Do you have any money?'

"When I told him no, he said, "What happened to that dollar I gave you?' He was kidding. He certainly wasn't cheap, it wasn't that he didn't care — he did as much as he was capable of — he just didn't think."

Young Hal briefly attended Douglas High School, where he played baseball (the local press made a big fuss when he hit a home run), but he was lonely and homesick in Arizona, and he went home after eight months.[47] Shortly after his return to California, in July 1926, the San Francisco Missions of the Pacific Coast League announced that they had signed him to a professional contract. Until he graduated from high school, the "lithe, bronzed lad of sixteen" would work out with the Missions on weekends and during vacations.

Both parties insisted that this "interesting experiment" was more than a publicity stunt. Young Hal announced that he was out to redeem the family name which his father had disgraced. "He has the same natural ability of his father," insisted the manager of the Missions, "and with the experience he will gain with us during the next two years, I expect him to develop into a valuable man."[48]

Young Hal's stated motivation in undertaking a baseball career — to clear the family name his father had besmirched — reportedly hurt Chase deeply. "I remember him coming to my office one day sobbing like a baby," wrote S. L. A. Marshall. "Hal hadn't lifted a finger for the boy in years, but he couldn't stand the indictment. 'You don't believe any boy would say that about his father, do you?' he blubbered." Marshall assured him that the story was probably false, and "Within two minutes he had forgotten the whole affair."[49]

In reality, young Hal was a good athlete, but not in the class of his father. His dream of a professional baseball career remained unfulfilled, which may have been for the best; the pressure of trying simultaneously to live up to and live down the accomplishments of such a father would almost certainly have been too much for any son.

More than fifty years later, however, the son was still trying to clear the family name, although he seemed to have changed his mind regarding his father's guilt. To a sportswriter who had written unflatteringly about his father, he stated flatly that he did not "believe that Hal Chase used his ability to corrupt a game that he loved." Instead, he argued, the magnates made Chase a scapegoat because he refused to bend to their paternalistic authority and because he dared to challenge the inviolability of the standard player's contract by jumping to the Federal League.

The son explained his father's jumping the Yankees for the California State League in 1908 on the grounds that Chase, "a bucolic young man," simply missed his native state. At one point he claimed "that Hal Chase was not only absolved of any guilt in the Black Sox scandal, but … one of the most admired men in baseball, John McGraw of the N.Y. Giants, felt [sufficiently] strongly about it to offer him a contract with his team as an indication of his feelings toward Hal Chase."

Much of the foregoing, of course, is either debatable or wrong. The description of Chase as "a bucolic young man," for example, certainly does not jibe with contemporary accounts of the Broadway boulevardier and habitué of New York's saloons and pool halls; and by the time the Black Sox affair was history, Chase's major league career was already over. Nevertheless, the son made some excellent points. "I can't believe … that you are so naive that you cater to the adolescent belief (prevalent among sportswriters) that baseball, organized baseball, is only a sport, operated by sportsmen because of their love of the 'game,'" he wrote in words almost identical to those of baseball historian Harold Seymour. "I am sure you know that organized baseball is big business & that any individual who acts against it in any regard is subject to villification [sic] & exile in any possible manner."[50]

Regardless, the Douglas Blues once again got off to a shaky start in 1926, winning only two of their first seven games. They lost three in a row to Fort Bayard when O'Connell hit a home run in the first game, Gandil hit one in the second game, and second baseman Irish Shannon hit three off Lefty Williams in the third game.

The Blues rebounded from this mauling and won eight of their next twelve games. They even received a bonus when the league president upheld their protest of that dreadful third loss to Fort Bayard on the grounds that the umpire had stopped a Fort Bayard overthrow and handed the ball to Gandil. As a result, despite their shaky start and lackluster 9-8 record, the Blues were in third place. But Douglas lost six of its next seven games, and by early June, Weaver had had enough of managing. He resigned and was replaced by second baseman Bunny Lindsay amid reports that the Blues were in serious financial straits again.[51]

Another possible explanation for Weaver's resignation was that Chase was up to his old tricks, and Weaver did not want to take the fall. S. L. A. Marshall later recalled that before the first game of a Douglas-Juarez series, Weaver told him, "Watch Hal. I think there's something up but I can't tell you why."

"Sure enough," wrote Marshall, "Chase went sour." Though Douglas won, Chase "looked impossible on at least four easy plays." After the game Marshall confronted Chase, who confirmed that he had tried to throw the game. When Marshall asked him why, Chase replied, "You know that Chinaman from Lordsburg (one of the local gamblers); well, he came up to me before the game and asked if I wouldn't boot a few and try to help Juarez. He's a nice fellow, and I said sure, but I didn't have any money on the game and he wasn't paying me."[52]

Marshall did not indicate whether this game was played before Weaver's resignation as manager, but if so it could have contributed to his decision. Though he was tarred with the same brush as were the other Black Sox players because he had known of the fix beforehand, Weaver apparently refused to go along with the scheme and played the 1919 World Series honestly. Perhaps Weaver felt that Chase had betrayed him and decided that he no longer wanted the responsibility of running the team.

Douglas was not the only Copper League team experiencing difficulties. The two stars of the Fort Bayard Veterans, Gandil and O'Connell, were not getting along. Matters came to a head one day when Gandil was ragging O'Connell, who had emerged as the best player in the league. O'Connell announced that one of them would have to go, and predicted that it would be Gandil. He then picked up a bat and chased the burly first baseman across the field and out of the ballpark. Gandil was quickly released, but within a week had signed on with Chino. Fort Bayard signed Lefty Williams, who had been completely ineffective for Douglas, to take Gandil's place on the roster.[53]

All this was sensational enough, but in late June such doings were completely overshadowed when evangelist Aimee Semple McPherson, who was believed to have drowned in California a month before, turned up in Douglas. The town became the center of national attention as McPherson spun a spellbinding (and implausible) tale of abduction, escape, and hardship.[54] Even at the time, many doubted her story,[55] but a couple of months later, in gratitude for the kindness shown her by the people of Douglas, she gave the town a Model 28 Radiola and loudspeaker.[56]

In late July, an item had appeared in the New York *Evening Journal*, in the column titled "Tad's Tidbits," which brought Chase back to the attention of New Yorkers. A letter from Joe Quinn, of Elmhurst, Long Island, appeared under the headline "Hal Chase Still a Star in Mexico." Quinn had recently returned from "Mexico" and reported that Chase was playing "as good as he ever did." Quinn elaborated: "He's running the Douglas team in the Frontier League and also a saloon and dance hall in El Preto, State of Sonora, called the Crystal Palace Café." Quinn enclosed a photo of Chase wearing his Douglas uniform, with lettering promoting M and O cigars prominently displayed on the chest. Quinn had been associating with another disgraced former major leaguer, Prince Hal's old sidekick on the Giants, which apparently gave him a certain entrée with Chase: "I told Hal that I was playing ball with Heinie Zimmerman's team at College Point and he made me right at home. He also told me to give his regards to John O'Reilly on Broadway."[57] If Chase expressed any regrets about his current situation, Quinn did not see fit to report them.

Meanwhile, the Blues had finished the first half of the season with a 16-19 record, but won nine of their first twelve games to begin the second half. Chase was again playing impressive baseball; he hit home runs in consecutive games on July 4–5, and "was in particularly exuberant spirits" as he stole three bases against the Chino Twins on July 23.[58]

The Blues' good fortune soon crashed to an end, however. When Lefty Williams went to Fort Bayard they lost one of their major gate attractions. Blues president Walter Alberts predicted that the team would finish the season $1,100 in the red.[59] On July 30 the team bus broke down near Silver City, New Mexico, forcing the players to walk eight miles into Hurley, where they were to play the Twins that afternoon. Chino coasted a 23-1 win over the "weary and footsore" Blues; "Hal Chase, aroused from his bed early Friday evening following the game, declared that there were no 'outstanding features except the fact that the Blues were all in before the game started.'"[60]

A few days later the Juarez Indians folded, only to be replaced by a new club made up of local amateurs. El Paso was reported to be $1,800 in the red. On August 11 came the news that the Copper League itself might fold as a result of the Blues' financial problems, but once again Douglas fans kicked in enough money to keep the team, and the league, afloat.

All this bad news was nothing compared to what happened on August 21, when Chase and McKenry nearly died after Chase's car overturned near Silver City. "According to McKenry, Chase was driving into Silver City and thought he had passed the last curve when he came unexpectedly to another curve which he was unable to negotiate.... Chase received severe lacerations about his head, arms, chest and legs in addition to painful bruises about the head. His attending physician stated ... that he was resting comfortably but that he would be unable to be up and about for at least two weeks."[61] Years later S. L. A. Marshall recalled that "a group of the boys were celebrating with a wild ride through the hills near Tyrone, N.M.... The car went over a cliff. The other boys crawled out of the wreck but they had to drag Prince Hal out. He had gone through the windshield — sliding feet first for the first time in his life — and the glass had severed the Achilles tendon in both feet."[62]

McKenry's claim that Chase had been driving was contradicted by other accounts, which also described Chase's injuries as somewhat less severe than Marshall indicated.[63] They were, however, serious enough to keep him from playing baseball during the 1927 season. According to Marshall, Chase tried to return the following spring; on his first time up he hit what looked like a sure triple over the left fielder's head, but fell down three times running to first base and walked off the field. "He was crying like a kid," wrote Marshall, "and there were many other eyes on that field and in the stands which were suspiciously moist."[64] His enforced absence from the game at which he excelled, and the only profession which he had ever known, must have been difficult, even though he seems to have remained the same happy-go-lucky Prince Hal on the outside. He took a job selling Marmon automobiles in Douglas in 1927 and 1928.[65] While his celebrity and personal charm would have been any salesman's dream, there is no reason to suppose that Chase took selling cars any more seriously than he did playing baseball. At any rate no record of his performance as a salesman survives.

By August 1927 his injuries had healed sufficiently for the El Paso Copper League team to pursue his services. According to Lynn Bevill, Chase finally and reluctantly joined El Paso for a three-game series. The record shows that Chase knocked out four singles in ten at bats, but he was virtually unable to run, and El Paso quickly dropped him.[66]

The next few years were restless ones for Chase. In 1928 he moved back to California, reportedly to run a chicken ranch for his brother-in-law Frank Topham in Lindsay, in central California.[67] If true, this represented a striking reversal of fortune, and symbolized Prince Hal's fallen state. Although a 1913 newspaper story had reported that Chase was the owner of a twenty-acre orange grove in Lindsay "to which he expects eventually to retire,"[68] his son later claimed that Chase had bought the property as a gift for his sister Jessie and her husband Frank Topham. Later, Chase bought them a house in San Jose, and also helped them buy a spread in Williams, California.[69] Jessie seems to have been a devoted sister, but Frank Topham made no secret of his dislike of his notorious brother-in-law, and must have relished having the upper hand in their relationship at last. While living in Lindsay, Chase played Sunday ball for nearby Porterville in the Valley League, where his colleagues included his former teammates Ezra Midkiff from the Highlanders and Limb McKenry from Cincinnati and Arizona.

In early 1930 Chase moved to Oakland, where he hooked up with a prospector. He migrated to the Sierra Nevada mountains to muck for gold, and continued to play Sunday baseball, this time for a team representing the Reno Garage.[70]

His prospecting career apparently did not pan out, and he reappeared in Williams, Arizona, where he found a job in a pool hall, in July 1930. Still agile at the age of forty-seven, he led the local baseball team to the Northern Arizona semipro championship with victories over seven other teams during the Labor Day weekend.[71] His problems with alcohol seem to have escalated, however; on December 8 the car he was driving crashed into two other vehicles in Nogales, and he was given the choice of paying a $75 fine or spending thirty days in jail after pleading guilty to driving while intoxicated.[72]

This was only one of several automotive misadventures for Chase, in addition to his 1926 crash in New Mexico. Aaron Gordon of Houston stopped to help Chase mend a flat tire on the side of a road near Tucson one December night. A third car, driven by O. K. Anderson of Tucson, struck their cars, and Gordon died of shock as a result of a mangled leg.[73] In Oakland in 1936, Chase suffered a concussion and body lacerations when he was hit by a car driven by Anton Geraci of Berkeley. Geraci told police that Chase had "stepped right in front of me," and no charges were filed.[74]

No record survives to indicate whether Chase played baseball in 1931, although he later claimed to have been in Nogales that year,[75] but in August 1932 he appeared in one game for Williams, collecting two hits in three at bats, before dropping from sight again.[76]

In the summer of 1932 he went to Tucson, where he worked for an oil company and in the lumber business,[77] but he was also seen in Holbrook and

Winslow over the next couple of years. In the latter town he filled in briefly for the local team's regular first baseman. At the age of fifty, he was "rusty but adequate" on defense and no longer capable of playing a full game, but hit the ball "a country mile" in his lone at bat.[78]

By now, the combination of age, alcohol, and his refusal to take adequate care of himself was beginning to wear Chase down. With his playing days ending, he had nothing to fall back on, and the Great Depression was in full swing. For a time he worked washing cars for fifty cents apiece, and he occasionally took other menial jobs through the Civil Works Administration, precursor of the Work Projects Administration.[79] Roy Drachman, who had played against Chase in the 1920s, befriended him in Tucson around this time. "He'd paint a barn, clean a yard, chop wood," recalled Drachman. "He would do anything to try and keep body and soul together." He also spent a good deal of time at Dooley's Pool Hall on Stone Street, though by now he preferred to watch and kibitz the college kids rather than to play himself.[80]

The depths to which Chase had fallen became public knowledge in late December 1933, when the Columbia University footbal team spent a week in Tucson preparing to face Stanford in the Rose Bowl game in Pasadena, California, on New Year's Day. On the day after Christmas, several New York sportswriters traveling with the team reported that they had seen a ghost.

Not a real ghost, of course. The apparition was all too clearly flesh and blood, the middle-aged shell of a man whom several members of the Lions' entourage remembered from happier days. When veteran Columbia trainer Charlie (Doc) Barrett first saw his old friend Hal Chase, however, he did not recognize him, and little wonder: one writer present at the scene described Chase as a "disheveled and broken figure" who "stumbled into the gorgeous lobby of the Hotel El Conquistador...."[81] Barrett introduced Chase to New York sportswriter Bill Corum, and asked Corum if he had ever seen Chase play first base.

In fact, Corum revealed to his readers in *The Sporting News,* Chase had been his boyhood idol. He recounted his emotional, unspoken response to Barrett's question: "Ever see him? Ever see him? How many times had I seen him. Hadn't I sat with my eyes glued on him in old Sportsman's Park [in St. Louis] until I could go back home to my own little country town and see him with them shut? Hadn't I put my glove under my pillow at night and dreamed of the time when I would spear 'em out of the dirt with one hand like Chase?"

Such memories were superseded by the image now before him. Chase's "once sharp, cunning mind was bobbing and weaving with his stumbling, shambling footsteps now," and Corum drew the obvious moral: "So this was Prince Hal? This relic, this wanderer through little one-street mining towns, playing ball with the Mexicans for a buck, or maybe just a shot when the game was over, was Chase, the Peerless One. What a wind-up for an athlete so perfect he was all but unbelievable.

"What an object lesson in square shooting, because nothing made a bum out of Hal Chase but Hal Chase himself. He was one of those strange characters

Ten—A Long Way to the So-Called "Big Town"

An older Chase, with ball and glove, perhaps pondering what might have been. *National Baseball Hall of Fame Library, Cooperstown, N.Y.*

who are going to outsmart everybody and wind up outsmarting only themselves."

Still, Corum could not deny Chase one moment of dignity. "Not until I asked him about first basemen," recalled Corum, "did he square his shoulders and look me in the eye.

"'Sisler was the next thing to me,' he said simply, and there was no hint of bragging in his words, 'but I could go get that old apple.'"[82]

Corum never got over this encounter with his boyhood hero; after Chase's death several years later he wrote about it again, although this time the details were different. Corum recalled his excitement at Barrett's announcement that he had just seen Hal Chase: "To a sports writer that was something like saying to a city side reporter, 'I have just seen Judge Crater.'" Barrett offered to take Corum to the "sort of semi-speakeasy night club" where he had met Chase, but when the two men arrived Chase was gone. "Maybe he will drop in tomorrow," said the bartender. "But don't count on it. He comes and he goes."

On the next day Corum went to the rooming house where Chase was supposed to be staying. A red-headed woman answered his knock on the door; when Corum asked if Chase lived there, she snapped "Ask him," and slammed the door in his face.

Corum returned to the saloon, but saw a man in overalls and a sweater enter a neighboring establishment. Corum followed and found the place empty except for himself, the man in overalls, and the bartender. Corum explained to the latter that he was a friend of Barrett's and was looking for Hal Chase; at that, the man in overalls rose and came over with his hand extended. "He moved easily and his back was straight and even in his sweater and open collar without a tie, there was the touch of the dandy."

Corum learned that Chase occasionally worked on the Mexican ranch owned by Tal Pendleton, a former football star at Princeton University, and "frequently went there when the going was extra rough" because "Mrs. Pendleton was particularly anxious to help him in every way."[83]

Like Corum, the other New York writers who rediscovered Chase in Tucson generally treated him sympathetically. The New York *Evening Post* was more discreet than most, reporting simply that "Chase has met with ill-fortune since his enforced retirement from baseball."[84] Joe Vila called him "a dilapidated figure," and added, "it would be easy to moralize about a genius gone to wrack and ruin, but it is easier and, perhaps, kinder merely to marvel that a man who began with so much could wind up with so little." Vila recalled the younger Chase as "a fine looking man — square-jawed, with deep-set blue eyes, strong, even white teeth and a flashing smile. He generally had a stubble of beard, for his beard was strong and his skin tender and he shaved only two or three times a week. Save when he was on the ball field and when he slept, he chewed a partially smoked cigar."[85]

Of course, how much credence to give such descriptions is a problem. Perhaps, in looking at Chase, the New York writers saw what they wanted or expected to see: a once-proud hero who had been brought low. Such a figure certainly made better copy than an unrepentant crook whose self-inflicted disgrace seemed to have had little effect on him. In one respect, however, Chase seemed not to have changed at all. When Barrett asked him how old he was, Chase responded, "Forty-six." The two shook hands and, wrote Harry Grayson, "the tramp who was once Hal Chase shuffled out into the blazing desert sun." A local sportswriter who happened to witness the encounter mentioned to Barrett that a few days earlier Chase had claimed to be forty-eight.

"Well, I happen to know that he's fifty-one," replied Barrett. "Even though he is down and out, he's still Hal."[86]

After this brief flurry of publicity Chase again dropped from sight. Just a few months later, Eddie Collins, the Hall of Fame second baseman and a contemporary of Chase's, wrote in the *Saturday Evening Post*, "It's a sad thing to recall Hal Chase, but in fairness to him, wherever he is, nothing can stop me from saying that he was the greatest of all first basemen."[87] Collins, now an executive with the Red Sox, had been a leader of the so-called "Clean Sox," those members of the 1919 White Sox whose honesty contrasted so strongly with that of their teammates, the Black Sox. Thus Collins could be expected to hold no brief for Chase, allegedly involved in the fix; but he recalled Prince Hal admiringly, while acknowledging his current obscurity.

Chase returned to California in 1934 and early 1935, living with his niece in Alameda, then moved back to Tucson during the latter year. He was listed in the 1935 Tucson city directory, giving his occupation as "ballplayer," and renting a room at 422 East Ninth Street. Another mystery surrounds this period of his life, for the city directory commonly listed the first names of wives in parentheses after each homeowner's or renter's name. Chase's name is followed by that of "Bernie," perhaps short for Bernice or Bernadette[88] and probably the redhead who slammed the door in Bill Corum's face. In Arizona, at least initially, Chase seems to have maintained his well-earned reputation as a womanizer; in recounting Prince Hal's outlaw days in the Southwest, baseball historian Bob Hoie wrote that "men whose wives and girlfriends were seduced by Chase were still in awe of him fifty years later."[89] By the mid–1930s, however, he had apparently settled down somewhat. In fact, Roy Drachman said that he never saw Chase with a woman.[90] Chase may or may not have married Bernie — one of those Rose Bowl–bound reporters had written that "He and his second wife live in tourist camps,"[91] although if his companion was in fact his wife she was his third, not his second — but nothing else is known of her, and she does not appear in any subsequent accounts.

Perhaps, however, the mysterious Bernie is the solution to another unsolved puzzle regarding Chase. In 1966 baseball historian Lee Allen received a letter from a J. L. May of Metairie, Louisiana. May had been moved to write after reading Allen's book *The National League Story*, which contained a discussion of Chase. "I was very interested," wrote May, "you see he was my father and my mother and all other relatives have never told me anything about him, the reason for this letter is to see if you would try and find a picture of him that I could have and let me know where I can get one."[92] No record exists of Allen's response to this remarkable communication, but it is possible that J. L. May's mother was the mysterious Bernie.

Chase had fallen quite a distance by now; his athletic talents were now put to use playing in pickup games with the local Mexican American kids.[93] Drachman, who managed a couple of Tucson movie theaters, recalled that Chase "was living in some hovel or shack someplace on the southwest side of Tucson, which was the poorer area of the community." Drachman said bluntly, "He was a bum," before adding more affectionately that when Chase asked him for spare change Drachman gave willingly, even though Chase "never paid anything back." They clung to the fiction that these transactions were loans, not outright gifts, because "It saved him a little embarrassment."[94] Drachman recalled one visit in detail: "He asked me for money and I told him I only had fifteen cents on me. We visited for a while, and when he got up to leave, he said, 'Roy, can I have that fifteen cents? I can buy a loaf of bread.' I gave it to him and couldn't help thinking that a man in the position of needing such a pittance was really near the end of the line."[95]

Despite his straitened circumstances, Chase never seemed bitter. "He would talk about baseball," but never about his own troubles, and his friends were too tactful to ask. "He didn't seem to be a guy who had a lot of resentment about him," recalled Drachman. "I don't recall him ever saying, 'Well, they picked on me, they made me the goat.'... He seemed like a happy-go-lucky guy. He didn't cry about his bad luck or anything."[96]

It was around this time that Bill Corum, inspired by his encounter with Chase in Tucson, wrote another article that was reprinted in *The Sporting News* and titled "A Mumbling Man Reads About First Basemen." The "mumbling, red-eyed man" of the title is sitting "in one of those little desert hideaways between Tucson, Ariz., and the Mexican border" on Christmas day. Another patron of the bar reads aloud a newspaper account of the founding of the baseball Hall of Fame, which notes that Sisler, Gehrig, and Foxx head the list of first basemen eligible for election. Meanwhile the mumbling man is "spinning his little glass in gnarled and dirty-nailed but somehow not clumsy fingers." The bartender tells him not to pay too much attention to the opinions of sportswriters, whereupon the man recalls getting five hits in a game against the Athletics but being robbed of one by the official scorer, a newspaperman. Eventually the mumbling man climbs into someone's car for a ride toward the Pendleton ranch, sitting in the front seat and mumbling, "Gehrig ... and Sisler ... and Foxx." The story concludes melodramatically: "And the name of the mumbling man would be Hal Chase."

In an afterword Corum admitted that his "impression" of Chase was "wholly imaginary," but even taking into account a certain amount of exaggeration it provides a glimpse of how far Prince Hal had fallen. Corum said that when he had seen Chase the former player had been "doing the best he could, which was something less than tops," but the writer insisted that his former idol was as deserving of recognition for his baseball ability as were Gehrig, Sisler, and Foxx: "Chase is a desert drifter now and perhaps he was never such a great first baseman. He was only the best."[97]

In fact, in the first balloting for election to the National Baseball Hall of Fame, held in 1936, five players received the minimum 170 votes needed for election: Ty Cobb, Babe Ruth, Honus Wagner, Christy Mathewson, and Walter Johnson. Chase received eleven votes, and eighteen the following year, when 151 were needed for election. Chase was one of seven players receiving votes in that 1936 election who have not subsequently been elected to the Hall; the others were Bill Bradley, Lou Criger, Joe Jackson, Johnny Kling, Nap Rucker, and Chase's old enemy Kid Elberfeld.[98] Coincidentally, Criger, whose major league career overlapped Chase's for seven years, also ended up in Tucson and died there in May 1934.

Corum was not the only writer of fiction inspired by the denouement of Chase's career. Jim Palana's story "Old-Timers," published in *Spitball* magazine in the early 1980s, concerns a barnstorming team from Arizona that comes to a California mining town to play the local semipro team in the spring of 1938. The visitors are led by an aging but still impressive ex–major league first baseman: "Word had it he creaked like a wagon running the bases, but he could still swing the bat, and in the field he was an absolute magician. Reflexes like a cat, even at his age." A traveling salesman, who had seen the Arizona team a few weeks earlier in Chico, confirms the rumors, and adds that after the game "the first baseman had taken on all comers at the pool hall, and nobody could whip him."

The Arizona team wins the first game from the local team, but loses the second when the first baseman, "after spearing everything else hit within ten feet of him," allows "an easy ground ball" to bounce between his legs. After the games the players crowd into the bar, and the narrator sees the first baseman for the first time.

"He was a big man and still looked trim, but the way the flesh hung on his face, I could tell he liked to drink more than he liked to eat.... But he had a merry twinkle in his eyes and a thick head of red hair, and our boys seemed taken by him.... They called the first baseman Harold and he bought his share of the rounds."

Soon Harold takes to the pool table, and in short order has beaten the locals out of their pocket money. "But he had such a winning personality, cracking jokes and keeping up a steady stream of patter, that no one got sore. Everyone was charmed by him and awed by his ability."

Eventually, after several more rounds, Harold begins reminiscing. He admits that he used to play in the majors, and tells stories about Cobb and Lajoie and the other stars of his day. One of the locals asks how long Harold stayed in the big leagues, and he answers that he quit during World War I. He was never more than a utility man, he says, because he "Never could get the hang of that pitching."

Suddenly an old drunken stranger who has been eavesdropping interrupts. "Why don't you tell them the truth?" he asks. The drunk points at Harold and claims to recognize him. Harold tries to make light of the situation, but the drunk persists.

"You haven't changed at all, have you? All these years and you're still a liar. And I hear you made an error today and cost your team a win. Well, let me guess how it happened. You let an easy ground ball go through your legs. Or the shortstop made a routine throw and somehow you got your legs tangled up around the bag and didn't catch it and it looked like a wild throw. Or maybe the pitcher was covering and you made a little toss to him, but it was off just enough so he couldn't reach it. Which one was it? Or have you found a new way to lose a game?"

The drunk then addresses the rest of the crowd. "This man was without a doubt the best first baseman I ever saw, and there's many who will admit he's the best who ever played the position. Better even than George Sisler. But he won't deny that he liked to make a quick dollar, just as he's done tonight. Only he bet against his own team to lose, and always found a way to help his own cause if he could. You won't deny it, will you? No doubt you had a few side bets on the games today. Why even Christy Mathewson swore that this man deliberately threw ballgames, and who would doubt Matty? There never was a fairer man. Oh, they cleared this feller's name in a court of law, but everyone knew what he was doing. John J. McGraw finally sent him packing. Ran him out of the game in 1919, right in the middle of the season. It wasn't the war now, was it? Why, they say he even helped to set up the Black Sox scandal in the World Series that year. You won't deny it, will you? Because you know that I know."

Harold remains silent, and the drunk finally identifies Harold as Hal Chase. Then Chase confesses that he does not recognize the man.

"I'll grant you I'm a damn sight poorer than you may remember me," responds his accuser. "But I remember you. I remember how you couldn't hit a good fastball on your fists. And I remember you were a better hitter than you've told your friends here.... Look at my eyes. Don't you recall the way they studied you? You were only sixty feet away. Try to picture me with a younger, smoother face. Don't you recall how, even in your championship year, you couldn't hit a foul ball off me? Because I had a fastball in my prime.... Three hundred and seventy-three games I won in my time and not a single one dishonestly. Your kind couldn't buy me off, could it?"

Finally Chase recognizes the drunk as "Old Pete," Grover Cleveland Alexander, and responds to the great pitcher's accusations. He calls Alexander a "bum" and a "drunken old fool," and says defiantly, "I've got money in my pocket and friends to spend it on. I'm welcome wherever I go. People are glad to see me. I can still play ball, and no one cares about some ancient history. But they care about a sloppy drunk in their midst. Travel with me, Pete, and I'll show you which one of us they turn away at the door. Who of your old friends will have you now?"

Alexander stiffens, then pulls out an envelope. "Here is something you will never have, Prince Hal. All your lying and scheming and cheating and gambling will never win you what is inside this envelope. And you could have had this if you'd only been honest." Inside the envelope, Alexander reveals, is a letter informing him of his election to the Hall of Fame. His trump card played, the old pitcher then shuffles back out of the bar. Chase gazes after him.

"That old son-of-a-gun," he says. "He always did have my number."[99]

Palana's description of Chase has the ring of truth, although it might more accurately have been applied to a younger Prince Hal; by the spring of 1938 Chase's health had probably deteriorated to the point that he resembled the Old Pete of the story more than he did the still-robust Harold. He had certainly given up playing ball by then; his last "public appearance" was at a softball game in Williams, California, about sixty miles northwest of Sacramento.[100] By then he was living with Jessie and Frank Topham. The bitterness with which Chase's son recalled Frank Topham years later is entirely understandable. Chase had been extremely generous to the Tophams, buying them the orange grove in Lindsay and a house in San Jose[101] and

An old-timer at bat. *The Sporting News Archives.*

paying for them to come to New York to watch him play ball,[102] as well as assisting them with the purchase of their five-acre Williams property. According to the son, Frank Topham "remained a bully all of his life" and resented Chase's generosity because "he never was very successful" on his own. He may also have resented Jessie's devotion to her family; Edgar, Chase's father, had also come to live with Jessie and Frank.[103] At any rate, Frank Topham refused to allow Chase in their house, instead exiling him to a one-room log cabin elsewhere on the property.

The last few years of Chase's life were miserable, as his health gave out almost completely. On October 6, 1940, he was admitted to Colusa County Hospital in Colusa, California, suffering from beriberi, a disease caused by a deficiency of thiamine and characterized by excruciating pain. It is often associated with alcoholism. He remained in the hospital for at least eleven months. Upon his release, he apparently tried to make a go of independent living again, but it was a failure. On the afternoon of July 29, 1942, Mrs. Irvin Wyman of 2621 Lincoln Avenue in Alameda complained to police that a "ragged and tattered man, apparently drunk," was reeling about her front lawn. The patrolmen who picked him up failed to detect the odor of alcohol, and he did manage to remember his address, 1026 Bella Vista Avenue, but his memory was spotty and he seemed disoriented.

Sgt. George Doren identified him as Hal Chase at police headquarters, and he was admitted to Highland Hospital, where Dr. W. W. Stadel diagnosed him as suffering from the aftereffects of a stroke. The newspapers reported that he had recently found a job as a welder's helper in an Alameda shipyard—during World War II the civilian population of the Bay Area grew by more than half a million, or 25.9 percent, due mostly to the presence of the Kaiser shipyards and other defense industries[104]—but had never reported for work. He had been under a doctor's care for swollen feet, legs, and arms, and admitted being "down on his luck."[105]

After this episode Chase returned to his cabin on the Topham place, where his grandnephew Frank Cloak Jr. brought him food and cigars and the occasional five or ten dollars from Jessie, and sometimes drove his grandmother out to the cabin to visit her brother.

Years later Cloak recalled playing catch with the sickly, solitary old man—they used oranges instead of baseballs—and being amazed by his still-evident reflexes and athletic ability. He also recalled that Chase's love of the game was undiminished; every Friday afternoon, when the local high school team played, Chase would watch from his customary seat on a tree stump behind first base.[106]

His physical woes continued, however. In April 1944 a Sacramento newspaper reported that Chase had been hospitalized in Colusa with an undisclosed leg ailment, but was expected to "be up and about in a few days."[107]

While Chase was recuperating he would have been cheered by the results of a nationwide poll of sportswriters, ballplayers, and servicemen—this was wartime, remember—conducted by *Esquire* magazine, with the aim of picking an all-time all-star team.

Lou Gehrig led all first basemen, being named by 68.10 percent of the respondents, but according to the poll Hal Chase was the second-best first baseman in baseball history, being named by 18.54 percent of the respondents. He received more than twice as many votes as George Sisler, in third place with 9.05 percent.[108] While the results of this poll are by no means definitive, they do serve to indicate how Chase's fame persisted despite his disgrace, even after he had fallen out of the public eye. Not many of the servicemen or ballplayers who voted in the poll could have been old enough to remember seeing Chase during his major league career.

Chase's physical problems seemed to have little effect on his character. In 1946 he occasionally journeyed from Colusa to Sacramento, where he frequented a bowling alley and bar owned by former San Francisco *News* sports editor Tom Laird. According to Sacramento sportswriter Bill Conlin, Laird was always glad to see Chase, but Laird's partner Johnny Bascou grumbled about Prince Hal's visits.

"He was a mooch," said Bascou. "He was dead broke, never spent a dime with us, but my partner enjoyed pumping him full of booze."[109]

By March 1947, Chase was back in the hospital, this time for what he described as a "mixup of the liver, kidney and heart." At one point he had reportedly been in a coma for thirty-five hours, and he was expected to be paralyzed if he survived.

It would hardly have been surprising had this series of disasters, such obvious intimations of mortality, inspired in Chase a desire to revisit the past and perhaps to right old wrongs. Such, at any rate, seemed to be their effect. Twice while he was hospitalized, in 1941 and 1947, he submitted to lengthy interviews which were published in *The Sporting News,* and in 1942 he wrote a letter to his old friend Sid Mercer, who published it in his column in the New York *Journal American.*

The letter is a remarkably sad and revealing document, despite Chase's transparent attempts at jocularity: "Getting along O.K. Not so much pep as I formerly had, but no complaint to register." He was apparently still following major league baseball, as he enclosed a clipping on the awards to be presented to Mercer and Ted Williams of the Boston Red Sox by the New York chapter of the Baseball Writers Association, and added, "I want to extend my heartiest congratulations to you.... Am also glad to know that Ted Williams has finally received his due. I have always pulled for him. Had quite a few arguments over Ted and Joe DiMaggio. Out here they think DiMag is the whole works."

The rest of the letter was uncharacteristically nostalgic, a sentiment which Chase had previously avoided. "Read awhile back that Larry Doyle was in poor health," he wrote. "I wonder if you could send me his address. I would like to drop him a line.

"Quite a few of our old friends and acquaintances have left us, Sid. Are Alan Sangree and Bill MacBeth still present? And is Bill Farnsworth still on that Atlanta paper? O, yes, do you remember the time I tried shaving you in Atlanta? Back in 1907, I think. Boy, I sure nicked you plenty. You had a tough beard.... Is Al Demaree in New York? Give him my best.

"Also if you run into Doc Barrett or Russ Ford or any of my old acquaintances, including the 'Head Office Boy' Mark Roth or Willie Hoppe, say Hello.... Run out of time and pretty near out of ink so will ring off now. With my kindest wishes.... Sincerely, HAL CHASE."

Mercer's response made clear just how far out of touch Chase had fallen. Mercer noted that he had heard nothing of Doyle or Ford, but that Demaree was living in Chicago, Farnsworth had been back in New York for some twenty-five years, and MacBeth and Sangree had died seven and fifteen years ago respectively.[110]

In both of the hospital interviews Chase sounded sincerely regretful in confessing to relatively minor trangressions while insisting that he was innocent of the worst allegations against him. A cynical interpretation would be that he was merely being his usual disingenuous self. His limited mea culpas were a distorted and completely self-serving version of events, and everything Chase said was a calculated attempt to win sympathy. A more generous interpretation would be that, convinced of his imminent death, he had finally decided to unburden his conscience and make a clean breast of his past mistakes, most of which were relatively minor, and prove that he had not been the corrupt monster he had been made out to be. No matter which view is correct, the Chase of these interviews was unquestionably a scared old man, and the spectacle of the once-defiant Prince Hal trying desperately to curry favor with the baseball establishment which he had bedeviled for so many years is almost unbearably pathetic.

The first interview took place in 1941, when Lester Grant, a young reporter with the Oakland *Post-Enquirer,* tracked Chase down in the Colusa County Hospital, where he was recovering from his attack of beriberi. Grant called Chase "The Anthony Adverse of the game," and was inclined to be sympathetic: "If, as he admits, his life has been a series of ghastly mistakes, then certainly he has paid dearly for every one of them." The extent of Chase's current degradation was painfully obvious; he admitted drinking heavily during the 1930s in an attempt "to drown his sorrows," but said that he had been on the wagon since October 6, 1940, when he had first been hospitalized. (This statement, of course, contradicts the memory of Johnny Bascou, the Sacramento saloonkeeper.) He was also in dire financial straits: "Where he'll get the money to pay for medical advice and treatment, he does not know."[111]

Despite Chase's reputation for venality, his interview with Grant seemed to confirm his son's assertion that "money never seemed to mean anything to him."[112] Indeed, Chase related a couple of instances in which he claimed that he had passed up a sure source of income for a more uncertain future. He said that, contrary to the accepted version of his departure from the major leagues, John McGraw had not only sent him a contract for the 1920 season, but had actually offered him a raise. "There was nothing wrong with that contract," he insisted. "I was perfectly satisfied with the terms. But I told the New York management that my marital difficulties were growing more and more complicated, that I was sick of the East, that I had good connections in the West and that I would be doing myself a favor by quitting the major league baseball scene. People wondered about my leaving the majors at the time, but they just shrugged it off and didn't think any more about it."

Similarly, Chase said that in 1920 Cy Moreing, his old boss in the California State League, had offered to get him a position with the Sperry Flour Company. Chase would have received $300 a month and had the opportunity to learn a new business, but he turned Moreing down to play Sunday baseball in San Jose.

The most poignant part of Chase's conversation with Grant involved Nellie Heffernan. "Life would have been smoother sailing all the way through had I appreciated my first wife," Chase admitted. "But I didn't appreciate her until it was too late. It was a fatal mistake that can never be corrected." About this, at least, there seemed little room for argument.[113]

The sentimental mood of the conversation continued as Grant asked Chase to name his all-time all-star team. Chase complied, but tactfully insisted on listing as well several other players at each position who "would be assets to any team." He was in a forgiving mood; he picked Christy Mathewson over Walter Johnson at pitcher, and picked Frank Chance as one of his reserve first basemen. He also had kind words for John McGraw, although he said that Bill Carrigan, who had guided the Red Sox to consecutive world championships in 1915 and 1916, was the best manager that he had ever seen.[114]

In 1947, the enterprising newspaperman who sought Chase out in the hospital was J. W. Sehorn of the Woodland (Calif.) *Daily Democrat*. The faithful Jessie was at Chase's bedside, charging that he was the victim of a conspiracy of lies. Chase himself insisted that he had been more innocent than guilty of the charges against him, although he admitted that he used to bet with players on opposing teams and with gamblers in the box seats because he was unhappy with his salary: "I could have made a million dollars out of baseball on bets and gambling.... My limit was $100 per game and I never bet against my own team. That was easy money. Certainly, I bet, and later on I drank too much. It's an old story now, but it's a sad one for a man whose name, I am told, is often linked with the greatest players."

Chase also acknowledged his estrangement from his son. Young Hal, then living in Port Angeles, Washington, had telegraphed him on March 31 to wish him a speedy recovery. "That was a happy day, hearing from my boy," said Chase. "I haven't seen him in a long time."[115]

The most dramatic part of these interviews concerned Chase's role in the Black Sox scandal. He insisted in both interviews that he had had nothing to do with arranging the fix, although he had known of it beforehand, and that his most serious mistake had been in keeping that knowledge to himself: "When Sleepy Bill Burns told me about the frameup, I should have reported immediately to John Heydler, president of the National League," he told Grant. "But I never had any use for a stool pigeon or squealer, and while I was debating this, the Series got under way and I felt it was too late then.

"Had I told Heydler about that scandal before it broke, I would have saved myself a lot of grief as far as organized ball is concerned."[116]

Similarly, in 1947 he told Sehorn, "I became implicated because I did not report the Series fix to either President Heydler or to my manager, John McGraw of the Giants.

"I did not want to be what I then called a 'welcher.' I had been involved in all kinds of bets with players and gamblers in the past, and I felt this was no time to run out. I had sat in on many games of chance, but this Series fix was big business."[117]

Chase did not help his credibility by telling two different versions of the scheme. He told Grant that Bill Burns had called him one evening late in the 1919 season and requested a meeting at the Ansonia Hotel in New York. At that meeting, said Chase, Burns hinted strongly that the upcoming games between the White Sox and the Reds could be fixed, whereupon Chase said, "Why, Bill, I'd say that if the World's Series could be fixed, someone would make a lot of money out of it." Burns smiled mysteriously, but nothing more was said on the subject that night.

Shortly thereafter, said Chase, he ran into Burns again, and this time the former pitcher made no attempt to conceal his machinations. "I've been talking to Arnold Rothstein," said Burns, "and I have given him a sure-fire proposition on the Series. I've got the thing all lined up. Everything is set. There can't be a slip-up. But Rothstein says he isn't interested." Chase claimed that he never saw Burns again, but that he heard from other sources that Burns had managed to find other backers for his scheme.[118]

In 1947, however, his story differed in a few significant details from the version he had told Grant six years before. This time, Chase said that Burns had come to his hotel room in Chicago (not New York) with another man (Sehorn or perhaps *The Sporting News*'s lawyers deleted the man's name, coyly identifying him as "a well known sports figure of the time"—Abe Attell?). Burns, said Chase, did all the talking, and asked Chase, "Would you like to make a lot of easy money?"

Chase responded that "somebody ought to make a lot of money if he could fix the Series, but that I didn't want to get mixed up in it because I had enough trouble at the moment, including another run-in with my second wife."

Chase said that he and his unnamed roommate (Jean Dubuc?) were to raise $100,000 in the plot, but both refused. Nevertheless, "My name was tossed around, and I received much of the blame for plotting the fix. That is a lie, but had I gone to President Heydler or to Manager McGraw, I could have helped baseball and myself. Later, it was too late. My name, because of my past, was implicated, and no one wanted to believe my story. That's when a bad name hurts."

In neither interview did Chase specifically mention his indictment and arrest in San Jose. Instead, he told Grant that he had offered to testify at the Black Sox trial if the investigators paid him $500 in expenses. He admitted, however, that he now regretted not paying his own way to Chicago to clear his name, because he had been irrevocably linked to the scandal as a result.

He added, with less than convincing piety, "Any form of gambling in baseball is bad and any player who thinks he can get by with it is badly mistaken."[119]

An intriguing sidelight of these interviews was the revelation of the correspondence between Chase and Judge Landis. Chase told Grant that he had written to Judge Landis from Nogales in 1931. "I asked Landis to tell me where I stood at that time with regard to organized ball. I admitted that I had made a mistake [in not reporting his knowledge of the Black Sox fix] and wondered if it was possible to clear up some of the misrepresentations connected with my name." Chase claimed that Landis had replied promptly to the effect that so far as he knew Chase was in good standing in organized baseball, but requested more information about the mistake to which Chase had referred.

"I showed Landis' answer to an attorney," said Chase, "and was advised not to reply and not to elaborate on the original statement. Then, before I could stop him, the attorney tore up Landis' letter. I'm sorry I don't have Landis' letter to show it to people who insist that I played a sinister role in the Black Sox scandal."[120] Six years later, however, Chase said merely that a friend in Arizona had lost Landis's reply, and that he himself "had neglected to answer as requested by Landis."

Sehorn revealed that he had written to Landis in 1943 about this correspondence. Landis confirmed that Chase had written him on October 29, 1931, but said only that Sehorn should ask Chase for copies of that letter and of Landis's reply, dated November 4, 1931. The judge added that he had never heard from Chase again.[121] The commissioner's office, however, still says that Chase was never officially banned from organized baseball.[122]

In 1941, Chase followed the story of his letter to Landis by fawning over the vain and autocratic commissioner: "I wonder how many people realize just what Landis has done for baseball? Where would the game be today without him? His consistent championing of the underdog and his determination to see that justice prevails, no matter what the cost, has made him, in my opinion, the most valuable member of the whole baseball fraternity."[123]

Chase added that baseball was now "a cleaner, healthier institution through and through" than it had been during his career. Of course the owners still saw the game as a business and cared little for the welfare of the players. "But today the ballplayer has Judge Landis on his side and if I talked all day and all night about the value of having a Judge Landis on the scene, I don't think I could do justice to the subject. Landis is the champion of the ballplayer, the greatest single individual in the game today. He stands for justice for the worker, the player who gets out there and makes those base hits and catches those long flies and pitches those victories."

Indeed, said Chase, "Because of Landis—and only because of Landis—baseball today holds a position in America's athletics second to none. Never before has the game been on such sound footing, even with the dangerous signs

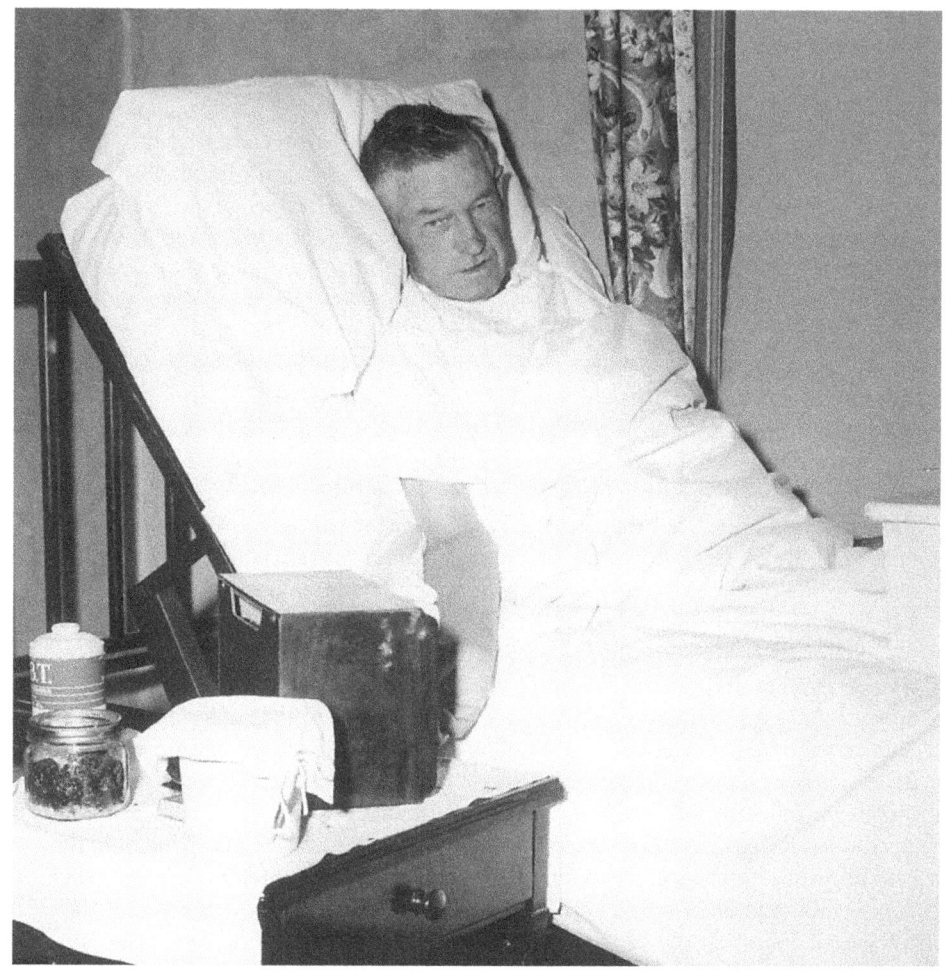

Chase in the hospital in Colusa, Calif., shortly before his death in 1947. He spent much of the last few years of his life battling various ailments. *The Sporting News Archives.*

on the political horizons and the upheavals in the world. It took a Landis to remake the character of baseball after the Black Sox scandal in 1919. And that same Landis is the game's greatest attribute today."[124]

Six years later Chase was still lavishing praise on the commissioner. Landis, however, had died in 1944, so the object of Chase's encomiums was Landis's successor, Happy Chandler. Chandler, whom Chase called "baseball's G-man," had suspended Brooklyn manager Leo Durocher for the 1947 season for consorting with gamblers, a decision of which Chase apparently approved. He recalled for Sehorn the prevalence of gambling in his playing days: "That wasn't a healthy condition. Once the evil started, there was no stopping it and club owners were not strong enough to cope with the evil. That's why Commissioner Chandler has to be the strong man today."[125]

Clearly Chase was still hoping that such statements would convince the commissioner to clear his name, but the overall tone of both interviews was decidedly downbeat. "You know, baseball was good to me, but I'm afraid I wasn't very good to baseball," he told Grant. "Most of the grief I had during my career as a player was of my own making. At least, if it wasn't of my own making, I could have prevented it had I acted more wisely."[126] Similarly, he told Sehorn, "I'd give anything if I could start in all over again. What a change there would be in the life of Hal Chase. I was all wrong, at least in most things, and my best proof is that I am flat on my back, without a dime."[127]

Chase died less than a month after the publication of the interview with Sehorn. The end came on May 18, 1947, and occasioned a great outpouring of obituaries that were simultaneously admiring and moralistic. In death, as on those occasions in the latter part of his life when he had been periodically rediscovered by the press, Prince Hal was held up as an example of great talent gone horribly wrong. His was a cautionary tale, a fable with an obvious moral. As Fred Lieb wrote, "What a waste of skill and artistry, and of a lifetime!"[128] Arthur Daley of the New York *Times* added, "It's the might-have-been which makes the career of Chase such an utter tragedy." Daley called Chase "One of the most gifted operatives the sport ever possessed," but added that he "lacked the moral stability to become the all-time standout his talents ordained."[129] Harry Grayson, who had made so much of his encounter with Chase in Tucson, wrote, "In grace and instinct, Chase was not inferior to Ty Cobb. He had no moral sense, however, toyed with the laws of life, was suspected and caught.... Hal Chase was a rogue whose genius carried him through to big things against a handicap that would have carried an ordinary criminal to silent obloquy."[130] S. L. A. Marshall, as one might expect from a man nicknamed "Slam," was less subtle: "Chase was completely and congenitally amoral. The man was born without a sense of right and wrong."[131]

By 1947 the National Baseball Hall of Fame in Cooperstown, New York, was fourteen years old. Enshrinement in the Hall is baseball's ultimate accolade. Many still believe that Joe Jackson deserves to be enshrined in Cooperstown. They argue that his achievements should count for more than his involvement in the Black Sox scandal, and that the illiterate, unsophisticated Jackson was a victim and a dupe who probably did not realize the gravity of the fix.

Yet in a larger sense Chase, for all his sophistication and worldliness, is no less a victim than Jackson. Was he corrupt? Did he throw games and offer bribes to other players? We may never know for sure, although the circumstantial evidence of his guilt is overwhelming. But upon examining Chase's life and career one conclusion is inescapable: he was only doing what others, including a number of the mighty magnates who condemned him, were doing. If he had pretended to more virtue than he possessed, as did so many of his peers and employers, he might have had his plaque in Cooperstown after all. His utter lack of discretion or remorse, however, ensured that organized baseball would repudiate him utterly. Joe Williams wrote that "No monuments to Chase will ever reach into the sky.... Baseball has its own personal Westminster Abbey of immortals, the Cooperstown shrine, but there is no niche reserved for Chase."[132]

Instead the only monument to the man who might have been the greatest first baseman in baseball history stands beneath a tree in San Jose's Oak Hill Memorial Park. The pink granite obelisk bears five names: those of Edgar and Mary Chase on the front, those of three of their sons on the sides. The name of Hal Chase is on the west side, beneath that of his brother Edwin.

How good a ballplayer was Chase — or, rather, would he have been, had he taken his ballplaying seriously? The question is ultimately unanswerable, because, despite the best efforts of thousands of dedicated baseball fans and sabermetricians, assessing the relative merits of various ballplayers remains largely a subjective pursuit. Perhaps the greatest tribute to his talent is that he could so impress those who saw him play, apparently while contriving to lose games at the same time.

But it is not his athletic ability alone that makes Chase such a fascinating character; it is the inscrutability of the man. He comes down to us as a shadowy, grinning figure, and we will never know what really went on behind the pale blue eyes that squint at us through a cloud of cigar smoke. Given the scarcity of proven facts about him, it is perhaps appropriate that arguably the best representation of his character to date occurs in a work of fiction, Eric Rolfe Greenberg's *The Celebrant*.

The novel concerns the relationship between a young New York jewelry designer and the baseball player he idolizes, Christy Mathewson of the New York Giants. Chase is Matty's dark twin, the sinister personification of deceit and corruption, and the narrator is justifiably concerned when his older brother Eli befriends Chase. During a discussion of Mathewson's earnings, Eli tells Chase, "You should make so much, Hal. Over the counter, I mean."

"Don't matter how it comes in, Kappy. It's all the same going out."

"You're a philosopher, Hal."

"No. I am a professional ballplayer. 'Professional' means only one thing. You do it for money.... I'm a professional ballplayer. I do it for money, and if there's more money in losing than winning, shit if I care."[133]

And yet, despite such statements, Chase emerges as a strangely sympathetic character. Just before the exchange quoted above, the narrator takes his young son Matthias to his first major league game at the Polo Grounds:

"Matthias was delighted to find his Uncle Eli in the box; I was something less enchanted to discover his guest, Hal Chase. Matthias, though, immediately took to the Yankee, whose huge hands held him gently.... Finally he fell asleep in Chase's arms, which charmed the player. I offered to take him, but Chase insisted he was no bother.... Matthias stirred, and he soothed the child by stroking his hair. 'Good-looking kid. I probably have a few of my own out west....'"[134]

Greenberg's fictional portrait, with its combination of hard-eyed cynicism, unexpected tenderness, and roguish charm, reminds us that its factual subject was not a mere symbol, a one-dimensional stick figure which we can label "scapegoat" or "villain." Rather, like all humans and all things human, including the institution of baseball itself, he contained within himself both good and evil. Perhaps it is enough to acknowledge him as the most complex, and thus the most compellingly human, character in the history of the grand old game.

Epilogue

In the course of my research for this book, I made several trips to San Jose. On one of those trips, in early 1999, I was in the public library absently searching the computerized *Mercury News* database for references to Hal Chase when I stumbled onto a more recent scandal involving the Chase family.

One of Hal Chase's grandsons, Jeff, was the president of the National Traffic Safety Institute (NTSI), a company based in Salem, Oregon, that had an exclusive contract with Santa Clara County to provide traffic school courses. In April 1995, the *Mercury News* reported in a front-page story that NTSI had underreported its earnings by more than one million dollars over the previous five years by buying supplies through an insider deal with one of Jeff Chase's other businesses.[1]

Subsequent stories unearthed more allegations of questionable practices by NTSI and by Jeff Chase. One story revealed that Jeff had paid his father, then eighty-five, $79,000 for "public relations and marketing," which NTSI had reported as an expense of the Santa Clara County program. A report prepared by an independent accounting firm concluded that the old man's services "did not directly benefit" the local program.

The Santa Clara County Municipal Court terminated its contract with NTSI, entrusting the county's traffic school program to a consortium of local community colleges.[2] Hal E. Chase Sr. died in February 1997. I never got the chance to talk to him about the NTSI scandal, for which I was grateful: he had always been quite cordial to me, though we disagreed on many issues concerning his infamous father, and I would not have enjoyed questioning him about his new notoriety.

I could not help wondering, however, about the black cloud which seemed to dog this family. Was this some divine retribution for the illicit activities of the first Hal Chase? Was it merely the manifestation of some rogue gene passed down from father to son to grandson?

I certainly don't know the answers to these questions, but there is little doubt that the Chase name, already so deeply tarnished by Prince Hal, has not been helped by the subsequent actions of his descendants. Certainly they could argue that the allegations, if true, amounted to a victimless crime. The citizens of Santa Clara County had received their driver safety courses, and no one had actually suffered as a result of the illegal contract.

The same argument, of course, could be applied to Prince Hal. If he threw games, bribed other players, or bet against his own team, the only people hurt were those who had bet illegally on the other team — and, of course, Prince Hal himself, once his reputation began to precede him. And in an environment where making under-the-table deals to get business done was commonplace, how can we single out one man for special opprobrium?

To think meaningfully about these issues raises some fundamental questions about what we have been taught about the American character. Perhaps we need to learn to think of ourselves, collectively and individually, in new, more realistic ways.

Chapter Notes

Introduction

1. Frank Cloak Jr. to Martin Kohout, Feb. 6, 1991 (interview).
2. Thomas J. Schlereth, *Victorian America: Transformations in Everyday Life, 1876–1915* (New York: HarperCollins, 1991), 28; Douglas Brinkley, *American Heritage History of the United States* (New York: Viking, 1998), 242; Ray Ginger, *Age of Excess: The United States from 1877 to 1914* (2nd ed.; New York: Macmillan, 1975), 97.
3. Page Smith, *America Enters the World: A People's History of the Progressive Era and World War I*, vol. VII (New York: McGraw-Hill, 1985), 9–10.
4. Robert H. Wiebe, *The Search for Order: 1877–1920* (NY: Hill and Wang, 1967), 40 (1st quotation); Judy Crichton, *America 1900: The Turning Point* (New York: Henry Holt, 1998), 115 (2nd quotation); Brinkley, *American Heritage History of the United States*, 249 (3rd quotation); Glenn Porter, "Industrialization and the Rise of Big Business," in Charles W. Calhoun (ed.), *The Gilded Age: Essays on the Origins of Modern America* (Wilmington, Del.: Scholarly Resources, 1996), 2 (4th quotation); William Leach, *Land of Desire: Merchants, Power, and the Rise of a New American Culture* (New York: Pantheon, 1993), 8 (5th quotation).
5. Thorstein Veblen, *The Theory of the Leisure Class: An Economic Study of Institutions* (1899; New York: Modern Library, 1934), 28 (1st quotation); Adams and George quoted in Smith, *America Enters the World*, 10, 76; Rice quoted in William A. Harper, *How You Played the Game: The Life of Grantland Rice* (Columbia: University of Missouri Press, 1999), 279; Chapman quoted in Ginger, *Age of Excess*, 19.
6. Brinkley, *American Heritage History of the United States*, 249 (2nd quotation), 251 (1st quotation); Ginger, *Age of Excess*, 20 (3rd quotation).
7. Ginger, *Age of Excess*, 20 (1st quotation), 332 (2nd quotation); Wiebe, *The Search for Order*, 40 (3rd quotation).
8. Edward Marshall, "The Psychology of Baseball," New York *Times*, Nov. 13, 1910 (1st quotation); Addington Bruce quoted in Nash, *The Call of the Wild*, 296–297 (2nd quotation); G. W. Axelson, *"Commy": The Life Story of Charles A. Comiskey* (Chicago: Reilly and Lee, 1919), 318 (3rd quotation). See also *Sporting Life*, Jan. 11, 1908 (cited hereafter as *SL*), in which William F. H. Koelsch argued that fans came to ballparks "not to gamble, but to see a manly clean game, free from the taint of corruption.... The enthusiasm of the school boy is blended with that of the merchant prince and true democracy prevails...."
9. Veblen, *Theory of the Leisure Class*, 274 (1st quotation); Harold Seymour, *Baseball: The Golden Age* (2nd ed.; New York: Oxford University Press, 1989), 90 (2nd quotation; cited hereafter as *Golden Age*).
10. *The Sporting News*, May 28, 1947 (quotation; cited hereafter as *TSN*). Gehrig, Terry, and Sisler, of course, are all members of the National Baseball Hall of Fame.

11. Bob Hoie, "More About Chase," *Grandstand Baseball Annual 1991* (Downey, Calif.: Joseph M. Wayman, 1992), 1. Cobb chose Sisler over Chase, but called Chase "the ace fielder of all time at that position," and later recalled a play on which he outsmarted Chase as his most satisfying moment in baseball. See Frank Graham, "One for the Book," *Sport* (May 1951), 30; Ty Cobb with Al Stump, *My Life in Baseball* (1961; reprint, Lincoln: University of Nebraska Press, 1993), 166; New York *World*, Dec. 13, 1924.

12. Richard Scheinin, "Hal Chase's Son, Grandson Say He's Being Treated Unfairly," Knight-Ridder Newspapers, March 1993 (1st quotation); unidentified clipping in possession of Hal E. Chase Sr. (2nd quotation); unidentified clipping, Mar. 23, 1916, in Hal Chase file, National Baseball Library, Cooperstown, N.Y. (3rd quotation; cited hereafter as NBL); Washington *Post*, May 20, 1947 (4th quotation). Others who considered Chase the best first baseman they had ever seen included Nick Altrock, Jimmy Austin, George Davis, Billy Evans, Kid Gleason, Willie Keeler, Connie Mack, Clyde Milan, Fred Tenney, and Edd Roush. See, for example, Lawrence S. Ritter, *The Glory of Their Times: The Story of the Early Days of Baseball Told by the Men Who Played It* (New York: Collier, 1966), 78; T. P. Harrison, "Tenney's All Star Team," *Baseball* (July, 1911), 61; Paul Green, *Forgotten Fields* (Waupaca, Wisc.: Parker, 1984), 31; Ira L. Smith, *Baseball's Famous First Basemen* (New York: A. S. Barnes, 1956), 78; *SL*, Nov. 17, 1906, Dec. 28, 1907; and *TSN*, Jan. 1, 1919, May 28, 1947.

13. Gehrig, at minus sixty, is one of them. The others, in alphabetical order, are Jim Bottomley, Dan Driessen, Ron Fairly (who played almost as many games in the outfield), Steve Garvey, Joe Kuhel, Ted Kluszewski, Candy LaChance, John Mayberry, Tony Perez, Eddie Robinson, and Gus Suhr. Chase played 1815 games at first base in his career, and his fielding runs total was minus forty-two. John Thorn, Pete Palmer, Michael Gershman, and David Pietrusza (eds.), *Total Baseball: The Official Encyclopedia of Major League Baseball* (6th ed.; New York: Total Sports, 1999). The fielding-runs statistic, a linear-weights measure of runs prevented beyond what a theoretical league-average player would have prevented, is not perfect, but it does seem to provide a somewhat more accurate measure of a player's defensive abilities than does fielding percentage alone. *Ibid.*, 2530. See Pete Palmer and John Thorn, "Sabermetrics," in *ibid.*, 630–637, for an explanation of linear-weights formulas.

14. Quoted in Lawrence Ritter and Donald Honig, *The 100 Greatest Baseball Players of All Time* (New York: Crown, 1981), 129–131.

15. Bob Hoie to Martin Kohout, Feb. 26, 1990 (1st quotation); *SL*, Aug. 4, 1906 (2nd quotation); Nick Altrock, quoted in Hoie, "More About Chase" (3rd quotation). Gib Bodet played ball while serving in the military in the mid–1950s. His coach, a master sergeant who had known Chase in Arizona in the 1920s, regarded Chase as "a cross ... between Clark Gable and Joe DiMaggio." Gib Bodet, "The Life and Times of Prince Hal Chase" (unpublished MS., 1991), 1.

16. Donald Honig, *The Greatest First Basemen of All Time* (New York: Crown, 1988), 7.

17. Ray Fisher to Jeff Mortimer, Oct. 20, 1975 (transcript in possession of John Leidy).

18. *TSN*, May 28, 1947 (quotation). See also, for example, Ritter, *The Glory of Their Times*, 75–76; unidentified clipping, Aug. 27, 1908, NBL.

19. Bodet, "The Life and Times of Prince Hal Chase," 2.

20. Bill James, *Whatever Happened to the Hall of Fame? Baseball, Cooperstown, and the Politics of Glory* (1994; New York: Fireside, 1995), 102.

21. Hal E. Chase Sr. to Martin Kohout, Sept. 18, 1994. To avoid confusion, I will refer to Hal E. Chase Sr. as "young Hal," even as an adult.

22. Bill James, *The Bill James Historical Baseball Abstract* (New York: Villard, 1986), 134–138.

23. Al Stump, *Cobb: A Biography* (1994; Chapel Hill, N.C.: Algonquin Books, 1996), 23–24; Charles C. Alexander, *Ty Cobb* (1984; reprint, New York: Oxford University Press, 1985), esp. 5, 155, 227.

24. Betsy Tunis, quoted in Los Gatos (Calif.) *Weekly*, May 28, 1986 (1st quotation); Bill Wambsganss, quoted in Green, *Forgotten Fields*, 44 (2nd quotation).

25. Gib Bodet to Martin Kohout, Sept. 25, 1990 (1st quotation); Lloyd Morris, *Incredible New York: High Life and Low Life of the Last Hundred Years* (New York: Random House,

1951), 226 (2nd quotation); M. R. Werner, *Tammany Hall* (Garden City, N.Y.: Doubleday, Doran, 1928), 487; Oliver E. Allen, *New York, New York: A History of the World's Most Exhilarating and Challenging City* (New York: Atheneum, 1990), 181–182, 225–226; Lothrop Stoddard, *Master of Manhattan: The Life of Richard Croker* (New York: Longmans, Green, 1931), 206–209.

26. Riess, *Touching Base*, 76 (1st quotation); Seymour, *Golden Age*, 390; Charles C. Alexander, *John McGraw* (New York: Viking, 1988), 229–230; Allen, *New York, New York*, 268 (2nd quotation). Stoneham operated a semilegal "bucket shop," or "an office where orders to buy or sell stock were taken but not executed; instead, the operator pocketed the customer's money and gambled on the possibility of buying the stock later at a lower price or selling it at a higher one." Seymour, *Golden Age*, 390; Alexander, *John McGraw*, 250, 266. The attorney who defended Stoneham against the charges of perjury and mail fraud was William J. Fallon, who was himself indicted for trying to bribe a federal juror and for taking part in the destruction of company records in the case. Fallon later resurfaced as Rothstein's attorney during the investigation of the Black Sox fix, and also defended McGraw on charges that the Giants manager had violated the Volstead Act. Alexander, *John McGraw*, 223, 250; Seymour, *Golden Age*, 142, 308–309.

27. Alexander, *John McGraw*, 71–72, 89–91, 105, 142, 198, 256–257, 263; Harold Seymour, *Baseball: The Early Years* (1960; reprint, New York: Oxford University Press, 1989), 321–322 (cited hereafter as *Early Years*); Seymour, *Golden Age*, 139–140, 142, 279 (quotation), 283–285, 378–379. McGraw's 1904 arrest came after he and a friend had reportedly made about $2,300 taking on all comers in pitching silver dollars at a basket on the grounds of the Eastman Hotel in Hot Springs, Arkansas. Alexander, *John McGraw*, 105.

28. Seymour, *Golden Age*, 9 (quotation), 279, 300–301.

29. Anne-Marie Kern, Office of the Commissioner, Major League Baseball, to Martin Kohout, Mar. 29, 1991.

30. Arizona *Daily Star*, Dec. 16, 1990 (1st quotation); Roy P. Drachman to Martin Kohout, Oct. 17, 1990 (interview) (2nd quotation); Bodet to Kohout, Sept. 25, 1990 (3rd quotation).

31. *TSN*, Sept. 18, 1941 (1st quotation), Apr. 23, 1947; San Francisco *Examiner*, May 19, 1947; Red Barber, *1947: When All Hell Broke Loose in Baseball* (Garden City, N.Y.: Doubleday, 1982) (2nd quotation). The title of the latter, of course, refers primarily to the controversy engendered by Jackie Robinson's debut as the first African American major leaguer in modern times.

32. Fred Lieb, *Baseball As I Have Known It* (New York: Coward, McCann and Geoghegan, 1977), 97 (1st quotation); S. L. A. Marshall, "An Amoral Man," n.d., NBL (2nd quotation). Lieb was quoting his editor at the New York *Press*, James Price.

33. Quoted in Honig, *The Greatest First Basemen of All Time*, 10.

Chapter 1

1. Josiah Royce, "Provincialism," *Putnam's Magazine* (Nov., 1909), 234.

2. For a more detailed discussion of Royce's social thought, see Bruce Kuklick, *The Rise of American Philosophy: Cambridge, Massachusetts, 1860–1930* (New Haven, Conn.: Yale University Press, 1977), 296–309. A number of historians have discussed the anxieties of late-nineteenth- and early-twentieth-century America; see, for example, Alan Trachtenberg, *The Incorporation of America: Culture and Society in the Gilded Age* (New York: Hill and Wang, 1982); Thomas Schlereth, *Victorian America: Transformations in Everyday Life, 1876–1915* (New York: HarperPerennial, 1992); T. J. Jackson Lears, *No Place of Grace: Antimodernism and the Transformation of American Culture, 1880–1920* (New York: Pantheon, 1981); Ray Ginger, *Age of Excess: The United States from 1877 to 1914* (New York: Macmillan, 1965); Samuel P. Hayes, *The Response to Industrialism, 1885–1914* (Chicago: University of Chicago Press, 1957); and Nell Irvin Painter, *Standing at Armageddon: The United States, 1877–1919* (New York: W. W. Norton, 1987).

3. Trachtenberg, *Incorporation of America*, 15.
4. Quoted in Paul Johnson, *A History of the American People* (New York: HarperCollins, 1997), 511.
5. Ellis A. Davis, *Davis' Commercial Encyclopedia of the Pacific Southwest: California, Nevada, Utah, Arizona* (Oakland: Ellis A. Davis, 1915), 411.
6. Stephen M. Payne, *Santa Clara County: Harvest of Change* (Northridge, Calif.: Windsor Publications in cooperation with County of Santa Clara Historical Heritage Commission, 1987), 108.
7. George G. Bruntz, *The History of Los Gatos: Gem of the Foothills* (Fresno, Calif.: Valley Publishers, 1971), 6–7, 20.
8. San Jose *Mercury News*, Jan. 25, 1960.
9. This information is recorded in the baby book of Chase's descendant Frank Cloak Jr. I am grateful to him and to his daughter, Corinne Kunkel, for sharing it with me.
10. Here again, there is a mystery about Chase. Most sources, including John Thorn and Pete Palmer (eds.), *Total Baseball: The Ultimate Encyclopedia of Baseball* (3rd ed.; New York: HarperPerennial, 1993), say his middle name was "Homer," and it appears as such on his gravestone. The respected baseball historian Bob Hoie, however, insists it was "Harris." See Robert C. Hoie, "The Hal Chase Case." And on various documents during his tenure at Santa Clara College, he was repeatedly listed as "Harold E. Chase."
11. San Jose *News*, n.d.; (Los Gatos?) *Times-Observer*, May 8, 1984.
12. U.S. Census, Santa Clara County, roll 110.
13. Hal E. Chase Sr. to Martin Kohout, Jan. 30, 1990 (interview); (Los Gatos?) *Times-Observer*, May 8, 1984.
14. *SL*, July 28, 1906; John E. Spalding, *Pacific Coast League Stars, Volume II: Ninety Who Made It in the Majors, 1903 to 1957* (n.p.: John E. Spalding, 1997), 9.
15. (Los Gatos?) *Times-Observer*, May 1, 1984.
16. Los Gatos *Times*, n. d. [May 19, 1947?] (quotation); Los Gatos *Weekly*, May 28, 1986. According to one account, Edgar himself was the owner of the fruit stand.
17. Quoted in Bruntz, *History of Los Gatos*, 79.
18. Hal E. Chase Jr. to Martin Kohout, Jan. 30, 1990 (interview). One researcher claims that Chase dropped out of high school after his sophomore year. Gib Bodet, "The Life and Times of Prince Hal Chase" (unpublished MS., n.d. [1991]), 6.
19. Quoted in unidentified clipping by Joe Williams, May 25, 1955, in National Baseball Hall of Fame files.
20. Jim Johnson, "Heroes and Villains: Santa Cruz Produced Baseball Stars and Baseball Scandals," http://www.cruzio.com/~sclibs/history/rec/heroes.html (originally published in the [Santa Cruz] *Mid-County Post*, Mar. 4–17, 1997); Jim Johnson, "Hometown Hardball: Local Baseball Heroes Went to Big Cities Bring [sic] Back Both Pride and Scandal," http://www.cruzio.com/~sclibs/history/rec/hardball.html (originally published in the [Santa Cruz] *Mid-County Post*, March 4–17, 1997) (quotation).
21. San Jose *Daily Mercury*, Feb. 15, 1903.
22. James D. Hart, *A Companion to California* (Berkeley: University of California Press, 1987), 453.
23. Gerald McKevitt, S. J., *The University of Santa Clara: A History, 1851–1977* (Stanford, Calif.: Stanford University Press, 1979), 145. Seven of those who attended Santa Clara around the turn of the century later went on to play in the major leagues, although Chase was the first and the best. Cappy Gagnon to Martin Kohout, n.d. (June 1990).
24. Santa Clara *Redwood*, Mar. 1903, 194.
25. San Jose *Daily Mercury*, Feb. 19, 1903.
26. McKevitt, *The University of Santa Clara*, 145.
27. Bodet, "The Life and Times of Prince Hal Chase," 6.
28. Julia O'Keefe, University Archivist, Santa Clara University, to Martin Kohout, Oct. 27, 1989; informational biography form on Hal Chase compiled by Santa Clara University athletic department (n.d.), in Hal Chase clipping file, Santa Clara University Archives.
29. *Santa Clara College Catalogue for the Year 1902–1903*, 71; *Santa Clara College Catalogue*

for the Year 1903–1904, 80; "Santa Clara College, Session of 1902-1903," in "Registration, 1902–1906," ledger book, Santa Clara University Archives.

30. John E. Spalding, *Always on Sunday: The California Baseball League, 1886 to 1915* (n.p.: John E. Spalding, 1992), 102–103; *Santa Clara College Catalogue for the Year 1904–1905,* 60, in Santa Clara University Archives.
31. McKevitt, *The University of Santa Clara,* 146.
32. *Redwood,* Mar. 1903, 194 (quotation), 197–200; San Jose *Daily Mercury,* Feb. 20, Mar. 2, 1903.
33. *Redwood,* May 1903, 334.
34. *Ibid.,* 336.
35. Geoff LaCasse, "Hal Chase in Victoria," *The National Pastime: A Review of Baseball History,* No. 15 (1995), 88–89.
36. Victoria *Daily Colonist,* Feb. 4, 1903.
37. Chicago *Daily Tribune,* July 13, 1913.
38. Gagnon to Kohout, n.d. (June 1990); Seymour, *Golden Age,* 82.
39. Chicago *Daily Tribune,* July 13, 1913.
40. Victoria *Daily Colonist,* Apr. 26, May 2, 1903.
41. *Ibid.,* May 10, 1903.
42. *Ibid.,* May 23, 24, 1903.
43. *Ibid.,* June 13, 14, 1903.
44. *Ibid.,* July 7, 8, 9, 1903.
45. *Ibid.,* July 11, 1903.
46. *Ibid.,* July 12, 1903.
47. *Ibid.,* July 16, 1903.
48. *Ibid.,* July 19, 1903.
49. *Ibid.,* Aug. 11, 1903.
50. See Chicago *Daily Tribune,* July 13, 1913.
51. Victoria *Daily Colonist,* Aug. 11, 1903. Cohn had had an opportunity to see Chase in action in late June, when he brought his Vancouver team, loaded with "ringers" he had recruited from Seattle of the Pacific Coast League, to Victoria. The *Daily Colonist* called the visitors, who won 8–5, "the strongest team that has ever played on the local diamond." *Ibid.,* June 28, 1903.
52. LaCasse, "Hal Chase in Victoria," 90. LaCasse says that Victoria compiled a record of 21-8-1 in 1903.
53. *Redwood,* Mar. 1904, 123.
54. New York *World-Telegram,* Dec. 26, 1933. Both Chase and Strub, however, said that the play had occurred while Strub was playing for the University of California. See unidentified clipping by Harry Grayson, n.d., National Baseball Hall of Fame files.
55. *Redwood,* Mar. 1904, 124–125.
56. *Ibid.,* 127.
57. *Ibid.,* 187–188.
58. Hoie, "The Hal Chase Case," in Robert L. Davids, ed. *The Baseball Research Journal: Volumes 1 through 3.* Cleveland: Society for American Baseball Research, 1998.
59. *Ibid.,* 191; Los Angeles *Times,* Mar. 6, 1904.
60. Los Angeles *Herald,* Mar. 8, 1904.
61. Bill O'Neal, *The Pacific Coast League: 1903–1988* (Austin, Tex.: Eakin Press, 1990), 6.
62. *SL,* Jan. 2, Feb. 13, 1904.
63. *TSN,* Mar. 12, 1904; *SL,* Feb. 20, 1904; Los Angeles *Herald,* Mar. 20, 1904.
64. *SL,* Feb. 27, 1904.
65. *Ibid.,* Mar. 5, 1904; *TSN,* Mar. 19, 1904.
66. *TSN,* Mar. 12, 1904.
67. Morley may have gotten the last laugh after all. As Brooklyn's regular first baseman in 1904, Dillon batted only .258 with no home runs and thirty-one runs batted in. The 1904 season was to be his last in the major leagues; in 1905 he was back in Los Angeles, where he replaced Chase as the Angels' first baseman.
68. Los Angeles *Times,* Mar. 18, 1904; Los Angeles *Herald,* Mar. 20, 21, 1904.

69. *Redwood,* May 1904, 250–251.
70. Los Angeles *Herald,* Mar. 28, 1904.
71. *SL,* Apr. 16, 1904.
72. *Ibid.,* May 7, June 25, 1904.
73. *Redwood,* May 1904, 250, 251.
74. Leo Moriarty (ed.), *Baseball Records: Pacific Coast League from 1903 to 1928* (Los Angeles: n. p., 1928), 35.
75. *TSN,* Nov. 26, 1904.
76. *SL,* Dec. 10, 1904.
77. Los Angeles *Herald,* Sept. 4, 6, 8, 1904.
78. *SL,* Mar. 4, 1905.
79. *Ibid.,* Oct. 15, 1904.
80. Eugene C. Murdock, *Ban Johnson: Czar of Baseball* (Westport, Conn.: Greenwood Press, 1982), 76; Riess, *Touching Base,* 71; Alexander, *John McGraw,* 85.
81. Seymour, *Early Years,* 322.
82. Fred Lieb, *The Baseball Story* (New York: G. P. Putnam's Sons, 1950), 159; Frank Graham, *The New York Yankees: An Informal History* (New York: G. P. Putnam's Sons, 1943), 5–6.
83. *TSN,* July 12, 1923.
84. Graham, *The New York Yankees,* 7–8; Riess, *Touching Base,* 90–91.
85. O'Neal, *The Pacific Coast League,* 6–7.
86. *SL,* Oct. 29, Nov. 5, 1904.
87. *Ibid.,* Oct. 15, 1904, Jan. 14, 1905.
88. *TSN,* Dec. 3, 1904.
89. Los Angeles *Times,* Sept. 25, 1904.
90. Quoted in *TSN,* Oct. 22, 1904.

Chapter 2

1. Robert Shackleton, *The Book of New York* (Philadelphia: Penn, 1917), 218.
2. Martin Gilbert, *A History of the Twentieth Century. Vol. I: 1900–1933* (New York: Avon, 1997), 217.
3. John C. Van Dyke, *The New New York: A Commentary on the Place and the People* (New York: Macmillan, 1909), 7 (1st quotation); Shackleton, *The Book of New York,* 70 (2nd quotation).
4. Morris, *Incredible New York,* 225 (1st quotation); Rupert Hughes, *The Real New York* (New York: The Smart Set, 1904), 75 (2nd quotation).
5. McAllister quoted in Henry Steele Commager and Allan Nevins (eds.), *The Heritage of America: Readings in American History* (rev. ed.; Boston: D. C. Heath, 1949), 890; Gates quoted in Stephen Longstreet, *Win or Lose: A Social History of Gambling in America* (Indianapolis: Bobbs-Merrill, 1977), 164; Edward Hotaling, *They're Off! Horse Racing at Saratoga* (Syracuse, N.Y.: Syracuse University Press, 1995), 177–178. Longstreet says Gates lost $400,000 at the track that afternoon, while Hotaling says $375,000.
6. Longstreet, *Win or Lose,* 166–172; Hotaling, *They're Off!,* 216–217; George Waller, *Saratoga: Saga of an Impious Era* (New York: Bonanza, 1966), 305; Richard Sasuly, *Bookies and Bettors: Two Hundred Years of Gambling* (New York: Holt, Rinehart and Winston, 1982), 92–95.
7. Hotaling, *They're Off!,* 139; Oliver E. Allen, *New York, New York: A History of the World's Most Exhilarating and Challenging City* (New York: Atheneum, 1990), 225; Ken Bloom, *Broadway: An Encyclopedic Guide to the History, People and Places of Times Square* (New York: Facts on File, 1991), 51 (quotation).
8. Longstreet, *Win or Lose,* 144.
9. Herbert Asbury, *Sucker's Progress: An Informal History of Gambling in America from the Colonies to Canfield* (New York: Dodd, Mead, 1938), 451–452; Longstreet, *Win or*

Lose, 143–144. Suzannah Lessard, *The Architect of Desire: Beauty and Danger in the Stanford White Family* (New York: Dial, 1996), provides a chilling portrait of her illustrious ancestor Stanford White, who was shot dead by Harry K. Thaw in 1906 while listening to a performance of "I Could Love a Million Girls" at the Roof Garden.

    10. Burt Solomon, *Where They Ain't: The Fabled Life and Untimely Death of the Original Baltimore Orioles, the Team That Gave Birth to Modern Baseball* (New York: Free Press, 1999), 239.

    11. Morris, *Incredible New York*, 226 (quotation).

    12. Longstreet, *Win or Lose*, 144.

    13. Morris, *Incredible New York*, 226; Werner, *Tammany Hall*, 404; Riess, *Touching Base*, 72.

    14. Gerald Kurland, *Seth Low: The Reformer in an Urban and Industrial Age* (New York: Twayne, 1971), 116.

    15. New York *Times*, Feb. 23, 24, 1901, July 30, Aug. 31, 1902. In 1901 the Tammany leadership began to distance itself from Devery, who had become a political liability: "His antics were amusing, but the alliance of the Deputy Commissioner of Police with vice and gambling was not profitable propaganda, and Tammany Hall lost votes because of Devery." Devery responded by running unsuccessfully for mayor against the Tammany candidate in 1903; after his defeat he retired from politics and moved to Far Rockaway, Long Island. In later years, he "always carried his gold police badge, whistle, and book of rules in his pocket, and he was fond of spending much time over his thirty-six scrapbooks of press clippings which he had cross-indexed elaborately." Devery died in 1919. Werner, *Tammany Hall*, 487 (1st quotation), 497 (2nd quotation).

    16. Arthur Ruhl, "The Caliph and His Court," *McClure's Magazine* (Aug. 1901), 394 (1st Quotation), 395 (2nd quotation).

    17. Kurland, *Seth Low*, 144.

    18. Solomon, *Where They Ain't*, 239, 241.

    19. Lewis Michels (born 1902) quoted in Jeff Kisseloff, *You Must Remember This: An Oral History of Manhattan from the 1890s to World War II* (New York: Harcourt Brace Jovanovich, 1989), 226.

    20. *SL*, Jan. 28, Feb. 11, 1905.

    21. *Ibid.*, Jan. 28, 1905; New York *Globe and Commercial Advertiser*, Mar. 8, 1905. Anderson, primarily an outfielder, played only thirty-two games for the Highlanders in 1905 before Griffith sold him to the Washington Senators in early June.

    22. New York *Times*, Mar. 1, 1905.

    23. *SL*, Feb. 18, 1905. According to Chase's son, Edwin was considered the best athlete in the family. He died of appendicitis on January 26, 1905. Hal E. Chase Sr. to Martin Kohout, Jan. 30, 1990 (interview).

    24. *SL*, Mar. 11, 1905.

    25. *Ibid.*, Feb. 4, Mar. 18, 1905.

    26. *Ibid.*, Mar. 18, 25, 1905.

    27. His son argued that Chase's homesickness for California was responsible for many of his problems during his fifteen-year major league career. Hal E. Chase Sr. to Martin Kohout, Jan. 30, 1990 (interview).

    28. New York *Times*, Mar. 18, 1905.

    29. *Ibid.*, Mar. 21, 22, 1905.

    30. *SL*, Mar. 25, 1905.

    31. New York *Times*, Mar. 22, 1905.

    32. *SL*, April 1, 1905.

    33. *Ibid.*, Mar. 25, 1905.

    34. *TSN*, Mar. 25, 1905.

    35. *SL*, Apr. 1, 1905.

    36. *Ibid*.

    37. *Ibid.*, Apr. 8, 1905.

    38. New York *Times*, Mar. 29, 1905.

39. *SL*, Apr. 8, 1905.
40. *Ibid.*, July 28, 1906 (quotation), Apr. 8, 1905.
41. Alexander, *John McGraw*, 101.
42. Michael Gershman, "The 100 Greatest Players," in John Thorn and Pete Palmer with Michael Gershman (eds.), *Total Baseball*, 3rd edition (New York: HarperCollins, 1993), 179 (1st quotation); Ray Robinson, *Matty: An American Hero, Christy Mathewson of the New York Giants* (New York: Oxford University Press, 1993), 5 (2nd quotation).
43. Eric Rolfe Greenberg, *The Celebrant* (New York: Everest House, 1983), 144–145, 166, 170–172, 178–179, 184–185, 198, 213, 219–222, 224–225.
44. Alexander, *John McGraw*, 102, 119 (quotation).
45. The musician David Frishberg, who once tried to write a musical about Mathewson and Chase, now owns Chase's signed copy of Mathewson's book. David Frishberg to Martin Kohout, July 29, 1990.
46. New York *Times*, Apr. 4, 6, 1905; *SL*, Apr. 15, 1905.
47. New York *Times*, Apr. 9, 1905.
48. *Ibid.*, Apr. 11, 1905.
49. *TSN*, Apr. 15, 1905.
50. New York *Times*, Apr. 23, 1905.
51. *TSN*, May 20, 1905; *SL*, May 13, 1905.
52. New York *Times*, May 21, 1905.
53. *SL*, May 27, 1905.
54. Mack Whelan, "Brains in Baseball," *Outing* (Sept. 1913), 653–663.
55. *SL*, June 10, 17, 1905.
56. *Ibid.*, July 22, 1905.
57. *Ibid.*, July 22, Aug. 5, 1905.
58. New York *Times*, Aug. 2, 1905.
59. *Ibid.*, Aug. 21, 22, 1905.
60. *SL*, Sept. 16, 1905.
61. *Ibid.*, Oct. 14, 1905.
62. *Ibid.*, Oct. 7, 1905, Jan. 13, 1906; *TSN*, Feb. 9, 1907.
63. *SL*, Dec. 9, 1905, Jan. 6, 1906.
64. *Ibid.*, Apr. 14, 28, 1906.
65. New York *Times*, Apr. 15, 1906.
66. *SL*, May 26, June 2, 1906.
67. *Ibid.*, June 9, 1906.
68. *Ibid.*, June 16, 23, July 21, 28, 1906.
69. Smith, *Baseball's Famous First Basemen*, 75–76.
70. New York *Times*, May 20, 22, July 22, 1906.
71. *Ibid.*, July 25, 1906.
72. *Ibid.*, July 26, 1906.
73. *Ibid.*, Aug. 21, 1906.
74. *Ibid.*, Sept. 4, 6, 1906.
75. *Ibid.*, Sept. 26, 1906.
76. Joe Vila later reported that Chase's 1907 contract called for a salary of $5,000, but Vila may have been trying to make his friend Farrell appear more generous than he really was. *TSN*, Jan. 9, 1908. Farrell himself later claimed that Chase's 1907 salary was $4,000, but this too is questionable. See note 94 below.
77. Esther Wright Madden to Martin Kohout, Feb. 10, 1991 (interview).
78. New York *Times*, Sept. 18, 1906.
79. *Ibid.*, Mar. 2, 1907.
80. San Jose *Daily Mercury*, June 8, 1913.
81. *SL*, Feb. 23, 1907.
82. Bob Hoie, "The Hal Chase Story," *Grandstand Baseball Annual 1991*, in National Baseball Hall of Fame files. This is an unabridged version of Hoie's article "The Hal Chase Case," originally published in the 1974 *Baseball Research Journal* by the Society for American Base-

ball Research and collected in SABR's 1981 *Baseball Historical Review*. See also Paul J. Zingg, *Harry Hooper: An American Baseball Life* (Urbana: University of Illinois Press, 1993), 50–53, for more on the St. Mary's baseball dynasty.
  83. Zingg, *Harry Hooper*, 53, 189 (quotation).
  84. New York *Times*, Mar. 2, 1907.
  85. New York *Globe and Commercial Advertiser*, Mar. 4, 11, 1907.
  86. Los Gatos *Times*, n. d. (May 19, 1947?).
  87. New York *Times*, Mar. 7, 1907.
  88. *Ibid.*, Mar. 9, 1907.
  89. *Ibid.*, Mar. 10, 1907.
  90. *Ibid.*, Mar. 11, 12, 1907; New York *Globe and Commercial Advertiser*, Mar. 9, 1907.
  91. New York *Times*, Mar. 23, 29, 30, 1907; Joseph M. Overfield, "Tragedies and Shortened Careers," in Thorn and Palmer (eds.), *Total Baseball*, 426, 429.
  92. New York *Globe and Commercial Advertiser*, Apr. 2, 1907.
  93. New York *Times*, Apr. 3, 1907.
  94. *TSN*, Feb. 9, 1907; New York *Times*, Sept. 4, 1908. A newspaper story at the time, however, said that Chase had been asking for a salary of $5,500, which would have made him one of the four or five highest-paid players in baseball. The same story suggested that Chase had gotten what he wanted. Unidentified clipping, n.d., National Baseball Hall of Fame files.
  95. New York *Times*, Apr. 8, 15, 1907; New York *Globe and Commercial Advertiser*, Apr. 15, 1907.
  96. New York *Times*, May 2, 1907.
  97. *Ibid.*, June 11, 1907.
  98. *Ibid.*, June 13, 1907.
  99. *Ibid.*, June 18, 1907.
  100. *Ibid.*, July 27, 1907.
  101. Hoie, "More About Chase"; New York *World*, July 27, 1907; New York *Sun*, July 27, 1907, all in National Baseball Hall of Fame files.
  102. New York *Times*, Aug. 31, 1907.
  103. *Ibid.*, Aug. 30, 1907.
  104. *Ibid.*, Sept. 13, 1907.

Chapter 3

  1. John E. Spalding, *Always on Sunday: The California Baseball League, 1886 to 1915* (n.p.: John E. Spalding, 1992), 92, 97.
  2. *SL*, Nov. 23, 1907.
  3. Seymour, *Golden Age*, 198; *SL*, Oct. 26, 1907.
  4. *SL*, Nov. 23, 1907.
  5. *Ibid.*, Jan. 4, 1908.
  6. *Ibid.*, Nov. 30, 1907; Bob Hoie, "The Hal Chase Story," *Grandstand Baseball Annual 1991*, in National Baseball Hall of Fame files.
  7. *TSN*, Jan. 9, 1908.
  8. *Ibid.*, Nov. 21, 1907.
  9. *Ibid.*, Jan. 30, 1908.
  10. *SL*, Jan. 25, 1908.
  11. New York *Times*, Sept. 4, 1908.
  12. Beston, "The Story of Hal Chase," 9.
  13. Chase file, NBL.
  14. *Ibid.*, Mar. 9, 1908.
  15. Unidentified clipping, n.d., National Baseball Hall of Fame files.
  16. Unidentified clipping, n.d., National Baseball Hall of Fame files; San Jose *Mercury News*, Feb. 7, 1997.

17. Esther Wright Madden to Martin Kohout, Feb. 10, 1991 (interview).
18. New York *Times*, June 22, 1908.
19. *Ibid.*, June 24, 1908.
20. New York *Globe and Commercial Advertiser*, June 25, 1908.
21. New York *Times*, June 25, 1908.
22. Seymour, *Golden Age*, 288.
23. Solomon, *Where They Ain't*, 249–250.
24. Chicago *Daily Tribune*, Oct. 28, 1908.
25. New York *Times*, June 25, 1908. Griffith, of course, went on to become first the manager and then, for thirty-five years, the owner of the Washington Senators.
26. *Ibid.*, June 27, 1908.
27. *Ibid.*, July 1, 8, 9, 11, 1908.
28. Smith, *Baseball's Famous First Basemen*, 76.
29. New York *Times*, July 26, 1908.
30. *TSN*, Sept. 10, 1908; New York *Times*, Sept. 4, 1908.
31. New York *Press*, Aug. 23, 1908.
32. New York *Times*, Aug. 19, 1908.
33. Unidentified clipping, Aug. 27, 1908, National Baseball Hall of Fame files.
34. New York *Press*, Sept. 4, 1908.
35. *Ibid.*; Spalding, *Always on Sunday*, 114.
36. New York *Press*, Sept. 6, 1908.
37. *TSN*, Sept. 10, 17, 1908.
38. New York *Globe and Commercial Advertiser*, Sept. 4, 1908.
39. Chicago *Daily Tribune*, Oct. 15, 1908; New York *Times*, Oct. 22, 1908.
40. Spalding, *Always on Sunday*, 114–115; San Francisco *Examiner*, Sept. 5, 19, 1908.
41. Spalding, *Always on Sunday*, 115.
42. Sacramento *Union*, Oct. 18, 1908.
43. J. C. Kofoed, "The California Comet," *Baseball* (July 1917), 369.
44. San Francisco *Examiner*, Sept. 3, 13, 1908; Sacramento *Union*, Oct. 12, 18, 1908; Spalding, *Always on Sunday*, 114.
45. San Francisco *Examiner*, Sept. 10, 1908.
46. *Ibid.*, Sept. 10, 11, 1908.
47. *Ibid.*, Oct. 14, 1908; New York *Times*, Oct. 14, 1908.
48. (Los Gatos?) *Times Observer*, May 1, 1984.
49. San Francisco *Examiner*, Dec. 18, 24, 1908.
50. Los Angeles *Times*, Jan. 3, 1909.
51. *TSN*, Sept. 18, 1941. According to Gib Bodet, Moreing's offer to Chase was actually $6,500. Bodet, "The Life and Times of Prince Hal Chase," 10.
52. Chicago *Daily Tribune*, July 13, 1913; *TSN*, Sept. 18, 1941. Chase also claimed that he had returned to California to be near his wife, who was ill. Beston, "The Story of Hal Chase," 12.
53. *TSN*, May 28, 1947; Seymour, *Golden Age*, 288.
54. One scholar has pointed out that during the first 15 seasons in which the American League and the National League went head-to-head in New York, the Highlanders outdrew the Giants only once, in 1906. Beston, "The Story of Hal Chase," 12–13.
55. New York *Globe and Commercial Advertiser*, Apr. 5, 1909; *TSN*, Dec. 31, 1908, Mar. 11, 1909; Augusta (Ga.) *Chronicle*, Apr. 4, 1909.
56. New York *Globe and Commercial Advertiser*, Apr. 6, 1909; New York *Daily Tribune*, Apr. 4, 1909; New York *Times*, Apr. 5, 1909.
57. New York *Times*, Apr. 6, 1909; Augusta (Ga.) *Chronicle*, Apr. 9, 1909.
58. New York *Globe and Commercial Advertiser*, Apr. 26, 1909; New York *World*, Apr. 9, 1909.
59. New York *Times*, Apr. 9, 10, 11, 25, 1909; *TSN*, Apr. 15, 1909.
60. New York *Press*, Apr. 24, 1909.
61. *Ibid.*, Apr. 26, 1909; New York *Sun*, Apr. 26, 1909.
62. New York *Press*, Apr. 26, 1909; New York *World*, Apr. 26, 1909.
63. New York *Globe and Commercial Advertiser*, May 3, 1909.

64. New York *Press*, May 4, 1909.
65. New York *Globe and Commercial Advertiser*, May 4, 1909.
66. New York *Herald*, May 4, 1909.
67. New York *Times*, Aug. 6, 1909.
68. Lieb, *Baseball As I Have Known It*, 248.
69. Smith, *Baseball's Famous First Basemen*, 77–78.
70. Pete Cava to Martin Kohout, April 30, 1990.
71. Christy Mathewson, *Won in the Ninth* (New York: R. J. Bodmer, 1910), 16, 35.
72. *Ibid.*, 116.
73. *Ibid.*, 191. The New York *Times* reported that in a game against the White Sox Chase prepared to face pitcher Fred Olmstead by taking his chewing gum from his mouth and sticking it on the button of his cap. New York *Times*, July 12, 1910.
74. Decades later the jazz musician David Frishberg, who once attempted to write a musical about Mathewson, found this copy of the book for sale in a Soquel, California, bookstore for twenty dollars. David Frishberg to Martin Kohout, July 29, 1990.
75. New York *Times*, Mar. 13, 26, 1910.
76. New York *Press*, July 5, 1910.
77. Chase reportedly was one of the few veterans who went out of his way to befriend young players. Chet Hoff, a rookie with the Yankees in 1911, recalled Chase as "a wonderful man," "a great person," and "very easy to get along with." Chet Hoff to Renwick W. Speer, 1991 (interview; transcript in possession of author). Jack Martin, a rookie with the Yankees in 1912, "loved" Chase. Hoie, "More About Chase."
78. New York *Times*, Oct. 1, 1909.
79. Ritter, *The Glory of Their Times*, 75–76. Chase apparently had a unique method of selecting bats, as was revealed a couple of years later, when he was reported with a splinter in his tongue. When asked what had happened, he replied, "Well, I'll tell you. I was downtown this morning, sampling new sticks. I can tell a new bat by tasting the wood." The story added, "The Yanks' bat boy declares that Hal has all the Highlanders' bats imprinted with his teeth." Unidentified clipping, Aug. 24, 1912, National Baseball Hall of Fame files.
80. *TSN*, May 28, 1947.
81. New York *Press*, July 30, 1910.
82. *Ibid.*, Aug. 2, 1910. It is possible, especially given Chase's reputation as a ladies' man, that he may have been suffering from a malady of a different nature. Baseball historian Harold Seymour has noted that the press often used "malaria" or "rheumatism" as code words for less savory diseases such as gonorrhea and syphilis. Seymour, *Golden Age*, 106–107.
83. New York *Press*, Aug. 2, 1910.
84. *TSN*, Aug. 4, 1910.
85. New York *Globe and Commercial Advertiser*, Aug. 9, 1910.
86. New York *Press*, Aug. 18, 1910.
87. Ritter, *The Glory of Their Times*, 75.
88. New York *Press*, Aug. 19, 1910.
89. New York *Globe and Commercial Advertise*r, Sept. 19, 20, 1910.
90. Chicago *Daily Tribune*, Sept. 20, 1910; New York *Times*, Sept. 20, 1910.
91. New York *Globe and Commercial Advertiser*, Sept. 20, 1910.
92. *TSN*, Sept. 29, 1910; Chicago *Daily News*, Sept. 20, 1910.
93. Chicago *Daily Tribune*, Sept. 22, 1910.
94. New York *Globe and Commercial Advertiser*, Sept. 21, 1910.
95. New York *Daily Tribune*, Sept. 22, 1910.
96. *Ibid.*, Sept. 23, 1910.
97. See Ritter, *The Glory of Their Times*, 75–76.
98. Frank Graham, *The New York Yankees: An Informal History* (G. P. Putnam's Sons, 1943), 14.
99. New York *Times*, Sept. 22, 1910.
100. New York *Globe and Commercial Advertiser*, Sept. 21, 1910.
101. New York *Tribune*, Sept. 26, 1910.

102. *TSN*, Oct. 6, 1910.
103. New York *Times*, Sept. 23, 1910; New York *Press*, Sept. 23, 1910 (quotation).
104. New York *Times*, Sept. 25, 1910.
105. Chicago *Daily Tribune*, Sept. 23, 1910.
106. New York *Tribune*, Sept. 27, 1910.
107. Seymour, *Golden Age*, 289.
108. New York *Press*, Sept. 26, 1910. Fred Knowles was the secretary of the New York Giants at the time, and had secretly signed John McGraw to a Giants contract during the 1902 season. Later Knowles became McGraw's partner in a pool hall. Alexander, *John McGraw*, 91, 142.
109. *TSN*, Sept. 29, 1910.
110. New York *Tribune*, Sept. 27, 1910. Years later, looking back on the whole episode, Jimmy Austin exclaimed, "God, what a way to run a ballclub!" Quoted in Ritter, *The Glory of Their Times*, 75.
111. Apparently not even his success in Boston could completely eradicate Stallings's bitterness over the events of 1910, however. In an article published shortly after his Braves swept the Athletics in the World Series, Stallings listed Chesbro, Elberfeld, and Keeler as the Yankees' principal stars during his tenure with the team, but did not even mention Chase. See George T. Stallings, "The Miracle Man's Own Story," *Collier's*, Nov. 28, 1914.
112. New York *Times*, Oct. 1, 1910.
113. *Ibid.*, Apr. 2, 1911.

Chapter 4

1. Solomon, *Where They Ain't*, 220–221.
2. New York *Globe and Commercial Advertiser*, Feb. 24, 1911.
3. *Ibid.*, Mar. 20, 1911.
4. New York *Times*, Mar. 2, 1911.
5. *Ibid.*, Mar. 6, 7, 1911.
6. *Ibid.*, Mar. 9, 1911.
7. *Ibid.*, Mar. 15, 1911.
8. New York *Globe and Commercial Advertiser*, May 13, 1911.
9. New York *Times*, Apr. 7, 1911.
10. *Ibid.*, Apr. 11, 1911.
11. *Ibid.*, Apr. 10, 11, 1911.
12. *Ibid.*, Apr. 22, 1911.
13. *Ibid.*, May 6, 1911.
14. *Ibid.*, May 13, 1911.
15. New York *Globe and Commercial Advertiser*, May 15, 16, 1911.
16. New York *Times*, June 2, 1911.
17. New York *Globe and Commercial Advertiser*, July 13, 1911.
18. *Ibid.*, July 17, 1911.
19. *Ibid.*, Aug. 5, 1911.
20. *Ibid.*, Aug. 31, 1911.
21. *Ibid.*, Aug. 9, 1911.
22. New York *Globe and Commercial Advertiser*, Sept. 6, 1911.
23. New York *Times*, Sept. 24, 1911.
24. *Ibid.*, Sept. 29, Oct. 5, 1911.
25. *Ibid.*, Oct. 6, 7, 1911.
26. *Ibid.*, Aug. 30, Sept. 21, 22, 1911.
27. *Ibid.*, Mar. 14, 20, 1911.
28. New York *Globe and Commercial Advertiser*, Sept. 9, 14, 1911.
29. *Ibid.*, Oct. 2 (emphasis added), 7, 1911.
30. *TSN*, May 28, 1947, July 16, 1914, July 13, 1916; New York *Times*, Dec. 12, 1911.

31. Chet Hoff to Renwick W. Speer, 1991 (interview; transcript in possession of the author).
32. New York *Globe and Commercial Advertiser*, Oct. 5, 11, 1911.
33. *Ibid.*, Oct. 18, 1911.
34. *Ibid.*, Oct. 20, 1911.
35. *Ibid.*, Oct. 23, 1911.
36. *Ibid.*, Oct. 25, 1911.
37. *Ibid.*, Oct. 28, 1911.
38. *Ibid.*, Oct. 27, 1911.
39. John J. McGraw, *My Thirty Years in Baseball* (1923; Lincoln: University of Nebraska Press, 1995), 113.
40. New York *Globe and Commercial Advertiser*, Oct. 28, 1911.
41. New York *World*, Nov. 4, 1911; New York *Times*, Nov. 22, 1911; New York *Tribune*, Dec. 12, 1911.
42. New York *Globe and Commercial Advertiser*, Nov. 6, 1911.
43. *Ibid.*, Nov. 17, 1911.
44. *Ibid.*, Nov. 21, 1911.
45. *Ibid.*, Nov. 23, 1911.
46. New York *World*, Nov. 22, 1911.
47. New York *Tribune*, Nov. 19, 1911.
48. New York *Times*, Nov. 22, 1911.
49. New York *Herald*, Nov. 22, 1911.
50. New York *Globe and Commercial Advertiser*, Sept. 18, Nov. 23, 24, 25, Dec. 5, 1911.
51. *Ibid.*, Dec. 12, 1911; *TSN*, July 16, 1914; New York *Times*, Dec. 12, 1911.
52. New York *Globe and Commercial Advertiser*, Dec. 5, 9, 1911.
53. *Ibid.*, Mar. 4, 1912.
54. New York *Times*, Mar. 3, 9, 1912.
55. New York *Globe and Commercial Advertiser*, Mar. 18, 1912.
56. New York *Times*, Mar. 16, 1912.
57. *Ibid.*, Mar. 16, 1912.
58. *Ibid.*, Mar. 21, 1912.
59. *Ibid.*, Mar. 27, 1912.
60. *Ibid.*, Apr. 4, 1912; New York *Globe and Commercial Advertise*r, Apr. 4, 1912.
61. New York *Times*, Apr. 7, 1912.
62. *Ibid.*, Apr. 12, 1912.
63. *Baseball* (June 1912), 12–14.
64. New York *Times*, Apr. 28, 29, 1912. Again, one might wonder whether this episode was concealing another, less savory malady. (See Chapter 3, note 82.)
65. *Ibid.*, May 12, 16, 17, 19, 1912.
66. *Ibid.*, May 19, 21, 1912.
67. *Ibid.*, May 22, 1912.
68. *Ibid.*, May 23, 24, 1912.
69. New York *Globe and Commercial Advertiser*, May 24, 1912.
70. New York *Times*, June 7, 1912.
71. New York *Globe and Commercial Advertiser*, June 13, 1912.
72. New York *Times*, June 10, 1912; New York *Globe and Commercial Advertiser*, June 10, 1912.
73. New York *Globe and Commercial Advertiser*, June 20, 21, 1912.
74. *Ibid.*, June 28, 1912.
75. *Ibid.*, June 29, 1912; New York *Times*, June 28, 1912.
76. New York *Times*, July 6, 9, 1912.
77. *Ibid.*, July 4, 1912.
78. *Ibid.*, July 21, 1912.
79. *Ibid.*, July 25, 1912.
80. *Ibid.*, Aug. 1, 1912.

81. *Ibid.*, Sept. 21, 1912.
82. *Ibid.*, Oct. 6, 1912.
83. *Ibid.*, Oct. 8, 1912.
84. *Ibid.*, Oct. 28, 29, 1912; Robert Peterson, *Only the Ball Was White: A History of Legendary Black Players and All-Black Professional Teams* (New York: McGraw-Hill, 1970), 64.
85. *Baseball* (Nov. 1912).
86. *Ibid.* (Dec. 1912).
87. *Ibid.* (Nov. 1912), 85.

Chapter 5

1. *Baseball* (Mar. 1913), 21.
2. *Ibid.* (Jan. 1913), 26, 27.
3. New York *Press*, Jan. 3, 1913.
4. Murdock, *Ban Johnson*, 78 (quotation); *Baseball* (Feb. 1913), 25; *Ibid.* (Mar. 1913), 17.
5. New York *Press*, Jan. 9, 1913 (1st quotation); *Baseball* (Mar. 1913), 20 (2nd quotation).
6. *Baseball* (Feb. 1913), 25.
7. New York *Press*, Jan. 8, 9, 1913; *TSN*, Jan. 16, 23, 1913.
8. *Baseball* (Mar. 1913), 17.
9. New York *Press*, Feb. 11, 1913.
10. New York *Tribune*, Feb. 11, 1913.
11. New York *Press*, Jan. 5, 1913.
12. *Ibid.*, Feb. 13, 1913; *TSN*, Mar. 11, 1920.
13. New York *Press*, Feb. 13, 15, 1913.
14. New York *Times*, Mar. 4, 1913; *TSN*, Mar. 6, 1913.
15. New York *Tribune*, Mar. 4, 5, 1913.
16. *Ibid.*, Mar. 9, 28, 29, 1913.
17. *Ibid.*, Apr. 4, 1913.
18. Will Irwin, "With Chance in Bermuda," *Collier's* (Apr. 19, 1913), 8.
19. Unidentified clipping, n.d., National Baseball Hall of Fame files.
20. New York *Tribune*, May 27, 1913.
21. Unidentified clipping, n.d., National Baseball Hall of Fame files.
22. New York *Tribune*, May 27, 1913; Robert Hoie, "The Hal Chase Case," in *Baseball Historical Review* (Manhattan, Kan.: Society for American Baseball Research, 1987), 36. The amount of alimony was one-third of what Nellie had originally sought. Unidentified clipping, n.d., National Baseball Hall of Fame files. Three years later, Chase's alimony was cut from $1,200 a year to $600 a year, supposedly because his income had fallen during his tenure with the Buffalo Federal League team. Unidentified clipping, June 7, 1915, National Baseball Hall of Fame files. When Chase first joined Buffalo in 1914, however, his salary actually rose. Thus, the reduction in alimony remains a mystery.
23. Esther Wright Madden to Martin Kohout, Feb. 10, 1991 (interview).
24. Tucson Arizona *Daily Star*, Dec. 16, 1990; Hal E. Chase Sr. to Martin Kohout, Jan. 30, 1990 (interview).
25. New York *Times*, Apr. 5, 1913.
26. New York *Tribune*, Apr. 8, 1913.
27. New York *Times*, Apr. 16, 1913.
28. New York *Tribune*, Apr. 11, 17, 18, 1913.
29. *Ibid.*, Apr. 19, 20, 28, 1913.
30. Quoted in *TSN*, May 28, 1947.
31. New York *Tribune*, Apr. 23, 1913.
32. New York *Times*, May 6, 1913.
33. *Ibid.*, May 18, 1913.
34. New York *Tribune*, May 18, 1913.

35. *TSN*, May 15, 1913.
36. Esther Wright Madden to Martin Kohout, Feb. 10, 1991 (interview).
37. New York *Herald*, Sept. 29, 1912; New York *Times*, Oct. 18, 1912; National Baseball Hall of Fame files.
38. New York *Tribune*, May 27, 1913; San Jose *Daily Mercury*, May 27, 1913.
39. *TSN*, Nov. 9, 1944.
40. Graham, *The New York Yankees*, 17–18.
41. Chicago *Daily Tribune*, June 2, 1913; *TSN*, June 5, 1913, Nov. 9, 1944.
42. Chicago *Daily Tribune*, June 3, 1913; New York *Tribune*, Apr. 30, 1913.
43. New York *Times*, June 2, 1913; New York *Tribune*, June 2, 1913.
44. *TSN*, June 12, July 24, 1913.
45. *Baseball* (Aug. 1913), 18.
46. *Baseball* (Sept. 1913), 68.
47. *Ibid*. (Nov. 1913).
48. New York *Globe*, June 2, 1913.
49. Chicago *Daily Tribune*, June 3, 1913.
50. *TSN*, June 5, 1913; Chicago *Daily Tribune*, June 2, 1913.
51. Chicago *Daily Tribune*, June 3, 1913.
52. *Ibid*., June 3, 1913; *TSN*, June 5, 1913.
53. Chicago *Daily Tribune*, June 6, 1913.
54. *Ibid*., June 9, 1913.
55. *Ibid*., June 8, 1913.
56. *Ibid*. June 10, 1913.
57. *Ibid*., June 24, 1913.
58. Quoted in Kenan Heise, *Chaos, Creativity, and Culture: A Sampling of Chicago in the Twentieth Century* (Salt Lake City: Gibbs-Smith, 1998), 27.
59. *TSN*, June 19, 1913.
60. Chicago *Daily Tribune*, July 9, 1913.
61. *Ibid*., July 18, 1913.
62. Lieb, *Baseball As I Have Known It*, 98; Chicago *Daily Tribune*, July 31, 1913.
63. Chicago *Daily Tribune*, July 31, 1913.
64. *Ibid*., July 24, 1913.
65. *Ibid*., Aug. 2, 1913.
66. *Ibid*., Aug. 15, 1913.
67. James T. Farrell, *My Baseball Diary* (New York: A. S. Barnes, 1957), 37.
68. Chicago *Daily Tribune*, Aug. 29, 1913.
69. *Ibid*., Sept. 3, 1913.
70. *Ibid*., Sept. 4, 1913.
71. *Ibid*., Sept. 25, 1913.
72. *Ibid*., Sept. 27, 28, 1913.
73. *Ibid*., Oct. 10, 1913.
74. *Ibid*., Oct. 14, 1913.
75. *Ibid*., Oct. 15, 1913.
76. *Ibid*., Oct. 26, 1913.
77. *Ibid*., Oct. 28, 1913, Oct. 29, 1913.
78. *Ibid*., Nov. 7, 1913.
79. *Ibid*., Nov. 12, 18, 1913.
80. *Ibid*., Nov. 16, 1913.
81. *Ibid*., Nov. 20, 1913.

Chapter 6

1. Chicago *Daily Tribune*, Feb. 27, 1914.
2. *Ibid*., Feb. 24, 25, 27, 1914.

3. *Ibid.*, Mar. 1, 1914.
4. Seymour, *Golden Age*, 6–7; Lee Lowenfish and Tony Lupien, *The Imperfect Diamond: The Story of Baseball's Reserve System and the Men Who Fought to Change It* (New York: Stein and Day, 1980), 18, 82, 142.
5. Chicago *Daily Tribune*, Mar. 4, 1914.
6. *Ibid.*, Mar. 5, 1914.
7. *Ibid.*, July 2, 1914.
8. *Ibid.*, Mar. 2, 3, 1914.
9. *Ibid.*, Mar. 5, 1914.
10. *Ibid.*
11. *Ibid.*, Mar. 6, 1914.
12. *Ibid.*, Mar. 8, 1914; *TSN*, Mar. 19, 1914.
13. Chicago *Daily Tribune*, Mar. 10, 1914.
14. *Ibid.*, Mar. 14, 1914.
15. *Ibid.*, Mar. 15, 1914; San Francisco *Examiner*, Mar. 15, 1914.
16. Chicago *Daily Tribune*, Mar. 23, 1914.
17. *Ibid.*, Mar. 24, 1914.
18. *Ibid.*, Apr. 3, 12, 1914.
19. *Ibid.*, May 13, 1914.
20. *Ibid.*, May 14, 25, 1914.
21. *Ibid.*, May 17, 18, 1914.
22. Seymour, *Golden Age*, 203; Chicago *Daily Tribune*, June 15, 1914.
23. Chicago *Daily Tribune*, June 15, 1914.
24. *Ibid.*, June 17, 1914.
25. Buffalo *Express*, June 20, 1914.
26. *Ibid.*, June 20, 1914.
27. *Ibid.*, June 22, 1914.
28. *Ibid.*, June 25, 1914.
29. *Ibid.*
30. *Ibid.*, June 26, 1914.
31. Lowenfish and Lupien, *The Imperfect Diamond*, 62–64, 71–72.
32. Buffalo *Express*, June 26, July 2, 7, 1914.
33. *Ibid.*, July 7, 16, 1914.
34. *Ibid.*, July 2, 1914.
35. *TSN*, July 2, 1914.
36. *Ibid.*, July 9, 1914.
37. New York *Times*, July 2, 1914.
38. *Ibid.*, July 2, 1914; *TSN*, July 16, 1914.
39. Buffalo *Express*, July 10, 1914.
40. *Ibid.*, July 18, 1914.
41. *Ibid.*, July 22, 1914.
42. *TSN*, July 30, 1914.
43. *Ibid.*, Sept. 3, 1914.
44. *Ibid.*, Aug. 6, 1914.
45. Buffalo *Express*, Aug. 18, 1914.
46. *Ibid.*, Aug. 11, 1914.
47. *Ibid.*, Aug. 18, 1914.
48. *Ibid.*, Aug. 19, Sept. 6, 7, 1914.
49. *Ibid.*, Sept. 8, 10, 11, 1914.
50. *Ibid.*, Sept. 13, 1914.
51. *TSN*, July 5, 1923.
52. Buffalo *Express*, Oct. 8, 1914.
53. *Ibid.*, Oct. 14, 1914.
54. *Ibid.*, Oct. 24, 1914.

55. Mark Goldman, *High Hopes: The Rise and Decline of Buffalo, New York* (Albany: State University of New York Press, 1983), 143–145.
56. Buffalo *Express*, Oct. 24, 1914.
57. *Ibid.*, Oct. 12, 14, 15, 16, 17, 1914.
58. *Ibid.*, Oct. 26, 1914.
59. Herbert Gehrig Coleman, "Judge Kenesaw Mountain Landis and the Chicago I.W.W. Trial" (M.A. thesis, University of Texas at Austin, 1992), 7–9.
60. Lowenfish and Lupien, *The Imperfect Diamond*, 88–90.
61. Buffalo *Express*, Feb. 20, 1915.
62. *Ibid.*, Feb. 20, 21, 25, 1915.
63. *Ibid.*, Feb. 26, 1915.
64. *Ibid.*, Mar. 3, 4, 6, 1914.
65. *Ibid.*, Mar. 7, 1915.
66. *Ibid.*, Mar. 8, 1915.
67. *Ibid.*, Mar. 12, 13, 1915.
68. *Ibid.*, Mar. 15, 1915.
69. *Ibid.*, Mar. 20, 21, 1915.
70. *Ibid.*, Mar. 26, 27, 1915.
71. *Ibid.*, Apr. 4, 6, 1915.
72. *Ibid.*, Mar. 28, 1915.
73. *Ibid.*, Apr. 11, 1915.
74. *Ibid.*, Apr. 12, 1915.
75. *Ibid.*, Apr. 23, 1915.
76. Unidentified clipping, May 1, 1915, National Baseball Hall of Fame files.
77. Buffalo *Express*, May 20, 1915.
78. *Ibid.*, May 24, 25, 1915.
79. *Ibid.*, May 30, 1915.
80. *Ibid.*, May 31, June 2, 1915.
81. *Ibid.*, June 4, 5, 1915.
82. *Ibid.*, June 14, 1915.
83. *Ibid.*, June 19, 1915.
84. *Ibid.*, July 6, 1915.
85. *Ibid.*, June 30, 1915.
86. *Ibid.*, June 30, 1915.
87. *Ibid.*, July 14, 1915; *TSN*, Aug. 12, 1915.
88. Buffalo *Express*, Aug. 6, 1915.
89. *Ibid.*, Aug. 8, 10, 1915.
90. *Ibid.*, Aug. 11, 1915.
91. *Ibid.*, Aug. 12, 1915.
92. *Ibid.*, Aug. 19, 1915.
93. *Ibid.*, Aug. 21, 22, 1915.
94. *Ibid.*, Aug. 25, 1915.
95. *Ibid.*, Aug. 16, 28, 1915.
96. *Ibid.*, Aug. 31, 1915.
97. *Ibid.*, Sept. 5, 7, 9, 12, 1915.
98. *Ibid.*, Sept. 14, 18, 1915.

Chapter 7

1. *TSN*, Oct. 14, 21, 1915.
2. Buffalo *Express*, Oct. 28, 1915.
3. *TSN*, Oct. 28, 1915.
4. Buffalo *Express*, Oct. 26, 1915.
5. *Ibid.*, Nov. 10, 1915.

6. *Ibid.*, Oct. 26, 28, Nov. 9, 10, 12, 1915.
7. *Ibid.*, Oct. 3, 1915.
8. *Ibid.*, Oct. 4, 1915.
9. *Ibid.*, Oct. 6, 11, 1915.
10. *Ibid.*, Oct. 25, 1915.
11. *Ibid.*, Dec. 15, 16, 1915; Seymour, *Golden Age*, 230–231.
12. Seymour, *Golden Age*, 232.
13. Buffalo *Express*, Dec. 20, 22, 23, 24, 1915.
14. *Ibid.*, Dec. 27, 1915; Lowenfish and Lupien, *The Imperfect Diamond*, 87.
15. Seymour, *Golden Age*, 206.
16. Buffalo *Express*, Jan. 1, 1916.
17. Seymour, *Golden Age*, 235–236.
18. Robert F. Burk, *Never Just a Game: Players, Owners, and American Baseball to 1920* (Chapel Hill: University of North Carolina Press, 1994), 233.
19. Cincinnati *Enquirer*, Feb. 6, 1916.
20. Daniel Okrent and Harris Lewine, eds., *The Ultimate Baseball Book* (Boston: Houghton Mifflin, 1979), 94.
21. *Ibid.*, Feb. 9, 1916.
22. Lowenfish and Lupien, *The Imperfect Diamond*, 105–107.
23. Cincinnati *Enquirer*, Feb. 10, 1916, Feb. 5, 1916.
24. *Ibid.*, Feb. 3, 1916.
25. Farrell, *My Baseball Diary*, 37.
26. Unidentified clipping, Mar. 23, 1916, National Baseball Hall of Fame files.
27. Unidentified clipping, n.d., National Baseball Hall of Fame files.
28. San Francisco *Chronicle*, Mar. 12, 1916; San Francisco *Examiner*, Mar. 17, 1916.
29. San Francisco *Examiner*, Mar. 10, 1916.
30. San Francisco *Chronicle*, Mar. 10, 1916.
31. *Ibid.*, Mar. 10, 1916.
32. *Ibid.*, Mar. 11, 1916.
33. *TSN*, Sept. 18, 1941.
34. Cincinnati *Enquirer*, Mar. 4, 8, 1916, Mar. 21, 1917.
35. *Ibid.*, Mar. 4, 1916.
36. *Ibid.*, Mar. 8, 1916.
37. *Ibid.*, Mar. 9, 1916.
38. *Ibid.*, Mar. 10, 1916.
39. *Ibid.*, Mar. 18, 1916.
40. *Ibid.*, Apr. 1, 1916; Seymour, *Golden Age*, 131.
41. Cincinnati *Enquirer*, Apr. 3, 1916.
42. *Ibid.*, Apr. 7, 1916.
43. *TSN*, Mar. 11, 1920.
44. Cincinnati *Enquirer*, Apr. 8, 1916.
45. *Ibid.*, Apr. 8, 1916.
46. *Ibid.*, Apr. 14, 1916.
47. *Ibid.*, Apr. 16, 1916.
48. *Ibid.*, Apr. 17, 1916; Lee Allen, *The Cincinnati Reds* (New York: G. P. Putnam's Sons, 1948), 114.
49. Cincinnati *Enquirer*, Apr. 17, 1916.
50. *Ibid.*, Apr. 19, 1916.
51. *Ibid.*, Apr. 23, 1916.
52. *Ibid.*, Apr. 30, 1916.
53. *Ibid.*, May 4, 1916.
54. One author described Zimmerman as "one of those ballplayers who watch batting statistics and little else — an indifferent fielder and base runner who did not play up to his great potential because he did not care enough to develop a rounded game." Jonathan Yardley, *Ring: A Biography of Ring Lardner* (New York: Random House, 1977), 135.

55. Cincinnati *Enquirer*, May 26, 1916.
56. *Ibid.*, Apr. 30, June 2, 6, 1916.
57. *Ibid.*, June 10, 1916.
58. *Ibid.*, June 16, 18, 1916.
59. *Ibid.*, June 23, 1916.
60. *Ibid.*, June 26, 1916.
61. *Ibid.*, June 30, 1916.
62. *Ibid.*, July 1, 1916.
63. *Ibid.*, July 2, 1916.
64. *Ibid.*, July 3, 8, 1916.
65. *Ibid.*, July 6, 1916.
66. *Ibid.*, July 10, 1916.
67. *Ibid.*, July 11, 1916.
68. *Ibid.*, July 13, 12, 1916.
69. *Ibid.*, July 13, 14, 1916.
70. *Ibid.*, July 16, 1916.
71. Cincinnati *Enquirer*, July 16, 1916.
72. *Ibid.*, July 17, 1916.
73. *Ibid.*, July 19, 20, 1916.
74. *Ibid.*, July 20, 1916.
75. *Ibid.*, July 21, 1916.
76. *Ibid.*, July 23, 24, 1916.
77. *Ibid.*, July 27, 1916.
78. *Ibid.*, July 30, Aug. 1, 1916.
79. *Ibid.*, Aug. 4, 5, 1916.
80. *Ibid.*, Aug. 5, 1916.
81. *Ibid.*, Aug. 8, 1916.
82. *Ibid.*, Aug. 14, 1916.
83. *Ibid.*, Aug. 23, 1916.
84. *Ibid.*, Sept. 2, 1916.
85. *Ibid.*, Sept. 4, 6, 1916.
86. *Ibid.*, Sept. 5, 1916.
87. *Ibid.*, Sept. 7, 1916.
88. *Ibid.*, Sept. 9, 1916.
89. *Ibid.*, Sept. 12, 1916.
90. *Ibid.*, Sept. 21, 1916.
91. *Ibid.*, Oct. 2, 1916.
92. *Ibid.*, Feb. 29, Mar. 3, 1917.
93. *Ibid.*, Mar. 5, 17, 1917.
94. *Ibid.*, Mar. 6, 8, 1917.
95. *Ibid.*, Mar. 12, 1917.
96. *Ibid.*, Mar. 26, 1917.
97. *Ibid.*, Apr. 3, 6, 1917.
98. *Ibid.*, Apr. 7, 8, 1917.
99. *Ibid.*, Apr. 12, 1917.
100. *Ibid.*, Apr. 14, 1917.
101. *Ibid.*, Apr. 21, 1917.
102. John Thorn, *Baseball's 10 Greatest Games* (New York: Four Winds Press, 1981), 26. Two other old Yankees were present at the game as well: Harry Wolter, a reserve outfielder watching from the Cubs' bench, and Al Orth, now a National League umpire.
103. *Ibid.*, 37–40.
104. Cincinnati *Enquirer*, May 9, 1917 (emphasis added).
105. *Ibid.*, May 21, 1917.
106. *Ibid.*, May 29, June 2, 1917.
107. *Ibid.*, May 29, 1917.

108. *Ibid.*, June 1, 1917.
109. Alexander, *John McGraw*, 197–198.
110. Cincinnati *Enquirer*, June 9, 1917.
111. *Ibid.*, July 2, July 13, 1917.
112. *Ibid.*, July 24, 1917.
113. *Ibid.*, July 15, Aug. 5, 1917.
114. *Ibid.*, Aug. 12, 1917.
115. *Ibid.*, Aug. 8, 1917.
116. *Ibid.*, Aug. 13, 1917.
117. *Ibid.*, Aug. 20, 21, 22, 1917.
118. *Ibid.*, Aug. 27, 30, 1917.
119. *Ibid.*, Aug. 29, 1917.
120. *Ibid.*, Aug. 31, 1917.
121. *Ibid.*, Sept. 6, 7, 1917.
122. *Ibid.*, Sept. 12, 1917.
123. *Ibid.*, Sept. 13, 1917.
124. *Ibid.*, Sept. 14, 1917.
125. *Ibid.*, Sept. 16, 1917.
126. *Ibid.*, Sept. 19, 1917.
127. *Ibid.*, Sept. 28, 30, 1917.
128. *Ibid.*, Oct. 12, 1917.
129. *Ibid.*, Oct. 13, 1917.
130. Hal Chase, *How to Play First Base* (New York: American Sports Publishing Company, 1917), 7, 9, 44.
131. J. C. Kofoed, "The California Comet," *Baseball* (July 1917), 369.
132. Hal Chase, "Doing the 'Come-Back' stunt," *Baseball* (Oct. 1917), 559–560.

Chapter 8

1. Cincinnati *Enquirer*, Mar. 6, 13, 1918.
2. *Ibid.*, Mar. 10, 1918.
3. *Ibid.*, Mar. 12, 1918.
4. *Ibid.*, Mar. 12, 26, 1918.
5. *Ibid.*, Mar. 24, 1918.
6. *Ibid.*, Apr. 2, 7, 1918.
7. *Ibid.*, Apr. 11, 1918.
8. *Ibid.*, Apr. 27, 1918.
9. *Ibid.*, May 3, 1918.
10. *Ibid.*, May 9, 1918.
11. *Ibid.*, May 14, 16, 1918.
12. *Ibid.*, May 17, 1918.
13. *Ibid.*, June 1, 1918.
14. *Ibid.*, June 11, 1918.
15. *Ibid.*, June 19, 1918.
16. *Ibid.*, June 23, 1918.
17. *Ibid.*, July 3, 5, 1918.
18. *Ibid.*, July 7, 1918.
19. *Ibid.*, July 18, 1918.
20. *Ibid.*, July 20, 1918.
21. *Ibid.*, July 21, 1918.
22. *Ibid.*, July 26, 1918.
23. Boston *Herald and Journal*, July 26, 1918.
24. Cincinnati *Enquirer*, July 27, 1918.

25. *Ibid.*
26. *Ibid.*, July 30, 1918.
27. *Ibid.*, Aug. 4, 1918.
28. *Ibid.*, Aug. 6, 1918.
29. *Ibid.*, Aug. 8, 1918.
30. *TSN*, Aug. 15, 1918.
31. Cincinnati *Enquirer*, Aug. 8, 9, 1918; *TSN*, Aug. 15, 1918.
32. Cincinnati *Enquirer*, Aug. 8, 1918.
33. *TSN*, Aug. 15, 1918.
34. Cincinnati *Enquirer*, Aug. 10, 1918.
35. Tom Swope to Lee Allen, June 23, 1960, in National Baseball Hall of Fame files.
36. Quoted in Lieb, *Baseball As I Have Known It*, 101.
37. Ray Fisher to Jeff Mortimer, Oct. 20, 1975 (transcript in possession of John Leidy).
38 Cincinnati *Enquirer*, Aug. 11, 1918.
39. *Ibid.*, Aug. 12, 1918.
40. *TSN*, Aug. 15, 1918; Cincinnati *Enquirer*, Aug. 13, 1918.
41. *TSN*, Aug. 22, 1918; Cincinnati *Enquirer*, Aug. 13, 17, 1918.
42. *TSN*, Aug. 22, 1918.
43. Cincinnati *Enquirer*, Aug. 19, 1918. Youngs, one of McGraw's particular favorites, was also implicated in the 1924 Jimmy O'Connell–Cozy Dolan scandal, but was exonerated by Judge Landis. See Alexander, *John McGraw*, 256–257.
44. *TSN*, Aug. 22, 1918.
45. *Ibid.*
46. *Ibid.*, Aug. 8, 22, 1918.
47. *Ibid.*, Aug. 22, 1918.
48. *Ibid.* In this, Phelon was either naive or disingenuous, as the activities of Arnold Rothstein and others would reveal.
49. *Ibid.*, Aug. 29, Sept. 5, 1918.
50. Garry Herrmann to John Heydler, Aug. 30, 1918, in National Baseball Hall of Fame files.
51. Cincinnati *Enquirer*, Aug. 23, 27, Sept. 17, 1918; *TSN*, Sept. 5, 1918.
52. Garry Herrmann to John Heydler, Aug. 29, 1918, Oct. 10, 1918, in National Baseball Hall of Fame files.
53. John Heydler to Garry Herrmann, Oct. 14, 1918, in National Baseball Hall of Fame files.
54. Garry Herrmann to John Heydler, Aug. 30, 1918; John Heydler to Robert S. Alcorn, Sept. 27, 1918, in National Baseball Hall of Fame files.
55. Cincinnati *Enquirer*, Aug. 18, 1918.
56. *Ibid.*, Sept. 8, 1918.
57. *Ibid.*, Oct. 22, 1918.
58. Seymour, *Golden Age*, 262–263.
59. *Ibid.*, 254–255.
60. Cincinnati *Enquirer*, Dec. 1, 1918.
61. *Ibid.*, Nov. 24, 25, 1918; Seymour, *Golden Age*, 263.
62. Cincinnati *Enquirer*, Dec. 4, 19, 1918.
63. Seymour, *Golden Age*, 261–264; Cincinnati *Enquirer*, Dec. 10, 1918.
64. Cincinnati *Enquirer*, Dec. 12, 13, 1918; Alexander, *John McGraw*, 208.
65. Cincinnati *Enquirer*, Jan. 26, 1919.
66. Frank Graham, *McGraw of the Giants: An Informal Biography* (New York: G.P. Putnam's Sons, 1944), 116.
67. Seymour, *Golden Age*, 253; Cincinnati *Enquirer*, Dec. 30, 1918, Jan. 7, 1919.
68. Seymour, *Golden Age*, 253; Cincinnati *Enquirer*, Dec. 12, 13, 1918, Jan. 26, 1919.
69. New York *Times*, Feb. 3, 1919.
70. Cincinnati *Enquirer*, Jan. 15, 1919; Alexander, *John McGraw*, 142, 192, 210; Seymour, *Golden Age*, 140.
71. Cincinnati *Enquirer*, Jan. 27, 1919.

72. New York *Globe*, Jan. 22, 1919.
73. *Ibid.*, Jan. 27, 31, 1919.
74. *Ibid.*, Jan. 31, 1919.
75. *Ibid.*, Jan. 27, 1919.
76. *TSN*, Feb. 6, 1919; New York *Globe*, Feb. 6, 1919.
77. New York *Globe*, Jan. 31, 1919.
78. *Ibid.*
79. New York *Times*, Jan. 31, 1919.
80. *TSN*, Feb. 6, 1919.
81. Cincinnati *Enquirer*, Jan. 27, 1921; Cincinnati *Commercial Tribune*, Jan. 27, 1921.
82. New York *Globe*, Jan. 31, Feb. 6, 1919; *TSN*, Feb. 13, 1919.
83. New York *Sun*, Jan. 31, 1919.
84. Cincinnati *Enquirer*, Feb. 6, 1919.
85. New York *Globe*, Feb. 6, 1919.
86. New York *Sun*, Feb. 6, 1919; *TSN*, Feb. 13, 1919.
87. John Heydler to Garry Herrmann, Feb. 5, 1919, in National Baseball Hall of Fame files.
88. *TSN*, Feb. 13, 1919; New York *Globe*, Feb. 6, 1919; Cincinnati *Enquirer*, Feb. 9, 1919.
89. Murdock, *Ban Johnson*, 185 (quotations); David Quentin Voigt, *American Baseball, Vol. II: From the Commissioners to Continental Expansion* (1970; reprint, University Park: Pennsylvania State University Press, 1983), 123; Bill Conlin to Martin Kohout, June 14, 1990. Fred Lieb wondered, "How many good young ballplayers may have said, 'Chase gets by with it, year after year, so why shouldn't we pick up a little extra money when the chance is offered us?' And how many, when tempted, fell?" Lieb, *Baseball As I Have Known It*, 103.
90. John Heydler, "A Defense of the Hal Chase Affair," *Baseball* (Dec. 1920), 328.

Chapter 9

1. Quoted in William K. Klingaman, *1919: The Year Our World Began* (1987; reprint, New York: Harper and Row, 1989), xix.
2. See Hofstadter, *The Age of Reform*, 280–281.
3. Klingaman, *1919*, 95–97, 250, 279–281, 288–289, 310 (quotation).
4. Painter, *Standing at Armageddon*, 367–380.
5. "The Second Coming," in *The Collected Poems of W. B. Yeats* (3rd edition; New York: Macmillan, 1956), 184.
6. Cincinnati *Enquirer*, Feb. 9, 1919.
7. *Ibid.*, Feb. 20, 22, 23, 1919.
8. Unidentified clipping, n.d., National Baseball Hall of Fame files.
9. New York *Globe*, Feb. 24, 1919.
10. *Ibid.*, Mar. 3, 1919.
11. *Ibid.*, Mar. 8, 1919.
12. *Ibid.*, Mar. 24, 1919.
13. Frank Graham, *The New York Giants: An Informal History* (New York: G. P. Putnam's Sons, 1952), 110.
14. New York *Globe*, Mar. 24, 28, 1919.
15. New York *Sun*, Apr. 20, 1919.
16. New York *Globe*, Apr. 5, 6, 1919; Robert W. Creamer, *Babe: The Legend Comes to Life* (New York: Simon and Schuster, 1974), 189–190.
17. Creamer, *Babe*, 190–191.
18. New York *Globe*, Apr. 12, 13, 1919.
19. *Ibid.*, Apr. 18, 1919.

20. New York *Sun*, Apr. 20, 1919.
21. *Ibid.*, Apr. 23, 1919.
22. New York *Globe*, Apr. 23, 1919.
23. New York *Sun*, June 3, 1919.
24. *Ibid.*, July 26, 1919.
25. *Ibid.*, Aug. 4, 1919.
26. According to one scholar of Cincinnati's German element during this period, about half of the city's population was of German descent. Don Heinrich Tolzmann, *The Cincinnati Germans After the Great War* (New York: Peter Lang, 1987), 7.
27. Alexander, *John McGraw*, 214; Cincinnati *Enquirer*, Aug. 4, 1919.
28. New York *Sun*, Aug. 9, 10, 1919.
29. *Ibid.*, Aug. 14, 1919.
30. *Ibid.*, Aug. 15, 1919.
31. New York *Herald*, Aug. 16, 1919; New York *Sun*, Aug. 16, 1919.
32. New York *Herald*, Aug. 10, 1919; New York *Sun*, Aug. 18, 1919.
33. New York *Globe and Commercial Advertiser*, Aug. 20, 1919.
34. New York *Sun*, Sept. 1, 5, 1919.
35. *Ibid.*, Sept. 12, 1919.
36. Alexander, *John McGraw*, 215.
37. Graham, *The New York Giants*, 115.
38. New York *Sun*, Sept. 28, 30, 1919.
39. *Ibid.*, Oct. 1, 1919.
40. *Ibid.*, Oct. 10, 1919.
41. *TSN*, Dec. 25, 1919.
42. *Ibid.*, Jan. 1, 1920.
43. *Ibid.*, Jan. 1, 22, 1920.
44. *Ibid.*, Jan. 1, Feb. 26, 1920.
45. *Ibid.*, Feb. 26, 1920.
46. *Ibid.*, Mar. 11, 1920.
47. *Ibid.*
48. *Ibid.*, Feb. 26, 1920.
49. *Ibid.*, Mar. 11, 1920.
50. *Ibid.*, Apr. 1, 1920; New York *Times*, Mar. 24, 1920. Magee never revealed who might have been turning tricks since 1906. The 1906 season, of course, was Chase's second in the majors.
51. New York *Times*, Mar. 28, 30, 1920.
52. Cincinnati *Enquirer*, Mar. 25, 1920.
53. *TSN*, Apr. 8, 1920.
54. New York *Times*, Apr. 15, 1920.
55. *Ibid.*; Cincinnati *Enquirer*, Apr. 15, 1920.
56. *TSN*, May 6, 1920.
57. *Ibid.*, May 13, 1920.
58. New York *Times*, May 21, 1920.
59. Cincinnati *Commercial Tribune*, June 8, 1920.
60. Cincinnati *Enquirer*, June 8, 1920.
61. Cincinnati *Commercial Tribune*, June 8, 1920.
62. Cincinnati *Enquirer*, June 9, 1920.
63. *Ibid.*
64. Cincinnati *Commercial Tribune*, June 9, 1920.
65. Cincinnati *Enquirer*, June 8, 1920.
66. Cincinnati *Commercial Tribune*, June 8, 1920.
67. *Ibid.*, June 9, 1920.
68. *Ibid.*
69. *Ibid.*, June 10, 1920.
70. New York *Times*, June 10, 1920.

71. *Ibid.*, June 9, 1920.
72. Los Angeles *Times*, May 13, 1920.
73. New York *Times*, June 10, 1920.
74. New York *Sun and Herald*, June 11, 1920.
75. *TSN*, June 17, 1920.
76. *Ibid.*, May 13, 20, 1920.
77. New York *Times*, Sept. 24, 27, 1920; Seymour, *Golden Age*, 300.
78. Los Angeles *Times*, Aug. 11, 1920; *TSN*, Aug. 12, 19, 1920.
79. Bob Hoie and Carlos Bauer, comps., *The Historical Register: The Complete Major & Minor League Record of Baseball's Greatest Players*, ed. L. Robert Davids, Bob McConnell, Ray Nemec, John Benesch Jr., William J. Weiss (1999; San Diego: Baseball Press Books, 1998), 54.
80. Los Angeles *Times*, Aug. 4, 1920.
81. *Ibid.*, Aug. 5, 8, 1920.
82. *Ibid.*, Aug. 9, 1920; *TSN*, Aug. 12, 1920.
83. *TSN*, Aug. 26, 1920.
84. Los Angeles *Times*, Aug. 13, 1920.
85. *Ibid.*, Aug. 5, 18, 1920.
86. New York *Times*, Sept. 5, 1920.
87. Eliot Asinof, *Eight Men Out: The Black Sox and the 1919 World Series* (New York: Holt, Rinehart and Winston, 1963), 149–150; Seymour, *Golden Age*, 297.
88. Chicago *Tribune*, Sept. 5, 1920.
89. *Ibid.*, Sept. 5, 1920.
90. *TSN*, Sept. 16, 1920.
91. Chicago *Tribune*, Sept. 12, 1920.
92. Asinof, *Eight Men Out*, 151; Chicago *Tribune*, Sept. 19, 1920.
93. The standard work on the fix is still Asinof, *Eight Men Out*, although Gib Bodet, who has researched the Black Sox fix, says that much of Asinof's book is speculation, especially since Asinof interviewed only one of the so-called Black Sox (Happy Felsch). Gib Bodet to Martin Kohout, Sept. 25, 1990. More recent works include Donald Gropman, *Say It Ain't So, Joe: The True Story of Shoeless Joe Jackson* (1979; revised ed., New York: Citadel Press, 1992); Irving M. Stein, *The Ginger Kid: The Buck Weaver Story* (Dubuque, Ia.: Elysian Fields Press, 1992); and Harvey Frommer, *Shoeless Joe and Ragtime Baseball* (Dallas: Taylor, 1992).
94. Chicago *Tribune*, Sept. 16, 1920.
95. *Ibid.*, Sept. 8, 1920.
96. *Ibid.*, Sept. 21, 1920.
97. New York *Sun*, Sept. 12, 1919; New York *Times*, Sept. 24, 1920; Seymour, *Golden Age*, 299–300.
98. Chicago *Tribune*, Sept. 24, 1920.
99. Chicago *Tribune*, Sept. 23, 1920.
100. When pressed about Herzog's testimony, Benton countered that he had won only $20 on the Series, but admitted that he had had advance knowledge of the fix. *Ibid.*, Sept. 24, 1920.
101. *Ibid.*, Sept. 27, 29, 1920.
102. Seymour, *Golden Age*, 300.
103. Heydler told writer Fred Lieb that when he got hold of an affidavit and copy of Chase's cancelled check from James Costello, he (Heydler) immediately showed them to Giants owner Charles Stoneham, telling him, "Please notify your manager that Chase will not play in any future game with the Giants." According to Heydler, Stoneham responded, "If that's the way it is, that's it," and added, "John, you had no other choice." Lieb, *Baseball As I Have Known It*, 102.
104. New York *Times*, Sept. 29, 1920.
105. Chicago *Tribune*, Sept. 25, 1920.
106. Philadelphia *North American*, Sept. 28, 1920. Several people, however, including Eliot Asinof, believed that Maharg was really a former journeyman catcher named George Frederick "Peaches" Graham ("Maharg" spelled backwards), who played part of the 1912

season, his last in the majors, with the Phillies. Maharg himself denied this in court. See Asinof, *Eight Men Out*, 162, 262.
   107. Philadelphia *North American*, Sept. 28, 1920.
   108. New York *Herald*, Oct. 6, 1920.
   109. *Ibid.*, Oct. 30, 1920.
   110. Seymour, *Golden Age*, 301.
   111. Farrell, *My Baseball Diary*, 37–38.
   112. Cincinnati *Enquirer*, Nov. 23, 1920; Cincinnati *Commercial Tribune*, Nov. 23, 1920.
   113. Cincinnati *Commercial Tribune*, Jan. 27, 1921.
   114. Cincinnati *Enquirer*, Jan. 27, 1921.
   115. Cincinnati *Commercial Tribune*, Jan. 27, 1921.
   116. *Ibid.*
   117. Bob Hoie to Martin Kohout, Feb. 26, 1990.
   118. Asinof, *Eight Men Out*, 225. Rachael Brown was apparently the pseudonym of Nat Evans, one of Rothstein's New York associates. *Ibid.*, 30–31.
   119. *Ibid.*, 231.
   120. New York *Times*, Apr. 9, 16, 1921.
   121. San Francisco *Examiner*, Apr. 26, 1921; San Francisco *Chronicle*, Apr. 26, 1921.
   122. San Francisco *Examiner*, Apr. 27, 1921. The Lambs' Club was the unofficial headquarters of the New York theatrical crowd. In August 1920 (not "only the other day"), following a bibulous evening there, McGraw had had a violent run-in with actor John C. Slavin. McGraw retained William J. Fallon to represent him and was acquitted of violating the Volstead Act. He also settled out of court with Slavin, who had brought suit against him. Seymour, *Golden Age*, 142.
   123. New York *Times*, Apr. 27, 1921.
   124. Chicago *Tribune*, May 28, 1921.
   125. Riess, *Touching Base*, 65. See n. 121 above.
   126. Asinof, *Eight Men Out*, 233.
   127. *TSN*, Sept. 18, 1941.
   128. Ray Robinson, "Hal Chase: Baseball's Black Prince," *Argosy* (1959), 98.
   129. Asinof, *Eight Men Out*, 28.
   130. *Ibid.*, 159; Seymour, *Golden Age*, 299–300.
   131. Frommer, *Shoeless Joe and Ragtime Baseball*, 149.
   132. New York *Times*, Oct. 5, 1920.
   133. *TSN*, Sept. 18, 1941, April 23, 1947.
   134. Alexander, *John McGraw*, 228; Seymour, *Golden Age*, 322–325, 387–388.

Chapter 10

   1. Hal E. Chase Sr. to Martin Kohout, Jan. 30, 1990 (interview). It is unclear whether Chase's visitor was Mrs. Harvey S. Firestone Sr., whom the industrialist's biographer described as having "fair hair, class, aristocratic features, and a very engaging personality," or Mrs. Harvey S. Firestone Jr., who married the son of the industrialist in 1921. Mrs. Harvey S. Firestone Sr., the former Idabelle Smith, would have been Chase's senior by about ten years. Alfred Lief, *Harvey Firestone: Free Man of Enterprise* (New York: McGraw-Hill, 1951), 49–50, 208.
   2. *TSN*, Sept. 18, 1941.
   3. Arturo Soto to Martin Kohout, Oct. 3, 1990.
   4. Quoted in Arizona *Daily Star* (Tucson), Dec. 16, 1990.
   5. Arizona *Republic* (Phoenix), June 14, 15, 1923.
   6. *TSN*, July 12, 1923; *SL*, Aug. 1923.
   7. *TSN*, July 12, 1923.
   8. Arizona *Republic* (Phoenix), June 22, 28, 1923.
   9. *Ibid.*, June 25, 1923.
   10. *Ibid.*, June 28, 1923.

11. *Ibid.*, July 10, 1923.
12. Robinson, *Matty*, 211–212.
13. Quoted in Arizona *Republic* (Phoenix), July 10, 1923.
14. *Ibid.*, July 18, 1923.
15. Quoted in A. Marguerite Peck to Martin Kohout, Sept. 26, 1990.
16. Lynn Bevill, "Outlaw Baseball in the Old Copper League," *Cochise Quarterly* (n.d.), 6.
17. Lynn Bevill to Martin Kohout, Oct. 16, 1990; *TSN*, Sept. 18, 1941.
18. Bevill, "Outlaw Baseball in the Old Copper League," 6.
19. Herbert V. Young, *They Came to Jerome: The Billion Dollar Copper Camp* (Jerome, Ariz.: Jerome Historical Society, 1972), 117.
20. New York *Times*, Mar. 11, 1925.
21. Writers Program, *Arizona: The Grand Canyon State* (New York: Hastings House, 1956), 180–182; Charles H. Dunning with Edward H. Peplow Jr., *Rock to Riches: The Story of American Mining ... Past, Present and Future ... as Reflected in the Colorful History of Mining in Arizona, the Nation's Greatest Bonanza* (Phoenix: Southwest Publishing, 1959), 193.
22. Quoted in Douglas *Daily International*, Mar. 16, 1925.
23. *Ibid.*
24. Quoted in *ibid.*, Mar. 27, 1925.
25. *Ibid.*
26. "Hal Chase, Talking 'Honesty,' Springs a New One," n.d., National Baseball Hall of Fame files.
27. St. Louis *Post-Dispatch*, Mar. 12, 1925.
28. During the previous season the Copper League had expelled former Detroit Tigers pitcher Red Oldham, who had signed with the Santa Rita team under the name of Miller. Douglas *Daily Dispatch*, Mar. 24, 1925.
29. *Ibid.*, Mar. 31, Apr. 2, 1925.
30. *Ibid.*, Apr. 3, 1925.
31. *Ibid.*
32. Nearly eighty years later, the building, which now housed a sporting-goods store, was still standing, once-secret gambling rooms and all. Mark Stewart to Martin Kohout, Feb. 4, 1991 (interview).
33. Douglas *Daily Dispatch*, Apr. 7, 1925.
34. Chase downplayed his expertise — "I do not pretend to be a Hugh Fullerton [the veteran sportswriter who had, incidentally, played a central role in exposing the Black Sox fix] and I've been too busy to look the field over thoroughly" — before offering his predictions, which seemed to be safe ones: "It looks like the two New York teams to me." *Ibid.*, Apr. 15, 1925. The Giants had won the pennant while the Yankees had finished second to the surprising Washington Senators in 1924. The 1925 season would prove a disappointment for both New York teams, however, as various ailments limited Babe Ruth to only ninety-eight games and knocked the Yankees down to seventh place, while the collapse of the Giants' pitching staff allowed the Pirates to edge them for first place.
35. Douglas *Daily Dispatch*, Apr. 28, 1925.
36. *Ibid.*, June 4, 1925.
37. *Ibid.*, June 13, 1925.
38. Bevill, "Outlaw Baseball in the Old Copper League," 12.
39. Douglas *Daily Dispatch*, Apr. 7, 1925.
40. *Ibid.*, July 11, 1925.
41. *Ibid.*, Aug. 10, 1925.
42. *Ibid.*, Aug. 28, 1925.
43. Bevill, "Outlaw Baseball in the Old Copper League," 14.
44. Hoie and Bauer (comps.), *The Historical Register*, 54.
45. *Ibid.*, 16.
46. O'Connell did not deny that he had offered a bribe to Philadelphia's Heinie Sand, but

claimed that in doing so he had only been following the instructions of McGraw's "man Friday," Giants coach Albert (Cozy) Dolan. O'Connell also implicated three other Giants players—George Kelly, Frankie Frisch, and Ross Youngs—but Landis exonerated them while banning O'Connell and Dolan. McGraw, of course, disclaimed any knowledge of the bribery scheme. Seymour, *Golden Age*, 378–379.

47. Arizona *Daily Star* (Tucson), Dec. 16, 1990.
48. Unidentified clipping, n.d., National Baseball Hall of Fame files.
49. Marshall, "An Amoral Man."
50. Quoted in column by Frank Freeman, n.d., National Baseball Hall of Fame files.
51. Douglas *Daily Dispatch*, June 3, 8, 1926.
52. Marshall, "An Amoral Man."
53. Bevill, "Outlaw Baseball in the Old Copper League," 20–21.
54. Two thousand people assembled in Douglas to see her off on the evening of June 25. She thanked them for their kindness, promised a build a church in Douglas, introduced her mother and children, led the singing of a hymn, read a Bible passage, and prayed, "Oh, Douglas, God bless you!" Lately Thomas, *The Vanishing Evangelist [The Aimee Semple McPherson Kidnaping Affair]* (New York: Viking, 1959), 3–9, 49–70, 87.
55. Eventually, the kidnapping story was exposed as an attempt to conceal her liaison with radio engineer Kenneth Ormiston. *Ibid.*, 170–171.
56. Douglas *Daily Dispatch*, Aug. 24, 1926.
57. New York *Evening Journal*, July 20, 1925. I am grateful to Steve Steinberg for sending me this clipping.
58. *Ibid.*, July 24, 1926.
59. Bevill, "Outlaw Baseball in the Old Copper League," 22.
60. Douglas *Daily Dispatch*, July 31, 1926.
61. *Ibid.*, Aug. 24, 1926.
62. Marshall, "An Amoral Man."
63. Bevill, "Outlaw Baseball in the Old Copper League," 22–24.
64. Marshall, "An Amoral Man."
65. Lynn Bevill to Martin Kohout, Oct. 16, 1990; Cindy Hayostek to Martin Kohout, Oct. 6, 1990.
66. Lynn Bevill to Martin Kohout, Oct. 16, 1990, Mar. 13, 1991; Hoie and Bauer (comps.), *The Historical Register*, 54.
67. *TSN*, Sept. 18, 1941.
68. Chicago *Daily Tribune*, July 13, 1913.
69. Hal Chase Jr. to Martin Kohout, Sept. 18, 1994 (interview).
70. *TSN*, Sept. 18, 1941.
71. Lynn Bevill to Martin Kohout, Oct. 16, 1990.
72. New York *American*, Dec. 10, 1930.
73. *Ibid.*, n.d.
74. Unidentified clipping, Apr. 20, 1936.
75. *TSN*, Sept. 18, 1941.
76. Bevill to Kohout, Oct. 16, 1990.
77. *TSN*, Sept. 18, 1941.
78. Bevill to Kohout, Oct. 16, 1990; Cindy Hayostek to Martin Kohout, Oct. 6, 1990.
79. New York *Evening Post*, Jan. 4, 1934.
80. Arizona *Daily Star* (Tucson), Dec. 16, 1990.
81. New York *World-Telegram*, Dec. 26, 1933.
82. *TSN*, Jan. 4, 1934.
83. New York *Journal American*, Apr. 3, 1947.
84. New York *Evening Post*, Dec. 26, 1933.
85. New York *Sun*, Dec. 29, 1933. See also New York *Herald Tribune*, Dec. 27, 1933.
86. New York *World-Telegram*, Dec. 26, 1933. The joke was on Barrett, for Chase was actually fifty at the time.

87. Eddie Collins with Boyden Sparkes, "Coaching with Connie Mack," *Saturday Evening Post* (July 28, 1934), 60.
88. *TSN*, Sept. 18, 1941; *Tucson City Directory* (Phoenix: Arizona Directory Co., 1935).
89. Hoie, "More About Chase."
90. Roy P. Drachman to Martin Kohout, Oct. 17, 1990 (interview).
91. New York *Evening Post*, Jan. 4, 1934.
92. J. L. May to Lee Allen, May 6, 1966, National Baseball Library files.
93. Mark Stewart to Martin Kohout, Feb. 4, 1991 (interview).
94. Roy P. Drachman to Martin Kohout, Oct. 17, 1990 (interview).
95. Arizona *Daily Star* (Tucson), Dec. 16, 1990.
96. Roy P. Drachman to Martin Kohout, Oct. 17, 1990 (interview).
97. *TSN*, Jan. 9, 1936.
98. Palmer and Thorn (eds.), *Total Baseball*, 299–307. Criger must have been a sentimental choice; in sixteen years in the major leagues he compiled a batting average of only .221 and hit a total of eleven home runs, and only once did he play in as many as one hundred games in a single season. Bert Randolph Sugar claimed erroneously that Chase, Jackson, and Criger were the only players receiving votes in 1936 never to be elected to the Hall. Bert Randolph Sugar (ed.), *Baseballistics* (New York: St. Martin's Press, 1990), 131.
99. Jim Palana, "Old-Timers," in T*he Best of Spitball: The Literary Baseball Magazine*, ed. Mike Shannon (New York: Pocket Books, 1988), 164–173. In fact, there is no record that Alexander, who was elected to the Hall of Fame in 1938, subsequently spent any time in Arizona. See Jack Kavanagh, *Ol' Pete: The Grover Cleveland Alexander Story* (South Bend, Ind.: Diamond Communications, 1996), 161-169.
100. New York *Times*, May 19, 1947.
101. Hal E. Chase Sr. to Martin Kohout, Sept. 18, 1994 (interview).
102. Frank Cloak Jr. to Martin Kohout, Feb. 6, 1991 (interview).
103. Hal E. Chase Sr. to Martin Kohout, Sept. 18, 1994 (interview).
104. Marilynn S. Johnson, *The Second Gold Rush: Oakland and the East Bay in World War II* (Berkeley: University of California Press, 1993), 33.
105. New York *Times*, July 30, 1942; San Francisco *Chronicle*, July 30, 1942, Aug. 1, 1942; San Francisco *Examiner*, July 30, 1942.
106. Frank Clark Jr. to Martin Kohout, Feb. 6, 1991 (interview). Cloak also recalled that Jessie Topham kept the letters Chase had sent her while he was playing ball and cut off the signatures to send to fans who wrote seeking Chase's autograph.
107. Sacramento *Union*, Apr. 22, 1944.
108. Results quoted in San Francisco *Chronicle*, Apr. 21, 1944.
109. Bill Conlin to Martin Kohout, June 14, 1990.
110. New York *Journal American*, Feb. 1, [1942?].
111. *TSN*, Sept. 18, 1941.
112. Hal E. Chase Sr. to Martin Kohout, Sept. 19, 1994 (interview).
113. *TSN*, Sept. 18, 1941.
114. *Ibid.*, Sept. 25, 1941.
115. *Ibid.*, Apr. 23, 1947.
116. *Ibid.*, Sept. 18, 1941.
117. *Ibid.*, Apr. 23, 1947.
118. *Ibid.*, Sept. 18, 1941.
119. *Ibid.*, Apr. 23, 1947.
120. *Ibid.*, Sept. 18, 1941.
121. *Ibid.*, Apr. 23, 1947.
122. Anne-Marie Kern, Office of the Commissioner, to Martin Kohout, Mar. 29, 1991.
123. *TSN.*, Sept. 18, 1941.
124. *Ibid.*, Sept. 25, 1941.
125. *Ibid.*, Apr. 23, 1947.
126. *Ibid.*, Sept. 25, 1941.
127. *Ibid.*, Apr. 23, 1947.

128. *Ibid.*, May 28, 1947.
129. New York *Times*, May 20, 1947.
130. Unidentified clipping, n.d., National Baseball Hall of Fame files.
131. Marshall, "An Amoral Man."
132. New York *World-Telegram*, May 20, 21, 1947.
133. *The Celebrant*, Greenberg, 172.
134. *Ibid.*, 170–171.

Epilogue

1. San Jose *Mercury News*, Apr. 23, 1995.
2. *Ibid.*, Apr. 26, 1995.

Bibliography

Books

Abrams, Roger I. *Legal Bases: Baseball and the Law*. Philadelphia: Temple University Press, 1998.
Adelman, Melvin L. *A Sporting Time: New York City and the Rise of Modern Athletics, 1820–70*. 1986; Urbana, Ill.: University of Illinois Press, 1990.
Alexander, Charles C. *John McGraw*. New York: Viking, 1988.
_____. *Ty Cobb*. 1984; New York: Oxford University Press, 1985.
Allen, Frederick Lewis. *The Great Pierpont Morgan*. New York: Harper and Brothers, 1949.
Allen, Lee. *The American League Story*. New York: Hill and Wang, 1962.
_____. *The Cincinnati Reds*. New York: G. P. Putnam's Sons, 1948.
_____. *Cooperstown Corner: Columns from* The Sporting News*, 1962–1969*. Cleveland: Society for American Baseball Research, 1990.
_____. *The National League Story: The Official History*. New York: Hill and Wang, 1961.
Allen, Oliver E. *New York, New York: A History of the World's Most Exhilarating and Challenging City*. New York: Atheneum, 1990.
Arbuckle, Clyde. *Clyde Arbuckle's History of San Jose*. San Jose: City of San Jose, 1986.
Asbury, Herbert. *Sucker's Progress: An Informal History of Gambling in America from the Colonies to Canfield*. New York: Dodd, Mead, 1938.
Asinof, Eliot. *Bleeding Between the Lines*. New York: Holt, Rinehart and Winston, 1979.
_____. *Eight Men Out: The Black Sox and the 1919 World Series*. New York: Holt, Rinehart and Winston, 1963.
Axelson, Gustav W. *"Commy": The Life Story of Charles A. Comiskey*. Chicago: Reilly and Lee, 1919.
Bailey, Lynn R. *Bisbee: Queen of the Copper Camps*. Tucson: Westernlore, 1983.
Bandini, Helen Elliott. *History of California*. New York: American Book, 1908.
Barber, Red. *1947: When All Hell Broke Loose in Baseball*. Garden City, N.Y.: Doubleday, 1982.
Barth, Gunther. *City People: The Rise of Modern City Culture in Nineteenth-Century America*. New York: Oxford University Press, 1980.
Bean, Walton. *California: An Interpretive History*. 2nd ed. New York: McGraw-Hill, 1973.
Beard, Charles A., and Mary R. Beard. *The Rise of American Civilization. Vol. II: The Industrial Era*. New York: Macmillan, 1927.
Beston, Greg. "The Story of Hal Chase: How Baseball Officials Allowed Corruption to Exist in the Game from 1905–1919." B.A. thesis, Princeton University, 1997.
Blake, Mike. *Baseball Chronicles: An Oral History of Baseball Through the Decades*. Cincinnati: Betterway, 1994.
Bloom, Ken. *Broadway: An Encyclopedic Guide to the History, People and Places of Times Square*. New York: Facts on File, 1991.

Bowman, Lynn. *Los Angeles: Epic of a City.* Berkeley: Howell-North Books, 1974.
Brinkley, Douglas. *American Heritage History of the United States.* New York: Viking, 1998.
Brown, Warren. *The Chicago White Sox.* New York: G. P. Putnam's Sons, 1952.
Bruntz, George G. *The History of Los Gatos: Gem of the Foothills.* Fresno, Calif.: Valley Publishers, 1971.
Burk, Robert F. *Never Just a Game: Players, Owners, and American Baseball to 1920.* Chapel Hill: University of North Carolina Press, 1994.
Calhoun, Donald W. *Sport, Culture, and Personality.* 2nd ed. Champaign, Ill.: Human Kinetics, 1987.
California Gazetteer. Wilmington, Del.: American Historical Publications, 1985.
Cashman, Sean Dennis. *America in the Age of the Titans: The Progressive Era and World War I.* New York: New York University Press, 1988.
Chadwick, Bruce. *Baseball's Hometown Teams: The Story of the Minor Leagues.* New York: Abbeville, 1994.
Chase, Hal. *How to Play First Base.* Spalding's Athletic Library. New York: American Sports Publishing, 1917.
Churchill, Allen. *The Upper Crust.* Englewood Cliffs, N.J.: Prentice-Hall, 1970.
Cleland, Robert Glass. *A History of California: The American Period.* New York: Macmillan, 1922.
Cobb, Ty, with Al Stump. *My Life in Baseball: The True Record.* 1961; reprint, Lincoln: University of Nebraska Press, 1993.
Coleman, Herbert Gehrig. "Judge Kenesaw Mountain Landis and the Chicago I.W.W. Trial." M.A. thesis, University of Texas at Austin, 1992.
Collett, Ritter. *The Cincinnati Reds: A Pictorial History of Professional Baseball's Oldest Team.* Virginia Beach, Va.: Jordan-Powers, 1976.
Commager, Henry Steele, and Allan Nevins, eds. *The Heritage of America: Readings in American History.* Rev. ed.; Boston: D. C. Heath, 1949.
Connor, Anthony J. *Voices from Cooperstown: Baseball's Hall of Famers Tell It Like It Was.* New York: Macmillan, 1982.
Cooper, John Milton, Jr. *Pivotal Decades: The United States, 1900–1920.* New York: W. W. Norton and Company, 1990.
Creamer, Robert W. *Babe: The Legend Comes to Life.* 1974; New York: Simon and Schuster, 1988.
_____. *Stengel: His Life and Times.* New York: Simon and Schuster, 1984.
Crepeau, Richard C. *Baseball: America's Diamond Mind, 1919–1941.* Orlando: University Presses of Florida, 1980.
Crichton, Judy. *America 1900: The Turning Point.* New York: Henry Holt, 1998.
Curran, William. *Mitts: A Celebration of the Art of Fielding.* New York: William Morrow, 1985.
Davis, Ellis A. *Davis' Commercial Encyclopedia of the Pacific Southwest: California, Nevada, Utah, Arizona.* Oakland: Ellis A. Davis, 1915.
Dedmon, Emmett. *Fabulous Chicago.* New York: Random House, 1953.
DeValeria, Dennis, and Jeanne Burke DeValeria. *Honus Wagner: A Biography.* 1995; Pittsburgh: University of Pittsburgh Press, 1998.
Dickey, Glenn. *The History of National League Baseball: Since 1876.* New York: Stein and Day, 1979.
Dodge, Phyllis B. *Tales of the Phelps-Dodge Family.* New York: New York Historical Society, 1987.
Donohoe, Patrick A. *The University of Santa Clara.* Princeton, N.J.: Newcomen Society, 1966.
Douglas, Ann. *Terrible Honesty: Mongrel Manhattan in the 1920s.* New York: Farrar, Straus and Giroux, 1995.
Douglas City Directory 1926. Long Beach, Calif.: Western Directory, 1926.
Drisko, George W. *Narrative of the Town of Machias: The Old and the New, the Early and the Late.* Machias, Me.: Press of the Republican, 1904.
Dunning, Charles H., with Edward H. Peplow Jr. *Rock to Riches: The Story of American Mining in Arizona, the Nation's Greatest Bonanza.* Phoenix: Southwest, 1959.

Durocher, Leo, and Ed Linn. *Nice Guys Finish Last.* New York: Simon and Schuster, 1975.
Durso, Joseph. *Baseball and the American Dream.* St. Louis: The Sporting News, 1986.
_____. *The Days of Mr. McGraw.* Englewood Cliffs, N.J.: Prentice-Hall, 1969.
Elder, Donald. *Ring Lardner.* Garden City, N.Y.: Doubleday, 1956.
Evans, Harold, with Gail Buckland and Kevin Baker. *The American Century.* New York: Alfred A. Knopf, 1998.
Faber, Charles F. *Baseball Ratings: The All-Time Best Players at Each Position.* Jefferson, N.C.: McFarland, 1985.
Farrell, James T. *My Baseball Diary.* New York: A. S. Barnes, 1957.
Faulk, Odie B. *Arizona: A Short History.* Norman: University of Oklahoma Press, 1970.
_____. *Land of Many Frontiers: A History of the American Southwest.* New York: Oxford University Press, 1968.
Federal Writers' Program. *Arizona: A State Guide.* New York: Hastings House, 1940.
Finch, Robert L., L. H. Addington, and Ben M. Morgan, eds. *The Story of Minor League Baseball.* Columbus, Oh.: Stoneman Press for the National Association of Professional Baseball Leagues, 1953.
Findlay, John M. *People of Chance: Gambling in American Society from Jamestown to Las Vegas.* New York: Oxford University Press, 1986.
Foote, H. S., ed. *Pen Pictures from the Garden of the World or Santa Clara County, California.* Chicago: Lewis, 1888.
Fowler, Gene. *The Great Mouthpiece: A Life Story of William J. Fallon.* New York: Covici-Friede, 1931.
Fox, Frances L. *Luis Maria Peralta and His Adobe.* San Jose, Calif.: Smith-McKay, 1975.
Fox, Stephen. *Big Leagues: Professional Baseball, Football, and Basketball in National Memory.* New York: William Morrow, 1994.
Frommer, Harvey. *Shoeless Joe and Ragtime Baseball.* Dallas: Taylor, 1992.
Gallen, David, ed. *The Baseball Chronicles.* New York: Carroll and Graf, 1991.
Gilbert, Martin. *A History of the Twentieth Century. Vol. I: 1900–1933.* New York: Avon, 1997.
Ginger, Ray. *Age of Excess: The United States from 1877 to 1914.* New York: Macmillan, 1965.
Ginsburg, Daniel E. *The Fix Is In: A History of Baseball Gambling and Game Fixing Scandals.* Jefferson, N.C.: McFarland, 1995.
Goldman, Mark. *High Hopes: The Rise and Decline of Buffalo, New York.* Albany: State University of New York Press, 1983.
Goss, Rev. Charles Frederic. *Cincinnati: The Queen City, 1788–1912.* 4 vols. Chicago: S. J. Clarke, 1912.
Graham, Frank. *McGraw of the Giants: An Informal Biography.* New York: G. P. Putnam's Sons, 1944.
_____. *The New York Giants: An Informal History.* New York: G. P. Putnam's Sons, 1952.
_____. *The New York Yankees: An Informal History.* New York: G. P. Putnam's Sons, 1943.
Grayson, Harry. *They Played the Game: The Story of Baseball Greats.* 1944; New York: A. S. Barnes, 1945.
Green, Martin B. *New York 1913: The Armory Show and the Paterson Strike Pageant.* New York: Charles Scribner's Sons, 1988.
Green, Paul. *Forgotten Fields.* Waupaca, Wisc.: Parker, 1984.
Greenberg, Eric Rolfe. *The Celebrant.* 1983; New York: Everest House, 1986.
Gropman, Donald. *Say It Ain't So, Joe! The Story of Shoeless Joe Jackson.* Boston: Little, Brown, 1979.
Guttman, Allen. *From Ritual to Record: The Nature of Modern Sports.* New York: Columbia University Press, 1978.
Hammack, David C. *Power and Society: Greater New York at the Turn of the Century.* New York: Russell Sage Foundation, 1982.
Hardy, Stephen. *How Boston Played: Sport, Recreation, and Community, 1865–1915.* Boston: Northeastern University Press, 1982.
Harper, William A. *How You Played the Game: The Life of Grantland Rice.* Columbia: University of Missouri Press, 1999.

Harris, Neil, ed. *The Land of Contrasts (1880–1901)*. New York: George Braziller, 1970.
Hart, James D. *A Companion to California*. Berkeley: University of California Press, 1987.
Hatch, Louis Clinton, ed. *Maine: A History*. 5 vols.; New York: American Historical Society, 1919.
Hays, Samuel P. *The Response to Industrialism, 1885–1914*. Chicago: University of Chicago Press, 1957.
Heise, Kenan. *Chaos, Creativity, and Culture: A Sampling of Chicago in the Twentieth Century*. Salt Lake City: Gibbs-Smith, 1998.
Historical Atlas Map of Santa Clara County, California. San Francisco: Thompson and West, 1876.
History of Santa Clara County, California; Including Its Geography, Geology, Topography, Climatography and Description.... San Francisco: Alley, Bowen and Company, 1881.
Hobsbawm, Eric. *The Age of Extremes: A History of the World, 1914–1991*. 1994; New York: Vintage, 1996.
Hofstadter, Richard. *The Age of Reform: From Bryan to F. D. R*. New York: Vintage, 1955.
_____. *The American Political Tradition: And the Men Who Made It*. 1948; New York: Alfred A. Knopf, 1983.
Hoie, Bob, and Carlos Bauer, comps. *The Historical Register: The Complete Major & Minor League Record of Baseball's Greatest Players*. Ed. L. Robert Davids, Bob McConnell, Ray Nemec, John Benesch Jr., William J. Weiss. 1999; San Diego: Baseball Press Books, 1998.
Honig, Donald. *Baseball America: The Heroes of the Game and the Times of Their Glory*. New York: Macmillan, 1985.
_____. *The Greatest First Basemen of All Time*. New York: Crown, 1988.
_____. *The New York Yankees: An Illustrated History*. New York: Crown, 1981.
Hornsby, Rogers, and Bill Surface. *My War with Baseball*. New York: Coward-McCann, 1962.
Hotaling, Edward. *They're Off! Horse Racing at Saratoga*. Syracuse, N.Y.: Syracuse University Press, 1995.
Hughes, Rupert. *The Real New York*. New York: The Smart Set, 1904.
Hynd, Noel. *The Giants of the Polo Grounds: The Glorious Times of Baseball's New York Giants*. New York: Doubleday, 1988.
James, Bill. *The Bill James Historical Baseball Abstract*. New York: Villard, 1986.
_____. *Whatever Happened to the Hall of Fame? Baseball, Cooperstown, and the Politics of Glory*. 1994; New York: Fireside, 1995.
James, George Wharton. *Arizona, the Wonderland*. Boston: Page, 1917.
Johnson, Curt, and R. Craig Sautter. *The Wicked City: Chicago from Kenna to Capone*. 1994; New York: Da Capo, 1998.
Johnson, Lloyd, and Miles Wolff, eds. *The Encyclopedia of Minor League Baseball*. Durham, N.C.: Baseball America, 1993.
Johnson, Marilynn S. *The Second Gold Rush: Oakland and the East Bay in World War II*. Berkeley: University of California Press, 1993.
Johnson, Paul. *A History of the American People*. New York: HarperCollins, 1997.
Jones, Howard Mumford. *The Age of Energy: Varieties of American Experience, 1865–1915*. New York: Viking, 1971.
Katcher, Leo. *The Big Bankroll: The Life and Times of Arnold Rothstein*. 1958; New Rochelle, N.Y.: Arlington House, 1969.
Kavanagh, Jack. *Ol' Pete: The Grover Cleveland Alexander Story*. South Bend, Ind.: Diamond Communications, 1996.
Kisseloff, Jeff. *You Must Remember This: An Oral History of Manhattan from the 1890s to World War II*. New York: Harcourt Brace Jovanovich, 1989.
Klingaman, William K. *1919: The Year Our World Began*. New York: Harper and Row, 1987.
Kuklick, Bruce. *The Rise of American Philosophy: Cambridge, Massachusetts, 1860–1930*. New Haven, Conn.: Yale University Press, 1977.
_____. *To Every Thing a Season: Shibe Park and Urban Philadelphia, 1909–1976*. Princeton, N.J.: Princeton University Press, 1991.
Kurland, Gerald. *Seth Low: The Reformer in an Urban and Industrial Age*. New York: Twayne, 1971.

Lansche, Jerry. *The Forgotten Championships: Postseason Baseball, 1882–1981*. Jefferson, N.C.: McFarland, 1988.
Lears, T. J. Jackson. *No Place of Grace: Antimodernism and the Transformation of American Culture, 1880–1920*. New York: Pantheon, 1981.
Lessard, Suzannah. *The Architect of Desire: Beauty and Danger in the Stanford White Family*. New York: Dial, 1996.
Leuchtenberg, William E. *The Perils of Prosperity, 1914–1932*. Chicago: University of Chicago Press, 1958.
Levine, Peter. *A. G. Spalding and the Rise of Baseball: The Promise of American Sport*. New York: Oxford University Press, 1985.
_____. *American Sport: A Documentary History*. Englewood Cliffs, N.J.: Prentice-Hall, 1989.
Lieb, Fred. *Baseball As I Have Known It*. New York: Coward, McCann and Geoghegan, 1977.
_____. *The Baseball Story*. New York: G. P. Putnam's Sons, 1950.
Lief, Alfred. *Harvey Firestone: Free Man of Enterprise*. New York: McGraw-Hill, 1951.
Lindberg, Richard. *Sox: The Complete Record of Chicago White Sox Baseball*. New York: Macmillan, 1984.
Link, Arthur S. *American Epoch: A History of the United States Since the 1890s*. New York: Alfred A. Knopf, 1955.
Longstreet, Stephen. *Chicago, 1860–1919*. New York: David McKay, 1973.
_____. *Win or Lose: A Social History of Gambling in America*. Indianapolis: Bobbs-Merrill, 1977.
Lord, Walter. *The Good Years: From 1900 to the First World War*. New York: Harper and Brothers, 1960.
Lowenfish, Lee, and Tony Lupien. *The Imperfect Diamond: The Story of Baseball's Reserve System and the Men Who Fought to Change It*. New York: Stein and Day, 1980.
Luhrs, Victor. *The Great Baseball Mystery: The 1919 World Series*. South Brunswick, N.J.: A. S. Barnes, 1966.
McCaffrey, Eugene V., and Roger A. McCaffrey. *Players' Choice*. New York: Facts on File, 1987.
McClellan, R. Guy. *The Golden State: A History of the Region West of the Rocky Mountains, Embracing California ... from the Earliest Period to the Present Time*. Philadelphia: William Flint, 1872.
McElvaine, Robert S. *The Great Depression: America, 1929–1941*. 1984; New York: Times Books, 1993.
McGraw, John. *My Thirty Years in Baseball*. New York: Boni and Liveright, 1923.
McKelvey, Blake. *The Urbanization of America, 1860–1915*. New Brunswick, N.J.: Rutgers University Press, 1963.
McKevitt, Gerald, S.J. *The University of Santa Clara: A History, 1851–1977*. Stanford, Calif.: Stanford University Press, 1979.
Mandell, Richard D. *Sport: A Cultural History*. New York: Columbia University Press, 1984.
Maranville, Walter "Rabbit." *Run, Rabbit, Run: The Hilarious and Mostly True Tales of Rabbit Maranville*. Cleveland: Society for American Baseball Research, 1991.
Mathewson, Christy. *Pitching in a Pinch, or Baseball from the Inside*. 1912; New York: Stein and Day, 1977.
_____. *Won in the Ninth*. New York: R. J. Bodmer, 1910.
May, Henry. *The End of American Innocence: A Study of the First Years of Our Own Time, 1912–1917*. 1959; Chicago: Quadrangle, 1964.
Miller, Donald L. *City of the Century: The Epic of Chicago and the Making of America*. 1996; New York: Touchstone, 1997.
Morgan, Ted. *A Shovel of Stars: The Making of the American West—1800 to the Present*. 1995; New York: Touchstone, 1996.
Moriarty, Leo, ed. *Baseball Records: Pacific Coast League from 1903 to 1928*. Los Angeles, 1928.
Morris, Lloyd. *Incredible New York: High Life and Low Life of the Last Hundred Years*. New York: Random House, 1951.
Mote, James. *Everything Baseball*. New York: Prentice Hall, 1989.
Mrozek, Donald J. *Sport and American Mentality, 1880–1910*. Knoxville: University of Tennessee Press, 1983.

Mumford, Lewis. *My Works and Days: A Personal Chronicle*. New York: Harcourt Brace Jovanovich, 1979.
_____. *Sketches from Life: The Autobiography of Lewis Mumford. The Early Years*. New York: Dial, 1982.
Murdock, Eugene C. *Ban Johnson: Czar of Baseball*. Westport, Conn.: Greenwood Press, 1982.
_____. *Baseball Players and Their Times: Oral Histories of the Game, 1920–1940*. Westport, Conn.: Meckler, 1991.
Nash, Roderick. *The Nervous Generation: American Thought, 1917–1930*. Chicago: Rand McNally, 1970.
_____, ed. *The Call of the Wild (1900–1916)*. New York: George Braziller, 1970.
Neft, David S., and Richard M. Cohen. *The Sports Encyclopedia: Baseball*. 8th ed. New York: St. Martin's Press, 1988.
Nemec, David. *The Great Encyclopedia of 19th Century Major League Baseball*. New York: Donald I. Fine, 1997.
_____. *A History of Baseball in the San Francisco Bay Area. San Francisco Giants Official 1985 Yearbook*. San Francisco: Woodford Associates, 1985.
Nevins, Allan. *Study in Power: John D. Rockefeller, Industrialist and Philanthropist*. 2 vols.; New York: Charles Scribner's Sons, 1953.
_____ and John A. Krout, eds. *The Greater City: New York, 1898–1948*. New York: Columbia University Press, 1948.
Newton, James D. *Uncommon Friends: Life with Thomas Edison, Henry Ford, Harvey Firestone, Alexis Carrel and Charles Lindbergh*. 1987; San Diego: Harvest/HBJ, 1989.
Nordhoff, Charles. *California: For Health, Pleasure, and Residence*. New York: Harper and Brothers, 1872.
Norton, Henry K. *The Story of California from the Earliest Days to the Present*. Chicago: A. C. McClurg, 1913.
Obojski, Robert. *Bush League: A History of Minor League Baseball*. New York: Macmillan, 1975.
Okkonen, Marc. *The Federal League of 1914-1915: Baseball's Third Major League*. Garrett Park, Md.: Society for American Baseball Research, 1989.
Okrent, Daniel, and Harris Lewine, eds. *The Ultimate Baseball Book*. Boston: Houghton Mifflin, 1988.
_____ and Steve Wulf. *Baseball Anecdotes*. New York: Oxford University Press, 1989.
O'Neal, Bill. *The Pacific Coast League, 1903–1988*. Austin, Tex.: Eakin Press, 1990.
Painter, Nell Irvin. *Standing at Armageddon: The United States, 1877–1919*. New York: W. W. Norton, 1987.
Payne, Stephen M. *Santa Clara County: Harvest of Change*. Northridge, Calif.: Windsor Publications in cooperation with County of Santa Clara Historical Heritage Commission, 1987.
Peterson, Robert. *Only the Ball Was White: A History of Legendary Black Players and All-Black Professional Teams*. 1970; New York: McGraw-Hill, 1984.
Pietrusza, David. *Judge and Jury: The Life and Times of Judge Kenesaw Mountain Landis*. South Bend, Ind.: Diamond Communications, 1998.
_____. *Major Leagues: The Formation, Sometimes Absorption and Mostly Inevitable Demise of 18 Professional Baseball Organizations, 1871 to Present*. Jefferson, N.C.: McFarland, 1991.
Pomeroy, Earl. *In Search of the Golden West: The Tourist in Western America*. New York: Alfred A. Knopf, 1957.
Reichler, Joseph L., ed. *The Baseball Encyclopedia*. 7th ed. New York: Macmillan, 1986.
Rice, Damon. *Seasons Past*. New York: Praeger, 1976.
Riess, Steven. *Touching Base: Professional Baseball and American Culture in the Progressive Era*. Westport, Conn.: Greenwood Press, 1980.
Ritter, Lawrence S. *The Glory of Their Times: The Story of the Early Days of Baseball Told by the Men Who Played It*. New York: Collier, 1966.
_____ and Donald Honig. *The 100 Greatest Baseball Players of All Time*. New York: Crown, 1981.
Robinson, Ray. *Matty: An American Hero*. New York: Oxford University Press, 1993.
Rodgers, Daniel T. *The Work Ethic in Industrial America, 1850–1920*. Chicago: University of Chicago Press, 1978.

Rust, Art, Jr. *"Get That Nigger Off the Field!" A Sparkling, Informal History of the Black Man in Baseball.* New York: Delacorte, 1976.
Sante, Luc. *Low Life: Lures and Snares of Old New York.* 1991; New York: Vintage, 1992.
Sasuly, Richard. *Bookies and Bettors: Two Hundred Years of Gambling.* New York: Holt, Rinehart and Winston, 1982.
Schlereth, Thomas. *Victorian America: Transformation in Everyday Life, 1876–1915.* New York: HarperPerennial, 1992.
Schoor, Gene, with Henry Gilford. *Christy Mathewson: Baseball's Greatest Pitcher.* New York: Julian Messner, 1953.
Seymour, Harold. *Baseball: The Early Years.* 1960; New York: Oxford University Press, 1989.
_____. *Baseball: The Golden Age.* 1971; New York: Oxford University, 1989.
Shackleton, Robert. *The Book of New York.* Philadelphia: Penn, 1917.
Shannon, Mike, ed. *The Best of* Spitball: *The Literary Baseball Magazine.* New York: Pocket Books, 1988.
Shatzkin, Mike, ed. *The Ballplayers: Baseball's Ultimate Biographical Reference.* New York: William Morrow, 1990.
Sklar, Robert, ed. *The Plastic Age (1917–1930).* New York: George Braziller, 1970.
Skolnick, Richard. *Baseball and the Pursuit of Innocence: A Fresh Look at the Old Ball Game.* College Station: Texas A&M University Press, 1994.
Smith, Henry Justin. *Chicago's Great Century, 1833–1933.* Chicago: Consolidated for a Century of Progress, 1933.
Smith, Ira L. *Baseball's Famous First Basemen.* New York: A. S. Barnes, 1956.
Smith, Leverett T., Jr. *The American Dream and the National Game.* Bowling Green, Ohio: Bowling Green University Popular Press, 1975.
Smith, Marion Jaques. *A History of Maine: From Wilderness to Statehood.* Portland, Me.: Falmouth Publishing House, 1949.
Smith, Page. *America Enters the World: A People's History of the Progressive Era and World War I.* Vol. VII. New York: McGraw-Hill, 1985.
Smith, Robert. *Baseball: A Historical Narrative of the Game, the Men Who Have Played It, and Its Place in American Life.* New York: Simon and Schuster, 1947.
_____. *Baseball in the Afternoon: Tales from a Bygone Era.* New York: Simon and Schuster, 1993.
_____. *Pioneers of Baseball.* Boston: Little, Brown, 1978.
Snelling, Dennis. *The Pacific Coast League: A Statistical History, 1903–1957.* Jefferson, N.C.: McFarland, 1995.
Solomon, Burt. *The Baseball Timeline: The Day-to-Day History of Baseball, from Valley Forge to the Present Day.* New York: Avon, 1997.
_____. *Where They Ain't: The Fabled Life and Untimely Death of the Original Baltimore Orioles, the Team That Gave Birth to Modern Baseball.* New York: Free Press, 1999.
Sonnichsen, C. L. *Tucson: The Life and Times of an American City.* Norman: University of Oklahoma Press, 1982.
Spalding, Albert G. *Base Ball: America's National Pastime.* Samm Coombs and Bob West, eds. 1911; San Francisco: Halo Books, 1991.
Spalding, John E. *Always on Sunday: The California Baseball League, 1886 to 1915.* N.p.: John E. Spalding, 1992.
_____. *Pacific Coast League Stars, Volume II: Ninety Who Made It in the Majors, 1903 to 1957.* N.p.: John E. Spalding, 1997.
Spink, J. G. Taylor. *Judge Landis and 25 Years of Baseball.* St. Louis: The Sporting News, 1974.
Starr, Kevin. *Americans and the California Dream, 1850–1915.* New York: Oxford University Press, 1973.
_____. *Inventing the Dream: California Through the Progressive Era.* New York: Oxford Universty Press, 1985.
_____. *Material Dreams: Southern California Through the 1920s.* New York: Oxford University Press, 1990.
Stein, Fred, and Nick Peters. *Giants Diary: A Century of Giants Baseball in New York and San Francisco.* Berkeley: North Atlantic, 1987.

Stein, Harry. *Hoopla*. New York: Alfred A. Knopf, 1983.
Stein, Irving. *The Ginger Kid: The Buck Weaver Story*. Madison, Wisc.: Brown and Benchmark, 1992.
Steiner, Jesse Frederick. *Americans at Play*. 1933; New York: Arno Press, 1970.
Stoddard, Lothrop. *Master of Manhattan: The Life of Richard Croker*. New York: Longmans, Green, 1931.
Stump, Al. *Cobb: A Biography*. 1994; Chapel Hill, N.C.: Algonquin Books, 1996.
Sugar, Bert Randolph, ed. *Baseballistics*. New York: St. Martin's Press, 1990.
Sullivan, Dean, comp. and ed. *Early Innings: A Documentary History of Baseball, 1825–1908*. Lincoln: University of Nebraska Press, 1995.
Sullivan, George, and John Powers. *The Yankees: An Illustrated History*. Philadelphia: Temple University Press, 1997.
Sullivan, Neil J. *The Minors: The Struggles and the Triumph of Baseball's Poor Relation from 1876 to the Present*. New York: St. Martin's Press, 1990.
Terkel, Studs. *My American Century*. New York: New Press, 1997.
Thomas, Henry W. *Walter Johnson: Baseball's Big Train*. Lincoln: University of Nebraska Press, 1995.
Thomas, Lately. *The Vanishing Evangelist [The Aimee Semple McPherson Kidnapping Affair]*. New York: Viking, 1959.
Thorn, John. *Baseball's 10 Greatest Games*. New York: Four Winds Press, 1981.
——— and Pete Palmer, eds. *Total Baseball: The Ultimate Encyclopedia of Baseball*. 3rd ed. New York: HarperPerennial, 1993.
———, Pete Palmer, Michael Gershman, and David Pietrusza, eds. *Total Baseball: The Official Encyclopedia of Major League Baseball*. 5th ed. New York: Viking, 1997.
Tolzmann, Don Heinrich. *The Cincinnati Germans After the Great War*. American University Studies, Series IX, History; vol. 16. New York: Peter Lang, 1987.
Trachtenberg, Alan. *The Incorporation of America: Culture and Society in the Gilded Age*. New York: Hill and Wang, 1982.
Trimble, Marshall. *Arizona: A Panoramic History of a Frontier State*. Garden City, N.Y.: Doubleday, 1977.
Tucson City Directory 1935. Phoenix: Arizona Directory, 1935.
Turner, Frederick Jackson. *The Significance of the Frontier in American History*. Ed. Harold P. Simonson. New York: Frederick Ungar, 1963.
Urdang, Lawrence, ed. *The Timetables of American History*. New York: Simon and Schuster, 1981.
Valentine, Alan. *1913: America Between Two Worlds*. New York: Macmillan, 1962.
Van Dyke, John C. *The New New York: A Commentary on the Place and People*. New York: Macmillan, 1909.
Veblen, Thorstein. *The Theory of the Leisure Class: An Economic Study of Institutions*. 1899; New York: Modern Library, 1934.
Veeck, Bill, with Ed Linn. *The Hustler's Handbook*. New York: G. P. Putnam's Sons, 1965.
Voigt, David Quentin. *American Baseball*. 3 vols. 1966–1970; University Park: Pennsylvania State University Press, 1983.
———. *Baseball: An Illustrated History*. University Park: Pennsylvania State University Press, 1987.
Walker, Donald E., and B. Lee Cooper, comps. *Baseball and American Culture: A Thematic Bibliography of Over 4,500 Works*. Jefferson, N.C.: McFarland, 1995.
Wallechinsky, David, and Irving Wallace. *The People's Almanac*. Garden City, N.Y.: Doubleday, 1975.
Waller, George. *Saratoga: Saga of an Impious Era*. New York: Bonanza, 1966.
Waller, Spencer Weber, Neil B. Cohen, and Paul Finkelman, eds. *Baseball and the American Legal Mind*. New York: Garland, 1995.
Wallop, Douglas. *Baseball: An Informal History*. New York: W. W. Norton, 1969.
Ward, Geoffrey C., and Ken Burns. *Baseball: An Illustrated History*. New York: Borzoi, 1994.
Weaver, John D. *Los Angeles: The Enormous Village, 1781–1981*. Santa Barbara, Calif.: Capra Press, 1980.

Wecter, Dixon. *The Hero in America: A Chronicle of Hero Worship*. 1941; New York: Charles Scribner's Sons, 1969.
Werner, Morris R. *Tammany Hall*. Garden City, N.Y.: Doubleday, Doran, 1928.
Wheeler, Lonnie, and John Baskin. *The Cincinnati Game*. Wilmington, O.: Orange Frazer Press, 1988.
White, G. Edward. *Creating the National Pastime: Baseball Transforms Itself, 1903–1953*. Princeton, N.J.: Princeton University Press, 1996.
Wiebe, Robert H. *The Search for Order, 1877–1920*. New York: Hill and Wang, 1967.
Writers Program. *Arizona: The Grand Canyon State*. New York: Hastings House, 1956.
Yardley, Jonathan. *Ring: A Biography of Ring Lardner*. New York: Random House, 1977.
Young, Herbert V. *They Came to Jerome: The Billion Dollar Copper Camp*. Jerome, Ariz.: Jerome Historical Society, 1972.
Zingg, Paul J. *Harry Hooper: An American Baseball Life*. Urbana: University of Illinois Press, 1993.
_____ and Mark D. Medeiros. *Runs, Hits, and an Era: The Pacific Coast League, 1903–58*. Urbana: University of Illinois Press for the Oakland Museum, 1994.
Zoss, Joel, and John Bowman. *Diamonds in the Rough: The Untold History of Baseball*. New York: Macmillan, 1989.

Articles

Barber, Frederick Courtenay. "The Star Ball-Players and Their Earnings." *Munsey's*, XLIX (May 1913).
Barrows, Robert G. "Urbanizing America." In Charles W. Calhoun, ed. *The Gilded Age: Essays on the Origins of Modern America*. Wilmington, Del.: Scholarly Resources, 1996.
Beasley, N. B. "Baseball — A Business, a Sport, a Gamble." *Harper's Weekly*, LVIII (Apr. 11, 1914).
Bevill, Lynn. "Outlaw Baseball in the Old Copper League." *Cochise Quarterly*, XX (Summer 1991).
_____. "Prince Hal and His Arizona Odyssey." In Mike Holden, ed. *Mining Towns to Major Leagues: A History of Arizona Baseball*. Cleveland: Society for American Baseball Research, 1999.
Blaisdell, Lowell D. "Legends as an Expression of Baseball Memory." *Journal of Sport History*, XIX (Winter 1992).
Bodet, Gib. "The Life and Times of Prince Hal Chase." Unpublished ms. N.d. (1991).
"The Business Side of Baseball." *Current Literature*, LIII (Aug. 1912).
Chase, Hal. "Doing the Comeback Stunt." *Baseball Magazine*, XIX (Oct. 1917).
Collins, Eddie, with Boyden Sparkes. "Coaching with Connie Mack." *Saturday Evening Post*, CCVII (July 28, 1934).
Crepeau, Richard C. "Urban and Rural Images in Baseball." *Journal of Popular Culture*, IX (Fall 1975).
Dexter, Pete. "Black Sox Blues." *Esquire*, CII (Oct. 1984).
Eaton, W. Clement. "Frontier Life in Southern Arizona, 1851–1861." *Southwestern Historical Quarterly*, XXXVI (Jan. 1933).
Fidler, Douglas K., George Coroneos, and Michael Tamburro. "Frederick Jackson Turner, the Revisionists, and Sport Historiography." *Journal of Sport History*, II (Spring 1975).
Franks, Joel. "California and the Rise of Spectator Sports, 1850–1900." *Historical Society of Southern California Quarterly*, LXXI (Winter 1989).
_____. "Organizing California Baseball, 1859–1893." In Peter Levine, ed. *Baseball History 4: An Annual of Original Baseball Research*. Westport, Conn.: Meckler, 1989.
Fullerton, Hugh S. "Freak Plays That Decide Baseball Championships." *American Magazine*, LXXIV (May 1912).

_____. "The Right and Wrong of Baseball: Tricks and Schemes, Blocking and Interfering; The Art of Balking." *American Magazine* (Oct. 1911).
Grella, George. "White Lines and Green Fields: A Meditation on Baseball and the West." In Alvin L. Hall, ed. *Cooperstown Symposium on Baseball and the American Culture (1990)*. Westport, Conn.: Meckler in association with the State University of New York College at Oneonta, 1991.
Grosshandler, Stanley. "Right-Left Players Are Rare Birds." *Toronto Scorebook*, II (1978).
Harrison, T. P. "Tenney's All Star Team." *Baseball*, VII (July 1911).
Hoie, Robert C. "The Hal Chase Case." In Robert L. Davids, ed. *The Baseball Research Journal: Volumes 1 through 3*. Cleveland: Society for American Baseball Research, 1998.
_____. "The Hal Chase Story." *Grandstand Baseball Annual 1991*. Downey, Calif.: Joseph Wayman, 1992.
_____. "More About Chase." *Grandstand Baseball Annual 1991*. Downey, Calif.: Joseph Wayman, 1992.
"In Douglas." *Time*, VI (Sept. 21, 1925).
Irwin, Will. "With Chance in Bermuda." *Collier's* (Apr. 19, 1913).
Johnson, Jim. "Heroes and Villains." (Santa Cruz) *Mid-County Post*, Mar. 4–17, 1997.
Kimmel, Michael S. "Baseball and the Reconstitution of American Masculinity, 1880–1920." In Peter Levine, ed. *Baseball History 3: An Annual of Original Baseball Research*. Westport, Conn.: Meckler, 1990.
Kohout, Martin Donell. "The Prince of Darkness." In John B. Holway, ed. *The National Pastime: A Review of Baseball History*. No. 11. Cleveland: Society for American Baseball Research, 1992.
LaCasse, Geoff. "From Amity Wolf to Vancouver Beaver: A History of Baseball in BC." *Dugout*. June 1994.
_____. "Hal Chase in Victoria." *The National Pastime: A Review of Baseball History*. No. 15. Cleveland: Society for American Baseball Research, 1995.
Lavoie, Steven. "St. Mary's Has Sent Players to Majors for 100 Years." In Norman Macht, ed. *Northern California Baseball History*. Cleveland: Society for American Baseball Research, 1998.
Lloyd, F. R. "The Home Run King." *Journal of Popular Culture*, IX (Spring 1976).
Macht, Norman L. "Playing for John McGraw." In Peter Levine, ed. *Baseball History 2: An Annual of Original Baseball Research*. Westport, Conn.: Meckler, 1989.
Mrozek, Donald J. "The Image of the West in American Sport." *Journal of the West*, XVII (July 1978).
Murdock, E. "The Tragedy of Ban Johnson." *Journal of Sport History*, I (Spring 1974).
Nardinelli, Clark. "Judge Kenesaw Mountain Landis and the Art of Cartel Enforcement." In Peter Levine, ed. *Baseball History: An Annual of Original Baseball Research*. Westport, Conn.: Meckler, 1989.
Nielsen, Monty, and George W. Schubert. "An Examination of Professional Baseball Players as Heroes and Role Models." In Alvin L. Hall, ed. *Cooperstown Symposium on Baseball and the American Culture (1989)*. Westport, Conn.: Meckler in association with the State University of New York College at Oneonta, 1991.
Porter, Glenn. "Industrialization and the Rise of Big Business." In Charles W. Calhoun, ed. *The Gilded Age: Essays on the Origins of Modern America*. Wilmington, Del.: Scholarly Resources, 1996.
Riess, Steven A. "The Baseball Magnates and Urban Politics in the Progressive Era: 1895–1920." *Journal of Sport History*, I (Spring 1974).
_____. "Race and Ethnicity in American Baseball, 1900–1919." In Paul J. Zingg, ed. *The Sporting Image: Readings in American Sport History*. Lanham, Md.: University Press of America, 1988.
_____. "Sport and the Redefinition of American Middle-Class Masculinity, 1840–1900." In Steven A. Riess, ed. *Major Problems in American Sport History*. New York: Houghton-Mifflin, 1997.
Robinson, Ray. "Hal Chase: Baseball's Black Prince." *Argosy* (1959).
Royce, Josiah. "Provincialism: Based Upon a Study of Early Conditions in California." *Putnam's Magazine*, VII (Nov. 1909).

Ruhl, Arthur. "The Caliph and His Court." *McClure's Magazine*, XVII (Aug. 1901).
Sanborn, Irving E. "The Dollar Demon and the National Game." *Everybody's Magazine*, XXXII (May 1915).
Scheinin, Richard. "Hal Chase's Son, Grandson Say He's Being Treated Unfairly." San Jose *Mercury News*.
_____. "The Story of Hal Chase." San Jose *Mercury News*.
Smith, Leverett. "Ty Cobb, Babe Ruth and the Changing Image of the Athletic Hero." In Ray B. Browne, Marshall Fishwick, and Michael T. Marsden, eds. *Heroes of Popular Culture*. Bowling Green, Ohio: Bowling Green University Popular Press, 1972.
Splitter, Henry Winfred. "Los Angeles Recreation, 1846–1900: Part II." *Historical Society of Southern California Quarterly*, XLIII (June 1961).
Stallings, George T. "The Miracle Man's Own Story." *Collier's* (Nov. 28, 1914).
Stewart, Charles D. "The United States of Base-Ball." *Century Magazine*, LXXIV (June 1907).
Van Loan, C. E. "Baseball as the Bleachers Like It." *Outing*, LIV (Sept. 1909).
Voigt, David Q. "Reflections on Diamonds: American Baseball and American Culture." *Journal of Sport History*, I (Spring 1974).
Weiss, Bill. "The California League in Professional Baseball." In Norman Macht, ed. *Northern California Baseball History*. Cleveland: Society for American Baseball Research, 1998.
Zingg, Paul J. "The Phoenix at Fenway: The 1915 World Series and the Collegiate Connection to the Major Leagues." *Journal of Sport History*, XVII (Spring 1990).

Newspapers and Periodicals

Arizona *Daily Star* (Tucson)
Arizona *Republic* (Phoenix)
Baseball Magazine
Boston *Globe*
Boston *Herald*
Buffalo *Express*
Chicago *Daily Tribune*
Cincinnati *Enquirer*
Douglas (Ariz.) *Daily Dispatch*
Douglas (Ariz.) *Daily International*
Los Angeles *Examiner*
Los Angeles *Times*
Los Gatos (Calif.) *Times-Observer*
Los Gatos (Calif.) *Weekly*
New York *American*
New York *Evening Journal*
New York *Evening Post*
New York *Evening World*
New York *Globe and Commercial Advertiser*
New York *Herald*
New York *Herald Tribune*
New York *Journal American*
New York *Sun*
New York *Times*
New York *Tribune*
New York *World-Telegram*
Sacramento *Union*
St. Louis *Post-Dispatch*
San Francisco *Chronicle*
San Francisco *Examiner*
San Jose *Mercury-Herald*
San Jose *Mercury-News*
San Jose *News*
Sporting Life
The Sporting News
Time Magazine
Washington *Post*

Index

Adams, Brooks 2
Addington, Keene H. 137, 139
African American baseball players 103, 154
Agler, Joe 141, 147
Ainsmith, Eddie 191
Alberts, Walter 260
Alcorn, Robert S. 199, 227–29, 232, 233
Alexander, Grover Cleveland 208, 236–37, 241, 268, 310n. 99
Allen, Lee 162, 265–66
"All-Stars" games 143, 144, 154
Altrock, Nick 102, 284n. 12
American Association 121, 153, 158, 175
American League 3, 22, 25, 30, 32–34, 36, 76, 153–57; *see also* Johnson, Byron Bancroft (Ban); and specific teams
Ames, Harry 256
Ames, Red 89
Anderson, Fred 130
Anderson, John 31, 32, 38, 289n. 21
Anderson, O. K. 261
Angels *see* Los Angeles Angels
antitrust legislation *see* Sherman Antitrust Act
Arellanes, Frank 46, 63, 157
Arizona: Chase in semipro ball in 7, 111, 123, 249–60; Douglas Blues 252–56, 258–60; Jerome baseball team 252; Nogales Internationals in 249–52; son Hal in 256–57; statehood for 249; Williams baseball team 252, 261
Arkansas Travelers 175
Arrington, R. G. 32
Asinof, Eliot 246, 248, 306n. 106

Athletics *see* Philadelphia Athletics
Atlanta Crackers 94
Attell, Abe 241, 242, 244, 245, 246, 274
Auburn University 188
Augspurger, Owen B. 134, 135, 137
Augusta baseball team 65
Aulick, W. W. 67–68, 70
Austin, Jimmy 71, 72, 74, 80, 81, 84, 284n. 12, 294n. 110

Bagby, Jim 183
Baird, Al 220
Baird, Doug 181
Baker, Frank 88, 111
Baker, Newton D. 191
Ball, Phil 153, 155
Baltimore 6, 31
Baltimore Feds (Terrapins) 130, 142, 146, 148, 151, 156
Baltimore International League team 153, 156
Baltimore Orioles 78, 131, 179, 217, 225
Bancroft, Dave 165
Bancroft, Frank 194
Barnes, Jess 214, 223
Barrett, Charlie (Doc) 109, 262, 264, 265, 272, 309n. 86
Barrow, Ed 4, 217
Barry, Jack 38–39, 89
Bascou, Johnny 271, 272
baseball: all-time all-star teams 270–71, 273; attendance statistics for 2–3, 38; as big business 90, 96, 258; black players in 103, 154; as exempt from antitrust legislation 139–40, 156; gambling and bribery in 3, 5–8, 89, 116–17, 156, 196–200, 202, 204–10, 223–46, 248, 268, 273–77; in Mexico 250,

253–54, 255; National Commission ruling against moonlighting 53–55; newspaper coverage of generally 60; players banned or blacklisted from 5; public image of 3, 283n. 8; reserve clause in 125; semi-professional teams during offseason 102–3; Sunday baseball games prohibited 102–3, 181, 204; ten-day clause in 129, 130, 131, 138, 139, 203; and World War I 178–79, 187, 188, 190, 191, 199, 200; *see also* Black Sox scandal; and specific teams and players
Baseball Hall of Fame *see* National Baseball Hall of Fame
Baseball Writers of America 237
batting statistics *see* Chase, Hal; and specific players
Baum, Charlie 235, 236
Baum, Spider 63, 157
Beaumont baseball team 234
Becker, Sheriff 135–36
Beckley, Jake 26
Bedient, Hugh 144, 146
Belmont 13
Benton, Rube 117, 214, 220, 235, 238–40, 246, 248, 306n. 100
Benz, Joe 131
Berger, Victor 211
beriberi 270, 272
Bernal, John 256–57
Berry, Henry 157–58
Bert, Eugene 21–22, 23
Bescher, Bob 176–77
betting *see* Gambling and bribery

325

Index

Betzel, Bruno 176–77
Bevill, Lynn 260–61
Bijur, Justice 112
billiards 127, 193, 256–57, 262
Birtch, Paul 143
Bisbee (Ariz.) baseball team 256
Bissell, Herbert P. 137, 139–40, 144
black baseball players 103, 154
Black Sox scandal: arrests of Chase and Gandil 245–46, 274; Burns's involvement in 15; Chase's involvement in 5, 7, 15, 116, 239–42, 244–46, 248, 258, 268, 273–75; and Comiskey 7, 244; early knowledge and rumors of 224–25, 238, 239, 240; expulsion of Black Sox from organized baseball 7, 116; and Fallon 246, 248, 285n. 26; and Gandil 97, 241, 244, 246; and Gedeon 210; impact of, on public sentiment 212; indictments in 244, 245, 274; legal proceedings on 7, 239–40, 244–48, 274–75; and Maharg 97, 241; newspaper coverage of 241–42; Rothstein as mastermind of 6, 285n. 26; sources for information on 306n. 93
Blackburne, Earl 171
Blackburne, Lena 131, 191–92
Blair, Walter 129, 147
Blake, "Ananias" 27
Blanding, Fred 140
Blankenship, Cliff 33
Block, Bruno 73
Blues *see* Buffalo Federal League team (Buffeds or Blues)
Bodet, Gib 284n. 15
Bodie, Ping 100, 102, 116, 129, 157
Boeckel, Norman (Tony) 240, 248
Boehling, Joe 119
Borton, Babe 113–14, 117–19, 126, 127, 148, 235, 236
Boston 212
Boston Braves: and Dolan's death 48; Holke's trade to 214; Mathewson as president of 251; 1916 season 165, 171, 174; 1917 season 178, 180–82, 183; 1918 season 190, 191–93; 1919 season 218–19, 219; and Perry case 200, 202; Stallings as manager of 146, 155, 171, 192; suspension of Stallings as manager of 171; Tenney as

first baseman for 37; trade of Nehf to New York Giants 220; and trade rumors about Herzog 169; in World Series of 1914 76, 294n. 111; and World War I 178
Boston Red Sox: Bedient as player for 144; Carrigan as manager of 273; Frazee as owner of 202; interest in trading for Chase 63; 1905 season 38, 40, 41; 1906 season 42, 45; 1908 season 56; 1910 season 72; 1911 season 81–82, 83, 84, 85; 1912 season 94, 99; 1913 season 110, 113, 117, 121; 1915 and 1916 seasons 157, 273; 1918 season 217; 1919 exhibition games and season 216, 217; Speaker's salary 155; and Stahl's suicide 48; and trade rumors about Chase 98, 114; in World Series of 1918 202
Bottomley, Jim 284n. 13
Bradley, Bill 267
Bradley, Hugh 98
Brady, Diamond Jim 28–29
Brashear, Norman (Kitty) 46
Braves *see* Boston Braves
Brennan, William 150
Bresnahan, Roger 30
bribery *see* gambling and bribery
bridge games 195
British Columbia Amateur Base Ball League 16
Brookfeds *see* Brooklyn Federals (Brookfeds)
Brooklyn Dodgers 3, 63, 103, 104, 110, 276
Brooklyn Federals (Brookfeds) 129, 141, 144, 146, 147, 148, 150–51
Brooklyn Superbas: Daubert as first baseman for 159, 180, 203–4, 225; Daubert traded to Cincinnati Reds 180; and Dillon case 22–23, 287n. 67; Giants' interest in Myers of 220; 1916 season 166–67, 169, 171, 172, 174; 1917 season 178, 180; 1918 season 191, 193, 197; 1919 season 223; and World War I 190
Broun, Heywood 113
Brouthers, Dan 225
Brown, Bill 110, 256
Brown, Mordecai (Three-Finger) 125, 130, 148, 173
Brown, Rachael 244, 245
Browns *see* St. Louis Browns
Buchanan, Jim 33
Buckley, May 174–75

Buckman, C. T. 236
Bucknell University 36
Buckout, Al 87
Buffalo 143
Buffalo Bisons 143, 145, 153, 155, 178
Buffalo Federal League Booster Club 153
Buffalo Federal League team (Buffeds or Blues): and "All-Stars" games 143, 144, 154; Chase as first baseman for 132, 141; Chase as pitcher in exhibition games 149, 151, 154; Chase's batting and fielding statistics 143, 146, 148, 149, 151, 152; Chase's contract with 129; Chase's debut in Buffalo 132, 134–38; Chase's first game with 132; Chase's injuries 145, 146, 148, 149, 150; Chase's salary 155, 296n. 22; Chase's trip from Canada before debut game in Buffalo 134–35; fans' responses to Chase 132, 135, 140–41, 143, 147; financial problems of 150, 153, 154; legal battle over Chase's contract 134–40; Lord as manager of 147–48, 149, 151; Lord as player for 129, 147; merger of, with Bisons 153; 1914 exhibition games and season 132, 135–36, 141–43; 1915 exhibition games and season 144–52; photographs of Chase with 133, 136; pitchers for 142, 148–49; players for 129–30; poem on Chase 150; positive comments on Chase by the press 134, 141, 143, 148, 150; pregame festivities of 142; reactions to Chase's contract with 131; Schlafly as manager of 144, 145, 146, 147; ticket prices for 150, 154; and trade rumors 147
Buffalo Simon Pures 143
Buffeds *see* Buffalo Federal League team (Buffeds or Blues)
Burns, Bill 15, 179, 240–46, 248, 273, 274
Burns, Ed 46
Burns, George 214, 215, 220, 221
Burrell, Lyman 10
Bush, Donie 82
Bush, Joe 217
Butte (Mont.) baseball team 15–16
Byron, Bill 171, 179

Index

Cady, Hick 219
Caldwell, Ray 142, 143
California: Chance's ranch in 106, 128; Chase family's arrival in 10–11; Chase's homesickness for 32, 47, 258, 289n. 27; Chase's later life in 1, 7–8, 9, 269–77; Chase's youth in 11–13; earthquakes in 109; lumber business in 10, 11; spring floods in 124; *see also* California State League; Pacific Coast League
California State League (CSL) 14, 46, 53–55, 59, 61–64, 126, 273
Callaghan, Policeman 147
Callahan, Jimmy 116–19, 121, 122, 126–29, 138, 172
Calvo, Jack 119
Campbell, Vin 141
Canavan, Hugh 192
Canfield, Richard 28
Cardinals *see* St. Louis Cardinals
Carrigan, Bill 273
Carroll, Laura 179
Carroll, Richard T. (Buck) 129, 134–37, 142, 143
Carter, Paul 188, 239
"Casey at the Bat" (Thayer) 149
Casinos *see* Gambling
Caton, Buster 191
Cava, Andy 67
Cavanagh, John 28
Cavenee, James 11
Cavenee, Mary 11
The Celebrant (Greenberg) 278–79
Chance, Frank: batting average of, with Yankees 121; Caldwell's dispute with 142; California ranch of 106, 128; and charges of "laying down" against Chase 113; and Chase as second baseman for Yankees 106, 108, 110–11; Chase on abilities of 273; Chase's mimicking of 113; Chase's relationship with 26, 108, 111, 113; on Chicago Colts 21, 23; deafness of 113; dismissal of as manager of Chicago Cubs 105; dispute with Callahan about Borton and Zeider 118–19; as first baseman for Yankees 105–6, 107, 111, 225; injuries of 105, 113; on Los Angeles Angels 24; as manager of Los Angeles Angels 157; as manager of Yankees 106, 108; in Mathewson's book 68, 70; photograph of 107; resignation of, as Yankee manager 142; salary of 106; on Stockton baseball team 46; and trade of Chase to Chicago White Sox 113–14, 117, 118–19; and trade rumors about Chase 112; and White Sox players in spring of 1914 124; as Yankee manager 24, 142
Chandler, Happy 276–77
Chapman, John Jay 2
Chapman, Ray 102, 183
Chappell, Larry 119
Chase, Albert (Bert) 11
Chase, Anna Marion Cherurg: and Chase's baseball career 145, 148, 180, 215, 216; divorce of 243–44; homes of 143, 194, 199; illness of 166; marriage of 112–13; in New York 146, 170, 173–74, 180; at spring training in 1917 175; sweater stolen from 176; trip from Canada before Chase's debut game in Buffalo 134–35
Chase, Clifford 11
Chase, Edwin 11, 31, 278, 289n. 23
Chase, Elmer 10, 11
Chase, Ephraim 11
Chase, Foster 10
Chase, Hal: as alcoholic 1, 9, 250, 261, 270, 271, 272, 273; arrest of, for Sunday baseball games 102–3; athletic abilities of generally 80, 142; in automobile accidents 260, 261; as bartender 123, 252, 259; beard worn by 188, 256, 264; Bernie as possible wife or girlfriend of 265–66; birth of 10, 11; brawling by 147; on California chicken ranch 261; as car salesman 260; as card-shark 195; on career possibilities after baseball career 96; children of 6, 9, 18, 55, 71, 110, 256–58, 273; church attendance by 191; confusion about age of 23, 26, 43, 265, 309n. 86; death of 7, 8, 9, 18, 277; disinterest in money 5, 272; divorce from Anna Cherurg 6, 9, 243–44; divorce from Nellie Heffernan 6, 9, 99, 110, 112, 296n. 22; education of 12–16, 96, 286n. 18; engagement and marriage to Nellie Heffernan 46, 47, 49, 51, 55, 99, 273; family background on 9–11; fiction on 266–69, 278–79; financial irresponsibility of 5; grandchildren of 18, 281–82; grave of 278; during Great Depression 262–270; health problems and illnesses of 1, 7, 63, 64, 65, 72, 83, 97, 98, 172, 188, 190, 270, 271, 272, 276, 293n. 82; home of, in Buffalo 143; home of, in Cincinnati 194, 199; homesickness for California 32, 47, 258, 289n. 27; and horse racing 43–44, 166, 184, 186, 196; and hunting 184; idealization of, by press 36; injuries of 40, 41, 42, 44, 45, 51, 56, 65, 70, 72, 84, 86, 92, 99, 100, 109, 110, 115, 117, 119–21, 123, 126, 127, 129, 145, 146, 148, 149, 150, 164–67, 171, 172, 178, 180, 183, 186, 188, 190, 193, 221, 223; in later life 1, 7–8, 9, 269–77; marriage to Anna Marion Cherurg 112–13; and Mathewson 36, 62, 70, 87, 95; Mathewson's book on 37, 67–68, 70; middle name of 14, 286n. 10; and mother's fatal illness 254; musical about 290n. 45, 293n. 74; New York lifestyle of generally 47, 109–10, 118, 258; not elected to National Baseball Hall of Fame 266–67, 310n. 98; personality of 5, 7, 9, 87, 95, 157, 184, 186, 284n. 15; photographs of 12, 15, 19, 35, 57, 69, 70, 76, 79, 82, 85, 93, 101, 133, 136, 160, 163, 263, 269, 276; poems on 66, 115, 150; as pool player 127, 193, 256–57, 262; as prospector 261; selfishness of 71; son Hal's living with, in Arizona 256–57; in Tucson 261, 265, 266; as womanizer 55, 99, 243, 249, 265, 293n. 82; youth of 11–13
baseball career: aggressive on-field conduct by Chase 43, 61–62, 88, 120; Arizona semiprofessional baseball 7, 111, 123, 249–60; banning and blacklisting of Chase from organized baseball 5, 7, 156–57, 235–36, 275; batting and fielding statistics 4, 16, 20, 24, 41, 45, 52, 54, 58, 62, 67, 72, 77, 81, 84, 96, 99, 100, 102, 111, 118, 122, 143,

Index

146, 148, 149, 151, 152, 172, 173, 174, 178, 180, 183, 190, 191, 193, 208, 217, 219, 221, 235, 255, 256, 284n. 13; Black Sox scandal 5, 7, 15, 116, 239–42, 244–46, 248, 258, 268, 273–75; book on playing first base by Chase 184, 185; bribery and fixing schemes by Chase 4, 5–9, 18, 89, 116–17, 194–200, 204–10, 223–24, 226–28, 230–36, 238, 239–46, 248, 268, 273–75, 277–78, 306n. 103; Buffalo Federal League team (Buffeds or Blues) 132–52; as business with Chase 90, 96; as catcher 17, 19–20, 23; Chase's reflections on 186, 215–16, 271–76; Chicago White Sox 107, 113–23, 126–29; Cincinnati Reds 158, 159–96; Douglas (Ariz.) team 252–56, 258–60; El Paso team 260–61; Federal League contract 124–26, 129–32; as first baseman 3–4, 8, 18, 24, 34, 36–39, 41, 44–45, 50, 84, 95, 110–11, 115, 118, 132, 141, 161–62, 164, 167, 170, 180, 184, 217–18, 220–21, 225–26, 253, 255, 264, 265, 267, 268, 271, 284nn. 11–12; hearing on gambling charges against Chase and his exoneration 205–10, 228, 232, 233, 234, 235, 238, 246; international baseball tour 122–23; Jerome (Ariz.) team 252; Los Angeles Angels 21, 23–24, 31; Los Gatos High School baseball team 12–13; managers' negative views of 157, 159; managers' relationships with Chase generally 157, 184, 186, 214–15; Mayer Brothers semi-pro team 12, 13; Mexican National Baseball League 253–54; National Commission ruling against moonlighting 53–55; New York Giants 203, 204–5, 207, 209, 212, 214–24, 226, 272–73; New York Highlanders/Yankees player 24–26, 31–72, 90–104; New York Highlanders/Yankees player-manager 5, 73–90, 138, 206; Nogales Internationals player-manager 249–52; as outfielder 18, 24, 40, 52, 56–57, 84, 90, 111, 164–66,

170, 188; as pitcher 17, 20, 21, 23, 54, 57–58, 81, 144, 149, 151, 173, 182–83, 183, 236, 255; St. Mary's College baseball coach 46–47; salary figures 16, 31, 42, 46, 47, 49, 64, 67, 73, 77, 90, 112, 124, 125–26, 127, 138, 139, 155, 290n. 76, 291n. 94, 296n. 22; San Jose Mission League club 234, 235–36; San Jose Prune Pickers 42, 46, 53–55, 61; Santa Clara College team 13–16, 15, 19, 20–21, 23, 286n. 23; as second baseman 14, 21, 24, 39, 84, 89, 99, 106, 108–11, 170, 171, 172; as shortstop 41, 54, 83; Soquel Giants semi-pro team 13; Stockton Millers 61–63; summary of 9; suspension from Reds for "indifferent playing" 193–200, 205, 207, 209, 238, 243–44; as third baseman 17; versatility of Chase 14, 17, 18, 23, 108–9, 154, 170; Victoria Baseball Club 16–20; Williams (Ariz.) team 252, 261; *see also* specific teams
Chase, Hal (grandson) 18
Chase, Hal (pitcher from Redwood City) 157
Chase, Hal E., Sr. (son): in Arizona with Chase 256–57; on athletic ability of Edwin Chase 289n. 23; baseball career considered by 257; birth of 55, 71; on Chase as womanizer 249; on Chase's disinterest in money 5, 272; on Chase's homesickness for California 47, 258, 289n. 27; on Chase's innocence of illegal doings 6, 18, 257–58; on Chase's lack of bitterness 7; childhood of 84, 110, 112; death of 281; estrangement of, from Chase 6, 9, 273; and parents' divorce 110, 112; payments from National Traffic Safety Institute (NTSI) to 281
Chase, Harold 11
Chase, Israel 11
Chase, James Edgar 10–11, 270, 278, 286n. 16
Chase, Jeff 281–82
Chase, Josiah W. 10
Chase, Mary Cavenee 11, 254, 278
Chase, Nellie Heffernan *see* Heffernan (Chase Brown), Nellie

Chase, Stephen Hall (Si) 10
Chase (S. H.) Company 10, 11
Chattanooga Lookouts 80–81
Cherlet, Harry 207
Cherurg, Anna Marion *see* Chase, Anna Marion Cherurg
Cherurg, Rudolph 112, 207
Chesbro, Jack 25, 31, 39, 48, 50, 57–58, 57, 294n. 111
Chicago 118, 212
Chicago Baseball League 245
Chicago Colts 21, 22
Chicago Cubs: Chance as player for Colts (later Cubs) 21; Chance's dismissal as manager of 105; and Federal League 126; and gambling scandals 227–34, 236–42, 246, 305n. 50; and Hendrix gambling scandal 237–38, 239, 242; and Magee's involvement in gambling 227–34, 238, 239, 240–41, 246, 305n. 50; Magee's suit against 228–33; Mollwitz as player for 170, 172, 191; 1916 season 162, 164, 165, 171–72, 173; 1917 season 177–78, 180, 181, 182; 1918 season 188, 190, 200, 218; 1919 season 221; 1920 season 236–37, 238; possible trade of Herzog to 169; release of Magee by 227, 231; salaries of 155–56; Seaton as player with 158; series with Chicago White Sox in 1913 122; and trade rumors about Chase 206; Weeghman as owner of 7, 153, 155–56, 178; in World Series 63, 202
Chicago Federals (Chifeds) 124, 126, 130, 132, 141, 142, 147, 148, 150–53, 155
Chicago Ladies' Club 61
Chicago Nationals 23, 122
Chicago White Sox: Callahan as manager of 116–19, 121, 122, 126–29, 138; Chase as first baseman for 118; Chase traded to 107, 113–17; Chase's batting and fielding statistics 118, 122; and Chase's contract with Federal League 124–26, 129, 130–35; Chase's injuries 119, 120–21, 123, 126, 127, 129; Chase's salary 126, 127, 138, 155; Comiskey as president of 3, 40, 111, 113, 119, 227; Duffy as manager of 147; errors committed by Chase 118, 119, 128; fans' responses to Chase 120, 127; Fournier

Index

as first baseman for 157; and Frank Chance Day 111; Gandil as player with 92; international tour in 1913 122–24; legal battle over Chase's contract 134–40; and "loaning" of Powers to Highlanders 40; Lord's departure from 128, 147; 1905 season 40, 41; 1906 season 43, 44, 45; 1907 season 51; 1910 season 72–73, 74, 293n. 73; 1911 season 83; 1912 season 97, 98, 99, 100; 1913 season 111, 116–23; 1914 exhibition games and season 126–29, 138; 1916 season 157; pitchers for 116, 128; players for, in 1913, 116; poem on Chase 115; positive comments on Chase by the press 118, 120, 121; Roush as player for 120, 121; rumors of players leaving for Federal League 131; St. Mary's College team playing 46; series with Chicago Cubs in 1913 122; sign-stealing charges against Highlanders by 71–72, 75; trade of Borton and Zeider to Yankees 113–14, 117, 118–19, 126; and trade rumors about Chase 91, 98; in World Series of 1906 116; in World Series of 1919 224–25, 265; and World War I 190; see also Black Sox scandal; and specific players and managers

Chifeds see Chicago Federals (Chifeds)

Chino (N.Mex.) Twins 256, 259, 260

Cicotte, Eddie 116, 120, 123, 224, 241, 244, 246

Cincinnati 194, 199, 220, 305n. 26

Cincinnati Reds: attendance figures for 219–20; and Black Sox scandal 7; and Blankenship 33; Chase acquired by 158, 159, 161; Chase as first baseman for 161–62, 164, 167, 170, 180; Chase as outfielder for 164–66, 170, 188; Chase as pitcher in exhibition games 173, 182–83; Chase as possible manager of 169–70; Chase as second baseman for 170, 171, 172; Chase's absence from, at beginning of 1916 season 161, 162; Chase's batting and fielding statistics 172–74, 178, 180, 183, 190, 191, 193, 208; Chase's debut game with 162; Chase's injuries and illnesses 164, 165–67, 171, 172, 178, 180, 183, 188, 190, 193; Chase's involvement in throwing games and gambling 194–200, 204–10, 223–24, 226–28, 230–32, 239–40; Chase's salary 243; Chase's suit against 199, 215; Daubert traded to, in 1919 180, 212; errors committed by Chase 171, 172, 180, 188, 190, 193; exhibition series against Cleveland Indians in 1917 183, 208; and failure of Federal League 158; fans' responses to Chase 170, 174–75, 183, 194, 220; fight between Magee and Neale 193; finances of 202–3; floral tribute to Chase 176; Herzog as manager of 158, 159, 161, 164–66; Herzog traded by 167, 169; Herzog's injury 165, 166; Johnson's departure for Federal League 139; lack of seriousness in ball playing 181–82, 192; Magee as player for 187, 191–93; Marsans' departure for Federal League 129; Mathewson as manager of 36, 167, 169, 170, 171, 174, 186; Mathewson as pitcher for 173; Mollwitz as first baseman for 158–59, 161, 162, 164, 165, 167, 170; Mollwitz's injury 158–59, 161; Bill Moriarty with 63; Murphy as owner of 105; 1916 exhibition games and season 158–75, 186; 1917 exhibition games and season 175–84; 1918 exhibition games and season 187–94, 199–200; 1919 season 219–21, 224; photographs of Chase with 160, 163; positive comments on Chase by the press 170–73, 178, 180, 181, 183, 184, 186; Roush as player for 120; rowdiness of games with New York Giants 219–20; sale of Mollwitz to Cubs 170; suspension of Chase for "indifferent playing" 193–200, 205, 207, 209, 238, 243–44; trade of Chase to New York Giants 212, 214; violation of Sunday baseball prohibition 181; in World Series of 1919 224–25; and World War I 178, 187, 188, 199; see also Black Sox scandal

Clarkdale Smelter (Ariz.) baseball team 252

Clarke, Tom 162, 170, 175

Cleveland Indians 155, 156, 176, 183, 198, 208

Cleveland Naps: 1905 season 39, 40, 41; 1906 season 44, 45; 1907 season 50, 51; 1911 season 84, 86; 1912 season 97, 98, 100, 102; 1913 season 120, 121

Cloak, Frank, Jr. 270, 310n. 106

Cobb, Ty: on catcher position as difficult 95; compared with Chase 6, 277; criticism of McGraw by 176; feud with Dubuc 218; and fight with Herzog 175–76; financial acumen of 5; as free agent after 1918 season 203; and Griffith's assault on fan 50; hitting by 58, 82, 84, 87; Jennings as manager of, with Detroit Tigers 4; and Mathewson 176; in National Baseball Hall of Fame 267; salary of 155; suspension of, for violence against fan 97, 117, 241; on Wolverton as manager of Yankees 94

Cohan, George M. 5

Cohn, L. H. 16, 19, 287n. 51

Collins, Eddie 129, 137, 265

Collins, Shano 116, 121

Colts see Chicago Colts

Columbia University 262

Columbus baseball team 94

Comiskey, Charles: and Black Sox scandal 7, 244; on Chase trade to White Sox 113, 119; and Chase's contract with Federal League 130, 131, 132, 134, 139, 140; as Chicago White Sox president 3; on crookedness and baseball 3; and Frank Chance Day 111; on gambling 202; and international tour for Chicago White Sox 122; on "loaning" of Powers to Yankees 40; popularity of 131; relationship with players 227; sixty-fourth birthday of 120; and World Series of 1919 224

Conlin, Bill 271

Connor, Joe 41

Conroy, Wid 40, 57, 63

Coolidge, Calvin 212

Copper League 259, 260–61, 308n. 28
Corbett, Jim 13
Corbett, Joe 13, 157
Corum, Bill 262, 264, 265, 266–67
Costello, Frank 28
Costello, James 230–33, 306n. 103
Coughlin, Bill 63
Coveleskie, Stan 183
Cox, George B. 7
Cox, James M. 178–79, 219
Crandall, Otis 149
Crane, William 135, 136
Crawford, Sam 44, 58, 68, 119, 122
Cree, Birdie 81, 86, 100
Criger, Lou 267, 310n. 98
Crockett, Davy 74
Croker, Boss 6, 29
Cross, Lave 43, 88, 120
Crowe, Robert E. 239, 244, 245–46
Cruise, Walton 177
Crusinberry, James 238
CSL *see* California State League (CSL)
Cuba Giants 154
Cubs *see* Chicago Cubs
Curtiss, Glenn 134
Cutshaw, George 167, 169, 180

Dahlen, Bill 30
Daley, Arthur 277
Daley, George Herbert 113
Dalker, Albert 243
Dalton, Jack 149
Daniel, Dan 209, 220, 221, 224, 234
Daniels, Bert 73, 74, 80, 98
Daubert, Jake 103–4, 159, 174, 180, 203–4, 212, 220, 221, 225
Davenport, Dave 138
Davis, George 41, 51, 284n. 12
Davis, Harry 59–60, 82
Davis, Tom 73, 74
Deal, Charlie 182
Delahanty, Frank 44, 135
Demaree, Al 272
Demmitt, Ray 131
De Passe, I. O. 207
Depression *see* Great Depression
Dernoga 154
Detroit Tigers: Cobb's salary with 155; and Cobb's suspension for violence against fan 97, 117, 241; feud between Cobb and Dubuc 218; interest in trading for Chase 63–64; Jennings as manager of 4, 157; 1905 season 38, 39, 40, 41; 1906 season 44, 45; 1907 season 50; 1908 season 57–58, 59; 1910 season 72; 1911 season 81, 82, 84; 1912 season 97, 117; 1913 season 111, 118, 119, 121; 1914 season 128; 1917 exhibition games 175–76; 1918 exhibition games of 188; Stallings as manager of 61, 76; Stallings's attempted sale of, to National League 76; and trade rumors about Chase 117; in World Series of 1908 63; *see also* Cobb, Ty; and specific players
Dever, William E. 244
Devery, William S. (Big Bill) 6, 25, 29–30, 74, 142, 289n. 15
Devore, Josh 102–3
Diamond, Legs 28
Dillon, Frank (Pop) 22–24, 26, 31, 33, 34, 287n. 67
DiMaggio, Joe 271
Dirnberger, Michael F. 137
Dodgers *see* Brooklyn Dodgers
Dolan, Albert (Cozy) 303n. 43, 309n. 46
Dolan, Father Albert O. 242
Dolan, Patrick 48
Donlin, Turkey Mike 30, 78, 96, 123, 175
Doren, George 270
Douglas, James 252
Douglas, Phil 220, 221
Douglas (Ariz.) Blues 252–56, 258–60
Downs, Red 63
Doyle, Charlie 61
Doyle, Dirty Jack 22, 31, 40, 78
Doyle, Larry 102–3, 172, 214–18, 220, 241–42, 271, 272
Drachman, Roy P. 250, 262, 265, 266
drafting of minor league players 26, 32–34
Dreyfuss, Barney 154, 202
Driessen, Dan 284n. 13
Driscoll, Dave 181
Drucke, Louis 102–3
Dubuc, Jean 117, 218, 240, 242, 246, 248, 274
Duffy, Hugh 71–72, 147
Dugdale, Dan 18–19
Dunn, Jack 91
Dunwell, J. W. 103–4
Durocher, Leo 276

earthquakes 109
Eastern League 49, 137
Ebbets, Charles 169, 180, 204, 220, 231

Ehmke, Howard 154
El Paso baseball team 254, 255, 256, 260–61
Elberfeld, Norman (Kid): Chase's dislike of 58, 64, 65; Chase's friendship with 65, 66–67; errors by, in 1907 season 50; injuries of 41, 48; as manager of Highlanders 56–60; and National Baseball Hall of Fame 267; in 1905 Highlander season 31, 32, 40, 41; in 1908 Highlander season 65; photograph of 57; Stallings on 294n. 111; suspensions of 40, 45, 51; on Washington Senators team 71, 77
Elias, Francisco 250
eligibility rules for college athletics 14
Eller, Hod 188, 191–92, 231, 234
Elliott, Gene 82, 86
Elliott, Rowdy 172
Emerson, Elmer 16, 18–19, 20, 53
Engle, Clyde 71, 82, 142, 144, 146, 150, 151
Enwright, Charlie 61, 62, 63
Essick, Bill 235
Evans, Billy 225–26, 284n. 12
Everett baseball team 17–18
Evers, Johnny 23, 105, 171

Fairly, Ron 284n. 13
Fallon, William J. 246, 248, 285n. 26, 307n. 122
Fanning, Skeeter 127
Farnsworth, Bill 271, 272
Farrell, Frank J.: and Chance's charges against Chase 113; and Chance's resignation as Yankee manager 142; and Chance's signing with Yankees 105, 106; and Chase as manager of Yankees 76, 89, 90, 138; and Chase as second baseman 109; and Chase's departure from Highlanders during 1908 season 59, 64; on Chase's injury 56; and Chase's managerial aspirations 74, 75; and Chase's moonlighting on San Jose team 54; and Chase's return to Yankees in 1909 64–65; and Chase's salary with Highlanders/Yankees 49, 54, 90, 126, 290n. 76; and dissension between Chase and Stallings 72–75; and Elberfeld as manager of Highlanders 56, 58, 60; and

Index

Elberfeld's suspension 51; and financial success of Highlanders 41; and free admissions for Highlander fans 38; gambling house of 6, 25, 29; and Griffith's resignation from Highlanders 56; and Highlanders' 1905 season 41; and Highlanders' 1907 season 48; as Highlanders' owner 6, 25, 30, 42; and horse racing 43–44, 54; patronizing attitude of toward baseball players 54; relationships between managers and 91; and Stallings as manager of Highlanders 60–61; and trade of Chase to Chicago White Sox 117; and trade rumors about Chase 98; and Wolverton as manager of Yankees 91
Farrell, James T. 120, 157, 242
Farry, Frank 53
Federal League 123–26, 129–32, 137–40, 144, 150, 153–57; *see also* specific teams
Feeney, Tom 14
Felsch, Happy 244, 255
Ferris, Hobe 71
Fields, Mamie 78
Firestone, Mrs. Harvey S., Sr. or Jr. 249, 307n. 1
first basemen *see* Chase, Hal; and other specific players
Fischer, Fred 144
Fisher, Bobby 166, 172
Fisher, Ray 5, 86, 120, 195
Fitzgerald, Justin (Wingo) 171, 193
Fitzpatrick, Ed 171
Flack, Max 169, 182
Fleischmann, Julius 202–3
Fletcher, Art 169, 176, 214, 217–21, 223
Fohl, Lee 183
Ford, Russ 85, 98, 100, 102, 129, 130, 142, 143, 145, 148–49, 272
Fort Bayard Veterans (N.Mex.) 254, 256, 258–60
Foster, John B. 215
Fournier, Jack 157
Foxx, Jimmie 266, 267
Franklin, Benjamin 245
Frazee, Harry 202
Freedman, Andrew 25, 30
Fresno baseball team 63
Friedman, Sam 250
Frisch, Frankie 220, 229, 309n. 46
Frishberg, David 290n. 45, 293n. 74

Frisk, Emil 33
Frontier League 254–56, 259
Frothingham, Magistrate 181
Fullerton, Hugh 308n. 34
Fultz, Dave 41

gambling and bribery: in baseball 3, 5–8, 89, 194–200, 202, 204–10, 223–46, 248, 268, 273–77; Chase's comments on, in later life 275–77; Chase's involvement in 4, 5–8, 9, 18, 89, 116–17, 194–200, 204–10, 223–24, 226–28, 230–36, 238, 239–46, 248, 258–59, 268, 273, 306n. 103; on Chicago Cubs–Philadelphia Phillies games in 1920 236–37, 238, 239, 242; in Frontier League 258–59; hearing on charges against Chase and his exoneration 205–10, 228, 232, 233, 234, 235, 238, 246, 304n. 89; by Hendrix of Chicago Cubs 237–38, 239, 242; by Magee of Chicago Cubs 227–34, 238, 239, 240–41, 246, 305n. 50; in New York 6, 25, 27–30, 204; newspapers on 237–39; by O'Connell and Dolan of New York Giants 256, 303n. 43, 308–9n. 46; in Pacific Coast League 234, 235–36, 238; players' response to exoneration of Chase 210, 304n. 89; in Saratoga 27, 28; on World Series 224–25; Zimmerman's involvement in 117, 123, 172, 223, 224, 226–27, 239–40, 241; *see also* Black Sox scandal; Horse racing
Gandil, Arnold "Chick": on Arizona semipro teams 255, 256, 258, 259; and Black Sox scandal 97, 241, 244, 246; on Chicago White Sox team 92, 227; as manager of Idaho team 227; photograph of 245; on Washington Senators team 92, 110
Ganzel, John 31, 37, 38, 39, 151, 156, 158, 175
Gardiner, Asa Bird 29
Gardner, Earle 84, 86, 100
Gardner, Larry 110
Garvey, Steve 284n. 13
Gary, Elbert 212
Gates, Charles 28
Gates, Edward E. 129, 137
Gates, John W. "Bet-a-Million" 27–28
Gedeon, Joe 117, 210

Gehrig, Lou 3, 4, 266, 267, 271, 283n. 10, 284n. 12
George, King of England 124
George, Henry 2
George, Lefty 192
Georgia Tech 145
Geraci, Anton 261
Getz, Gene 176–77
Giants *see* New York Giants
Gilmore, James A. 123, 125–26, 131, 144, 150, 153, 154, 155
Gleason, Kid 124, 126, 127, 128, 225, 284n. 12
golf 80, 181
Gonzalez, Mike 218
Gooch, Mary 11
Gordon, Aaron 261
Gordon, Joseph W. 25, 30
Gordon, Waxey 28
Gould, Jay 2
Gowdy, Hank 178, 219
Graham, Charlie 13, 15, 63
Graham, Frank 3, 71, 113
Graham, George Frederick "Peaches" 306–7n. 106
Grant, Lester 272, 274
Grayson, Harry 265, 277
Great Depression 262–270
Greenberg, Eric Rolfe 278–79
Greene, Carolyn 28
Gregg, Vean 97
Griffith, Clark: and alcohol use by players 55; and Anderson sold to Washington Senators 289n. 21; and Chase's absences from Highlanders at beginnings of seasons 31–34, 47–49; and Chase's batting 42; and Chase's 1907 contract 46, 47; dissatisfaction of Highlander players with 50; and drafting of Chase for Highlanders 26; and Highlanders' 1905 season 37–41; and Highlanders' 1907 season 48–51; and Highlanders' 1908 season 55–56; as manager and owner of Washington Senators 92, 175, 292n. 25; physical assault against fan by 50; as pitcher for Washington Senators 102; as player-manager of Highlanders 25, 184; praise for Chase by 4, 39, 41–42; resignation of, from Highlanders 55–56
Griffith, Mrs. Tommy 175
Griffith, Tommy 164, 165, 171–72, 182, 184, 191
Griven, Henry J. 136
Groh, Heinie 166, 171, 172, 175, 181–84, 190, 197, 199, 219
Grover Gulch Wildcats 13

Index

Hall of Fame *see* National Baseball Hall of Fame
Handford, Charlie 136
Hanlon, Ned 22–23, 31
Hanna, William B. 221
Harrington, E. D. 250–52
Harris, Henry 21–22
Harrison, Pete 173
Hart, James A. 22
Hartley, Grover 103
Hartzell, Roy 81, 86, 100, 108, 118, 120
Haywood, Big Bill 211
Healley, J. J. 134, 135
Heffernan (Chase Brown), Nellie: alimony for 110, 112, 296n. 22; and Chase with smallpox 65; Chase's regrets about 273; children of 55, 71, 99, 110; divorce from Chase by 99, 110, 112, 296n. 22; engagement of, to Chase 46, 47, 49; family of 46; and illegal disposal of body of infant 51; marital problems of 99; marriage of, to Bill Brown 110; marriage of, to Chase 55; move to California by 110
Heffernan, May 46
Heffernan, Mr. and Mrs. Thomas 46
Hemphill, Charlie 80
Hempstead, Harry 169, 170, 202, 204
Hendrix, Claude 125, 236, 237, 239, 242
Henriksen, Olaf 98
Henry Grays 173
Herne, John F. 150
Herrmann, August (Garry): and Chance's sale to Yankees 105; and charges against Chase for gambling on Cincinnati Reds 198, 199, 204, 207, 209–10; and Chase's contract 159, 161; and Chase's suspension from Cincinnati Reds 194, 195, 196, 199, 244; and finances of Cincinnati Reds 202–3; gambling by 7; and Magee's release 231; and Magee's suit against Chicago Cubs 229, 233; and Marsans' departure to St. Louis Feds 129, 139; as National Commission member 7, 105, 200, 202; and signing of contract jumpers after end of Federal League 156; and trade of Herzog 167, 169, 170; and war against gambling on baseball 225; and World War I 178–79; *see also* Cincinnati Reds
Herzog, Buck: on Boston Braves team 191, 192; on Chicago Cubs team 237, 239; cleared of suspicion on throwing game 176; Cobb's fight with 176; consequences of association with Chase generally 117; gambling charges against 235, 239–40, 241; injury of 165, 166; as manager of Cincinnati Reds 158, 159, 161, 164–66, 240; on New York Giants team 170, 176; testimony of, on gambling charges before grand jury 240, 306n. 100; trade rumors about 169; trade to New York Giants 170
Heydler, John A.: and Benton-Herzog hearing on gambling charges 240; and Benton's charges against Chase and Herzog 235; and Black Sox scandal 273–74; and Chase's dismissal of Chase from New York Giants 306n. 103; and hearing on gambling charges against Chase and his exoneration 205–10, 212, 232–35, 238, 244, 246; and Herrmann's comments on gambling charges against Chase 199; and Magee's involvement in gambling 227–33, 240–41; and Perry case 200; photograph of 201
Highlanders *see* New York Highlanders (later Yankees)
Hildebrand, George 46
Hill, Carmen 162
Hodges, Frank H. 254
Hoff, Chet 87, 293n. 77
Hogg, Bill 31, 56, 57
Hogg, Brad 219
Hoie, Bob 5, 265, 286n. 10, 290n. 82
Holke, Walter 203, 204, 212, 214, 216
Hollywood High School baseball team 244
Holmes, Oliver Wendell, Jr. 211
Holness, Jimmy 17, 20
home run hitters 152, 174, 216–17; *see also* specific players
Hooper, Harry 46, 47
Hoppe, Willie 193, 272
Hornsby, Rogers 177, 220
horse racing 27, 28, 43–44, 54, 89, 166, 184, 186, 196, 197
horseback riding 80
Hoskins, Doc 166
How to Play First Base (Chase) 184, 185
Howell, Watkins F. 10
Hoyne, Maclay 239
Huff, George 91
Hughes, Rupert 27
Hunter, Herb 172
hunting trip 184

Indianapolis baseball team 81, 94
Indianapolis Feds 130, 141, 142, 153
Indians *see* Cleveland Indians
Interborough Subway Guards 218
International baseball tours 122–24
International League 89, 91, 118, 131, 132, 137, 143, 145, 153, 155, 156, 158, 221
Internationals *see* Nogales Internationals
Irwin, Arthur 91, 108, 109, 142
Irwin, Charlie 21
Isaminger, Jimmy 241

Jackson, Joe 190, 212, 244, 245, 256, 267, 277, 310n. 98
Jackson baseball team 34
Jacobson, Merwin 172
Jarman, Al 61
Jennings, Hughie 4, 84, 91, 157, 225
Jerome, William Travers 29
Jersey City baseball team 37, 71, 109, 181
Johnson, Byron Bancroft (Ban): American League founded by 25; banning of Chase and Stovall from American League 156–57; and Black Sox scandal 246; California State League and National Agreement 64; and Chance's signing with Yankees 105, 106; and charges of "laying down" against Chase 76; and Chase as player-manager of Nogales Internationals 250; and Chase's betting on Cincinnati Reds 199; and Chase's Federal League contract 131–32, 134; and Chase's involvement in gambling 234, 242, 250; and Chase's replacement for Yankee manager 91; and Chase's return to Yankees from California 64; Cobb suspended by, for violence against fan 97; and dissension between

Stallings and Chase 73, 75–76, 132; Elberfeld suspended by 40; and Federal League 131, 154; feud between Stallings and 61, 76; and Gedeon's expulsion from baseball 210; importance of New York Highlanders for 25, 30, 54, 59; and Mexican National Baseball League 254; and Pacific Coast League 22, 32, 34; and Perry case 200; and shortened 1918 season 200; and sign-stealing charges against Highlanders 71–72; and Stallings's attempted sale of Detroit Tigers to National League 76; and World Series of 1918 202; and World War I 200; and Yankees' trade of Chase for Borton and Zeider of Chicago White Sox 119
Johnson, Ernie 235
Johnson, George (Chief) 139, 140
Johnson, Otis 81, 86
Johnson, Walter 4, 91–92, 95–96, 98, 103, 123, 129, 137, 175, 267, 273
Johnston, Doc 102
Jolson, Al 5, 175, 187
Jones, Davy 44, 84, 125, 130
Jones, Fielder 91
Joss, Addie 85
Juarez Indians 255–56, 258, 260

Kaiser, Al 141
Kansas City Blues 153, 175
Kansas City Feds (Kawfeds) 139, 148–51, 153, 154, 156
Kauff, Benny 117, 155, 180, 190, 214, 219, 221
Kawfeds *see* Kansas City Feds (Kawfeds)
Keating, Ray 117
Keefe, Bobby 14–15, 179
Keefe, Mrs. Bobby 179
Keeler, Willie 31, 36, 41, 42, 49, 57, 91, 225, 284n. 12, 294n. 111
Kelly, George 4, 221, 229, 309n. 46
Kelly, Jack 149
Kerr, Dickie 224
Killefer, Wade 63, 164, 170
Killifers, Bill 140
King, Lee 220
Kinkaid, Ellis G. 134, 135, 137
Kitson, Frank 50
Kleinow, Red 32, 48
Klem, Bill 219
Kling, Johnny 267

Kluszewski, Ted 284n. 13
Knetzer, Elmer 178
Knight, Jack 71, 74, 81, 86, 91
Knowles, Fred 76, 294n. 108
Koelsch, William F. H. 25–26, 34, 37–40, 42, 283n. 8
Kofoed, J. C. 184, 186
Kohler 182
Konetchy, Ed 165
Kopf, Larry 177, 182, 219, 220
Krapp, Gene 130, 144
Krause, Harry 48
Krotel, Magistrate 103
Kuhel, Joe 284n. 13

labor strikes 211, 212
LaChance, Candy 284n. 13
Laird, Tom 271
Lajoie, Napoleon 4, 43, 68
Lake, Fred 91
Lambs' Club 307n. 122
Landis, Kenesaw Mountain: as baseball commissioner 7, 116, 248, 275–76; and Black Sox scandal 7, 210, 244; and Chase on Nogales Internationals team 250; Chase's praise for 275–76; correspondence between Chase and 275; failure to ban Chase after Black Sox scandal 7, 248, 275; and Federal League suit 144, 156; and O'Connell-Dolan scandal 303n. 43, 309n. 46; photograph of 247; and Sedition Act 211; and Standard Oil antitrust violations 144
Lane, F. C. 94–97
Lange, Bill 26
Lange, Frank 97
Lanigan, Ernest J. 58, 59, 72, 138, 140
Lansky, Meyer 28
LaPorte, Frank 48, 57, 81, 130
Lapp, Jack 88
Lardner, Ring 76, 115, 117, 119, 126, 130
League of Nations 211
Leavell, Harry (Ha Ha) 154
Leifield, Lefty 46
Lesher, J. C. 236
Leverenz, Walt 236
Levi, Ben 245
Levi, Louis 245
Lewis, Duffy 82
Lexow Committee 29
Lieb, Fred 108, 113, 216, 218, 219, 221, 277, 304n. 89, 306n. 103
Lincoln Giants 103
Linde Airs 154
Lindsay, Bunny 258
Lindsay, Pinky 45
Lobert, Hans 123, 169

Logansport (Ind.) Ottos 182–83
Lohman, Pete 26
Lomoor baseball club 236
Long, Danny 26
Long, Tommy 166, 176
Loomis, Fred 238–39
Lord, Harry 116, 121, 127–30, 147–49, 151
Los Angeles Angels: Chance as manager of 157; Chase with 21, 23–24, 31; Dillon as first baseman for 22, 287n. 67; and Dillon's contract dispute 22–23, 26, 33, 34; exhibition series between Chicago Colts and 21, 22; loss of Newton and Chase from 24, 26; Morley's prevention of Chase's move to Highlanders 31–34; and 1903 pennant 22; 1904 season 24
Louden, Billy 130, 144, 149, 151, 156, 158, 161–62, 166, 172, 174
Low, Seth 30
Loyola Marymount University 21
Luciano, Charles (Lucky) 28
lumbago 148, 149
lumber business 10, 11
Luque, Adolfo (Dolf) 192, 220
Lusitania 126
lynchings 212

MacBeth, Bill 271, 272
Mack, Connie 38, 59–60, 84, 91, 184, 200, 284n. 12
Mackall, J. L. 242
Macon baseball team 48
Madden, Esther Wright 55
Madera baseball team 236
Madison baseball team 121
Magee, Lee: and betting scandal 227–34, 237, 238, 239, 240–41, 246, 305n. 50; on Cincinnati Reds team 187, 191–93; consequences of association with Chase generally 117; fight with Neale 193; photograph of 189; as player-manager of Brookfeds 144, 146, 151; release of, by Cubs 227, 231; suit against Chicago Cubs 228–33; as umbrella-toting barnstormer 123, 144
Magee, Sherwood "Sherry" 187, 197, 200, 234
Maggert, Harley 157, 236
Maharg, Billy 97, 241, 242, 306–7n. 106
Maisel, Fritz 120

malaria 72, 293n. 82
Maloney, Pat 100
Mamaux, Al 190
Mann Act 188, 218
Maranville, Rabbit 155, 169, 218–19
Marcy, William H. 137
Marquard, Rube 88, 193
Marriott, Bill 182
Marsans, Armando 129, 138, 139, 140
Marshall, Cy 151
Marshall, S. L. A. 257, 258–59, 260, 277
Martin, Carmel 53
Martin, Ethel Monroe 51
Martin, Jack 4, 100, 293n. 77
Martin, Mike 51, 53, 58–59
Mason, Walter C. 145, 147–50
Massey, Roy 191–92
Mathewson, Christy (Matty): as bridge player 195; Chase on pitching abilities of 273; and Chase's betting on Cincinnati Reds games 194–95, 198, 208, 268; and Cobb 176; compared with Chase 36, 62, 251; compared with Johnson 95–96; departure of, from Cincinnati Reds 199, 203; fiction on 278; health problems of 251; injury of 216; and Jolson 175; and Magee's involvement with betting scandal 230–31; as manager of Cincinnati Reds 36, 167, 169, 170, 171, 174, 175, 186; and McGraw 37, 167, 169, 203; musical about 290n. 45, 293n. 74; in National Baseball Hall of Fame 267; as New York Giants coach 203, 215, 223; on New York Giants team 30, 36–37, 88; photograph of 168; as pitcher for Cincinnati Reds 173; as president of Boston Braves 251; statistical record for 95; suspension of Chase for "indifferent playing" 193–96, 205, 207, 238, 244; *Won in the Ninth* written by 37, 67–68, 70, 290n. 45, 293n. 74; in World Series of 1911 87–88; in World War I 199, 251
May, J. L. 265–66
Mayberry, John 284n. 13
Mayer, Emil 13
Mayer Brothers semi-pro team 12, 13, 20
McAleer, Jimmy 85, 98, 114
McAllister, Ward 27
McAvoy, Thomas F. 30

McBeth, W. J. 106, 108–9, 111–12, 114
McBride, George 110, 119
McCamant, T. J. 254, 255
McCarthy, Alex 164
McCarthy, William 235, 236
McCarty, Lew 214, 215, 221, 226
McConnell, George 100
McCormick, Moose 103
McDonald, Charles A. 239
McDonald, Tex 146
McGinnity, Joe 30
McGraw, Blanche 37
McGraw, John: and accusations against Chase for throwing games 223–24, 246; on betting on baseball 89; and Black Sox scandals 274; charges against, of violation of Volstead Act 285n. 26, 307n. 122; on Chase as first baseman 218; and Chase's attempted bribe of Perritt 197, 204; and Chase's contract in 1920 272–73; and Chase's departure from Giants 226, 228, 240, 241; Chase's kind words for 273; Cobb's criticism of 176; and conflict between Herzog and Chase 165; contract-breaking move to New York Giants 6, 179, 294n. 108; gambling by 6–7, 246, 285n. 27; handling of Chase by 214–15; and hearing on gambling charges against Chase 207, 208, 246; home of 37; and interest in Chase for Giants team 203, 204–5, 207, 209, 212, 258; and international tour for Giants 122; as manager of New York Giants 6, 30–31, 37, 86, 91, 106, 158, 171, 214–15, 285n. 26; and Mathewson 37, 167, 169, 203; and O'Connell-Dolan bribery scandal 309n. 46; photograph of 213; physical assault on umpire by 179; and reacquiring Herzog 167, 169, 170; and rowdiness of games with Cincinnati Reds 220; rumor on purchase of Cincinnati Reds by 203; saloon owned by 78; Slavin's suit against 307n. 122; suspension of Zimmerman for throwing games 223, 224, 229, 240, 241; and trades of infielders 172; and World Series of 1919 224; *see also* New York Giants

McGuigan, Paddy 147
McGuire, Jim 32
McHale, Jim 63
McInerney, Jack 141
McInnis, Stuffy 103, 111, 225
McKechnie, Bill 110, 130, 156, 158, 169, 170, 172, 173, 175, 182, 183
McKenry, Limb 255, 260, 261
McKevitt, Gerald 13, 14
McMillan, Frederick 191
McMulin, Fred 244
McNally, Mike 217
McNeill, Norman 144
McPherson, Aimee Semple 259, 309n. 54
McQuade, Francis X. 204
McRoy, Robert B. 114, 134
Meadows, Lee 173
Memphis Chicks 175
Mencken, H. L. 118
Mercer, Sid 48, 60, 204–8, 271–72
Merkle, Fred 123, 182, 206, 239
Mesa baseball team 251, 252
Mexico 250, 252, 253–54, 255, 259, 264
Meyer, Benny 147, 149
Michigan City (Ind.) Grays 121
Midkiff, Ezra 102, 261
Milan, Clyde 128, 284n. 12
Miller, Dots 177
Milwaukee Brewers 121
Mission League 234, 235
Mitchell, Clarence 166, 170, 182
Mitchell, Fred 206, 236, 239
Mitchell, Mike 46
Moeller, Danny 119
Mollwitz, Fred (Zip) 158–59, 162, 164, 165, 170, 172, 191
Monroe, Ethel *see* Martin, Ethel Monroe
Montgomery, Eliza 11
Montgomery baseball team 32, 41
Moore, Earl 50
Moot, Sprague, Brownell and Marcy 135, 137
Moran, Pat 203, 219, 224
Moreing, Cy 59, 61, 64, 273
Morgan, J. P., Jr. 211
Moriarty, Bill 63
Moriarty, George 48, 49, 54, 57, 63, 66
Morley, James 21–23, 24, 26, 31–34, 287n. 67
Moskiman, Doc 63
Mullen, Walter 134–35
Mullin, George 63, 68
Multnomah Athletic Club (Portland) 17
Murphy, Charles W. 105, 106

Murphy, Danny 51, 125
Murphy, Michael G. 30
Murray, Jimmy 143
Murray, Red 103
musical about Chase 290n. 45, 293n. 74
Myers, Hy 167, 220

Naps *see* Cleveland Naps
National Agreement 26, 32, 33–34, 53, 64
National Association of Minor Leagues 22, 200
National Baseball Hall of Fame 3, 4, 5, 18, 120, 266–67, 277, 283n. 10
National Commission of Baseball: and Dillon case 23; Herrmann on 7, 105, 200, 202; Lanigan's criticism of 138; outmoded structure of 200, 202; and Pacific Coast League 22, 32–34; and Perry case 200; and reinstatement of Chase after departures from Yankees 64; ruling against moonlighting 53–55; and shortened 1918 season 203; and Stallings 61; and World Series of 1918 202; and Yankees' trade of Chase for Borton and Zeider of White Sox 119
National League 3, 21, 25, 34, 36, 76, 153–56, 200, 206–7; *see also* specific teams
National Traffic Safety Institute (NTSI) 281
Nattress, Natty 143
Navin, Frank J. 117
Neale, Greasy 164, 167, 172, 190, 193, 197, 204, 207, 208, 232, 244
Nealon, James J. 235, 236
Nealon, Joe 62, 63
Nehf, Art 192, 220
New Brunswick Skeeters 109
New Orleans Pelicans 159
New York: Chase's lifestyle in 47, 109–10, 118, 258; gambling in 6, 25, 27–30; population of 27; wealth of 27–30
New York Giants: accusations against Chase for throwing games 223–24, 226–27, 244, 246; attendance figures for 220; ballpark for 30; Chase as first baseman for 217–18, 220–21; Chase traded by Cincinnati Reds to 212, 214; Chase's attempted bribe of Perritt 197, 198, 204, 205, 206; Chase's batting and fielding statistics 217, 219, 221; and Chase's contract in 1920 272–73; Chase's departure from 226, 238, 240, 306n. 03; Chase's injuries 221, 223; Chase's salary 243; Doyle as player with 31; Dubuc as pitcher for 218; errors committed by Chase 220, 221; exhibition games with Yankees in 1912 94, 102; fight between Douglas and Fletcher 221; Freedman as owner of 25, 30; Herzog as player for 171, 176; Highlanders as competition for 3, 30, 54; Holke's departure from 203, 212, 214; interest trading for Chase 203, 204–5, 207, 209; international tour in 1913 122–24; Kelly as first baseman of 4; Mathewson as coach for 203, 215, 223; Mathewson as player with 16, 30, 36–37, 88; Mathewson's injury 216; McGraw as manager of 6, 30–31, 37, 86, 91, 158, 171, 214–15, 285n. 26; McGraw's contract-breaking move to join 6; McKechnie as player for 158; negative comments on Chase by the press 221; 1902 season 294n. 108; 1910 postseason game with Highlanders 77; 1916 season 167, 170–71, 172; 1917 exhibition games and season 175–76, 178, 179, 180, 181, 183; 1918 season 190, 191, 193, 200; 1919 exhibition games and season 214, 215–24; 1920 season 226, 229; 1924 and 1925 seasons 308n. 34; and O'Connell-Dolan bribery scandal 256, 303n. 43, 308–9n. 46; pitchers for 214, 218; players for in 1919 214; rowdiness of games with Cincinnati Reds 219–20; Sinclair's purchase of 153; stars of 30–31; Stoneham as owner of 6, 204, 224, 306n. 103; Terry as first baseman for 175; Toney's sale to 191; trade of Herzog to 167, 169, 170; and trade rumors about Chase 159, 203, 204–5; and trade rumors about Daubert 203, 204; violation of Sunday baseball prohibition 181, 204; in World Series 87–89, 102, 122; Zimmerman's suspension from, for throwing games 223, 224, 226–27, 229, 238, 239–40, 241; *see also* McGraw, John; and specific players
New York Highlanders (later Yankees): attendance figures for 38; ballpark for 25, 30; bats for Chase 71, 293n. 79; Chance as manager of 106, 108; Chance's salary 106; Chance's signing with 105–6, 108; Chase as captain of in 1910, 70; Chase as first baseman for 34, 36, 37, 38–39, 41, 42, 44–45, 50, 84, 95, 110–11, 115; Chase as outfielder for 40, 52, 56–57, 84, 90, 111; Chase as pitcher for 57–58, 81; Chase as player-manager of 5, 73–90, 138, 206; Chase as second baseman for 39, 84, 89, 99, 106, 108–11; Chase as shortstop for 41, 83; Chase drafted by 24, 32; Chase on 24; and Chase with smallpox 65–66; Chase's absences from, at beginnings of seasons 31–33, 46–48; Chase's aggressive on-field conduct 43, 88, 120; Chase's batting and fielding statistics 37–43, 45, 52, 58, 67, 72, 77, 81, 84, 96, 98, 99, 100, 102, 111, 114, 116; Chase's contract with 32; Chase's departure from, during 1908 season 58–60, 64, 292n. 52; Chase's friendships with rookies 87, 293n. 77; Chase's injuries and illnesses 40, 41, 42, 44, 45, 51, 56, 63, 64, 65, 70, 72, 83, 84, 86, 92, 97, 98, 99, 100, 109, 110, 115, 117; Chase's managerial aspirations 56, 58, 59, 72, 73, 75, 108; Chase's mimicking of Chance 113; and Chase's moonlighting on San Jose team 42, 46, 53–55; Chase's popularity with teammates 36; Chase's return to in 1909 64–65; Chase's rookie season of 1905 34–41; Chase's salary 31, 42, 46, 47, 49, 67, 73, 77, 90, 112, 139, 290n. 76, 291n. 94; criticisms of Chase as manager of 81, 83–84, 86–87, 90, 91; dissatisfaction with Griffith 50; dissension between Elberfeld and Chase 58, 64, 65; dissension between Stallings and Chase 72–76, 95, 131, 132, 294n. 111; Elberfeld as manager of 56–60; Elberfeld's

Index

suspension from 51; errors committed by Chase 34, 38, 41, 44, 45, 49, 52, 74, 83, 97, 98, 99, 110; fans' responses to Chase 42, 43, 51, 65–66, 67, 98, 99, 100, 111, 115, 117–18; Farrell and Devery as owners of 6, 25, 30; finances of 41; floral tributes to Chase as player-manager 76–77, 81; Ganzel as holdout in 1905 season 31; Griffith's praise for Chase 4, 39, 41–42; Griffith's resignation from 55–56; and Hal Chase Day 65, 66; and horse racing 43–44; insinuations against Chase for "laying down" 50, 60, 73–76, 98, 113; known as Yankees 3, 49, 79; negative comments on Chase by the press 38, 45, 58–59, 60, 98, 103, 112, 114–15; 1903 and 1904 seasons 25, 31; 1905 exhibition games and season 31–41; 1906 season 42–46; 1907 exhibition games and season 46, 47–52; 1908 season 55–60; 1909 season 65–67, 143; 1910 exhibition games and season 70–77; 1911 exhibition games and season 80–87; 1912 exhibition games and season 92–103; 1913 exhibition games and season 105–14, 117–18, 120, 121, 142; 1914 season 138, 142; 1915 season 142; 1916 exhibition games of 159; 1924 and 1925 seasons 308n. 34; pennants won by 76, 105, 216–17; photographs of Chase with 35, 57, 69, 70, 79, 82, 85, 93, 101; photographs of team 57, 70, 79; pitchers for 48, 50, 57–58, 85; player's attempted attack on umpire 45; poem on Chase 66; positive comments on Chase by the press 37, 38, 39, 40, 42–43, 51, 65, 75, 81, 84, 95, 100, 102, 103, 108–10, 115; Powers "loaned" to 40; resignation of Chance as manager of 142; resignation of Chase as manager of 90; selfishness of Chase 71; sign-stealing charges against 71–72, 75; Stallings as manager of 60–61, 65–67, 70–76, 78, 80; survival of, because of Chase 3; trade of Chase to Chicago White Sox 107, 113–17, 118–19, 126; and trade rumors about Chase 91–92, 98, 112; Wolverton as manager of 91, 92, 94, 97, 98, 99, 100, 157; *see also* specific players and managers

New York National Guard 181

New York Yankees *see* New York Highlanders (later Yankees)

Newark baseball team 37, 41, 49

Newark Indians 89

Newport Trojans 178

Newton, Eustace James (Doc) 24–26, 31–33

Niehoff, Bert 208

Nogales Internationals 249–52

Northern San Joaquin Valley League 236

NTSI *see* National Traffic Safety Institute (NTSI)

Oakland baseball team 23, 26, 33, 34

Oakland Oaks 89, 126

O'Connell, Jack 23

O'Connell, Jimmy 256, 258, 259, 303n. 43, 308–9n. 46

O'Day, Hank 162

O'Grady, Tommy 135

Oldham, Red 308n. 28

Oldring, Rube 41

"Old-Timers" (Palana) 267–69

O'Leary, Charley 44, 50

Olmstead, Fred 293n. 73

O'Loughlin, Silk 45, 59, 97

Olson, Ivy 178

O'Reilly, John 259

Orioles *see* Baltimore Orioles

Orth, Al 48, 301n. 102

outfielders *see* Chase, Hal; and specific players

Overall, Orval 15

Owen, Frank 45

Oxnard baseball team 234

Pacific Coast League (PCL): all-star team of 46; banning of Chase from 235–36; and California State League 53, 61, 64; Chase as player in 23–26, 31–34, 157–58; and Dillon case 22–23; exhibition games by 126–27; gambling and bribery in 234, 235–36, 238; as independent league 21–22; and National Commission 22, 32–34; players for 157; salaries of 64, 158; son Hal as player with 257; *see also* specific teams

Pacific National League 15, 18

Packard, Gene 150

Palana, Jim 267–69

Palmer, A. Mitchell 211

Palmer, Pete 286n. 10

Paskert, Dode 183

Patrick, J. Keeler 144

PCL *see* Pacific Coast League (PCL)

Peck, John W. 229–30

Peckinpaugh, Roger 4, 8

Pendleton, Mr. and Mrs. Tal 264

Perez, Tony 284n. 13

Perritt, William Dayton "Pol" 157, 180, 197, 198, 204–7, 214, 218

Perry, Scott 200, 202

Phelon, William A. 106, 131, 193, 194, 197, 198

Philadelphia Athletics: Collins's interest in Brooklyn Federals 129; and "loaning" of Powers to Highlanders 40; Mack as manager of 84, 91, 200; McInnis as star player of 103; 1905 season 38–39, 40; 1906 season 44, 45; 1907 season 50, 51–52; 1910 season 71; 1911 season 80, 81, 83, 85; 1912 season 94, 97, 99; 1913 season 111, 113, 121; 1914 season 129, 130; Oldring as outfielder for 41; as pennant-winning team 116; and Perry case 200, 202; and trade rumors about Chase 59–60; in World Series 87–89, 122, 294n. 111

Philadelphia Phillies: Duffy as manager of 147; 1916 season 165, 170, 171, 174; 1917 season 178, 181, 183–84; 1918 season 191, 193; 1919 season 219, 224; 1920 season 236–37, 238

Phoenix Tigers 250–51, 252

Pirates *see* Pittsburgh Pirates

pitchers *see* Chase, Hal; and other specific pitchers

Pittsburgh Pirates: Callahan as manager of 172; Dreyfuss as owner of 154; Herrmann's gambling on 7; Nealon as player with 63; 1916 season 162, 164, 165, 166, 172, 174; 1917 season 183, 207; 1918 season 188, 190–91; 1919 season 221; 1925 season 308n. 34; and trade rumors about Zimmerman 226; Wagner as player with 61, 66

Pittsburgh Rebels 130, 135, 147, 149, 151
Plank, Eddie 130
Players Protective Association 137
poems about Chase 66, 115, 150
poker games 195
Pooley, Justice 135
population statistics 1–2
Port Angeles baseball team 19
Porterville (Calif.) baseball team 261
Portland baseball team 24, 31, 235
Portland Multnomah Athletic Club 17
Powell, Ray 180, 190
Powers, Mike 40
Powers, Pat 159
Price, James 113
Princeton University 264
prostitution 29
Pulliam, Harry 64
Purviance, Dorsey 11

Quigley, Ernie 179
Quinn, Billy 147
Quinn, Jack 73, 85, 97, 130
Quinn, Joe 259

race riots 211, 212
racist humor 91
Ragland, Howard 199, 243, 244
Ramirez, Felix 255
Rankin, W. M. 75
Rariden, Bill 179, 214
Rath, Morrie 219
Rawlings, Johnny 192
Red Sox see Boston Red Sox
Reddy, Al 89
Reds see Cincinnati Reds
Reese, John D. "Bonesetter" 159
Regan, Mike 191, 195, 204, 205, 207, 208, 244
Rehg, Wally 181–82, 183
Reichow, Oscar C. 227, 229
Reliance Club 20
Reno Garage baseball team 261
Replogle, Hartley L. 239
reserve clause 125
Rice, Grantland 2
Rich, L. E. 207
Ring, Jimmy 177, 192, 204–9, 232, 233, 244
Ripley, Robert 206
Risberg, Swede 157, 241, 244, 245, 248
Roach, Roxey 145, 148
Robertson, Bill 11, 47
Robertson, Dave 170

Robertson, William E. 147, 148–49, 154, 155
Robinson, Eddie 284n. 13
Robinson, Jackie 103, 285n. 31
Rochester baseball team 118
Rochester Nationals 154
Rockefeller, John D. 211
Rogers, Will 5, 187
Roosevelt, Theodore 33, 49
Rosoff, Sam 28
Rossman, Claude 58, 63
Roth, Braggo 152
Roth, Mark 55, 78, 80, 83–84, 86, 88–92, 94, 96, 98, 99, 107, 115, 119, 272
Rothstein, Arnold 6, 7, 28, 198, 204, 241, 242, 246, 248, 274, 285n. 26
Roush, Edd 120, 121, 130, 169, 170, 183, 192, 220, 230, 231, 284n. 12
Rowland, Clarence (Pants) 203, 214–15
Royce, Josiah 9
Rucker, Nap 267
Rudolph, Dick 190, 219
Ruether, Dutch 181
Rumler, Bill 235
Russell, Lillian 28
Russell, Reb 116, 128, 131
Ruth, Babe 3–4, 152, 216–17, 267, 308n. 34
Ryan, John W. 135, 137
Ryan, Rosie 215
Ryder, Jack 156, 159, 161, 162, 164–67, 169–76, 178–84, 188, 190–96, 199, 200

S. H. Chase Company 10, 11
Sacramento Senators 61–62, 63
Sacramento Wolves 127, 179
Saier, Vic 122
St. Denis, Walter 48, 207, 225
St. Louis Browns: and Frisk 33; Gedeon as player with 210; Magee traded to Cincinnati Reds by 187; merger of Sloufeds with 155; 1905 season 40; 1906 season 45; 1908 season 56; 1910 season 71, 73, 74; 1911 season 80, 81, 84, 85, 86; 1912 season 100, 102; 1913 season 121; 1916 season 148
St. Louis Cardinals: Beckley as first baseman for 26; Enwright as player with 63; Giants' interest in Hornsby of 220; merger of, with St. Louis Feds 153; 1916 season 164, 165–66, 173, 174; 1917 season 176–77, 181, 182; 1918 season 188, 190, 196; trade of Gonzalez by 218; and

trade rumors about Zimmerman 226; Wingo's departure from 145
St. Louis Feds (Sloufeds) 148, 149, 151, 153, 155
St. Mary's College 14, 46–47
St. Vincent's College 20, 21
salaries: in American and National Leagues 155–56; of Chance 106; of Chase 16, 31, 42, 46, 47, 49, 64, 67, 73, 77, 90, 112, 124, 125–26, 127, 138, 139, 155, 243, 290n. 76, 291n. 94, 296n. 22; of Daubert 203–4; in Federal League 124, 125, 129, 155; in Frontier League 256; of Pacific Coast League 158; and shortened 1918 season 203–4
Salt Lake City baseball team 218, 235
San Francisco Independents 15
San Francisco Missions 257
San Francisco Seals 13, 21, 126–27, 157–58, 161, 179, 197, 235, 251
San Joaquin Valley Baseball League 236
San Jose All-Stars 15
San Jose Mission League club 234, 235–36
San Jose Prune Pickers 14, 42, 46, 53–55, 61
Sanborn, I. E. 114, 115–18, 120–21, 126–29, 238, 251
Sand, Heinie 308–9n. 46
Sangree, Alan 271, 272
Santa Clara College 13–16, 15, 19, 20–21, 23, 109, 157, 179, 286n. 23
Santa Rita team 308n. 28
Saratoga 27, 28
Schaefer, Germany 50, 58, 102, 122
Schalk, Ray 116, 119, 225
Schick, Morrie 182
Schlafly, Larry 144, 145, 146, 147
Schneider, Pete 170, 176–77, 182, 183, 188, 191, 230, 231, 234
Schroeder, Bill 244
Schulte, Frank 122
Schultz, Dutch 28
Schulz, Al 141, 144, 156, 158, 174
Schumacher, Harry 20, 206, 208, 214, 215, 217
Schupp, Ferdie 214, 218
Schwab, Matty 179
Schwengers, Bernie 18, 20
Scott, Jim 116, 119, 129, 131
Scranton baseball team 81

Seals *see* San Francisco Seals
Seasongood, Murray 230
Seaton, Tom 125, 155, 156, 158, 234, 251–52, 255
Seattle baseball team 18–19, 24, 33, 34, 235
second basemen *see* Chase, Hal; and specific players
Sedition Act 211
Sehorn, J. W. 273–77
Senators *see* Sacramento Senators; Washington Senators
Sepulveda, Louis 127
Sex, James P. 236
Seymour, Cy 102–3
Seymour, Harold 3, 125, 155, 203, 240, 258, 293n. 82
Shannon, Irish 258
Shay, Danny 46, 63
Shean, Dave 182
Sheehan, Tommy 46
Sheridan, John B. 42, 102
Sherman Antitrust Act 129, 137, 138, 139–40
Shires, Art 111
Shotton, Burt 84
Shreveport Gassers 159, 175
Sidway, Ralph 135
Simmons, Hack 99, 100, 130
Simon, Mike 146
Sinclair, Harry 153, 154, 155, 157, 158, 159
Sisler, George 3, 4, 202, 264, 266–68, 271, 283–84nn. 10–11
Slavin, John C. 307n. 122
Sloufeds *see* St. Louis Federal League team (Sloufeds)
smallpox 65
Smith, Casey 234
Smith, Earl 214
Smith, Fred 141, 146
Smith, George 204
Smith, Heinie 143
Smith, Idabelle 307n. 1
Smith, Ira 43–44
Smith, Jack 17, 164, 166, 173, 177
Smith, Jimmy 214, 220
Smith, Milton 2
Smith, Red 171
Snodgrass, Fred 88
Snyder, Frank 177, 221
socialists 211
Soden, E. D. 103
Soquel Giants 13
South Atlantic League 65, 66
Southern Arizona League 252, 254
Southern Association 175
Southern League 41, 159
Spalding, Albert 3, 122
Spalding, John E. 11
Speaker, Tris 88, 98, 122, 155, 176, 183

Stadel, W. W. 270
Stahl, Chick 48
Stahl, Jake 114
Stallings, George Tweedy: attempted sale of Detroit Tigers to National League 76; and Buffalo Federal League team (Buffeds) 146; dissension between Chase and 72–76, 95, 131, 132, 294n. 111; dissension between Johnson and 61, 76; on Elberfeld 294n. 111; as manager of Boston Braves 146, 155, 171, 192; as manager of Detroit Tigers 61, 76; as manager of New York Highlanders 60–61, 65–67, 70–76, 78, 80; photograph of 62; popularity of, with Buffalo fans 131, 134; suspension of, as manager of Braves 171; and World Series of 1919 224
Stanage, Oscar 176
Standard Oil Company 144
Stanford University 13, 15, 16, 20, 21, 46, 262
Starbird, Ray 245
Steele, Bob 218
Steffens, Lincoln 7, 60
Stengel, Casey 167, 188
Sterrett, Charlie 99
Stifel, Otto 153
Stock, Milt 226
Stockton Millers 46, 61–63
Stoneham, Charles A. 6, 28, 204, 224, 285n. 26, 306n. 103
Stovall, George 39, 85, 88, 125, 156–57, 158
Strange, Gladys 188
Street, Gabby 97, 100, 195
Stricklett, Elmer 46, 63
Stroud, Ralph 235
Strub, Charles (Doc) 13, 20, 287n. 54
Stumpf, Bill 100
Sugar, Bert Randolph 310n. 98
Suhr, Gus 284n. 13
suicide 48
Sullivan, Billy 43, 88, 120
Sullivan, Sport 244, 245, 246
Sunday baseball games 102–3, 181, 204
Superbas *see* Brooklyn Superbas
Supreme Court case 156
Swacina, Harry 146
Sweeney, Ed 83, 86, 113
swimming 80
Swope, Herbert Bayard 28
Swope, Tom 194–95

Tacoma Athletic Club 17
Tacoma baseball team 24
Taft, Charles 202
Taft, William Howard 202
Tammany Hall 6, 25, 29, 30, 181, 204, 289n. 15
Tarbell, Ida M. 60
Tausch, J. Franklin 207
Taylor, Harry Leonard 137
Tebeau, Pat 225
Tellez, Manuel 250
ten-day clause 129, 130, 131, 138, 139, 203
Tener, John K. 200
Tennes, Monte 7
Tenney, Fred 37, 225, 284n. 12
Terrapins *see* Baltimore Feds (Terrapins)
Terry, Bill 3, 4, 175, 283n. 10
Texas League 175, 188, 234
Thaw, Harry K. 289n. 9
Thayer, Ernest 149
Thomas, Major 216
Thompson, Frog 242
Thoreau, Henry David 10
Thorn, John 286n. 10
Thorpe, Jim 177
ticket prices 150, 154
Tigers *see* Detroit Tigers
Tinker, Joe 124, 125–26, 130, 144, 155, 158, 172
Titanic 94
Toledo Rail-Lights 172, 175
Toney, Fred 170, 171, 175, 177, 178, 180–83, 187, 191, 208, 214, 218, 220, 223
Toole, John Conway 207
Topham, Frank 261, 269–70
Topham, Jessie Chase 1, 261, 269–70, 273, 310n. 106
Trachtenberg, Alan 9
Tragresser, Ed 180–81
Treaty of Versailles 211–12
Tri-State League 254–56
Tucker, Tom 225
Tucson Motive Power team 251
Turner, Frederick Jackson 9
Tuthill, Harry 176

umpires: Chase as Yankee manager on 81; Chase's arguments with 94, 171; Elberfeld suspended for fighting with 40; Evers ejected by 171; fans' disagreement with 42, 97; McGraw's ejection for hitting 179; Mollwitz's ejection from game by 162; players' attempted attacks on 45; Wolverton's anger at 94; Yankees' arguments with 82–83
University of Alabama 188

University of California 13, 15, 46, 287n. 54
University of Cincinnati 190
University of Georgia 70, 145
Untermyer, Alvin 110, 112

Valley League 261
Van Haltren, George 26
Van Wyck, Robert A. 29
Vancouver Terminals 16, 19, 287n. 51
Vanderbilt, William H. 2
Vaughn, Jim "Hippo" 72, 73, 85, 86, 122, 177–78, 182
Veblen, Thorstein 2, 3
Veeck, William L. 227, 229–33, 236–38, 240
venereal diseases 293n. 82
Venice baseball team 127–28
Vernon Tigers 235, 236
Vicksburg baseball team 32
Victoria Baseball Club 16–20
Victoria Hillside Intermediates 17
Victoria Wanderers 17
Vila, Joe 25, 30, 33, 37, 38, 60, 65, 66, 87, 108, 161, 206–9, 225, 226, 229, 237–38, 264, 290n. 76
Volstead Act 285n. 26, 307n. 122

Waco Navigators 188
Waddell, Rube 51–52
Wagner, Honus (Hans) 61, 66, 103, 267
Wallace, Bobby 85
Walsh, Ed 45, 98, 100, 128
Ward, Robert B. 153
Ward family 155
Washington, D.C. 145, 211
Washington Senators: Anderson as player with 289n. 21; Gandil as player with 92; Griffith as manager and owner of 4, 92, 292n. 25; 1905 season 38; 1906 season 43, 45; 1907 season 49, 50; 1909 season 66; 1910 season 71, 76–77; 1911 season 81, 85; 1912 season 97, 100, 102, 141; 1913 season 110, 119; 1914 season 128, 129; 1917 exhibition games of 175; 1919 exhibition games 217–18; pitchers for 91–92; and trade rumors about Chase 91–92
Watson, Mule 177, 181
wealth 1–2, 27–30
Weaver, Buck 116, 123, 128, 131, 212, 244, 255, 256, 258–59
Weeghman, Charles 7, 126, 153, 155–56, 178
Whalen, Bill 14, 20–21
Wheat, Zack 169, 174
Whelan, Mack 38
White, Doc 127
White, Stanford 6, 29, 289n. 9
White, Henry 212
White Sox see Chicago White Sox
Whitman, Burt 192
Whitted, Possum 219
Wickland, Al 149, 191–92
Widrig, Louis C. 167
Williams, Cy 177, 182
Williams, Harry 120, 123, 129
Williams, Jimmy 39, 48, 49, 56
Williams, Joe 278
Williams, Lefty 224, 244, 245, 256, 258–60
Williams, Ted 271
Williams (Ariz.) baseball team 252, 261
Wilson, Art 177–78, 182, 240, 248
Wilson, Woodrow 145, 176, 178, 211
Winchester Mystery House 10
Wingo, Ivy 145, 165, 170, 172, 175
Winslow (Ariz.) baseball team 262
Wolter, Harry 46, 63, 86, 100, 109, 157, 301n. 102
Wolverton, Harry 89, 91, 92, 94, 97, 98, 99, 100, 127, 157, 158
Won in the Ninth (Mathewson) 37, 67–68, 70
World Series of 1906 116; 1908 63; 1911 87–89; 1912 102; 1913 122; 1914 76; 294n. 111; 1918 200, 202; 1919 224–25; *see also* Black Sox scandal
World War I 141, 175, 176, 178–79, 187, 188, 190, 191, 199, 200, 211
Wortman, Chuck 172
Wray, John 253
Wright, Chick 127
Wyman, Mrs. Irvin 270

Yale University 218
Yankees *see* New York Highlanders (later Yankees)
Yeats, William Butler 212
Young, Cy 42, 56
Youngs, Ross 197, 214, 217, 219, 303n. 43, 309n. 46

Zeider, Rollie 98, 100, 113–14, 117, 118–19, 126, 130
Zelser, David 245
Zimmerman, Heinie: batting statistics 172, 174, 183, 214, 300n. 54; on Chicago Cubs team 122, 164, 172; and Cobb's fight with Herzog 176; and College Park baseball team 259; consequences of association with Chase generally 117, 123, 172; on New York Giants team 190, 214, 215, 218–19, 223; and 1919 season with Giants 215; photograph of 222; suspension of, for throwing games 223, 224, 226–27, 238, 239–40, 241; trade of, to New York Giants 172, 204; trade rumors about 220, 226
Zinn, Guy 99, 130
Zork, Carl 245